THE CALL TO WRITE

Preliminary Edition

John Trimbur
Worcester Polytechnic Institute

 LONGMAN

An Imprint of Addison Wesley Longman, Inc

New York • Reading, Massachusetts • Menlo Park, California • Harlow, England
Don Mills, Ontario • Sydney • Mexico City • Madrid • Amsterdam

Manager of Addison Wesley Longman Custom Books: Caralee Woods
Production Administrator: Kathleen Kollar
Cover Design: Paul Agresti

THE CALL TO WRITE
Preliminary Edition

ISBN: 0-201-45653-2

98 99 00 3 2 1

CONTENTS

PART
ONE

WRITING AND READING

PART
ONE

INTRODUCTION

THE CALL TO WRITE

People write in response to situations that call on them to put their thoughts and feelings into words. The call to write may come from a teacher who assigns a paper or from within yourself when you have ideas and experiences you want to write down. In any case, as you will see throughout this book, people who write typically experience some sense of need that can be met by writing. And accordingly what a person writes will be shaped by the situation that gave rise to the need.

The situations that call on people to write are as various as social life itself. Here are a few examples:

- Someone you know dies, and you want to write a letter of sympathy to the family.

- A friend transfers to another college, and you decide to stay in touch through e-mail.

- Your boss asks you to write a report on how to market a new product line.

- Your company wants to have a home page on the World Wide Web, and you offer to help design it.

- You belong to a campus organization and need to publicize your group's activities.

- You belong to an advocacy group (such as Amnesty International or the Sierra Club) and you need to inform the public about the issues—and to call on your readers to write to government officials.

- As a college student, you are assigned book reviews, critical analyses, research papers, case studies, and lab reports as part of your coursework.

As you can see, writing takes place in many different settings and for many purposes. By thinking about these various occasions, you can deepen your understanding of your own and other people's writing and develop a set of strategies that will help you become a more effective writer. The three chapters in Part One of this textbook offer a way of looking at why and how people respond to the call to write. In the next chapter, we'll look more closely at four contexts in which writing occurs—everyday life, the workplace, the public sphere, and school. The second chapter focuses on how writers read in order to develop their own writing projects. The third chapter considers what makes writing persuasive and how you can build a responsible and persuasive argument. But first we look at how writers identify the call to write and determine whether and how to respond to it.

IDENTIFYING AND RESPONDING TO THE CALL TO WRITE

In some situations, identifying the call to write seems like a straightforward matter. An example is your instructor assigning a term paper in history or a lab report for biology. In other situations, however, the call to write can be far less straightforward. Suppose, for example, you've just heard that next year there will be major cuts in student financial aid. Is this a situation you feel a need to respond to? And should your response take the form of writing?

In the case of financial aid cuts, you'll have to analyze and interpret the situation. By doing so, you'll know whether you want to respond and will begin to see how you can shape an effective response. Your analysis will involve asking questions about the situation: What's going on? What has happened? Who is involved? What seems to be at stake? What needs to be done?

Just because a situation seems to call for writing doesn't necessarily mean that people will respond in writing, however. You can probably think of times when you could have written something but, for one reason or another, let the occasion go by. Maybe you thought of writing to a friend who was going through hard times but decided to make a phone call instead. Or maybe you thought of writing a letter to the editor of your local newspaper but never quite got around to it.

Situations that seem to call for writing, after all, don't automatically put writers into motion.

If, however, you do respond to a situation by writing, your response should grow out of your analysis of the situation. That is, you will construct a writing task for yourself that seems appropriate to the situation. Like analyzing the situation, constructing a writing task can be relatively straightforward or it can be a more complicated matter. For example, if you decide to send written invitations to a party you're planning (instead of calling on the phone), your writing task is largely dictated by the situation: you need to buy some invitations (or design one on your computer), include the pertinent information (date, time, place, and so on), and ask people to RSVP.

In other cases, however, responding to the call to write can be more complicated. For example, to express your concern about cuts in financial aid, a range of responses might be appropriate: you could write a leaflet proposing that fellow students take action together to stop the cuts; you could write a letter of protest to the officials who made the cuts; you could write a letter to the editor of the local newspaper to explain the signficance of the impending cuts; or you could send a fact sheet to a public official to inform him or her about the cuts.

The fact that student financial aid is going to be cut, then, doesn't in itself determine your writing task or the form your response will take. In this and many other situtations, responding effectively to the call to write means thinking about several crucial factors: your purpose; your readers and the relationship you want to establish with them; the appropriate voice, or tone, of your writing; and the relationship of your writing to the larger social and cultural context. The type (or genre) of writing you choose—whether a leaflet, letter, or fact sheet—will depend in large part on the decisions you make about these factors.

FACTORS THAT WRITERS TAKE INTO ACCOUNT

Let's look more closely at each of the factors writers typically take into account when they identify a call to write and turn it into a writing task:

- Purpose: Writers need to clarify what they are trying to accomplish with their writing. How do they want to influence the situation that gave rise to the call to write? What effect does the writer intend to have, and how will the writing achieve this effect?

Let's return to the cuts in student financial aid. If you decide to respond to this situation, what kind of change will you be trying to bring about—a total reversal of the decision to cut financial aid? a reduction of cuts? Is your purpose to rally students to oppose the cuts or to call on the decisionmakers directly to change the new policy. Depending on your purpose, what genre of writing can best accomplish your goals?

- Relationship to readers: Closely related to decisions about purpose are decisions about readers. As you can see, part of clarifying your purpose involves clarifying who your primary readers will be. The way a writer constructs a writing task will depend in part on whom the writer chooses as the intended readers and on what the writer knows about them, about their familiarity with the situation, and about their interests and opinions.

As writers determine who their readers will be, they also make decisions about their relationship to these readers. For example, if you are trying to convince students to demonstrate against the financial aid cuts, you can appeal to your relationship as peers and emphasize your common interests. On the other hand, if you are writing to decisionmakers in positions of authority, you are probably addressing readers who have more power that you. Do you want to approach these readers as a humble petitioner, a concerned student, a morally outraged victim, a threat, or something else?

- Voice: The tone of voice in a piece of writing will vary depending on the purpose and the kind of relationship writers want to establish with their readers. The writer's voice is basically the attitude he or she wants to project to readers. Should the tone be formal or informal, intimate or distanced? Is it appropriate to express concern, sarcasm, or anger? Decisions such as these hinge on what the writer wants to achieve and whom the writer is addressing.

In the case of the financial aid cuts, a tone that's appropriate for a piece of writing intended to call on students to take action may not be appropriate for a piece of writing intended to persuade decisionmakers or to inform the public. An important part of responding to the call to write is knowing how to modulate your voice, to take on the right tone for the situation.

- Relationship to the culture and its social institutions: Like everything we say and do, writing both reflects our cultural knowledge and puts us into a certain relationship with our culture and its social institutions. In the example of the financial aid cuts, the cultural and institutional context is easy to identify—a college or university within the larger system of higher education in the United States. And it's also easy to see in this case how writers draw on their knowledge of such contexts to shape their writing tasks accordingly.

What may not be so obvious, however, is how the act of writing itself connects writers to the culture and its social institutions in different ways, depending on the situation and the writer's purposes. Writing an exam, for instance, is very different from writing flyers to rally students against the cuts in financial aid. And both differ from writing doodles on the margins of your notes during a dull lecture. Although the institution in which the writing takes place is the same, each instance of writing expresses not only a different purpose but also a different relationship to the institutional context—whether as an academic performer trying to get a good grade, an activist trying to change the direction of the institution, or a bored student trying to make class time pass more easily.

- Genre of writing: Genres are the different types of writing people draw on to respond to the call to write. As you can see from the genres listed in the discussion of financial aid cuts— leaflets, letters of protest, letters to the editor, and fact sheets—genres of writing have characteristic features that enable readers to recognize the writer's purpose and to understand the type of relationship the writer wants to establish with them.

There are, of course, many genres of writing. Part 2 in this book treats eight of the most familiar ones—letters, memoirs, public documents, profiles, reports, commentary, proposals, and reviews. Each of these genres offers a distinct strategy to deal with typical writing situations.

WORKING TOGETHER: Identifying and Responding to a Call to Write

1. Choose a piece of writing you've done at some time in the past. It could be a writing assignment in school, a note to a friend, something you wrote at work, a diary entry, a letter, an article for a student newspaper or community newsletter, a petition, flyer, or leaflet for an organization you belong to. Whatever the writing happens to be, write a page or two in which you describe the call that prompted you to write.

    - What was it about the situation that made you feel a need to respond in writing?

    - Why did you decide to respond by writing instead of taking some other action or not responding at all?

    - How did you construct your writing task? How did you determine your purpose, the relationship you wanted to establish with your readers, and the tone of voice in your writing? How did the writing connect you to the cultural context and its social institutions? What type or genre of writing did you use to communicate your purpose?

2. In a group with two or three other students, take turns reading aloud what you have written. Compare the situations that gave rise to the call to write and the way each of you responded. What, if anything, was similar about the way you identified and responded to the call to write? What was different? How would you account for the differences and similarities?

CHAPTER ONE

THE CALL TO WRITE IN CONTEXT

Learning to write involves understanding your own experience as a writer—to see how various situations have called on you to write, how you have shaped your writing tasks accordingly, and the success and failure of your writing to meet the need that called for it. This chapter looks at how people respond to the call to write in four contexts:

- writing in everyday life

- writing in the workplace

- writing in the public sphere

- writing in school

The chapter presents a wide range of writing samples for you to investigate various kinds of writing you and others have done and to see how writing differs in genre, purpose, intended readers, and tone, depending on the writer's context. This knowledge about writing can help you understand the role writing plays in your life. And it can help you become a more flexible writer who can fit what you want to say to the occasions that call on you to write.

The four contexts you will be looking at are not self-contained or mutually exclusive categories. In fact, they may overlap at times. For example, writing may be done in the workplace but intended for the public sphere. Moreover, various kinds of writing are done in each context, so that a particular piece of writing done in school may be more like some writing done in the workplace than it is like other school writing.

Throughout the chapter, Writing Inventories ask you to take stock of the kind of writing you have done in the four different contexts. These Writing Inventories can be used for various purposes:

- for classroom discussion

- as short writing assignments

- to write a literacy narrative about a telling episode in your life that involved writing (Directions for writing a literacy narrative appear at the end of the chapter.)

- to incorporate into a portfolio to submit at the end of the term.

You will also find Writing Inventories at the end of each chapter in Part Two to draw on for a portfolio (See Chapter X "Reviewing Your Writing Inventories" for more information about how to integrate Writing Inventories into a portfolio.)

WRITING IN EVERYDAY LIFE

Writing in everyday life is embedded in our daily routines and private purposes. Much of the writing that takes place in everyday life can be described as self-sponsored writing because it is up to the individual to decide whether, why, and how to write.

The call to write in everyday life emerges from a range of situations. People respond by drawing on various genres to carry out their purposes: They write lists to remember things and organize their daily activities. They write notes for friends or family members to ask for a ride home, to remind someone about a dentist's appointment, to jot down a phone message. People use writing to maintain social relationships—whether by means of a letter of condolence, a thank-you card for a birthday present, or a note passed between friends in a class. Some people keep personal diaries to record their experiences—and to let off steam, put their feelings in perspective, and cope with the stresses of life. Others write poetry or fiction for similar purposes and for the pleasure of using language to create imaginary worlds.

These purposes have in common a tendency to be personal rather than public. Similarly, intended readers are generally limited to people the writer knows well, intimate acquaintances such as friends and family—or even to just the writer. Not surprisingly, the tone is characteristically informal and familiar. And although these writings are personal, they are, like everyday life itself, tied to the larger social and cultural context.

Analysis of Writing in Everyday Life: A Shopping List

Nothing could be more ordinary than a shopping list. But this makes a shopping list ideal for our analysis of writing in everyday life. Shopping lists reveal one of the most powerful aspects of writing: writing frees us from having to commit everything to memory. It's easier and more efficient to write items down on paper, to let a list remind us of what we want.

A typical shopping list might look something like this:

apples	butter	rice
spaghetti	meat for Sunday dinner	
bananas	milk	hot dog rolls
eggs	bread	cat food
chicken	two cans of tomatos	
paper towels	salad stuff	

Notice that only the writer could actually bring home exactly what he or she wants. Someone else wouldn't know, for example, how many apples or what kind of meat to buy. The voice in the writing is imprecise and self-referential, the kind of private code that works when you want to talk to yourself. If, however, someone else were to do the shopping, the writer would need to be much more specific, to make the voice more precise and clear.

With some small changes, the shopping list could be written to be an organizing tool as well as a memory aid. The shopper could compose the list so that it corresponds to the aisles in the grocery store:

apples	bananas	salad stuff
chicken	meat for Sunday dinner	
two cans of tomatos		
spaghetti	rice	
paper towels		
butter	milk	eggs
breadhot dog rolls		
cat food		

This analysis points out how purpose and audience do indeed shape the writing task. Even as simple and straightforward a piece of writing as a shopping list can be written to serve different purposes and to be appropriate for different intended readers. From a broader perspective, these lists also express the shopper's relationship to other common cultural activities, such as planning meals, entertaining guests, packing children's lunches, caring for pets, and cleaning and managing a household. The act of writing a shopping list also locates private homes in relationship to social institutions, such as the larger economic order of food production and distribution that includes agribusiness, cattle ranches, dairy farms, bakeries, supermarket chains, and the huge corporations that make everything from lasagna to light bulbs.

WRITING SAMPLES

These two writing samples come from everyday life, but they differ greatly. The first is easy to recognize: an invitation to a party to celebrate a couple's 25th wedding anniversary. The second requires more explanation. It is a sample of the special code invented by Noah John Rondeau to keep a personal diary. Famous regionally as the Adirondack hermit, Rondeau lived alone at his hermitage in the Cold River valley on and off from the 1930's until 1950, hunting and trapping, reading philosophy and astronomy, and writing poetry, letters, and his diary. Rondeau boasted that experts would never decipher his code, and this has proved true, though his letters, poems, and portions of his diary written in conventional script have been published.

As you read each writing sample, consider the purpose it serves, the intended audience, the tone, and how it expresses the writer's relationship to social institutions and the larger cultural context.

JOIN US

TO CELEBRATE

ANDREA MARTIN & TIM BIENVENUE'S 25TH WEDDING ANIVERSARY

SATURDAY, JULY 14
3:30 - ???

14 SANDY HILL LANE
POTTSTOWN

(TAKE EXIT 7 OFF HIGHWAY 65, TURNING LEFT AT THE END OF THE RAMP ONTO FALLEN SPARROW BOULEVARD. SANDY HILL LANE IS THE THIRD STREET. TURN LEFT. OUR HOUSE IS AT THE BOTTOM OF THE HILL ON THE RIGHT.)

BRING KIDS & BATHING SUITS.
(WE'RE A HALF-BLOCK FROM OSTRICKER'S POND.)

R.S.V.P.
578-0954

NO PRESENTS PLEASE. YOU CAN MAKE DONATIONS AT THE PARTY TO THE ENVIRONMENTAL DEFENSE FUND AND THE POTTSTOWN RAPE CRISIS CENTER.

WRITING INVENTORY

Make a list of writing have you done in the context of everyday life. Try to come up with a wide range of writing. After you have listed the writings, think about them in terms of genre, purpose, intended reader (even if you are the only reader), tone of voice, and relationship to cultural activities and social institutions. What conclusions, if any, can you draw about the role writing plays in everyday life?

ETHICS OF WRITING

People sometimes think that learning to write amounts largely to acquiring a skill—to get your point across clearly and correctly. Now, certainly a writing class is concerned with how writers can effectively communicate their messages. But learning to write also involves considering the writer's responsibilities and the ethics of communication—not just what works but what is right and wrong, good or bad.

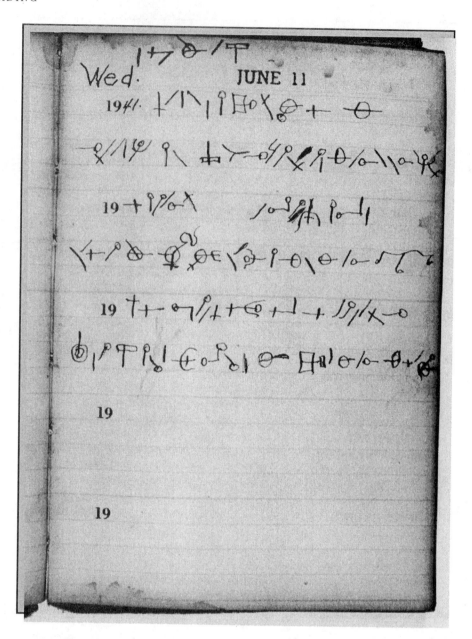

Some of the ethical principles responsible writers take into account can be summarized briefly: writers should be trustworthy, using the best information available and presenting it accurately; writers should be honest, acknowledging the sources of their information; writers should be fair, treating opposing views seriously; writers should keep in mind the best interests of individuals and groups they write about; writers should be reasonable, approaching their readers to persuade rather than manipulate them.

Listing these principles, however, does not fully describe the ethical issues raised by situations that call on people to write. The ethics of writing is always a matter of applying such principles in actual writing situations where ethical conflicts can arise. Writers may find, for example, that some of the evidence they have uncovered challenges a social or political belief they share with others and value deeply. (For example, an advocate of the death penalty might find data that suggests capital punishment does not deter violent crimes.) Is it dishonest to ignore the evidence out of loyalty to others and a shared cause? Or would it be disloyal to present the evidence?

Because ethical issues are so embedded in particular writing situations, you will find them treated throughout this textbook. As you will see, the ethics of writing can be complex, especially when writers encounter conflicts of interest, loyalty, and values.

HERE ARE THREE EXAMPLES OF WRITING SITUATIONS THAT RAISE ETHICAL ISSUES:

A. Cigarette advertising. Cigarette manufacturers are obliged by federal law to print Surgeon General warnings about the health risks of smoking on their advertising. Critics of the tobacco companies have argued that while the companies have abided by the law, they have sometimes done so by making the warnings difficult to read. Notice in the example how the warning from a billboard advertising cigarettes uses a thick frame and all capital letters with little white space in between to create a cluttered look. Do you agree with critics that this is unethical? Why or why not? Can you think of other instances where information has been made difficult to read?

> **SURGEON GENERAL'S WARNING: SMOKING CAUSES LUNG CANCER, HEART DISEASE, EMPHYSEMA, AND MAY COMPLICATE PREGNANACY**

B. Passing notes. Passing notes in class is one way students carry on their social lives even when they are supposed to be doing schoolwork. This note was written by an eighth-grader to a friend sitting nearby. Kelly presumably thinks Aubrey is trying to impress the teacher by holding up her hand to answer questions and seems to suggest that Aubrey is "really mean" even though she acts "so nice to everybody." Consider the ethics of passing notes in school. Think of your own experience in school and what purposes passing notes served. Notes are means of communication to maintain social relationships, but they can also include some while excluding others. Do you think passing notes might pose ethical problems? What do you think of this note?

Dear Martha,
    Hi! How are you? I'm okay. I feel sorry for Aubrey. I wish she'd take her hand down. Some people, not mentioning names, are really mean. You can ⬛ probably guess who they are? Aubrey's so nice to everybody. Do you know why people do that? I'm running out of things to say, so bye.

                                        Kelly

C. Graffitti. Graffiti has become an omni-present feature of contemporary urban life. Spraypainted on walls and subway cars, graffiti can perform a number of functions: marking a gang's turf, putting forth political messages, expressing the individual writer's identity, expressing grief for someone killed or anger at an enemy. Of course, people's reactions to graffiti differ dramatically. Some see it as simply a crime—an anti-social act of vandalism—while others believe grafffiti is a form of artistic expression and political statement by disenfranchised inner city youth. What ethical issues are raised for you by such examples of graffiti as the two printed here? Do you consider graffiti a justified form of writing even though it is illegal? Why or why not?

WRITING IN THE WORKPLACE

In many respects, the world of work is organized by acts of writing. Government agencies, for example, cannot exist without enabling legislation and funding, nor can corporations exist without articles of incorporation.

The call to write emerges repeatedly in the workplace. For financial and legal reasons, companies need to keep careful records of all their transactions, their inventory and sales, the contracts they enter into with customers or clients, and their dealings with unions and federal and state regulatory agencies.

Equally important is written communication among the members of an organization. Such writing serves to establish a sense of shared purpose, a clear chain of command, and procedures to evaluate performance. Writing helps manage the flow of work and the progress of individual projects.

Companies, moreover, need to make their goods and services known to potential customers and clients, and advertising and public relations have become major industries in their own right.

Today writing in the workplace is undergoing great change as a result of computerization. Inventory, sales figures, and other records are now immediately available on line. E-mail links employees through local area networks, and electronic communication has replaced the traditional memo and letter. In addition, companies and agencies can communicate with customers and clients through the Internet, and the World Wide Web is increasingly becoming a key advertising site.

Writing in the workplace is often specialized. Many of the professions are defined by the genres of writing practitioners are called on to do—the legal briefs, contracts, and wills written by lawyers, the diagnostic reports of doctors and psychologists, the case reports of social workers, the proposals and surveys of engineering and architectural firms, and so on. All show how specialized writing is crucial to the professions. A professional's ability to master the specialized genres of writing in his or her particular field will determine in large part that person's success in the world of work.

NIKE Code of Conduct

Nike, Inc. was founded on a handshake.

Implicit in that act was the determination that we would build our business with all of our partners based on trust, teamwork, honesty and mutual respect. We expect all of our business partners to operate on the same principles.

At the core of the NIKE corporate ethic is the belief that we are a company comprised of many different kinds of people, appreciating individual diversity, and dedicated to equal opportunity for each individual.

NIKE designs, manufactures and markets products for sports and fitness consumers. At every step in that process, we are driven to do not only what is required, but what is expected of a leader. We expect our business partners to do the same. Specifically, NIKE seeks partners that share our commitment to the promotion of best practices and continuous improvement in:

1. Occupational health and safety, compensation, hours of work and benefits.

2. Minimizing our impact on the environment.

3. Management practices that recognize the dignity of the individual, the rights of free association and collective bargaining, and the right to a workplace free of harassment, abuse or corporal punishment.

4. The principal that decisions on hiring, salary, benefits, advancement, termination or retirement are based solely on the ability of an individual to do the job.

Wherever NIKE operates around the globe, we are guided by this Code of Conduct. We bind our business partners to these principles. While these principles establish the spirit of our partnerships, we also bind these partners to specific standards of conduct. These are set forth below:

1. **Forced** ... (Contractor) certifies that it does not use any forced labor - prison, indentured, bonded or otherwise.

2. **Child Labor.** (Contractor) certifies it does not employ any person under the age of 15 (or 14 where the law of the country of manufacturing allows), or the age at which compulsory schooling has ended, whichever is greater.

3. **Compensation.** (Contractor) certifies that it pays at least the minimum wage, or the prevailing industry wage, whichever is higher.

4. **Benefits.** (Contractor) certifies that it complies with all provisions for legally mandated benefits, including but not limited to housing; meals; transportation and other allowances; health care; child care; sick leave; emergency leave; pregnancy and menstrual leave; vacation, religious, bereavement and holiday leave; and contributions for social security, life, health, worker's compensation and other insurance.

5. **Hours of Work/Overtime.** (Contractor) certifies that it complies with legally mandated work hours; uses overtime only when employees are fully compensated according to local law; informs the employee at the time of hiring if mandatory overtime is a condition of employment; and, on a regularly scheduled basis, provides one day off in seven, and requires no more than 60 hours of work per week, or complies with local limits if they are lower.

6. **Health and Safety.** (Contractor) certifies that it has written health and safety guidelines, including those applying to employee residential facilities, where applicable; and that it has agreed in writing to comply with NIKE's factory/vendor health and safety standards.

7. **Environment.** (Contractor) certifies that it complies with applicable country environmental regulations; and that it has agreed in writing to comply with NIKE's specific vendor/factory environmental policies and procedures, which are based on the concept of continuous improvement in processes and programs to reduce the impact on the environment.

8. **Documentation and Inspection.** (Contractor) agrees to maintain on file such documentation as may be needed to demonstrate compliance with this Code of Conduct, and further agrees to make these documents available for NIKE or its designated auditor's inspection upon request.

Analysis of Writing in the Workplace: NIKE Code of Conduct

NIKE is one of the most visible companies in the world today. Michael Jordan is featured in NIKE ads, and the company has become famous for its trademark slogan "Just Do It!" Concern has been raised recently, however, about the working conditions in NIKE manufacturing plants in China, Vietnam, and Indonesia. Some critics have called NIKE's labor practices into question, charging that its plants are really sweatshops, where workers are abused by managers. This bad publicity prompted NIKE to hire Andrew Young, former United Nations Ambassador and long-time civil rights activist, to assess whether NIKE plants were in fact complying with NIKE's Code of Conduct.

The NIKE Code of Conduct lays out general principles NIKE expects all the contractors who run NIKE plants to abide by. As you read it, consider the specific standards of conduct the Code sets forth.

GOING ON-LINE

Andrew Young's Report on the NIKE Code of Conduct

You can find Andrew Young's final report and recommendations, as well as NIKE's response, by visiting www.nike.com. As you read Young's report, notice how he seeks to establish the credibility of the report. Notice too his explanation of why he doesn't treat wages and living standards.

Do you find these two sections persuasive? Why or why not?

The Vietnam Labor Watch and and the Vietnamese Political Action Committee have chronicled what they believe to be labor abuses at the NIKE plant in Vietnam. For their side, visit www.vietnamlaborwatch.org and www.vpac-usa.org.

WRITING SAMPLES

The two following writing samples come directly from the workplace. The first "Properly Dispose of Confidential Information" was posted by management to remind workers to treat confidential documents carefully. The second is a memo written by one worker to her colleagues. What seems in each case to call for writing? Explain how you think each piece of writing fits into the workplace. Consider how the voices, or tones, of these samples relate to the writer's purpose and readers. What does this tone of voice indicate about the relationship the writer seeks to establish with readers? Do you think these pieces are effective? Why or why not?

WRITING INVENTORY

List some types of writing you have done in the workplace. Include even simple genres of writing, such as filling out forms. What kinds of situations called on you to do these particular kinds of writing at work? How did the writing fit into the overall organization of work? If you have had various jobs, has the writing you've done differed? In a workplace, people fill various roles—workers, supervisors, clients, and so on. How did your writing relate to the roles you played. How did it position you in relation to those in other roles? What conclusions, if any, can you draw about the role of writing in the workplace? How does the call to write in the workplace differ from calls to write outside the workplace?

WRITING IN THE PUBLIC SPHERE

In the broadest sense, writing in the public sphere refers to all the writing we encounter in public places—official signs (street names, building names and addresses, parking signs, and so on), notices put out by companies and groups (posters announcing meetings and concerts, billboards advertising movies and products, leaflets seeking support for causes, and so on), books, newspa-

MEMORANDUM

TO: The thief that has been stealing pens from the IBM.

FROM: A very angry phone receptionist who is constantly putting more pens near
               the IBM and who is perpetually frustrated with the fact that whenever
               he/she goes to use them they are missing

RE: A way to remedy this situation.

DATE: The summer

Over the course of the summer it has come to my attention that pens were mysterioulsy
vanishing from the IBM computer. This action causes significant trouble when one tries
to take a PHONE MESSAGE or attempts to take a START and commit it to memory.
Instead of philosofizing about the possible criminals who insist on making my life harder (i
know who you are!), I simply ask that if you, per chance, notice the absence of a pen or
pencil near the IBM that you take it upon yourself to correct this mishap and replace one
immediately.

I thank you for your time and efforts in this matter.

pers, and magazines, and even the graffiti spray-painted on the sides of buildings and subway cars.
In addition to being enormously wide ranging, public writing in this sense obviously overlaps with
writing done in other contexts.

This section focuses on a particular use of writing in the public sphere—namely, writing intended to inform and influence members of the public on matters of concern to all. In this sense
of the term, the public sphere can be understood as the context in which people deliberate on the
important issues of the day and seek to shape the direction of society.

Writing produced and disseminated by the mass media—books, newspapers, magazines, journals of opinion, radio, and television—is an important element of writing in the public sphere. The
media, after all, links us to others in society, provides information, and helps shape opinions and
attitudes.

Also important contributors to writing in the public sphere are the many advocacy groups.
These include environmental groups, animal rights groups, labor unions, business groups, political parties, groups that oppose abortion and groups that support abortion rights, groups for and
against gun control—the list goes on and on. Some of these advocacy groups are concerned with
a single issue; others have a broad agenda. Some are active at the local level; others at the national
level. What these diverse groups share is a concern with social issues that leads them to writing
and other actions that can shape public opinion and change society.

People can also contribute as individuals to writing in the public sphere. For example, a person may feel moved to write a letter to the editor of a newspaper or to a Senator or Congressman.

Make a difference through citizen involvement 3 Welfare Reform: Is the glass half full? 4

What's Up with Volunteers 6 Walk For Literacy Results 6 Coming Events 8

Pathfinder

A bimontly newsletter for friends and supporters of Dorcas Place

Winter 199

The faces of welfare reform

A sea-change is transforming the American societal landscape and the Dorcas Place community is standing squarely in the vanguard of that change. On Aug. 22, when President Clinton signed into law a bill eliminating the AFDC and reversing six decades of federal guarantees of cash assistance to low-income families with children, the response throughout the human services community was fear and deep concern for the populations we serve.

At Dorcas Place, we focus on the half-full glass, not the half-empty one. For 16 years, the our mission has focused on helping adults learn how to read and write, incorporating these literacy lessons into basic life skills that lead to employment, self-respect and self-sufficiency. If these are the stated goals of welfare reform, Dorcas Place is well ahead of the curve and positioned to help our students meet this new challenge.

In this special edition of our newsletter, we put a fac on welfare reform. The stories you will read in these pages are typical of the students who come through our doors. And it validates our conviction that when given the tools to learn and the encouragement to se achievable goals, our students can and will find the way to a better life for themselves and their children.

Electronic communication is greatly increasing people's access to the public sphere. With news-groups and web sites devoted to social and political issues, it is now possible for individuals to exchange views with people in other parts of the country or the world.

Writing in the public sphere poses special challenges. The broad purpose of such writing is to influence opinion—often precisely on the issues that most divide society. Moreover, in contrast to writing in other contexts, where the intended readers are familiar to the writer, writing in the public sphere is often addressed to a large and unknown audience. Writers need to imagine this audience in their minds in order to figure out what relationships to establish with readers, how to establish this relationship, what voice to use, and what genre. These challenges, of course, are inseparable from the considerable benefits of writing in the public sphere: writers have the opportunity to inform and influence their readers on issues they truly care about.

Analysis of Writing in the Public Sphere: Newsletter

The following is the cover page of a bi-monthly newsletter Pathfinder for students, staff, friends, and supporters of Dorcas Place, a non-profit adult literacy center in Providence, Rhode Island that provides educational services, job training, and parenting advice for poor and low-income women. Dorcas Place is typical of many non-profit organizations that operate in the public sphere. Formed to address particular social needs, Dorcas Place works with both government and business but is independent of both. It has a paid staff but also relies extensively on volunteers—including high school and college students—and its own fund raising.

As you can see, the cover story concerns changes in the welfare system signed into law by President Clinton in August 1996. What does Dorcas Place's attitude toward welfare reform seem to be? How does the newsletter explain the relation between Dorcas Place's mission and changes in the welfare system? Why do you think the writers of the newsletter felt called on to address these changes? From reading the table of contents that appears above the newsletter's title, what other purposes do you think the newsletter is intended to serve? Do you think it has different purposes for different readers? Explain your answer.

WRITING SAMPLES

Consider these two samples of writing in the public sphere. The first is a flyer from the Teamsters union urging shoppers not to buy from a business that purchases non-union products. The second is a wall mural from East Los Angeles that comes from a strong Chicano mural tradition in California and the Southwest that goes back to the Mexican Revolution of 1910-1917 and the work of muralists such as Diego Rivera and David Siqueiros. Unlike graffiti, wall murals are considered to be public art whose messages celebrate Chicano
history and speak for the Chicano community.

Notice key differences in how these two examples of public writing are disseminated. The flyer was handed to individuals by Teamster members in front of a business establishment, while the mural is painted on a wall for all passers-by to see. Taking these differences into account, consider how each writing responds to a call to write. Who are the intended readers? What sorts of relationships do the writers establish with readers? Do these writings differ from the other writing samples you've looked at? How would you account for these differences?

WRITING INVENTORY

What, if any, writing in the public sphere are you doing currently or have you done in the past? Think of occasions when you gave a speech or wrote a leaflet or contributed to a newsletter or circulated a petition. Explain what set of circumstances called on you to write and what you were trying to accomplish by writing. How did you know what to do in the writing—what genre to use and what tone of voice?

WRITING IN SCHOOL

At first glance it may appear that writing in school is a relatively uncomplicated matter—a call to write that comes from a teacher, who is also the audience, with the purpose of showing how well the student understands the material. From this perspective, school writing fits into the context of schooling in which students are in the role of performers, teachers in the role of evaluators, and writing serves as the basis for ranking students according to the prevailing reward system of grades.

Writing in school, however, is more complex than this description allows us to see. For one thing, students do lots of writing for their own purposes that is not directly evaluated by teachers—taking notes in lectures, for example, or writing summaries of textbook chapters to study for tests. And papers that students turn in to teachers for grades may not include all the writing—of research notes, outlines, first drafts, false starts, and so on—a student has done to complete the assignment.

Second, even when students are writing for grades, they are not just displaying knowledge of the material. They must also take into account how the different academic fields call for different genres of writing—a lab report in chemistry, for example, or a critical essay on a poem for English. Just as the various professions require different genres of writing, so do different subjects in school. For this reason, learning a subject is in part learning how chemists, literary critics, historians, psychologists, engineers, and so on use writing in their respective fields of study.

Analysis of Writing in School: Samples from Grade 3

Before we look at the kind of writing college teachers ask students to write, let's stop for a moment and think about whether writing as a display of learning is the only kind of writing you have been called on to do in school.

Here are two samples of writing drawn from a student in a recent third grade class.

SAMPLE ONE:

I will not forget my name and number.
I will not forget my name and number.
I will not forget my name and number.
I will not forget my name and number.
I will not forget my name and number.

SAMPLE TWO:

Dear Dad,

I had to stand in the lunch room today. I am very, very
sorry. Mrs. Bailey is horrified. I love you.
Love,
Martha

In both instances, the writing is intended not to show what the student knows but to punish and to change the student's behavior. The teacher-student relationship is essentially that of disciplinarian and culprit. The second one, addressed to the student's father, puts the student in a relationship both to teacher and parent in an act of remorse.

The same student also wrote the following piece:

SAMPLE THREE:

My Big and Small Dream

One morning when I woke up I was a monster with pink eyes, purple faded hair, a green body, and a fluorescent yellow face. I went downstairs and ate the stove, the fridg, and all the food. I started shrinking. I was so surprised, then for the next five days I stopped eating. Then to my surprise I was as big and as high as the sky. Since I was big I bumped into a tree that was smaller than me. Also, by mistake, I stepped on a house with people having a party. Then I went to bed and the next morning I woke up and was myself again.

Here, of course, the point of the call to write is neither to punish nor to show mastery of subject matter. Instead, this is a piece of creative writing, in which the student was called on to use her imagination and her sense of what a story should sound like.

WRITING SAMPLES

The following two pieces were both written by the same student, the first in freshman year in high school and the second in freshman year in college. As you read, compare the two pieces of writing. How does the writer seem to understand the assignments? What does the writer's purpose seem to be in each instance? How kind of relationship does she establish with her reader and her subject? Are there features that seem to distinguish college from high school writing? Does the college writing seem to be more "mature" or "advanced" than the high school writing?

The revival of the modern Olympic Games was influenced by the politics of the late nineteenth century. The Baron de Coubertin had two motives in reviving the Olympic Games. After France lost the Franco-Prussian War, a gloom set over all of France. The Baron wanted to revive the games to inspire the youth of France. In the lycees of France, the intellectual aspects dominated the school There were not physical education classes and very little, if any, athletic training. The Baron wanted both athletics and education in the schools. When creating these perfect schools of France, he used the ephebes of ancient Greece and the public schools of England. When education and athletics played a major role in the young boy's lives, there would be a perfect school. The Baron's other purpose in recreating the Olympics was to promote world peace by gathering all the countries together.

Though the Baron's intentions were to produce world amity he did the opposite. Instead of peaceful relations the games created many conflicts. In 1936, for example, there was much conflict at the summer games in Berlin. The problem of the games was racism. Adolf Hitler wrote the following in Mein Kampf, while in prison in 1924. "Americans ought to be ashamed of themselves for letting their medals be won by Negroes. I myself would never even shake hands with one of them." Adolf Hitler, the leader of Germany at the time was clearly very racist. When Jesse Owens, a black American won the gold medal in the 100 meter dash Hitler was infuriated. Hitler refused to congratulate him. Political incidents like these increased over the course of the Olympic Games.

In 1968 the politics shifted from racism to protests against racism. Before the games sprinter Tommie Smith and other students suggested to boycott the Olympics because of the racial conditions in the United States. Although Tommie Smith went to the Mexico City, he expressed his feelings on racism there as well. During the ceremony for the two hundred meter dash the "Star Spangled Banner" was played. At that time, both and John Carlos staged a protest. They were suspended by the International Olympic Committee and ordered to leave the country.

Another incident that politics played a major role in was the boycott of the Moscow Olympics in 1980. After Russian troops were sent into Afghanistan in 1979, President Jimmy Carter proposed that the games be rescheduled and moved to another location. The response of the International Olympic Committee was that "politics should be of no influence in the Olympic Games." After failing to reschedule and move the games to another location, the President and sixty-four other countries boycotted. Of the one-hundred and forty-five nations that were invited to take part in the games, only eighty-one entered. Some nations that boycotted the games were West Germany, China, Japan, Canada, Kenya, Australia, New Zealand, Great Britain, France, and Italy. Though many athletes within the United States protested that politics should be of no factor in the games, Carter refused to reconsider. By boycotting the Olympics, Carter did not get the troops out of Afghanistan, but simply increased the tension between the United States and the Soviet Union.

In 1984, in response to the boycott four years earlier, Russia, along with East Germany, Czechoslovakia, Poland, Hungary, Bulgaria, and Cuba, declined the invitation to participate in the summer games in Los Angeles. The Soviets denied the boycott was revenge, but argued that the publicity and ten billion dollar cost of the games were outrageous. They also argued that the security in Los Angeles was not sufficient.

In the most recent games, politics as usual, influenced the games. The games were held in South Korea. Though the bid was won fairly by South Korea, North Korea felt they deserved to be the co-hosts. Fearing what North Korea might do out of jealousy, South Korea had 120,000 specially trained antiterroist fighters, 700,000 men of the Republic of Korea's armed forces, 40,000 permanently stationed United States soldiers and marines, and 100,000 United States sailors aboard aircraft carriers patrolling the Korean shores. In addition, there was 63 armed personnel for each of the 13,000 athletes. Both the United States and South Korea had to take drastic measures to secure the safety of the athletes. If politics played no role in the Olympics none of those measures would be necessary

When Baron de Coubertin revived the Olympic Games he had nothing but good intentions. His hope was that the Olympics could be a place where people from all over the world could gather together in peace doing what they all had in common. Though his intentions were good, politicians took advantage of the Olympics. They used the games as chances to boycott what they thought was wrong and, in other cases, as revenge. Jesse Owens and all the athletes that were not able to go to the 1980 and 1984 Olympics suffered from politics. The purpose of the Olympics has changed into something that is not right. Let's leave the politics to the politicians and competition to the athletes.

1. What is the role of   rtrayed through the
worship of the Mador   nic identity of the
Italian community of

As I read through the Madonna of 115th Street; Faith and Community in Italian Harlem, 1880-1950, and the important role that popular religion played in the role of defining ethnic identity in the Italian community of East Harlem, I could not help but to think of my hometown, Cranston and the similarities that popular religion played there as well. As I read about the feasts of the Madonna of 115th street I was reminded of the Feast of St. Mary in Cranston and the almost identical origins of the feasts. In Cranston, the feast of St. Mary was started to honor La Madonna della Citta or the Madonna of the city, who was from a small village in southern Italy where many of the first Cranstonians originated. It also served as a distinguishing feature from other Catholics in the area; in essance serving as an ethnic identity. Both of the creations of the Madonnas and the feasts in their honor were popular religion. Popular religion was an important role in shaping ethnic identities in Italian communities.

Both of the feasts in Cranston and East Harlem's purpose were to honor the Madonnas, each from a specific place in Italy, where many of the honorees were from. The Madonna served as a shared history in the new world and gave immigrants something to serve as a reference point. Each immigrant could relate to the Madonna and trusted her with their most sacred prayers. The Madonna listened to the needs of the newly arrived immigrants. As quoted from the work, The Madonna of 115th Street, the author says of immigrant Italians, "the Italian feels safer when he plays homage to the patron saint of his hometown or village who in the past was considerate to the people."

The feast of the Madonna of 115th Street began in the summer of 1881 when immigrants from the town of Polla formed a mutual aid society. One of the functions of the mutual aid society was to give unemployment and burial benefits to immigrants. But a larger function of the mutual aid societies and the feasts that it started was to gather immigrants and preserve as well as observe traditional customs in the new world. Because mutual aid societies were unique to Italian Roman Catholics they served as an model for ethnic identity. Furthermore, Catholics of other ethnic backgrounds such as Irish Catholics, were hostile to feasts of the Madonna of 115th street. Orsi speaks of an attack published in the Catholic World in 1888. The attack criticized the shrines, holy cards and pagan superstitions and "devotions" of the Italian Roman Catholic and the ignorance for "great faith of religion." These attacks on Italian Catholics served to further separate Italians from other Catholics and create a stronger ethnic identity.

In addition the building of certain specifically Italian churches, (chiesa), which again, is popular religion, in East Harlem served as another ethnic identity. Italians as a group gathered to build their own churches. The building was a gathering of everyone, of an ethnic group to create something that they could call their own. As the book noted, junkmen and icemen donated their carts and horses to help manage the burden of building materials as people prepared refreshments for the workers. This act was substantial in the creation of ethnic identity.

During the late nineteenth century, popular religion served as an ethnic identity for Italians in East Harlem, Cranston, RI, as well as in other parts of the eastern seaboard. The creation of Madonnas from hometowns as well as feas:s for their honor were the most unique feature and distinguishing characteristic. The separation of Italian Catholics from other Catholics such as Irish Catholics provided further ethnic identity in the America.

ETHICS OF WRITING

The Problem of Cheating

Cheating in school refers to various types of academic misconduct: copying from someone's paper during a test; sneaking a cheat sheet into an exam; presenting as your own work something written by a friend or relative, lifted from a book or article, purchased from a term paper company, or pulled out of a file of old papers at a fraternity or sorority house; falsifying lab results or other research data; failing to acknowledge sources you have used; doing other students' work for them so that they get the credit.

These forms of academic misconduct, of course, are wrong not simply because if you get caught you will be punished. More important, such misconduct violates the principles of trust and honesty that intellectual work and public deliberation depend on. Whether readers are teachers, professional colleagues, or fellow citizens, they assume that what they are reading—whether they agree or disagree with it, think it is of high or

inferior quality—is the honest result of the writer's work. Otherwise there can be no genuine engagement between writers and readers, no real joint effort of writers and readers to think through intellectual issues and public problems. In this sense, cheating is ethically wrong because it makes it impossible for people to cooperate with each other and to negotiate the differences that divide them.

At the same time, a number of recent surveys on college campuses show that while students understand what cheating is and know that it is wrong, they are often willing to tolerate it on the part of others (and sometimes to engage in it themselves). One of the most striking results of such surveys is that a majority of students believe reporting students who cheat is just as bad as cheating itself—a form of disloyalty to peers. What do you see as the ethical issues involved here? Can you imagine any circumstances in which cheating is justified? Should college honor codes oblige students to report others who cheat?

WRITING INVENTORY

Make a list of the different kinds or genres of writing that you've done in school. Think back to grammar school and junior high as well as to high school. Were you ever called to write as an act of punishment? Did teachers assign creative writing? Did teachers ever ask you to keep a journal as part of your coursework? Did you ever do "free writing" or brainstorming in class? What kinds of essays, reports, and research papers were you assigned? Did you make posters or collages? Did you use the Internet or the World Wide Web? And don't forget the notes you took in class or from your reading.

Look at the list you've written. How much variety do you see in this writing—more or less than you would have expected? How do your purposes vary among the examples you've listed? What relationship did your writing put you into with your teachers? To what extent did you do writing not assigned by the teacher? What kind of writing did you do where the teacher was not the intended reader? How much did the tone of your writing vary and what accounted for these variations in tone? How did your writing patterns change from elementary school to high school and college? Compare the writing you have done in school with the writing you have done in everyday life, in the workplace, and in the public sphere. How would you explain differences and similarities?

The next section offers another way to reflect on a particular writing experience and what it meant to you.

LITERACY NARRATIVES: Telling Writing Stories

Literacy narratives are stories of how people encounter and make sense of writing. You can find literacy narratives in memoirs and autobiographies, such as the passage from The Narrative of the Life of Frederick Douglass reprinted here.

Literacy narratives offer rich descriptions of the various settings in which writing occurs, the various ways people use writing, and the various social purposes writing can serve. Some writing teachers, such as Linda Brodkey, have composed their own literacy narratives. A selection from her essay "Writing on the Bias" is included in the following readings. Literacy narratives are sometimes called "autoethnographies" because they are self-studies ("auto") of the cultural context and meaning ("ethnography") of writing.

Writing teachers have also started to ask students to compose their own literacy narratives— to recall a particular moment in which writing figured prominently and to reflect on its meaning. Included in the readings is student Russell Kim's narrative "Petitioning the Powers."

Writing a literacy narrative is one way to pull together some of the ideas in this chapter. If you have responded to the Writing Inventories throughout the chapter, you can use these responses to start thinking of a story about writing you want to tell.

From Narrative of the Life of Frederick Douglass

Very soon after I went to live with Mr. and Mrs. Auld, she very kindly commenced to teach me the A, B, C. After I had learned this, she assisted me in learning to spell words of three or four letters. Just at this point of my progress, Mr. Auld found out what was going on, and at once forbade Mrs. Auld to instruct me further, telling her, among other things, that it was unlawful, as well as unsafe, to teach a slave to read. To use his own words, further, he said, "If you give a nigger an inch, he will take an ell. A nigger should know nothing but to obey his master—to do as he is told to do. Learning would *spoil* the best nigger in the world. Now," said he, "if you teach that nigger (speaking of myself) how to read, there would be no keeping him. It would forever unfit him to be a slave. He would at once become unmanageable, and of no value to his master. As to himself, it could do him no good, but a great deal of harm. It would make him discontented and unhappy." These words sank deep into my heart, stirred up sentiments within that lay slumbering, and called into existence an entirely new train of thought. It was a new and special revelation, explaining dark and mysterious things, with which my youthful understanding had struggled, but struggled in vain. I now understood what had been to me a most perplexing difficulty—to wit, the white man's power to enslave the black man. It was a grand achievement, and I prized it highly. From that moment, I understood the pathway from slavery to freedom. It was just what I wanted, and I got it at a time when I the least expected it. Whilst I was saddened by the thought of losing the aid of my kind mistress, I was gladdened by the invaluable instruction which, by the merest accident, I had gained from my master. Though conscious of the difficulty of learning without a teacher, I set out with high hope, and a fixed purpose, at whatever cost of trouble, to learn how to read. The very decided manner with which he spoke, and strove to impress his wife with the evil consequences of giving me instruction, served to convince me that he was deeply sensible of the truths he was uttering. It gave me the best assurance that I might rely with the utmost confidence on the results which, he said, would flow from teaching me to read. What he most dreaded, that I most desired. What he most loved, that I most hated. That which to him was a great evil, to be carefully shunned, was to me a great good, to be diligently sought; and the argument which he so warmly urged, against my learning to read, only served to inspire me with a desire and determination to learn. In learning to read, I owe almost as much to the bitter opposition of my master, as to the kindly aid of my mistress. I acknowledge the benefit of both.

I had resided but a short time in Baltimore before I observed a marked difference, in the treatment of

If you believe family folklore, I began writing the year before I entered kindergarten, when I conducted a census (presumably inspired by a visit from the 1950 census taker). I consider it a story about writing rather than, say, survey research because while it has me asking the neighbors when they were going to die, in my mind's eye I see myself as a child recording their answers—one to a page—in a Big Chief tablet. As I remember, my mother sometimes told this story when she and her sister were of a mind to reflect on their children's behavior. Since in my family the past provided the only possible understanding of the present, the story was probably my mother's way of talking about her middle daughter's indiscriminate extroversion and perfectionism. On the one hand, these inborn traits would explain my performance in school, for teachers like gregarious children who approach all tasks as worth their full attention. On the other hand, my mother, who claims to have found me engaged in conversations with strangers on more than one occasion, would have been worrried about such wholesale friendliness. Innocence was not first among the virtues my mother admired in her children. That I view the census story as my mother's does not erase faint outlines I also see of myself as a little girl who leaves her mother's house to travel the neighborhood under the protective mantle of writing.

Writing was the girl's passport to neighbors' houses, where she whiled away the long and lonely days chatting up the grown-ups when the older children were at school, and otherwise entertained herself with this newfound power over adults, who responded to her even if they did not also answer her question. As naive as the question may seem, as startling and by some standards even unmannerly, a child asking grown-ups when they were going to die was probably considered a good deal less intrusive in the white, working-class neighborhood in the small Midwestern city where I grew up than the federal government's sending a grown man to ask questions about income, education, and religion. Forty-some years later, stories are all that remain of that childhood experience. I remember nothing: not if I ever met an official census taker, not if I believed grown-ups *knew* when they would die, not if I was a four-year-old preoccupied by death, not even if I took a survey. And while it seems to me of a piece with other family narratives explaining human behavior as inborn, whether it is a "true" story interests me a good deal less than how it may have affected me and my writing.

I would like to think that the story of my preschool experience sustained me through what I now remember as many lean years of writing in school. Yet when I look back I see only a young girl intent on getting it right, eager to produce flawless prose, and not a trace of the woman who years later will write that school writing is to writing as catsup is to tomatoes: as junk food is to food. What is nutritious has been eliminated (or nearly so) in processing. What remains is not just empty but poisonous fare because some people so crave junk that they prefer it to food; and their preference is then used by those who, since they profit by selling us catsup as a vegetable and rules as writing, lobby to keep both on the school menu. Surely a child possessed of a Big Chief tablet would be having a very different experience of writing than the one who keeps her lines straight and stays out of margins, memorizes spelling and vocabulary words, fills in blanks, makes book reports, explicates poems and interprets novels, and turns it all in on time. In the neighborhood I was fed food and conversation in exchange for writing. At school I learned to trade my words for grades and degrees, in what might be seen as the academic equivalent of dealing in futures—speculation based on remarkably little information about my prospects as an academic commodity.

"Petitioning the Powers"

Russell Kim

I think I really started to understand something about how writing actually works in the world when I was in the eighth grade. If you can remember what eighth grade is like, you might recall what hot shits kids think they are at that age. They've left childhood and are briefly at the top of the world before they go to high school and begin all over again as freshmen. That's how we were. And one of the things we got into was knowing our rights. This was a combination of what we heard on Clash albums and what we learned in American history. We knew that grownups couldn't just walk all over us. We knew we had rights and could petition the powers that be to change things.

Along with my friend Mike, I was a member of our junior high school chorus. This was a big deal because the chorus director, Mr. DeSouza, was a legendary figure in our community. Every year for the past fifteen years or so, he took the chorus on a trip to an international competition, held in places like Toronto, Miami, San Francisco, and once in London. Every year the chorus won a gold medal. But Mike and I thought Mr. DeSouza was getting out of step with the times and that our repertoire of songs needed some updating. We mentioned this to him but he was not responsive. So, naturally, knowing our rights, we took the logical next step.

We went over to Mike's house after school and wrote a petition that asked Mr. DeSouza to add a few contemporary songs to the chorus's repertoire. We printed the petition on Mike's dad's laser printer and circulated it the next day among chorus members and other students as well to sign, figuring the chorus belonged to the school and the added names would make us look good.

We thought that Mr. DeSouza would see the numbers and meet right away to negotiate a settlement. We weren't asking for all that much, so we didn't think it would be a hassle. Wrong. The day after we left the petition in Mr. DeSouza's box Mike and I got called into the principal's office. Mr. Boisvert the principal said we had a big problem. Mr. DeSouza was totally offended and insulted by the petition and had threatened to quit as chorus director, which would be a disaster because he was one of the most successful chorus directors in the country. And it was all our fault. We had "gone too far this time." When Mike and I said it was our right—and the American way—to petition to change things peacefully, Mr. Boisvert looked right through us and said we weren't being fair to Mr. DeSouza, to the chorus, or to the school. We could write petitions later, when we were adults and could "accept responsibility for our actions" (whatever that meant). We had a choice: we could either apologize and stay on the chorus or quit the chorus. No deals.

The fact that Mike and I quit, missing a great trip the chorus took that year to Puerto Rico, isn't exactly the point. Looking back on it, I'm interested in how writing a petition created such a crisis. Neither Mike nor I had imagined that Mr. DeSouza would react as he did. We certainly didn't intend to hurt his feelings or insult him. We thought we were just acting on our rights. But more important the principal showed us that in fact we didn't have any rights. To him, we were still little kids and while we were expected to learn all about the Declaration of Independence and the Bill of Rights, we were really dependents. Knowing your rights was, as he said, for "later."

WRITING ASSIGNMENT

This can be a short writing assignment—one to two pages—or longer, depending on your teacher's instructions. To understand the call to write and your purpose, think of the word "telling" in "Telling Writing Stories" in a double sense: you need to tell a good story that makes a telling point.

Select a particular moment or episode in your experience that involves writing. You may have been in the role of a writer or a reader or both. Tell the story of this literacy event and explain what it reveals about the meaning and use of writing.

DIRECTIONS

1. Read the sample literacy narratives. Notice how each tells a story and the extent to which each also makes a telling point that explains something about the meanings and uses of reading and writing.

   As you can see, literacy narratives deal with particular moments in which people encounter writing. They focus on moments that, for one reason or another, are especially revealing about an individual's personal experience with writing—when something about the nature and function of writing came to light in a dramatic way. They do not attempt to give an overall history of an individual's development as a reader and writer. Nor do they give advice about learning to write. Instead, they analyze and interpret a particular event involving writing.

2. Select a particular encounter with writing. To do this, begin by reviewing any responses you have written to the Writing Inventories. Then, make a list of three or four moments or events involving writing that seem interesting to you, whether or not they appear in your responses.

   Look for encounters with writing that reveal powerful feelings or strong responses on the part of the people involved. Look for misunderstandings, conflicts, resolutions, or alliances in which writing plays a key role. Look for instances of writing that assert or impose personal and group identities and consider what role these identities play in social institutions.

   If you have time, discuss the three or four moments you are considering with a partner. See what seems most interesting to another person. Use this information to help you make a decision about the writing story you want to tell.

3. Analyze the particular encounter with writing. Here are some questions to take into account:

   - What is the setting of the encounter with writing? Who was involved? What type of writing did the encounter center around? What was your role? Were you primarily a reader or a writer or both?
   - What relationships to other people did the writing involve? What role did writing play in establishing, maintaining, or changing these relationships?
   - What relationships to cultural activities and social institutions did the writing involve? What role did writing play in organizing cultural activities and in maintaining or disrupting social institutions?

4. Write an account of the literacy event. Weave into your literacy narrative an explanation of what the moment reveals about the meaning and use of writing.

CHAPTER
TWO

READING AND WRITING:
THE CRITICAL CONNECTION

Part of learning to write involves learning how to read in a special way. There are, of course, many purposes for reading—reading a novel for enjoyment, consulting a user's manual to program a VCR, checking the newspaper for today's weather report. The reading strategies presented in this chapter are typical of those used by working writers, when the purpose of reading is to find out what others have said about a topic or an issue the writer plans to write about.

Whether the writing task is completing a research paper in a history class, preparing a marketing strategy for a new product, or writing a flyer for or against a controversial law, you need to gather the best information available and include in your thinking a wide range of views on the topic at hand. The reading strategies presented in this chapter can help you handle these and many other kinds of writing tasks. Here is a quick overview of the strategies and their purposes:

- Previewing: to identify the type of writing, the writer's purposes, and what you can expect from the reading.

- Organizing information: to make sure you understand what you are reading and to create a written record you can return to when you start to write.

- Responding: to find what is personally meaningful for you, to raise questions, and to clarify your own sense of the issues.

- Analyzing: to examine how the writer seeks to accomplish his or her purposes and how the parts of a piece of writing fit together.

- Evaluating: to determine the value of what you are reading—whether it is credible, authoritative, and persuasive.

PREVIEWING

Getting the most out of what you read depends in part on identifying the genre of writing and the writer's purposes—whether to explain concept, argue a point, or provide an artful re-creation of experience. As readers get a sense of what the writer is up to, they adjust their reading strategies accordingly.

Take, for example, textbooks, encyclopedias, and other reference books intended to present the best currently available information on a subject. Because you recognize this type of well-researched informative writing, you expect to find a reliable account of what experts consider to be the present state of knowledge—at least at the time the writing was published. And you quite likely already know some of the reading strategies that can help you understand this kind of writing—underlining, taking notes, and summarizing.

You may also have noticed when you read the newspaper that different types of writing require different reading strategies. You can read a front page report on the 1997 flood of Grand Forks, North Dakota or a story in the business section on recent tele-communications mergers, for example, as informative accounts of these events—and use the strategies just listed to organize the information you find. In these instances, the purpose of reading is largely to extract information.

When you read an editorial on the op-ed page of the newspaper, however, you are likely to recognize that you have entered the realm of public debate. Although an editorial may provide information, like a news report does, it also puts forth an arguable position that relies on interpretation of that information. Thus, as you read, you need to figure out why the writer takes a particular position and whether you agree with it. To do that, you'll want to analyze the argument the writer presents and evaluate the underlying assumptions the writer makes.

A first step toward knowing what reading strategies to use, then, is to identify the genre of writing you are about to read by drawing on your prior experience. Putting what you are reading into a category—such as textbook chapter, encyclopedia article, news report, or editorial—can help you figure out what reading strategies are likely to be useful. (Part 2 contains discussion of various genres of writing and their characteristic features.)

1. What does the writer's purpose seem to be? What does the title convey to you? Is there a statement that describes the writer's purpose explicitly? Or is it implied?
2. What does the genre of writing seem to be? Can you put the reading into a category of writing you are familiar with? What other writings does it remind you of? What features do they have in common?
3. If the reading seems unfamiliar, how can you get a handle on it? Are there any editorial comments, prefaces, author notes, or blurbs on book covers that provide background information for your reading? Is there someone you can talk to for more information—another student, your teacher, a librarian, etc.?
4. What is your purpose for reading? What use are you planning to make of your reading?
5. What kind of reading strategies best fit the writer's purpose as you understand it?

Preview the first page of "Out of Africa Again . . . and Again?" to see how much you can figure out its genre and purpose.

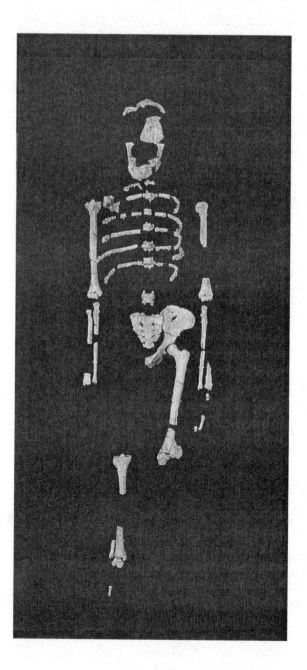

"LUCY" skeleton represents the best-known species of early hominid, or human precursor, *Australopithecus afarensis*, often characterized as a "bipedal chimpanzee." The 3.18-million-year-old skeleton is from the Hadar region of Ethiopia.

Out of Africa Again... and Again?

Africa is the birthplace of humanity.
But how many human species evolved there?
And when did they emigrate?

by Ian Tattersall

It all used to seem so simple. The human lineage evolved in Africa. Only at a relatively late date did early humans finally migrate from the continent of their birth, in the guise of the long-known species *Homo erectus,* whose first representatives had arrived in eastern Asia by around one million years ago. All later kinds of humans were the descendants of this species, and almost everyone agreed that all should be classified in our own species, *H. sapiens.* To acknowledge that some of these descendants were strikingly different from ourselves, they were referred to as "archaic *H. sapiens,*" but members of our own species they were nonetheless considered to be.

Such beguiling simplicity was, alas, too good to last, and over the past few years it has become evident that the later stages of human evolution have been a great deal more eventful than conventional wisdom for so long had it. This is true for the earlier stages, too, although there is still no reason to believe that humankind's birthplace was elsewhere than in Africa. Indeed, for well over the first half of the documented existence of the hominid family (which includes all upright-walking primates), there is no record at all outside that continent. But recent evidence does seem to indicate that it was not necessarily *H. erectus* who migrated from Africa—and that these peregrinations began earlier than we had thought.

A Confused Early History

Recent discoveries in Kenya of fossils attributed to the new species *Australopithecus anamensis* have now pushed back the record of upright-walking hominids to about 4.2 to 3.9 million years (Myr) ago. More dubious finds in Ethiopia, dubbed *Ardipithecus ramidus,* may extend this to 4.4 Myr ago or so. The *A. anamensis* fossils bear a strong resemblance to the later and far better known species *Australopithecus afarensis,* found at sites in Ethiopia and Tanzania in the 3.9- to 3.0-Myr range and most famously represented by the "Lucy" skeleton from Hadar, Ethiopia.

Lucy and her kind were upright walkers, as the structures of their pelvises and knee joints particularly attest, but they retained many ancestral features, notably in their limb proportions and in their hands and feet, that would have made them fairly adept tree climbers. Together with their ape-size brains and large, protruding faces, these characteristics have led many to call such creatures "bipedal chimpanzees." This is probably a fairly accurate characterization, especially given the increasing evidence that early hominids favored quite heavily wooded habitats. Their preferred way of life was evidently a successful one, for although these primates were less adept arborealists than the living apes and less efficient bipeds than later hominids, their basic "eat your cake and have it" adaptation endured for well

ORGANIZING INFORMATION

The strategies in this section can help you read virtually any genre of writing. Underlining, note taking, and summarizing are particularly useful when you want to make sure you understand the key concepts and major examples in what you are reading. When you are doing research, these basic reading strategies can help you compare and contrast the main ideas from diverse sources

• **Underlining** Underlining the writer's key points helps you identify and keep track of main ideas and important information. Underlining also enables you to return to a piece of writing and use the marked phrases to reconstruct its meaning quickly.

Underlining should be done selectively. If you underline everything, you will not be able to use your underlinings to recall the overall meaning of the writing. Selective underlining should enable you to identify where the writer presents important information, claims, evidence, interpretations, and conclusions.

In the following passage on Alfred Binet and the birth of IQ testing, notice how the underlinings in the first paragraph draw attention to Stephen Jay Gould's main ideas.

Stephen Jay Gould. "Alfred Binet and the Original Purpose of the Binet Scale."

This selection is taken from Stephen Jay Gould's book The Mismeasure of Man, an acclaimed study of the history of psychometrics, the science of measuring intelligence. As you will see, the passage describes how the French psychologist Alfred Binet developed IQ testing in the early 1900s.

There are a number of reasons you might want to learn about the birth of IQ testing. You could be doing research in a psychology course for a report on the various types of intelligence testing currently in use. Or in an American history course you might be trying to understand how cultural forces influenced intelligence testing in the early twentieth century. Or you could be developing an argument for or against the validity of IQ testing to influence a local school committee debate about the measures used to track students and whether they are culturally biased.

Notice that although the passage is part of the larger argument Gould makes about the theoretical inconsistencies and misuse of data in psychometrics, his purpose in the two paragraphs is largely informative. The reading strategies you use should follow accordingly.

WORKING TOGETHER: Underlining

Work together with two or three other students. Follow these directions:

1. On your own, underline the major ideas in the second paragraph in the passage.
2. Compare what you have underlined to the underlining others in your group have done. What are the main similarities and differences? Don't argue about who is right or wrong. Instead, explain to each other the decisions you have made in choosing phrases to underline. What do your underlinings bring to light? How do they compare to the emphases in others' underlinings?

• **Note Taking** Most students have a good deal of experience taking notes from lectures or readings. The purpose of taking notes is to record key points, whether to study for a test or compile research on a particular topic.

Good note taking involves organizing information in a form that makes it useful to you. When you take notes to create your own record of what you are reading, a list of phrases or short sentences should be enough, particularly if you arrange the list so that main points are displayed prominently and the major supporting evidence is clearly linked to the main point.

Notice in the sample notes how the reader has grouped the information under main headings and then uses dates to highlight key points.

In 1904 Binet was commissioned by the minister of public education to perform a study for a specific, practical purpose: to develop techniques for identifying those children whose lack of success in normal classrooms suggested the need for some form of special education. Binet chose a purely pragmatic course. He decided to bring together a large series of short tasks, related to everyday problems of life (counting coins, or assessing which face is "prettier," for example), but supposedly involving such basic processes of reasoning as "direction (ordering), comprehension, invention and censure (correction)" (Binet, 1909). Learned skills like reading would not be treated explicitly. The tests were administered individually by trained examiners who led subjects through the series of tasks, graded in their order of difficulty. Unlike previous tests designed to measure specific and independent "faculties" of mind, Binet's scale was a hodgepodge of diverse activities. He hoped that by mixing together enough tests of different abilities he would be able to abstract a child's general potential with a single score. Binet emphasized the empirical nature of his work with a famous dictum (1911, p. 329): "One might almost say, 'It matters very little what the tests are so long as they are numerous.'"

Binet published three versions of the scale before his death in 1911. The original 1905 edition simply arranged the tasks in an ascending order of difficulty. The 1908 version established the criterion used in measuring the so-called IQ ever since. Binet decided to assign an age level to each task, defined as the youngest age at which a child of normal intelligence should be able to complete the task successfully. A child began the Binet test with tasks for the youngest age and proceeded in sequence until he could no longer complete the tasks. The age associated with the last tasks he could perform became his "mental age," and his general intellectual level

was calculated by subtracting this mental age from his true chronological age. Children whose mental ages were sufficiently behind their chronological ages could then be identified for special educational programs, thus fulfilling Binet's charge from the ministry. In 1912 the German psychologist W. Stern argued that mental age should be divided by chronological age, not subtracted from it,* and the intelligence *quotient*, or IQ, was born.

SAMPLE NOTES ON "ALFRED BINET AND THE ORIGINAL PURPOSE OF THE BINET SCALE":

Binet's test
1904 — commissioned by minister of public education to identify **children in need of special education**
> Binet designs a series of everyday tasks to measure processes of reasoning instead of learned skills
>
> key assumption: tests results depend on using numerous activities rather than on a type of test

Developing the scale
1905 — tasks arranged in order of difficulty
1908 — Binet assigns age levels to each task mental age = highest task performed
calculates general intelligence by subtracting mental age from chronological age: gap indicates need for special education
1912 — Stern proposes dividing mental age from chronological age result: intelligence quotient or IQ

• **Summarizing**   A summary condenses what you have read in a clear and accurate way. Writing a good summary involves identifying the main idea and important supporting material, much in the way note taking does. But summaries go beyond notes because summaries call on you to explain the connections among points.

TO WRITE AN EFFECTIVE SUMMARY, FOLLOW THESE STEPS:

1. Read the text carefully, noticing its main point and supporting details.
2. If you have not done so already, underline and then use your underlinings to write notes.
3. Consult your underlinings and notes to identify the main point. If you can't find one, write your own.
4. Start writing your summary with a statement that identifies the writer and expresses the main point in your own words. Often by explaining the writer's purpose, you can capture the main idea.
5. Then consult your underlinings and notes to identify the most important supporting details. Rewrite these details in your own words, combining ideas when you can.
6. Check your summary to see if it holds together as a coherent piece of writing (and is not simply a series of unconnected statements). Add transitions where needed to make connections between parts of the summary.

Writing a summary can be quite useful, especially when you are reading difficult material, because it asks you to see the writer's point of view and to understand why he or she has arranged the material in a particular order. And when it comes to your own writing, there will be occasions when you'll need to incorporate summaries of other writer's ideas into your work.

Notice how the sample summary opens by explaining the author's purpose and then provides selected details on key developments in the test, using a series of parallel phrases—"In the original edition," "In the second edition," and "In 1912"—to open sentences and order the information.

SAMPLE SUMMARY OF "ALFRED BINET AND THE ORIGINAL PURPOSE OF THE BINET SCALE":

In The Mismeasure of Man, Stephen Jay Gould traces the origins of the IQ test to 1904, when the French psychologist Alfred Binet was asked to identify children in need of special education. To measure children's reasoning abilities, Binet developed a series of intelligence tests based on practical problems instead of learned skills. Binet believed that numerous short tasks could provide a single score to represent children's intellectual potential. In the original edition of the test (1905), Binet used a scoring scale that ranked the tasks in order of difficulty. In the second edition (1908), Binet gave each task an age level at which a normally intelligent child could perform it. Binet then used these age levels to determine a child's general intelligence by subtracting mental age (or the most difficult task a child could do) from chronological age. In 1912, the idea of an intelligence quotient or IQ appeared when Stern suggested mental age be divided by chronological age instead of subtracted from it.

ETHICS OF READING

BOREDOM AND PERSISTENCE

Going to college means that you will encounter a wide range of academic and professional writing, some of which may be specialized and technical. You may find at times that the reading you're assigned is intimidating and hard to follow. You may wonder what the writer is trying to prove or feel that he or she is splitting hairs. The writing may seem abstract, detached from the real world.

These are all symptoms of boredom, and the danger is that readers will give up at this point and say they weren't really interested in the first place. What is often the case, though, is not that readers aren't interested but rather that they are unfamiliar with the particular type of writing, its forms, specialized vocabularies, and ways of reasoning.

To act responsibly in college, the workplace, and the public domain, you need to read the writing that is pertinent and carries weight. An ethics of reading holds that readers need to give difficult material a chance. It's not simply a matter of being fair to the writer. By working on new and difficult material, you also, in effect, refuse to be alienated from it. And in this regard, you avoid the threat of boredom leading to the premature closure of communication.

RESPONDING

If the point of organizing information from your reading is to give you an accurate record of what the writer has said, responding to reading is meant to give you a record of your own reaction to what you are reading. Reading is not just a matter of extracting and organizing information. You can also make your reading personally meaningful by using the following strategies to write your way into the text.

• **Annotation** Annotations are comments that readers write in the margins of a piece of writing. The purposes of annotation are to help you engage what you are reading in an active way and to create a record of your experience as you come to grips with what you are reading.

There are no rules about annotation. You might

• write brief notes on what you see as major points

• agree or disagree with what the writer is saying

• refer to what the writer is doing at a particular point (making

a claim, giving an example, presenting statistical evidence,

refuting an opposing view, and so on)

• raise questions or voice confusion about something you need

to clarify

• draw connections to other things you have read or know about.

Notice how the annotations of the first paragraph of the passage from Gould both highlight the writer's key points and draw connections to the reader's ideas.

Sample annotation:

In 1904 Binet was commissioned by the minister of public education to perform a study for a specific, practical purpose: to develop techniques for identifying those children whose lack of success in normal classrooms suggested the need for some form of special education. Binet chose a purely pragmatic course. He decided to bring together a large series of short tasks, related to everyday problems of life (counting coins, or assessing which face is "prettier," for example), but supposedly involving such basic processes of reasoning as "direction (ordering), comprehension, invention and censure (correction)" (Binet, 1909). Learned skills like reading would not be treated explicitly. The tests were administered individually by trained examiners who led subjects through the series of tasks, graded in their order of difficulty. Unlike previous tests designed to measure specific and independent "faculties" of mind, Binet's scale was a hodgepodge of diverse activities. He hoped that by mixing together enough tests of different abilities he would be able to abstract a child's general potential with a single score. Binet emphasized the empirical nature of his work with a famous dictum (1911, p. 329): "One might almost say, 'It matters very little what the tests are so long as they are numerous.'"

Binet published three versions of the scale before his death in 1911. The original 1905 edition simply arranged the tasks in an ascending order of difficulty. The 1908 version established the criterion used in measuring the so-called IQ ever since. Binet decided to assign an age level to each task, defined as the youngest age at which a child of normal intelligence should be able to complete the task successfully. A child began the Binet test with tasks for the youngest age and proceeded in sequence until he could no longer complete the tasks. The age associated with the last tasks he could perform became his "mental age," and his general intellectual level

was calculated by subtracting this mental age from his true chronological age. Children whose mental ages were sufficiently behind their chronological ages could then be identified for special educational programs, thus fulfilling Binet's charge from the ministry. In 1912 the German psychologist W. Stern argued that mental age should be divided by chronological age, not subtracted from it, and the intelligence *quotient*, or IQ, was born.

• **Exploratory Writing**   Exploratory writing offers you a chance to explore your thoughts and feelings about the ideas in a piece of writing. You can use what you have read as a springboard to see where your thoughts lead you.

The only direction is that you begin with what you have just read and write non-stop for a pre-determined amount of time, say five or ten minutes. The idea is to build up momentum, so don't stop to revise, edit, or correct anything you have written. Don't worry about whether your ideas are consistent or contradictory. Just see where your writing takes you.

Sample Exploratory Writing:

IQ tests have this mystique about measuring people's intelligence and finding out who is a genius. You hear kids in school talking about who has a high IQ and who doesn't. So I was interested to read that the origins of the IQ test had a much more modest purpose, namely to identify students in need of special education. It seems that Alfred Binet just put together these tasks in a kind of scattergun way to get some insight about children's potential. This seems to me very different than the way IQ tests are being used today, as if they were this standard, objective measure of intelligence.

ANALYZING

Analysis means breaking something down into its constituent parts and determining how the parts fit together to make up the whole. Chemists, for example, break down water molecules into their constituent parts—two atoms of hydrogen and one of oxygen or H O—and they use this information to study how the chemical bonds that hold the parts together are formed. In similar fashion, you can analyze a piece of writing to identify the parts and what holds them together.

The purpose of analyzing written texts is to help you see
what connections exist between the paragraphs or sections of text, what lines of reasoning connect the facts and generalizations, and what assumptions underlie the piece as a whole. Analyzing these connections can deepen your understanding of the writer's purpose and position.

"Distancing the Homeless."

Jonathan Kozol.

The following passage from Jonathan Kozol's essay "Distancing the Homeless," which appeared in the Yale Review, consists of eight paragraphs. Not only is it longer than the passage from The Mismeasure of Man, it also makes an argument. As you will see, Kozol begins with the common belief that homelessness results from the release of mental patients from state hospitals in the 1970s and then counters this view with an alternative explanation of the cause of homelessness and the argument that the "deinstitutionalization" explanation amounts to a self-serving myth.

Because Kozol is asking his readers to reconsider how we think about the causes of homelessness, his passage calls for a certain kind of attention beyond just acquiring and organizing information.   The reading strategies already presented—underlining, note taking, and summarizing—are good methods to start a close reading of Kozol's argument. But, as you read, notice that Kozol's passage also calls on you as a reader to weigh alternative explanations, to consider the evidence he presents to support his argument, and to come to grips with his conclusions.

Following the reading selection are strategies to analyze it.

1 It is commonly believed by many journalists and politicians that
the homeless of America are, in large part, former patients of
large mental hospitals who were deinstitutionalized in the
1970s—the consequence, it is sometimes said, of misguided liberal opinion that favored the treatment of such persons in com-
munity-based centers. It is argued that this policy, and the subsequent failure of society to build such centers or to provide them
in sufficient number, is the primary cause of homelessness in the
United States.

2 Those who work among the homeless do not find that explanation satisfactory. While conceding that a certain number of
the homeless are or have been mentally unwell, they believe that,
in the case of most unsheltered people, the primary reason is economic rather than clinical. The cause of homelessness, they say
with disarming logic, is the lack of homes and of income with
which to rent or acquire them.

3 They point to the loss of traditional jobs in industry (2 million every year since 1980) and to the fact that half of those who
are laid off end up in work that pays a poverty-level wage. They
point out that since 1968 the number of children living in poverty
has grown by 3 million, while welfare benefits to families with
children have declined by 35 percent.

4 And they note, too, that these developments have occurred
during a time in which the shortage of low-income housing has
intensified as the gentrification of our major cities has accelerat-
ed. Half a million units of low-income housing are lost each year
to condominium conversion as well as to arson, demolition, or
abandonment. Between 1978 and 1980, median rents climbed 30
percent for people in the lowest income sector, driving many of
these families into the streets. Since 1980, rents have risen at
even faster rates.

5 Hard numbers, in this instance, would appear to be of
greater help than psychiatric labels in telling us why so many
people become homeless. Eight million American families now
use half or more of their income to pay their rent or mortgage. At
the same time, federal support for low-income housing dropped
from $30 billion (1980) to $7.5 billion (1988). Under Presidents
Ford and Carter, 500,000 subsidized private housing units were
constructed. By President Reagan's second term, the number had
dropped to 25,000.

6 In our rush to explain the homeless as a psychiatric problem even the words of medical practitioners who care for homeless people have been curiously ignored. A study published by
the Massachusetts Medical Society, for instance, has noted that,

with the exceptions of alcohol and drug use, the most frequent illnesses among a sample of the homeless population were trauma (31 percent), upper-respiratory disorders (28 percent), limb disorders (19 percent), mental illness (16 percent), skin diseases (15 percent), hypertension (14 percent), and neurological illnesses (12 percent). Why, we may ask, of all these calamities, does mental illness command so much political and press attention? The answer may be that the label of mental illness places the destitute outside the sphere of ordinary life. It personalizes an anguish that is public in its genesis; it individualizes a misery that is both general in cause and general in application.

7   There is another reason to assign labels to the destitute and single out mental illness from among their many afflictions. All these other problems—tuberculosis, asthma, scabies, diarrhea, bleeding gums, impacted teeth, etc.—bear no stigma, and mental illness does. It conveys a stigma in the United States. It conveys a stigma in the Soviet Union as well. In both nations the label is used, whether as a matter of deliberate policy or not, to isolate and treat as special cases those who, by deed or word or by sheer presence, represent a threat to national complacence. The two situations are obviously not identical, but they are enough alike to give Americans reason for concern.

8   The notion that the homeless are largely psychotics who belong in institutions, rather than victims of displacement at the hands of enterprising realtors, spares us from the need to offer realistic solutions to the deep and widening extremes of wealth and poverty in the United States. It also enables us to tell ourselves that the despair of homeless people bears no intimate connection to the privileged existence we enjoy—when, for example, we rent or purchase one of those restored town houses that once provided shelter for people now huddled in the street.

• **Topical Outline**   Outlining is similar to taking notes in that both create records of the main points in a piece of writing. But outlining can do more than just record important information for use later. It can also help you analyze how writers arrange their material—why the parts come in a certain order and what the connections are among the parts.

The sample below is a topical outline that marks off main sections with Roman numerals (I, II, and III), identifies important ideas within the sections with capital letters, and finally notes evidence that supports these ideas with Arabic numerals (1, 2, 3 . . .). The benefit of using such an organizational scheme is that it gives you a clear, concise record of what the piece of writing says. It also can help you begin your analysis by visualizing the relationships among the various parts.

The following topical outline shows how Kozol has organized his argument.

Sample Topical Outline:

Main point: The cause of homelessness is the lack of homes and of income with which to rent or acquire them.

I. Introduction
   A. Common view: deinstitutionalizing the mentally ill.
   B. Kozol's view: the lack of homes and income.

II. Main Body
   A. Lack of income
      1. Loss of traditional jobs in industry.
      2. Increase in poverty-level wages.
      3. Increase in children living in poverty.
      4. Decrease in welfare benefits.
   B. Shortage of low-cost housing.
      1. Loss to condiminium conversion, arson, demolition, and abandonment.
      2. Increase in rents.
   C. Other revealing statistics.
      1. Eight million Americans use half or more of their income for rent or mortgage.
      2. Drop in federal support for low-income housing.
      3. Decrease in subsidized private housing.
   D. Statistics on most frequent illnesses among homeless.

III. Conclusion
   A. Stigma of mental illness.
   B. Distancing from plight of homeless.

• **Identifying Sections and Describing Their Function**

As you have seen, a topical outline helps you identify the ideas and the order in which they appear. The next step is to analyze the organization by describing more explicitly how the parts are connected to each other.

This reading strategy asks you to identify the main sections in a piece of writing and to explain what function each section performs (instead of just recording what the writing says, as in a topical outline). This strategy focuses on the writer's technique—how he or she connects the sections and thereby constructs a whole piece of writing. What you read, after all, results from a series of decisions writers make about how to present their main point and connect the supporting material to it. Describing the function of the main sections can help you identify these decisions and the part each section is intended to play. In this way, you can deepen your understanding of the writer's purposes and line of reasoning.

FOLLOW THESE STEPS TO IDENTIFY AND DESCRIBE THE FUNCTION OF THE MAIN SECTIONS:

1. Write a statement that describes the writer's overall purpose. What is the writer trying to accomplish—provide information (as Stephen Jay Gould does about the birth of IQ testing), challenge a common

view (as Jonathan Kozol does of the causes of homelessness), or something else? You can probably think of a number of other purposes writers have: profiling a person or place, rendering personal experience, endorsing a policy, reviewing a book or movie, interpreting an event, explaining a concept, and so on.

2. Divide the writing into what seem to be the main sections, grouping paragraphs that seem to go together. (This step is similar to marking the main sections with Roman numerals in a topical outline.) Look for an opening section that introduces the topic or main idea, a middle section or sections that develop the writer's subject, and an ending.

3. Label the function each of the major sections performs. Your label should explain how the section fits into the writing as a whole. Consider how the opening section introduces the topic or main idea, how a middle section or sections develop it, and how the writing ends.

4. Label the parts within each main section, according to the function they perform. (Notice that you are analyzing here the parts marked by A., B., C., . . . and 1, 2, 3, . . . on a topical outline.) Explain how each part develops the main idea of the section in which it appears.

To label the parts, you'll need a language of analysis to describe what the function of the main sections and their parts. Consult the box that lists strategies writers often use but, if necessary, be prepared to invent your own terms.

WRITING STRATEGIES

- narrates, tells a story, relates an anecdote or incident
- describes things, people, places, processes
- illustrates by using examples, details, data
- defines key terms, problems, issues, trends
- compares and/or contrasts one thing, idea, person, place to another

- classifies things, ideas, people, places, processes into categories
- explains causes and effects
- gives reasons
- offers evidence (statistics, established facts, expert testimony, etc.)
- cites other writers
- makes concessions
- refutes opposing views

Sample of Identifying the Main Sections and Describing Their Functions in "Distancing the Homeless":

Notice how the following sample divides the writing into three main sections by grouping paragraphs together according to the function they perform—introducing the argument, providing supporting evidence, and explaining the consequences of the argument.

As you can see, these sections correspond to the Introduction, Main Body, and Conclusion in the topical outline. But instead of referring to the content of the writing, notice how the sample analysis uses labels that explain how the main sections build Kozol's argument and how the parts of each section develop it main idea. ¶ 1-2: Introduces the main idea

Replaces a common belief about the cause of homelessness
    with an alternative view

¶ 3-6: Provides supporting evidence for the main idea
Offers the testimony of experts, statistical evidence, and
    medical study to refute the common view
Raises a question about why the common view commands
    attention and offers an answer

¶ 7-8: Explains the consequences of the argument
Offers a second reason for the common view
Compares how the common view operates in the United
    States and the Soviet Union
Explains an important effect of the common view

• Distinguishing Facts and Claims

Readers justifiably expect that when writers make arguments they will back up their claims with factual evidence. This makes sense because facts have tremendous authority. They refer to items of information that are well-established and generally accepted. But the facts do not speak for themselves. They are used by writers to achieve particular effects, most often to support a claim the writer wants to make. For this reason, an important reading strategy is distinguishing between facts and claims. By making this distinction, you can identify how writers link the use of factual information to the arguable positions they take.

Some facts are expressed in the form of numbers, statistics, or other unit of measurement (the number of industrial jobs lost since 1980, the percentage of millionaires who pay no income taxes, or the length of the Mississippi River). Others describe in words what is known (DNA has a double-helical structure, Morocco is located in North Africa, the Soviet Union collapsed in 1989). In either case, the facts can be verified by reliable sources.

Facts are basically statements that no one calls into question. Facts have to be established to acquire such authority, and journalists, scientists, legal experts, historians, economists, engineers, and so on have developed methods to certify what counts as a fact and what remains in doubt. We know, for example, that John F. Kennedy was assasinated on November 22, 1963, and we can verify that fact by consulting newspapers and historical records. On the other hand, there is less certainty about whether the assasin Lee Harvey Oswald acted alone or with others.

The facts, moreover, don't necessarily tell us what to do with the information they contain. The fact that Kennedy was killed on a particular date doesn't tell us much about the meaning of his death, why it happened, or what the consequences are. These are questions that fall into the domain of interpretation, and as you may know, there are hundreds of books and articles that offer more or less plausible claims about the Kennedy assasination.

As a reading strategy, distinguishing between facts and claims can help you identify what the writer assumes readers will accept as the available information and what the writer assumes readers will need explained. By separating facts and claims, you can begin to ask whether the writer makes persuasive use of the available information to back up a claim. (See Chapter 5 for a fuller discussion of how writers connect facts to claims.)

SAMPLE ANALYSIS OF FACTS AND CLAIMS

Jonathan Kozol's essay "Distancing the Homeless" offers a good opportunity to distinguish the use of facts from the making of claims. By "Identifying Sections and Describing Their Function," you have already seen how Kozol uses statistical data and the results of a study published by the Massachusetts Medical Society to support his claim that the cause of homelessness is not the release of mental patients but rather the lack of income and affordable housing. The next step is to look more closely at how Kozol connects facts and claims. Here are some examples:

Fact	*Claim*
Loss of jobs (2 million a year since 1980) and poverty-level wages	Homelessness caused by lack of income
35% decline in welfare benefits to families with children	Homelessness caused by lack of income
Loss of low-income housing	Homelessness caused by lack of affordable housing
Rents have increased 30%	Homelessness caused by lack of affordable housing
Mental illness accounts for 16% of illness among homeless	Homelessness not caused by mental illness

As you can see, while the facts Kozol presents do not automatically lead to the claims he makes, the connections are arguable ones. In other instances, however, the connection is less clear. What, for example, are we to make of the fact that since 1968 the number of children living in poverty has increased by 3 million? This may indeed point to a deplorable situation that requires action, but whether this fact supports Kozol's central claims is another matter.

WORKING TOGETHER: Practicing Analysis

Work together in a group with two or three other students. Pick a short piece of writing that makes an argument. A good source for this assignment is the editorial page of a newspaper—whether it's a student, local, or national newspaper (such as the New York Times or USA Today). Look for something that is five to ten paragraphs long. Then follow these steps:

1. Working together as a group, compose a topical outline of the writing. Follow the sample, using Roman numerals, capital letters, and Arabic numerals to identify the parts. Use phrases to capture the meaning of each part.
2. Now use the topical outline you have written to identify the main sections of the argument and to describe their function. Follow the directions in the section "Identifying Sections and Describing Their Function."
3. Identify the facts the writer presents. What claims does the writer make based on these facts?

EVALUATING

The strategies of outlining and analyzing can be used to read in virtually any circumstance. They provide methods of reading closely to understand the meaning and to analyze how the parts relate to each other and form the whole.

What they don't do, however, is tell you much about the value of the writing—whether it can hold up to critical questioning, whether it provides a useful way of looking at the issues involved, and whether it has the power to persuade you.

Most people, of course, do a good deal of reading without consciously evaluating it—reading sports scores, recipes, weather reports, gossip columns, and so on. But there are occasions when evaluation is important. You may, for example, be called on in an essay exam in a psychology course to evaluate differing explanations of autism or schizophrenia. In this case, to be successful, you can't just summarize what the competing explanations say. You need to make a judgment about their relative strengths and weaknesses.

At election time, you are called on to evaluate the differing claims the candidates make and the arguments for or against ballot measures. Or you may be faced at work with making decisions based on competing arguments—whether, say, a company should open a new store or institute new forms of organization in the workplace.

In situations such as these, the reading you do has real consequences. The purpose of reading is to enable you to make a sound decision. The goal is for you to make up your mind—to know where you want to stand on the issues that face you and others.

In this section, you will find strategies to help you evaluate what you are reading.

• Using Background Information

Background information about the writer and the publication where the writer's work appears can be useful in identifying the writer's point of view and evaluating the writer's argument.

As you will see, the information you turn up about the writer and the place of publication does not speak for itself. You need to interpret this information in order to determine what it means to you and how it will influence your evaluation.

The writer. Information about the writer—his or her education, credentials, experience, politics, prior publications, awards, institutional affiliations, reputation, and so on—is often summarized briefly in an author note following an article or on the dust jacket of a book.

In evaluating a writer's argument, ask yourself if the available information indicates why and how the writer is qualified to speak on the topic at hand. What might this information tell you about the perspective the writer is likely to bring to the topic? Here are some questions you may find useful:

1. Based on what you know about his or her background, how much authority and credibility can you attribute to the writer? Is there reason to believe the writer will provide informed accounts and responsible arguments, whether you agree with them or not?
2. What political, cultural, social, or other commitments is the writer known for? How are these commitments likely to influence the writer's argument?
3. How do these commitments relate to your own views? How is this relationship likely to influence your evaluation of the writer's argument?

WORKING TOGETHER: Using Background Information on the Writer

The following background information on Jonathan Kozol is excerpted from the standard reference source Contemporary Authors, New Revision Series, Volume 45. It includes biographical information and discussion of Kozol's first book Death at an Early Age (1968) and his more recent book on homelessness Rachel and Her Children. Working together, use this information to answer the questions suggested for evaluating a writer's background.

The publication. Place of publication can also provide you with some useful background information. Readers are likely to form very different impressions based on the type of publication in which a writer's work appears.

Although there are certainly loyal readers of the National Inquirer and the Weekly World, supermarket tabloids do not have the same reputability and legitimacy as, say, the Wall Street Journal or the New York Times. By the same token, readers may well draw key distinctions between these last two newspapers, characterizing the Wall Street Journal as pro-business and the New York Times as the voice of the Eastern liberal establishment.

Here are some questions to ask about the place of publication:

1. What do you know about the publication? Who is the publisher? Is it a commercial publication? Does it have an institutional affiliation—to a college or university, an academic field of study, a professional organization, a church? Does it espouse an identifiable political, social, cultural, economic, or religious ideology?
2. If the publication is a periodical, what other writers—and types of writing and topics—appear in the issue?
3. Who would be likely to read the publication?

KOZOL, Jonathan   1936-

PERSONAL: Born September 5, 1936, in Boston, MA; son of Harry (a physician) and Ruth (a psychiatric social worker; maiden name, Massell) Kozol. *Education:* Harvard University, B.A. (summa cum laude), 1958; graduate study, Magdalen College, Oxford, 1958-59. *Politics:* Independent. *Religion:* Jewish.

ADDRESSES: Home—Byfield, MA. *Agent:* Lynn Nesbit, Janklow & Nesbit, 578 Madison Ave., New York, NY 10022.

CAREER: Author of works on poverty, race, and education. Elementary school teacher in Boston, MA, 1964-65, and in Newton, MA, 1964-68; Storefront Learning Center (alternative school), Boston, educational director and teacher of secondary level English, 1968-71; Center for Intercultural Documentation Institute, Cuernavaca, Mexico, instructor in alternatives in education, 1969, 1970, and 1974; South Boston High School, Boston, remedial writing and reading instructor, 1979; former director of National Literacy Coalition, Boston.

Visiting instructor, Yale University, 1969, University of Massachusetts—Amherst, 1978-79, and Trinity College, Hartford, 1980; visiting lecturer in literature and education at hundreds of colleges and universities, 1971—, including Antioch University, Vassar College, University of Wisconsin, University of Minnesota, Brown University, Boston University, Columbia University, Harvard University, and Princeton University. Trustee, New School for Children, Roxbury, MA. Consultant to U.S. Office of Economic Opportunity, 1965 and 1966, Pima County Board of Education, Tucson, AZ, 1974, Chicago Board of Education, 1975, Maryland State Penitentiary, Baltimore, MD, 1979, Connecticut Board of Education, Hartford, 1980, Rhode Island Board of Education, Providence, 1980, Cleveland Foundation, 1980—, Cleveland Public Library, 1980—, Edmonton Public Schools, Vancouver School Board, Syracuse University, University of Massachusetts, and others.

MEMBER: Fellowship of Reconciliation, Association of American Rhodes Scholars.

AWARDS, HONORS: Rhodes Scholar, 1958-59; Olympia Award, 1962; Sexton fellowship in creative writing from Harper & Row, 1962; National Book Award, 1968, for *Death at an Early Age: The Destruction of the Hearts and Minds of Negro Children in the Boston Public Schools;* Guggenheim fellow, 1970 and 1984; Field Foundation fellow, 1972; Ford Foundation fellow, 1974; Rockefeller fellow, 1978 and 1983; Robert F. Kennedy Book Award, 1988; Conscience in Media Award, American Society of Journalists and Authors, 1988; Christopher Award, 1988, for *Rachel and Her Children: Homeless Families in America;* New England Book Award, and National Book Critics Circle Award finalist, both 1992, both for *Savage Inequalities: Children in America's Schools.*

* * *

SIDELIGHTS: Until *Illiterate America* was published, Jonathan Kozol was probably best known for his first work of nonfiction, *Death at an Early Age: The Destruction of the Hearts and Minds of Negro Children in the Boston Public Schools,* which won him a National Book Award in 1968. *Death at an Early Age,* an account of the months Kozol taught in Boston's ghetto schools during the mid-1960s, was written after the author was fired from his fourth-grade teaching position, ostensibly for using in class a poem by Langston Hughes that was not on the approved curriculum material list. Most of his writings since *Death at an Early Age* have pertained to his career as a radical educator and his experience as an activist regarding issues related to education. *Free Schools,* for instance, recounts his experiences in setting up a free school in Roxbury, a black district of Boston, not long after his firing; he documents the methods he and his associates used to ensure that the institution would establish a solid community backing, a viable financial base, and a workable power structure. *Illiterate America,* a culminating work in Kozol's exploration of illiteracy, draws on the author's background as a grass-roots organizer to outline his proposal for dealing with the problem of illiteracy in the United States, which he estimates to be of colossal proportions. In *Rachel and Her Children: Homeless Families in America* Kozol looks closely at homeless families living in a shelter in New York City, but he returns to the subject of education in *Savage Inequalities: Children in America's Schools,* published in 1991.

Speaking to Paul Galloway of the *Chicago Tribune* about his interest in education, Kozol recounted his privileged childhood; attending a prep school, Harvard, and later Oxford as a Rhodes Scholar; and then living in poor neighborhoods in Paris while he wrote a novel. This latter experience was a lesson in how ordinary people live, and he returned to the United States in 1963 somewhat confused about his next step but planning finally to get a doctorate and teach English in a university. By chance in 1964 he learned of a need for tutors in a summer program in Roxbury, and he volunteered. As Galloway reports, "He found that he loved teaching; he loved being with children. In September [1964] he became a teacher in the Boston school system."

Death at an Early Age, Kozol's first book, is in large part a product of its times. Written several years before the integration of Boston public schools, much of the book relates to concerns which arose out of the desegregation debate that was taking shape while Kozol taught, as well as to civil rights conflicts that transpired in the South during the mid-1960s. The book documents the repressive teaching methods Kozol's colleagues used, techniques he believed were designed to reinforce a system that would keep the children separate and unequal.

Specifically, Kozol discusses the widespread practice of punishing disobedient or unlikable children with rattan whips, analyzes the irrelevant and often racist curriculum material, and describes the dirty, overcrowded, unsafe conditions of the buildings in which he taught. He also chronicles specific cases of incompetence and paternalism, along with instances of blatant racism. Robert Coles writes in the *New York Times Book Review* in 1967 that "what emerges is an unsparing picture of American education as it exists today in the ghettos of our major Northern cities."

Some reviewers think the work is open to criticism, however. As Charles R. Moyer states in *Carleton Miscellany,* the author's "rather romantic primitism blinds Mr. Kozol to his own brand of condescension which prevents him from ever seeing the black children in any role other than that of innocent victims." And Kozol's descriptions of "white teachers and agents of the system (with the possible exception of himself) are stereotyped and totally negative," Elizabeth M. Eddy says in *Harvard Educational Review.* "In contrast, there is no unsympathetic sketch of a Negro child or adult."

Others, however, believe *Death at an Early Age* provides a real public service. Kozol's book "eloquently describes the consequences of this system for both child and teacher, and Kozol himself is a dramatic example of the way in which the teacher is often discouraged from initiating creative learning activities in the classroom," Eddy reports, noting that "in addition, the book presents insightful material relevant to the pathological adaptations made by many teachers who remain in the slum school rather than moving elsewhere."

Shortly before Christmas of 1985, Kozol spent an evening at the Hotel Martinique in New York, which was serving four hundred of the city's homeless families, including 1,400 children, as a temporary shelter. There he began to talk with some of the residents, and returned many times in the course of writing *Rachel and Her Children: Homeless Families in America.* Sam Roberts comments on the book in the *New York Times:* "Individually, the voices of the pseudonymous Rachel and other residents of the Martinique are unsettling. Taken together, they represent a searing indictment of a society that has largely chosen to look the other way, to neglect a natural confluence of compassion and enlightened self-interest, and of people in government who may have done their best but whose best too often has not been good enough."

William J. Drummond, writing in *Tribune Books,* declares that "Kozol's major achievement in *Rachel and Her Children* is to dispel the media-fashioned stereotype of the homeless and force the reader to look into their faces and listen to their voices." Teresa Funiciello, in the *Nation,* see Kozol's method in another light. Though she believes Kozol "effectively uses the homeless to describe their own plight," she goes on to say that "he falls into the same trap that he warns others against: He can't quite hear what they are saying. He refuses to rely on them for prescriptive measures, instead choosing to derive political definitions primarily from the professional 'advocates.' " In the *New*

York Times, reviewer Christopher Lehmann-Haupt complains that, though Kozol "successfully humanizes his subject" and "even rises to an occasional pitch of eloquence," he notes that "there is something distinctly irritating and occasionally even infuriating about the tone of voice in which Mr. Kozol presumes to lecture us." Kai Erikson of the *Nation* observes that the people described in Kozol's book are "numbed by what happened to them and . . . they see the world around them as brittle, precarious, dangerous." Erikson notes that the author has "no way of knowing what kind of shape these men and women were in before they were set adrift. . . . But what is clear to Kozol, and he makes clear to us, is that homelessness *itself* damages the people who experience it, no matter what resources they bring to it."

WORKING TOGETHER: Using Background Information on the Publication

The two following entries appear in Magazines for Libraries, a standard reference source that describes the intended audience and editorial slant of many magazines and newspapers. Notice how the background information provided on Scientific American and U.S. New & World Report seeks to establish the credibility and point of view of articles that appear in these publications. Working together, pick a current periodical (e.g. Discover, Rolling Stone, Wired, Ms., Nation, National Review, New Yorker, Vanity Fair, etc.) and prepare a brief report on what it covers, its intended audience, and its point of view, using the entries from Magazines for Libraries as models.

6163. *Scientific American.* [ISSN: 0036-8733] 1845. m. $36. Jonathan Piel. Scientific American, 415 Madison Ave., New York, NY 10017. Illus., index, adv. Refereed. Circ: 622,806. Vol. ends: Dec. Microform: MIM, UMI. Online: DIALOG.

Indexed: AcadInd, ASTI, BioAb, ChemAb, GSI, RG. *Bk. rev:* 3, 1,000 words, signed. *Aud:* Hs, Ga, Ac, Sa.

This long-established magazine offers a broad range of articles covering archaeology, astronomy, earth science, medicine, psychology, technology—anything even remotely considered science. Its regular departments are up to date and newsy. "Science and the Citizen" covers current news developments such as restoration of the Hubble telescope; "Science and Business" deals with matters like research into ocular implants for the blind, and recent trends in computer technology. "50 and 100 Years Ago" recalls scientific advances in the past, as gleaned from the magazine's back issues. "Mathematical Recreation" is an imaginative feature that once discussed "Why Tarzan and Jane Can Walk in Step with the Animals That Roam the Jungle," and the "Amateur Scientist" tells how to count the number of species that live on your lawn. The illustrations, many in color, are informative and decorative; the book reviews are just about the right length. However, the layperson would find a solid scientific background helpful in understanding some of the articles. High school, academic, and special libraries need this journal. Public libraries will also want it because of its reputation, extensive indexing, and complete coverage.

5431. *U.S. News & World Report.* [ISSN: 0041-5537] 1933. w. $41. Merrill McLaughlin & Michael Ruby. U.S. News & World Report, 2400 N St. N.W., Washington, DC 20037-1196. Illus., adv. Circ: 2,400,000. Vol. ends: June. Microform: MCA, MIM. Online: DIALOG, Mead Data Central.

Indexed: MI, PAIS, RG. *Aud:* Hs, Ga, Ac.

This is the third of the major U.S. newsweeklies. Although *U.S. News & World Report* has the smallest circulation of the three, it tends to be as highly regarded as the other two. Considered by some to be more objective and reliable than *Time* or *Newsweek*, *U.S. News* is also regarded as more conservative. This perception is not totally inaccurate, but the editors also believe in calling them as they see them, sometimes resulting in unexpected opinions. *U.S. News* is written more for the person interested in serious reporting and issues discussed with thought. In addition to the excellent news coverage, *U.S. News* includes a section called "News You Can Use" that contains consumer, environmental, and other types of useful information for its readers. Other notable features are the occasional "Special Reports," discussions of topics that are even more in-depth than the regular reporting, and the magazine's availability through CompuServe. The positive attributes of this publication make it an excellent choice for all libraries.

BOX: THE LOOK OF THE PAGE

Even when you don't know much about a publication, you can make informed guesses about its credibility. One factor to consider is the look of the publication. Notice how the Weekly World News has a very different appearance than the Wall Street Journal. List features about each front page that gives you clues to the reputation of each publication.

• Evaluating the Writer's Evidence

The value of a writer's argument depends in many respects on the sources of information the writer uses to provide evidence for his or her argument. The following list includes the most common forms of evidence and criteria for evaluating how writers use them:

Examples. Examples generally serve the purpose of illustrating a point the writer wants to make. Examples can be drawn from a number of sources: anecdotal accounts of personal experience, observations in field research and case studies, or reading about the topic.

To evaluate a writer's use of examples, ask yourself whether the example is truly representative of the point the writer wants to establish. Imagine that a letter to the editor of your local newspaper uses the example of a bad encounter the writer recently had with the police to call for the establishment of a civilian review board. In this case, as a reader you need to determine whether the writer's personal experience really furnishes a convincing example of the need for the review board. Is the example truly representative? Does the writer fit it into a pattern of police abuse? Or does the example stand as an isolated instance leading to a hasty and unjustifiable conclusion?

Statistics. Statistics have taken on an unquestioned authority, in part because they seem to provide hard and incontestable evidence. The stock market index tells which companies are performing well, batting averages show who the top hitters in baseball are, and public opinion polling reveals what the American people think and believe. And there is no question that statistics can be enormously useful to writers, whether they are looking at the unemployment rate or the incidence of AIDS.

Nonetheless, there are some good reasons to be skeptical about the use of statistics in what you read and to have some questions at hand to evaluate them. In advertisements, for example, you may read that nine out of ten successful runners wear a certain brand of running shoe. To evaluate the use of statistics, you need to ask what the numbers actually mean. Did the person who designed the ad only talk to ten runners? This is hardly a large enough sample size to suggest that 90% of all successful runners wear the brand of shoe.

You should ask too whether the statistics are complete. For example, a writer calling for a get-tough approach to crime may cite the statistic that the city you live in had 182 homicides last year—a chilling figure that averages one murder every other day. On the face of it, these statistics seem to back up the writer's argument for a crackdown on crime. In this case, however, last year's number of murders actually represents a 15% decline over the previous year and a 30% decline over a five year period. Any claim that ignores this larger pattern must be considered a dubious one. As a reader, stay alert to such possible distortions in the writer's use of sources.

Statistics can be misleading, whether intentionally or not, unless the writer gives you a full and accurate picture. The current debate about teenage pregnancy is a good case in point. Journalists, politicians, and policymakers have claimed that an unsettling increase in teenage pregnancies has become a national problem. However, the number of teenagers who become pregnant has not gone up in decades. This statistic has remained relatively constant since the 1950s. What has in fact increased is the number of unmarried teenagers having children.

Research. Colleges and universities, the federal government, professional societies, independent research institutes, and corporations all conduct research in a range of fields. As you have seen, Jonathan Kozol draws on a study by the Massachusetts Medical Society as evidence that homelessness is not caused by mental illness. Citing such published studies from reputable sources adds credibility to the writer's case.

The question for you as a reader, though, is what published studies in fact provide reputable evidence. Let's say you are investigating the published literature on the addictive properties of nicotine, whether for academic purposes or to develop policies on cigarette advertising. One of the things you should pay attention to is who sponsored the research studies—the tobacco companies, the National Institutes of Health, the American Cancer Society. The fact that the tobacco companies have sponsored research on the properties of nicotine should not automatically disqualify the findings. At the same time, you should note that the tobacco companies can hardly be considered impartial sponsors and you should look for possible biases in the studies.

A second question to ask about research studies concerns how up to date they are. In general, the most recent studies will be more authoritative than older ones.

Expert testimony. Writers often cite experts to support their argument. The experience and professional credentials of people who are close to the issue at hand can certainly lend credibility to the writer's case. In "Distancing the Homeless," Jonathan Kozol uses the testimony of people who work among the homeless to introduce the main point in his argument.

To evaluate the use of expert testimony as evidence, you can ask the same questions you asked about the writer: What experience and background make these people experts? What reason is there to believe they will offer informed accounts? What political, cultural, social, or other commitments are likely to influence what the experts have to say?

• Identifying the Writer's Allegiances

The purpose of identifying the writer's allegiances is to understand where the writer is coming from. Whose interests does the writer represent? With whom does the writer align himself? What does the writer oppose, differ with, or distance himself from? What common ground is the writer asking readers to share? Asking these questions can help you see what it would mean to agree with the writer's argument.

In the case of "Distancing the Homeless," notice how Kozol quickly locates himself in opposition to the common belief on the part of journalists and politicians that the homeless are mainly former mental patients. Instead, he aligns himself with people "who work among the homeless" and believe that the cause of homelessness is the lack of homes and income. In this sense, he hopes to speak on behalf of the homeless, whom, he believes, have been unfairly represented in the media and politics.

After presenting evidence for his counter-interpretation of the causes of homelessness, notice that Kozol shifts in the sixth paragraph to speak in the collective voice of first person plural ("we may ask"). At this point, it seems he believes he has offered enough compelling evidence about the actual causes of homelessness to assume that readers may now be prepared to join with him on common ground to ask why the mental illness label has been persistently applied to the homeless.

As you can see in the passage from "Distancing the Homeless," writers seek points of identification with readers—to establish the common ground that joins individuals together as "we." And, as the passage illustrates, forming a "we" can often imply the existence of a "they" from whom "we" are somehow distinguished, different, perhaps antagonistic. For these reasons, identifying allegiances is an especially important reading strategy in instances where the issues under consideration are contested and the writer is attempting to line you up on one side or another. It can help you figure out where you stand on the issues, where your own allegiances reside, and what it would mean for you to be persuaded by the writer.

Here are some questions to help you identify the writer's allegiances:

1. Based on what you have read and the background information you have available on the writer, can you identify on whose behalf the writer is speaking? Whose interests does the writer seem to represent? Where do the writer's loyalties seem to reside?

2. Does the writer seem to align himself or herself against certain groups, individuals, points of view, institutions, values? If so, for what reasons? What does the writer find lacking or objectionable?

3. What would it mean to agree with the writer? How would agreement position you in relation to what the writer and others have said about the topic? What would you have to believe to agree with the writer? What allegiances would incline you to the writer's perspective?

GOING ON-LINE

Evaluating Web Sites

Evaluating information on the World Wide Web and Internet poses special problems for readers to take into account. Unlike most printed material such as newspapers, magazines, government documents, academic journals, and books, Web sites are not necessarily the result of a process of editing and peer review that filters out unreliable and unsubstantiated information. Instead, what appears on the Web is largely unregulated and sometimes of questionable credibility. After all, anyone can put up a Web site and include in it whatever they wish. This is, of course, part of the attraction of the Web but also the primary reason that readers need to approach Web sites with care. Here are some basic suggestions for evaluating the reliability and authority of information found on the Web.

READING A WEB DOCUMENT

Web documents contain three main elements: header, body, and footer. (See the diagram of the History of "Race" in Science, Medicine, and Technology Web site.) Knowing where to look in the document should enable you to answer the following questions as a starting point to evaluate the Web site:

- Who is the author or contact person? Usually located in the footer.

- What institution or Internet provider supports the Web site? Usually located in header or footer. (.edu indicates an educational institution; .org a non-profit organization; .gov a government institution; and .com a commercial source.)

- When was the Web site created or updated? Usually located in footer.

- What is the purpose of the information contained in the Web site? Determined by examining the body.

- Who is the intended audience? Determined by examining the body.

EVALUATING WEB SITES

You can use the information you have gathered to ask the following questions. Your answers should enable you to evaluate the reliability of the information at the Web site:

- What do you know about the author? Does he or she list an occupation, institutional affiliation, years of experience, or other information on qualifications? Does the author seem to be qualified to write and present information on the topic at hand?

- What do you know about the institution or Internet provider that supports the Web site? What influence, if any, is the author's affiliation to this particular organization, institution, or provider likely to have on the information presented at the Web site?

- What seems to be the purpose of the Web site—to inform, explain, persuade, or some combination? Who is the site's audience likely to be? What uses are visitors likely to make of the site?

- How much of the information at the Web site has the author created? How much is already existing material that the author has organized? Where does such information come from? Do these sources seem reliable? Is the Web site linked to other sites? Do linked sites seem to be reliable and authoritative? How can you tell?

```
┌─────────────────────────────────────────────┐
│                                             │
│               H E A D E R                   │
│                                             │
└─────────────────────────────────────────────┘

┌─────────────────────────────────────────────┐
│                                             │
│                                             │
│                                             │
│                                             │
│               B O D Y                       │
│                                             │
│                                             │
│                                             │
│                                             │
│                                             │
│                                             │
│                                             │
│                                             │
└─────────────────────────────────────────────┘

┌─────────────────────────────────────────────┐
│               F O O T E R                   │
└─────────────────────────────────────────────┘
```

Exercise: Use the questions to visit and evaluate the two Web sites reproduced here—the History of "Race" in Science, Medicine, and Technology and the Drudge Report. How do they differ in terms of credibility? What has shaped your judgment?

• Evaluating the Writer's Language

Reading closely the actual words the writer uses can give you some clues to understand where the writer is coming from and what his or her allegiances are. It is one thing, after all, to refer to business executives as "fat cats" or "robber barons" and quite another to call them "corporate leaders" or "entrepreneurial visionaries." The terms reveal the writer's attitude and perspective.

Words and phrases carry powerful associations that can sway readers to share or reject what a writer is saying. For this reason, it is useful to look at some of the ways writers use language to influence their readers.

 **History of "Race"
In Science, Medicine, and Technology**

Bibliography| Announcements| Links| Gallery| Syllabus Sampler | Primary Documents

This website is a forum, research, and teaching tool for scholars, students, and others interested in the **History of the Concept of "Race" in Science, Medicine, Public Health, and Technology,** with a focus on 19th and 20th century American, European and Colonial histories.

- **Bibliographies** of current scholarly literature.

- **Announcements:**
    - Race and Science Workgroup.
    - Fellowships, conferences and calls for papers.
    - Race and Science In the News.
    - **Science, Technology, and Race Conference** Calls for papers for Georgia Tech Conference. Due March 17, 1998. *NEW*
    - American Anthropological Association. Call for comments on the draft of their Official Statement on Race.
    - Social Science Knowledge on Race, Racism, and Race RelationsCall for help from the American Sociological Association Project.

- **Links** to other related web sites.

- **Syllabus Sampler** of university-level courses.

- **Primary Document Bibliography** useful for beginning research or teaching in the history of race and science in the U.S.

- **Gallery** of image exhibitions on the History of Race and Science. Do you have an image exhibition you'd like to contribute? Email us at race-sci@mit.edu!!**Under Construction!**

We are eager to make this site comprehensive. Please send bibliography entries, links, and general comments to race-sci@mit.edu. *Please send syllabi and other long documents as an **attached file.***

This Web site is edited by Prof. Evelynn Hammonds (MIT) and Michelle Murphy (Harvard University) and sponsored by MIT S.T.S. (Thanks to Babak Ashrafi). Complete Mailing Addresses:

Evelynn Hammonds
Assoc. Prof. of History of Science
Program in Science, Technology and Society
MIT
Cambridge MA 02139

Michelle Murphy
Ph.D. Candidate
History of Science Dept.
Harvard University
Cambridge MA 02138

Bizarre biological threat disclosed

DRUDGE REPORT

AP WORLD
AP NATIONAL
AP WASHINGTON
AP ON THE HOUR
AP HEADLINES
AP BREAKING
Search

Headline:
Date Range:
    Within 1 Day
Any word(s) in article:

[AP]

REUTERS ODD
BLOOMBERG
BLOOMBERG PAPERS
BBC
BBC AUDIO
SKY NEWS
NATIONAL ENQUIRER
STAR
U.K. TABLOIDS
W'KLY WORLD NEWS
US INFO WIRE
U.S. NEWSWIRE
SHOWBIZ PR
WorldNetDaily
JEWISH WORLD REVIEW
ABC NEWS

MATT DRUDGE
BOB NOVAK
HELEN THOMAS
MAUREEN DOWD
BILL SAFIRE
PAGE SIX
ARMY ARCHERD
LIZ SMITH
MIKE MCCURRY
JEANNIE WILLIAMS
BILL GERTZ
WES PRUDEN
NEAL TRAVIS
HARRY KNOWLES
CINESCAPE INSIDER
MICHAEL FLEMING
RUSH/MOLLOY
SUE SCHMIDT
FREE REPUBLIC
SHOWBIZWIRE
ARIANNA
PAGLIA
STEVE DUNLEAVY
TONY SNOW
TY SHOPTALK
MICHAEL SNEED
KUPCINET
PAT BUCHANAN
HOWIE KURTZ
DICK MORRIS
MONA CHAREN
MICHAEL KELLY
CAL THOMAS
TY COLUMN
AL KAMEN
THOMAS SOWELL

Former Israeli PM admits to nukes...

Dick Morris to Clinton: 'Call off the dogs!'

UPI SPOTLIGHT
UPI ON THE HOUR
UPI NATIONAL
UPI LOCAL
REUTERS ROUNDUP
REUTERS WORLD
REUTERS WASHINGTON
REUTERS BUSINESS
SEARCH

[UPI/REUTERS]

FOX NEWS WIRE
WORLDWIRES

x x x x x

DRUDGE NATIONAL PRESS CLUB SPEECH...
• REAL AUDIO
• TRANSCRIPT

WEATHER ACTION
QUAKE SHEET

CALL IN A STORY TO THE DRUDGE REPORT...

Denotation/Connotation. Words have precise meanings which you can find in the dictionary. These are their denotative meanings. For example, the denotative meaning of "virus" is a microscopic organism that can replicate only within the cells of a living host, and "nationalism" means a feeling of loyalty to a particular country.

Nonetheless, the meaning of these terms is not exhausted by their denotation. They also conjure up connotative meanings depending on the circumstances in which they are used. Connotation means that words take on certain coloring and emotional force based on how writers use them. The term "nationalism," for example, might call up images of unity and belongingness, but it can also release fears of war and ethnic antagonisms. "Virus" may lead the reader to think of new and mysterious "killer diseases" invading the country from the Third World.

Notice, for example, how denotation and connotation work in Kozol's comparison of the United States and the Soviet Union, particularly in regard to the latter name. At the level of denotation, the Soviet Union simply refers to a government system instituted by the Bolshevik Revolution in 1917—and one that collapsed in 1989, just after Kozol published "Distancing the Homeless." At a connotative level, however, the term Soviet Union has negative associations for many Americans, conjuring up images of a totalitarian police state. Kozol, of course, is quite aware of these negative connotations, and he uses them to indict the United States by way of comparison.

Figures of speech. Figures of speech compare one thing to another. You have probably learned that similes use the words like or as to make a comparison. ("My love is like a red, red rose." "He is happy as a clam.") Metaphors make an implicit comparison, as though one thing is actually another. ("She was a thin reed of a girl." "The long arm of the law grabbed him and brought him to trial.") Often figures of speech are used to describe—to set a scene or create a mood—as in the following instance:

If buildings could shiver, this Camden, N.J., tenement would have the shakes. (Jason DeParle, "Learning Poverty Firsthand")

Figures of speech, however, are not simply decorative. They also provide ways of thinking and carry judgments on the writer's part. In "Distancing the Homeless," for example, Kozol writes:

Hard numbers, in this instance, would to be of greater help than psychiatric labels in telling us why so many people become homeless.

Numbers, of course, are neither hard nor soft but their "hardness" here is meant to invest authority in the evidence Kozol presents, in contrast to "psychiatric labels."

The notion that the homeless are largely psychotics who belong in institutions, rather than victims of displacement at the hands of enterprising realtors . . . .

Literally this sentence says that "enterprising realtors" physically displaced the homeless. Kozol, of course, does not believe that realtors actually ejected people from their homes. But to say the homeless were displaced at the hands of realtors accentuates the sense of responsibility Kozol assigns to gentrification in causing homelessness.

Stereotypes. Stereotypes are oversimplified representations that fit people into unvarying categories. These broad generalizations break down under careful scrutiny but appear to carry powerful (and often self-serving) explanations.

"Women are more emotional than men" is a classic stereotype that justifies why women won't do well under the stress of positions of authority (and therefore shouldn't be promoted over men). Along the same line, stereotypes of poor and working-class people and racial and ethnic minorities have created popular images (of "white trash," "drunken Indians," "welfare queens," and so on) that make subordination of one group to another seem necessary and inevitable. They are used to shame people who fall under the stereotype.

In this sense, stereotyping people, events, and behaviors can, as Kozol says concerning the stereotype of homeless people as mentally ill, stigmatize others and thereby distance us from their fates.

WORKING TOGETHER: Practicing Evaluation

Work together in the same group you were in to do the "Practicing Analysis" exercise. Use the same piece of writing and the analysis you have already done to evaluate the writing. Evaluative issues are likely to have already come up in your discussion, but now is an opportunity to treat them systematically. Follow these steps:

1. What kind of background information do you have available on the writer and publication? What kind of inferences, if any, can you draw from this information?
2. Evaluate the writer's use of evidence. Note the types of evidence the writer provides and test them by the criteria suggested.
3. What do the writer's allegiances seem to be? Use the questions in the "Identifying Writer's Allegiances" section.
4. Evaluate the writer's language.
5. Taking all these considerations together, what is your evaluation of the writing? Do you think it succeeds at its purposes? Does it persuade you? Why or why not?

LOGICAL FALLACIES

A logical fallacy is a flaw in reasoning that weakens the legitimacy of a writer's argument. Statements that contain logical fallacies nevertheless can appear to be plausible and may have persuasive effects. Logical fallacies are sometimes meant intentionally to distort the issues and mislead readers. (Advertising and political campaigns offer examples here.) But other times logical fallacies appear not to deceive readers but because the writer has misstated the point. As you will see, this can be a matter of oversimplification, poor word choice, and unclear connections among the parts of a statement.

Faulty cause-and-effect relationship. This problem in reasoning mistakes a sequence of events for a causal relationship. It assumes that because one event happened after another, the first event caused the second.

Children and adolescents who watch Beavis and Butthead are more prone to anti-social behavior.

This statement might be true, but it is hard to accept on its own terms. Readers would be justified to think the writer needs at least 1) to explain why and how watching Beavis and Butthead leads to anti-social behavior (do people automatically imitate what they see on television?), and 2) to account for all those children and adolescents who watch Beavis and Butthead and are not prone to anti-social behavior. All cause and effect arguments should be analyzed carefully to make sure A in fact does arguably cause B. After all, in this case, the cause and effect could run in the opposite direction—that is, it might be that children and adolescents already "prone to anti-social behavior" are drawn to watching Beavis and Butthead. Or it could be that some third factor is responsible for both.

False analogy. Analogies are based on comparisons. To tell readers, for example, that the evolution of biological species resembles a branching tree can be useful and clarifying because the analogy is apt. In false analogies, the writer assumes that because things resemble each other in certain respects, conclusions about one thing can automatically be applied to the other.

Sending troops to Bosnia is going to get us into the same quagmire the government blundered into in Vietnam.

The writer's assumption that Bosnia is an identical situation to Vietnam is not a safe one. There are, to be sure, some similarities in the two cases: both were civil wars, both involved guerrilla forces, both raised the question of U.S. intervention. But the statement ignores many dissimilarities that the writer would need to take into account in order to make a persuasive case that commiting troops to Bosnia will necessarily lead to the same quagmire as occurred in Vietnam.

Slippery slope. In this type of reasoning, a writer predicts a chain of events that is inevitable and quite often catastrophic. The slippery slope argument is often used against an opponent's proposal to argue that it will have disastrous consequence, unforeseen by its advocates.

> If we decriminalize marijuana, people who smoke pot as a recreational drug will start experimenting with heroin and in no time we'll have a nation of junkies.

The writer assumes a disastrous chain of events will eventuate as the inevitable consequence of the first step—decriminalizing marijuana. Critical readers will not be persuaded by such a sweeping scenario unless the writer can explain why and how the chain of events is going to unfold in the way described.

Red herring. A red herring is something thrown into the argument that distracts readers from the real issues.

> The argument that women in the military should take part in combat just as their male counterparts do sounds fair in principle but actually violates one of the most fundamental laws of nature—the division of labor between men and women. People who do not recognize this law are most likely to be homosexuals, and they are probably the prime violators of the laws of nature in America today.

The writer begins with a position that is reasonable, whether you agree with it or not. But the second sentence does not follow logically and, worse, it takes off in a whole other direction to attack people with whom the writer differs.

Ad Populum.   Ad populum means "to the people." It refers to arguments that seek to mobilize readers' biases and prejudices instead of using principled reasoning.

> We need to limit the number of immigrants admitted into the United States annually. They are taking jobs away from real Americans. Go to your local convenience store and see if you can understand the English the employees are speaking. Koreans, Indians, Pakistanis, Russians. It's out of control. How would you like your daughter or sister to marry one of these people.

The writer has taken the controversial issue of immigration and begins by arguing that the United States needs a new policy. But then instead of explaining why, the writer launches off on a line of scare tactics, to evoke fears of foreigners.

Ad hominem. Ad hominem means literally "to the person" and refers to personal attacks on an opponent rather than rational debate on the issues.

> Councilman Roberts voted against needed increases in school aid. That's no surprise. After all, he sends his children to private school and doesn't care about public education. He's just another rich guy who drives a Mercedes, wears Armani suits, and eats at the most expensive restaurants every chance he gets.

Councilman Roberts may have used bad judgment to oppose school aid. At least, this writer thinks so. And the fact that he sends his children to private school may help explain what his priorities are and why he voted as he did. So up to a certain point, it may be principled and useful to look at an opponent's personal situation and motives in order to cast doubt on his credibility. But the car Roberts drives, the clothes he buys, and the kind of restaurant where he eats don't really fit the line of reasoning developed here.

Bandwagon appeal. The bandwagon appeal tries to persuade us on the grounds that everyone already believes in an idea or holds a particular view or supports a certain policy. The reason we should "join the bandwagon" in these cases does not have to do with the rational merits of an argument but the fact that everyone else is already on board.

Isn't the fact that the Ford Taurus is the best-selling American-made automobile proof enough when it comes to considering your next car purchase? How could so many satisfied customers be wrong?

Advertising relies a good deal on the bandwagon appeal, playing in part on people's anxieties about being left out. Notice in this case how the argument seeks to replace independent judgment with a sense of belonging to a group of "satisfied customers."

Begging the question. Arguments beg the question when they assume as a given what in fact they are supposedly trying to prove. This line of reasoning is sometimes called circular reasoning because it tries to support an assertion with the assertion itself.

We need to institute a policy of mandatory registration of handguns because it is up to the government to make sure it has complete records of exactly who own handguns.

Since "registering handguns" actually means "keeping complete records of who own guns, the argument really says, "We should register handguns because we should register handguns."

Either/Or. Either/or reasoning turns issues into false dilemmas by oversimplifying things, making it appear there only two polarized positions

Either you support a free-market, free enterprise system like the one we have in the United States or you are an enemy of democracy.

Notice two things here. First, the argument makes it seem that there are only two possible positions—for or against a free-market, free enterprise system—thereby reducing the complexity of the situation drastically. Second, not only is the dilemma posed a false one. The term used in opposition to support of a free-market system—"enemy of democracy"—is itself inaccurate because it falsely conflates capitalism and democracy as the same.

WORKING TOGETHER: Logical Fallacies

1. Working together in a group with two or three other students, choose five of the informal fallacies presented above and write an example of each kind of argument. One or two sentences are likely to be enough. Do not label the arguments you write according to type of fallacy.
2. Exchange the informal fallacies you have written with another group. Discuss the five arguments the other group wrote. What seems to be the problem in reasoning with each argument? What would it take to put the argument on more solid ground? What revisions or new support would you suggest for each argument?

CHAPTER
THREE

ARGUMENT, PERSUASION AND RESPONSIBILITY

Imagine you are taking a walk and encounter an elderly man whose car has broken down in the middle of the street. His request "Can you give me hand?" requires no explanation. What makes his request persuasive is the shared belief that people should help each other in times of need. Persuasion seems to occur spontaneously, based largely on a mutual understanding that goes without saying.

You can probably think of other occasions when persuasion took place as a spontaneous meeting of the minds. A friend suggests you go to the basketball game together Friday night, and you agree. A neighbor asks if you can feed their cat when they are away for the weekend. You laugh when a family member tells a story about your uncle's eccentricities. Woven into the fabric of social life, persuasion refers to moments when people reach agreements and join together to accomplish a wide range of purposes and activities.

Moments such as these require no elaborate explanation. You don't need an explicit argument to convince you to go to the basketball game of feed your neighbor's cat. And everybody knows your uncle is one strange guy. The reasons are implied in the situation and the shared understandings of the people involved.

In many other instances, however, people do need to make explicit arguments—to give reasons and explanations—to persuade others. Here are some situations that call on people to make explicit arguments:

- A Jewish man and a Catholic woman fall in love and want to get married. Both families are very devout and always imagined their children would marry someone of their faith in a religious ceremony. Grandchildren, of course, would be raised in the family religion. The couple, however, decides the best way to handle their different religious backgrounds is to get married in a civil ceremony and let their children make their own decisions about religion. Since the couple is of legal age, they could just go ahead and get married, but they want their parents' blessing. Clearly, they have a problem of persuasion and need to come up with some good arguments.

- Persuasion poses a problem for a public relations executive assigned to write a news release explaining why her company has decided to lay off a quarter of the work force. She knows her audience consists of different interests—stockholders concerned with the company's profit margin, company executives responsible for the layoffs, the individuals who have lost their jobs, the public and its low opinion of downsizing and corporate restructuring. What reasons can she give that will present the public image of the company in the best way?

- As part of a campaign to increase childhood immunization, a group of health workers have been commissioned to develop public service announcements for television. They have some decisions to make about the pitch of their publicity. What is the most persuasive approach? Should they emphasize the health risks and what can happen if children are not inoculated? Or should they appeal instead to positive images of good parents taking care of their children? Should they target mothers as the primary audience?

- Students know from experience that essay exams amount to exercises in persuasion. The point is to convince the teacher you have mastered the material and can intelligently answer questions about it. Part of learning in any course involves knowing what counts as a good answer, what kinds of statements teachers find persuasive, and the supporting evidence they expect. How can you use this understanding to prepare for tests and perform well on them?

As you see, situations that call for explicit arguments to persuade others can be complicated. Part of learning to write is learning how to deal with such situations. And that is precisely the purpose of this chapter. The chapter is arranged to help you

- understand the nature of argument,
- analyze issues to write about,
- develop a persuasive position,
- plan convincing arguments, and
- negotiate differences with others.

WORKING TOGETHER: Successful Persuasion

Work together in a group with two or three other students. Before the group meets, write a short description of three occasions you know about when someone or something persuaded someone else. Then follow these directions:

1. Take turns reading aloud the descriptions. Working together, choose one example from each group member. As much as possible, select examples that differ so that you wind up with three or four instances that describe different situations, interactions, and types of persuasion.
2. Working together, analyze the examples you have chosen. In each case, what calls on someone to persuade someone else? Who is trying to influence whom? For what purpose? By what means (written, spoken, visual)? Does the persuasion rely on an explicit argument or on something else? What makes the persuasion successful? What common ground, shared values, mutual understandings are involved?
3. Prepare a report, written or oral depending on your teacher's directions, to present to the class. Use the group reports to identify similarities and differences in the acts of persuasion.

WHAT IS ARGUMENT?: Dealing with Reasonable Differences

People often think of arguments as heated moments when tempers flare and discussion degenerates into a shouting match. There is no question such arguments can be seen frequently on television, whether on daytime talk shows like Rikki Lake and Sally Jessy Raphael or on political commentaries like Crossfire and Firing Line.

For our purposes, however, such images of argument are not very useful We want to think of argument instead as a particular type of persuasion writers and speakers turn to when people have reasonable differences about the issues that face them. This definition may sound obvious. If people didn't disagree, there would be nothing to argue about. Still, the idea that argument occurs when people have reasonable disagreements is worth examining.

After all, there are disagreements among people that are not, properly speaking, reasonable ones. Two people might disagree, for example, about the driving distance between New York City and Buffalo, New York or about the chemical composition of dioxin. These are not altogether reasonable disagreements because they can be resolved by consulting a road atlas or a chemistry book. There are available sources to settle the matter so there's really no point to arguing.

On the other hand, people might reasonably disagree about the best route to drive to Buffalo or about the best policy concerning the production and use of dioxin. In disagreements such as these, there are no final, definitive answers available. One person may prefer a certain route to Buffalo because of the scenery, while another wants only the fastest way possible. By the same token, some may argue that policy on dioxin needs above all to take risks to the environment and public health into account, while for others the effect of policy on the economy and workers' jobs must also be a prime consideration.

ETHICS OF ARGUMENT: The Writer's Responsibility

The recognition that argument begins when people have reasonable disagreements is not simply a technical definition of the term. It also carries important ethical implications about the writer's responsibilities in making arguments.

Genuine argument (as opposed to a shouting match) is devoted to understanding the reasonable differences that divide people and using this understanding to clarify the issues. Arguing is not just a matter of stating your position and scoring points. To argue responsibly means responding to others.

Whether you are making an argument about public policy on dioxin, how to reform the welfare system, or the long term consequences of the Vietnam War, the most persuasive argument is likely to be one that takes into account conflicting interests and differing views. Treating differing views as reasonable (instead of, say, malicious, ignorant, or deviant) makes the goal of argument that of expanding your readers' understanding of the issues so they can see exactly how and why your position fits into a controversy and what the merits of your thinking are.

This view of argument does not mean that you can't hold strong positions or find weaknesses in the views of people who differ with you. It means that you need to take them seriously—to see them not as obstacles to your views but as reasonable human beings. Arguments often polarize all too quickly into "us" arguing against "them." However, to think of arguing responsibly as responding to others can help you see that when you argue you are entering a   relationship with others that seeks mutual understanding, even if agreement is not possible. In this sense, arguments involve working with as much as against others. Reasonable disagreements amount to a collective effort to understand what is at stake and what the best course of action may be.

Exchange of letters.

Darcy Peters and Marcus Boldt.

This is an exchange of letters between Darcy Peters, a homemaker from Camas, Washington, and her representative in the state legislature, Marcus Boldt, a recently elected Republican. As you will see, Peters wrote to Boldt, asking him to oppose a plan to eliminate the state's Readiness to Learn program, which supports the Family Learning Center, an adult education and pre-school program Peters and her three sons attended in Camas. Included here are Peters' letter and the response from Representative Boldt.

Representative Marcus Boldt:

Please do not cancel funding for the Readiness to Learn Family Learning Center.

Our family came to the learning center frustrated. Barely self-supportive, we were struggling but living with no outside assistance. My husband was frequently laid off from work, and I was a full-time mother, not working outside the home. With four-year-old twins and another child, age three, we couldn't afford to pay for a preschool program. When I went to the Head Start program, I was told that we were ineligible because we made too much money. I felt like a victim of the system.

I was thrilled to find out we were eligible for the Readiness to Learn program. My children could all attend, and so could I. My sons, Caleb, Zachary, and Nathan, have learned so much at the center. They constantly surprise me with skills I didn't even know they had. I am so proud of their success. I myself have learned a great deal as well. Being challenged academically has sparked a thirst for learning that I never knew existed in me. I have seen the world open up before me, and I feel capable of meeting any academic challenge. Furthermore, using one of the agencies I learned of at the center, my husband is making a career change, having decided to leave the construction business to become an electrician.

This has been such a valuable experience that I hope many other families are able to attend the center. Abolishing Readiness to Learn might rob another family of the chance to improve itself and reach its long-term goals. We need this program in our area.

Sincerely,
Darcy Peters

Dear Ms. Peters:

Thank you for writing to me about your concerns regarding funding for the Family Learning Center. Your letter goes to the heart of the matter in the area of budgetary reform. My positions on budget expenditures are well-known, and served in large measure to assure my election to this office.

I see that you have three children, ages three and four. You wrote that your husband is subject to frequent layoffs. You indicate that you are a "full-time mother, not working outside the home."

The concerns expressed by the taxpayers over your situation are as follows:

a. If your situation was subject to so much financial instability, then why did you have three children?

b. Why is your husband in a line of work that subjects him to "frequent layoffs"?

c. Why, in the face of your husband's ability to parent as a result of his frequent layoffs, are you refusing to work outside the home?

d. Since there is no state or federally mandated requirement that children attend these programs, why should the taxpayer foot the bill for them?

e. Since your family apparently makes too much money for assistance, why should you receive subsidies of any kind?

f. How much of the situation outlined in your letter should be the responsibility of the people of this state?

g. What arrangements have you made to re-pay this program at some future date?

I do not necessarily agree with all of these perspectives. But I must contend with the expectations of a constituency that is tired of paying for so many programs without any discernible return.

The voters have made it clear that, in this era of personal responsibility, life must become a more "pay-as-you-go" proposition. To put it bluntly, the taxpayers' perspective says, "This program is something that Darcy *wants* to have, and not something that she *must* have."

Thank you for your time.

Marcus Boldt
State Representative

FOR CRITICAL INQUIRY

1. What argument is Darcy Peters making? What differences are at issue? Do they seem to be reasonable ones? On whose behalf is she writing? How does she seem to imagine her relationship to Representative Boldt? How can you tell?

2. How does Boldt seem to identify differences? On whose behalf is he writing? How does he seem to imagine his relationship to Peters? How can you tell?

3. Peter's letter, clearly, did not persuade Boldt or lead to a meeting of the minds. By the same token, it is not likely that Boldt's letter persuaded Peters either. Here, then, is a situation in which arguments have failed to achieve their intended aims. How would you explain this failure? Does the exchange seem to clarify the differences that divide the two? Can you imagine some common ground on which agreement might take place? Why or why not?

ENTERING A CONTROVERSY: Analyzing the Issues

The idea that argument takes place when there are reasonable disagreements among people means that writers do not just start arguments from scratch. Rather they enter a field of debate—or a controversy—where some positions have already been staked out and people are already arguing.

Entering a controversy is like coming into a room where a heated conversation is taking place. Let's say you know some of the people talking but not all of them. You need to listen for awhile, to find out what the various speakers are saying and what the issues seem to be. You may find yourself drawn toward some of the views argued and skeptical about others. Some speakers may be throwing out facts and figures, but you may not be quite sure what they are trying to prove. Some may be taking jabs at other speakers' reasoning.

Gradually, as you listen, you find you agree with some of the speakers' views but oppose others. The controversy begins to make sense to you, and you start to speak . . . .

Entering a controversy, as this scenario reveals, is a matter of coming into the middle of something, and it takes some time to learn your way around and figure out what is going on. It might well be considered rude or presumptuous if you started arguing the moment you entered the room. You need to listen first, to see how you can fit your own views into the stream of debate.

A second point this scenario illustrates is that people enter controversies through their relations to others. As the scenario reveals, your sense of what the debate is about depends on what others have said, what they value, what they propose to do.   For this reason, when you do step forward to speak, you are also articulating your relationship to others—whether it is agreement, qualified support, or counter-argument. Entering a controversy inevitably draws a person into alliances with some people and differences with others.

ANALYZING ISSUES

Listening to and reflecting on the heated conversation going on around you amounts to analyzing the issues. To take part in a controversy—to have your say—you need to understand first of all why speakers disagree and what is at stake for them. This can be complicated—and sometimes confusing—because people do not always agree on what they are arguing about.

Take the following argument about the meaning of Ronald Reagan's presidency:

- One person claims that Reagan's economic policies produced an unprecedented budget deficit and a polarization of the rich and the poor.

- A second person responds that the main achievement of Reagan's presidency is that it brought the country out of a crisis of self-confidence prompted by Vietnam, Watergate, and the Iran hostage episode and thereby restored a sense of national purpose and pride.

- A third person chimes in, claiming that Reagan started a revolution against "big government," public regulation, and the welfare state that should be continued today.

These people might argue all night long, but their argument is likely to be fruitless and unproductive unless they can agree on what they are arguing about. In fact, a person could hold all of the views and agree with each of the speakers, though we sense that in fact some real differences divide them. The problem is they have not sufficiently clarified what they disagree about.

To enter a controversy and argue responsibly means that your arguments (unlike the speakers' in this example) do in fact respond to the issues already posed in dispute. Otherwise, as in the case of the arguments about Reagan's presidency, you cannot possibly engage with others. You will simply get a sequence of claims but little productive debate about how and why people differ in their assessment of Reagan.

But let's not give up on the three people trying to argue about Reagan's presidency. They need to do some work, some sorting out, to understand what is at stake in the various claims they have made. They might still be able to engage each other and find out where and how they differ. But first they need to agree on what the issues are.

TYPES OF CLAIMS

Claims are arguable points that people make when reasonable differences exist. The statement "Ronald Reagan was elected president in 1980" isn't a claim because no one would dispute it. Instead, most people would agree the statement is an established fact. On the other hand, the statement "Ronald Reagan violated the law when he traded guns for the release of hostages in Iran and channeled the funds to buy weapons for the Contras in Nicaragua" is a claim because in this case the facts remain disputed and in doubt. Did Reagan actually authorize the shipment of weapons to the Contras? If so, what law did he violate and how?

To return to our three speakers, we can see that there are three different and distinct types of claims made in their argument about the Reagan presidency. Each of these claims offers a place to begin a productive argument.

1. Claims that can be substantiated: These claims refer to questions of disputed facts, definitions, causes, and consequences. They involve asking whether something actually happened, what it is, what brought it about, and what its effects are. The first speaker makes a claim that can be substantiated by asserting that Reagan's economic policies caused certain things to happen. This is a claim that can be supported or refuted by using the available evidence.

As it turns out, the claim that Reagan violated the law in the Iran-Contra affair is a complicated one because it actually contains two claims that require substantiation: 1) given the disputed facts in the case, the person making the claim needs to show that it was probable that Reagan authorized the arms shipments to the Contras, and 2) assuming Reagan did authorize the shipments, the person would still need to show that the case fits into a particular category—that is, there is the definitional question of explaining how Reagan's action violates an existing law.

Claims that call for substantiation occur regularly in ongoing arguments: Did Microsoft violate anti-trust laws by pressuring PC manufacturers to include its Web navigator (question of disputed fact)? What kinds of actions amount to sexual harrassment? (question of definition)? Are environmental carcinogenic responsible for the increase in breast cancer (question of cause)? Has expansion of pro football into new cities diluted the quality of the game (question of consequences)?

2. Claims based on evaluation: These claims refer to questions of whether something is good or bad, right or wrong, desirable or undesirable, effective or ineffective, valuable or worthless. The second speaker makes a claim based on evaluation when he says that Reagan's presidency was important because it restored a sense of national pride and purpose. In this case, support or refutation of the speaker's claim will necessarily rely on a value judgment.

Claims based on evaluation appear routinely in all spheres of life: Is a Macintosh or a DOS-based computer system best suited to your computing needs? Are day-time talk TV programs such as Jenny Jones and Sally Jessy Raphael a national scandal or do they provide a needed public forum for controversial issues? Is affirmative action unfair to white males? What novels should be included in an American literature course?

3. Claims that propose or endorse policy: These claims refer to questions of what we should do and how we should implement our aims. The third speaker makes a claim that endorses Reagan's policies to dismantle or scale down many government functions. Support or refutation of policy claims will typically focus on how well the policy solves an existing problem or addresses a demonstrable need.

Claims that endorse or propose policy are pervasive in public discussions. Typically, they use the terms "should," "ought," or "must" to signal the courses of action they recommend: Should the federal government implement a single income tax for all people? Or ought it substitute a national sales tax? Must all students be required to take a first-year writing course?

Identifying what type of issue is at stake in a speaker's claim offers a way to cut into an ongoing controversy and get oriented. This does not mean, however, that controversies come neatly packaged according to type of claim. The three claims are tools of analysis to help you identify how and why people disagree. As you prepare to enter an ongoing controversy, you are likely to find that the three types of claim are connected and lead from one to the next.

Here is an example of how the three types of claims can be used to explore a controversy and invent arguments.

CONTROVERSY: SHOULD HIGH SCHOOLS ABOLISH TRACKING AND ASSIGN STUDENTS TO MIXED-ABILITY CLASSROOMS INSTEAD?

1. Claims that can be substantiated: How widespread is the practice of tracking? When did it begin? Why was tracking instituted in the first place? What purposes was it designed for? What are the effects of tracking on students? What experiments have taken place to use mixed-ability groupings instead of tracking? What have the results been?
2. Claims based on evaluation: What educational values are put into practice in tracking? Are these values worthy ones? Is tracking fair to all students? Does it benefit some students more than others? What values are embodied in mixed-ability classrooms? How do these compare to the values of tracking?
3. Claims that endorse or propose policy: What should we do? What reasons are there for maintaining tracking? What reasons for implementing mixed-ability groupings? Can mixed-ability classrooms succeed? What changes would be required? What would the long-term consequences be?

TAKING A POSITION: Crafting a Rhetorical Stance

The point of analyzing the issues in any ongoing controversy is to clarify your own thinking and determine where you stand. Taking a position amounts to entering into the debate to have your own say. Determining your position means you have an arguable claim to make—an informed opinion, belief, recommendation, or call to action you want your readers to consider.

Look at the following two statements:

Tracking was recently dismantled in a local school district.
Tracking has become a very heated issue.

As you can see, these sentences simply describe a situation. They aren't really arguable claims because no one would reasonably disagree with them. They don't tell readers what the writer believes or thinks should be done. Now take a look at these two statements:

For the dismantling of tracking to be successful, our local school district should provide teachers with in-service training in working with multi-ability groups.
Tracking has become such a heated issue because parents of honors students worry unnecessarily that their children won't get into the best colleges.

Notice that in each statement you can see right away what the writer's stand on the issue is. The first writer treats an issue of policy, while the second treats an issue of interpretation. What makes each claim arguable is that there can be differing views regarding the issue the writer considers. Readers could respond, for example, that in-service training is a waste of money because teachers already know how to teach different levels of students or that the real reason tracking is so controversial is because it holds back the brightest students. To make sure a claim is arguable, ask yourself whether someone could reasonably disagree with it—whether there could be at least two differing views on the issue on which you've taken a position.

Both writers have successfully cued readers to their positions, in part by using key words that typically appear in position statements. Notice that in the first sentence, the writer uses should (but could have used similar terms such as must, ought to, needs to, and has to) to signal a proposed solution. In the second, the writer uses a because statement to indicate to readers there is evidence available to back up the claim. Writers also use terms such as therefore, consequently, thus, it follows that, the point is, and so on to signal their positions.

STEPS TOWARD A TENTATIVE POSITION

Take a current controversy that you know something about, where reasonable differences divide people. It could be the death penalty, drug testing for high school or college athletes, censorship of music lyrics, curfews for adolescents under eighteen. The main thing is that the controversy interests you and that you believe it is an important.

1. State the controversy in its most general terms in the form of a question. "Should colleges routinely conduct drug tests on varsity athletes?" "Do we need a rating system for television shows, similar to the one used for movies?"
2. Then use the three types of claims—of substantiation, evaluation, and policy —to generate a list of more specific questions. ("How do drug tests work?" "Why were drug tests developed in the first place and what are their consequences?" "Do drug tests violate constitutional freedoms?" "Is drug testing sound policy?")
3. Pick one set of questions from your list of types of claims. (For example, you might pick the interrelated questions "Do drug tests actually work?" "Are they reliable?" "Can they be circumvented?") Develop a tentative position that responds to the question or questions. Make sure it presents an arguable claim.
4. Consider whether your tentative position is an informed claim. At this point, you may need more information to analyze the issues responsibly and develop an arguable claim with sufficient evidence.

RHETORICAL STANCE: Developing a Persuasive Position

Once you have a tentative position in mind, you can begin to think about how to present it to your readers in the most persuasive way possible. One powerful set of persuasive strategies is known in classical rhetoric as the appeals. The three appeals—ethos, pathos, and logos—offer three different but interrelated ways to influence your readers by appealing to their ideas and values, sympathies and beliefs.

- Ethos: ethos refers to the character of the writer as it is projected to the reader through the written text. The modern terms "personality" or "attitude" begin to capture the meaning of ethos and how readers build an impression of the kind of person the writer is—how credible, fair, and authoritative.

- Pathos: pathos refers to the readers' emotions and the responses a piece of writing arouses in them. Pathos should not be associated simply with emotional appeals to readers' fears and prejudices. Instead, it offers a way to analyze their state of mind and the intensity with which they hold various beliefs and values.

- Logos: logos refers to what is said or written. Its original meaning was "voice" or "speech," though the term later took on association with logic and reasoning. For our purposes, the term offers a way to focus on the writer's message and the line of reasoning the writer develops.

RHETORICAL STANCE

Rhetorical stance refers to the way writers coordinate ethos, pathos, and logos as interrelated components in persuasive writing. To see how this coordination of the three appeals works in practice, let's look at a passage from one of Malcolm X's most famous speeches "The Bullet or the Ballot," delivered to a largely black audience in 1964. At the time Malcolm gave his speech, the Senate was debating the Civil Rights Act of 1964, which passed later in the year following a filibuster by its opponents.

Malcolm X. from "The Bullet or the Ballot."

I'm not a politician, not even a student of politics; in fact, I'm not a student of much of anything. I'm not a Democrat, I'm not a Republican, and I don't even consider myself an American. If you and I were Americans, there'd be no problem. Those Hunkies that just got off the boat, they're already Americans; Polacks are already Americans; the Italian refugees are already Americans. Everything that came out of Europe, every blue-eyed thing, is already an American. And as long as you and I have been over here, we aren't Americans yet.

Well, I am one who doesn't believe in deluding myself. I'm not going to sit at your table and watch you eat, with nothing on my plate, and call myself a diner. Sitting at the table doesn't make you a diner, unless you eat some of what's on that plate. Being here in America doesn't make you an American. Why, if birth made you American, you wouldn't need any legislation, you wouldn't need any amendments to the Constitution, you wouldn't be faced with civil-rights filibustering in Washington, D. C. right now. They don't have to pass civil-rights legislation to make a Polack an American.

No, I'm not an American. I'm one of the 22 million black people who are the victims of Americanism. One of the 22 million black people who are the victims of democracy, nothing but disguised hypocrisy. So, I'm not standing here speaking to you as an American, or a patriot, or a flag-saluter, or a flag-waver—no, not I. I'm speaking as a victim of this American system. And I see America through the eyes of the victim. I don't see any American dream; I see an American nightmare.

Notice in this passage how ethos, pathos, and logos are not separate aspects of the speech but rather work together in fashioning Malcolm X's rhetorical stance.

Analysis of Persuasive Appeals in "The Bullet or the Ballot"

• Ethos. Malcolm X identifies himself first by explaining what he is not—a politician, a student of politics, a Democrat, or a Republican. In fact, he does not even consider himself an American. Instead, he identifies himself as "one of the 22 million black people who are victims of Americanism."

Malcolm X presents himself here as someone who is willing to look at the racial situation in America without illusions. "I am one," he says, "who doesn't believe in deluding myself." Just being in America, he argues, doesn't make black people Americans. Otherwise, black people would not need civil rights legislation to achieve equality.

The tone and attitude Malcolm X projects are militant and unrelenting, chosen in part to distinguish his appeal from civil rights leaders such as Martin Luther King who emphasized racial reconciliation and working through the system. For Malcolm X, there is no point in appealing to American democratic values, as King often did, because the system has always been a hypocritical one—not a dream but a nightmare.

• Pathos. By locating a stance outside the system, Malcolm X is inviting his audience to join him in rejecting the moderation of civil rights leaders and to share a new, more militant politics.

He is seeking, on one hand, to mobilize his black listeners' feelings about what it means to be an American. By offering an explanation of how black people have been systematically excluded from the American dream, Malcolm X is seeking to redirect the intensity of his black listeners' emotions—away from the hope of racial integration toward a new identity based on the power and self-reliance of black people united in struggle. He is offering a way to see themselves not as humble petitioners to the white power structure but as a power in their own right.

On the other hand, it may well appear that Malcolm X has written off white listeners. His use of ethnic slurs such as "Hunkies" and "Polacks" are offensive and can hardly have endeared him to his white audience. Many whites did indeed reject his message as anti-white and potentially dangerous. But for others, Malcolm X's unflinching analysis of race relations in America brought with it the shock of recognition that white skin privilege is a pervasive feature of American life. In fact, Malcolm X did gain a wide audience of whites who came to admire his unyielding insistence on "telling it like it is" and who were thereby led to rethink the consequences of racism in America.

• Logos. As you have just seen, Malcolm X established a relationship to his listeners by projecting an attitude and a message that elicited powerful responses. If anything, the way he presents himself (ethos) and his listeners' responses (pathos) are inseparable from the form and content of his message (logos). Still, it is worth noting how cogently reasoned this message is.

Malcolm X's reasoning is simple yet devastating. It all revolves around the issue of how people get to be considered Americans. According to Malcolm X, people who came from Europe are already considered Americans. They don't need civil rights legislation. At the same time, the fact of being born in America is not necessarily enough to be considered an American. Otherwise black people born in American would not need civil rights legislation. Put these two propositions together and you get the unavoidable conclusion: the fact that black people need civil rights legislation proves in effect that they are not considered Americans. The implication is that they are therefore something else—not the inheritors of the American dream but the victims of an American nightmare.

"Another Hit Job on Ethnic Cuisine"

This editorial appeared in the *Adirondack Daily Enterprise* on August 1, 1994. It is a response to a report issued by the Center of Science in the Public Interest, a non-profit organization that had previously reported on the high fat and sodium content of food served in Chinese and Italian restaurants.

Editorial

Another hit-job on ethnic cuisine

The Center for Science in the Public Interest is at it again. The same folks who helped bring the Alar scare and, more recently, dietary fright-stories regarding Chinese and Italian foods have done another hit-job on ethnic cuisine. This time it's Mexican food on the Center for Pseudo-Science's growing NON list.

CSPI, whose staffers seem to spend their days worrying about everything that tastes good, say those wonderful enchiladas, tacos, salsa, chips and assorted dips and beans are full of fat and salt. Somehow we don't think too many people think they're avoiding fatty calories when they drop a nice big glop of sour cream on top of their chiles rellanos.

The worry-warts at CSPI are undeterred by common sense, however. They conveniently ignore the fact that many Mexican dishes have a lot of vegetables and fiber in them, and thus contribute to a balanced diet. Certainly people south of the border would be surprised to discover their native food, developed over centuries, is terrible.

Before you toss out your taco shells, you may want to take note of the fact that CSPI has an agenda: It rarely has met a regulation it hasn't liked. CSPI also doesn't much care for food that tastes good.

CSPI, of course, is anything but a moderate organization. And even though its "studies" of restaurant foods are shoddy, the media attention they garner has done great damage to the targeted restaurants. After its hit-job on Chinese foods, Chinese restaurants saw their business drop 25 to 35 percent, according to the New York Times.

So we have a suggestion for all you who are getting a bit weary of the grass-eating food police: For your next meal out, go Mexican. Load up on the refried beans and other dishes of CSPI's ire. After that, move on to Italian and Chinese feasts. Bon appetit!

FOR CRITICAL INQUIRY

1. Describe the attitude of this editorial. What impression does the editorial seem to want to make on readers? How can you tell?
2. What response does the editorial seek to elicit from readers? What does it seem to assume the writer and reader have in common? How does this shared ground position writer and reader in relation to the Center for Science in the Public Interest's report?
3. The final section contains the advice, "For your next meal out, go Mexican. Load up on the refried beans and other dishes of CSPI's ire. After that, move on to Italian and Chinese feasts." Describe the reasoning the led to this claim. Is it responsible and logically argued?

CONSTRUCTING THE APPROPRIATE RHETORICAL STANCE

Experienced writers know that to make persuasive arguments they need to construct an appropriate rhetorical stance. Whether the rhetorical stance you construct is appropriate will, of course, depend on the situation that calls for writing, your purposes, and the beliefs of your readers. Arguments that are appropriate and persuasive in one situation may not necessarily be appropriate and persuasive in another.

Two Letters of Application

The following letters were written by a student applying for a summer internship at a cable television station—Greater Worcester Media Cable Company. As you read, notice that the student is making an arguable claim, namely, ìyou should hire me as an intern.î The question is whether the rhetorical stance he develops is appropriate to the occasion.

Letter #1:

Dear _____ ,

I would like to apply for a summer internship at Greater Worcester Media Cable Company. I've just switched my major from pre-med to mass communication, and I'm really excited about getting out of those boring science classes and into something that interests me. I just finished this great video production class and made a short documentary called "Road Kill," about all the animals that get run over on Highway 61. It was pretty arty and punk, with a sound track dubbed from Sonic Youth.

I want to learn everything I can about television. I'd love to eventually be an anchorman on the national news, like Dan Rather or Peter Jennings or Tom Brokaw. I've always known that television is one of the most influential parts of American life, and I think it would be awesome to be seen nightly by millions of viewers. Think of all the influence—and fun—you could have, with everyone watching you.

Of course, if I do get the internship, I won't be able to go home this summer, and that will be kind of a bummer because my parents and girl friend are pretty much expecting I'll be around. But still, it would be worth it to get into television because that's where I see myself going long term.

Letter #2

Dear _____ :

I would like to apply for a summer internship at Greater Worcester Media Cable Company. As my resume indicates, I am a Mass Communication major in my sophomore year, with course work in video production, mass communication theory, and the history of television. In addition, I have a strong background in the natural sciences.

I believe that my studies in Mass Communication have given me skills and experience that would be valuable in a summer internship. In my video production class, I filmed and edited a short documentary, and I am eager to gain more experience in production and editing.

A summer internship would be a wonderful opportunity for me to learn how the day-to-day world of cable television works. This kind of practical experience would be an invaluable complement to my coursework in the history and theory of the media.

WORKING TOGETHER: Rhetorical Stance

You have probably concluded that the first letter would be inappropriate as a letter of application to Greater Worcester Media Cable Company and that the second letter has a greater chance of success. Your task now is to explain why. Work together with two or three other students. Follow these directions:

1. Compare the two letters in terms of the rhetorical stance the writer has constructed in each case. Be specific here and point to words, phrases, and passages that reveal how the writer coordinates ethos, logos, and pathos.

2. The first letter may be inappropriate to apply for a summer internship. But that doesn't mean it is not as well written as the second. Notice that in certain respects it has more life, more telling details, and more of a sense of the writer's personality than the second letter. Can you think of a situation in which the first letter would be appropriate to the writer's purposes and the interests of readers?

CRAFTING AN ARGUMENT: Persuasive Appeals

Use the information in the two letters to write a third letter, addressed to either the writer's parents or his girl friend. The letter should explain why the writer wants to apply for the summer internship and to persuade the reader this is a good idea, even though it would mean not being able to come home for the summer. Consider how an appropriate and persuasive rhetorical stance would coordinate the three appeals—ethos, pathos, and logos.

MAKING AN ARGUMENT: Looking at the Parts

Good arguments aren't found ready to use. They have to be made. To make a persuasive argument, you need to develop an effective line of reasoning. To do that, it is helpful to look at the parts that go into making an argument. In this section, we draw on a model of argument developed by the philosopher Stephen Toulmin, although we use somewhat different terms. Here is a quick sketch of the parts of argument we'll be considering in more detail in this section:

Claim	Your position, the basic point you want readers to accept
Evidence	The supporting material for the claim
Enabling Assumption	The line of reasoning that explains how the evidence supports the claim
Backing	Reasons that show the enabling assumption is valid
Differing views	Disagreements with all or part of your argument
Qualifiers	Words that modify or limit the claim

Claims, Evidence, and Enabling Assumptions

As you have seen, you can't have a responsible argument unless you have an arguable claim, and you've looked at some ways to develop claims by analyzing issues and constructing an appropriate rhetorical stance. In this section, we look in detail at the three basic parts of an argument—claims, evidence, and enabling assumptions. Taken together, these terms give us a way to think about the line of reasoning in an argument. Readers justifiably expect writers to provide evidence for the claims they make. Moreover, they expect the evidence a writer offers to have a clear connection to the claim. As you will see, enabling assumptions are explanations of how the evidence supports a writer's claim.

To see how these connections work, take a look at the two following evaluations students wrote of their composition instructor:

1. Ms. Smith is probably the worst teacher I've had so far in college. I've never been so frustrated. I could never figure out what the teacher wanted us to do. She didn't grade the papers we turned in but instead just wrote comments on them. Then we had to evaluate each others' writings. How are students qualified to judge each others' writing? This is the teacher's job. We had to revise some of our writing to put in a portfolio at the end of the term. How were we supposed to know which papers were any good?

2. Ms. Smith is probably the best teacher I've had so far in college. I really liked how she organized the work. By not grading our papers, she gave us the opportunity to select our best writing and revise it for a portfolio at the end of the term. The comments she offered on drafts and the evaluations we did of each others' papers really helped. I found this freed me to experiment with my writing in new ways and not worry about getting low grades. This system made me realize how important revision is.

In one sense, both evaluations are persuasive. It's hard not to be convinced, at the level of lived experience, that the first student did not like the class, while the second student did. But what are we to make of these differences? What do they tell us about the teacher and her way of teaching writing?

In this case, to understand why the two students differ, it will help to see how they differ. Each has made an argument, and we can analyze how the arguments have been made. Each consists of the same basic parts.

- Claims. In the two student evaluations, the competing claims are easy to find: Ms. Smith is either the best or the worst teacher in the student's experience. Each of the claims, moreover, meets the test for writing arguable claims.
  Reasonable differences. The claims are both matters of judgment that can't be decided by referring to an established, authoritative source. The question of whether Ms. Smith is a good teacher is worth arguing about.
  Plausibility. Both claims could be true. Each has a certain credibility that a claim like "An invasion of flyer saucers will take place next week" doesn't have.
  Sharable claims. Both claims can be argued on terms that can be shared by others. There's no reason to argue, for example, that blue is your favorite color or that you love the feel of velvet because such a claim refers to a personal preference based on subjective experience and can't really be shared by others.

- Evidence. The evidence is all the information available in a particular situation. Just as detectives do in the investigation of a crime, writers begin with the available evidence—data, information, facts, observations, personal testimony, statistics, common knowledge, or any other relevant material. (Chapter Four has information on the main types of evidence and how to evaluate the way writers use them.)

Writers use this evidence to construct a sense of what happened and what the unresolved issues are. Notice in the two evaluations of Ms. Smith that the students do not seem to differ concerning what happened in class. Both describe the same teaching strategies: students wrote papers which were not graded; they received comments from the teacher and from other students; they were required to revise a number of the papers for a final portfolio. The difference is how each uses this evidence. (See the box "Questions to Ask About Evidence.")

BOX QUESTIONS TO ASK ABOUT EVIDENCE

To make a persuasive argument, you need evidence for your claim—and you also need some guidelines to evaluate whether the evidence you turn up will work for your argument. Here are some questions to ask yourself:

- Is the evidence clearly related to the claim? As you plan an argument, you are likely to come up with lots of interesting material. Not all of it, however, will necessarily be relevant to the claim you want to support. For example, if you are arguing about how Darwin's theory of evolution influenced fiction writers in the nineteenth century, it doesn't make sense to give a lot of biographical details on Darwin. They may be interesting, but it's unlikely they will help you explain the influence of his theory.

- Do you have enough evidence? Making a claim based on one or two instances is hardly likely to persuade your readers. They are likely to dismiss your argument as a hasty and unjustifiable conclusion based on insufficient evidence. For example, the fact that two people in your neighborhood were laid off recently from their construction jobs is not enough evidence to claim the construction industry is in crisis. You would need to establish a pattern by showing, say, a decline in housing starts, the postponement of many major building projects, layoffs across the country, bankruptcies of construction companies, and so on.

- Is your evidence verifiable? Readers are likely to be suspicious of your argument unless they can check out the evidence for themselves. For example, let's say you are using examples of how corporate donations influenced politicians' voting to support an argument for campaign finance reform. If you don't tell readers who the politicians and corporations are, they will have no way to verify your evidence.

- Is your evidence up to date? Readers expect you to do your homework and provide them with the latest information available. If your evidence is dated, readers may well suspect that newer information has supplanted it and thereby find your argument unpersuasive. For example, if you are arguing for gender equity in medical education, citing figures on the enrollment of women in medical schools in the 1960s (around 10%) will be quickly dismissed because women currently represent around 50% of entering medical school classes. (A better case for gender equity might be built by looking at possible patterns of discrimination in residency assignments or the specializations women go into.)

- Does your evidence come from reliable sources? You would probably not make an argument based on The Weekly World's latest Elvis-sighting. As mentioned in Chapter 2, the evidence needs to be evaluated and interpreted in light of its sources. Scientific studies, government reports, and research by academics, professional associations, and independent research institutes are likely to carry considerable authority for readers. Partisan sources—magazines such as the conservative National Review or the left-liberal Nation—often contain important evidence you can use persuasively, especially if you acknowledge the bias and ask readers to consider the merits of the information in the context of your argument.

- **Enabling assumptions.**

Consider how the two students get from the available evidence—the facts that neither disputes—to their differing claims. There is a crucial move here that each argument relies on. For an argument to be persuasive, readers need to know how and why the evidence cited by the writer entitles him or her to make a claim. This link—the connection in an argument between the evidence and the writer's claim—is called the enabling assumption because if refers to the line of reasoning that explains how the evidence supports the claim. Such assumptions are often implied rather than stated explicitly.

Notice in the two student evaluations that the enabling assumptions are implied but not directly stated. To find out how the two students connect the evidence to their claims, let's imagine we could interview them, to push them to articulate this missing link in their arguments:

Student #1

Q. How was your writing teacher?

A. She was the worst teacher I've had so far. (claim)

Q. What makes you say that?

A. The teacher never graded our papers. We had to evaluate each others' papers and then revise a few and put them in a portfolio. (evidence)

Q. So why was that so bad?

A. Well, because good teachers give you lots of graded evaluations so you know exactly where you stand in a class. (enabling assumption)

Student #2

Q. How was your writing teacher?

A. She was great, best I've had so far. (claim)

Q. What makes you say that?

A. The teacher never graded our papers. We had to evaluate each others' papers and then revise a few and put them in a portfolio. (evidence)

Q. So why was that so good?

A. Well, because good teachers help you develop your own judgment by experimenting without worrying about grades. (enabling assumption)

Of course, we could push each writer further to explore the assumptions that underlie the one they have articulated. If we pushed far enough, we are likely to find fundamental beliefs each holds about the nature of education and learning. For example, in the case of the second student, an exploration of assumptions might look like this:

Assumption 1: Good teaching helps students develop judgment by experimenting and not having to worry about grades.

Assumption 2: Too much emphasis on grades can get in the way of learning judgment through trial and error.

Assumption 3: Education should emphasize the development of individual judgment as much or more than the learning of subject material.

Assumption 4: Students naturally want to learn and will do so if given the chance.

This process could continue indefinitely, and it can be a useful exercise for writers to explore the assumptions underlying assumptions. The practical question in making an argument is to decide which of these assumptions—or some combination of them—are likely to be shared by your readers and which can best clarify differences you have with others.

WORKING TOGETHER: Analyzing Claims, Evidence, and Enabling Assumptions

To work with the terms introduced here, analyze the statements that appear below. Identify the claim each statement makes. Identify the evidence that each statement relies on. Finally, explain how an enabling assumption, which may or may not be stated explicitly, connects the evidence to the claim.

1. Robert Dole made a fatal miscalculation in his bid for the presidency in 1996 by resting on his record as Senator and failing to present a compelling vision to the American people.
2. When the Chicago Bulls acquired power forward Dennis Rodman before the 1995-96 basketball season, they guaranteed themselves a shot at the NBA title.
3. The current increase in cases of tuberculosis can be attributed to new strains of the disease that are resistant to treatment by antibiotics.
4. The fact that both parents have to work just to make ends meet is destroying the American family.
5. It is reasonable that the CEOs of American corporations make over one hundred times in salary and bonuses what the average worker in the company earns.

GOING   ON-LINE

Following a Thread

The three messages that follow were posted at Wired magazine's web site in April 1996, when Congress was considering the Communications Decency Act (CDA). The bill, with its provisions to regulate "indecent" material on the Internet, was passed but subsequently ruled unconsitutional by the Supreme Court.

Wired was one of the leading opponents of the CDA, and as you can see, the thread of discussion seems to assume that readers are opposed to the bill as well. Notice that each of the messages instead seeks to offer a pesuasive explanation of the motivation behind the CDA.

As you read, identify the main claim each writer is making. What evidence does he offer? What enabling assumptions connect the evidence to the claim?

Visit a discussion at a web site, news group, or listserv on a topic that interests you where people are posting messages about a controversial issue. (See "Finding Forums" in Chapter XX for suggestions about locating discussions.) Follow a thread, noticing how the messages make arguments and seek to persuade readers. Do you notice ways that electronic argument and persuasion differ from more traditional forms of print literacy?

Andy Rozmiarek (drew) on Thu, 4 Apr 96 22:56 PST

1. **The unWIRED Majority**
   Mark Baum (silverhawaiian) on Wed, 10 Apr 96 22:48 PDT

```
I find that the CDA is the most supressive way of
silencing a new medium akin to Gutenberg's
printing press.  And, the shocking fact is that
the only people who aren't turning a blind eye to
the CDA are those who actually have computers,
modems and a link into this wellspring of
information known as the "Internet".

You need not look at the many propaganda-tasting
movies based on what the 'net is to figure out how
paranoid the unWired populace has become. With all
the media bloat governing the fears surrounding
what one can do to harm another person with a
computer.

As for price for the equipment, if you're willing
to sacrifice the graphics, you can grab a 2400
baud modem and an 8088 IBM PC with a monochrome
card and monitor plus the right terminal software
to surf the WWW via Unix's Lynx. So price is no
object.

And, as ironic as it sounds, the people who aren't
currently wired are making most of these laws
based on the paranoia of widespread sex, libel,
slander and other "attrocious" acts. I'm referring
to the majority of congressmen and possibly even
the President.

Let's face it.  There is a lot of information out
there already in print which may offend many
citizens.  And all _print_ material is offered
First Amendment protections.  The Internet is
different.  It's all a bunch of ones and zeroes
blasted through the ISDN and analog lines to
computers around the world.  And, like print
material, we choose what we want to view.  And if
you're online, you don't even have to go out in
public and risk going to that seedier place down
the street.

The CDA refuses to acknowledge the "human
curiosity" aspect of the equation.  I'm sure that
maybe at least a few of us has stooped to the
level of looking for those dirty magazines buried
```

underneath dad's underwear in his drawer. Just
for curiosity in the throes of our adolecence.
Who's to blame? Our parents for having those
magazines in the first place or the publisher for
making that magazine readily available to the
adults? The kids are naturally curious at that
age not because of "evil" from "pornography" but
hormones.

Sex is everywhere. There is no way that they'll
contain it all. Plus, to think that this bill was
sponsored by the Christian Coalition is also
ironic in itself. If sex is so bad in their eyes,
how the Hell are they multiplying?

Me, I have an open mind. Sex is not the evil. The
kids will learn all about it eventually. The evil
in their eyes stems from the publicity of
Internet-connected online services which, in the
eyes of the writers of the CDA, are _the
Internet_. They assume that the Internet has a
point of control. There is only one point and that
is via the user's terminal. The user has the
control; not the Internet.

These people have to get a clue and stop comparing
porn BBSes and online services to the Internet.
The Internet is not as simple as an online
service. The Internet is a connection _means_. A
standard. A way of getting diverse system
configurations to communicate with each other.
There is no centralized point of control in that
aspect.

In diversity comes choice. We choose what we, the
people, want.

POSTS-FIRST-PREVIOUS-NEXT-SINCE-INDEX-TOPICS

2. Ours is a fearful generation
Mark Libby (phroggity) on Thu, 11 Apr 96 16:27 PDT

In scanning all the posts related to the
"crackdown" on the internet, a simple, yet
profound scenario is panning itself out.

It helps to keep in mind that our society has long
ago embraced fear as its underlying philosophy.

The feminine concept of "security" has pervaded
our society. The press, law, politics, schooling,
business, and just walking down the street are
currently driven by fear. Anything that is
unknown, not_of_the_mainstream, not "secure", not
under someone's_control must be brought under
someone's management before it can be regarded as
"safe".

Of course, politics and the press are programmed
to sensationalize and dramatize anything "unsafe",

however absurd. Lawyers see "unsafe" as a wallet
opportunity - encouraging fear at every turn. They
all encourage fear to justify the need for
"control".

This obsession with fear (and its symptom,
"security") creates two equally predictible
results: a) A strident resolve to control
everything or destroy the uncontrollable. b) The
destruction of creativity, growth, and
self-expression, which cannot exist in a
controlled environment.

We are served by a VERY careful balance between
"control" and "self-expression".

If you realize the scope of the Internet -
crossing city, county, state, and national
boundaries - you must also recognize how it plays
on the fears of control groups. Those that regard
themselves the guarantors of "safe" to society AND
those that think information is power are very
strongly motivated to bring the internet under
"control" - all for our own safety, you
understand.

6. **Who decides what is indecent?**
   bill haynes (custodian) on Thu, 18 Apr 96 14:42 PDT

The problem with this bill is; who is going to
decide what is indecent? IMHO those who cry
the loudest for censorship have the dirtiest
minds on earth. They are the people who look
for smut in the clouds of a disney movie.
These anal-retentive folks could find smut
in a class of water, they seem to see filth
everywhere and of course filth is forbidden.
What amazes me is that in our society, violence
is AOK, but show any of the "forbidden" parts of
the body and all heck breaks loose. The human
body is of itself dirty of course, we don't
want anyone looking at that. There are already
plenty of tools out there for worried parents
to shield their children from "smut". I think
that parental control goes a long way toward
addressing the problem. Our intellectually
bankrupt legislators just leap on the bandwagon
to "protect the children" without ever having
browsed the net or joined a newsgroup in thier
life. Of course not knowing anything about a
given subject has never in the past stopped them
from writing restrictive legislation, why would
it now?

• **Backing** Backing refers to evidence and explanations that show an enabling assumption in an argument is valid and reliable. If your readers accept your enabling assumption, whether you state it explicitly or leave it implied, there is probably no reason to provide backing for it. But, as in the case of the two student evaluations, where enabling assumptions differ, writers need to explain why their enabling assumption is preferable or more important than competing ones.

As you have seen, the differences that divide the two student evaluations of Ms. Smith hinge on the different enabling assumption each uses to connect the evidence to the claim. Only by identifying these unstated assumptions can we really understand what is at stake for them. For the two writers to construct responsible arguments that can clarify their differences, they need to make these enabling assumptions explicit. Here is what the opening of the first student's evaluation might look like, if it made the enabling assumption explicit:

> One of the marks of good teaching is giving students frequent graded evaluations of their work so that they understand the teacher's expectations and know where they stand in the class. I just had a composition teacher who demonstrates the disaster that can happen when teachers don't take this basic principle of teaching into account.

This is certainly a clearer version of what the writer is trying to argue, but it still leaves open the question of whether giving frequent grades is a "mark of good teaching" and a "basic principle." Is this a safe assumption to make, one that readers will find a reliable measure of good teaching? We may or may not be persuaded, depending on our own assumptions about teaching. In fact, as you can see, the enabling assumption itself is arguable and therefore needs support if the student hopes to persuade readers.

For this reason, the writer could strengthen the argument further by adding backing to the enabling assumption. The student could provide supporting evidence and explanations (such as research studies about the level of student anxiety in classes where there is little graded work; expert testimony on the subject of what constitutes good teaching; statistics showing students learned more in classes with frequent grades; personal accounts from other students about how they slacked off when their work wasn't graded, and so on) to bolster the persuasiveness of the enabling assumption.

WORKING TOGETHER: Backing an Argument

Work together in groups of two or three. What kind of backing can you think of that would support the following enabling assumptions? What sources would you turn to?

1. In the final analysis, the state of the economy determines presidential elections.
2. To win in the NBA, a team needs an intimidating power forward.
3. In time, we will see that most diseases are hereditary.
4. We must strengthen the American family.
5. Big business is greedy.

• **Differing Views** To argue responsibly, you can't pretend no one disagrees with you or that there are no alternative perspectives. To note these differences is not, as students sometimes think, to undermine your own argument. In fact, it can strengthen your argument by showing that you are willing to take all sides into account and that you can refute objections to your argument and, when necessary, concede the validity of differing views.

Summarize differing views fairly and accurately. Readers can often detect when writers handle differing views in a distorted way. In fact, readers' impressions of a writer's credibility and good character—the writer's ethos—depends in part on how reasonably the writer deals with differences. For this reason, the ability to summarize fairly and accurately is quite important to the success of an argument. By summarizing fairly and accurately, you can show readers you have anticipated reasonable differences and intend to deal with them in a responsible manner.

This can help avoid readers jumping into your argument with objections you've overlooked: "Sure the government creating jobs for people on welfare sounds like a good idea but what about the cost? And what about personal responsibility? Doesn't this just make people dependent in a different way?" Or rushing to the defense of objections you have characterized unfairly: "Not all conservative Christians believe women should be barefoot and pregnant." (See the section "Summary" in Chapter 4.)

Refuting differing views. Summarize views that differ from yours briefly, fairly, and accurately. Then explain what's wrong with them. Your best chance of persuading readers that your position is preferable to others is to clarify the differences that divide you and explain what you see as the weaknesses in other lines of reasoning.

To return to the student evaluations, the first student could strengthen his argument about what good teaching is by anticipating, summarizing, and refuting elements in the second student's argument. He might argue, for example, that while peer response to others' written work may sound like a good idea, in fact it doesn't really help students improve their writing and then explain why. It would enhance the persuasiveness of the argument, of course, if the explanation consisted of more than personal anecdotes (why peer review didn't help me)—for example, references to research studies on the effects of peer review. (Note: the author of this textbook does not endorse the view that peer review doesn't work but does recognize it as an arguable claim.)

Conceding to Differing Views. When differing views have merit, don't try to avoid them. Remember your readers will likely think of these objections, so you're better off taking them head on. Summarize the differing view and explain what you concede. Such concessions are often signaled by words and phrases such as admittedly, granted, while it may is true, despite the fact, of course, she is right to say, and so on.

The purpose of concession is not to give up on your argument but to explain how it relates to differing views. In this sense, it's another means of clarifying differences and explaining your position in the fullest possible way. To make a concession effectively, you need to follow it up right away with an explanation of how your position relates to the point you have conceded. Otherwise, you may give readers the impression you endorse the point.

In the case of the student evaluations, the first student could make good use of concession. For example, he might concede the second student's point that an important goal of education is developing independent judgment. And then he could go on to show that in practice the teacher's methods don't really lead to independent judgment but instead leave students to flounder on their own. In fact, conceding the point offers the student a line of reasoning he could pursue to strengthen his argument by explaining how the development of independent judgment depends on constant interaction with and regular evaluation from a more experienced and knowledgeable person.

Negotiating differing views. Negotiating differences means a writer seeks to find points of agreement in differing views. Once again, the purpose is not to give up on your views but to see if you can find any common ground with those who hold differing positions. Negotiating differences may sound like unnecessarily compromising what you believe or giving in just to make other people happy. But negotiating differences doesn't have to lead to such results. It's better to think of negotiating differences as trying to combine elements in reasonable differences to come up with new solutions and perspectives. Sometimes, this is possible but not always. Still, it's worth trying because negotiated differences can strengthen your argument by broadening its appeal and demonstrating your desire to take into account as many views as possible.

Back to the student evaluations. The first student might concede that the teacher's portfolio system of evaluation has some merit because it bases grades on student improvement. But from his perspective, it still has the problem of not providing enough evaluation and information on the teacher's expectations. To negotiate these differences, the student might propose that the teacher grade but not count the first writing assignment so students can see the teacher's evaluative standards in practice. He might also suggest that the teacher give each student a mid-term progress report on where they stand in the class and again grade but not count one paper between mid-term and the end of class.

Such a solution may not satisfy everyone, but it is likely to enhance the reader's impression of the student as someone who doesn't just criticize but tries to deal with differences constructively. (For more on this strategy, see the next "Negotiating Differences.")

• **Qualifiers.** Qualifiers modify or limit the claim in an argument by making it less sweeping, global, and categorical. For most claims, after all, there are exceptions that don't necessarily disprove the claim but need to be noted. Otherwise, you will needlessly open your claim to attack and disbelief. In many instances, a qualifier is as simple as saying "Many students at Ellroy State drink to excess" instead of "The students at my school get drunk all the time." Qualifiers admit exceptions without undermining your point, and they make statements harder to refute with a counter-example—"I know students who never drink" or "Some students drink only occasionally" or "My friends drink moderately."

You can qualify your claim with words and phrase such as in many cases, often, frequently, probably, perhaps, may or might, maybe, likely, usually, and so on. In some instances, you will want to use a qualifying clause that begins with unless to limit the conditions in which the claim will hold true: "Unless the DNA evidence proves negative, everything points to the accused as the murderer."

PUTTING THE PARTS TOGETHER

To see how the various parts of argument we've just discussed can help you make an argument, let's look at the notes a student wrote to plan an argument opposing a recent proposal to the local school committee that would require students to wear uniforms at Middlebrook High School. No one contests the fact that there are some real problems at Middlebrook—declining test scores, drug use, racial tensions, lack of school spirit, a growing sense of student alienation. But, as you will see, the student doesn't think school uniforms can really address these problems.

Claim: Middlebrook High School should not require students to wear uniforms.

Evidence: School uniforms don't have the intended effects. I could use examples from schools that require uniforms to show they don't increase discipline, improve self-esteem, or alleviate social tensions.

Teachers oppose requiring uniforms because it would make them into cops. I could get some good quotes from teachers.

Even if they are required to wear uniforms, students will figure out other ways to show what group they are in. Jewelry, hair styles, shoes, jackets, body piercing, tattoos, and so on will just become all the more important.

Uniforms violate students' right to self-expression. I could call the American Civil Liberties Union to see if they have any information I could use.

Requiring uniforms will make students hate school. I could get more on this by talking to students.

Enabling assumption: A uniform requirement doesn't really address the problems at Middlebrook. Instead, it would make things worse.

Backing: The uniform proposal is based on a faulty view of what influences student behavior. More rules will just lead to more alienation from school.

To address Middlebrook's problems, students must be given more responsibility, instead of given regulations from above. They need to brought into the decisionmaking process so they can develop a stake in what happens at school.

The proposal to require uniforms is based on the desire to return to some mythic age in Middlebrook's past, when students were orderly, disciplined, filled with school spirit—namely, all the same kind of white middle-class students. Middlebrook has changed, and the proposal doesn't deal with these changes.

Differing views: Some uniform supporters claim the success of Catholic and private schools is based on the fact students are required to wear uniforms. I need to show the causes of success are not uniforms but other factors.

I'll concede that there are real problems at Middlebrook but maintain my position uniforms aren't the way to deal with them.

I could also concede that what students wear sometimes gets out of hand but argue that the best way to deal with this is to get students involved, along with teachers and parents, in writing a new dress code. In fact, I could extend this argument to say that the way to deal with some of the problems is for the school to get the different groups—whites, Latinos, blacks, and Cambodians—together to look at the problems and propose some solutions.

Qualifers: My position is set. I'm against uniforms, period. But maybe I should state my claim in a way that takes uniform supporters' views into account. For example, I could say, "Admittedly there are a number of problems at Middlebrook that need attention, but requiring uniforms will not solve these problems."

As you can see, using the parts of argument has given this students a lot of material to work with and some leads about where to get more. Just as important, using the parts of argument offers a way to see the connections among the available material and how it might fit together in developing the writer's line of reasoning. Not all of this material will necessarily turn up in the final version of the student's argument, of course. This can only be determined through the process of drafting and revising. In fact, the student might turn up new material and new arguments as she composes.

WORKING TOGETHER: Analyzing the Making of an Argument

The following ad from the International Ladies' Garment Workers Union (ILGWU) seeks to influence public opinion about the "corporate greed" of Leslie Fay and to persuade people to join in a boycott of their products.

The Price of Corporate Greed at Leslie Fay

As you read, notice the evidence presented and how it is connected to the ad's central claim.

FOR CRITICAL INQUIRY

1. The central claim of the ILGWU ad comes across clearly in boldface type: "Don't buy Leslie Fay." What evidence does the ad present to support this claim? What are the enabling assumptions that connect this evidence to the claim?
2. Does the ad present any backing to explain and support the enabling assumptions? What backing can you imagine that would be persuasive?
3. Consider how the ad uses concession and refutation to bolster its argument.
4. What qualifiers, if any, does the ad use?
5. The ad refers to Leslie Fay's search for sources of cheap labor as a "formula for disaster—for all of us." Who is the "we" in this phrase? Who does the term include? Who does it exclude?

NEGOTIATING DIFFERENCES

Newspapers, talk shows, and political debates often treat disagreements as arguments that have two sides—pro/con, for
and against. You are either pro-choice or anti-abortion, for or against the death penalty, a tax-and-spend liberal or a budget-slashing conservative.

Knowing how to argue persuasively and responsibly for your side is an important skill. Without it, people would be powerless in many situations. Unless you can make an effective argument, there may well be occasions when your perspective will go unheard and your views will be unrepresented. Moreover, if you do not argue for what you and others with shared values hold in common, it is quite likely someone else will do your talking for you.

There is little question, then, that arguing for your side is a crucial means of participating in public life and influencing public opinion. Still, as important as argument is, we need to look carefully at how arguments are conducted and what happens to the character and quality of public discussions when issues are polarized into pro and con, for and against positions.

Consider, for example, the following three ways pro/con, for and against arguments can limit discussion.

- Adversarial stance. One of the limits of pro/con arguments is that they put people in an adversarial stance toward those with whom they disagree. Instead of clarifying the issues and reaching mutual understandings, the goal of argument can turn into defeating your opponent.

- Limited perspectives. By polarizing issues along adversarial lines, pro/con arguments frequently limit the perspectives available in public debate to two—and only two—sides, those for and those against. This may well restrict who is entitled to be heard to the members of rival camps and thereby limit the alternatives considered in making decisions.

- Common ground. The pro/con, winner-take-all style of adversarial argument makes it nearly impossible for participants to identify points of agreement and common ground they might share with others. The search for common ground does not assume that everyone is going to drop their differences and harmonize their interests. Instead, common ground looks for areas of agreement and shared understanding, large or small, that people can use as the basis to talk about their differences.

BEYOND PRO/CON

The following strategies offer approaches to reasonable differences that divide people. These strategies enable writers to remain committed to their own goals and values but at the same time to avoid some of the limitations of simply arguing for or against, pro/con, in an adversarial relation to others.

These strategies seek to engage people with whom you may differ—to enter into a dialogue that seeks not a victory in debate but a clarification of the issues that may ultimately make it easier for you and others to live together and perhaps to locate common ground.

As you will see, the strategies do not deny differences in the name of everyone getting along for the common good. Nor do they assume that people can easily reconcile their differences or harmonize conflicting interests. Too often, some members of society

—women, minorities, working people, seniors, teenagers, and children—have been asked to keep quiet and sacrifice their interests to create what is in fact a false unity. Instead of setting aside differences, these strategies want to use differences constructively in order to take more interests and perspectives into account.

The strategies that follow seek to bring differences out into the open—only not in an adversarial way. Instead of an adversarial stance that imagines issues in terms of warring camps, the following strategies are attempts to negotiate—to understand how others feel about the issues, why people might be divided in their views, and what is thereby at stake for all involved. Negotiating differences does not mean abandoning the goal of influencing others but it does recognize that we need to be open to influence from others—if not to change our minds, at least to deepen our understanding of others' views and ways of thinking

• **Dialogue with Others** It is difficult to think of people negotiating their differences unless they recognize each other as reasonable beings in the first place. To recognize another person means to see him or her not as an opponent to be defeated in debate or as someone to overwhelm with convincing arguments or manipulate with emotional appeals. It means to start by listening to what they have to say—to put yourself in their shoes and imagine how the world looks from their perspective. It is presumptuous, of course, to think that you can be totally successful in understanding those with whom you differ. (Just assuming you can understand them, after all, may well imply a sense of your own superiority.) But it is the engagement with others that counts—to keep talking and trying to understand.

The reading selection that follows illustrates how recognizing others can lead people into dialogue and open the possibility of mutual understanding. As you read, notice that the strategy of recognizing others differs in important respects from the standard move of adversarial argument—acknowledging and refuting opposing views or making concessions to them. The writer's point here is not so much to strengthen his particular line of argument as to reach understanding.

Storm in the Mountains: A Case Study of Censorship, Conflict, and Consciousness.

James Moffett

In the following passage, the educator and textbook author James Moffett is engaged in a dialogue with Reverend Ezra Graley, who was one of the leaders of a movement in West Virginia in 1974 to ban Interactions, a series of elementary and high school reading and language arts textbooks that Moffett had helped develop. This textbook controversy was tumultuous, involving school boycotts, strikes, demonstrations, bombings, and shootings. Notice that though Moffett clearly disagrees with Graley's line of thinking, Moffett nonetheless continues to pursue a dialogue that seeks clarification and avoids turning the encounter into a debate.

GRALEY: We had a lot of people come in that we didn't invite in like the KKK and the NAACP. They come in. When we started off it was just a couple ministers, or three ministers trying to get good textbooks in our schools, and it growed and growed and finally it went nationwide and probably news of it, I know, went worldwide, but it grew into a big thing and then some of the more radical groups got into it, see. A lot of them didn't pretend to be Christians, but they was interested in their school, their children's education, and there's none of us in West Virginia, and still I don't know of *anybody*, that really thinks them four-letter words

and all that cussing belongs in a classroom, or in textbooks. . . . They haven't give them any education. It's taught them anti-everything. Just about everything in the textbooks was *anti*—anti-authority, government, parents, or any kind of authority. So we was against that 100 percent, and still are.

MOFFETT: You felt free in your struggle, though, to resist authority too didn't you, in the sense that you didn't accept the decision of the School Board and you did break some injunctions and so on. I'm not saying it was wrong, I'm saying you felt that there are times when you're right in challenging authority.

GRALEY: Oh yes, there's times that you're right. You know, a lot of people say that it says in the Bible, "Obey the laws of your land," but I never found that in the Bible and I'm a minister of twenty-five years. I've never found where it said, "Obey the laws of your land," because in the old Bible, Moses he defied the king, and Daniel defied the king's decree, and the Hebrew children did, and then you come on down into the New Testament, Paul, when they tried to get him not to speak, that it was against their law, he said, "What's better—for me to mind God or man?" And I think that we are to obey laws as long as them laws don't conflict with our worship of God or try to do away with our God.

MOFFETT: I think there are a lot of people who would accept that principle of obeying a spiritual law over a human law. The problem comes that equally sincere people have different notions of spiritual law, and then you get into conflict. This is what concerns me.

GRALEY: Yeah now, I think though it's people more or less don't know what the Bible says. They're good Christian people, seem like, but they said, "Well we'll do ours a-praying, we'll pray about ours, we'll pray about our problems and let *God* work them out." Well I'm sure Joshua prayed about his problem, but he had to march around Jericho seven times, you know, and Gideon prayed about his problems, but he also went then. . . .

MOFFETT: Well, Christians can agree that the Bible is an inspired work of God, but they go to it and they come back with different things. I can see it's partly maybe because people are at different stages of their development.

GRALEY: I think it's just a lack of understanding really, cause I know a lot of things that I stood for or against back when I first started out for God, I have studied more deeply in the Bible and I've changed my mind on a lot of things, you know, that I would have died for back then.

MOFFETT: A lot of people have said this, that the reason that they do Bible study year after year is the Bible deepens in meaning as they mature and as they study and they grow, but what it means is that people are going to interpret it differently at different times. It seems to me the practical problem is what do we do about this? Is there something we should learn from the book controversy about how to get along with people who interpret the Bible differently?

GRALEY: I really believe that if everybody that's truly been borned again—like Jesus said, "You must be borned again"—I believe if they're truly borned again, I think they'll see the word of God just about the same, because I don't think that it was written to cause divisions; it was written to—and Jesus prayed in his prayer, "Father, make them one, even as you and I are one." And I think these people don't want to see it, or don't see it in a holy light, is just people who don't want to live a good life, just wants to play around the banks, you know. [Laughs.]

MOFFETT: You're saying then that if the interpretation is different that they're not being really serious?

GRALEY: I don't believe that they're really serious if their interpretation—now, I know some of these people up here that was against us and fought, stood up against us, they went along and blessed homosexuals and everything else. He said he didn't marry them, but he blessed their relationship. [The Episcopalian minister, the Rev. James Lewis.]

FOR CRITICAL INQUIRY

1. Moffett is persistent in his questioning of Reverend Graley. It seems that he really wants to get inside Graley's thinking, to understand why he opposed the textbooks. It would be easy enough for Moffett to explain Graley away as a dangerous religious fundamentalist and bookburner, but he does not take this approach. What does Moffett seem to be seeking from Graley? What is Moffett's purpose in this interview? How can you tell?

2. How would you describe the dialogue between Moffett and Graley? What, if anything, does it seem to have accomplished? Do you think it accomplished the same thing for Moffett and Graley? Is there a sense of mutual understanding between them? Explain your answer.

• **Recognizing Ambiguities and Contradictions** To negotiate differences is to recognize ambiguities and contradictions. Recognizing ambiguities and contradictions goes beyond acknowledging that there are differing sides, perspectives, and interests that divide people over particular issues. It suggests further that the positions people hold may themselves contain internal differences—that things may not be as simple as they seem at first glance, with views neatly arranged for and against.

To recognize the ambiguities or contradictions in your position does not mean that you are abandoning what you believe in. Instead, it means that you hold your views but are willing to talk about gray areas, troubling aspects, conflicting loyalties.

The following reading illustrates how the ambiguities and contradictions writers recognize may be both internal—in the writers own thinking—and a result of the contradictory character of the world and how it repeatedly resists being organized in neat categories.

"Abortion Is Too Complex to Feel All One Way About."

Anna Quindlen.

Anna Quindlen is a newspaper columnist and fiction writer. The following essay was first published in her column at the New York Times. As you read, notice that how Quindlen writes about the abortion debate by expressing a range of contradictory feelings.

It was always the look on their faces that told me first. I was the freshman dormitory counselor and they were the freshmen a women's college where everyone was smart. One of them come into my room, a golden girl, a valedictorian, an 800 ver score on the SATs, and her eyes would be empty, seeing only busted future, the devastation of her life as she knew it. She failed biology, messed up the math; she was pregnant.

That was when I became pro-choice.

It was the look in his eyes that I will always remember, They were as black as the bottom of a well, and in them for a minutes I thought I saw myself the way I had always wished be—clear, simple, elemental, at peace. My child looked at me I looked back at him in the delivery room, and I realized that of a sea of infinite possibilities it had come down to this: a cific person born on the hottest day of the year, conceived on a Christmas Eve, made by his father and me miraculously from scratch.

Once I believed that there was a little blob of formless proto-plasm in there and a gynecologist went after it with a surgical in-strument, and that was that. Then I got pregnant myself—eagerly, intentionally, by the right man, at the right time—and I began to doubt. My abdomen still flat, my stomach roiling with morning sickness, I felt not that I had protoplasm inside but instead a complete human being in miniature to whom I could talk, sing, make promises. Neither of these views was accurate; instead, I think, the reality is something in the middle. And there is where I find myself now, in the middle, hating the idea of abortions, hat-ing the idea of having them outlawed.

For I know it is the right thing in some times and places. I re-member sitting in a shabby clinic far uptown with one of those freshman, only three months after the Supreme Court had made what we were doing possible, and watching with wonder as the lovely first love she had had with a nice boy unraveled over the space of an hour as they waited for her to be called, degenerated into sniping and silences. I remember a year or two later seeing them pass on campus and not even acknowledge one another because their conjoining had caused them so much pain, and I shuddered to think of them married, with a small psyche in their unready and unwilling hands.

I've met 14-year-olds who were pregnant and said they could not have abortions because of their religion, and I see in their eyes the shadows of 22-year-olds I've talked to who lost their kids to foster care because they hit them or used drugs or simply had no money for food and shelter. I read not long ago about a teen-ager who said she meant to have an abortion but she spent the money on clothes instead; now she has a baby who turns out to be a lot more trouble than a toy. The people who hand out those execrable little pictures of dismembered fetuses at abortion clin-ics seem to forget the extraordinary pain children may endure after they are born when they are unwanted, even hated or simply tolerated.

I believe that in a contest between the living and the almost living, the latter must, if necessary, give way to the will of the former. That is what the fetus is to me, the almost living. Yet these questions began to plague me—and, I've discovered, a good many other women—after I became pregnant. But they became even more acute after I had my second child, mainly because he is so different from his brother. On two random nights 18 months apart the same two people managed to conceive, and on one occasion the tumult within turned itself into a curly-haired brunet with merry black eyes who walked and talked late and loved the whole world, and on another it became a blond with hazel Asian eyes and a pug nose who tried to conquer the world almost as soon as he entered it.

If we were to have an abortion next time for some reason or another, which infinite possibility becomes, not a reality, but a nullity? The girl with the blue eyes? The improbable redhead? The natural athlete? The thinker? My husband, ever at the heart of the matter, put it another way. Knowing that he is finding two children somewhat more overwhelming than he expected, I asked if he would want me to have an abortion if I accidentally became pregnant again right away. "And waste a perfectly good human being?" he said.

Coming to this quandary has been difficult for me. In fact, I believe the issue of abortion is difficult for all thoughtful people. I don't know anyone who has had an abortion who has not been haunted by it. If there is one thing I find intolerable about most of the so-called right-to-lifers, it is that they try to portray abortion rights as something that feminists thought up on a slow Saturday over a light lunch. That is nonsense. I also know that some people who support abortion rights are most comfortable with a monolithic position because it seems the strongest front against the smug and sometimes violent opposition.

But I don't feel all one way about abortion anymore, and I don't think it serves a just cause to pretend that many of us do. For years I believed that a woman's right to choose was absolute, but now I wonder. Do I, with a stable home and marriage and sufficient stamina and money, have the right to choose abortion because a pregnancy is inconvenient right now? Legally I do have that right; legally I want always to have that right. It is the morality of exercising it under those circumstances that makes me wonder.

Technology has foiled us. The second trimester has become a time of resurrection; a fetus at six months can be one woman's late abortion, another's premature, viable child. Photographers now have film of embryos the size of a grape, oddly human, flexing their fingers, sucking their thumbs. Women have amniocentesis to find out whether they are carrying a child with birth defects that they may choose to abort. Before the procedure, they must have a sonogram, one of those fuzzy black-and-white photos like a love song heard through static on the radio, which shows someone is in there.

I have taped on my VCR a public-television program in which somehow, inexplicably, a film is shown of a fetus in utero scratching its face, seemingly putting up a tiny hand to shield itself from the camera's eye. It would make a potent weapon in the arsenal of the antiabortionists. I grow sentimental about it as it floats in the salt water, part fish, part human being. It is almost living, but not quite. It has almost turned my heart around, but not quite turned my head.

FOR CRITICAL INQUIRY

1. Although Quindlen characterizes the abortion debate as a "quandary," she nonetheless takes a position. What is it? What evidence does she use to support her position?
2. How does Quindlen describe the two sides in the debate? What does her attitude toward them seem to be? How does Quindlen locate her own position in relation to the two sides? How can you tell?
3. What do you think Quindlen is trying to accomplish by exploring the "quandary" of the abortion debate? How are readers likely to respond?

- **Locating Common Ground** Locating common ground is built on the strategies we have just looked at but seeks to go one step further by identifying how people can join together in spite of their differences.

The strategy of locating common ground depends on the sense that you do not have it all figured out or have reached absolute certainty on an issue or controversy. Instead, something remains incomplete, and you are seeking the participation of others, even with their differences. Locating common ground involves finding ways out of the impasse of polarized debate. It seeks to loosen people from rigid positions and to get them talking to each other. Common ground, in this regard, cannot be identified before hand but rather must be discovered through negotiation and interaction.

"Nobody in America Escaped the Vietnam War."

This ad appeared during the 1992 presidential campaign when Bill Clinton ran against the incumbent George Bush. The ad is a response to politicians who sought at the time to make the Vietnam War a test case of the candidates' character (and thereby an attack on people like Clinton who had evaded military service). The signers include people who served in the military as well as those who resisted the draft and served time in jail. As you read, notice the common ground that joins together people who made very different decisions.

Nobody in America escaped the Vietnam War

Nobody.

Why is it that around election time, some people always seem to have a problem remembering what the Vietnam War was about?

Mostly, they are politicians who want us to believe that Vietnam was a test. Those who went, passed. Those who refused, failed. And that's all there was to it.

Our generation knows better.

We know Vietnam was not World War II. In the forties, a generation of brave and loyal Americans fought against fascism the only way they could. In the sixties, a generation of brave and loyal Americans defended our nation's heritage the best way they knew how.

Some of us went into the military. Some of us went to jail. A lot of us managed to avoid the draft. None of us was able to escape the war.

Vietnam was a crucible that shaped our generation. Everyone who lived through that sad, awful time had to confront it, examine his or her conscience, and make a choice.

Whatever choice we made then, we can agree on one thing now. It is past. It is done.

Our generation bore the burden of that tragedy. Our generation learned to live with the choices we made. And our generation understands that it is over.

Other challenges remain. We have to care for our wounded who still suffer the ravages of war. We must find real peace with Vietnam.

What we cannot and will not do is tolerate yet another cynical attempt to stir the angry ashes of this dead conflict in hopes of lighting a fire under today's voters.

Daniel Boone, USN 1968-70
William Brochett, USN 1963-67
George Certa, USAIC 1967-70
Daniel Harris
John Kehrt, USAIC 1965-67
Tina Kehrt
Ellen Klotznick

Harry Kressler
Jerry Lubenow
Joan Lubenow
Vincent Lubenow, Jr., USAF 1967-73
Nicholas Proffitt, USA 1961-64
Barbara Klune
Henry Ross, USAIC 1965-68
Jack McClosky

Dee Samuels
Joel Simsom
John Terzano, USN 1970-74
Dorian Weinberg
Will Weinstein
Betty Zhukhin
Carl Zhukhin

FOR CRITICAL INQUIRY

1. What position does the ad take? What arguments does it make in support of the position?
2. Explain what you see as the common ground this ad seeks to establish. What does the ad mean when it says, "Our generation knows better"? What do they know? What is this knowledge better than?
3. What effect is the ad trying to have? How do the signers want readers to respond? What would it mean to agree to the statement, "Nobody in America escaped the Vietnam War"? How would such agreement position readers in relation to the politicians who "want us to believe the Vietnam War was a test"?

WRITING ASSIGNMENTS

1. Write an account of an argument you witnessed or took part in that polarized into opposing sides. Describe what happened and explain why the polarization took place. The point of this exercise is not to condemn the people involved but to understand what happened and why. Remember that polarization is not necessarily a bad thing. It may be unavoidable as people begin to identify their differences or involve a matter of principle, where a person finds no alternative but to make a counterargument and take a stand. Your task here is to analyze what took place and to consider whether the polarization was inevitable or could have been avoided.
2. Watch a television talk program such as Nightline or Crossfire that presents opposing views. Prepare a report that analyzes the speakers' presentations and interactions. On whose behalf did they seem to be speaking? How did they define the issues and make their arguments? What perspectives and alternatives, if any, did they ignore? Depending on your instructor's direction, this can be an oral or written report, an individual or group project. If you are presenting an oral report and your instructor agrees, tape the program and show in class short clips to illustrate your points.
3. Identify someone who is knowledgeable about and can speak for a position with which you disagree. Use James Moffett's interview as a model to enter a dialogue with the person. The point of the interview is not to argue with or seek to persuade the other person. Rather your task is ask questions that can help you understand where the person is coming from and why. If you can, tape and transcribe the interview. Follow a presentation of the interview with your own account of what you learned about the differences that divide you and the other person. Indicate how or whether you changed your mind in any respect.

PART
TWO

WRITING PROJECTS

INTRODUCTION:

GENRES OF WRITING

The mail has just arrived, and you glance through it, putting letters in one pile, magazines in another, and junk mail in still another. You may do this automatically, but sorting the mail is based on some very real experience with the written materials of print culture. That is why people can distinguish immediately between, say, an L.L. Bean catalog and the recent issue of Newsweek—to identify one as advertising and the other as journalism. The same is true of the letters they receive—a personal letter from a friend, a fund raising appeal from Amnesty International, a library overdue notice, and junk mail advertising storm windows or aluminum siding.

Each type of writing is likely to have a different appearance—a four-color catalog, a slick news magazine, handwritten stationery, a form letter with profiles of human rights abuse, a computer printout, and a promotional flyer addressed to "resident." People use such visual cues to make sense of the written material they receive and what they should do with it.

People are likely to notice, for example, how the different types of writing address them in different ways. A personal letter may call for a reply, whether a letter, a phone call, or e-mail message. A library notice calls for prompt action, if you want to avoid running up a fine. A fund-raising letter may lead to a financial contribution to support a particular cause. A catalog from L.L. Bean may lead to placing an order or just to fantasy reading about the life styles of the outdoorsy middle classes.

This example of sorting the mail is meant to illustrate how people classify different types of writing into categories in order to get a handle on what they are reading—to know what to expect from it and how to respond. Based on their past experience with written texts, people fit what they read into patterns. For example, when you read (or hear) the phrase "Once upon a time," you are likely to recognize right away that you are in the realm of fairy tales. The familiar opening line is an immediate giveaway that prepares you for the story that follows, whether it's about Cinderella, Snow White, or Jack and the Beanstalk.

The same is true for many other types—or genres—of writing. Based on their familiarity with various genres of writing, people browsing at a bookstore can easily distinguish, say, science fiction from Westerns, cookbooks from dictionaries, or poetry from biography. This is the same kind of knowledge that enables you to distinguish between different types—or genres—of movies. You probably know that you can expect something very different from a Jackie Chan kung-fu action adventure, a Disney cartoon version of Hercules or Pocahontas, and a romantic comedy starring Julia Roberts—and you are likely to make your viewing choices accordingly.

Genres of Writing

Just as knowing about various movie genres can help you make informed decisions about what you want to see, understanding the various genres of writing can help you make sense of situations that call on you to write. As writers identify a call to write, they typically draw on past experience to help them determine the genre best suited to the current occasion. To do this, they look for recurring patterns: How is this writing situation similar to ones I've encountered in the past? How well do genres of writing I've used in the past match the demands of the present? What genre best fits my purposes, given the situation and the intended readers?

In the following chapters, you'll see how writers use various genres to respond to recurring writing situations. You'll see how writers' choice of genre takes into account the occasion that calls for writing, the writer's purposes, and the relationship the writer seeks to establish with readers.

While writing teachers do not always agree on how best to classify genres of writing, the chapters in Part Two offer practical examples of how writers use eight of the most familiar genres:

- letters
- memoirs
- public documents
- profiles
- reports

- commentary

- proposals

- reviews

This, of course, is by no means a comprehensive list of all genres of writing. Nor are the genres of writing fixed once and for all. New genres are always emerging in response to new conditions. Witness, for example, the proliferation of e-mail messages, newsgroups, and web sites with the appearance of new electronic communications technologies. The genres in the following chapters have been selected to illustrate some of the most common ones writers use to respond to the call to write—genres you will find helpful when you are called on to write in college, in the workplace, and in public life.

As you will see, some of the genres are broader than others. The genre of letters, for example, can be further divided into personal letters, business letters, letters to the editor, letters of appeal, and so on. Nonetheless, each of the genres has distinctive features that readers will recognize—whether, for example, the recreation of personal experience in a memoir or the evaluative judgment of a review. Studying and experimenting with the eight genres can help you expand your repertoire of writing strategies, so that you can respond flexibly and creatively to a range of situations that call on you to write.

The Arrangement of the Chapters

The chapters are arranged according to the purpose writers bring to their writing tasks and the focus of attention they thereby establish for their readers.

In the first three chapters—"Letters," "Memoirs," and "Public Documents"—the dominant purpose is to express individual and group identities, whether by rendering personal experience or codifying communal beliefs and norms of conduct. In the next two chapters—"Profiles" and "Reports"—the focus of attention shifts from presentation of self and community to the subject matter being investigated and analyzed, and the writers' main purposes are to inform and explain. In the final three chapters—"Commentary," "Proposals," and "Reviews"—the main focus shifts once again, this time from an emphasis on the topic under consideration to an emphasis on the writer's own interpretations and judgments, and writers explicitly seek to persuade readers to a particular point of view.

It is important to understand that the differences in purpose and focus are matters of emphasis rather than absolute ones. All writing, after all, involves a presentation of the writer's identify, even if it is subordinated to other purposes, such as informing readers. By the same token, a convincing commentary, proposal, or review often relies on extensive background information and analysis. So it's best to understand the arrangement of the chapters as a continuum, in which the emphasis shifts depending on the writer's purpose and focus of attention.

Your instructor may ask you to read some or all of the chapters. You may want to consult chapters you haven't been assigned for advice about writing tasks you face in and out of school.

CHAPTER FOUR

LETTERS:
Establishing and Maintaining Relationships

Looking at the Genre

Letters are easy to recognize. Whether handwritten, typed, word processed, or composed as e-mail, letters have a predictable format that usually includes the date of writing, a salutation that addresses the reader directly ("Dear Jim"), a message, a closing (such as "Sincerely" or "Yours truly"), and a signature. There are many different occasions for and purposes of letter-writing, and the genre of letters can be divided into a number of subgenres, such as personal letters, business letters, letters to the editor, letters of appeal, and so on. Nonetheless, letters are easy to identify because of the way they appear on the page or computer screen.

But it's not only the form of the writing that makes letters a distinct genre. Just as important is the way letters address their readers, and establish a relationship between the writer and the reader. In part because of two elements of their form—the salutation and the closing and signature—letters is the genre that comes closest in feeling to conversations between people. The letters you receive—whether a postcard from a friend on vacation, an invitation to a party, a notice from an organization you belong to, or a grade report from your college—are addressed to you and come from someone.

This relationship established between writer and reader is one of the main attractions of the genre of letters. It's also one of its most basic functions: Letters are important links that help you maintain your networks of personal and social relations.

When you read a letter, you can almost hear the voice and feel the presence of the person writing to you. This is particularly true of personal letters, which often convey the immediacy and intimacy of face-to-face conversation, but it is also true of other letters as well. Think, for example, of the correspondence you have received from your college. Such letters address you directly but in your role as a student or a citizen. The voice you hear sounds official and institutional—not entirely unlike the voice you would hear if you spoke to a school administrator you didn't know about some official business.

Letters are also like conversation in that the writer seeks to engage the reader in an ongoing interaction. Letters often call for a response from their readers—whether it's to RSVP to a party invitation, attend a meeting, donate to a worthy cause, pay an overdue bill, or just write back.

One way that letters differ from conversation is that the person you're writing to can't talk back, at least not immediately. As a writer with something to say, you therefore have certain advantages. In a letter, you can talk directly to someone without being interrupted. And you know that the reader can return several times to your letter and reflect on its message before responding to you.

Thus, permanence is also a difference between letters and conversation. Once you've sent a letter, you can't take your words back as easily as you can in conversation. By expressing thoughts and feelings in a letter and sending it to someone, the letter writer may be taking a greater risk than by talking face-to-face or on the phone.

Although from one perspective a disadvantage, permanence, and the greater risk it entails, is actually another of the attractions of letters. G.K. Chesterton once described the mailbox as "a sanctuary of the human heart" and the letter as "one of the few things left entirely romantic, for to be entirely romantic, a thing must be irrevocable." Many people save the letters they receive from relatives, friends, lovers, and other correspondents as a personal record of what their life was like at a particular time. There is a long tradition of letters in which writers reveal their deepest, most intimate thoughts to readers in a language that is unimaginable in conversation—love letters, letters of advice, letters of friendship, letters of condolence, letters of despair, and letters written on the eve of death.

Although we've focused on personal letters, other kinds of letters play just as important a role. They share with personal letters the basic function of maintaining the social networks that link people together. Business letters serve a wide range of indispensable functions for businesses and government, going to clients and customers, suppliers and contractors, employees, and the general public in order to advertise products and services, discuss policy changes, request payment, and negotiate agreements.

"To My Beloved Wife"

It has been serveral autums now since your dull husband left you for a far remote alien land. Thanks to my hearty body I am all right. Therefore stop your embroidering worries about me.

Yesterday I received another of your letters. I could not keep tears from running down my checks when thinking about the miserable and needy circumstance3s of our home., and thinking back to the time of our separation.

Because of our destitution I went out, trying to make a living. Who could know that the Fate is always opposite to man's design? Because I can get no gold, I am detained in this secluded corner of a strange land. Furthermore, my beauty, you areimplicated in an endless misfortune. I wish this paper would console you a little. This is all what I can do for now.

Letters written for the public realm are equally wide ranging in their functions and, taken together, are crucial to a democratic society. For example, individuals and groups write to politicians to influence the direction of public policy. Letters to the editor, which are included in most newspapers and magazines, give readers a chance to respond to news stories, feature articles, editorials, and other letters, as well as to raise neglected issues.

Letters of appeal have several different purposes. For example, advocacy groups such as the Sierra Club or the National Rifle Association, historical restoration groups, arts groups, and community groups write fund-raising letters appealing for memberships and donations. Another kind of letter of appeal, often called an open letter because it is circulated widely, is a political tradition in democratic cultures. Sent out through the mail or Internet and sometimes appearing as a paid advertisement in a magazine or newspaper, this letter of appeal calls on its readers to support a cause, protest a policy, or otherwise take action.

The readings in this chapter include personal letters, an e-mail exchange that represents a new subgenre, letters to the editor, and an open letter. As you read these letters, look at what calls on people to write letters and at the particular relationships that the letters establish between writers and readers.

LETTERS HOME

The two following personal letters were written during the Vietnam war. The first is from Cathleen Cordova, who worked as a club director for Army Special Services in Vietnam. The second letter is from Richard Marks, who   . Both letters were published in the book Dear America, which became the basis for a PBS special. Notice that, although both are letters to family written from Vietnam, they differ significantly in purpose, content, and tone.

BASE CAMP: WAR AT THE REAR

25 November 1968
Tay Ninh

Dear Mom and Dad,

"Happy birthday to me. Happy birthday to me!" Thanks for your pretty card. The girls gave me a "surprise" party at the club—they got one of the cooks on the American side to bake a birthday cake. It was fun. The officers fixed me an "American" breakfast the next day. Instead of the usual cold rice and dried fish heads, they gave me corn flakes with chocolate milk! Oh, well—it's the thought that counts, right?

1st Cav moved in here a few weeks ago, and what a rowdy bunch. They came here from the DMZ and apparently these guys have been out in the mud and the boonies for months. They've caused lots of trouble on post. We weren't sure we could handle it. But they were no trouble at the club! For the first 20 minutes or so, they just wandered around staring at everything, trying out all the chairs, flushing the toilets, etc. It was funny to watch. But I guess when you've had to do without clean clothes, good food, and shelter for as long as they have, you might not believe your eyes either. They kept telling us they didn't believe anything like the club existed in Vietnam. It must be awful for them out there. . . .

So "Tricky Dick" will really make a difference, huh? Do you think the war will be over soon? I doubt it, but even if it does happen, the troops won't be pulled out that fast. I'd be willing to bet we'll be here for quite some time yet.

Last night we got a special treat. One of the officers was in Saigon and brought back a movie projector. We showed an old John Wayne movie on a sheet stapled to the side of the building (very primitive, huh?). Actually, it's not really a building—more like a carport, open air but with a roof. It was *weird* to sit and watch an old WW II movie, surrounded by GIs, in a war zone!

This is all for now. Did Grandma and Grandpa get my letter? I'm well. Hope both of you are too.

> Love always,
> "Me"

Last Will & Testament
of PFC Richard E. Marks
December 12, 1965

Dear Mom,

I am writing this in the event that I am killed during my remaining tour of duty in Vietnam.

First of all I want to say that I am here as a result of my own desire—I was offered the chance to go to 2nd Marine Division when I was first assigned to the 4th Marines, but I turned it down. I am here because I have always wanted to be a Marine and because I always wanted to see combat.

I don't like being over here, but I am doing a job that must be done —I am fighting an *inevitable* enemy that must be fought—now or later.

I am fighting to protect and maintain what I believe in and what I want to live in—a democratic society. If I am killed while carrying out this mission, I want no one to cry or mourn for me. I want people to hold their heads high and be proud of me for the job I did.

There are some details I want taken care of. First of all, any money that you receive as a result of my death I want distributed in the following fashion.

If you are single, I want you and Sue to split it down the middle. But if you are married and your husband can support you, I want Sue and Lennie to get 75% of the money, and I want you to keep only 25%— I feel Sue and Lennie will need the money a lot more.

I also want to be buried in my Marine Corps uniform with all the decorations, medals, and badges I rate. I also want Rabbi Hirschberg to officiate, and I want to be buried in the same cemetery as Dad and Gramps, but I do not want to be buried in the plot next to Dad that I bought in mind of you.

That is about all, except I hope I never have to use this letter—

I love you, Mom, and Sue, and Nan, and I want you all to carry on and be very happy, and above all be proud—

> Love & much more love,
> Rick

ANALYSIS: Maintaining Family Ties

Letters home offer a good example of how people use writing to maintain social relations. Part of this is simply the responsibility family members feel to stay in touch, to use the available means of communication (telephone and e-mail as well as letters) to keep up family ties when someone is away from home. One of the main functions of these letters home, as you can see, is to reaffirm the importance of the family. Just writing these letters reaffirms family ties, but notice too how the two letters talk about family business. Thus, Cathleen Cordova mentions Grandma and Grandpa, her letter to them, and her parents' birthday card to her. Richard Marks mentions Sue, Lennie, and Nan, as well as his dead father and grandfather, and also refers to the cemetary plot he bought his mother.

While both writers pay homage to home and family, they do so in very different ways. Cathleen Cordova does so through informality—her chatty tone conveys a sense that she feels comfortable with and close to her family. Richard Marks does so through formality—his serious tone conveys a sense of respect. The difference is quite obviously related to the difference in purpose between the letters.

FOR CRITICAL INQUIRY

1. Compare the purposes of the two letters home. What appears to have called on Cordova and Marks to write these letters home? What is each writer trying to accomplish?
2. What are the topics in each letter? How is each letter structured or organized into parts?
3. Describe the tone of voice in each letter. For each, give examples of specific words and phrases that help convey the tone, and explain how these words and phrases convey the tone. Based on these letters, what sense do you have of the personalities of Cordova and Marks?
4. What kind of relationship do these letters establish between the writers and their readers at home? How do you imagine the readers responded?

AN E-MAIL CORRESPONDENCE

This e-mail correspondence differs markedly from the letters home. Here the correspondents are strangers, a gay teacher and a Vietnam vet joined together in conversation by the new electronic technology of the Internet. While the two writers do not know each other personally, they are nonetheless engaged, as you will see, in deeply personal discussion. The fact that each chooses to reveal so much of himself raises interesting questions about the kind of communication that can—and does—take place in cyberspace.

Do you have any idea what it is like to be gay? To have to hide the most important thing about yourself, even though you had no choice about it? To live in terror of discovery? To be laughed at, isolated and beaten up? To live around people who hide their children from you? Who wouldn't let you teach them if they knew? Because I am a teacher who dreads every call to the principal's office. I always wonder if it will be my last. How can you love a country that finds you too disgusting to serve? That permits people to attack you and your friends, throw things at them from car windows, deny them the right to be married, have families? Can you conceive of that? Does this get through to you on any level at all?

Two years ago, my lover and I walked through the French Quarter of New Orleans. We vacationed there because we knew it to be a tolerant place. We left a restaurant just off Bourbon Street, and three men jumped out of their cars. They knocked my lover and me down. They kicked us in the face, in the kidneys, in the groin. They knocked four of my teeth out, broke my jaw. Then they urinated on us. They laughed and said they were soldiers. That they'd love to have us in the military. I couldn't tell the police what happened. I was afraid the school district might find out back home.

—From the computer bulletin
board Compuserve

And a reply: I was very touched by your message, buddy. What happened to you was horrible, unsupportable. That's not what I lost three toes for in Vietnam, for scum to beat up on people like you and your friends. I fought so you could do whatever you wanted so long as you didn't hurt anybody or break the law. You and I have no quarrel. But we do have these problems, and I'll be straight with you about it, just like you were with me. Do you have any idea what it's like to be in a field or jungle or valley with bullets and shells blowing up all around you? With your friends being cut down, ripped apart, bleeding, dying right next to you screaming for their moms or kids or wives? Do you know how much trust and communication it takes to get through that? Do you have any idea what it's like to go through that if there's tension among you?

I'm not saying this can't be worked out. I'm saying, go slow. Don't come in here with executive orders and try to change things in a day that should take longer. Don't make me into a bigot because I know it takes an unbelievable amount of feeling to crawl down there into a valley of death. It takes love of your buddy. And that's something both of us can understand, right? But if you hate him, or fear him or don't understand him — how can you do it?

ANALYSIS: Talking Intimately to Strangers

Whereas Cordova and Marks wrote their letters to the people they were most intimate with, these writers are writing to strangers. In fact, the teacher's letter isn't even written to a particular person. Yet the content of these letters is truly intimate. Notice that the gay teacher is talking about things he ordinarily cannot reveal for fear of losing his job—that is, he is in a sense more intimate with strangers than he evidently can be with many friends and co-workers. The veteran similarly reflects on memories that are extremely painful and that must be difficult to talk about.

While these letters are intimate, they're clearly not personal letters. The writers focus on a single topic, and don't try to present all the aspects of themselves, nor can they include the sorts of familiar references you have seen in the first two letters. In a way these letters are more like public letters such as letters to the editor and open letters. In the end, it's probably most accurate to say that they combine features of personal letters with features of public letters and that in some ways they differ from both—most strikingly, perhaps, in their anonymity.

FOR CRITICAL INQUIRY

1. Describe the gay teacher's purpose. What seems to be calling on him to write? What is he trying to accomplish? Why do you think he has chosen to write to a bulletin board on the Internet (instead of, say, writing a letter to the editor of a newspaper or just talking to people)?
2. Summarize the content of the two letters, and describe the structure of each letter. Why is the veteran's use of a structure similar to that of the first letter especially effective?
3. What is the vet getting at when he says, "You and I have no quarrel. But we do have these problems"? What common ground does he see as a possible basis for working on the problems?
4. Do you see these letters as being more like personal letters or more like public letters? Explain your answer, using specific language from the letters to support it.
5. Imagine how you would have replied to the teacher. What would you have said to him? Take into account the fact that you do not know each other personally and that you are corresponding by e-mail. How would this influence what you might say or not say?

GOING ON-LINE

Electronic Discussion Groups

Electronic discussion groups have their own unique characteristics. Discussion groups are generally groups of people with a common interest who post messages to an on-line public forum on a general topic. Specific topics are denoted by use of a "subject line." Several messages on the same topic are called "threads."

In order to explore electronic discussion groups, identify a group that is devoted to a topic that interests you. Tile.Net/Lists: The Reference to Internet Discussion Groups is a search engine you can use to find information on Internet listservs and discussion groups—http://tile.net/listserv/.

You will notice how some postings spur further messages to create threads. Follow the discussion for a week, noting what threads develop an exchange of ideas. After you have followed the discussion, send your own posting in response to one of the threads. Notice the kinds of replies you receive.

Now write a short description that could serve as an introduction to the discussion group for someone who was not familiar with it. Explain what the general purpose of the discussion group is. Describe the types of messages that are posted and the threads that are followed. Comment on the exchange of ideas that takes place, paying particular attention to how writers respond to each other and the tone of their postings. Finally, explain what happened when you posted to the group.

Depending on your teacher's directions, you can do this assignment individually or in groups.

the technology explain the characteristics of these letters discussed in the analysis section? How might the technology diminish the differences between letters and conversations discussed in the introduction to this chapter?

LETTERS TO THE EDITOR

The newspaper column and letters to the editor presented in this section follow a cycle of writing that is common in newspapers—a pattern of call and response where the writers respond to the views of those who wrote before them. First, newspaper columnist Mark Patinkin of the Providence Journal-Bulletin wrote a column on an item in the news: The authorities in Singapore had sentenced Michael Fay, an American teenager who lived there, to be caned as a punishment for spray-painting cars. (As you'll see, Patinkin's column was actually itself inspired by a column.) Patinkin's column, which supported the caning, led to a round of letters, many of them condemning him for taking that position. The letter from Kristin Tardiff was among those published at this point. There followed a second round of letters, responding to Patinkin and the first round of letters. Many of these supported Patinkin, including the letter from John N. Taylor.

THE COLUMN

Commit a crime, suffer the consequences

MARK PATINKIN

At their best, columnists are supposed to leave people thinking, "That's just how I feel and didn't know it until reading that." Well, it took reading a column by an 18-year-old student to crystallize my own feelings about an issue I've been perusing day to day.

The Singapore caning case: The American teenager who's about to be flogged because he spray-painted several cars. From the start, I'd viewed it as a barbaric punishment for a poor kid who just did a little mischief. Then I read a column by an 18-year-old telling Michael Fay, the convicted American, to take it like a man, and learn from it.

Something in me instantly said, "She's right."

Yes, I know caning is harsh, but am I the only one who's tired of Michael Fay's whining? Am I the only one who feels President Clinton has better things to do than to write letters appealing for leniency?

Singaporeans get caned all the time for vandalism. Are we Americans supposed to be exempt when we break their laws? What are we — princes?

I'll tell you what else I'm tired of: Michael Fay's father — his biological father here in America — traveling the country insisting his precious boy didn't do it.

It's a setup, the father says. Supposedly, he says, Michael only pleaded guilty as a bargain with the police — after the local cops leaned on him — with the promise of little punishment. But suddenly the judge sentenced him to six strikes with a cane.

Not once have I read Michael's parents

saying their child was out of line. They just make excuses. Gee, I wonder if a life of such excuse-making is part of why he's so troubled.

See, that's the other line here. First, the father says he didn't do it. Then he says, well, Michael also has personal problems, like Attention Deficit Disorder. I happen to think that's a legitimate syndrome, but not for excusing crimes like vandalizing cars.

All this is just part of the new American game of always saying, "It's not my fault." No one, when caught, seems ready to admit having done wrong anymore. They just whine and appeal. As in: "Your honor, the stabbing was not my client's fault. He had a bad childhood. And was caught up in a riot at the time. In fact, he's not a criminal at all, he's one of society's victims."

That's Michael Fay. All those cars he spray-painted? Not his fault. He's had a hard life.

I might have had sympathy for him if he'd only said, "I admit it. I did a dumb thing. I was with the wrong crowd and crossed the line into criminality. I deserve to pay. And I'm truly sorry for the victims."

But we're not hearing that.

There's another thing: Many articles on this — including a paragraph in a column I wrote — have referred to what Michael Fay did as "mischief." Well, it's not. It's hardcore vandalism. He spray-painted a bunch of cars.

Michael Fay might want to think about what it feels like to the car owners. Anyone whose car has been vandalized knows. Personally, I've had about four car stereos stolen. I still remember the shock — each time — of seeing the broken window and the damage. I remember having to take a good half day out of work to deal with it. And during the times I had little money, I remember how badly it pinched to have to pay the deductible on the insurance.

Finally, I remember how creepy and unnerving it was. It took weeks before I could approach my car again without feeling nervous. It erodes your trust in the world. And it's worse for women, I think, who feel a heightened vulnerability to crime in the first place.

In short, it's beyond mischief, beyond obnoxious — it's vandalism. A violation. And it's downright mean-spirited.

But after he was caught, Michael Fay and his family have been telling the world that he — not the car owners but HE — is the victim.

Sorry, Michael, you're not the victim. You're the criminal. Caning may well be rough.

But if you do the crime, you've got to pay the price.

Mark Patinkin is a Journal-Bulletin columnist. His column appears in Lifebeat each Tuesday and Thursday, and in the Metro section each Sunday.

To the Editor,

I wonder why I continue to read Mark Patinkin's columns. At best they bore me, at worst they anger me. I've thought before of responding to his maudlin whining or self-righteous hypocrisy, but this time I really had to put pen to paper.

Mr. Patinkin has chosen this time to attack Michael Fay, the 18-year-old boy who has been accused of spray-painting some cars in Singapore. Mark, jury of one, has decided that Fay is unequivocally guilty, and that his sentence of jail term, fine, and caning is fitting punishment. "Stop whining, take it like a man," he says.

I find it interesting that Mr. Patinkin has completely ignored the statements of those who may have a little more experience with the Singaporean police than he does. What about the Navy officer who said that our military police were under order to immediately take into custody any American soldier who was going to be arrested by the Singaporean police to protect them? Did he make that up? What about those who have had the experience of being detained in Singapore and tell of torture and forced confessions? Are they just wimpy bleeding hearts in Mark's eyes?

Perhaps as a teenager Mr. Patinkin never made a mistake, never did anything considered wrong in the eyes of the law. Hard to believe, but I'll give him the benefit of the doubt. Had he, however, ever been caught and punished for some infraction,

that punishment certainly would not have involved being tied up with his pants around his ankles while someone split his cheeks the opposite way with a water-soaked cane. Nor do I think he would have considered that just. The punishment should fit the crime.

Michael Fay is willing to serve his time in jail and make restitution. He has already suffered physically and psychologically, and has, I'm sure, seen the error of his ways. Is this not enough punishment? Have we become so warped by the violence of our society that we now see justice as incomplete without the imposition of physical pain? Do we really want to see the young graffiti artist in our neighborhood caned? (I hear some saying yes, but what if it turns out to be your child? Think about it.) Is this really the way we want society to turn? What comes next? Amputation for thieves and maybe prolonged torture and death for drug dealers? Should we just kill all the "bad" people? Why can't we for once work on the causes instead of lashing out blindly at the symptoms?

Just one more thing. Regarding Mr. Patinkin's criticism of Fay's parents' pleas for leniency for their son, as a parent he should have more empathy. What else can parents do when they truly feel that their child is being unjustly treated?

I hope Mark's children all turn out as perfect as their dad. Maybe he should send to Singapore for a cane. Just in case.

KRISTIN TARDIFF
Providence

denouncing Mark Patinkin's support for caning Michael Fay ("Patinkin should know better than to advocate caning," 5/3) are no different from any of the other whiny, moralizing claptrap we hear from those mawkish people who fear more for Mr. Fay's buttocks than for those who are victimized everyday by the crimes of young punks like Fay. The arguments of all three are laden with the rancid, canting self-righteousness common to all opposing Fay's caning, and evince concern only for the criminal while telling crime victims to go eat cake.

From Ms. Tardiff, we get a lot of sarcasm, a lot of questions, and no answers. If she can't propose any semblance of an idea for controlling crime, then neither she (nor anyone else) has the moral authority to condemn a nation which has come up with its own means of dealing with criminals.

Singapore has in recent years carried out canings of 14 of its own citizens who were convicted of offenses similar in nature to those of Mr. Fay. Why should Fay be treated any differently from these people? Just because Fay is an affluent white American with many powerful supporters in America (like President Clinton) doesn't mean he should be above the law of the nation where he resides. To let Fay out of the caning simply because he has the support of powerful leaders is an affront to the people of Singapore, who have abided by the law or taken their lumps for violating same. Clemency for Fay would effectively divide Americans and Singaporeans into separate, unequal classes, whereby the former avoid punishment because of America's political and economic clout while the latter, who do not enjoy such powerful connections, suffer the consequences.

The caning of Fay is simply an affirmation of the principle that, all people, whether they are wealthy white Americans or poor Chinese Singaporeans, are equal in the eyes of the law.

It has much to do with upholding Singaporean mores and nothing to do with Fay being American or U.S. political traditions; these sanctions, as applied to crimes like vandalism and other non-political offenses, are designed to discourage repetition of criminal behavior. And they succeed in this goal. How many drive-by shootings go down in Singapore?

Like American authorities, the Singaporeans perceive crimes to be the individual act and choice of the perpetrator.

There is no doubt Singapore is a non-democratic nation which punishes even peaceable political dissent, and there is no doubt that Singapore's criminal laws are harsh. But Michael Fay knew what the laws were like and freely assumed the risks of getting punished when he engaged in his spree of vandalism. It is the height of arrogance and folly for Americans living or traveling abroad to expect to be protected by the Bill of Rights when they break other nations' laws.

Americans have no right demanding a blanket exemption from foreign laws they violate, or that foreign governments give them easier treatment than they would give their own people under similar circumstances.

And if caning is immoral, is not the American criminal justice system itself laden with unfairness? Where is the morality in releasing quadruple murderer Craig Price into the community after only four years? Is it right that in the U. S., a murderer draws an average sentence of only about six years? Is it right that dangerous criminals are dumped onto communities simply because the prisons don't meet the standards of some soft-headed judge? We in America sacrifice the lives of innocent people in the name of criminals' civil rights, and then have the gall to denounce Singapore as harsh and oppressive! If anyone's justice is extremist, it is America's.

America's approach to crime is to do nothing and let the community be damned, while Singapore has opted to let the offender be damned. What the Michael Fay fan club here in America conveniently forgets while moaning about Singaporean tyranny is the everyday tyranny of violence and fear imposed on millions of Americans by violent criminals in our inner cities and suburbs. These people are oppressed by a dictatorship of criminals and their rights are violated on a massive scale every day. Yet I see more concern for Michael Fay's rear end than I do for people who bear the scars of bullets and knives of criminals.

My heart will not bleed if Fay's read end does. Given the carnage on America's streets, and in Rwanda Bosnia and Haiti, the supporters o Michael Fay will just have to excus me if I fail to shed a tear.

JOHN N. TAYLOR JR
North Providence

ANALYSIS: A Public Forum

Like a lot of newspaper columnists, Mark Patinkin uses short paragraphs, an informal, conversational tone, and a commonsensical man-in-the-street approach to his readers. Notice he speaks to his readers as an equal, not as someone who is more knowledgeable or somehow above them. This approach in effect positions the column as something that readers can and should respond to. The controversial nature of the topic—and of some of Patinkin's comments about the topic—make it all the more likely that readers will respond.

In the letters to the editor, the writers argue a position in response to what they've read. The letters to the editor all reveal an intensity of feeling, and at times they resort to logical fallacies and other questionable tactics. These tactics include name-calling: Kristin Tardiff refers to Patinkin's "maudlin whining" and "self-righteous hypocrisy." By the same token, John N. Taylor says Tardiff's letter contains the "whiny, moralizing claptrap" of "mawkish people." The writers use exaggeration: "What comes next? Amputation for thieves and maybe prolonged torture and death for drug dealers?" (Tardiff). They are not always completely accurate: "in the U.S., a murderer draws an average sentence of only about six years" (Taylor). At times, they beg the question instead of explaining the point: "What else can parents do?" (Tardiff) and make questionable comparisons: "if caning is immoral, is not the American justice system laden with unfairness?" (Taylor). The letters are definitely opinionated, and finally that is the point: Letters to the editor give people the chance to talk back, to take strong positions, to have their say in a public forum.

FOR CRITICAL INQUIRY

1. Re-read Mark Patinkin's column, underlining his main points. Write a summary of the position he takes in his column. Your purpose is to state fairly and accurately what Patinkin is saying. Next, comment on any problems of argument such as those discussed in the analysis section.

2. Re-read the letter to the editor from Tardiff. What is it about Patinkin's column that seems to call on her to respond? How does she define her own position in relation to what Patinkin has written? To what extent does her letter respond directly to Patinkin's column? To what extent does it introduce other issues? Again, comment on any problems such as those discussed in the analysis section.

3. Re-read the letter from Taylor. How would you describe the call to write he responds to? How does he define his own position in relation to Patinkin and Tardiff? Comment on any problems of argument.

4. Write an overview of the exchange of letters. The overview shouldn't just be a summary of what each letter writer says. Although the letters are ostensibly about Michael Fay, his punishment doesn't really seem to be the main issue. Try to distill the main issues that emerge and explain how the letters relate to these issues and to each other.

5. Apart from the salutation and the name at the bottom, do these two letters to the editor seem to you like letters? What if anything distinguishes them from the column that precedes them? How are they different from the letters in the preceding section? The salutation reads "To the editor"—in your opinion, who are these letters actually addressing?

OPEN LETTER

This letter from the writer James Baldwin to his nephew was published as part of the book-length essay *The Fire Next Time*, which appeared in 1962. *The Fire Next Time* is an extended analysis of black-white relations in the United States, written with the passion and eloquence characteristic of Baldwin's prose. In this letter, Baldwin speaks directly to his nephew in what appears to be a traditional letter of advice from an older family member to a younger one. At the same time, Baldwin is using the intimacy of family relations to instill a personal intensity into an open letter on race relations.

Dear James:

I have begun this letter five times and torn it up five times. I keep seeing your face, which is also the face of your father and my brother. Like him, you are tough, dark, vulnerable, moody—with a very definite tendency to sound truculent because you want no one to think you are soft. You may be like your grandfather in this, I don't know, but certainly both you and your father resemble him very much physically. Well, he is dead, he never saw you, and he had a terrible life; he was defeated long before he died because, at the bottom of his heart, he really believed what white people said about him. This is one of the reasons that he became so holy. I am sure that your father has told you something about all that. Neither you nor your father exhibit any tendency towards holiness: you really *are* of another era, part of what happened when the Negro left the land and came into what the late E. Franklin Frazier called "the cities of destruction." You can only be destroyed by believing that you really are what the white world calls a *nigger*. I tell you this because I love you, and please don't you forget it.

I have known both of you all your lives, have carried your Daddy in my arms and on my shoulders, kissed and spanked him and watched him learn to walk. I don't know if you've known anybody from that far back; if you've loved anybody that long, first as an infant, then as a child, then as a man, you gain a strange perspective on time and human pain and effort. Other people cannot see what I see whenever I look into your father's face, for behind your father's face as it is today are all those other faces which were his. Let him laugh and I see a cellar your father does not remember and a house he does not remember and I hear in his present laughter his laughter as a child. Let him curse and I remember him falling down the cellar steps, and howling, and I remember, with pain, his tears, which my hand or your grandmother's so easily wiped away. But no one's hand can wipe away those tears he sheds invisibly today, which one hears in his laughter and in his speech and in his songs. I know what the world has done to my brother and how narrowly he has survived it. And I know, which is much worse, and this is the crime of which I accuse my country and my countrymen, and for which neither I nor time nor history will ever forgive them, that they have destroyed and are destroying hundreds of thousands of lives and do not know it and do not want to know it. One can be, indeed one must strive to become, tough and philosophical concerning destruction and death, for this is what most of mankind has been best at since we have heard of man. (But remember: *most* of mankind is not *all* of mankind.) But it is not permissible that the authors of devastation should also be innocent. It is the innocence which constitutes the crime.

Now, my dear namesake, these innocent and well-meaning people, your countrymen, have caused you to be born under conditions not very far removed from those described for us by

Charles Dickens in the London of more than a hundred years ago. (I hear the chorus of the innocents screaming, "No! This is not true! How *bitter* you are!"—but I am writing this letter to *you*, to try to tell you something about how to handle *them*, for most of them do not really know that you exist. I *know* the conditions under which you w¯re born, for I was there. Your countrymen were *not* there, and haven't made it yet. Your grandmother was also there, and no one has ever accused her of being bitter. I suggest that the innocents check with her. She isn't hard to find. Your countrymen don't know that *she* exists, either, though she has been working for them all their lives.)

Well, you were born, here you came, something like fourteen years ago; and though your father and mother and grandmother, looking about the streets through which they were carrying you, staring at the walls into which they brought you, had every reason to be heavy-hearted, yet they were not. For here you were, Big James, named for me—you were a big baby, I was not— here you were: to be loved. To be loved, baby, hard, at once, and forever, to strengthen you against the loveless world. Remember that: I know how black it looks today, for you. It looked bad that day, too, yes, we were trembling. We have not stopped trembling yet, but if we had not loved each other none of us would have survived. And now you must survive because we love you, and for the sake of your children and your children's children.

This innocent country set you down in a ghetto in which, in fact, it intended that you should perish. Let me spell out precisely what I mean by that, for the heart of the matter is here, and the root of my dispute with my country. You were born where you were born and faced the future that you faced because you were black and *for no other reason*. The limits of your ambition were, thus, expected to be set forever. You were born into a society which spelled out with brutal clarity, and in as many ways as possible, that you were a worthless human being. You were not expected to aspire to excellence: you were expected to make peace with mediocrity. Wherever you have turned, James, in your short time on this earth, you have been told where you could go and what you could do (and *how* you could do it) and where you could live and whom you could marry. I know your countrymen do not agree with me about this, and I hear them saying, "You exaggerate." They do not know Harlem, and I do. So do you. Take no one's word for anything, including mine—but trust your experience. Know whence you came. If you know whence you came, there is really no limit to where you can go. The details and symbols of your life have been deliberately constructed to make you believe what white people say about you. Please try to remember that what they believe, as well as what they do and cause you to endure, does not testify to your inferiority but to their inhumanity and fear. Please try to be clear, dear James, through the storm which rages about your youthful head today, about the reality which lies behind the words *acceptance* and *integration*. There is no reason for you to try to become like white people and there is no basis whatever for their impertinent assumption that *they* must accept *you*. The really terrible thing, old buddy, is that *you* must accept *them*. And I mean that very seriously. You must accept them and accept them with love. For these innocent people have no other hope. They are, in effect, still trapped in a history which they do not understand; and until they understand it, they cannot be released from it. They have had to believe for many years, and for innumerable reasons, that black men are inferior to white men. Many of them, indeed, know better, but, as you will discover, people find it very difficult to act on what they know. To act is to be committed, and to be committed is to be in danger. In this case, the danger, in the minds of most white Americans, is the loss of their identity. Try to imagine how you would feel if you woke up one morning to find the sun shining and all the stars aflame. You would be frightened because it is out of the order of nature. Any upheaval in the universe is terrifying because it so profoundly attacks one's sense of one's own reality. Well, the black man has functioned in the white man's world as a fixed star, as an immovable pillar: and as he moves out of his place, heaven and earth are shaken to their foundations. You, don't be afraid. I said that it was intended that you should perish in the ghetto, perish by never being allowed to go behind the white man's definitions, by never being allowed to spell your proper name. You have, and many of us have, defeated this intention; and, by a terrible law, a terrible paradox, those innocents who believed that your imprisonment made them safe are losing their grasp of reality. But these men are your brothers—your lost, younger brothers. And if the word *integration* means anything, this is what it means: that we, with love, shall force our brothers to see themselves as they are, to cease fleeing from reality and begin to change it. For this is your home, my friend, do not be driven from it; great men have done great things here, and will again, and we can make America what America must become. It will be hard, James, but you come from sturdy, peasant stock, men who picked cotton and dammed rivers and built railroads, and, in the teeth of the most terrifying odds, achieved an unassailable and monumental dignity. You come from a long line of great poets, some of the greatest poets since Homer. One of them said, *The very time I thought I was lost, My dungeon shook and my chains fell off.*

You know, and I know, that the country is celebrating one hundred years of freedom one hundred years too soon. We cannot be free until they are free. God bless you, James, and Godspeed.

Your uncle,
James

ANALYSIS: Private and Public Audiences

Of all the genres of writing gathered in this book, letter writing may appear the most personal and the most intimate. As James Baldwin writes to his nephew, "I keep seeing your face."

But as the opening lines of Baldwin's letter indicate—"I have begun this letter five times and torn it up five times"—writing on such intimate terms can bring with it certain complications, especially in this case because Baldwin actually has two audiences, his nephew and a public audience of readers.

On the one hand, Baldwin represents himself as a concerned and loving uncle writing a letter of advice to his namesake nephew, thereby invoking the sacred institution of the family as the ground to speak. On the other hand, the advice he offers his nephew—to accept white people without accepting their definitions of him—is meant to be overheard by Baldwin's other audience.

When Baldwin explains to his nephew that white people are trapped in a history of race relations they don't understand and can't escape, he is also explaining to his white readers how their own identities have been based on a belief in the inferiority of African Americans. By using the letter of advice from one family member to another, Baldwin is simultaneously offering his white readers a way to reposition themselves in relation to their own history and identities.

FOR CRITICAL INQUIRY

1. James Baldwin's letter consists of six paragraphs. To get a sense of how Baldwin establishes his relationship to his nephew and a sense of the issues, annotate each of the paragraphs. Summarize briefly what each paragraph says and what function it performs in the letter. Where in the letter does Baldwin first indicate his main point and reason for writing to his nephew? Mark this passage and explain why you think Baldwin locates his main point here. How does this passage connect to what comes before and what follows?

2. A good deal of the long fifth paragraph involves Baldwin's admonition to his nephew "to be clear . . . about the reality that lies behind the words acceptance and integration." What is the reality Baldwin alludes to here? What does he see as the relation between "acceptance" and "integration"? What assumptions have led him to this view?

3. Baldwin wrote a number of novels and essays concerning race relations in the United States. In this instance, however, he has chosen the more personal form of a family letter addressed directly to his nephew but published for all to read. How does this traditional letter of advice from an older family member to a younger one influence the way you read the letter? What advantages do you see in Baldwin's strategy of addressing his nephew instead of the more anonymous audience of people who read The Fire Next Time, in which "My Dungeon Shook: Letter to My Nephew" appeared? Are there things Baldwin can say to his nephew that he can't say directly to this audience?

LOOKING AT THE GENRE: LETTERS

1. List the kinds of letters you write and receive (letters you receive means anything that comes to you personally addressed, printed form letters along with personal letters). Classify the letters according to the relationship they are based on—letters to and from family, letters to and from friends, love letters, letters to you as a consumer or a potential donor, letters from your college, and so on. Are there particular letters you wrote or received that are especially important to you? What makes these letters important? Do you save letters? If so, what kinds of letters and why? Compare your answers to those of your classmates.

2. The letters you have read in this chapter appeared originally in very different places. The first two are private letters to family members (though later published with the writers' permission). The rest of the letters are public ones—from the Internet, a newspaper, and Baldwin's book The Fire Next Time. Pick two of the letters that appeared in different places and compare them. Identify key differences and similarities in the kind of relationship the

writer is seeking to establish with readers. Explain how these differences and similarities are influenced by the writer's understanding of where the letter will appear and who will read it.

3. Like Henry Louis Gates, Jr.'s memoir "In the Kitchen," which appears in Chapter Seven (pages 000-000), James Baldwin's letter to his nephew, "My Dungeon Shook" calls up memories of family life. Nonetheless, Baldwin's piece clearly belongs to the genre of letters, not memoir. To understand why and how this is so, compare the use Baldwin and Gates make of family memories. Explain how their purposes for recreating scenes from a family's past differ. What is each writer trying to accomplish by invoking the past? What kind of relationship to his readers is each writer seeking to establish by drawing on family history?

DESIGNING DOCUMENTS: Letter from Doctors Without Borders

This letter is from Doctors Without Borders, an international organization that sends volunteer nurses, doctors, and other health care workers to war-torn countries such as Bosnia, Rwanda, Afghanistan, and Liberia. It is a fund-raising letter, which is a type of letter of appeal. It is typical of fund-raising letters in many respects, including a number of design-related aspects. Notice these key design features:

- Organization name and logo. The organization's name and logo appear at the top left in what is often called letterhead. Logos are symbols or icons that companies, organizations, and institutions use to identify themselves visually. Think, for example of the logos of the television networks—the CBS eye or the NBC peacock. Logos are meant to stick in the mind as a graphic representation of an organization and to suggest something about the ethos of the organization.

- Listing of Board of Directors and Advisory Board. Running down the left side of the page are the names of Doctors Without Borders' Board of Directors and Advisory Board, along with identifying titles and affiliations. Because board members are often prominent people, such listings give a letter of appeal a certain legitimacy and authority in the reader's eye.

- Focusing quote. A quote from surgeon and volunteer Angie Saridakis appears centered above the text of the letter. Any quote used in this way can focus the reader's attention by establishing a sense of urgency and the main theme of the letter.

- Selective underlining. To emphasize the central theme of the letter, one sentence in the body of the letter has been underlined.

- Clinching P.S. You will notice that the letter does not end with Joelle Tanguy's signature but contains a final P.S. to underscore the urgency of its appeal.

DISCUSSION AND ACTIVITIES

1. Discuss how each of the design features contributes to making the Doctors Without Borders letter more effective as a letter of appeal:
   - What does the logo seem to represent? What does it suggest about the organization? What is the effect of the inclusion of both English and French in the letterhead?
   - What credentials do the people on these boards have? Why might this combination of people impress potential donors?
   - In addition to centering, what makes the initial quote stand out? Why did the people who wrote this letter of appeal choose to use this particular quote and to quote this particular person?
   - How would the first page of the letter be different without the underlined sentence? What effect does the underlining have on you as a reader? Why was this particular sentence, rather than another on the page, chosen for underlining?
   - How would the letter be different without the P.S. and why is this particular content used in it?

DOCTORS WITHOUT BORDERS
MEDECINS SANS FRONTIERES

*"Over here, there is no such thing
as minor surgery..."*

— *American surgeon Angie Saridakis
Doctors Without Borders Rwanda volunteer*

Dear Friend:

You have read the horrifying stories. You have seen the gruesome pictures. You have heard of the unspeakable atrocities. By now, the wars in Bosnia, Rwanda, Afghanistan, Liberia and other tortured regions may seem sadly familiar.

Yet every day, men, women and children are fighting to stay alive. Thousands of them are being saved by volunteer physicians of Doctors Without Borders: the surgeons of war.

Who are these incredibly skilled men and women who freely give up time from their secure practices to work at the center of the violence, often in abhorrent conditions? Why do they do it?

They are people like you. And they do it because they care.

Like you, they have been moved by the immeasurable pain of the victims of war. They feel they must act to help save lives, restore hope and dignity and bear witness to an often indifferent world about genocide, torture and other atrocities that must be stopped.

The surgeons of war often work at the front lines, under deplorable conditions. They repair the devastating injuries of war: the bullet wounds, the missing limbs from mine explosions, the bodies hacked by hand-held knives.

I know how crucial their work is. I have seen them myself, working in Somalia and Bosnia. <u>Arriving promptly at the site of a medical emergency, they may start operating in a local hospital, then perhaps move to a makeshift operating room in the basement if the shells and bombs begin to fall.</u> Or they may work in a temporary tent hospital set up by Doctors Without Borders, under lights provided by our emergency generators and with clean water supplied by a system we rushed to the battlefield.

You should be proud of their successes. Because in part, <u>your</u> support makes it possible for them to be there.

Today, we need your support more than ever to keep the volunteer surgeons of war working where they are needed most, saving lives.

Please help us.

Your continued support helps make possible Doctors Without Borders outreach to more than 70 countries in crisis.

Every surgeon, anesthetist, doctor and nurse that we can send, every surgical kit we can provide, every antibiotic we will administer increases the odds that more lives will be saved.

$35 can provide a basic suture kit. **$50** brings infection-fighting antibiotics to treat more than 20 wounded children in Bosnia. **$120** supplies a volunteer surgeon with a basic surgery kit for an unlimited number of operations. **$175** provides anesthesia for 25 patients. **$220** supplies a specialized surgical kit to perform six lifesaving amputations a day for the length of an entire mission. **$600** gives a doctor the necessary tools to perform emergency abdominal surgery.

As you can see, your contributions have a direct, positive effect. You help save lives through your generosity.

Please, won't you continue to help Doctors Without Borders bring desperately needed medical aid—and hope—to the victims of violence and disease? On behalf of our surgeons of the war and our other volunteers, I thank you so much for your support!

Most gratefully,

Joelle Tanguy
Executive Director

P.S. If you are following the news, you know that now, more than ever, your help is <u>urgently</u> needed!

2. Notice that the actual appeal for contributions appears on the bottom of the first page of the letter. Why do you think it is located at the bottom of that page? Why is it given as a three-word paragraph? How does it divide the letter into two parts? How does the writing that precedes it set up the appeal, and what is the function of the writing that follows it?

3. From the salutation through the closing and the P.S., what sort of relationship does this letter try to establish between writer and reader? What tone is used to establish this relationship? How is the use of pronouns especially effective here? Why does this letter try to establish this kind of relationship?

4. What kinds of appeals are used to convince the reader? Which of these do you find most effective?

5. Design the letterhead for a club, organization, or institution that you belong to or know about. You can use the Doctors Without Borders letter as a model, modifying the design to fit your organization. The letterhead should include the name and a logo that represents the spirit and aims of the organization. If appropriate, list the names of board members (or officers or sponsors).

ASSIGNMENTS

WORKING TOGETHER: Writing and Designing A Letter of Appeal

Use the letter from Doctors Without Borders as a model to write a letter of appeal. As a group, you will need first to identify an issue, a cause, or an organization you want your readers to support. Then you need to decide exactly what you will ask your readers to do. Here are some possibilities:

- You could write a fund raising letter for a worthy organization or a particular cause (for example, a fund for victims of a recent flood, hurricane or earthquake).
- You could call on your readers to write government, business, or education officials asking them to change a policy or implement a new one, to release a prisoner who has been unjustly jailed (as appeals from Amnesty International do), to support or oppose impending legislation.
- You could call on readers to donate their time to a project worth supporting (for example, mentoring at-risk teenagers, volunteering in a soup kitchen or food pantry, attending a demonstration or rally).

Once you have determined the purpose of your letter, consider to whom you will send the letter. Who is most likely to respond to your appeal? Based on your sense of who your readers will be, consider what arguments are most likely to persuade them to take the action you call for. What information will prove persuasive? What appeals to shared values?

Use this information to design the letter of appeal. Part of the letter's persuasiveness, of course, will depend on its design. How do you want the letter to look? What features of document design will make it more likely that the letter will get a sympathetic reading?

CALL TO WRITE: LETTERS

WRITING ASSIGNMENT

For this writing assignment, compose a letter. In the pages that follow, you will find exercises and ideas for deciding the kind of letter you'll write, what the letter will be about, to whom you will send it, and how your letter should be presented. The possibilities are endless; you can write to someone you know, to the editor of a newspaper, to a politician, or a to a local community group concerning an issue of public concern. Here are some other letters you might find yourself called to write:

- A letter to your parents explaining your plans for the future and your reasons for undertaking a particular course of action, such as majoring in a certain field, choosing a career, devoting yourself to community service organization, or starting a business.

- A letter of advice to a younger relative or student. You might use James Baldwin's letter to his nephew as a model here. That is, you can address your letter and speak directly to the younger person, but your letter might raise issues that would interest other readers as well. You might explain what it takes to survive in college or how to handle particular kinds of peer group pressures, such as drinking, drugs, and sex. Or you might explain what it's like to be a scholarship athlete, a woman, an African American, a gay or lesbian, a Latino, or a working-class student in a white, middle-class college.
- A letter to the editor of a newspaper or magazine that responds to a news story, feature article, editorial, or column that particularly moved you. Or you might raise an issue that's important to you but hasn't yet appeared in the media.
- A letter of appeal, calling on readers to take an action or make a contribution. You can identify an organization or cause that you believe deserves support, and design a letter that presents the aims and activities of the organization and that calls on readers to do something—to become a member, to send a donation, to write a letter. You may want to design this letter of appeal for the Internet.
- A posting to an electronic discussion group. To do this, you will need first of course to follow the discussion for a week or so to catch on to the concerns and tone of the group. See the directions above in "Going On-Line: Electronic Discussion Groups" for further advice.

INVENTION

IDENTIFYING THE CALL TO WRITE

Because this assignment is relatively open-ended, the first thing you'll need to do is identify something that moves you to write. Obviously, one thing that is calling on you to write is the fact that you've just been given a writing assignment in a composition course. But to write a letter that you can be proud of you'll need to find your own reasons and your own motivation to write. Make this assignment work for you. After all, here's a chance to use the familiar form of the letter to do something you've been wanting to do anyway.

If nothing immediately springs to mind, work through the following exercise. In this way, you can identify a topic you feel strongly about or find a person you've been wanting to write.

EXERCISE

Follow as many of the steps below as you like.
- Is there a particular subject that has been making you curious, or angry, or grateful? If so, you can use this letter as a way to express your opinions, or to learn more about the subject, or to respond to something someone else has written about that subject. Is there something that you are learning in one of your courses that you want to tell someone about? Write it in a letter.
- Is there a person that you want to write to? Do you need to settle a score, or clear up confusion, or work out a problem? Do you want to let someone know about the impact they have had on your life? Do you want someone to know more about the way you approach your life? Is there a friend with whom you don't want to lose contact? Any of these options might provide your call to write.
- Is there a public issue in your community, either on campus, at home, or in the national or international scene that has captured your interest and made you want to participate? If so, you can become involved in that issue by participating in online conversations, by talking with local agencies about writing something for them, by starting a conversation in any of the forums you have open to you.

Throughout this chapter there have been examples of different kinds of letters people have written. As you can see, there is a broad range of types of letters that are possible. Is there a sub-genre of letters that you would like to try writing? Do any of those sub-genres of letters make you think of something you have been meaning to do? If so, you can choose to do it now. For a list of the sub-genres with which you are familiar, look through any Writing Inventories you may have created if you worked through Chapter 1.

If none of these exercises have helped you identify a call to write, try listing all of your hobbies, family members, friends, and the organizations to which you belong (or have belonged to in the past). Next to each item you list, think of ways that you can reach that person (or people) through writing.

Once you have worked through these exercises, go back through them and note those calls to write that you find most compelling. Which interest you the most? Which would actually change your life, or someone else's life, in a positive way? Choose the option that most interests you.

EXERCISE

Write a statement of purpose, using these questions to guide you:
- To whom are you writing?
- What calls on you to write?
- What are you going to say?
- What do you want to accomplish in your letter?
- How do you want your reader to respond?

UNDERSTANDING YOUR READER

How successful you will be in eliciting the response you want from your reader depends in part on how well you understand your reader and your relationship to your reader. If you are appealing for something—whether it's money from your parents or donations to a cause you believe in—you need to figure out what might persuade your reader. If you want to irritate someone or get under their skin, you need to know what buttons to push. To influence a politician, you need to know his or her interests and how you can tap into them.

EXERCISE

To gather ideas about how you can most effectively address your reader, respond to these questions:
- On what terms do you know your reader—family, personal, institutional? Describe your relationship to the person. Is it formal or informal? How does this relationship affect what you can and cannot say in your letter? If you are writing on-line, how does the electronic forum of the Internet affect your relationship to readers?
- What is an effective way to present yourself to your reader? What will it take to establish the credibility and authority of what you have to say? What kind of personality or attitude is your reader likely to respond to?
- What attitude is your reader likely to have toward your letter? What is your reader's interest in what you have to say? Will your reader care personally or read your letter as part of work?
- What is your reader likely to know about the message you are sending? How much shared information is involved? How much do you need to explain?
- What values and beliefs do you think your reader might hold about the subject of your letter? What common ground can you establish? What shared values can you appeal to?

(For information on how writers can use the classical appeals—ethos, logos, and pathos—to approach their readers, see the section Rhetorical Stance in Chapter 5.)

E T H I C S   O F   W R I T I N G

Using the Internet

One of the most exciting aspects of the Internet is its capacity to open up new public forums for the exchange of ideas. A posting from an individual to a mailing list or newsgroup can connect him or her to people all over the world with an that promotes rapid feedback and response. But precisely because e-mail offers such exciting possiblities for transmitting information and ideas, it is important to use it properly—to understand what can be sent to whom under what conditions
.

- Author's permission. Communicating on the Internet requires the same attention to copyright and intellectual property as print communication. In other words, you need

to cite your sources, and if you want to forward a message written by someone else, you need to secure permission first.

- Reader's permission. Don't just asume that people will want to be added to a regular mailing list or newsgroup. You need to secure peopleís permission before adding their names. Readers are likely to resent unsolicited e-mail and feel imposed upon. Be careful not to flood cyberspace with junk e-mail.

Carnegie Mellon Universityís Internet offers a collection of articles on Internet issues such as copyright, access, and politics, as well as Internet protocols. The address is http://eng.lss.cmu.edu/internet/.

EXERCISE

Another step in understanding your readers is to understand the forum in which your readers communicate with one another. After all, readers do bring certain expectations with them when they open a letter in the mail, or read a newsletter, or log in to read their email. Find some models that you can use to guide your decisions as you write your letter. Think about the following issues:

- How long do these types of letters tend to be?
- How do readers address one another? Do they use first names only, or last names only, or is there some other way?
- Do paragraphs tend to be short or long? Or do they vary greatly?
- What level of formality do these writers tend to use?
- If the writers are giving someone else credit for a quote or an idea, how do they handle the citation (if there is one)?

PLANNING

ESTABLISHING THE OCCASION

Letters often begin by establishing their timeliness: why they're written at that moment, in response to what call to write, to what person or people, on the basis of what relationship. Notice the ways writers establish the occasion in the reading selections:

- Acknowledging a letter or card (Cathleen Cordova).

- Providing instructions in case of death (Richard Marks).

- Making a complaint, expressing sympathy (e-mail correspondence).

- Establishing authority to speak and familiarity with the topic (Kristine Tardiff, regular reader of Mark Patinkin's column).

- Characterizing an opponent's position, expressing sense of outrage (John N. Taylor, "whiny, moralizing claptrap").

- Invoking family ties as the right to speak (James Baldwin).

The need to establish the occasion of a letter—the grounds for writing in the first place—is also true of business letters, job application letters ("I am interested in applying for the position you have advertised . . ."), letters to politicians and public officials ("I write to urge you to . . ."), letters of sympathy and condolence ("I know this is a difficult time, and I wanted you to know . . ."), letters of congratulations ("Congratulations, you really deserve . . ."), and letters of gratitude ("Thanks for the birthday present . . .").

In some instances, writers will make explicit their relationship to the reader—for example, in letters to politicians ("I have been a registered Democrat in the Third Ward for thirty years, and like my neighbors I am concerned about . . .") or letters of complaint ("I bought one of your [name of product]) and . . ."). In letters where the reader knows you personally, relationships are often implied rather than stated.

In your letter, you need to design an opening that treats the occasion of the letter and your relationship to the reader. How explicitly you do this will depend on what your reader needs to hear. Politicians, business people, government officials, and newspaper editors all appreciate letters that get right to the point. In letters home and other personal letters, staying in touch (as much or more than the letter's content) may be the main point of writing.

ARRANGING YOUR MATERIAL

List the points you want to make and the information you want to include in your letter. Arrange the material in an outline that consists of three sections:

- Opening: to establish occasion, relationship, point of letter.
- Main body: to explain and develop the point of the letter, whether that means concentrating on one main topic or including a number of separate topics.
- Closing: to reiterate main point of the letter, whether that involves calling for action, firing a final salvo, reaffirming the writer's relationship to the reader, sending regards, or thanking the reader for his or her time.

Notice how even a letter that appears loosely structured, like Cathleen Cordova's, still has a discernible order and pattern to it:

- Opening: marks occasion of the letter, sends thanks, tells a story—all centered on a moment, the writer's birthday.
- Main body: offers observation (about "1st Cav"), opinion (about "Tricky Dickî), and an anecdote (about a John Wayne movie). Cordova does not connect the three paragraphs to each other explicitly but at the same time they each mark an aspect of the writer's experience in wartime.
- Closing: announces ending ("This is all for now"), inquires about grandparents, sends best wishes.

WORKING DRAFT

Once you have a list of the main points you want to make, the next step is to write a working draft. As you write, new ideas may occur to you. That's only natural. Don't censor them out by trying to rigidly follow your list of points. Instead try to incorporate new points by connecting them to the ones you have already listed. If you can connect them, the new points probably belong in the letter. If you can't, then you need to think carefully about whether they really fit your letter. As you write your working draft, keep in mind the overall movement you want in your letter—from an opening that sets the occasion to a main body that explains your key points to a closing that wraps things up for the reader.

Writing a working draft often means revising the words you have written based on your own sense of what might need to change. Below are some possibilities for reshaping or revising your draft before you share it with others. After you have written your main ideas into a working draft, you might want to develop parts of your letter more fully by using some paragraph development strategies. Below are some exercises for describing your subject in more depth. For other paragraph development ideas, look at the strategies discussed in the context of other genres. Depending on your purpose and your audience, some of these paragraph development strategies might be more useful and appropriate than others. For example, personal letters often contain longer paragraphs with significant amounts of descriptive detail, while letters of appeal often have shorter paragraphs with a more topical focus. Consider your options, try a few, and choose those that work for you in this situation.

see Narrating (page XXX in Memoirs) to tell a story within a time sequence

see Defining (page XXX in Public Documents) to make sure your readers share your meanings of important terms

see Offering Reasons with Supporting Facts and Evidence (page XXX in Reviews) to make a persuasive argument

PARAGRAPH DEVELOPMENT: Describing

One option for developing certain paragraphs, and an option that most readers will immediately recognize, is to describe your subject. Describing allows you to create a picture for your readers by providing detail about an important place or object, or to portray a person in depth.

EXERCISE:

To generate description for a place or an object, try to illustrate your subject in terms of your five senses. If you like, set a timer for five minutes per sense. In that time, write as much as you can about the way your subject looks, feels, smells, tastes, and sounds. Use the most appropriate description in your letter.

To generate description for a person, try to imagine him or her in time segments. Write as much as you can about that person through different points in time, remembering stories if you can. Select a time frame based on the duration of your relationship with that person; for example, if you have known him or her a long time, spend at least five minutes writing about each five year period. On the other hand, if you have known him or her only a few months, break your brainstorming into one-week segments. Next, ask yourself what has remained the same about this person? What has changed through time? Use the description that best fits your purpose; in other words, use the description that provides evidence for the points you are making. Notice here that you are describing the person at various points in time rather than telling stories about that person (if you are interested in telling stories in time sequences, see Narrating on page XXX in Memoirs).

Now that you have more information about your subject and your paragraphs are more fully developed, you might want to reconsider the overall organizational structure of your letter. You may also want to check through some of the options described in Chapter 2, particularly the section on Planning (pages XXX). After thinking about your organization, you might want to consider some different techniques for opening and closing your letter. You can read below about using an ìecho effectî to frame your letter, and in other chapters you can find additional options.

- see Pointing Out Significance (page XXX in Memoirs) if you hope to persuade someone to act
- see Using Facts, Statistics, and Background Information (page XXX in Public Documents) if you need to establish your credibility from the outset
- see Forecasting What Is to Come (page XXX in Reports) if you want to set up clear expectations from the beginning of the letter.

BEGINNINGS AND ENDINGS: Using an Echo Effect to Reframe

One effective way to end your letter may be to loop back to the issues raised in your opening. One aspect of a satisfying closure for readers is the sense that the writing ends where it began, only now in the light of what the writer has said in between. This is commonly called an echo effect, when the ending echoes the concerns of the opening. This echo effect gives a text a kind of symmetry that readers will recognize.

Joelle Tanguy uses an echo effect in her letter on behalf of Doctors Without Borders. In the opening, after explaining the connection between the surgeons of war and the people receiving this letter: she writes, "They are people just like you . . . and they do it because they care." At the end of the letter, Tanguy reinforces the idea that the recipient can be just as active as the surgeons by giving financially to Doctors Without Borders. Near the end of the letter, she spells out exactly what certain dollar amounts might buy, allowing readers to choose their giving levels according to the actions they want to support. In the final two paragraphs before her signature, Tanguy again reminds readers of their ìdirect, positive effect.î The connection between the volunteers in war-torn countries and the readers at home is echoed throughout Tanguy's letter.

You may want to try this echo effect in your own writing. Take a look back at your opening, and see if there are threads that you would like to recur in your closing. Or think about adding the suggestion of a theme to your introduction, and return to it at the end of your letter.

PEER COMMENTARY

Exchange working drafts with a classmate. Depending on your teacher's direction, you can do this peer commentary electronically, via e-mail or a class listserv. In classes without computer access, however, you will probably want to write your comments either on your classmateís paper itself, or on a separate sheet of paper. Comment on your partner's draft by responding to these questions:

1. Who is the writer addressing? What is the occasion of the letter? Where in the letter did you become aware of the writer's purpose? Be specific. Is there a particular phrase, sentence, or passage that alerted you to the writer's purpose? If not, where would you like this information to be?
2. What kind of relationship does the writer seem to want to establish with the reader? How does the writer seem to want the readers to respond? How can you tell? Are there places you think the writer should make the relationship or the desired response more explicit?
3. Does the writer address the reader in a way that makes a positive response likely or possible? Explain your answer. What could the writer do to improve the chances of making the impression he or she wants?
4. Describe the tone of the letter. What kind of personality seems to come through in the letter? What identity does the writer take on in the letter? Do you think the intended reader will respond well to it? If not, what might you change?

REVISING

Review the commentary from your peers. Based on their response, do your think you accomplished your purpose with your letter? Have you clearly defined the occasion and your purpose? Have you addressed any concerns your reader might have? Does the letter establish the kind of relationship with your reader or readers that you want? Do you think your readers will respond well to the way you present yourself?

If you are comfortable with these aspects of your letter, it is probably time to fine-tune your writing. You will find revision strategies Connections and Coherence in each chapter of Part II. Connections and Coherence sections can help you make sure you have provided your readers all the signposts they need to follow the flow of your writing. In this chapter, you will be asked to check your writing for coherence using topic sentences. You might also want to check for other types of coherence devices discussed in other chapters.

- see Temporal Transitions (page XXX in Memoirs) to signal divisions by time segments

- see Spatial Transitions (page XXX in Profiles) to signal geographical divisions

- see Topical Chains (page XXX in Reviews) to construct a series of arguments that build on one another with repeated words.

CONNECTIONS AND COHERENCE: Direct and Implied Topic Sentences

Writers have a number of strategies for helping their readers make links between sections in their writing. These strategies can be called connections, or they can be called coherence devices. They often function as connective tissue, to hold the pieces of your writing together, and to guide readersí expectations. One of the most common ways to establish coherence in a letter (or any other genre of writing, for that matter), is to use topic sentences.

As you have already seen, beginnings and endings have different issues for you to address as you are writing (for example, how you will grab the readerís attention, or establish your credibility; likewise, how you will leave the reader with your strongest appeal in mind). The other paragraphs, often called topical paragraphs because they cover specific information about the topics in your letter, generally focus on a single idea or a sequence of related ideas. They often have a fairly conventional structure that links the parts together to form a coherent whole. In general, topical paragraphs have three well-defined parts:

TOPIC SENTENCE: establishes the reader's focus of attention by identifying the writer's point in the opening sentences. Often draws on an issue from the previous paragraph and explains how the writer will treat it.

DISCUSSION: explains, describes, illustrates, or otherwise develops the focus of attention established in the opening sentences. Shows readers how the evidence provided is linked to the writer's main point.

ENDING (optional): some paragraphs use an ending that can perform a number of different functions. Sometimes the topic statement follows rather than precedes the Discussion. In other cases, endings summarize or draw conclusions from the Discussion or offer a different perspective from that in the topic sentence.

There are, of course, many exceptions to this pattern, as you saw throughout the letters in this chapter. However, if you do not already know how to work with topic sentences, they can be an important part of your repertoire. Depending on the kind of letter you are writing, they may help strengthen your writing. The key to writing topical paragraphs is to establish your main point with a topic sentence, usually at the beginning of each paragraph.

When readers encounter a paragraph break, they expect there is a reason. The indentation that marks the beginning of a new paragraph carries with it the anticipation that the writer will be presenting something new—a new topic or perspective—that the reader will need to fit into the larger pattern of the passage. Topic sentences are the most common means of guiding readers through this transition. Notice, for example, how each of the following paragraphs uses topic sentences to describe the main point of each paragraph.

Topic sentences establish a focus of attention at the beginning of a paragraph. In a well-designed paragraph, the reader should be able to anticipate what is to come in the rest of the paragraph. Topic sentences orient readers by identifying what the paragraph is about and how it will be developed. When writers stay within the limits they establish, paragraphs are easier to follow. They feel unified, since they donít seem to digress or run off the point. Notice how Mark Patikin uses a topic sentence in the following paragraph in his column about the Micheal Fay caning. The first sentence (the topic sentence) establishes the focus of the paragraph, and the rest of the sentences explain it more fully:

All of this is just part of the new American game of always saying, "It's not my fault." No one, when caught, seems ready to admit having done anything wrong anymore. They just whine and appeal. As in: "Your honor, the stabbing was not my client's fault. He had a bad childhood. And was caught up in a riot at the time. In fact, he's not a criminal at all, he's one of society's victims."

Topic sentences link paragraphs together. To keep readers oriented to the writer's train of thought as it moves from paragraph to paragraph, writers often show how a particular paragraph's focus of attention is linked to the paragraphs that precede and follow. Richard Marks' letter to his mother, for example, uses the topic sentence in one paragraph to set up the expectation that the following paragraphs will contain specific instructions for dealing with his death. The next several paragraphs, then, do just that.

There are some details I want taken care of. First of all, any money that you receive as a result of my death I want distributed in the following fashion.
If you are single . . . .
I also want to be buried . . . .
That is about all, except I hope I never have to use this letter—

Sometimes topic sentences are implied. Not all paragraphs have topic sentences; in some cases, the topic or focus of attention in a paragraph is implied rather than explicitly stated upfront. Implied topic sentences often work well when the paragraph appears in a piece of writing that provides enough context for the reader to know the main point without having to read it. Since readers need to be able to recognize the main point, and to see how it fits into the flow of the writing, implied topic sentences can be very effective when the preceding paragraph has already set up the point. James Baldwin uses an implied topic sentence effectively in the following paragraph, because an explicit topic sentence might distract from the powerful presentation of Baldwin's experience, diluting the points he is making.

I have known both of you all your lives, have carried your Daddy in my arms and on my shoulders, kissed and spanked him and watched him learn to walk. I donít know if youíve loved anybody that long, first as an infant, then as a child, then as a man, you gain a strange perspective on time and human pain and effort. Other people cannot see what I see whenever I look into your fatherís face, for behind your fatherís face as it is today are all those other faces which were his .
. . .

By the end of this paragraph, Baldwin works his way from a loving tribute about his brother to a painful critique of society's destruction. Baldwin does this without a topic sentence, and he moves quite gradually from the first sentence (where the topic sentence most often appears) to the last. You might want to try this technique in your own letter.

WRITERS WORKSHOP

Michael Brody wrote the following letter to the editor in a first-year writing class after he read Mark Patinkin's column "Commit a crime, suffer the consequence" that appeared in the Providence Journal-Bulletin on April 19, 1994 and letters to the editor that followed on May 3 and May 9, 1994. As you will see, entering the caning debate at this point enables Brody to summarize positions people have already taken as a way to set up his own main point. The letter to the editor is followed by a commentary Brody wrote to explain his approach to the issue.

LETTER TO THE EDITOR

May 12, 1994

To the Editor:

Mark Patinkin's column "Commit a crime, suffer the consequences" (4/19) has generated heated responses from readers and understandably so. For some, the sentence of six strokes of the cane, at least by American standards, does indeed seem to be "cruel and unusual punishment," no matter what Patinkin writes about Michael Fay's "whining." On the other hand, Patinkin and those readers who side with him are right that Michael Fay is the criminal in this case, not the victim, and that he deserves to suffer the consequences of his actions.

I happen to agree with readers who argue for leniency. Let Michael Fay pay for his crime by fines and a jail sentence. It worries me that some readers are willing to tolerate or even endorse caning. Obviously, these sentiments show how fed up Americans are with the problem of crime in our society. But there is a tendency in some of the pro-Patinkin letters to idealize Singapore's strong measures as a successful get-tough solution to crime. As readers point out, the crime rate in Singapore is low, the streets are safe, and there are no drive-by shootings. While this picture of Singapore may appear to be reassuring to some readers, it hides the fact that beneath a polished, secure, and business-like facade Singapore is ruled by a brutal dictatorship that keeps its people in fear by punishing not only vandalism and spraypainting but chewing gum as antisocial crimes.

Readers need to understand how the Michael Fay case is being used by the Singapore government as a lesson to its own people about the decadence of American ways. The leaders of Singapore are portraying Michael Fay as a living illustration of all that's flawed about American values of freedom and individual rights, and his admittedly immature and illegal actions are held up as direct consequences of the American way of life. Mark Patinkin and his supporters have failed to see how the Michael Fay incident is more than a matter of whether America, unlike Singapore, is soft on crime, coddles law breakers, and ignores the true victims. For the Singapore government, the caning of Michael Fay is a stern warning to the people of Singapore against the dangers of American democracy.

What is ironic about this attempt to use Michael Fay for anti-American purposes is the fact that caning is itself not a traditional Singapore means of punishment. It's tempting to think of caning as the barbaric practice of cruel Asian despots, but in reality Singapore learned about caning from the British colonial powers who once ruled the country. The British Empire, as I'm sure Mark Patinkin is well aware, took a tough stand on law and order in the colonies and routinely crushed native movements for freedom and independence. I wish Mark Patinkin and others who are properly concerned about crime would consider the lessons Singapore leaders learned from their former masters about how to control and intimidate those they rule. Caning is not a matter of different national customs, as some people make it out to be. Nor is it an extreme but understandable response to crime in the streets. In Singapore, caning is part of both a repressive judicial system and a calculated propaganda campaign to discredit democratic countries and silence dissent.

Michael Brody

Worcester, MA

Michael Brody's Commentary

When I read Mark Patinkin's column, I got angry and wanted to denounce him as a fascist. Then I read the letters readers had written opposing or supporting Patinkin's point of view, and they made me realize that I didn't want to follow them because they all seemed to be too emotional, just gut responses. I wanted to find a different approach to the whole caning incident so that I could raise an issue that was different or had been overlooked.

Now I must admit that when I first heard about the sentence of caning, I thought it was barbaric, probably something typical of Asian dicatatorships. I thought of the massacre at Tienamien Square, and I dimly recalled what I had heard when I was young about how the Chinese Communists tortured Catholic missionaries, stuff like bamboo slivers under the finger nails. Then I read somewhere that caning was brought to Singapore by the British in colonial days, and I started to think along new lines. It occurred to me that maybe the caning wasn't just about crime but had something to do with how governments ruled their people.

As I read more in the newspapers, Time, and Newsweek about the incident, I was shocked to discover how Michael Fay was being used by Singapore leaders to build up anti-American sentiment, to paint America as a permissive society that coddled its criminals. I decided that I'd try to write something that looked at how the case was being used by Singapore's rulers. The more I thought about it, this seemed to give me an angle to go beyond agreeing or disagreeing with Patinkin's column and still have something interesting to say.

When I was getting ready to write, I made a quick outline of my points. I wanted to sound reasonable so I decided to concede that both sides, for or against caning, had some valid points. I decided to show this in my opening and wait until the second paragraph to indicate where I was coming from. I wanted to create the effect that there's this debate going on, which I figured readers would know about and already have their own opinions about, but that I had an angle people maybe hadn't thought about. So I tried to get this point to emerge in the second paragraph and then drive it home at the beginning of the third paragraph with the sentence that starts "Readers need to understand . . . . "

That sentence set me up to give my own analysis of the incident and of how Patinkin and the pro-caning people failed to see the full political picture. I decided to leave the idea that caning came from British colonial powers until the end as my clincher. I figured this would do two things. First, it would surprise people, who like me thought caning was a barbaric Asian punishment. Second, it would have an emotional charge because I assumed most people would be against colonialism, especially British colonialism, given that America had to fight England for our independence. Besides I'm Irish, and I know a lot of people where I live are against the British in Ireland, and I knew they'd be against anything associated with the British empire.

I'm not totally sure the irony I talk about in the opening line of the last paragraph works. I remember learning about irony in English class in high school, and how funny or odd it is when things don't turn out the way you expected. So I wanted to throw that in, to make readers feel, well I thought it was one way but when you look at it again, it's another way. I thought this might work in the very end to show that caning is not just this (a barbaric national custom) or that (an extreme form of punishment) but also a form of political intimidation.

WORKSHOP QUESTIONS

1. When you first read Michael Brody's letter to the editor, at what point did you become aware of his own position in the caning debate? Note the sentence or passage that enabled you to see where Brody is coming from. What was your initial response? Explain how you responded as you followed Brody's line of reasoning in the rest of the letter. Why do you think you responded as you did?

2. Brody devotes considerable space in the first two paragraphs to presenting positions people have already taken in the caning debate. What kind of relationship does he seem to want to establish with his readers by doing so? Do you think his relationship to readers will vary, depending on whether they are pro-caning or anti-caning? Do you consider Brody's presentation of positions in the debate an effective strategy? Why or why not?

3. Describe the tone Brody uses in the letter. How does it compare to the tone in Mark Patinkin's column and in the letters to the editor from Kristin Tardiff and John N. Taylor? Do you think Brody's tone works well? Explain your response.

4. Re-read Brody's commentary. If you could talk to him, how would you respond to what he says about composing his letter? Notice that Brody seems a bit uncertain about his ending and whether it works to point out the irony that caning comes from the British. Does this provide the clincher that Brody wants?

WRITER'S INVENTORY

Use the commentary Michael Brody wrote as a model to write your own account of how you planned and composed the letter you wrote. Explain how you defined the call to write and how you positioned yourself in relation to your readers, your topic, and what others had already said about your topic (if that applies to your letter). Notice how Brody explains how he developed his own position by considering what others had said and reading newspapers and magazines on the Michael Fay incident. Explain, as Brody does, in a step-by-step way how you composed your letter, what effects you were trying to achieve, and what problems or issues emerged for you along the way. Indicate any aspects of the letter that you're not certain about. Add anything else you'd like to say.

A CLOSING NOTE

The point of writing a letter is to communicate with someone. While your instructor and classmates can be helpful readers, they may not be the real audience for the letter you have written. This audience may be located outside your writing classroom. If this is the case, send your letter to the audience it is intended for.

CHAPTER
FIVE

MEMOIRS:
Recalling Personal Experience

LOOKING AT THE GENRE

Writing memoirs, as the word itself suggests, involves memory-work. Memoirists draw on their past, looking back at events, people, and places that are important to them, in order to recreate, in written language, moments or episodes of lived experience. This recreation of particular experiences distinguishes memoirs from the genre of autobiographies, which seek to encompass an entire life instead. But memoirists don't just recreate moments of experience—they seek to imbue them with a significance readers will understand.

The call to write memoirs comes in part from the desire people have to keep track of the past and to see how their lives have intersected with public events. This impulse to remember is what leads people to take photographs, compile scrapbooks, and save letters and keepsakes of all sorts. Long after a particular experience is over, these objects help remind us of how things were at that moment. They also help remind us of how we were. You may have experienced how objects you've saved give you a sense of connection to your past.

This sense of connection between present and past is at the center of memoir writing. By recreating experiences from the past and exploring their significance, memoirists can begin to identify the continuities and discontinuities in their own lives. Writing memoirs is always, at least in part, an act of self-discovery, of clarifying where the writer has come from and what he or she has become. The writer of a memoir is both participant and observer: On the one hand, the writer often appears as a character in the memoir, a participant in the events that unfold. On the other hand, the writer is also an observer who comments on and interprets these unfolding events, giving them a shape and meaning for the present. Writing memoirs thereby puts the writer in a complicated relationship to his or her own experience.

Because memoirs are not simply reports from the past, in which the events speak for themselves, writing memoirs also puts the writer in a complicated relationship to readers, a relationship that carries certain risks. For one thing, self-disclosure leaves the writer vulnerable to the judgments of readers. For another, there is the risk of seeming self-indulgent or sentimental. The memoir writer, after all, is asking readers to devote time and attention to his or her reminiscences.

The solution to this last potential problem lies in an aspect of memoirs already mentioned: successful memoirs make personal experiences significant to others. Thus, the reader of the memoir isn't a mere voyeur, peering at intimate details of the writer's past, but rather is gaining insights into other times and places, as well as the writerís personality. A memoir aims for understanding—to help readers come to terms with the writer's experience of the past and its meanings for the present.

One strategy memoir writers often use to this end is to focus on details that reveal deeper meanings to themselves and to readers. For memoirist Patricia Hampl, details such as a "black boxy Ford" in a photograph, a "hat worn in 1952," an aunt polishing her toenails, and the "booths of the Gopher Grill" at the University of Minnesota can move writers to recover and convey to readers what might otherwise be overlooked in their pasts—the "intimate fragments . . . that bind even obscure lives to history." Memoir writers can take an incident from, say, childhood or adolescence that readers will recognize immediately—such as visiting grandparents, going on a first date, moving to a new town, or going away to college—and bring out meanings that readers may not have suspected were there. Writers may focus on moments of revelation, showing how crises and insights have challenged and changed their perceptions, expectations, and values.

Another strategy that writers typically use in memoirs is to put their experience in a larger historical or cultural context. That is, writers present their past in part as exemplifying and shedding light on something larger—what it meant, say, to grow up in the Great Depression or during the sixties. Thus, as you'll see, Henry Louis Gates, Jr., begins "In the Kitchen" with a personal scene from childhood that seems unimportant but anchors a larger discussion and comes to evoke a whole way of life in African-American communities.

The point here is that as detailed, specific, and filled with sensory impressions as successful memoirs typically are, it is the larger context that gives these details their significance. To put it another way, memoirs offer writers a way to show how the details of everyday life take on wider meanings when located in a wider framework.

Ultimately, people are called on to write memoirs, not only to establish a connection to the past and to inform readers about the past and entertain them, but also from a sense of responsibility to the past, from a desire to bear witness to things that might otherwise be overlooked or forgotten. Amy Tan says of the people she sees in her family's photographs—people she tells of in "Lost Lives of Women"—that they "never let me forget why stories need to be told." In many respects, memoirs derive their unique power to move readers from the way writers position themselves in the present in order to bear witness to the past, thus revealing the secrets and unsuspected meanings of ordinary lives that turn out to be not so ordinary after all.

"Black Hair."

Gary Soto.

Gary Soto is a poet and essayist who teaches at the University of California at Berkeley. His books of poetry include The Elements of San Joaquin (1991), Black Hair (1985), and Home Course in Religion: New Poems (1991). The following selection appears in his book of essays Living Up the Street (1985) and like many of the essays that appear in Small Faces (1986) and A Summer Life (1990) recounts incidents in his Chicano childhood and adolescence, growing up in the Central Valley of California.

Black Hair

There are two kinds of work: One uses the mind and the other uses muscle. As a kid I found out about the latter. I'm thinking of the summer of 1969 when I was a seventeen-year-old runaway who ended up in Glendale, California, working for Valley Tire Factory. To answer an ad in the newspaper I walked miles in the afternoon sun, my stomach slowly knotting on a doughnut that was breakfast, my teeth like bright candles gone yellow.

I walked in the door sweating and feeling ugly because my hair was still stiff from a swim at the Santa Monica beach the day before. Jules, the accountant and part owner, looked droopily through his bifocals at my application and then at me. He tipped his cigar in the ashtray, asked my age as if he didn't believe I was seventeen, but finally, after a moment of silence, said, "Come back tomorrow. Eight-thirty."

I thanked him, left the office, and went around to the chain-link fence to watch the workers heave tires into a bin; others carted uneven stacks of tires on hand trucks. Their faces were black from tire dust, and when they talked — or cussed — their mouths showed a bright pink.

From there I walked up a commercial street, past a cleaners, a motorcycle shop, and a gas station where I washed my face and hands; before leaving I took a bottle that hung on the side of the Coke machine, filled it with water, and stopped it with a scrap of paper and a rubber band.

The next morning I arrived early at work. The assistant foreman, a   5
potbellied Hungarian, showed me a time card and how to punch in. He showed me the Coke machine and the locker room with its slimy shower, and also pointed out the places where I shouldn't go: the ovens where the tires were recapped and the customer service area, which had a slashed couch, a coffee table with greasy magazines, and an ashtray. He introduced me to Tully, a fat man with one ear who worked the buffers that resurfaced the whitewalls. I was handed an apron and a face mask and shown how to use the buffer: Lift the tire and center it, inflate it with a foot pedal, press the buffer against the white band until cleaned, and then deflate and blow off the tire with an air hose.

With a paintbrush he stirred a can of industrial preserver. "Then slap this blue stuff on." While he was talking a coworker came up quietly behind him and goosed him with the air hose. Tully jumped as if he had been struck by a bullet and then turned around cussing and cupping his genitals in his hands as the other worker walked away calling out foul names. When Tully turned to me, smiling his gray teeth, I lifted my mouth into a smile because I wanted to get along. He has to be on my side, I thought. He's the one who'll tell the foreman how I'm doing.

I worked carefully that day, setting the tires on the machine as if they were babies, because it was easy to catch a finger in the rim that expanded to inflate the tire. At the day's end we swept up the tire dust and emptied the trash into bins.

At five the workers scattered for their cars and motorcycles while I crossed the street to wash at a burger stand. My hair was stiff with dust and my mouth showed pink against the backdrop of my dirty face. I ordered a hotdog and walked slowly in the direction of the abandoned house where I had stayed the night before. I lay under the trees and within minutes was asleep. When I woke my shoulders were sore, and my eyes burned when I squeezed the lids together.

From the backyard I walked dully through a residential street, and as evening came on, the TV glare in the living rooms and the headlights of passing cars showed against the blue drift of dusk. I saw two children coming up the street with snow cones, their tongues darting at the packed ice. I saw a boy with a peach and wanted to stop him but felt embarrassed by my hunger. I walked for an hour, only to return and discover the house lit brightly. Behind the fence I heard voices and saw a flashlight poking at the garage door. A man on the back steps mumbled something about the refrigerator to the one with the flashlight.

I waited for them to leave but had the feeling they wouldn't because there was a commotion of furniture being moved. Tired, even more desperate, I started walking again with a great urge to kick things and tear the day from my life. I felt weak and my mind kept drifting because of hunger. I crossed the street to a gas station where I sipped at the water fountain and searched the Coke machine for change. I started walking again, first up a commercial street, then into a residential area where I lay down on someone's lawn and replayed a scene at home — my mother crying at the kitchen table, my stepfather yelling with food in his mouth. They're cruel, I thought, and warned myself that I should never forgive them. How could they do this to me?

When I got up from the lawn it was late. I searched out a place to sleep and found an unlocked car that seemed safe. In the backseat, with my shoes off, I fell asleep but woke up startled about four in the morning when the owner, a nurse on her way to work, opened the door. She got in and was about to start the engine when I raised my head to explain my presence. She screamed so loudly when I said "I'm sorry" that I sprinted from the car with my shoes in hand. Her screams faded, then stopped altogether, as I ran down the block, hid behind a trash bin, and waited for a police siren to sound. Nothing. I crossed the street to a church where I slept stiffly on cardboard in the balcony.

I woke up feeling tired and greasy. It was early and a few streetlights were still lit, the east growing pink with dawn. I washed myself from a garden hose and returned to the church to break into what looked like a kitchen. Paper cups, plastic spoons, a coffee pot littered on a table. I found a box of Nabisco crackers and ate until I was full.

At work I spent the morning at the buffer, but was then told to help Iggy, an old Mexican who was responsible for choosing tires that could be re-capped without the risk of exploding at high speeds. Every morning a truck would deliver used tires, and after I unloaded them Iggy would step among the tires to inspect them for punctures and rips on the sidewalls.

With yellow chalk he marked circles and Xs to indicate damage and called out "junk." Tires that could be recapped got a "goody" from Iggy, and I placed them on my hand truck. When I had a stack of eight I kicked the truck at an angle and balanced off to another work area, where Iggy again inspected the tires, scratching Xs and calling out "junk."

Iggy worked only until three in the afternoon, at which time he went to the locker room to wash and shave and to dress in a two-piece suit. When he came out he glowed with a bracelet, watch, rings, and a shiny fountain pen in his breast pocket. His shoes sounded against the asphalt. He was the image of a banker stepping into sunlight with millions on his mind. He said a few low words to workers with whom he was friendly and none to people like me.

15

I was seventeen, stupid because I couldn't figure out the difference between an F78 14 and a 750 14 at sight. Iggy shook his head when I brought him the wrong tires, especially since I had expressed interest in being his understudy. "Mexican, how can you be so stupid?" he would yell at me, slapping a tire from my hands. But within weeks I learned a lot about tires, from sizes and makes to how they are molded in iron forms to how Valley stole from other companies. Now and then we received a truckload of tires, most of them new or nearly new, and they were taken to our warehouse in the back, where the serial numbers were ground off with a sander. On those days the foreman handed out Cokes and joked with us as we worked to get the numbers off.

Most of the workers were Mexican or black, though a few redneck whites worked there. The base pay was a dollar sixty-five but the average was three dollars. Of the black workers, I knew Sugar Daddy the best. His body carried 250 pounds and armfuls of scars, and he had a long knife that made me jump when he brought it out from his boot without warning. At one time he had been a singer and had cut a record in 1967 called *Love's Chance*, which broke into the R & B charts. But nothing came of it. No big contract, no club dates, no tours. He made very little from record sales, only enough for an operation to pull a steering wheel from his gut when, drunk and mad at a lady friend, he slammed his Mustang into a row of parked cars.

"Touch it," he smiled at me one afternoon as he raised his shirt, his black belly kinked with hair. Scared, I traced the scar that ran from his chest to the left of his belly button, and I was repelled but hid my disgust.

Among the Mexicans I had few friends because I was different, a *pocho*° who spoke bad Spanish. At lunch they sat in tires and laughed over burritos, looking up at me to laugh even harder. I also sat in tires while nursing a Coke and felt dirty and sticky because I was still living on the street and had not had a real bath in over a week. Nevertheless, when the border patrol came to round up the nationals, I ran with them as they scrambled for the fence or hid among the tires behind the warehouse. The foreman, who thought I was an undocumented worker, yelled at me to run, to get away. I did just that. At the time it seemed fun because there was no risk, only a good-hearted feeling of hide-and-seek, and besides, it meant an hour away from work on company time. When the police left we came back, and some of the nationals made up stories of how they were almost caught — how they outraced the police. Some of the stories were so convoluted and unconvincing that everyone laughed and shouted *"mentiras,"*° especially when one described how he overpowered a policeman, took his gun away, and sold the patrol car. We laughed and he laughed, happy to be there to make up such a story.

---

pocho   Mexican slang meaning "outsider."
mentiras   Spanish: "lies."

If work was difficult, so were the nights. I still had not gathered enough   20
money to rent a room, so I spent the nights sleeping in parked cars or in the church balcony. After a week I found a newspaper ad for a room for rent, phoned, and was given directions. Finished with work, I walked the five miles down Mission Road looking back into the traffic with my thumb out. No rides. After eight hours of handling tires I was frightening to drivers, I suppose, since they seldom looked at me; if they did, it was a quick glance. For the next six weeks I would try to hitchhike, but the only person to stop was a Mexican woman who gave me two dollars to take the bus. I told her it was too much and that no bus ran from Mission Road to where I lived, but she insisted that I keep the money and trotted back to her idling car. It must have hurt her to see me day after day walking in the heat and looking very much the dirty Mexican to the many minds that didn't know what it meant to work at hard labor. That woman knew. Her eyes met mine as she opened the car door, and there was a tenderness that was surprisingly true — one for which you wait for years but when it comes it doesn't help. Nothing changes. You continue on in rags, with the sun still above you.

I rented a room from a middle-aged couple whose lives were a mess. She was a schoolteacher and he was a fireman. A perfect setup, I thought. But during my stay there they would argue for hours in their bedroom.

When I rang at the front door both Mr. and Mrs. Van Deusen answered and didn't bother to disguise their shock at how awful I looked. But they let me in all the same. Mrs. Van Deusen showed me around the house, from the kitchen and bathroom to the living room with its grand piano. On her fingers she counted out the house rules as she walked me to my room. It was a girl's room with lace curtains, scenic wallpaper of a Victorian couple enjoying a stroll, a canopied bed, and stuffed animals in a corner. Leaving, she turned and asked if she could do laundry for me. Feeling shy and hurt, I told her no; perhaps the next day. She left and I undressed to take a bath, exhausted as I sat on the edge of the bed probing my aches and my bruised places. With a towel around my waist I hurried down the hallway to the bathroom where Mrs. Van Deusen had set out an additional towel with a tube of shampoo. I ran water into the tub and sat on the closed toilet, watching the steam curl toward the ceiling. When I lowered myself into the tub I felt my body sting. I soaped a washcloth and scrubbed my arms until they lightened, even glowed pink, but I still looked unwashed around my neck and face no matter how hard I rubbed. Back in the room I sat in bed reading a magazine, happy and thinking of no better luxury than a girl's sheets, especially after nearly two weeks of sleeping on cardboard at the church.

I was too tired to sleep, so I sat at the window watching the neighbors move about in pajamas, and, curious about the room, looked through the bureau drawers to search out personal things — snapshots, a messy diary, and high-school yearbook. I looked up the Van Deusen's daughter, Barbara, and studied her face as if I recognized her from my own school — a face that said "promise," "college," "nice clothes in the closet." She was a skater and a member of the German Club; her greatest ambition was to sing at the Hollywood Bowl.

After a while I got into bed, and as I drifted toward sleep I thought about her. In my mind I played a love scene again and again and altered it slightly each time. She comes home from college and at first is indifferent to my presence in her home, but finally I overwhelm her with deep pity when I come home hurt from work, with blood on my shirt. Then there was another version: Home from college she is immediately taken with me, in spite of my work-darkened face, and invites me into the family car for a milkshake across town. Later, back at the house, we sit in the living room talking about school until we're so close I'm holding her hand. The truth of the matter was that Barbara did come home for a week but was bitter toward her parents for taking in boarders (two others besides me). During that time she spoke to me only twice: Once, while searching the refrigerator, she asked if we had any mustard; the other time she asked if I had seen her car keys.

But it was a place to stay. Work had become more and more difficult. I   25
worked not only with Iggy but also with the assistant foreman, who was in charge of unloading trucks. After they backed in I hopped on top to pass the tires down, bouncing them on the tailgate to give them an extra spring so they would be less difficult to handle on the other end. Each truck was weighted down with more than two hundred tires, each averaging twenty pounds, so that by the time the truck was emptied and swept clean I glistened with sweat and my T-shirt stuck to my body. I blew snot threaded with tire dust onto the asphalt, indifferent to the customers who watched from the waiting room.

The days were dull. I did what there was to do from morning until the bell sounded at five; I tugged, pulled, and cussed at tires until I was listless and my mind drifted and caught on small things, from cold sodas to shoes to stupid talk about what we would do with a million dollars. I remember unloading a truck with Hamp, a black man.

"What's better than a sharp lady?" he asked me as I stood sweaty on a pile of junked tires. "Water. With ice," I said.

He laughed with his mouth open wide. With his fingers he pinched the sweat from his chin and flicked at me. "You be too young, boy. A woman can make you a god."

As a kid I had chopped cotton and picked grapes, so I knew work. I knew the fatigue and the boredom and the feeling that there was a good possibility that you might have to do such work for years, if not for a lifetime. In fact, as a kid I had imagined a dark fate: to marry Mexican poor, work Mexican hours, and in the end die a Mexican death, broke and in despair.

But this job at Valley Tire Company confirmed that there was something   30
worse than fieldwork, and I was doing it. We were all doing it, from the foreman to the newcomers like me, and what I felt heaving tires for eight hours a day was felt by everyone — black, Mexican, redneck. We all de-

spised those hours but didn't know what else to do. The workers were unskilled, some undocumented and fearful of deportation, and all struck with uncertainty at what to do with their lives. Although everyone bitched about work, no one left. Some had worked there for twelve years; some had sons working there. Few quit; no one was ever fired. It amazed me that no one gave up when the border patrol jumped from their vans, batons in hand, because I couldn't imagine any work that could be worse — or any life. What was out there, in the world, that made men run for the fence in fear?

Iggy was the only worker who seemed sure of himself. After five hours of "junking," he brushed himself off, cleaned up in the washroom, and came out gleaming with an elegance that humbled the rest of us. Few would look him straight in the eye or talk to him in our usual stupid way because he was so much better. He carried himself as a man should — with Old World "dignity" — while the rest of us muffed our jobs and talked dully about dull things as we worked. From where he worked in his open shed he would now and then watch us with his hands on his hips. He would shake his head and click his tongue in disgust.

The rest of us lived dismally. I often wondered what the others' homes were like; I couldn't imagine that they were much better than our workplace. No one indicated that his outside life was interesting or intriguing. We all looked defeated and contemptible in our filth at the day's end. I imagined the average welcome at home: Rafael, a Mexican national who had worked at Valley for five years, returned to a beaten house full of kids dressed in mismatched clothes and playing kick the can. As for Sugar Daddy, he returned home to a stuffy room where he would read and reread old magazines. He ate potato chips, drank beer, and watched TV. There was no grace in dipping socks into a washbasin where later he would wash his cup and plate.

There was no grace at work. It was all ridicule. The assistant foreman drank Cokes in front of the newcomers as they laced tires in the afternoon sun. Knowing that I had a long walk home, Rudy, the college student, passed me waving and yelling "Hello" as I started down Mission Road on the way home to eat out of cans. Even our plump secretary got into the act by wearing short skirts and flaunting her milky legs. If there was love, it was ugly. I'm thinking of Tully and an older man whose name I can no longer recall fondling one another in the washroom. I had come in cradling a smashed finger to find them pressed together in the shower, their pants undone and partly pulled down. When they saw me they smiled with their pink mouths but didn't bother to push away.

How we arrived at such a place is a mystery to me. Why anyone would stay for years is an even deeper concern. You showed up, but from where? What broken life? What ugly past? The foreman showed you the Coke machine, the washroom, and the yard where you'd work. When you picked up a tire, you were amazed at the black it could give off.

ANALYSIS: A Moment of Revelation

Much of the power of memoirs, as Gary Soto's "Black Hair" illustrates, is their capacity to bring to life a moment of personal experience. Notice that Soto provides little information about why he was a runaway or how his experience at the Valley Tire Factory ended. Instead, he concentrates the reader's attention on the physical experience of work—the dirt, the noise, the smells, the sweat and bodily exhaustion of a day's labor. Soto seems to want us as readers to feel as intensely as he does this remembered moment. But he also wants the intensity of his recalled experience to unlock its significance—for readers and for himself. As the best memoirs do, Soto's "Black Hair" turns a moment of personal experience into a moment of revelation. Looking back on himself as a seventeen-year-old, Soto uses his account of this moment in the past to explain what he found out about work.

FOR CRITICAL INQUIRY

1. In the opening lines of his memoir, Gary Soto explains that there are "two kinds of work" and that he found out about work that "uses muscle" when he was a seventeen-year-old runaway. Most of the memoir then consists of Soto's account of his experience working at the Valley Tire Factory, and he seems to be telling a story more than explaining a point. When you reach the end of the memoir do you feel he has adequately explained his point? How does Soto's account of his experience develop the point about work with which he begins? To answer these questions, divide the memoir into sections by grouping paragraphs together. Describe what function the sections perform in the memoir. How does each contribute to Soto's explanation?

2. The final six paragraphs seem to offer Soto's closing evaluation of his experience. Explain the conclusions he appears to reach at the end. Do they seem justified based on his account of his experience?

3. Soto does not tell us why he was a runaway or how his experience working at the Valley Tire Factory ended. Why do you think he has decided not to provide this information? How does it affect the way you read his memoir?

4. Soto offers quick sketches of a number of characters he encounters at work and in the home where he stayed. What role do these characters play in Soto's memoir? What does Soto's attitude toward them seem to be? How does he seem to want us as readers to understand them?

5. Consider the title of the memoir "Black Hair." What are the various meanings this title might hold?

6. Write a paragraph summary of "Black Hair." Compare your summary to those of classmates. Notice the extent to which they are similar and how they differ. How would you account for the differences? To what extent is it possible for such short summaries to capture the experience in Soto's memoir? What, if anything, is lost by summarizing? What, if anything, is gained?

"Lost Lives of Women."

Amy Tan.

Amy Tan is the author of the best-selling novels The Joy Luck Club and The Kitchen God's Wife. These novels recreate the world of the Chinese-American community in California, the world of Tan's childhood (Tan was born shortly after her parents emigrated from China). The photo-essay that follows was originally published in Life in 1991. Here, as in her novels but more explicitly, Tan is preoccupied with her responsibilities, as a writer, to her family's past. Thus, as you will see, the family photo she looks at and tells about connects her to her family's past and helps clarify her responsibilities as a writer in the present.

When I first saw this photo as a child, I thought it was exotic and remote, of a faraway time and place, with people who had no connection to my American life. Look at their bound feet! Look at that funny lady with the plucked forehead!

The solemn little girl is, in fact, my mother. And leaning against the rock is my grandmother, Jingmei. "She called me Baobei," my mother told me. "It means Treasure."

: picture was taken in Hangzhou, and my mother believes the year was possibly spring or fall, judging by the clothes. At first glance, it appears ___ omen are on a pleasure outing.

But see the white bands on their skirts? The white shoes? They are in mourning. My mother's grandmother, known to the others as Divong, "The Replacement Wife," has recently died. The women have come to this place, a Buddhist retreat, to perform yet another ceremony for Divong. Monks hired for the occasion have chanted the proper words. And the women and little girl have walked in circles clutching smoky sticks of incense. They knelt and prayed, then burned a huge pile of spirit money so that Divong might ascend to a higher position in her new world.

This is also a picture of secrets and tragedies, the reasons that warnings have been passed along in our family like heirlooms. Each of these women suffered a terrible fate, my mother said. And they were not peasant women but big city people, very modern. They went to dance halls and wore stylish clothes. They were supposed to be the lucky ones.

Look at the pretty woman with her finger on her cheek. She is my mother's second cousin, Nunu Aiyi, "Precious Auntie." You cannot see this, but Nunu Aiyi's entire face was scarred from smallpox. Lucky for her, a year or so after this picture was taken, she received marriage proposals from two families. She turned down a lawyer and married another man. Later she divorced her husband, a daring thing for a woman to do. But then, finding no means to support herself or her young daughter, Nunu eventually accepted the lawyer's second proposal— to become his number two concubine. "Where else could she go?" my mother asked. "Some people said she was lucky the lawyer still wanted her."

Now look at the small woman with a sour face. There's a reason that Jyou Ma, "Uncle's Wife," looks this way. Her husband, my great-uncle, often complained that his family had chosen an ugly woman for his wife. To show his displeasure, he often insulted Jyou Ma's cooking. One time Great-Uncle tipped over a pot of boiling soup, which fell all over his niece's four-year-old neck and nearly killed her. My mother was the little niece, and she still has that soup scar on her neck. Great-Uncle's family eventually chose a pretty woman for his second wife. But the complaints about Jyou Ma's cooking did not stop.

Doomma, "Big Mother," is the regal-looking woman seated on a rock. (The woman with the plucked forehead, far left, is a servant, remembered only as someone who cleaned but did not cook.) Doomma was the daughter of my great-grandfather and Nu-pei, "The Original Wife." She was shunned by Divong, "The Replacement Wife," for being "too strong," and loved by Divong's daughter, my grandmother. Doomma's first daughter was born with a hunchback—a sign, some said, of Doomma's own crooked nature. Why else did she remarry, disobeying her family's orders to remain a widow forever? And why did Doomma later kill herself, using some mysterious means that caused her to die slowly over three days? "Doomma died the same way she lived," my mother said, "strong, suffering lots."

Jingmei, my own grandmother, lived only a few more years after this picture was taken. She was the widow of a poor scholar, a man who had the misfortune of dying from influenza when he was about to be appointed a vice-magistrate. In 1924 or so, a rich man, who liked to collect pretty women, raped my grandmother and thereby forced her into becoming one of his concubines. My grandmother, now an outcast, took her young daughter to live with her on an island outside of Shanghai. She left her son behind, to save his face. After she gave birth to another son she killed herself by swallowing raw opium buried in the New Year's rice cakes. The young daughter who wept at her deathbed was my mother.

At my grandmother's funeral, monks tied chains to my mother's ankles so she would not fly away with her mother's ghost. "I tried to take them off," my mother said. "I was her treasure. I was her life."

My mother could never talk about any of this, even with her closest friends. "Don't tell anyone," she once said to me. "People don't understand. A concubine was like some kind of prostitute. My mother was a good woman, high-class. She had no choice."

I told her I understood.

"How can you understand?" she said, suddenly angry. "You did not live in China then. You do not know what it's like to have no position in life. I was her daughter. We had no face! We belonged to nobody! This is a shame I can never push off my back." By the end of the outburst, she was crying.

On a recent trip with my mother to Beijing, I learned that my uncle found a way to push the shame off his back. He was the son my grandmother left behind. In 1936 he joined the Communist party—in large part, he told me, to overthrow the society that forced his mother into concubinage. He published a story about his mother. I told him I had written about my grandmother in a book of fiction. We agreed that my grandmother is the source of strength running through our family. My mother cried to hear this.

My mother believes my grandmother is also my muse, that she helps me write. "Does she still visit you often?" she asked while I was writing my second book. And then she added shyly, "Does she say anything about me?"

"Yes," I told her. "She has lots to say. I am writing it down."

This is the picture I see when I write. These are the secrets I was supposed to keep. These are the women who never let me forget why stories need to be told.

ANALYSIS: Bridging a Cultural Gap

Amy Tan is quite explicit about the sense of responsibility she feels for the past. For Tan, the "secrets and tragedies" contained in the photograph of her mother, grandmother, and aunts seem to call on her to tell these women's stories—to keep faith with her family's history and to bear witness to a past from which she is separated not only by time but also by culture. As Tan looks at her family's past from the perspective of the present, she is also looking across cultures, from the perspective of "my American life" to what initially appeared to be "exotic and remote, of a faraway time and place." Tan's memoir represents her effort to bridge this cultural gap by connecting her own life to what seemed alien and unfamiliar in the lives of her relatives. Thus, the revelation in Tan's memoir involves her act of repositioning herself in relation to her family's history—to tell the stories her mother had kept secret.

FOR CRITICAL INQUIRY

1. Amy Tan opens this essay by saying, "When I first saw this photo as a child, I thought it was exotic and remote, of a faraway time and place, with people who had no connection to my American life." Why do you think she begins this way? How has Tan's relationship to the photo changed? Mark specific passages in the essay that, either explicitly or implicitly, show this change. How would you explain the change?

2. In an exchange recounted in the essay, Tan tells her mother that she understands her grandmother's concubinage, but her mother responds angrily: "How can you understand? You did not live in China then. You do not know what it's like to have no position in life." What is going on in this exchange? Is Tan able to understand, as she claims she does, or is her mother right that no one can understand who did not live through this tragedy? How do these difficulties in understanding affect the reader of the essay?

3. The story of the funeral has within it the story of another funeral. These funerals begin and end the discussion of the photo. What are the two funerals? What are some things that tie the two funerals together? What is an important difference between them? Why is the inclusion of the second funeral effective?

4. In a sense, this memoir consists of two dialogues—between mother and daughter and between writer and reader—with the photo at their center. How does the photo make these two dialogues possible? How does the dialogue between mother and daughter enhance that between writer and reader?

5. How do the final four paragraphs of the memoir, which go beyond the photo only to return to it, provide a kind of perspective and larger context? What is the significance of Tan's encounter with her uncle?

"In the Kitchen."

Henry Louis Gates, Jr.

This selection from Henry Louis Gates, Jr.'s memoir Colored People first appeared as an essay in the New Yorker. Gates is Professor of English and Chairman of Afro-American Studies at Harvard University and one of the leading literary and cultural critics of our time. As you will see, this memoir takes Gates from the fifties to the present and from the kitchen of his childhood home in Piedmont, West Virginia, to the island of Zanzibar, off the coast of east Africa. Throughout the essay, Gates offers memories and reflections about the cultural meanings of hair-straightening in African-American communities.

IN THE KITCHEN

From a childhood view of a mother's home beauty parlor to adolescent dreams of a perfectly greased flat head, a history unfolds of the politics of the hairdo.

BY HENRY LOUIS GATES, JR.

WE always had a gas stove in the kitchen, in our house in Piedmont, West Virginia, where I grew up. Never electric, though using electric became fashionable in Piedmont in the sixties, like using Crest toothpaste rather than Colgate, or watching Huntley and Brinkley rather than Walter Cronkite. But not us: gas, Colgate, and good ole Walter Cronkite, come what may. We used gas partly out of loyalty to Big Mom, Mama's Mama, because she was mostly blind and still loved to cook, and could feel her way more easily with gas than with electric. But the most important thing about our gas-equipped kitchen was that Mama used to do hair there. The "hot comb" was a fine-toothed iron instrument with a long wooden handle and a pair of iron curlers that opened and closed like scissors. Mama would put it in the gas fire until it glowed. You could smell those prongs heating up.

I liked that smell. Not the smell so much, I guess, as what the smell meant for the shape of my day. There was an intimate warmth in the women's tones as they talked with my Mama, doing their hair. I knew what the women had been through to get their hair ready to be "done," because I would watch Mama do it to herself. How that kink could be transformed through grease and fire into that magnificent head of wavy hair was a miracle to me, and still is.

Mama would wash her hair over the sink, a towel wrapped around her shoulders, wearing just her slip and her white bra. (We had no shower—just a galvanized tub that we stored in the kitchen—until we moved down Rat Tail Road into Doc Wolverton's house, in 1954.) After she dried it, she would grease her scalp thoroughly with blue Bergamot hair grease, which came in a short, fat jar with a picture of a beautiful colored lady on it. It's important to grease your scalp real good, my Mama would explain, to keep from burning yourself. Of course, her hair would return to its natural kink almost as soon as the hot water and shampoo hit it. To me, it was another miracle how hair so "straight" would so quickly become kinky again the second it even approached some water.

My Mama had only a few "clients" whose heads she "did"—did, I think, because she enjoyed it, rather than for the few pennies it brought in. They would sit on one of our red plastic kitchen chairs, the kind with the shiny metal legs, and brace themselves for the process. Mama would stroke that red-hot iron—which by this time had been in the gas fire for half an hour or more—slowly but firmly through their hair, from scalp to strand's end. It made a scorching, crinkly sound, the hot iron did, as it burned its way through kink, leaving in its wake straight strands of hair, standing long and tall but drooping over at the ends, their shape like the top of a heavy willow tree. Slowly, steadily, Mama's hands would transform a round mound of Odetta kink into a darkened swamp of everglades. The Bergamot made the hair shiny; the heat of the hot iron gave it a brownish-red cast. Once all the hair was as straight as God allows kink to get, Mama would take the well-heated curling iron and twirl the straightened strands into more or less loosely wrapped curls. She claimed that she owed her skill as a hairdresser

to the strength in her wrists, and as she worked her little finger would poke out, the way it did when she sipped tea. Mama was a southpaw, and wrote upside down and backward to produce the cleanest, roundest letters you've ever seen.

The "kitchen" she would all but remove from sight with a handheld pair of shears, bought just for this purpose. Now, the kitchen was the room in which we were sitting—the room where Mama did hair and washed clothes, and where we all took a bath in that galvanized tub. But the word has another meaning, and the kitchen that I'm speaking of is the very kinky bit of hair at the back of your head, where your neck meets your shirt collar. If there was ever a part of our African past that resisted assimilation, it was the kitchen. No matter how hot the iron, no matter how powerful the chemical, no matter how stringent the mashed-potatoes-and-lye formula of a man's "process," neither God nor woman nor Sammy Davis, Jr., could straighten the kitchen. The kitchen was permanent, irredeemable, irresistible kink. Unassimilably African. No matter what you did, no matter how hard you tried, you couldn't de-kink a person's kitchen. So you trimmed it off as best you could.

When hair had begun to "turn," as they'd say—to return to its natural kinky glory—it was the kitchen that turned first (the kitchen around the back, and nappy edges at the temples). When the kitchen started creeping up the back of the neck, it was time to get your hair done again.

SOMETIMES, after dark, a man would come to have his hair done. It was Mr. Charlie Carroll. He was very light-complected and had a ruddy nose—it made me think of Edmund Gwenn, who played Kris Kringle in "Miracle on 34th Street." At first, Mama did him after my brother, Rocky, and I had gone to sleep. It was only later that we found out that he had come to our house so Mama could iron his hair—not with a hot comb or a curling iron but with our very own Proctor-Silex steam iron. For some reason I never understood, Mr. Charlie would conceal his Frederick Douglass-like mane under a big white Stetson hat. I never saw him take it off except when he came to our house, at night, to have his hair pressed. (Later, Daddy would tell us about Mr. Charlie's most prized piece of knowledge, something that the man would only confide after his hair had been pressed, as a token of intimacy. "Not many people know this," he'd say, in a tone of circumspection, "but George Washington was Abraham Lincoln's daddy." Nodding solemnly, he'd add the clincher: "A white man told me." Though he was in dead earnest, this became a humorous refrain around our house—"a white man told me"—which we used to punctuate especially preposterous assertions.)

My mother examined my daughters' kitchens whenever we went home to visit, in the early eighties. It became a game between us. I had told her not to do it, because I didn't like the politics it suggested—the notion of "good" and "bad" hair. "Good" hair was "straight," "bad" hair kinky. Even in the late sixties, at the height of Black Power, almost nobody could bring themselves to say "bad" for good and "good" for bad. People still said that hair like white people's hair was "good," even if they encapsulated it in a disclaimer, like "what we used to call 'good.'"

Maggie would be seated in her high chair, throwing food this way and that, and Mama would be cooing about how cute it all was, how I used to do just like Maggie was doing, and wondering whether her flinging her food with her left hand meant that she was going to be left-handed like Mama. When my daughter was just about covered with Chef Boyardee Spaghetti-O's, Mama would seize the opportunity: wiping her clean, she would tilt Maggie's head to one side and reach down the back of her neck. Sometimes Mama would even rub a curl between her fingers, just to make sure that her bifocals had not deceived her. Then she'd sigh with satisfaction and relief: No kink . . . yet. Mama! I'd shout, pretending to be angry. Every once in a while, if no one was looking, I'd peek, too.

I say "yet" because most black babies are born with soft, silken hair. But after a few months it begins to turn, as inevitably as do the seasons or the leaves on a tree. People once thought baby oil would stop it. They were wrong.

Everybody I knew as a child wanted to have good hair. You could be as ugly as homemade sin dipped in misery and still be thought attractive if you had good hair. "Jesus moss," the girls at Camp Lee, Virginia, had called Daddy's naturally "good" hair during the war. I know that he played that thick head of hair for all it was worth, too.

My own hair was "not a bad grade," as barbers would tell me when they cut it for the first time. It was like a doctor reporting the results of the first full physical he has given you. Like "You're in good shape" or "Blood pressure's kind of high—better cut down on salt."

I spent most of my childhood and adolescence messing with my hair. I definitely wanted straight hair. Like Pop's. When I was about three, I tried to stick a wad of Bazooka bubble gum to that straight hair of his. I suppose what fixed that memory for me is the spanking I got for doing so: he turned me upside down, holding me by my feet, the better to paddle my behind. Little *nigger*, he had shouted, walloping away. I started to laugh about it two days later, when my behind stopped hurting.

When black people say "straight," of course, they don't usually mean literally straight—they're not describing hair like, say, Peggy Lipton's (she was the white girl on "The Mod Squad"), or like Mary's of Peter, Paul & Mary fame; black people call that "stringy" hair. No, "straight" just means not kinky, no matter what contours the curl may take. I would have done *anything* to have straight hair—and I used to try everything, short of getting a process.

Of the wide variety of techniques and methods I came to master in the challenging prestidigitation of the follicle, almost all had two things in common: a heavy grease and the application of pressure. It's not an accident that some of the biggest black-owned companies in the fifties and sixties made hair products. And I tried them all, in search of that certain silken touch, the one that would leave neither the hand nor the pillow sullied by grease.

I always wondered what Frederick Douglass put on *his* hair, or what Phillis Wheatley put on hers. Or why Wheatley has that rag on her head in the little engraving in the frontispiece of her book. One thing is for sure: you can bet that when Phillis Wheatley went to England and saw the Countess of Huntingdon she did not stop by the

Queen's coiffeur on her way there. So many black people still get their hair straightened that it's a wonder we don't have a national holiday for Madame C. J. Walker, the woman who invented the process of straightening kinky hair. Call it Jheri-Kurled or call it "relaxed," it's still fried hair.

I used all the greases, from sea-blue Bergamot and creamy vanilla Duke (in its clear jar with the orange-white-and-green label) to the godfather of grease, the formidable Murray's. Now, Murray's was some *serious* grease. Whereas Bergamot was like oily jello, and Duke was viscous and sickly sweet, Murray's was light brown and *hard*. Hard as lard and twice as greasy, Daddy used to say. Murray's came in an orange can with a press-on top. It was so hard that some people would put a match to the can, just to soften the stuff and make it more manageable. Then, in the late sixties, when Afros came into style, I used Afro Sheen. From Murray's to Duke to Afro Sheen: that was my progression in black consciousness.

We used to put hot towels or wash-rags over our Murray-coated heads, in order to melt the wax into the scalp and the follicles. Unfortunately, the wax also had the habit of running down your neck, ears, and forehead. Not to mention your pillowcase. Another problem was that if you put two palmfuls of Murray's on your head your hair turned white. (Duke did the same thing.) The challenge was to get rid of that white color. Because if you got rid of the white stuff you had a magnificent head of wavy hair. That was the beauty of it: Murray's was so hard that it froze your hair into the wavy style you brushed it into. It looked really good if you wore a part. A lot of guys had parts *cut* into their hair by a barber, either with the clippers or with a straightedge razor. Especially if you had kinky hair—then you'd generally wear a short razor cut, or what we called a Quo Vadis.

We tried to be as innovative as possible. Everyone knew about using a stocking cap, because your father or your uncle wore one whenever something really big was about to happen, whether sacred or secular: a funeral or a dance, a wedding or a trip in which you confronted official white people. Any time you were trying to look really sharp, you wore a stocking cap in preparation. And if the event was really a big one, you made a new cap. You asked your mother for a pair of her hose, and cut it with scissors about six inches or so from the open end—the end with the elastic that goes up to the top of the thigh. Then you knotted the cut end, and it became a beehive-shaped hat, with an elastic band that you pulled down low on your forehead and down around your neck in the back. To work well, the cap had to fit tightly and snugly, like a press. And it had to fit that tightly because it *was* a press: it pressed your hair with the force of the hose's elastic. If you greased your hair down real good, and left the stocking cap on long enough, voilà: you got a head of pressed-against-the-scalp waves. (You also got a ring around your forehead when you woke up, but it went away.) And then you could enjoy your concrete do. Swore we were bad, too, with all that grease and those flat heads.

My brother and I would brush it out a bit in the mornings, so that it looked—well, "natural." Grown men still wear stocking caps—especially older men, who generally keep their stocking caps in their top drawers, along with their cufflinks and their see-through silk socks, their "Maverick" ties, their silk handkerchiefs, and whatever else they prize the most.

A Murrayed-down stocking cap was the respectable version of the process, which, by contrast, was most definitely not a cool thing to have unless you were an entertainer by trade. Zeke and Keith and Poochie and a few other stars of the high-school basketball team all used to get a process once or twice a year. It was expensive, and you had to go somewhere like Pittsburgh or D.C. or Uniontown—somewhere where there were enough colored people to support a trade. The guys would disappear, then reappear a day or two later, strutting like peacocks, their hair burned slightly red from the lye base. They'd also wear "rags"—cloths or handkerchiefs—around their heads when they slept or played basketball. Do-rags, they were called. But the result was straight hair, with just a hint of wave. No curl. Do-it-yourselfers took their chances at home with a concoction of mashed potatoes and lye.

THE most famous process of all, however, outside of the process Malcolm X describes in his "Autobiography," and maybe the process of Sammy Davis, Jr., was Nat King Cole's process. Nat King Cole had patent-leather hair. That man's got the finest process money can buy, or so Daddy said the night we saw Cole's TV show on NBC. It was November 5, 1956. I remember the date because everyone came to our house to watch it and to celebrate one of Daddy's buddies' birthdays. Yeah, Uncle Joe chimed in, they can do shit to his hair that the average Negro can't even *think* about—secret shit.

Nat King Cole was *clean*. I've had an ongoing argument with a Nigerian friend about Nat King Cole for twenty years now. Not about whether he could sing—any fool knows that he could—but about whether or not he was a handkerchief head for wearing that patent-leather process.

Sammy Davis, Jr.,'s process was the one I detested. It didn't look good on him. Worse still, he liked to have a fried strand dangling down the middle of his forehead, so he could shake it out from the crown when he sang. But Nat King Cole's hair was a thing unto itself, a beautifully sculpted work of art that he and he alone had the right to wear. The only difference between a process and a stocking cap, really, was taste; but Nat King Cole, unlike, say, Michael Jackson, looked *good* in his. His head looked like Valentino's head in the twenties, and some say it was Valentino the process was imitating. But Nat King Cole wore a process because it suited his face, his demeanor, his name, his style. He was as clean as he wanted to be.

I had forgotten all about that patent-leather look until one day in 1971, when I was sitting in an Arab restaurant on the island of Zanzibar surrounded by men in fezzes and white caftans, trying to learn how to eat curried goat and rice with the fingers of my right hand and feeling two million miles from home. All of a sudden, an old transistor radio sitting on top of a china cupboard stopped blaring out its Swahili music and started playing "Fly Me to the Moon," by Nat King Cole. The restaurant's din was not affected at all, but in my mind's eye I saw it: the King's magnificent sleek black tiara. I managed, barely, to blink back the tears. ◆

ANALYSIS: An Insider's Perspective

Henry Louis Gates, Jr.'s memoir "In the Kitchen" begins as a loving and nostalgic evocation of the hair-straightening he witnessed as a child in his mother's kitchen and proceeds to an elaborate cataloguing of hair-straightening methods. By the end of his essay, however, we realize that Gates is not simply reminiscing or reporting on the intricacies of African-American hair style but, rather, is reconstructing a way of life and affirming his loyalty to his memories of growing up and to the people from his past. Particularly striking, perhaps, is how Gates resists representing hair-straightening as an acceptance of white standards of beauty by African Americans. Though he acknowledges the famous criticism of the "process" in Malcolm X's autobiography, Gates does not seek to position himself as a critic in relation to the people from his past he is writing about. Instead, Gates reveals, from an insider's perspective, how the ritual of hair straightening, far from simply the product of a desire to look white, reflects a uniquely African-American style and sensibility.

FOR CRITICAL INQUIRY

1. You may have noticed that Henry Louis Gates, Jr., has broken his essay into three sections. Annotate and write a summary of each section. Now consider how the sections connect to each other to form a whole. What does each section contribute to the whole? What links are there in each section to the other sections? Why did Gates organize his essay into the three sections?—how would the essay have been different without the breaks?

2. Memoirs depend in part on recreating scenes from the past so that readers can share the lived experience of the writer. Mark passages in the essay where you think Gates is especially effective in using specific detail and sensory impressions to recreate the past. What makes these passages work effectively? Many of the details, naturally, relate to hair and hair-straightening techniques and products. List some of these details. How are they crucial to the essay?

3. In the final lines of the essay, as Gates remembers Nat King Cole's "magnificent sleek black tiara," he says, "I managed, barely, to blink back the tears." One of the issues memoirists face is avoiding sentimentality in explaining to readers how they feel looking back on the past. How does Gates handle the problem of potential sentimentality at the close of the essay? Consider the final lines in the context of the entire essay.

4. The essay combines purely personal references with broader cultural references. Give some examples of each. Why is this combination effective?

5. The essay spans a long period of time—from the fifties to the present. Why is this more effective than if the author had looked at a single point in time? Note also that the presentation is not chronological. For example, in the last section, Gates goes back to 1956 and then to 1971, a point farther back than the eighties, discussed earlier. Consider first why putting together these particular scenes from 1956 and 1971 is effective. Then consider generally why the presentation is more effective than a purely chronological presentation would have been.

LOOKING AT THE GENRE: MEMOIRS

1. Amy Tan and Henry Louis Gates each use a feature of popular culture—family photos and hair styles—to focus the writer's recreation of the past. In each case, the writer invests the feature chosen with personal meaning. What aspects of popular culture could you use to focus your memories? Write a list of things that somehow capture an important moment or period in your life. Photos and hair styles are, of course, possible categories for items for your list, as are popular songs, articles of clothing, movies, posters, stuffed animals, toys, letters, cards, newspaper clippings, school or team uniforms, art objects, souvenirs, and so on. Compare your list to those that others in your class have written. What generalizations can you make about the capacity of things to hold and evoke memories? Why are things

ETHICS OF WRITING:

Bearing Witness

Part of a memoirist's authority derives from the fact of his or her having been there as an eyewitness to the events recounted. In effect, by offering an eyewitness account, the memoirist is claiming a privileged perspective on what took place. But unlike, say, news reporters, who, if also there, present themselves as detached observers, memoirists are typically central characters in the events they retell. They are participants as well as observers. For these reasons, memoirists face some important ethical issues concerning their responsibility as witnesses to the past. How does the memoirist represent other people involved? What are the memoirist's responsibilities to these people? What is the memoirist entitled to divulge about their private lives? What are the memoirist's loyalties to those he or she writes about? Might such loyalties conflict with obligations to readers? What impact will the memoir have on the writer's relationship with others in the present and does this potential impact affect the retelling? In cases where the memoirist feels hurt, angry, or offended by what took place, can he or she nonetheless be fair? These are questions that memoirists invariably struggle with, and there are no easy answers, especially when a memoir treats situations that are difficult or painful. The memoir, don't forget, is an act of self-discovery, and yet memoirs are written for the public to read. As witnesses to the past, successful memoirists can handle their responsibility to others in an ethical way by seeking to understand the motives and character of those involved, including themselves.

so effective as the focus of memories? Of the items in your list, which do you think would be particularly good as the basis for a memoir? Why?

2. What ethical issues of bearing witness do you think the authors of each of the three memoirs in this chapter faced in writing the memoir? What do their allegiances to other people seem to be? How have they handled their ethical responsibility to others involved in the memoir? How, if at all, has their own involvement as characters posed ethical issues? What do you see as the major differences and similarities?

3. How do the three memoirs here differ as far as (1) the role the author plays as a character in the memoir and (2) the relationship between the author's present-day self and the author as a character in the memoir?

4. Successful memoirs appeal to readers because they invest the personal with a greater significance. Compare and contrast the three memoirs with regard to the greater significance they convey and how they go about conveying this significance. Do you find that the three memoirs speak to you? Why or why not?

5. A photo figures prominently in Amy Tan's "Lost Lives of Women." Indeed, memoirs often include photos, although the photos generally do not play as pivotal a role as they do here. Find another example of a photo that plays a prominent role in a written account of any sort. Bring the photo and accompanying text to class. Depending on your teacher's directions, work together in small groups or as a whole class. Identify the genre of writing in which the various photos appear and describe the role they seem to play in that genre. How do these uses of photos compare to the way Tan uses a photo in her memoir? What do these different uses indicate about the purposes of the various genres?

DESIGNING DOCUMENTS: VISUAL MEMORIES

As you saw in Amy Tan's memoir, a photograph can help a writer evoke a moment in the past. Likewise, individuals and families often put together photo albums, scrapbooks, and collages to create their own record of the past, using visual memories of all sorts—photos, newspaper clippings, report cards, certificates of achievement, concert tickets, pressed flowers, letters, and other souvenirs and keepsakes. High schools and colleges publish annual yearbooks to capture a year in the life of the institution, its students and faculty.

4yrs

ART 5-

3yrs   4yrs

Zayante, cal.

May 30, 1950

Oct 31, 1950

Dec. 25, 1950

275

Like written memoirs, visual memories have the power, years later, to bring the past back to life, and just as we can analyze how written memoirs are composed, we can do the same with visual memories. Consider, for example, the differences between photo albums and scrapbooks. Photo albums, of course, consist of photographs, while scrapbooks are often multi-media, employing virtually every type of material you can think of to cut and paste on the page.

The following examples offer a look at these differences. The first is from a young boy's photo album. The second is a high school student's scrapbook page. Notice that the two pages are composed in quite different ways. The young boy's scrapbook is arranged in rows. Visually, the rows create an orderly sense of sequence in which one thing seems inevitably to lead to the next, telling the story of a life as it unfolds over time. In contrast, the scrapbook page is composed as a collage. It uses the association of visual memories rather than temporal sequence as the principle of composition, linking disparate images and materials together to create a moment in time.

DISCUSSION AND ACTIVITIES

1. How do the visual elements on the photo album and scrapbook pages interact to tell a story? What difference does the arrangement of the material make? What can you infer about each of the people from the scrapbook page? How effective is each in creating an impression of a person at a moment in time?

2. If you keep or have kept a scrapbook, what have you put in it? What determines your selection and the arrangement of materials? How do you feel when you look again at the scrapbook after time has passed? Do you find your feelings remain the same over the years or have they changed? If they have changed, how would you account for the change?

3. How do high school and college yearbooks bring together varied materials to create a sense of people at a particular moment in time? Work together in small groups. Gather three or four yearbooks. If you have your own high school yearbook available, you can use it. Otherwise, use yearbooks from your college. You can usually find these in the library; ask a librarian where they are. You could work with college yearbooks from different decades.
   - Survey the yearbooks' contents. How are they divided? What standard features do they all have? What differences are there?
   - Now focus on design. How are the yearbooks similar and different in their design? What is the effect on the reader of the differences in design?
   - Next, consider the yearbooks as repositories of memories. How do the yearbooks shape people's high school or college experience? How effective are they as memoirs—what are their strengths and weaknesses in this regard? To what extent do the yearbooks reflect the history of the times?
   - If you are using your own yearbooks that friends and teachers have written in, consider what people write in the yearbooks. How does this writing seem similar to and different from the actual yearbook text in the picture it creates?

3. Compose a page or two for a scrapbook. Include things that will remind you of what it's like to be you at the present moment. You can use many different kinds of material—photos, printed matter, drawings, pressed flowers, and so on. Consider the different arrangements of your material that are possible.

When you have completed the assignment, bring your pages to class. Discuss with classmates how the process of composing differs from producing written texts and how it is similar.

GOING ON-LINE

Visiting Others' Home Pages

Personal home pages might be thought of as another type of visual memory—a cyber-scrapbook that uses multimedia to create a sense of a person at a moment in time. Find three personal home pages that, for one reason or another, interest you. Try to find ones that differ in their use of text, graphics, photos, sound, video, and links to other sites. Work in a group with two other students at a computer screen. Take turns showing the three home pages you have chosen. Using the guidelines in the "Document Design" chapter and any other considerations that seem relevant to you, work together as a group to select three home pages from the nine you've visited—one that you think is good or outstanding, one that is fair, and one that is not as good as the other two. Write a short report or make an oral presentation that explains the reasoning that led to these judgments.

ASSIGNMENTS

WORKING TOGETHER: Creating a Time Capsule

Time capsules contain items that are meant to represent a particular moment or period of history. The term "time capsule" was coined in 1938, for a cylinder the Westinghouse Electrical Company filled with over 100 articles used for scientific, industrial, or everyday purposes, along with microfilms and newsreels, and buried on the grounds of the New York World's Fair of 1939, to be opened in 6939. Sometimes time capsules are buried in the foundations of buildings for future generations (or aliens visiting the planet Earth) to excavate as archaeological evidence about the culture that lived in times past.

Work together in groups of four or five to create a time capsule that can serve to capture the present moment in history. To do this, select 25 things that in your judgment best represent what it means to be alive in the late 1990s. Write a list of the items with brief explanations of why you have included each. Make enough copies of the list for other members of class or circulate them on a class listserv.

Compile the items on each group's list in a master list. You should have a considerable number. Now work together as a class to narrow the items down to 25 that the majority can agree on. Provide a rationale for each item: What does it represent about the present culture that would help future generations (or aliens) understand current ways of life? Put another way, how would it be effective as the focal point of a memoir of our times?

CALL TO WRITE: MEMOIRS

WRITING ASSIGNMENT

Recall a person, a place, or an event from your past and write a memoir. You will want to use detail and sensory impression to recreate the moment for your readers. Remember that the point of a memoir, as you have seen, is to reveal the meaning of the past so that readers can understand the significance your memories hold for the present. Since memoirs function to help both writers and their readers understand the past, this assignment can be a good time for you to probe significant times in your life, revisiting them now that you have some distance from them. You can learn more about yourself in the present by looking into events in your past. You might decide to begin with some of the ideas listed below, or you might try some of the exercises that follow this list.

- Focus on a job have held at some time in the past, as Gary Soto does. How could you reconstruct the experience of work in order to reveal something about its significance to you and others?
- Pick a photograph that holds memories and emotional associations. You might, as Amy Tan has done, unlock the "secrets and tragedies" contained in photos from your family's past in order to explore how your family's history intersects larger social and historical forces.

- Recall a particular family ritual, such as visits to grandparents, Sunday dinners, summer vacations, holiday celebrations, weddings, and so on, as a way to focus on an event or a person that is especially significant to you.
- Follow the directions in Question 1 in "Looking at the Genre" to list aspects of popular culture that might unlock memories.
- Consider some aspect of your own cultural ancestry—whether it is the language your ancestors spoke, a kind of food or music, a family tradition, an heirloom that has been passed down from generation to generation—to explain how the past has entered your life and what it reveals about your relationship to the culture of your ancestors.
- Focus on an incident in the past that, for one reason or another, reveals something about the history of the time and how private lives of ordinary individuals are linked to public meanings. Perhaps you remember a friend or relative in the military who participated in the Persian Gulf crisis in 1990-91, or a friend or relative who lost his or her job during troubled economic times.
- Look through an old diary or journal, if you have kept one at times during your life. Look for moments when you faced an occasion that challenged your values, had a difficult decision to make, a situation that turned out unexpectedly, or a time when you were keenly disappointed. Consider using these memories as the starting point for your memoir, in which you can reflect upon the experience and put it in a larger context.

INVENTION

Sketching

Consider what moves you to write. The call to write often begins with the memory of a single detail or an image from everyday life. The seemingly mundane memory of an old bicycle, the refrain from a song, or the smell of your grandparents' kitchen can unlock a series of emotional associations worth exploring. To see what such memories hold for you, do some sketching of scenes or memories from the past.

Just as artists often sketch as preliminary work, you can use sketching as exploratory writing to recall the details, sensory impressions, emotional associations, and social allegiances that moments in the past contain for you. Here's an example of what a sketch might look like:

It was a green ten-speed Schwinn bike that I remember, a gift for my eleventh birthday. It was sleek and racy-looking, with handbrakes that could stop you on a dime and the exotic-sounding derailleur with its levers to change gears. This was no child's bike, this was an instrument of speed and effortless motion. When I rode this ten-speed, I felt weightless and free, an anonymous blur of cycling energy zooming through my neighborhood and beyond. I could go, and the bike brought me a mobility I had never imagined before. I named my bike The Green Wind and rode out of my childhood and into the adventure of adolescence and parts of town my parents would have been horrified to know I visited. The Green Wind took me many places and I learned to be silent about my travels.

Another way to approach sketching is to take a mental walk through the house in which you grew up. Begin by drawing a floor plan of that house, making it as specific as you like. Next, think of a strong memory associated with that house. Once you have chosen a particular memory for further reflection, mark the room on your map in which this memory took place. Sketch out as full a picture as you can of the memory, and of the room. Describe the room as you narrate the memory, and try to draw connections between the two of them. You can use this information in your memoir.

EXERCISE

1. Using the guidelines below, sketch a scene, memory, event, or incident from the past, something you can recall in reasonable detail that has important associations for you.

2. Exchange your sketch with a classmate. Read your partner's sketch.

3. Take turns interviewing each other. Ask your partner about the sketch you wrote:
   • what is most interesting about the sketch?
   • what would your partner like to know more about?
   • what themes or issues does your partner see in the sketch?

GUIDELINES FOR SKETCHING

• Visualize the moment in the past. Imagine you are photographing or videotaping. What exactly do you see? List as many specific items and details as you can. Think about the time of day, the season of the year, and what the weather was like. If your memoir is located mostly indoors, try to recall what particular rooms looked like—the furniture, the color of the walls or the design of wallpaper, anything hanging, such as pictures, posters, photographs, and so on. Recall too the movement of people. How do they move through the physical space in which your memoir is located? What are they doing?

• Note other sensory perceptions, such as sounds, smells, tastes, and textures. What do you hear in the physical space you're writing about? What produces the sounds—people's voices, people's work, animals, machines, city traffic, the wind? Are there characteristic smells associated with the place? If there is a meal or food involved in your memoir, what do things taste like? Are there particular textures to objects that you can recall?

• Describe the people involved in your memoir. What do they look like? How do they move? What are they doing? What are they wearing? Recreate conversation among the people in your memoir. What are they talking about? Can you capture particular ways of speech? Can you use snatches of dialogue to define people and issues?

EXPLORING PAST AND PRESENT PERSPECTIVES

To clarify the purpose of your memoir and what you want it to mean to readers, consider what your feelings were at the moment things were taking place in the past and what they are now as you look back from the perspective of the present.

In the sketch about the ten-speed bicycle, the writer has recreated the excitement and sense of adventure he felt as an eleven year old. However, as the writer reflected on the importance of the bike from the perspective of the present, he realized that his travels to the "wrong side" of town not only opened up a whole new world of class and cultural differences but also created a barrier of silence between him and his parents that is still partially in place. Some of the work ahead for this writer is to decide how much he wants to emphasize the physical freedom, mobility, and new knowledge he acquired and how much he wants to emphasize what the consequences of his silence have been for his relationship with his parents.

Considering the memory you're writing about from past and present perspectives can help you clarify the double role of the memoir writer—as a participant and as an observer—and decide what relative emphasis each of the two perspectives will take on in your memoir.

EXERCISE

1. Past perspective. Recall in as much detail as possible what your feelings were at the time. Spend five minutes or so responding to these questions in writing:
   - What was my initial reaction to the moment in the past I'm writing about? What did I think at the time? How did I feel? What did other people seem to think and feel?
   - Did I share my reaction with anyone at the time? If so, how did they respond?
   - Did my initial reaction persist or did it change? If it changed, what set of feelings replaced it? What caused the change? Were other people involved in this change?

2. Present perspective. Now think about your present perspective. Write for another five minutes or so in response to these questions:
   - Looking back on the moment in the past, how do the feelings you experienced at the time appear to you today? Do they seem reasonable? Why or why not?
   If you were in the same situation today, would you act the same way? Why or why not? If you would act differently, what would you change? How? Why?
   - What are your present feelings about the event you're describing? Have your feelings changed? Do things look different from the perspective of the present? If so, how would you explain the change?
   - As you compare your feelings from the past and your feelings in the present, what conclusions can you draw about the significance of the memory for you? Are your feelings resolved or do they seem unsettled and changing? In either case, what do you think has shaped your current perspective?

3. Review the two writings. Use them to write a third statement that defines what you see as the significance of the memory you're writing about and what your purpose is in recreating it for your readers. What does the memory reveal about the past? How do you want to present yourself in relation to what happened in the past? If there is conflict or crisis, what are your loyalties toward the people and the events?

Exploring Cultural and Historical Perspectives

Just as you have looked into your past and present for new insights, you can also try exploring by considering broader cultural and historical implications of the event or events you are examining. In other words, you can place your own memories and experience within a broader context, linking your life with social movements and political events happening around you at the time.

You may want (or need) to look in the library and on the Internet for more help in responding to these questions. Check, for example, the New York Times Index for that particular year, or the Facts on File Yearboook. Weekly periodicals such as Time, Newsweek, and U.S. News and World Report have an end-of year issue that can help provide both cultural and historical perspective. In addition, you can browse on the Internet to find all kinds of information. As a starting point, take a look at the following sites:

- The White House Virtual Library. This links to the White House, to government organizations, and provides historical documents online. Address: http://www2.whitehouse.gov/WH /html/library-plain.html

- EINet Galaxy. This site is a good starting point if you are searching for a specific subject.

Address: http://www.einet.net/galaxy.html

- WWW Virtual Library. Like the site listed above, this one is also a good starting point for specific subjects.

Address: http://www.w3.org/pub/DataSources/bySubject/Overview.html

- Check your own institution's resource section. There may be one off of the main home page, or there may be a section for writing and learning resources through your campus Writing Center.

EXERCISE

1. Cultural Perspective. Isolate the year that this event happened. If your are examining a ritual that occurred many times, pick one such instance and focus only on that. In answering the following questions, you might need to ask family members or friends for their impressions, insights, and suggestions.
   - What is the year in question? Was anything remarkable about that year in the context of national and world events? Is that year "famous" for anything?
   - Who was President that year? Was the United States involved in any wars or conflicts? What international figures were seen as the "villains" that year?
   - How was the economic outlook that year? How has it been characterized in retrospect? How did your event match the national economic scene?
   - What generation is known for that year (WWII veterans, baby boomers, generation X)? Was any particular ethnic or racial group prominent during this time?
   - What were the major social conflicts that year? Were there important political demonstrations, social movements, or riots in any part of the country? If so, what were they about? Were there any natural disasters that captured national attention that year?
   - What was the "news story of the year"? What was the "success story of the year"? Who were the heroes that year?
   - What were the new technological innovations?
   - What kind of music was most popular, or notable? Did that music represent anything about society? Was it a reaction to anything?

2. Historical Perspective. If any of your responses in the above section seem like they might shed some light on the event or ritual you are examining, it might be useful to put those responses in historical perspective. Choose three of the responses above that seem most promising, and answer the following questions about them. Again, you might want to enlist the help of someone who can provide some historical context for you.
   - If the time you are looking at was particularly turbulent, what preceded it? What led to the conflicts? What characterized the previous generation? Why the differences?
   - If the time you are looking at seemed particularly calm and trouble-free, why might this be? What had happened in the preceding years to foster a sense of peace and stability? Have there been comparable times in history? If so, what are the similarities and differences?
   - If you are looking at a time in which a social, ethnic, or racial group achieved prominence, what is that group's history? Where had they come from, how had they come together, and what was their urgency?
   - What is the historical significance of the event or ritual you are exploring? Did it grow from a meaningful story that happened hundreds (or even tens) of years ago? If so, what is that story? If not, where might it have come from?

3. Review your writings so far. Now you may be able to see some of the links between your own experience and the experiences that others have had through time, and those others may have been having at the same time ñ nationally and internationally. Record your impressions of the cultural and historical contexts that might be illuminating in your memoir.

PLANNING

Arranging your material

One thing you have seen from the memoirs gathered in this chapter is that memoir writers may tell a story in chronological order, as Gary Soto does. Or, instead, as Henry Louis Gates does, they may present a sequence of memories as separate sketches that create one dominant impression. And they may also use a single object, such as the photograph in Amy Tan's memoir, to unfold the stories of the people represented. All of these options are open to you in arranging your material.

Here are some questions to help you design a working draft:
- How will you begin? Do you want to ease into the moment from the past or state it outright? How can you capture your readers' interest? Do you need to establish background information? How will you present yourself—as a participant in the past or as an observer from the perspective of the present?
- What arrangement best suits your material? If you are telling a single story, how can you keep the narrative crisp and moving? Do you need to interrupt the chronology with commentary, description, interpretation, asides? If you are using selected incidents, what order best conveys the point you want them to make? Do the separate incidents create a dominant impression?
- How will you set up the moment of revelation that gives your memoir its meaning and significance? Do you want to anticipate this moment by foreshadowing that gives readers a hint of the revelation that is to come? Or do you want it to appear suddenly?
- How will you end your memoir? Do you want to surprise readers with an unsuspected meaning? Or do you want to step back from what has taken place to reflect on its significance? Is there a way in which you can echo the opening of the memoir to make your readers feel they have come full circle?

Selecting Detail

Memoirists often use techniques you can find in fiction: scene-setting, description of people, action, and dialogue. These techniques enable memoirists (like fiction writers) to recreate the past in vivid and convincing detail. Designing a memoir (like fiction writing) involves decisions about the type and amount of detail you need to make your recreation of the past memorable to readers.
- Scene-setting: use vivid and specific description to set the scene; name particular objects; give details about places and things; use description and detail to establish mood.
- Description of people: use description of people's appearance to highlight their personality in your memoir; name the clothes they are wearing; give details about a person's physical presence, gestures, facial features, hairstyle; notice personal habits; use description and detail to establish character.
- Dialogue: put words in your characters' mouths that reveal their personality; invent dialogue that is faithful to people's ways of speaking (even if it is not their exact words); use dialogue to establish relationships between characters.
- Action: put the characters in your memoir in motion; use narrative to tell about something that happened; use narrative to develop characters and reveal the theme of your memoir.

WORKING DRAFT

Review the writing you have done so far. Draw on the sketching you have done, the writing that compares past and present perspectives, and your analysis of cultural and historical contexts. Decide tentatively on an opening that will establish the mood and theme of your memoir using some of the strategies above for selecting detail. Write a working draft with the understanding that you can go back and add details and commentary.

PARAGRAPH DEVELOPMENT: Narrating

You have already tried sketching some of your memories, and you have seen suggestions for selecting detail. Another way to approach developing your memoir is to try narrating, or telling stories and anecdotes to recreate an event. To some extent, this means thinking about your subject chronologically. What happened first? Then what? Tell your story in order, as it happened, punctuating it with observations as they occur to you. Several of the readings in this chapter use this development strategy. Notice that Henry Louis Gates, Jr. uses short narratives throughout "In the Kitchen," creating a sense of multiply woven stories all intersecting through his analysis of hair styles.

"Mama would wash her hair over the sink, a towel wrapped around her shoulders, wearing just her slip and her white bra. (We had no shower ñ just a galvanized tub that we stored in the kitchen ñ until we moved down Rat Tail Road into Doc Wolversonís hourse, in 1954.) After she dried it, she would grease her scalp thoroughly with blue Bergamot hair grease, which came in a short, fat jar with a picture of a beautiful colored lady on it."

If you find that you have already done a good job with the narration in your memoir, take a look at some of the paragraph development ideas in other chapters.

- see Describing (page XXX in Letters) to another approach to filling in detail on your sketches

- see Comparing and Contrasting (page XXX in Profiles) to explore connections between events and rituals that can make your memoir more meaningful

- see Moving from Old Information to New Information (page XXX in Proposals) to sort and organize the information you present in each paragraph

BEGINNINGS AND ENDINGS: Pointing out the Wider Significance or Consequences

You have already started with a tentative idea of how you might begin your memoir to establish the themes and tone of your writing. One possibility is to either begin or end by pointing out the wider significance of your memories. Since you have been exploring their significance through the invention exercises in this chapter, you probably have a good idea about the broader significance of the memories you are describing.

Amy Tan uses this strategy to conclude her essay. Having described her initial reaction to the photograph, and having provided background information on each of the women that shows their complexity and their strength, Tan completes her essay by explaining why she has written it. Her final words seem to challenge the reader to do as she does.

This is the picture I see when I write. These are the secrets I was supposed to keep. These are the women who never let me forget why stories need to be told.

Although none of the writers in this chapter begin their memoirs by explaining the wider significance or consequences of their insights, you might want to try it with your own writing and see if you like the results. If not, it might be helpful to look at other beginning and ending strategies discussed in other chapters.

- see Using an Echo Effect to Reframe (page XXX in Letters) to illustrate how your perceptions have altered over time
- see Setting Up with a Metaphorical Anecdote (page XXX in Profiles) to establish a theme like Gates does with his concept of the ìkitchenî
- see Replacing a Common View with an Alternative Perspective (page XXX in Commentary) to cement the social significance of your memories

PEER COMMENTARY

Now that your working draft is in pretty good shape, and now that you have put most of your finished thoughts down on paper, you are ready to get feedback from other writers. Before exchanging papers, work through the following exercise. Then, you can guide your partner or group members how to best help you. If you find it helpful, look through the suggestions for peer commentary described in Chapter 3 (see pages XXX).

EXERCISE

1. Write an account of your working draft:
   - What made you want to write this memoir? Describe in as much detail as you can what you experienced as the call to write.
   - What is your purpose in the working draft? What are you trying to reveal about the moment in the past? What significance does this moment hold for you?

- What problems or uncertainties do you see in your working draft? Ask your readers about particular passages in the draft so that you can get specific feedback.

2. Your readers can offer you feedback, either oral or written, based on your working draft and the commentary you have written. Here are questions for your readers to take into account:
   - Does the writer's purpose come across clearly? Are you able to see and understand the significance of the moment in the writer's past? If the significance of the moment is not revealed clearly enough, what suggestions can you offer?
   - Is the memoir organized effectively? Does the moment of revelation appear in the best place? Does the essay begin with sufficient background information and scene setting? Comment on the ending of the memoir. Does the writer pull things together in a way that is satisfying to the reader?
   - Is the writing vivid and concrete in recreating particular scenes and moments from the past? Point to passages in the memoir that are particularly vivid. Are there passages that are too vague, obscure, or abstract? Do the narrative passages move along crisply or do they seem to drag?

REVISING

Use the commentary you have received to plan a revision. Does your purpose come across clearly to readers? Is there a moment of revelation that gives the memoir significance? Can readers easily follow what happened? Are the events and people in the memoir vivid? Do you need more detail? What, if anything, should you cut? What do you need to add? After you have taken the peer response into consideration, work through the sections suggested below, checking for yourself to see if you can improve your transitions, vary your sentences, and check your verb tenses.

CONNECTIONS AND COHERENCE: Temporal Transitions

In narrative passages, temporal transitions are useful to indicate the sequence of events that takes place and the passage of time. Some useful temporal transitions writers often use to indicate how and when time has passed include: next, later, after, before, earlier, meanwhile, immediately, soon, shortly, often, frequently, again, during, finally, at last.

Several of the writers in this chapter use temporal transitions to build coherence from one paragraph to the next. Consider, for example, the way Gary Soto begins many of the paragraphs in his narration:

¶ 5 The next morning, I arrived early at work.

¶ 7 I worked carefully that day . . . .

¶ 8 At five the workers scattered . . . .

¶ 9 From the backyard I walked dully through a residential street, and as evening came on . . . .

¶ 11 When I got up from the lawn it was late.

¶ 13 At work I spent the morning at the buffer . . . .

¶ 15 Iggy worked only until three in the afternoon . . . .

Transitions indicating time sequences are one of the options for making connections within your writing to increase coherence. If they don't seem fruitful for you, look at some of options described in other chapters

- see Enumerative Order (page XXX in Public Documents) to establish a sequence of events

- see Spatial Transitions (page XXX in Profiles) help you describe a geographical area

- see Parallelism of Ideas (page XXX in Proposals) to forge stronger links between your memory and your analysis

WRITERS WORKSHOP

Jennifer Plante wrote the following two pieces in response to a assignment in her composition class that called on students to write a memoir.

The first piece is Jennifer's commentary on an early working draft of a short memoir based on her recollections of Sunday afternoon visits to her grandparents. In this commentary, Jennifer describes the call to write that got her started on the piece in the first place and her own sense of both the potential and the problems of her work in progress. You'll notice that Jennifer wrote her commentary as a kind of interim report—to explain what she was trying to do and to request feedback, constructive criticism, and suggestions from her readers.

The second piece of writing is the working draft itself, before Jennifer went on to revise it. As you read, remember that Jennifer's memoir is still work in progress. Try to read it through her commentary, to see what advice or suggestions you would give her concerning revision.

JENNIFER PLANTE'S COMMENTARY

What got me started on this piece of writing is exactly what I begin with—the smell of over-cooked pot roast. For some reason, when I was thinking about a memoir I might write, this smell suddenly seemed to leap out at me and bring me back to the Sunday afternoons we spent at my grandparents. In one way, I wanted to remember these days because I loved them so much. I felt so safe and secure and loved, with not only my parents but my grandparents surrounding me. I tried to find images of warmth, light, and enclosure to recreate this feel. I wanted the opening to have a Norman Rockwell-like, almost sentimental feel to it—of the "typical" American family living out the American dream of family gatherings. A ritualistic feel.

But I also wanted the paragraphs to serve as a set-up for what was to come, which is really the point of the memoir. It was on a typical Sunday when I was ten that my father and grandfather argued, and my grandfather made these incredibly racist and homophobic comments. I didn't understand at the time exactly what my grandfather meant but I did understand the look on my father's face—and that something had happened that was going to change things.

I think I've done a decent job of setting this scene up, but I don't think it fully conveys what I want it to. So I had to add the final section reflecting back on it and how I now feel betrayed by my grandfather. I think this last part is probably too obvious and maybe even a little bit preachy or self-righteous, though I try to explain how my grandfather is a product of his upbringing. I want readers to understand how my feelings toward my grandfather went from completely adoring to totally mixed and contradictory ones. I don't think this is coming out clearly enough and I would appreciate any suggestions about how to do it or to improve any other parts of the essay.

Jennifer Plante

EN 2211

The smell of over-cooked pot roast still magically carries me back to Sunday afternoons at my grandparents' house. I was all of ten years old; a tom-boyish, pig-tailed girl who worshipped the ground that her elders walked on. Back then, my grandfather seemed like an enormous man, every bit as intimidating as he was loving. He knew what he wanted, what he believed in, he thought that President Reagan was a demigod, and he thought that his only granddaughter was one of the biggest joys of his life. I remember that every time my family went over to my grandparents' humble home, I would run into my grandfather's warm arms and get swallowed up in a loving hug. Then, he'd sweep me off of my feet and twirl me around in the air until I was giggling so hard that I could no longer breathe.

After we ate the charcoaled roast, I would follow my grandfather into the living room. Light always seemed to radiate from the huge picture window spreading warmth into the living room; it <u>never</u> seemed to rain while I was at my grandparents' house. I would proceed to sit on my grandfather's lap while he stretched out in his La-Z Boy and flipped through the T.V. channels to find the New England Patriots' football game. He would often shout at the players as if he was their coach, and trying to emulate him, I would shout equally as loud not knowing what the hell I was talking about (face-masking means nothing to a ten year-old girl). This is how every Sunday afternoon of my childhood was spent; the sequence of events was very ritualistic, the only thing distinguishing one Sunday from another was which meal my grandmother would decide to burn.

One Sunday afternoon, my grandfather and I had assumed our normal positions on the brown, beat-up chair and found our Patriots losing to some random team. I'm not exactly sure how the subject came up, but my grandfather and my dad began discussing politics and our society. My grandfather and my dad held different opinions about <u>both</u> topics, so as usual, the debate had gotten pretty heated. I began feeling a bit uncomfortable as the discussion wore on; they talked for what seemed like hours and they must have discussed every issue that was of importance to our society. To numb my discomfort, I became focused on the T.V. screen- Steve Grogan had just completed a 30-yard touchdown pass, but the referee had called that "face-masking" thing on the offense, sending Patriot fans into a frenzy. Then, just as quickly as it had started, the debate ended in dead silence. My father sat, open-mouthed, in disbelief at what he'd just heard; my grandfather had finally spoken his mind.

"What is this interracial marriage garbage? Decent white people shouldn't be marrying those blacks. And what is this perverted gay business? All the gays should go back into the closet where they belong!"

I didn't understand what my grandfather had said at the time, but I did notice the look on my father's face. It was as if my grandfather had just slapped him, only I somehow knew that what he'd said had hurt my father much more than any slap ever could have. And I did notice that, for the first time ever, a hard rain began to fall outside.

*   *   *   *   *   *   *   *   *   *   *

I look back on that day now and I understand why my father looked so hurt. I also understand now what my grandfather had said, and can't help but feel betrayed that a man that I admired so much had managed to insult over half of the population in one breath. I do feel bitter towards my grandfather, but I can't really blame him for his ignorance; he is a product of his time, and they were taught to hate difference. But ever since that day, I have vowed that, when my grandchildren come to visit me on Sunday afternoons, they will never see a hard rain falling outside of my picture window.

WORKSHOP QUESTIONS

1. Do you agree with Jennifer Plante that she has done a "decent" job of scene-setting in the opening sections of her memoir? Does it effectively recreate the "ritualistic feel" of family gatherings? Plante notes that she wants the scene to have a Norman Rockwell-like character. Does it achieve this effect? Does it become too sentimental? Explain your responses to these questions and make any suggestions you might have for strengthening the opening.

2. Plante's memoir relies on a moment of revelation—in this case, when her grandfather makes racist and homophobic remarks and the effect these remarks have on her father. In many respects, the memoir hinges on this moment. Does it have the dramatic value and emotional force it needs as the pivotal point in the memoir—the moment that "changed things"? Do you have questions about what happened or things you want to know more about? In your response to these questions, take into account the fact that Plante is recreating the moment from the perspective of a young girl who doesn't fully understand what is happening but knows nonetheless that it is important. What suggestions, if any, would you offer to strengthen this crucial point in the memoir?

3. Plante seems dissatisfied with the final section of the memoir, in which she writes from the perspective of the present reflecting back on a moment in the past. She worries, for one thing, about seeming "obvious," "preachy," and "self-righteous" is describing her sense of betrayal. Do you think this is a problem in the draft? If so, what sentences, phrases, words create the problem? Do you think Plante explains sufficiently how and why her feelings about her grandfather changed from "completely adoring" to "mixed and contradictory"? What advice would you offer to strengthen this section of the memoir?

WRITERS INVENTORY

Write an account that explains how you handled the dual role of the memoir writer as a participant and as an observer. How did you recreate yourself as a character in your memoir? How does this re-creation fit with your current perspective on the incident you wrote about? To what extent are you the same self in both cases? To what extent does your self in the past and in the present differ in your memoir? If memoirs are in part acts of writing that bear witness to and thereby take responsibility for the past, how do the selves you created and re-created express loyalties and social allegiances?

A CLOSING NOTE

Events and people from the past worth writing about often contain powerful emotional associations for the writer—associations that may not have been put into words before. Part of the work of writing a memoir is to bring such associations forward to explain why they are so powerful and what influence they continue to have on the writer. For this reason, bringing a memoir to closure is likely to involve work creating a mood and portraying the writer's attitude. Memoirists want readers to get a sense of what it felt like to be there, and at the same time they know readers expect a memoir to have its revelations—to make a point as well as tell a story or describe a moment.

CHAPTER
SIX

PUBLIC DOCUMENTS:
Codifying Beliefs and Practices

LOOKING AT THE GENRE

People in contemporary society rely on public documents to organize and carry out a wide range of social activities. In fact, an individual's life can be charted by following the documents that mark key moments. Notice how the following documents describe the course of a life as it is entered into the public record:

- birth certificate

- religious records (baptism, first communion, confirmation, bar mitzvah, and so on)

- school records (report cards, standardized test results, high school and college diplomas, awards and scholarships)

- driver's license

- social security card

- marriage license

- employment contracts

- mortgage

- tax returns

- last will and testament

- death certificate and obituary

If anything, people are so surrounded by public documents that they may well take this form of writing for granted. After all, documents just seem to appear out of a file in school, at work, in a bank or a government office as though they were always there. In fact, nowadays, many public documents are available on-line, and people can fill out their tax forms on a home computer. Documents seem to be natural parts of the bureaucratic maze of contemporary life, and so people get used to documents like you get used to a piece of furniture that's always been in your grandparents' house.

No one seems to have written these documents. You just use them, fill in the blanks and sign, like you'd sit in a familiar chair. But precisely because written documents are an ever present part of our social reality, it's worthwhile taking a closer look at the purposes documents serve.

Public documents serve to codify the beliefs and practices of a culture, a community, an organization—any group of people who share a mutual concern. Unlike many of the genres of writing in this textbook, public documents derive their authority from collective sources, instead of from the individual who wrote them. Public documents speak on behalf of a group of people, to articulate the principles and procedures that organize their purposes and guide their way of life.

Some public documents, such as the Ten Commandments or the Declaration of Independence, have taken on a sacred or nearly sacred character because they codify principles of morality and political liberty that are considered fundamental to a whole way of life. Their power resides in the authority people have invested over time in these documents as basic accounts of what they believe and hold most dear.

These documents shape public life. For example, the Commandment that the Sabbath be a day of rest is evident in state laws that prohibit the sale of alcohol or regulate hours of business on Sunday. By the same token, the Fourth of July was established as a national holiday to commemorate the Declaration of Independence and the birth of the United States.

Other public documents serve to codify customary behavior and conventional social arrangements. Marriage vows, contracts, wills, and other agreements commit parties to binding relationships that are publicly and legally recognized. Articles of incorporation enable companies to do business, while documentation of not-for-profit status enables civic and arts groups to carry out their purposes. The professions have codes of ethics that govern the practice of medicine, law, scientific research, engineering, social work, teaching, and so on.

Still other documents charter the mission and activities of voluntary associations people have formed to respond to particular needs—organizations such as student clubs, neighborhood associations, trade unions, advocacy groups, and community service projects. Writing a constitution for such a group literally constitutes it as a public entity by giving the group a name and a statement of purpose. Not only does this establish an identity for members of the group, it also enables them to be heard in the public record and to shape public opinion.

The call to write public documents grows out of a culture's need to establish institutions, social order, and predictable patterns of interaction among people. Since written words take on visible shape in documents, they can be stored as a relatively permanent and authoritative account of a culture's beliefs and practices so that people can consult them in order to consider and reconsider their meanings. Public documents create an archive, the collective memory of a culture.

The public documents that form a culture's archive themselves do not change, though their meanings can and often do. The words on the page remain the same, for written documents serve as a kind of external memory to preserve what people or institutions want to commit to writing at a particular time. This is in part what gives documents such as the Ten Commandments or the Declaration of Independence or the Bill of Rights their special authority—their language seems to be fixed once and for all.

At the same time, however, the judgments readers draw from these documents can change over time. Readers will return repeatedly to documents such as the Bill of Rights to invoke its authority to interpret new situations. The language of the First Amendment guaranteeing Americans freedom of speech defines one of the fundamental principles of a democratic society. Nonetheless, even though the language of the First Amendment seems to be fixed and precise, its meanings remain in flux as citizens debate how its principles should be applied to cases of violence in the media, pornography, or hate speech. Likewise, Jews and Christians continually debate what the commandment "You shall not kill" means and whether factors such as self-defense or war modify the meaning of the commandment.

The reading selections in this chapter offer a range of documents to consider. The first selection from My Own Country, Abraham Verghese's account of his work with HIV positive and AIDS patients in Tennessee, shows how public documents such as wills and family records affect people's everyday life. The next selection, WPI Policy for Students with HIV Infection, offers a good example of how institutions set standards of practice in response to new situations. The final two readings concern legal documents, in this case English Only legislation. The first document is Proposition 63, an English Only amendment to the California state constitution, passed by voters in 1986. This is followed by a leaflet from the Conference on College Composition and Communication that includes the organizationís policy statement on English Only legislation.

Public documents can tell us a lot about the culture we're living in. But just as important, you can write and use documents on your own behalf to accomplish your ends—to establish new voluntary associations and their purposes, to define policies and procedures you're willing to live by, to recruit sympathizers to a cause you believe in, to articulate new social identities, and to define new directions for the future.

My Own Country.

Abraham Verghese.

This selection is taken from Abraham Verghese's book My Own Country, an account of his experience as a doctor working with HIV positive and AIDS patients in Johnson City, Tennessee. Verghese is Professor of Medicine and Chief of Infectious Diseases at Texas Tech Health Sciences Center. A graduate of the Iowa Writer's Workshop, Verghese has published in Esquire, New Yorker, and Sports Illustrated, as well as in medical journals such as the Annals of Internal Medicine and the American Journal of Medicine. This selection recounts a medical emergency when Verghese had to determine whether to put a patient on life support machines. As you will see, legal documents concerning both the patient's wishes and who will make the decision play prominent roles in shaping the outcome. You will judge for yourself whether the decision was the right one.

BOBBY KELLER called me in the office as I was about to leave for home. He sounded shrill and alarmed.

"Doc? Ed is *very* sick! He is *very, very* short of breath and running a fever. A hundred and three. Dr. Verghese, he's turning blue on me."

"Bobby, call the emergency ambulance service—tell them to bring you to the Johnson City Medical Center."

Ed Maupin, the diesel mechanic, had had a CD4 count of 30 the previous week when I had seen him in clinic; Bobby Keller's was 500. At that visit, Ed's oral thrush had cleared up but he was still feeling tired and had been missing work. When I had examined Ed, the lymph nodes in his neck, which had been as big as goose eggs, had suddenly shrunk: I had thought to myself that this was either a good sign or a very bad sign; his immune system had either given up the fight or successfully neutralized the virus. The latter was unlikely.

Bobby, at that visit, had looked well and continued to work in the fashion store. I hoped now that Bobby's description of the gravity of the situation was just histrionics.

I was at the Miracle Center well ahead of the ambulance. Soon it came roaring in, all its lights flashing. When the back door opened, I peeked in: Ed's eyes were rolled back in his head, and he was covered with a fine sheen of sweat. Despite the oxygen mask that the ambulance crew had on, his skin was the color of lead. His chest was making vigorous but ineffective excursions.

Bobby, who had ridden in the front, was scarcely able to stand up. His face was tremulous; he was on the verge of fainting.

"Don't put him on no machines, whatever you do," Bobby begged me. "Please, no machines."

"Why?"

"Because that's what he told me. He doesn't want it."

"When did he tell you? Just now?"

"No. A long time ago."

"Did he put it in writing? Does he have a living will?"

"No . . ."

In the emergency room, I stabilized Ed as best I could without intubating him. I took his oxygen mask off momentarily and looked at his mouth. His mucous membranes were loaded with yeast again—it had blossomed in just a week. But I was examining his mouth to try to decide how difficult it would be to intubate him. His short, receding lower jaw, which the beard concealed well, could make this a tricky intubation. I asked him to say "aaah." He tried to comply: his uvula and tonsils just barely came into view, another sign that he would be a tough intubation.

Ideally, an anesthetist would have been the best person to perform intubation. But I didn't want to call an anesthetist who, given the patient, might or might not be willing to do this procedure. Time was running out.

Ed was moaning and muttering incomprehensibly; his brain was clearly not getting enough oxygen. His blood pressure was 70 millimeters of mercury systolic over 50 diastolic. This was extremely low for him, because he had baseline hypertension. His cold, clammy extremities told me that the circulation to his arms and legs had shut down in an effort to shunt blood to the brain; even so, what blood got to the brain was not carrying enough oxygen. Ed's chest sounded dull in the bases when I percussed it; on listening with my stethoscope, he was wet and gurgly. The reason he was not oxygenating his blood was clear: his lungs were filled with inflammatory fluid. I ordered a stat chest x-ray and arterial blood gases. I had only a few minutes before I had to either breathe for him, or let him go. I needed more guidance from Bobby as to Ed's wishes.

I had an excellent nurse assisting me; she had already started an IV and brought the "crash cart." The respiratory therapist was administering oxygen and had an Ambu bag ready. I asked them to get goggles and masks in addition to their gloves, and to get a gown, mask and gloves ready for me. They were to put theirs on and wait for me. The curtains were pulled and Ed's presence was largely unnoticed in the bustle of the ER. An orthopedist was putting a cast on an individual in the next room, and patients were waiting in the other cubicles.

I came out to the waiting room, but Bobby was not there!

I hurried outside.

Bobby and three other men and one woman were near the ambulance entrance, smoking. The men bore a striking resemblance to Ed Maupin—the same sharp features, the slightly receding chin. One of them, the oldest, wore a green work uniform. I recognized his face as a familiar one, someone who worked in an auto parts store where I had ordered a replacement bumper for the rusted one that had fallen off my Z. Bobby Keller, still trembling, introduced me to Ed's brothers, all younger than Ed. The woman was the wife of one of the brothers.

"Bobby," I asked, "can I tell them what's going on?"

"Tell them everything," Bobby said, the tears pouring down uncontrollably, his body shaking with sobs.

I addressed the brothers: "Ed is very sick. A few months ago we found out he has AIDS." (There was no point in trying to make the distinction between HIV infection and AIDS. If Ed had not had AIDS when I saw him in the clinic, he most certainly did now.) "Now he has a bad pneumonia from the AIDS. I need to put him on a breathing machine in the next few minutes or he will die. I have a feeling that the pneumonia he has can be treated. If we put him on the breathing machine, it won't be forever. We have a good chance of getting him off. But Bobby tells me that Ed has expressed a desire *not* to be put on the machine."

The assembled family turned to Bobby who nodded vigorously: "He did! Said he never wanted to be on no machines."

The family was clear-eyed, trying to stay calm. They pulled hard at their cigarettes. The smoke rose quietly around their weathered faces. They looked like a Norman Rockwell portrait—small-town America's citizens in their work-clothes in a hospital parking lot, facing a family crisis. But this situation was one that Norman Rockwell hadn't attempted, one he had never dreamed of. I felt they were fond of their oldest brother, though perhaps disapproving of his relationship with Bobby. Yet judging by how they had all been standing around Bobby when I walked out, I didn't think they had any strong dislike for Bobby—it was almost impossible to dislike him. They had had many years to get used to the idea of Bobby and Ed, the couple, and it was only the idea, I sensed, that they had somehow not accepted.

"We need to discuss this," the older brother said.

"We have no time, I need to go right back in," I said.

They moved a few feet away from Bobby and me. I asked Bobby, "Do you have power-of-attorney or anything like that to make decisions for Ed?" Bobby shook his head.

We looked over to where the family was caucusing. The oldest brother was doing all the talking. They came back.

"We want for you to do everything you can. Put him on the breathing machine, if you have to."

At this a little wail came out of Bobby Keller and then degenerated into sobs. I put my hand on Bobby's shoulder. He shook his head back and forth, back and forth. He wanted to say something but could not find a voice.

The oldest brother spoke again. His tone was matter-of-fact and determined:

"*We* are his family. *We* are legally responsible for him. We want you to do *everything* for him."

We are his family. I watched Bobby's face crumble as he suddenly became a mere observer with no legal right to determine the fate of the man he had loved since he was seven years old. He was finally, despite the years that had passed and whatever acceptance he and Ed found together, an outsider.

I took him aside and said, "Bobby, I have to go on. There is no way for me not to at this point. There's a really good chance that I can rescue Ed from the pneumonia. If I thought it would only make Ed suffer, I wouldn't do it. If this is *Pneumocystis*, it should respond to treatment."

Bobby kept sobbing, shaking his head as I talked, fat tears rolling off his eyes onto the ground, onto his chest. He felt he was betraying Ed. He could not deliver on his promise.

I had no time to pacify Bobby or try to convince him. I rushed back in. Ed looked worse. As I went through the ritual of gowning and masking (it was reassuring to have rituals to fall back on, a ritual for every crisis), it struck me that the entire situation had been in my power to dictate. All I had to do was to come out and say that the pneumonia did not look good, that it looked like the end. *I* mentioned the respirator, *I* offered it as an option. I could have just kept quiet. I had, when it came down to the final moment, given Ed's brothers the power of family. Not Bobby.

But there was no time to look back now.

ANALYSIS: Defining Legal Responsibility

Notice how the absence of two crucial public documents shapes the outcome of this event. First, there is no "living will" to express Ed's wishes about medical treatment. Second, there is no document, such as a marriage license or power of attorney, entitling Bobby legally to make decisions on Ed's behalf—no record of their relationship.

The "living will" or Directive to Physicians is recognized by doctors as a binding statement of a patient's wishes and legal ground to withhold emergency treatment in certain life-threatening situations. (An example of a "living will" appears below, in the section "Analyzing Public Messages.") In the absence of a "living will," Verghese defers to Ed's family, even though he knows Ed would have wanted Bobby to make the decision.

The tableau of Bobby, Ed's three brothers, and his sister-in-law standing outside the hospital near the ambulance entrance is a telling one. "We are his family. We are legally responsible for him," Ed's oldest brother tells Verghese. It is precisely because the brothers' relationship to Ed can be documented in the public record that they have the legal right to make decisions. Family ties can be verified while Bobby and Ed's relationship remains private and unofficial, neither legally recognized nor culturally sanctioned.

FOR CRITICAL INQUIRY

1. Describe how the decision to put Ed on the respirator was made. What authorized the decision? Notice that Verghese indicates he is conflicted by the decision and might have acted differently. What is Verghese's conflict? Do you think he could or should have acted differently given the circumstances?

2. Here is the main text of a sample "living will," which Ed Maupin did not have on record. What protections does it offer a patient, and from whom?

DECLARATION

If I should have an incurable and irreversible condition that has been diagnosed by two physicians and that will result in my death within a relatively short time without the administration of life-sustaining treatment or has produced an irreversible coma or persistent vegetative state, and I am no longer able to make decisions regarding my medical treatment, I direct my attending physician, pursuant to the Natural Death Act of California, to withhold or withdraw treatment, including artificially administered nutrition and hydration, that only prolongs the process of dying or the irreversible coma or persistent vegetative state and is not necessary for my comfort or to alleviate pain.

If Ed had had a signed living will, do you think Verghese's decision about putting him on a respirator would have been different? Why or why not?

3. Gay and lesbian organizations have urged states and cities to recognize same-sex partners for purposes of insurance coverage, death benefits, adoption of children, and so on. If same-sex relationships were legally recognized, Bobby would have had the right to make decisions for Ed. What prevents such legal recognition? What, if anything, would happen if same-sex relationships did become matters of the public record?

4. This selection illustrates how public documents enter into people's lives and can have dramatic consequences. Can you think of other instances—from your own experience, what you have read, or what you have heard about—in which the presence or absence of particular public documents plays a prominent role in people's everyday lives?

WPI POLICY FOR STUDENTS WITH HIV INFECTION

WPI Policy for Students with HIV Infection appears in a manual of policies and procedures that all WPI students receive. The manual also includes other policy statements (such as Trustee's Statement on Student Responsibility and Conduct, WPI Campus Code, Academic Honesty Policy, WPI Drug and Alcohol Policy, WPI Harassment Policy, and Hazing Policy) and the Constitution of the WPI Campus Judicial System and the procedures of the Campus Hearing Board. The purpose of the manual, as the Introduction notes, is to document "policies" of the institution and "the code of conduct all WPI students are expected to observe." Most colleges and universities publish such documents to inform students of their rights and responsibilities.

VI. WPI Policy for Students With HIV Infection

Background

Acquired Immune Deficiency Syndrome (AIDS) is caused by a fragile virus known as the Human Immunodeficiency Virus (HIV). The best scientific evidence available supports the position that the AIDS virus is not transmissible by casual contact. Epidemiological studies show that HIV is transmitted in three ways. These include: 1) "unsafe" sexual contact, 2) the exchange of contaminated blood or blood products, and 3) from mother to unborn infant. To date, there have been no known cases of HIV transmission through daily social contact with people testing positive for HIV. Sharing classrooms, study areas, libraries, theaters, bathrooms, residential living spaces, or sports and recreation facilities, etc., with HIV infected persons has not been shown to pose a health threat.

Policy

The Worcester Polytechnic Institute policy on HIV infection is similar to the policy developed in the Commonwealth's schools by the Governor's Task Force on AIDS. This policy is based on recommendations from the Department of Public Health, Center for Disease Control (1985), and the American College Health Association (1988). The policy and its guidelines serve as a framework for protecting our students' civil rights and the public's health. These guidelines draw heavily on current knowledge of infectious disease epidemiology and on well-established principles of disease prevention.

Individuals who have been infected by the AIDS virus may attend WPI. As with any personal medical problem and/or handicapping condition, every effort will be made to protect the individual's legal rights and privacy. Students with HIV infection, because of the physical and psychological effects of the virus, are encouraged to utilize support services on campus that are provided to help students with a wide array of handicapping conditions.

In some areas of the country, students with HIV infection or those suspected of being infected with HIV have been subjected to emotional and/or physical abuse. Administrative officials at WPI are keenly aware of the fear, anxiety and anger that some people feel in response to AIDS. WPI condemns any harassment or abusive behavior directed at WPI students and will use all means at its disposal to deal swiftly with such occurrences.

Guidelines

Since there is no medical evidence of viral transmission by sharing classrooms, study areas, bathrooms, residential living spaces, or sports and recreation facilities, etc., with people who test positive for HIV, infected persons are not thought to pose a health threat. The following guidelines will govern attendance at WPI by students of the Institute who are infected with HIV.

1. A student with clinical evidence of HIV infection will be allowed to attend classes, use all facilities, and participate in all phases of WPI life as long as the student is able. For those students with special living requirements, the Office of Residential Services will address student needs on a case-by-case basis.

2. The WPI Health Service will not routinely ask students to respond to questions about the existence of HIV infection. Students who know they have tested positive for HIV, however, are encouraged to contact and inform a WPI Health Service physician so appropriate medical care, support, counsel and education can be provided. HIV positive status, like any other medical information, will be handled in a strictly confidential manner as mandated by Massachusetts statute and the Massachusetts Department of Public Health. The WPI Health Service is an acute health care facility. WPI students suffering from any chronic medical condition must obtain medical services from a primary care physician at home or in the Worcester community. The WPI Health Service will assist the student in finding a primary care physician if the student so wishes. The WPI Health Service can be contacted by calling 831-5520.

3. Since individuals with compromised immune systems may have a greater risk of encountering infection within an institutional setting, the WPI Health Service will inform students with HIV infection of any outbreak of communicable disease (such as chicken pox or measles), allowing students to take proper precautions so as to minimize their risk of infection.

4. HIV screening is a blood test for detecting the presence of antibodies to the AIDS virus. WPI does not support HIV blood screening of its students other than that necessary in the practice of good medical care as determined by the student's physician, or as a standard practice by health care organizations such as the American Red Cross. Results of HIV antibody tests are confidential and will not be reported to any agency other than those prescribed by law.

5. College students may find the psychosocial consequences of HIV infection or fear of such infection to be a source of emotional stress. The WPI Student Counseling Center (831-5540) will provide counseling and assistance in locating their support resources for any student wishing help.

Analysis: Standards of Practice

WPI Policy for Students with HIV Infection is a good example of the way institutions, government agencies, task forces, panels of experts, and professional associations set standards of practice for health workers, educators, lawyers, insurance agents, stock brokers, and so on. Based on authoritative, up to date knowledge and the best thinking of experts in the field, standards of practice such as WPI Policy for Students with HIV Infection provide guidelines for the delivery of professional services.

In this case, WPI Policy for Students with HIV Infection was written by a group of faculty, administrators, and campus health workers in response to a new situation, the spread of HIV and the growing public alarm about risks of infection. The statement responds to the call for WPI to clarify its policy concerning HIV positive students by assessing the public health risks and establishing the right of students with HIV infection to attend WPI and participate in all aspects of campus life.

FOR CRITICAL INQUIRY

1. Describe in a sentence or two what you see as the overall purpose of the document. Now look at each of the three sections—Background, Policy, and Guidelines—and describe what each section contains and what the function of each section is in the document.
2. Notice the document makes reference to various authoritative bodies, such as the Governor's Task Force on AIDS. Mark each reference to a government agency, professional association, or other organization. How does the document use these references to enhance its own authority?
3. What does the document oblige WPI to do? What standards of practice does it set? What reasons does the document offer to justify these practices?

Proposition 63. California State Ballot, 1986.

Proposition 63 is a voter initiative that appeared on the 1986 California state ballot. Passed by voters, Proposition 63 amended the California state constitution by making English the official language. Notice that two pairs of supporting and opposing statements are included on the ballot—first an argument for Proposition 63, followed by rebuttal, and then an argument against Proposition 63, followed again by rebuttal. At first glance, this may seem redundant. But the ballot uses the conventions of formal debate, which gives each side an opportunity to make its own presentation and to reply to its opponent's case.

Text of Proposed Law

This initiative measure is submitted to the people in accordance with the provisions of Article II. Section 8 of the Constitution.

This initiative measure amends the Constitution by adding sections thereto; therefore, new provisions proposed to be added are printed in *italic type* to indicate that they are new.

PROPOSED AMENDMENT TO ARTICLE III

Section 1. Section 6 is added to Article III of the Constitution to read as follows:

SEC. 6. (a) <u>Purpose</u>.

English is the common language of the people of the United States of America and the State of California. This section is intended to preserve, protect and strengthen the English language, and not to supersede any of the rights guaranteed to the people by this Constitution.

(b) <u>English as the Official Language of California</u>.

English is the official language of the State of California.

(c) *Enforcement*.

The Legislature shall enforce this section by appropri-
ate legislation. The Legislature and officials of the State of
California shall take all steps necessary to insure that the
role of English as the common language of the State of
California is preserved and enhanced. The Legislature
shall make no law which diminishes or ignores the role of
English as the common language of the State of California.

(d) *Personal Right of Action and Jurisdiction of Courts*.

Any person who is a resident of or doing business in the
State of California shall have standing to sue the State of
California to enforce this section, and the Courts of record
of the State of California shall have jurisdiction to hear
cases brought to enforce this section. The Legislature may
provide reasonable and appropriate limitations on the
time and manner of suits brought under this section.

Section 2.   Severability

If any provision of this section, or the application of any
such provision to any person or circumstance, shall be held
invalid, the remainder of this section to the extent it can
be given effect shall not be affected thereby, and to this
end the provisions of this section are severable.

Argument in Favor of Proposition 63

The State of California stands at a crossroads. It can
move toward fears and tensions of language rivalries and
ethnic distrust. Or it can reverse that trend and
strengthen our common bond, the English language.

Our immigrants learned English if they arrived not
knowing the language. Millions of immigrants now living
have learned English or are learning it in order to participate in our culture. With one *shared* language we learn to
respect other people, other cultures, with sympathy and
understanding.

Our American heritage is now threatened by language
conflicts and ethnic separatism. Today, there is a serious
erosion of English as our common bond. This amendment
reaffirms California's oneness as a state, and as one of fifty
states united by a common tongue.

This amendment establishes a broad principle: English
is the official language of California. It is entitled to legal
recognition and protection as such. No other language can
have a similar status. This amendment recognizes in law
what has long been a political and social reality.

Nothing in the amendment prohibits the use of languages other than English in unofficial situations, such as
family communications, religious ceremonies or private
business. Nothing in this amendment forbids teaching foreign languages. Nothing in this amendment removes or
reduces any Californian's constitutional rights.

The amendment gives guidance to the Legislature, the
Governor and the courts. Government must protect English:

- by passing no law that ignores or diminishes English;
- by issuing voting ballots and materials in English only
  (except where required by federal law);
- by ensuring that immigrants are taught English as
  quickly as possible (except as required by federal
  law);
- by functioning in English, except where public

health, safety and justice require the use of other languages:

- by weighing the effect of proposed legislation on the role of English; and
- by preserving and enhancing the role of English a our common language.

Californians have already expressed themselves decisively. More than a million Californians asked to place this measure on the ballot, the third largest number of petition signatures in California history. In 1984, 70+ percent of California voters, 6.300.000, approved Proposition 38 "Voting Materials in English *ONLY*."

This amendment sends a clear message: English is the official language of California. To function, to participate in our society, we must know English. English is the language of opportunity, of government, of unity. English, in a fundamental sense, is *US*.

Every year California's government makes decisions which ignore the role of English in our state; some may cause irreversible harm. Government's bilingual activities cost millions of taxpayers' dollars each year. This amendment will force government officials to stop and think before taking action.

The future of California hangs in the balance—a state divided or a state united—a true part of the Union. *YES* is for unity—for what is right and best for our state, for our country, and for all of us.

PLEASE VOTE *YES* ON PROPOSITION 63—ENGLISH AS THE OFFICIAL LANGUAGE OF CALIFORNIA.

S. I. HAYAKAWA, Ph.D.
United States Senator, 1977–1982

J. WILLIAM OROZCO
Businessman

STANLEY DIAMOND
Chairman, California English Campaign

Rebuttal to Argument in Favor of Proposition 63

Proposition 63 doesn't simply make English our "official" language; it seeks to make it California's *only* language. It does *nothing positive* to increase English proficiency. It only punishes those who haven't had a fair opportunity to learn it.

Proposition 63 threatens to isolate those who haven't yet mastered English from essential government services such as 911 emergency operators, public service announcements, schools, and courts. By preventing them from becoming better, more involved citizens while making the transition into American society, Proposition 63 will *discourage* rather than encourage the assimilation of new citizens.

Worse yet, because Proposition 63 amends the *Constitution*, its harmful effects will be virtually *permanent* and *unchangeable*. All governmental bodies, from the State Legislature to local school boards, police and hospitals will be powerless to meet the changing and varying needs of the public.

Proposition 63 is inflexible. It does not contain the exceptions the proponents claim. It has *no* exception for use of foreign languages where public health, safety and justice require.

Inevitable disputes over the meaning of Proposition 63's sweeping language will mean our government will be dragged into countless, costly lawsuits at taxpayers' expense.

America's greatness and uniqueness lie in the fact that we are a nation of diverse people with a shared commitment to democracy, freedom and fairness. *That* is the common bond which holds our nation and state together. It runs much deeper than the English language.

Proposition 63 breeds intolerance and divisiveness. It betrays our democratic ideals.

Vote NO on Proposition 63!

> **THE HONORABLE DIANNE FEINSTEIN**
> *Mayor, San Francisco*
>
> **ART TORRES**
> *State Senator, 24th District*
>
> **STATE COUNCIL OF SERVICE EMPLOYEES**

Argument Against Proposition 63

This summer we celebrated the 100th anniversary of the Statue of Liberty. That glorious 4th of July brought all Americans together. Now, four months later, Proposition 63 threatens to divide us and tarnish our proud heritage of tolerance and diversity.

This proposition, despite its title, does not preserve English as our common language. Instead, it undermines the efforts of new citizens of our state to contribute to and enter the mainstream of American life.

English is and will remain the language of California. Proposition 63 won't change that. What it *will* do is produce a nightmare of expensive litigation and needless resentment.

Proposition 63 could mean that state and local government must eliminate multilingual police, fire, and emergency services such as 911 telephone operators, thereby jeopardizing the lives and safety of potential victims.

It could mean that court interpreters for witnesses, crime victims, and defendants have to be eliminated.

It could outlaw essential multilingual public service information such as pamphlets informing non-English-speaking parents how to enroll their children in public schools.

Even foreign street signs and the teaching of languages in public schools could be in jeopardy.

We can hope that sensible court decisions will prevent these consequences. But Proposition 63 openly invites c ʿly legal attempts to seek such results. It is certain to set Californian against Californian with tragic consequences.

What makes this especially troubling is that the overwhelming majority of immigrants *want* to learn English. In fact, a recent study shows that 98% of Latin parents say it is essential for their children to read and write English well.

Asians, Latinos and other recent immigrants fill long waiting lists for English courses at community colleges and adult schools. But this initiative does nothing *positive* to help. For instance, it provides for no increase in desperately needed night and weekend English classes.

The Los Angeles County Board of Supervisors, when faced with a negative local measure like this one, firmly and wisely rejected it by a unanimous, bipartisan vote. On April 21, 1986, they said in part:

"English as the official language resolutions will not help anyone learn English. They will not improve human relations, and they will not lead to a better community. They will create greater intergroup tension and ill will, encourage resentment and bigotry, pit neighbor against neighbor and group against group. They reflect our worst fears, not our best values.

"In many areas . . . non-English-speaking persons have sometimes represented a problem for schoolteachers, service providers, law enforcement officers, who are unable to understand them. The problem will be solved over time as newcomers learn English. It has happened many times before in our history. In the meanwhile . . . common sense . . . good will, sensitivity, and humor will help us through this challenging period."

Well said by public officials representing both sides of the political spectrum.

Proposition 63 is unnecessary. It is negative and counterproductive. It is, in the most fundamental sense, un-American. Vote NO on Proposition 63!

JOHN VAN DE KAMP
Attorney General

WILLIE L. BROWN, JR.
Speaker, California State Assembly

DARYL F. GATES
Police Chief, Los Angeles Police Department

Rebuttal to Argument Against Proposition 63

When this country was founded, immigrants from all over the world streamed to our shores with one hope—a chance at success. People with divergent backgrounds were forced into close contact, yet the assimilation of these cultures was remarkably constructive. This assimilation into one nation gave us a diversity, a strength and a uniqueness that today we treasure. Every schoolchild learns to marvel at the miracle of the American melting pot.

But the melting pot was not an accident. There was a common thread that tied society together. The common thread in early America and current California was the English language. Proposition 63 will strengthen the English language and invigorate our melting pot. It will not eliminate bilingual police and fire services. It will not prohibit the teaching of foreign languages in our schools. In-

stead, Proposition 63 will serve as a directional marker towards which we as society can point our new immigrants.

The official language proposition is not an attempt to isolate anyone. Indeed, it is the opposite. We want all immigrants to assimilate into our country. We believe to be a success in California and in the United States, you must be proficient in English. We want to cherish and preserve the ethnic diversity that adds strength and fiber to our society. Yet we remember the common thread binding us together as Americans is the English language. The melting pot has served this nation for 200 years. The ingredients may have varied, but this is no time to change the recipe. Vote yes on Proposition 63.

FRANK HILL
Member of the Assembly, 52nd District

Analysis: Finding Common Ground

When it passed in the 1986 general election, Proposition 63 became the first English language amendment to a state constitution in U.S. history. Since then, a number of other states have declared English the official language, and a Constitutional amendment to make English the national language is currently being considered by Congress. The issues posed by English Only legislation are serious and divisive ones. You can get a sense of the issues in the arguments and rebuttals in favor of and against Proposition 63, which appeared following the text of the amendment on the 1986 ballot.

One of the most interesting features of this debate is that both sides use similar arguments to different ends. Both talk about "our common bonds," and both invoke the immigrant experience as a shaping moment in American history. Both sides, in other words, seek to establish a common ground with their readers.

FOR CRITICAL INQUIRY

1. Examine closely the Text of Proposed Law. It is written in the formal and legalistic style of government documents and needs careful attention. Consider SEC. 6. How does (a) Purpose express the intent of the amendment? What assumptions does it seem to make? Now look at (c) Enforcement. What does the amendment entitle the state of California to do? What would "all steps necessary" actually look like in practice? Who would it affect? What are the consequences likely to be? Finally, consider (d) Personal Right of Action and Jurisdiction of Courts. This section gives individuals the legal grounds to bring suit over breach of enforcement. Can you imagine a situation which would call for such legal action? Try to think of concrete instances of what suing would involve.

2. Consider the first round of argument and rebuttal. Notice that the argument in favor of Proposition 63 and the rebuttal both invoke the notion of "our common bond" to make their case. But do they agree on what this common bond is or who the "we" in "our" common bond might be? What is the significance of your answers in explaining why the sides support or oppose Proposition 63?

3. Notice in the second round of argument and rebuttal that both prominently feature monuments and metaphors of immigration, namely the Statue of Liberty and the "melting pot." Notice, however, that each statement tells the story of immigration to the United States in different ways. Describe the underlying narrative of immigration in each case. What purposes are these differing accounts of immigration meant to serve?

Conference on College Composition and Communication. "The National Language Policy."
The Conference on College Composition and Communication (CCCC) is the leading professional association of college and university faculty who study and teach writing. The following statement is the official policy of the organization, passed unanimously by both its executive committee and the membership at the annual meeting in 1988. It offers a good example of policy statements in which organizations take stands on controversial issues. As you read, think about its intended audience and purpose and how these might have influenced its content.

ANALYSIS: Responding to a Controversy

As its opening section shows, the CCCC statement "The National Language Policy" is a "response to efforts to make English the 'official' language of the United States." The organization clearly feels called on to clarify its own position on the rise of the English Only movement and to propose an alternative policy to its members, other educators, and policymakers.

As you see, the policy statement provides background on the English Only movement and explains why CCCC opposes it. The statement also provides a sketch of a National Language Policy that CCCC does endorse, one that the organization presents as vastly preferable to English Only. By presenting an alternative National Language Policy, the authors are taking a positive and constructive position. They're taking responsibility for their beliefs by providing what they see as a workable alternative to English Only.

Lugha भाषा لُغَة Langue

語言 Lenguaje ɔɔɔɔɔ

Tiẽng nói ภาษา ēde язык

THE NATIONAL LANGUAGE POLICY

CONFERENCE ON
COLLEGE
COMPOSITION
AND
COMMUNICATION

Lenguaje Language Sprache

언어 ēde язык भा

Dinébizaad ภาษา Lang

BACKGROUND

The National Language Policy is a response to efforts to make English the "official" language of the United States. This policy recognizes the historical reality that, even though English has become the language of wider communication, we are a multilingual society. All people in a democratic society have the right to education, to employment, to social services, and to equal protection under the law. No one should be denied these or any civil rights because of linguistic differences. This policy would enable everyone to participate in the life of this multicultural nation by ensuring continued respect both for English, our common language, and for the many other languages that contribute to our rich cultural heritage.

CCCC NATIONAL LANGUAGE POLICY

Be it resolved that CCCC members promote the National Language Policy adopted at the Executive Committee meeting on March 16, 1988. This policy has three inseparable parts:

1. To provide resources to enable native and nonnative speakers to achieve oral and literate competence in English, the language of wider communication.

2. To support programs that assert the legitimacy of native languages and dialects and ensure that proficiency in one's mother tongue will not be lost.

3. To foster the teaching of languages other than English so that native speakers of English can rediscover the language of their heritage or learn a second language.

Passed unanimously by both the Executive Committee and the membership at the CCCC Annual Meeting in March 1988, the National Language Policy is now the official policy of the CCCC.

What raised the need for the Language Policy?

The English Only movement, which began in 1981 when Senator S. I. Hayakawa sponsored a constitutional amendment to make English the official language of the United States. Variations on his proposal have been before Congress ever since; there were five proposals in 1988 and three in 1990. The Language of Government Act has been pending before the House and Senate since 1991.

In 1983 an organization called "U.S. English" was founded by Senator Hayakawa and Dr. John Tanton, an ophthalmologist. That organization promotes English Only legislation, both in Congress and state legislatures. By June 1992, sixteen states had declared English the official language.

Some states, however, have taken stands against language protectionism. In 1989, New Mexico, Washington, and Oregon passed "English Plus" laws that protect the use of languages other than English and encourage the study of foreign languages. Both Hawaii and Louisiana have official policies aimed at preserving languages and cultures.

In February 1990, a federal district judge in Arizona ruled that the state's constitutional amendment making English the official language violated the First Amendment's protection of free speech.

What's wrong with English Only?

■ **It's unnecessary.**
English, the global lingua franca and the language of wider communication in this country, is not threatened. For two centuries, most immigrants learned English within a generation without any laws compelling them. Current immigrants are doing the same.

■ **It's unrealistic.**
Thousands of people are on waiting lists to enroll in English classes. Laws making English the official language do nothing to increase the number of such classes, nor do they teach a single person English.

■ **It's educationally unsound.**
English Only opposes bilingual and similar programs that help students build on their linguistic skills. When students cannot use their strengths, they experience alienation and failure. Prohibiting or discouraging diversity limits rather than expands learning opportunities.

■ **It's unfair and dangerous.**
When we pass laws that forbid health and safety information, street signs, court trials, and marriage ceremonies in languages people can understand, we deny them legal protection and social services.

■ **It's invasive.**
English Only laws violate the privacy of speakers of other languages. When Filipino hospital employees are told they cannot speak Tagalog in the lounge, or when a college employee is told he must not speak Spanish during lunch break, they are denied free expression.

■ **It's counterproductive.**
As members of the global community, we need speakers of different languages. It's shortsighted, anti-immigrant, and racist to demean and destroy the competencies of bilingual people.

■ **It's unconstitutional.**
The First Amendment guarantees freedom of speech. The Fourteenth Amendment forbids abridging the privileges and immunities of naturalized citizens. English Only laws violate these constitutional rights.

Who else opposes English Only?

The English Plus Information Clearinghouse (EPIC) was born in the fall of 1987. Housed at t headquarters of the Joint National Council on L guages in Washington, D.C., EPIC serves as a n tional repository for information helpful to the increasing number of scholarly, ethnic, and civil liberty organizations that oppose English Only legislation. *EPIC Events*, a bimonthly newsletter keeps subscribers informed. According to EPIC' Statement of Purpose, the English Plus concept "holds that the national interest can best be serve when all persons of our society have access to ctive opportunities to acquire strong English ficiency *plus* mastery of a second or multiple languages."

More than forty civic, religious, and professional organizations have passed resolutions opposing the English Only movement and supporting English Plus. Supporters include NCTE, NEA, TESOL, MLA, American Council of Teachers of Foreign Languages, the Center for Applied Linguistics, the American Psychological Association, the National Council for Black Studies, and the National Council of Churches of Christ. Both NCTE and NEA have published books that explain their positions on English Only legislation and that provide background material necessary to guard against language restrictionism (see Selected Titles). For more information, contact EPIC, 220 I Street, NE, Suite 220, Washington, DC 20002.

SUPPORT THE NATIONAL LANGUAGE POLICY: WHAT YOU CAN DO

Strive to include all citizens of all language communities in the positive development of our daily activities.

Provide education, social services, legal services, medical services, and protective signing for linguistic minorities in their own languages so that basic human rights are preserved.

Emphasize the importance of learning second and third languages by all Americans so that we can:

- participate more effectively in worldwide activities
- unify diverse American communities
- enlarge our view of what is human

Recognize that those who do not speak English need time and encouragement to learn, but that their ability to prosper over the long term requires facility in the dominant American language.

Encourage immigrants to retain their first languages, to pass them on to their children, and to celebrate the life-supporting customs of their parents in the company of other Americans of differing backgrounds.

SELECTED TITLES

Adams, Karen L., and Daniel T. Brink, eds. *Perspectives on Official English: The Campaign for English as the Official Language in the USA.* New York: Mouton de Gruyter, 1990.

Baron, Dennis E. *The English Only Question.* New Haven: Yale University Press, 1990.

Butler, Melvin A., chair, and the Committee on CCCC Language Statement. "Students' Right to Their Own Language." Special Issue of *College Composition and Communication* 25 (Fall 1974): 1–32.

Crawford, James, ed. *Language Loyalties: A Source Book on the Official English Controversy.* Chicago: The University of Chicago Press, 1992.

Daniels, Harvey A., ed. *Not Only English: Affirming America's Multicultural Heritage.* Urbana, IL: NCTE, 1990.

Official English/English Only: More than Meets the Eye. Prepared for the National Education Association by John Trasviña. Washington, DC: National Education Association, 1988.

Piatt, Bill. *Only English? Law and Language Policy in the United States.* Albuquerque: University of New Mexico Press, 1990.

Smitherman-Donaldson, Geneva. "Toward a National Public Policy on Language." *College English* 49.1 (1987): 29–36

Readers who already oppose English Only legislation are likely to find good reasons to bolster their position and to make them more effective and knowledgeable advocates of the CCCC's proposed policy. (That's why the authors of the statement have included a brief bibliography of further readings.) For those who are uncertain of their position or inclined to support English-Only legislation, the statement provides reasons and an alternative policy that can't be dismissed simply as a politically-motivated attack on the English Only movement.

FOR CRITICAL INQUIRY

1. Summarize the position that the CCCC statement "The National Language Policy" takes, some of the reasons it gives for taking this position, and the desirable consequences that it indicates could result.
2. How does the policy statement convey a sense of urgency?
3. Notice how the CCCC statement "The National Language Policy" is divided into sections. For each section, describe what it contributes to the document—what effects its contents could have on readers who agree and on those who don't. In what ways does this sectioning enhance the document's readability? Is the order of the sections an effective one? Why or why not?
4. Consider the section "What's wrong with English Only?" What evidence does it offer to support its claim that there is something wrong? Do you find this critique of the English Only movement persuasive? Why or why not?
5. Does the policy statement attribute motives to those who support the English Only movement? What effect, if any, does attributing motives or refraining from doing so have on the way readers will likely respond to the document?
6. What values and beliefs does the statement seem to appeal to? How can you tell? Point to particular words, phrase, or passages that make clear the appeal to these values and beliefs.

ETHICS OF WRITING

Accessibility of On-Line Documents

One of the key features of a healthy democracy is all citizens having access to information about their government. Currently, the Library of Congress and other federal agencies are putting public documents on line, and readers can find everything from the Declaration of Independence to the intricacies of this year's income tax rules on the World Wide Web. In many respects, such documents are more public on the Web than they are in government archives. More people have access to them.

But access works two ways. It's not simply a matter of making documents available. It's also a matter of people having computers capable of accessing the documents. Without the necessary technology, citizens have no greater access to public documents than they did before.

The ethics of democratic communication is based in part on the wide availability of information to all citizens. Consider who owns computers and spends time on-line. While home computers are certainly proliferating rapidly, the audience for the Web remains basically students and people with some knowledge of computers. Demographically, the world of cyberspace is inhabited by white, middle- to upper-income males, ages 20-35. What needs to happen to realize the potential of an informed citizenry? Can you imagine ways in which electronic communication media can heighten democracy? Are there ways in which the new media may restrict democratic participation?

LOOKING AT THE GENRE: PUBLIC DOCUMENTS

1. List as many documents from your college or university as you can that involve students. Pick one of these documents that in your view reveals something interesting about the student's relationship to others. It could be your college's Honor Code or its policy on sexual harassment, a student loan form or a job description. Analyze the relationship the document seeks to establish between the individual student and others. Describe what the document covers. What rights and responsibilities does it assign to the individual student? What rights and responsibilities does it assign to others? What beliefs does the document attempt to put into practice?

2. You have already read the section in the CCCC statement "The National Language Policy" that gives the organization's views on "What's Wrong with English Only." How do you imagine supporters of Proposition 63 would respond to the language proposed by CCCC? What rebuttals might they make? What concessions? Do you think the English Only debate is hopelessly polarized, with the differing sides deeply entrenched in their views? Can you imagine any common ground they might share?

3. The selection you have read from Abraham Verghese's book *My Own Country* involves memory work, as it calls up a telling incidence from his medical practice with AIDS patients. Nonetheless, it seems to differ in important respects from the reading selections in Chapter "Memoirs." Pick one of the memoirs to compare to Verghese's account. Explain what you see as the most important differences and similarities. Consider in particular each writer's purpose in recreating a scene from the past.

DESIGNING DOCUMENTS: The Preamble to the United Nations Charter

The charter or constitution that serves as the founding document for a group, club, organization, or government body typically begins with a preamble that presents the general goals of the organization. It may also explain who is forming the new organization, and what gives them the authority to do so. Notice how the Preamble to the United Nations Charter identifies that it is "we the people of the united nations," through the power invested in their respective governments to represent them, who are founding the organization. By invoking the will of the people of all nations to "combine our efforts," the Preamble takes on a moral authority that goes beyond a simple diplomatic agreement among governments. As you read the Preamble, consider how the design of the document helps you mentally organize the founders' reasons for establishing the UN and the goals it sets forth.

THE PREAMBLE TO THE UNITED NATIONS CHARTER

WE THE PEOPLE OF THE UNITED NATIONS DETERMINED

to save succeeding generations from the scourge of war, which twice in our lifetime has brought untold sorrow to mankind, and

to reaffirm faith in fundamental human rights, in the dignity and worth of the human person, in the equal rights of men and women and of nations large and small, and

to establish conditions under which justice and respect for the obligations arising from treaties and other sources of international law can be maintained, and

to promote social progress and better standards of living in larger freedom,

AND FOR THESE ENDS

to practice tolerance and live together in peace with one another as good neighbors, and

to unite our strength to maintain international peace and security, and to ensure, by the acceptance of principles and the institution of methods, that armed force shall not be used, save in the common interest, and to employ international machinery for the promotion of the economic and social advancement of all peoples,

HAVE RESOLVED TO COMBINE OUR EFFORTS TO ACCOMPLISH THESE AIMS.

Accordingly, our respective Governments, through representatives assembled in the city of San Francisco, who have exhibited their full powers found to be in good and due form, have agreed to the present Charter of the United Nations and do hereby establish an international organization to be known as the United Nations.

DISCUSSION AND ACTIVITIES

1. What effects does the use of the three phrases written in upper case letters have on you as a reader? What do they cause you to do as you read?
2. Notice that the first two parts of the Preamble comprise a single long sentence, which, if printed in the usual way, might be difficult to keep straight. What specific text and design features of the document establish a predictable order that the reader can anticipate in reading the sentence?
3. The United Nations was established in 1945, and its founders took advantage of the existing technology—the typewriter—to design the Preamble. Since then, computer technology has dramatically increased the capability to design documents effectively. Given whatever kind of software you use, whether it be a word processor or a more sophisticated design program, what other kinds of design features or layout could be used if the Preamble were being designed today? Describe in writing changes you might make, sketch a rough layout, or actually re-design the Preamble on your computer.

ASSIGNMENTS

WRITING ASSIGNMENT

Here are three options for this writing assignment:

1. Work together as a class to write a class charter.
2. Design and write your own public document, either individually or with others, depending on your teacher's directions.
3. Write an essay that explains how a public document has affected your life or the life of someone you know, using the reading selection from Abraham Verghese for hints on how to approach this assignment.

OPTION 1: WRITING A CLASS CHARTER

For this assignment, you will be working together as a whole class to design and produce a charter for the writing course you are currently taking. One way to do this assignment is to break the class into working groups of four to six, depending on the size of the class, with each group responsible for drafting one section of the charter. Here is one possible way of dividing the charter into sections. Your class, however, may decide to modify this plan.

- Preamble. The preamble to a charter explains the purposes and goals of an organization or, in this case, of a writing course. (See the Preamble to the Charter of the United Nations below for an example.)
- Rights and responsibilities of the teacher to the students. This section explains the role of the teacher in the writing course and what students can legitimately expect from the teacher.
- Rights and responsibilities of the students to the teacher. This section explains the role of students in their relationship to the teacher in a writing class and what teachers can legitimately expect from them.

- Rights and responsibilities of the students to each other. This section explains the relationship among students in a writing class and what students can legitimately expect from each other.
- By-laws governing classroom life. While the first three sections will be somewhat general in their explanations of the goal of the course and individuals' roles within it, this section should be more specific, presenting the policies that will govern classroom life. By-laws often appear in charters as numbered points. Here are some things you will likely want to consider in the by-laws section—attendance, timely completion of work, how to ensure everyone is heard in class discussion, how to handle differences of opinion, how to make group work productive, and so on. There are probable other things, depending on the circumstances, that you will want to cover in this section.

The class as a whole will need to discuss collectively what it wants to see appear in each of the sections. Then the working groups can draft sections, make sufficient copies, and bring them to class for revision. Or the class can work on and respond to the sections electronically through a listserv or Web page.

OPTION 2: DESIGNING A PUBLIC DOCUMENT

For this assignment, design and write your own public document. As you have seen from the reading selections in this chapter, there are a number of different types of public documents for you draw on:

- Codes. There are well known codes, such as the Ten Commandments or the Boy Scout Law (to be "trustworthy, loyal, helpful, friendly, courteous, kind, obedient, cheerful, thrifty, brave, clean, and reverent") to use as a model. Your college may have an honor code or a statement of standards students are expected to abide by. Imagine a specific community or group of people you know. Make a list of rules or principles to govern their behavior and relationships.
- Contract or agreement. As you have seen, public documents such as directives to physicians and marriage vows commit people to binding relationships that have a recognized legal status. You could use one of these or other agreements, contracts, or declarations you have signed or know about as a model to design your own document. Or you could re-write one of these documents to redefine relationships, agreements, and courses of action. Imagine a situation that calls for a specification of individuals' rights and obligations toward others.
- Law, statute, or Constitutional amendment. Currently there are movements afoot for balanced-budget and prayer-in-school amendments to the United States Constitution and state and municipal laws for gay rights or to secure a living wage (above the minimum wage) for workers whose employers have state or city contracts. Imagine a situation that requires a new law, statute, or constitutional amendment. Write a law, statute, or Constitutional amendment. Include an argument for your legislation, using the 1986 California ballot as a model.
- Policy statement. Imagine you have been commissioned by an advocacy group, professional association, student organization, or other body to write a policy statement that puts your group on record on an issue of public concern. Use the "The National Language Policy" statement as a model.
- Charter or constitution. Imagine a group you would like to form on campus or in your community. Write a preamble or mission statement that explains why the group has come into being and what its tasks and goals will be.

OPTION 3: WRITING AN ESSAY

One way to approach the genre of public documents is to look at the affects a public document has had on an individual life. As you have seen in the selection from Abraham Verghese, public documents can play a determining role at critical moments. Of course, you may not have faced the kind of situation Verghese describes, but there are nonetheless likely to be moments in your life or in the life of someone you know where public documents (or their absence) helped shape the outcome. The task here is to go beyond a simple description of, say, how you got a speeding ticket or a bad report card and your parents grounded you. You need to analyze and explain how the document entered into the situation and what its significance was to those involved.

The Invention, Planning, and Drafting sections that follow can be helpful no matter which assignment you are doing.

INVENTION

DEFINING THE NEED FOR THE DOCUMENT

Public documents address some very real social needs — to regulate behavior, to recognize the roles and status of individuals, to constitute organizations and associations, to codify beliefs and values, and to specify rights, responsibilities, and benefits. In addition to these more abstract functions, public documents also determine the ways in which many of us have access to certain segments of our communities; conversely, they can prevent us from having that access. With this assignment, you have the opportunity to change that. You may want to create your own public document delineating a groupís mission or membership; you may opt to redesign a public document that has prevented you from succeeding in some way in the past. Regardless of your choice, at some point you will need to clearly define the need your document will fulfill.

EXERCISE

Work through the following exercises to give yourself plenty of options. Afterwards, select the public document that most excites you, or the one that will allow you a chance to help others (or yourself) the most, the one that might have the most significant impact.

- Think through the stages of your life. What public documents have defined you to others at various times throughout your life? Which ones define you now? Keep track of those that impact you the most, and consider working to officially change them.

- Go through your files of official documents at home. What functions do they serve? Are there any functions that you find position you in undesirable or uncomfortable ways? Is there a power structure implied in these documents that you find troublesome? How might you like to shift the power structure in one of these documents? Now, how would you do it if you were to revise and redesign the text?

- Look again at the list you generated on page XX. Of those public documents that you interact with in college, have any of them caused you problems? Which ones, and in what way? If you can identify what makes particular forms difficult for you to navigate, perhaps you can make it easier for others. These, then, might be good documents to change, with the consent of your institution.

- Think ahead to your future. What public rituals, social movements, or community organizations do you think you will be involved with? What texts accompany positions in those groups? If there are no public documents, consider creating one.

- Talk with parents and friends about public documents that have affected their lives in positive or negative ways. Is a labor union renegotiating a contract at the factory where a relative works? Is a friend getting married in the near future? Do you have an acquaintance working on a political campaign or with a public interest research group? If so, try to get copies of some of the public documents included in those enterprises. Do they need you to help create one for them?

- Throughout this chapter you have seen suggestions for public documents that are either missing or are somehow problematic (for example, the lack of legally-binding agreements for same-sex couples). Skim back through the chapter, and see if any of those missing pieces provide you with the call to write your own public document.

If you are working on this project within a group, it will probably work best at this stage if each group member tries each exercise. Your group could also decide to complete the exercises together, and use the time as an opportunity to get to know one another better.

EXERCISE

This next exercise helps you focus your options down to one or two viable choices, and it will enable you to explicitly define the need that your document will address. Work through the advice below, and check your statement with your writing partners; offer them advice on theirs as well.

- Once you have generated a useful list from the exercise above, select three or four situations, relationships, or problems where a written document seems to be called for—whether to regulate, codify, or change the present state of affairs. Who is involved in the situation? What needs clarification or change? How would your document be used?

- Pick one of the situations, relationships, or problems that seems particularly urgent or that you are especially interested in. Write a one-page statement that describes the situation, defines the need for a document, and explains the type of document you plan to write.

- Exchange the one-page statement with a classmate. Take turns asking your partner what he or she sees as the need your statement establishes for the document you propose. Ask your partner if the proposed document seems to meet the need. If so, why? If not, why not?

FINDING A MODEL

Public documents often seem to follow a set pattern and formula; many times they look and sound remarkably similar. In part, this feature of public documents makes them easily recognizable to readers and easily reproducible by writers to account for new situations. Different types of documents—whether a law, a contract, or an organization's charter—have their own typical look, and one good way to begin designing your own document is to find one or more examples of the type of document. Bring several models to class, and work through the following exercise with your writing partners.

EXERCISE

Consider the following features of the model or models you have found. As your group works together, notice the similarities and differences in the models you have in front of you.

- Layout. Notice first of all the general layout of the document. Does it use a letterhead, logo, or other design feature? How many sections does it have? How does it organize the material it includes? Does it use blank spaces to be filled in each time the document is used?

- Presentation of key points. Does the document use headings, numbered lists, bullets, or other features that highlight key points? Does it use other devices, such as repetition or parallelism, to emphasize key points?

- Tone and language. Does the document use specialized or technical language, such as legal or medical terms? How would you describe the type of language in the document? Does it seem to be the formal language of a specific community or discipline? Is it meant to sound impersonal and official, or does it strike its own characteristic tone? What would you say is the level of formality in the document? What are the implications of this level and tone?

- Signature. Is the document signed? If so, by whom? What does signing commit people to? How can you tell from the document? Will signers be clear about what they are agreeing or committing themselves to?

PLANNING

BLOCKING OUT THE MAIN SECTIONS OF THE DOCUMENT

To help you determine what order you will use to present your main points, block out the main sections. Not all documents have a beginning, middle, and end, as other genres of writing do. Consider the models you have found.

GOING ON-LINE

Finding On-Line Documents at Your College

Colleges and universities increasingly are making important documents available on-line. Many now have on-line catalogues and course announcement bulletins. In some cases, students can register for classes on-line. In addition, many departments and programs have designed Web sites that students can visit to get information about courses, majors, and faculty interests. Work together in groups of three or four to explore what your college, its programs, and departments offer on-line. Do a search and bring your results to class.

The purpose of this exercise is first to find out what information is available to you and your classmates. Next, once the class has inventoried what is on-line, consider whether there are other documents or types of information that would be useful to put on-line. Finally, if you have suggestions to make, you may want, as a class, to write a letter proposing something be put or created on-line and explaining why it would be helpful to students. You will need, of course, to figure out who the proper person is to receive the letter.

- Do you need a preamble that explains the occasion of the document you are designing and its general principles (such as the preamble to the U.N. Charter), or a background sections that present information (as in the WPI Policy for Students with HIV)? Or can you simply begin by listing main points?

- Are the main points you plan to highlight clearly distinct from each other and roughly equivalent in terms of scope and importance? Can you combine two or more of the points? Is one point actually an aspect of another point?

- Does the document need a conclusion or some type of formal ending? Is the ending of the document the section where people will sign it, as in the "living will"? Or does the ending explain what people can do to support a policy, as in The National Language Policy?

DESIGNING FOR EMPHASIS

As you have seen in the "Designing Documents" section above, documents such as the Preamble to the United Nations Charter use page layout and design features to emphasize key points and make the document easier for the reader to process. Here are some considerations to take into account (for more information, see Chapter   Document Design):

- White space. Are there ways you can use white space (or sections of the page that are blank) to separate sections in the document and to emphasize key points? How can you use white space to create a document that is not cluttered but is easy to read?

- Headings and subheadings. Are there ways to break the document into sections by using headings and subheadings? How can such divisions make the document easier to read?

- Fonts. Are there ways to use capitals, italics, boldface, underline, or designer fonts to emphasize key words or phrases? How can you use these features selectively to gain the maximum effect?

- Balance. Are there ways that equally important sections can occupy approximately the same amount of space on the page? How can the use of space cue readers to the importance of points and sections?

- Parallelism. Are there ways to use parallelism to make the document easy to follow? You might want to use devices such as numbered or bulleted series to highlight parallel items. You can also make sure the items in a series all use the same type of grammatical structure (for more on parallelism, see). Here are some of the most commonly used structures:

Infinitives: "to save," "to reaffirm," "to establish," and so on (from Preamble to United Nations Charter)

Noun phrases: "Purpose," "English as the Official Language of California," "Enforcement," "Personal Right of Action and Jurisdiction in Courts" and "Severability" (from Text of the Proposed Law of Proposition 63)

Imperative verbs: "strive," "provide," "emphasize," and so on (from The National Language Policy)

Repeated subject: "It's unnecessary," "It's unrealistic," "It's educationally unsound" and so on (from The National Language Policy)

WORKING DRAFT

Once you have the main sections and points of your document blocked out, you can begin drafting. As you write, try to use parallelism where it seems called for, to make your document easy to follow. Keep in mind the way your document will look on the page. Once you have a draft you are fairly comfortable with, try revising certain sections with the development strategies discussed below: defining and forecasting what is to come.

PARAGRAPH DEVELOPMENT: Defining

One way you clarified your own thinking at the beginning of this assignment was to define your problem in order to either justify the need for your new (or revised) public document, or to explain why you found a particular document worthy of writing about in an analytical essay. Using that strategy, you built a stronger sense of purpose for yourself. At this point in your working draft, you can focus on building a stronger sense of purpose for your readers. Definitions of key concepts and new terms can help you develop your paragraphs so that your readers not only feel your sense of urgency, but that they also understand exactly what it expected of them. Several of the readings in this chapter use definitions as support for their calls to act, and you can use them to rally your call to write.

Clear definitions might help you develop your paragraphs more fully and appropriately. If you are designing a form that people have to fill out, are all of the terms understandable? Do you need to add some definition to make your form more accessible? In the strictest sense of the term "definition," the writers of the WPI Policy for Students with HIV Infection actually define AIDS, to ensure that all readers know whether or not the policy applies to them. As a part of this definition, the writers also state how AIDS is transmitted, so that those not infected will have appropriate responses to those who are.

"Acquired Immune Deficiency Syndrome (AIDS) is caused by a fragile virus know as the Human Immunodeficiency Virus (HIV). The best scientific evidence available supports the position that the AIDS virus is not transmissible by casual contact. Epidemiological studies show that HIV is transmitted in one of three ways . . . ."

The writers make efforts to invoke scientific authority in their definitions of AIDS and HIV. Since AIDS can be a controversial subject, the writers of the policy needed to make sure their definition established that they had researched the topic adequately, and that the position advocated in the policy was a responsible and ethical one. Had they defined AIDS in some other way, perhaps using language that a conservative religious group might use in discussing HIV, the policy would have had different implications. You, too, will need to consider how you craft the definitions most important to your subject, and from where you get your information.

Here are some steps you can take in crafting useful definitions for your document or essay.

1. Consult authorities on your subject. Clearly, the writers of the WPI policy invoked the scientific community. What communities will help you establish your credibility and knowledge? What kind of background information is crucial to defining your issues for your readers? You may need to consult books and magazines, or you may need to get on the phone to obtain written information from relevant organizations.
2. Look in the dictionary. Perhaps the most prevalent source of definitions, the dictionary might provide you with some leads for crafting your own.
3. Consider the definitions offered in similar documents. Since you may be gathering a variety of public documents related to your subject, use the information offered in them to shape your own. Note places where you disagree, or where you think their definitions are vague or unsatisfactory. Your task, then, will be to improve upon your predecessors.

If you are writing a public document or essay in which definitions might not be an issue, take a look at some of the Paragraph Development options discussed elsewhere.

- see Using Summaries (page XX in Reports) to help provide the relevant information that will set the context for your document or essay

- see Moving from General to Particular and from Particular to General (page XX in Proposals) to guide your readers to a heightened level of commitment

- see Offering Reasons with Supporting Facts and Evidence (page XX in Reviews) to develop paragraphs containing information that will support the position you are staking in your document

BEGINNINGS AND ENDINGS — USING FACTS, STATISTICS, AND BACKGROUND INFORMATION

One way to alert readers to the scope and importance of your document (or your essay about public documents) is to provide some background information. Citing striking facts and statistics can also be a way to grab your readersí attention. Consider The National Language Policy, in which the writers begin their statement by offering background they feel will be important for their readers to know:

"The National Language Policy is a response to efforts to make English the ëofficialí language of the United States. This policy recognizes the historical reality that, even though English has become the language of wider communication, we are a multilingual society."
— Conference on College Composition and Communication. The National Language Policy

This type of contextual information, or background information, is necessary for the readers of the language policy to understand why such a public document was created. You may want to make sure that you have provided the necessary background information in the document you are writing, as well. If you are writing an essay about your experience with a public document, consider including some facts about that document, or some statistics about the numbers of people that document effects.

As you create and revise your document, decide whether or not you think it might be effective to begin with a striking fact, statistic, or some other piece of relevant background information. In addition, this might also be a good time to read (or re-read) the material presented in Chapter 2 on Using Background Information, especially the sections on Examples, Statistics, and Expert Testimony (see pages XXX). If you do not think such a strategy would set the right tone for your document, consider some of the options presented in other chapters.

- see Pointing Out the Significance or Wider Consequences (page XXX in Memoirs) to state the purpose of your document, or the main point of your essay, from the outset

- see Forecasting What Is to Come (page XXX in Reports) let your readers know precisely what they can expect in this piece of writing

- see Offering a Recommendation or Solution (page XXX in Proposals) to clarify any expectations you might have at the end of your document or essay

PEER COMMENTARY

EXERCISE

Exchange drafts of the document you have designed with a classmate. Respond to the following questions:

1. Format. Is the purpose of your partner's document easy to find? Will readers understand what its uses are? What suggestions can you offer to improve or strengthen the format of the document? Consider its layout, organization, use of numbered or bulleted items, and other design features.

2. Language and tone. Is the language of the document precise and easy for readers to understand? How would you characterize the level of formality the writer has used? Does this level seem appropriate for this document? Underline words, phrases, or passages that might be written more clearly. Explain why you marked them. Is the tone appropriate for the type of document your partner has designed? Why or why not? Circle words, phrases, or passages where you think the tone does not work well. Explain.

REVISING

Review the peer commentary you have received. Is the purpose of your document easy for the reader to identify? Have you ordered your points in a way that is easy to follow? Check at this point to make sure similar points are parallel in structure. Is each point clearly separate from other points? Consider the feedback you have received on the tone of the document. After you have revised based on your writing partners' feedback, check Connections and Coherence. You may decide that the particular features discussed in this chapter don't provide the instruction you need for this assignment; if so, choose a section in another chapter to apply to your revising process (some suggestions for specific places to look are included in the section below).

CONNECTIONS AND COHERENCE: Enumerative Order

One way to establish the links between one section and another is to mark the connections by numbering them. In some cases, this can mean that whole paragraphs are set off with numbers, as in WPI Policy for Students with HIV Infection:

1. A student with clinical evidence of HIV infection will be allowed to attend classes . . . .
2. The WPI Health Service will not routinely ask students . . . .
3. Since individuals with compromised immune systems may have a greater risk of encountering infection within an institutional setting, the WPI Health Service will inform . . . .

[and so on].

In other texts, such as the Republican platform for the 1994 Congressional elections, "Contract with America," the numbers are spelled out, but they still function to establish an order and a connection among items.

First, require all laws that apply to the rest of the country to apply equally to Congress;

Second, select a major independent auditing firm to conduct a comprehensive audit of Congress for waste, fraud, or abuse;

Third, cut the number of House committees, and cut committee staff by one-third;

[and so on].

These examples show how enumerative order can be used to mark transitions from one paragraph or section to the next. Enumerative order can also be used within a more traditional-looking paragraph. If you want to use enumerative order, all you need to do is mark your points with "First . . . ," "Second . . . ," "Third . . . ," and so on. By using a numeric transition like this, you can indicate that you are moving on to a new issue before developing it, thus helping readers recognize the points of emphasis in the paragraph so they can pay attention accordingly. Such a paragraph might look like this one below:

The death of the "People's Princess" holds a number of implications for those working in mainstream media. First, it requires that members of the media confront their own role in the accident. Even if they weren't one of the particular paparazzi following Diana's car, they still need to examine their own responsibility in perpetuating the thirst for scandalous stories. Second, it requires that they take an active stance in deciding how to deal with the photographs that were taken at the scene of the accident. It is one thing to condemn the actions of the paparazzi; it is another to run the grisly photographs anyway. Third, it offers an opportunity for the media to handle Diana's death in a different, perhaps less sensationalized, way than they handled her life. Given that Mother Teresa's death followed within a week of Diana's, it will be interesting to see how much coverage—and coverage of what kind —is granted to each woman.

Try organizing your main ideas this way, and signal them using enumerated order, either in a traditional-looking paragraph, or with easy-to-read lists. If this technique does not seem applicable to your writing assignment, try some of the coherence devices discussed in other chapters.

- see Using Direct and Implied Topic Sentences (page XXX in Letters) to begin each section of your document with clear expectations

- see Linking the Parts to the Proposition (page XXX in Commentary) to reinforce the main points you are making throughout your document

- see Parallelism of Ideas (page XXX in Proposals) to set a pattern of expectations for the organization and presentation of your thoughts

After your coherence devices and transitions are in place, read through your document again to make sure it uses inclusive language (see Pages XXX in Guide to Editing). If not, you may be unintentionally excluding certain groups of people from hearing and participating in your statement.

WRITERS WORKSHOP

The web site of the Grand Prix Foundation at Purdue University is, as its creators note on the home page, "currently under construction." A group of students in a technical writing course at Purdue has taken on the task of documenting and publicizing the activities of the Grand Prix Foundation. Below you'll see three screens from the web site—home page, "Other Grand Prix Facts," and "Scholarship Information." Keep in mind the Purdue students are well aware that the web site is still in the process of creation ("if you couldn't tell"). As you view the three screens, consider what suggestions you might offer them.

WORKSHOP QUESTIONS

1. Given the information on the three screens, what does the purpose of the Grand Prix web site seem to be? Who does the audience seem to be? How can you tell? Point to particular passages and design features.
2. Consider how the information is organized and presented on the three screens. Does the home page contain the right type and amount of information to introduce viewers to the mission and activities of the Grand Prix Foundation? Do "Other Grand Prix Facts" and "Scholarship Information" provide further needed information? Is "Other Grand Prix Facts" a good screen title? Do you have questions about the foundation or ideas about other information you think would strengthen the web site? Are there any passages you think should be revised?
3. Screen print-outs, of course, don't give you the full visual sense of the web site—how, for example, the black and old gold (Purdue's school colors) P with the crossed racing flags scrolls onto the screen. But from what you can see here, how well do the visuals fit the document? Do they seem to be good choices? Do you have any suggestions?

Home Page

Other Grand
Prix facts

Senior Board
Members

Past Winners

Scholarship
Information

This Year's
Drivers

This Year's
Qualifiers

This Year's
Race Results

Links to
suppliers and
other Grand
Prix sites

Purdue
University

Welcome to Purdue University's Grand Prix Web Site

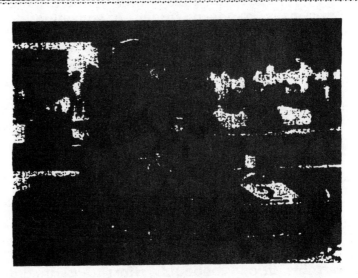

The Purdue Grand Prix is known as the "Greatest Spectacle in College Racing", it is an annual event used to raise money for student scholarships. Through the Grand Prix Foundation effort, twenty-three scholarships were awarded last year totaling $11,000. The Grand Prix Foundation is a non-profit organization run entirely by students for students. The foundation consists of a President, a nine member Senior Board, a Junior Board of approximately 50 members, the trackworkers, the Safety and Security workers, and all the participants of the many Grand Prix activities.

For further information or general comments, please drop us a line.
grand@expert.cc.purdue.edu

This site is currently under construction if you couldn't tell!!

Best if viewed by

The Grand Prix was first run in 1958. At that time, karts were built from scratch and powered by lawnmower engines. In 1968, the existing track was built on the Northwest corner of campus at the cost of over $25,000. The track is carefully modeled after the World Kart Championship in Japan.

The Gramd Prix is scored by one of the most advanced computer scoring systems anywhere in the world of racing. Once again the Grand Prix Foundation will be testing the autoscoring system. This system allows us to provide up-to-date information to the media, kart crews, and the public.

The karts cost approximately $5,000 to build from scratch. This money comes partially from a team sponsor such as a business, housing unit, or private individual. The drivers are required to run the race with a Yamaha KT-100s engine.

Any Purdue Student may enter the race. Usually fraternities, residence halls, co-ops, or student organizations enter. Last year approximately 45 karts entered with 33 karts qualifying for the race.

Because of the efforts of the Safety and Security workers and the Track workers, the Grand Prix race is one of the safest races run anywhere in the world.

Each year the Grand Prix Foundation sponsors the Black and Gold Spring Classic and the classic Les Filles Prix Bed Race.

Scholarship Information

The purpose of Purdue Grand Prix is to raise funds for student scholarships. In our continuing effort to assist students scholastically we are once again offering scholarships to those individuals who have contributed to the welfare and advancement of their fellow students. Our objective is to recognize those individuals, and assist them in their future endeavors

1997 Grand Prix Scholarship Recipients

$12,000 dollars was awarded to these students and another $2,000 was awarded to the two Old Gold Student Ambassadors, Jill Hossenlopp and Edwin Williams, for their scholarship and contributions to the Purdue Community.

Abigail Igarta
Amy Roberts
Andrew Hayes
Chad Curts
Cory Sickafoose
Cynthia Mahler
Dan Colpi

Eric McClish
Jason Evans
Jillian Olsen
Kara Elliot
Katherine Swit
Kathrine Gapinski
Kimberly Lojewski
Lindsay Dreiman
Maggie Grant
Matt Brady
Matt Heckaman
Molly Peelle
Peter Schenk
Rebecca Figler
Rona Stewart
Shawn Richardson
Stacy Demerly
Tracy Williamson
Tyonia Puckett
Wendy Dorfman

The Grand Prix Foundation would like to congratulate all the recipients and thank everyone who participated. Winners will be notified of the amount of their scholarships in a congratulatory letter. Any questions or comments may be directed to Jim Niehoff at the Grand Prix office at 494-7771. Race day is April 26 and we hope everyone will attend the 40 anniversary running of the "Greatest Spectacle in College Racing."

4. Thinking about the overall effect of these three screens, what image of the Grand Prix Foundation does the web site project? Does this image seem appropriate for a public document that explains and publicizes the mission of the organization? What suggestions, if any, would you make for further construction?

WRITER'S INVENTORY

Write a short account of your experience composing a public document. Take into account what authority you drew on to write the document. On whose behalf did you write the document? What problems or issues did you encounter writing the document? Explain how you dealt with them.

A CLOSING NOTE

Read the draft of the document you have designed. Remember that the purpose of a document is in its uses. Make sure it will be clear to readers what use the document is for, what it commits people to, and how it regulates their relationship to others.

SEVEN

PROFILES:
Creating a Dominant Impression

LOOKING AT THE GENRE

Talking about other people—describing them, analyzing their personalities, trying to understand why they do the things they do—is one of the main topics of conversation in most people's lives. Think for a moment about how and why you talk or write about other people in the course of everyday life—whether you're telling your parents what your new roommate is like, discussing with co-workers why your boss supervisor acts the way he or she does, or writing a letter to a friend trying to explain why someone you both know is leaving school or changing majors. This impulse to describe, to analyze, and to understand what people are all about seems to grow out of a genuine need to come to terms with our social experience and our relationships with others.

It's not surprising, then, that a genre of writing—the profile—is devoted to describing and analyzing particular people or that this genre is extremely popular in magazine and newspaper writing. Profiles are a regular feature in publications such as Rolling Stone, Sports Illustrated, Ebony, Ms., and the Wall Street Journal, as well as in local newspapers. Many profiles are of well-known people, and the call to write profiles undoubtedly has a lot to do with readers' fascination with the famous and the powerful. Profiles offer readers a behind-the-scenes look at people they've heard so much about. But the call to write has at least as much to do with our general curiosity about and desire to understand other people and their lives.

One way to understand profiles is to consider how they differ from another genre that focuses on individual people, the biography. While biographies are often long, profiles tend to be relatively brief. Whereas biographies give full chronologies, profiles usually seek to capture their subject at a moment in time (even though they often include information about other times in the subject's life). In fact, the immediate call to write a particular profile often comes because events in that moment in time have brought the person into the public eye. A first-time director makes a movie that becomes the box office hit of the year. A Wall Street investment banker is under investigation for illegal trading. A sports star unexpectedly retires. In such cases, profile writers seek to fill in the human details behind the headlines.

Note that at times the events are larger than the person profiled. Thus, Dr. Susan M. Love, profiled in Molly O'Neill's "A Surgeon's War on Breast Cancer," although already a prominent physician, became newsworthy to a wider audience because of growing national attention to breast cancer. When an issue moves to the forefront, ordinary people affected by that issue often become the subject of profiles—for example, a family supported by public assistance when changes in welfare are being debated. Such profiles of ordinary people supplement statistical and analytical treatments of issues, illuminating social issues and cultural patterns in a way they cannot, making concrete and personal what would otherwise remain abstract and impersonal. And working on people's natural curiosity about others, they take readers beyond their preconceptions to explore the remarkable variety of people, backgrounds, life styles, and experience that are frequently reduced to a single category like "welfare mothers," "the elderly," or "blue-collar workers."

Not only are profiles often focused on a present moment in time, but they also in many cases seem to take place in real time. That is, they may tell what the person does over the course of a day or during characteristic activities. As a result, another characteristic of profiles is that they create a sense of immediacy and intimacy, as though the reader were there on the spot, watching and listening to what's going on. Readers of profiles have come to expect that they will be able to visualize the person (what does she look like? what is she wearing? what are her surroundings?), to hear the person's voice (what does she sound like? how does she talk to the people around her?), and to witness revealing incidents (what is she doing? how and why does she do it? what does this show about her?).

To be able to convey this sense of immediacy and intimacy, writers of profiles often rely heavily on two special research techniques: interviewing and observation. This doesn't mean, of course, that library research isn't involved. On the contrary, consulting written sources with pertinent background information not only supplements interviewing and observation but also makes them much more effective.

But no matter how immediate profiles seem to be, we are not seeing the people directly, but rather through the eyes of the writer. The way people appear in a profile—and the impact their story has on readers—depends as much on the writer as the people profiled. Profiles express, explicitly or implicitly, the author's point of view, or dominant impression. No profile will really work for its readers unless it creates this dominant impression—a particular and coherent sense of its subject. Writers of profiles don't just write up the results of their observations and interviews. Instead, they choose the descriptive details, events, daily routines, anecdotes, and quotes and reported speech that will show why and how its subject is unique. A good profile is meaningful as well as vivid.

In some profiles, a dominant impression emerges gradually from the writer's observations. As you'll see, this is what happens in Molly O'Neill's profile of Dr. Susan Love. In other profiles, the writer explicitly states a main point. An example is Mike Rose's "I Just Wanna Be Average," where profiles of three students illustrate his point that academic tracking affects students intellectually, emotionally, and socially.

Profiles take many forms. O'Neill's is a newspaper article, whereas Rose's profiles appear in a chapter of a book. Jon Garelick's "Kurt Cobain 1967-94" is a special type of profile, the eulogy. A eulogy differs from a newspaper obituary in the same way that profiles in general differ from biography. Garelick's eulogy doesn't try to give all the biographical details of Cobain's life, but rather tries to bring the meaning of his life into focus and to offer a kind of final judgment. As you'll see, brief profiles can even be used in advertising and publicity.

"A Surgeon's War on Breast Cancer"

Molly O'Neill.

Molly O'Neill is a staff writer for the New York Times, where her profiles, feature stories, and food columns appear regularly. The following profile is of Dr. Susan M. Love, a prominent surgeon, biomedical researcher, and activist. O'Neill effectively uses the techniques of observation and in-

By MOLLY O'NEILL

LOS ANGELES

THREE mammography films were clipped to the light box on the wall of a sleek conference room at the U.C.L.A. Breast Center. The different perspectives of a woman's breast looked like black and white photographs of the earth taken from a satellite. From each angle, the dark shadow of a tumor hovered like a storm cloud near the center of the gray sphere.

A woman born 50 years ago had, on the day of her birth, a 1 in 20 chance of being diagnosed with breast cancer in her lifetime. A woman born today has a 1 in 9 chance, partly due to a longer life expectancy. The U.C.L.A. Breast Center, part of the U.C.L.A. Medical Center, is one of about a dozen clinics in the country that both treat and research the disease. And Dr. Susan M. Love, the director of the U.C.L.A. program, is a leading crusader in the war against breast cancer.

A radiologist used a pointer to outline the tumor for a group of radiologists, oncologists, pathologists and surgeons. Dr. Love stood in the back of the conference room, rocking in her bone-colored pumps. Her brown eyes were narrowed behind red-frame glasses.

The lab coat she wore was a bulletin board of buttons. "Keep abreast," read one. "Get a second opinion." On another: "T.G.I.F. (Thank God I'm Female)." Under the string

In search of a malevolent gene.

of fat white pearls around her neck was a gold chain with an ankh, an ancient symbol of life. Above one of the gold Chanel-style earrings was a tiny labrys, the mythical double-bladed ax used by Amazons.

Dr. Love is not without contradictions.

She is a traditionally trained surgeon; yet, she believes political action, not surgery, is the only real hope for stemming the increase in breast cancer. She is a feminist, but is skeptical of self-help techniques like breast self-examinations. She was raised Irish Catholic, at one point entered a convent and is now a lesbian mother.

With patients, she is funny, warm and accessible. With peers, "Dr. Love constantly challenges dogma," said Dr. Jay Harris, a radiation oncologist and professor at Harvard University, who has known and worked with Dr. Love since her residency at Beth Israel Hospital in Boston nearly 15 years ago. "Surgeons aren't supposed to do that. Susan makes many surgeons uncomfortable."

Even the staff of Dr. Love's clinic say that the surgeon's approach is not for every patient. "Some women want to be told what to do," said Sherry Goldman, a nurse practitioner at the U.C.L.A. center. "Options make them nervous."

Even before she published "Dr. Susan Love's Breast Book" (Addison Wesley. 1990), a down-to-earth guide that has become the bible of women with breast cancer, she stirred controversy. In Boston, where she practiced before accepting the U.C.L.A. appointment in 1992, Dr. Love questioned the necessity of radical mastectomies and was an early champion of conservative surgeries like lumpectomies and partial mastectomies.

She is critical about what she sees as condescending and paternalistic attitudes among traditional breast surgeons. She is indefatigable in raising money — and political consciousness — for breast cancer research and prevention.

In 1991, Dr. Love helped found the National Breast Cancer Coalition, a federation of nearly 200 support and advocacy groups that helped raise the national budget for breast cancer research and prevention from $90 million to $420 million. "Thanks to Anita Hill," she likes to say "After that debacle, congressmen were all looking for a nice, noncontroversial women's issue."

Dr. Love, who is 46, is known as a brilliant surgeon. She is also known for her bluntness.

She grins puckishly when she describes conventional breast cancer treatment, as "slash, poison and burn." She hopes that hers will be the last generation of surgeons to treat breast cancer with radical and invasive methods. Meanwhile, she performs surgery eight times a week.

The woman whose mammogram she was regarding would probably wind up in her operating room.

Her tone is kindly, forever big sister. The faint arc of freckles across her nose seems to expand as she smiles. Hers is the sort of open, guileless face that is hard to refuse. But as she rattled off studies, statistics and personal experience to support her recommendations for treating patients, she sounded indomitable.

A minute later, as she was entering another examining room, however, her tone was alternately jovial and intimate. "Is it lethal?" asked the 32-year-old patient. The surgeon laughed, pulled up a chair, plunked down and leaned toward the patient, elbows resting on her knees.

"Driving in L.A. is lethal," she said.

"Your mammogram doesn't say anything about death. We're not talking doom."

For the next 40 minutes, using her own left breast to demonstrate each point, Dr. Love discussed the basic purpose of a breast ("it's like a milk factory"), how, under certain circumstances, cells build up on the wall of the duct, "like rust in a pipe," she said, "reversible."

The patient was laughing by the time Dr. Love told her: "When those cells break out into the surrounding fatty tissue, that's cancer. It is not reversible. We need to find out where you are on this continuum before we can really talk about options. But there *are* options. And you have *time* to think about it."

"And you'll take care of me?" the patient asked as they stood.

"I will take good care of you," said the surgeon, hugging the patient.

In the last 50 years, one-third of women diagnosed with breast cancer died of breast cancer. Dr. Love doesn't claim a better survival rate. She claims to take better care of women, and her patients generally agree.

Born in Long Branch, N.J., the oldest of five children, Susan Margaret Love was raised to change the world by doing good work. After two years as a pre-med student at the College of Notre Dame of Maryland in Baltimore, Dr. Love joined a convent but left after four months.

"I wanted to save the world," she said, "but they wanted to save their own souls." She enrolled at Fordham University and continued her pre-med studies. In 1970, she applied to medical school.

She wasn't fazed by the quota that limited women to 10 percent of the student body in most medical schools.

"I wasn't political, I was a nerd," she said. "I've always been mainstream, pretty conservative."

After graduating fourth in her class from the State University of New York, Downstate Medical Center, in Brooklyn, she entered the surgical residency program at Beth Israel Hospital in Boston. "The program was modeled after the military," she said. "Most women who survived paid a price. They lost their marriages, or their minds. I did it by being totally out of touch with myself, a good old Irish Catholic."

Besides, she loved surgery. "It's so pragmatic, so tactile," she said. "You can fix things."

Breast surgery, though, isn't a sure-fire fix. And initially, it didn't interest Dr. Love. "I didn't want to be ghettoized in a women's specialty," she said. But when she established her practice in Boston, doctors referred breast cancer patients to her. "I started to see that this was an area where I could make a difference." Within two years, she had become the breast surgeon for the Dana Farber Cancer Institute in Boston.

At the same time, she said, after mounting a "massive find-a-man campaign," she faced her own sexuality. For years, she had avoided another surgeon, Dr. Helen Cooksey, who was gay. "I thought it might be catching," Dr. Love said. "It was."

The couple have been together for 13 years. Five years ago, by artificial insemination, Dr. Love had a daughter, Katie Love Cooksey. Dr. Cooksey left surgery to stay home with the child. Last September, the couple won a legal battle that allowed Dr. Cooksey to adopt Katie. "Helen and I have money and privilege, so it's our obligation to pave the way." Dr. Love said.

The noblesse oblige theme also rises when she discusses the move from private practice to U.C.L.A.

"I was this little person in private practice, and now I have a whole medical school behind me," Dr. Love said. "Of course that means a huge responsibility. I have to get this clinic up and running and then build an equally serious research effort."

At 7 A.M. every weekday, Dr. Love takes her daughter to preschool and goes to the hospital, where she performs any surgeries by 10 A.M. She then dashes down one flight of stairs to the Breast Center to confer, teach and work on grants before patients arrive. One patient was worried. Her aunt had died of breast cancer. "Not close enough to worry," Dr. Love said briskly. She examined the patient,

found nothing and said, "Now, what else can I do for you?"

"Can you, uh, show me how to do, uh, one of those things?" the patient asked.

"Breast self-exam?" Dr. Love responded. "Sure, but it's an overrated activity. The medical establishment would like you to believe that breast cancer starts as a grain of sand, grows to be the size of a pea and on and on until it becomes a grapefruit. Breast cancer doesn't work like that. It grows slow and it's sneaky. You could examine yourself every day and suddenly find a walnut."

A 55-year-old patient with a small tumor had been advised by another surgeon to have a complete mastectomy, immediately. "Give me a break," Dr. Love told the patient. "Using a mastectomy to treat a lesion like yours is like using a cannon to shoot a flea."

Yet another patient, a 48-year-old woman, had an aggressive cancer but was hesitant to have a mastectomy. Was it possible to save her breast?

"Look, breast cancer is like mental health," Dr. Love said. "The early forms are neurotic and can be treated. The later forms are psychotic, and it's more difficult. You have a lot of pre-cancer, a little bit that's crossed the line. I can probably go in and take a wedge out of your breast; it's sort of like taking a dart.

"I think I could do it, but I may not get it all. You'll have a 50-50 chance of having to come back for a mastectomy. Go home, sleep on it. The good news is this is not an emergency."

The next patient was not so lucky. A 64-year-old who had had a partial mastectomy 10 years previously and had been cancer-free since had found a new lump. Subsequent tests found cancerous lesions in the chest wall, the stomach, the liver, the kidneys and the skull. "It doesn't make any *sense*," Dr. Love said to the team in the conference room. "Where have these cells been for 10 years?"

"Quiescent," said Dr. Dennis Slamon, the chief of oncology.

"Why can't we make then *all* quiescent?" Dr. Love asked. She repeated the question several times as she packed a bulging briefcase, exchanged her lab coat for a smart silk jacket and, after a typical 13-hour workday, walked down the long, cool hall and headed home.

The Breast Center is one of a handful of such centers that offer an interdisciplinary approach, using medical specialists and psychologists to care for patients from diagnosis through treatment. The force of Dr. Love's personality is the glue that holds the staff of 30 together. Still, Dr. Love is impatient.

"Research is the only way we are going to solve this thing, and I don't mean research into new chemo formulas, I mean research into the cause of breast cancer," she said, as she walked through an empty parking lot to a new Volvo station wagon.

"And we're so close," she said. "We know it's genetic. Some people are born with the gene, others develop the gene. We don't know what causes the gene to change. Pesticides? Pollution? Food additives? They are all possibilities. All we know is that a gene is involved. And we are very close to finding it. Unbelievably close."

Sliding behind the steering wheel, she distilled the latest breast cancer research with the same kind of down-to-earth similes that she uses to explain the disease to patients.

"You see, the gene is like a robber in the neighborhood," she said. "We have the neighborhood roped off. Now all we have to do is knock on every single door."

ANALYSIS: Open Form to Create Dominant Impression

Molly O'Neill never directly indicates what she wants readers to think of Dr. Susan M. Love. The profile doesn't state and then support a main idea; this isn't the basis of its organization. Nonetheless, the profile effectively conveys a dominant impression of Dr. Love. It does so because the information, description, scenes, conversations, and quotes it contains vividly and consistently contribute to this impression.

Moreover, the information, description, and so on are carefully organized into sections. Each section clusters together a particular kind of information or discussion, contributing to the dominant impression in a specific way. If, as in this profile, sections are carefully designed, they can resonate with each other, suggesting connections a reader can make, so that the dominant impression created by the whole is that much stronger. (If the sections are not carefully designed, readers will likely experience the piece as incoherent and frustrating.)

The pattern of organization used in this profile is called open form; it can be characterized as having an implicit center of gravity around which parts revolve, rather than an explicit main point which parts develop.

If you re-read the profile, you can see that it divides into the following sections:

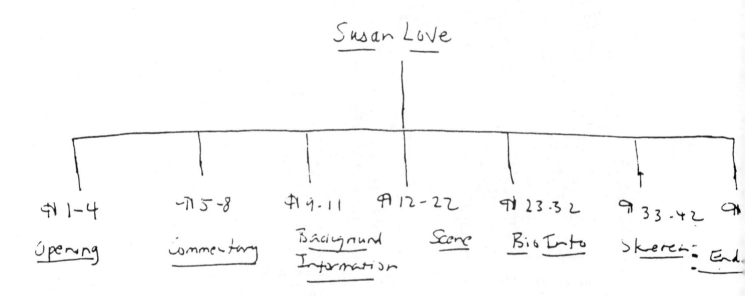

¶s 1-4: Opening scene at UCLA Breast Center
¶s 5-8:   Commentary on Love
¶s 9-11: Background information
¶s 12-22: Scenes from Love's practice
¶s 23-32: Biographical information
¶s 33-42: Sketch of typical day
¶s 43-47: Ending

To see how a section can contribute to a dominant impression, consider the opening scene of the profile (¶s 1-4). Effective profiles usually rely on a powerful opening that establishes a perspective for readers. This profile begins in a conference room where a radiologist is showing mammography films to a group of doctors. Readers are immediately immersed into Dr. Love's world. Dr. Love herself is initially in the back of the room, and O'Neill takes her time introducing her.

First O'Neill describes the mammography films, using metaphorical language (they "looked like black and white photographs of the earth taken from a satellite" and "the dark shadow of a tumor hovered like a storm cloud") to put what may be unfamiliar to readers into more familiar terms, and then she quickly sketches in statistics on the rising incidence of breast cancer.

It is only after this extended scene that Love appears, "a leading crusader in the war against breast cancer," as though O'Neill were using a camera to zoom in on her subject. Dr. Love is seen "rocking in her bone-colored pumps. Her brown eyes were narrowed behind red-frame glasses." The opening concludes with a description of Dr. Love. As in most successful profiles, this is by no means a full description. Instead, O'Neill describes only a couple of details—the buttons Dr. Love has on her lab coat and the jewelry she wears. Note that these are key details, revealing something important about Dr. Love. Like Dr. Love's posture and gaze, they point to characteristics that are part of the dominant impression the profile goes on to establish.

FOR CRITICAL INQUIRY

1. Re-read the profile, paying attention to how your perceptions of Dr. Susan Love develop and perhaps change over the course of the profile. Annotate the profile by indicating what your impression of Love is in the opening scene, at three or four points in the middle, and at the end. Now read back over your annotations to see how your impression of Love has developed. Is your final impression basically similar to your initial one? Are there any changes or shifts along the way? Explain why you think your impressions developed as they did. Compare your experience reading the profile to that of others in your class. How would you account for differences and similarities in the way you have responded to the profile?

2. What dominant impression does the profile seem to create? How do you think O'Neill wants readers to see Love? How does O'Neill establish such a perspective for readers?

3. Point to words (nouns, verbs, adjectives, adverbs), phrases, sentences, and passages that indicate the perspective O'Neill offers to readers. Locate also examples of the different kinds of evidence—quotes from Dr. Love, quotes from others, dialogue, observed details, background information—O'Neill uses to build this perspective. Why is this use of different kinds of evidence particularly effective?

4. In a few sentences each, summarize the sections listed in the analysis section. Indicate briefly for each how it contributes to the dominant impression.

5. Which sections make use of a chronological arrangement? Explain how and why the effect of this chronological arrangement within sections is very different from the effect of an overall chronological arrangement (as would be found in a biography).

6. Focus on a particular passage in the profile that you feel is especially revealing about the kind of person Dr. Love is. What is it about the passage that you find effective in characterizing Dr. Love? What effect do you think the passage has on readers? Compare the passage you have selected to those chosen by other students in class. Use these comparisons to develop a list of effective strategies for characterizing people in profiles.

Mike Rose. "I Just Wanna Be Average"

Mike Rose is a teacher, poet, scholar, and associate director of the UCLA Writing Programs. The following selection, which in effect contains three profiles, was taken from his award-winning book *Lives on the Boundary*. Rose's book is in part a telling critique of the failures of American schooling to address the needs of all students and in part an affirmation of the educability of all Americans. And, as this selection shows, it is also in part autobiographical, drawing on Rose's own experience growing up in a working-class neighborhood in Los Angeles. Notice that this selection differs significantly from the previous one both in how the information used was obtained and in how the profiles are organized.

1 Students will float to the mark you set. I and the others in the vocational classes were bobbing in pretty shallow water. Vocational education has aimed at increasing the economic opportunities of students who do not do well in our schools. Some serious programs succeed in doing that, and through exceptional teachers—like Mr. Gross in *Horace's Compromise*—students learn to develop hypotheses and troubleshoot, reason through a problem, and communicate effectively—the true job skills. The vocational track, however, is most often a place for those who are just not making it, a dumping ground for the disaffected. There were a few teachers who worked hard at education; young Brother Slattery, for example, combined a stern voice with weekly quizzes to try to pass along to us a skeletal outline of world history. But mostly the teachers had no idea of how to engage the imaginations of us kids who were scuttling along at the bottom of the pond.

2 And the teachers would have needed some inventiveness, for none of us was groomed for the classroom. It wasn't just that I didn't know things—didn't know how to simplify algebraic fractions, couldn't identify different kinds of clauses, bungled Spanish translations—but that I had developed various faulty and inadequate ways of doing algebra and making sense of Spanish. Worse yet, the years of defensive tuning out in elementary school

had given me a way to escape quickly while seeming at least half alert. During my time in Voc. Ed., I developed further into a mediocre student and a somnambulant problem solver, and that affected the subjects I did have the wherewithal to handle: I detested Shakespeare; I got bored with history. My attention flitted here and there. I fooled around in class and read my books indifferently—the intellectual equivalent of playing with your food. I did what I had to do to get by, and I did it with half a mind.

3 But I did learn things about people and eventually came into my own socially. I liked the guys in Voc. Ed. Growing up where I did, I understood and admired physical prowess, and there was an abundance of muscle here. There was Dave Snyder, a sprinter and halfback of true quality. Dave's ability and his quick wit gave him a natural appeal, and he was welcome in any clique, though he always kept a little independent. He enjoyed acting the fool and could care less about studies, but he possessed a certain maturity and never caused the faculty much trouble. It was a testament to his independence that he included me among his friends—I eventually went out for track, but I was no jock. Owing to the Latin alphabet and a dearth of *R*s and *S*s, Snyder sat behind Rose, and we started exchanging one-liners and became friends.

4 There was Ted Richard, a much-touted Little League pitcher. He was chunky and had a baby face and came to Our Lady of Mercy as a seasoned street fighter. Ted was quick to laugh and he had a loud, jolly laugh, but when he got angry he'd smile a little smile, the kind that simply raises the corner of the mouth a quarter of an inch. For those who knew, it was an eerie signal. Those who didn't found themselves in big trouble, for Ted was very quick. He loved to carry on what we would come to call philosophical discussions: What is courage? Does God exist? He also loved words, enjoyed picking up big ones like *salubrious* and *equivocal* and using them in our conversations—laughing at himself as the word hit a chuckhole rolling off his tongue. Ted didn't do all that well in school—baseball and parties and testing the courage he'd speculated about took up his time. His textbooks were *Argosy* and *Field and Stream*, whatever newspapers he'd find on the bus stop—from *the Daily Worker* to pornography—conversations with uncles or hobos or businessmen he'd meet in a coffee shop, *The Old Man and the Sea*. With hindsight, I can see that Ted was developing into one of those rough-hewn intellectuals whose sources are a mix of the learned and the apocryphal, whose discussions are both assured and sad.

5 And then there was Ken Harvey. Ken was good-looking in a puffy way and had a full and oily ducktail and was a car enthusiast . . . a hodad. One day in religion class, he said the sentence that turned out to be one of the most memorable of the hundreds of thousands I heard in those Voc. Ed. years. We were talking about the parable of the talents, about achievement, working hard, doing the best you can do, blah-blah-blah, when the teacher called on the restive Ken Harvey for an opinion. Ken thought about it, but just for a second, and said (with studied, minimal affect), "I just wanna be average." That woke me up. Average?! Who wants to be average? Then the athletes chimed in with the clichés that make you want to laryngectomize them, and the exchange became a platitudinous melee. At the time, I thought Ken's assertion was stupid, and I wrote him off. But his sentence has stayed with me all these years, and I think I am finally coming to understand it.

6   Ken Harvey was gasping for air. School can be a tremendously disorienting place. No matter how bad the school, you're going to encounter notions that don't fit with the assumptions and beliefs that you grew up with—maybe you'll hear these dissonant notions from teachers, maybe from the other students, and maybe you'll read them. You'll also be thrown in with all kinds of kids from all kinds of backgrounds, and that can be unsettling—this is especially true in places of rich ethnic and linguistic mix, like the L.A. basin. You'll see a handful of students far excel you in courses that sound exotic and that are only in the curriculum of the elite: French, physics, trigonometry. And all this is happening while you're trying to shape an identity, your body is changing, and your emotions are running wild. If you're a working-class kid in the vocational track, the options you'll have to deal with this will be constrained in certain ways: You're defined by your school as "slow"; you're placed in a curriculum that isn't designed to liberate you but to occupy you, or, if you're lucky, train you, though the training is for work the society does not esteem; other students are picking up the cues from your school and your curriculum and interacting with you in particular ways. If you're a kid like Ted Richard, you turn your back on all this and let your mind roam where it may. But youngsters like

Ted are rare. What Ken and so many others do is protect themselves from such suffocating madness by taking on with a vengeance the identity implied in the vocational track. Reject the confusion and frustration by openly defining yourself as the Common Joe. Champion the average. Rely on your own good sense. Fuck this bullshit. Bullshit, of course, is everything you—and the others— ear is beyond you: books, essays, tests, academic scrambling complexity, scientific reasoning, philosophical inquiry.

7   The tragedy is that you have to twist the knife in your own gray matter to make this defense work. You'll have to shut down, have to reject intellectual stimuli or diffuse them with sarcasm, have to cultivate stupidity, have to convert boredom from a malady into a way of confronting the world. Keep your vocabulary simple, act stoned when you're not or act more stoned than you are, flaunt ignorance, materialize your dreams. It is a powerful and effective defense—it neutralizes the insult and the frustration of being a vocational kid and, when perfected, it drives teachers up the wall, a delightful secondary effect. But like all strong magic, it exacts a price.

ANALYSIS: Claim and Evidence

Mike Rose's profiles of three students are part of a larger piece: they are the third through fifth paragraphs in a selection with seven paragraphs, which is itself an excerpt from a book. Notice that the first two paragraphs in the selection establish a main idea, or claim, that the three profiles then support. In the final two paragraphs the author in effect generalizes from the profiles and draws conclusions related to the main point. In contrast to O'Neill's piece, which uses open form, this selection uses an organization familiar from argumentative writing: claim and evidence:

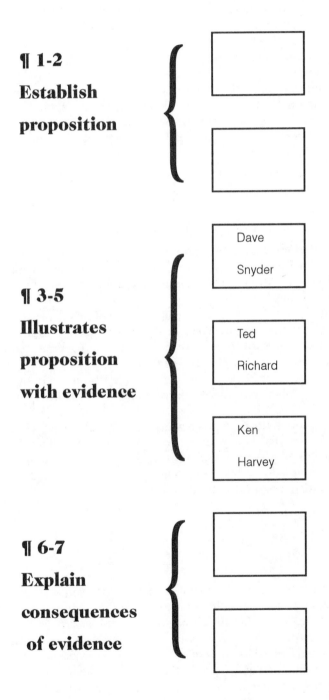

¶ 1-2
Establish proposition

¶ 3-5
Illustrates proposition with evidence

Dave Snyder

Ted Richard

Ken Harvey

¶ 6-7
Explain consequences of evidence

Whereas the success of O'Neill's article comes from the way sections establish a dominant impression, the success of a piece with claim and evidence organization comes from the way the evidence supports the claim and serves as a basis for conclusions that say something significant. (If these parts and their relationships to one another aren't clear, readers will find the piece hard to follow.)

Notice that Rose's piece is just as effective as O'Neill's but in a way that is appropriate to the type of organization he uses. He begins with two memorable sentences that help establish the main idea: "Students will float to the mark you set. I and the others in vocational classes were bobbing in pretty shallow water."

Notice also that the high school students Rose then profiles are much more that just evidence to support this main idea. He sketches Dave Snyder, Ted Richard, and Ken Harvey in vivid detail. Each appears to the reader as a unique individual, with his own characteristics and idiosyncrasies. Yet there is also a sort of shared dominant impression that emerges, an impression that is linked to Rose's main idea. For Rose is showing us, through their experience, a central problem in American schooling: it produces students who, in Ken Harvey's unforgettable words, "just wanna be average." Interpretation on the part of the author, inevitable in any profile, is made explicit in a piece like this one, occurring from the beginning sentences, quoted above, to the final judgment that the "powerful and effective defense" vocational education students develop "like all strong magic, . . . exacts a price."

FOR CRITICAL INQUIRY

1. Work together with two or three other students to write a short summary—two or three sentences—of what you see as Rose's main point as it is expressed in the two opening paragraphs. Compare your summary to ones written by other groups. What differences, if any, do you see in what the summaries emphasize?

2. For these profiles to work, they need to be more than just illustrations of Rose's controlling theme of what happens to students tracked into Voc. Ed. They also need to capture the individuality of each student. How does Rose do this? Point to particular passages, sentences, or words in the text that provide revealing characterization.

3. How does Rose connect evidence to his central claim? What does the enabling assumption seem to be? Does Rose make it explicitly? What backing, if any, does he provide to support his enabling assumption?

4. In the final two paragraphs of this selection, Rose wants to generalize from the experience of the three students he has profiled—to develop further his controlling theme about the effects of schooling by making some final points. What points exactly is Rose making in the final two paragraphs? Do they seem to be justified and to flow naturally from the three profiles? Explain how these points seem to grow logically out from the profiles (or why in your view they don't).

Jon Garelick. "Kurt Cobain 1967-94"

Jon Garelick is a music critic who wrote this tribute to Kurt Cobain shortly after Cobain had committed suicide. Cobain was the lead singer and guitarist in the rock group Nirvana, whose smash hit album Nevermind—and its single "Smells Like Teen Spirit"—brought them and the grunge rock scene in Seattle to national prominence in1988. To many, Nirvana's combination of punk rage, heavy metal guitars, and pop melodies returned rock to its authentic roots in teenage working-class rebellion. To others, Nirvana epitomized all that had gone wrong with young people in America. In any case, Cobain's self-inflicted death presented a moment of cultural reckoning, when people felt compelled to come to terms with Cobain and the meaning of his death.

Nirvana had just finished a majestic performance of "Smells like Teen Spirit" at the Wallace (MA) Civic Center last November when bassist Krist Novoselic burst into a sudden tantrum aimed at a member of the audience. "I saw you grab that girl! Why don't you come up here, you weenie!"

Guitarist/singer/songwriter Kurt Cobain then took a seat to play the ballad "All Apologies," first lecturing the audience about girl groping in the mosh pit. "We've hired goons," he said calmly, "and if we find anyone groping girls' breasts or pinching their asses, they'll throw them out . . . and then beat the shit out of them."

Musically it was a masterful show, perfectly paced, every segue showing off each song to its best advantage, with none of the dead spots that can stall a set at mid ballad. Through it all, Novoselic was a towering behemoth, hopping and banging out his bass lines. Cobain, by comparison, was a fragile waif. On stage, the band's personal dynamic was as clear as their musical dynamic: with David Grohl's fierce, precise drumming behind them, Novoselic was the kinetic genial giant, Cobain the soft-spoken introvert shuffling across stage in his permanent slouch, emitting howls of vocal and guitar noise mixed with touching, tender melodies. It wasn't hard to imagine that if anyone ever laid a hand on the singer, Novoselic would kill him.

If you've followed Nirvana's career at all over the past three years, it was difficult not to feel protective of Cobain. There was reported weirdness and with guns, drugs, petulant faxes sent to various publications (including this one) — exploits that made Cobain and wife Courtney Love a notorious rock-and-roll couple.

And yet, in interviews and in live performances, Cobain was invariably lucid, modest, intelligent. He denigrated his image as a "pissy, complaining, freaked-out schizophrenic who wants to kill himself." That came from an interview with *Rolling Stone*'s David Fricke after the release of 1993's *In Utero*. Cobain said he looked forward to the development of the band and considered tinkering with extended song forms, allowing that "I don't know if we're capable of it — as musicians." But the set at Wallace Civic Center was not the performance of a band on the verge of breaking up, and there were none of the signs of a frontman who can't, or wouldn't, perform.

Even so, when Cobain's shotgun-blasted body was found last week in his Seattle home, the shock wasn't merely at his death. We had been prepared for that (if by none of the other signs) by the "Rome coma" of a month before. And there were hints through his whole career of instability — an incident where he climbed a bank of amplifiers and appeared ready to jump off, his comment to writer Michael Azerrad that if he hadn't "cured" his mysteriously recurring stomach ailment with heroin, he would have blown his brains out.

Perhaps we were most shocked by our own sense of shock. At the time, I couldn't imagine another rock star's death that would affect me as profoundly. Bono? Eddie Vedder? Paul Westerberg? Is it simply because I like his songs the most? That I've written the most about him, "studied" him the most in my own rock-crit way? What other comparisons were there? We were more or less prepared for Frank Zappa's death. The jazz gods I worshipped — Mingus, Ellington, Dizzy Gillespie — were likewise in physical decline when they died.

But maybe this particular loss is part of the mystery of pop stardom. When it was confirmed that Cobain was dead, I was surprised at my own sense of loss, and of disbelief. The disbelief continued through the Friday-night MTV rebroadcast of the *Unplugged* session, through listening to DJs hopelessly trying to play amateur psychologist to distraught fans. Even the next morning, the shock was still there. There's his face on the front page of the *Times* — he must really be dead.

The "unwilling spokesman for a generation" line doesn't exactly fit either. At 41, I'm at least two generations removed from Cobain's. (Gertrude Stein once said that every five years makes a generation, and I didn't grow up in the '70s or the '80s.) The only parallel that fits, and the one that Baby Boom rock crits have been throwing at Gen Xers all week, is that of John Lennon. It's a more unlikely and awkward parallel than the Boomers will allow, but there it is. Cobain himself told Fricke that Lennon was his favorite Beatle, saying with a laugh, "He was obviously disturbed." Cobain wasn't nearly as famous (it was painful to have to listen to NPR explain who he was to a general audience). Nirvana's influence has been massive but not on a par with the Beatles'. And yet it's that same loss, that same sense of disbelief, and the shock at the violence of his passing.

There is, of course, anger as well. Lennon didn't choose his death. The self-destruction of Janis Joplin and Jim Hendrix can nonetheless be seen as accidents. There's compassion for a suicide, but also dismay over the selfishness of the act. A suicide leaves behind guilt for his survivors. And in Cobain's case, a fatherless daughter who'll have to deal with the anger and sense of abandonment for the rest of her life.

There is no good answer to the question "Why?" People scoff at the notion that fame alone can do someone in, no matter how sensitive or vulnerable the star. Cobain had access to treatment, he could have "retired," as John Lennon did in order to become a house husband. Cobain's troubled childhood in a broken home, his being shuttled from one guardian to the next, has been well enough documented in band biographies as well as in his own songs. In "Sliver" there's the primal scream of "Grandma take me home!" In "Serve the Servants" there's the ironic self-observation "Oh no, that legendary divorce is such a bore," followed by "I tried to have a father/ but instead I had a Dad."

None of which excuses Cobain's suicide or makes it completely comprehensible. There's only the understanding that his feelings of shame ran so deep that he finally lost all sense of himself. (In his suicide note, he apparently called himself a "faker.") There were stories that Cobain and Love were in danger of losing custody of their child because of their problems with drugs. There were published reports that in the last couple of weeks of his life he'd fled a rehabilitation center, that Love had called police because of suicide threats. And there was the purchase of the shotgun. It looks as though he went to great effort to isolate himself, so that this time no one could talk him out of it, remind him of the world outside himself, remind him about his daughter.

For some, Cobain's suicide validates a portion of his art — the demons in his songs were real after all. But his music was an affirmation. It was about survival. He turned the internalized demons outward and released them as squalling guitar rage and affecting melodies. It was proof that you could emerge from an unbearable isolation and connect, as he did on "Something in the Way," with only two chords and that delicate whisper of a voice. Even at their roughest and most abrasive, he made sense of chaotic feelings.

In hindsight, critics talked about the inevitability of Nirvana's success — the surefire mix of metal, punk, and pop that knocked Michael Jackson out of number one on the charts and made Seattle a brand name. But Cobain's art was no formula. His musical style was as personal as his oblique, powerful lyrics. He invented his own language, found his own voice. In the world of pop music — that mass commodity — he was that rare thing: an original. □

ANALYSIS: Eulogy as Profile

Eulogies traditionally play a ceremonial role at funerals and memorial services, when people gather to pay their last respects to someone who has died and to come to terms with the meaning of the person's life to the community. The practice of delivering eulogies dates back to ancient Greece, but as Jon Garelick's profile of Kurt Cobain shows, this type of profile still has relevance to contemporary life.

Eulogies have as much to do with understanding a person's character as journalistic profiles. Their function is an ethical one, to interpret the meaning of an individual's life and to clarify what it tells us about our own communities. Eulogies come from what the ancient Greeks called epideictic rhetoric, the ceremonial use of language to praise and blame. For this reason, as you can see in Garelick's eulogy, eulogies are centered as much on the judgments and perceptions of the writer or speaker as they are on the person eulogized.

Notice there is nothing simple about a eulogy, nothing about how "he was a nice person, a hard worker, a good father and husband, an active member of the community." Rather because Kurt Cobain was a complicated and controversial figure, the judgments offered by Garelick are complex and at times ambivalent. What is telling here is that while Garelick praises his subject, he does not dodge Cobain's flaws or evade criticisms. He is looking for the meaning of the person's life, whatever its strengths and weaknesses and contradictions might be, to come to terms with what the person's death represents to the larger community and how we might remember him. And in this sense, the ambitions of the eulogy are sweeping and powerful ones, because they strive to shape the historical memory of a community.

FOR CRITICAL INQUIRY

1. Jon Garelick opens with an anecdote from a Nirvana concert. How does he use the incident to provide the reader with a perspective on Kurt Cobain? In what light does the anecdote portray Kurt Cobain?

2. What dominant impression of Kurt Cobain emerges? Trace how this impression develops from the opening anecdote to the end of the eulogy. List some of the words, phrases, and sentences that are central to conveying this dominant impression.

3. In structure, which of the two previous selections does this one most resemble? Explain.

4. Like the other profiles, this eulogy can be divided into sections. The first five paragraphs can be seen as the opening section—with the first three presenting the anecdote and the next two indicating the anecdote's significance. Into what other sections would you divide this eulogy? For each section, indicate what the topic is and summarize what is said about it. Indicate also how the section contributes to the eulogy as a whole. Compare your answers with those of classmates.

5. Garelick spends part of his tribute to Cobain looking for explanations for Cobain's suicide. To what extent is he successful? Do you think Garelick has a plausible explanation? Does he think he does? Garelick, then, in the next-to-the-last paragraph, turns to the question of whether Cobain's music is consistent with his death. How does he seem to answer this question? What does his answer say about the plausibility of his explanation?

6. As the last paragraph makes clear, Garelick praises Cobain above all for his uniqueness as an artist. But the eulogy says little about his specific achievements or, for that matter, about his music in general. Why do you think this is the case? Would such a eulogy be more or less effective than the one Garelick has written?

7. How does this selection differ from the other two profiles you've read? To what extent do you think the differences relate to the fact that this selection is a eulogy? Based on the differences between this selection and the others, how would you characterize eulogies?

ETHICS OF WRITING:

Responsibility to the writer's subject

What is a writer's responsibility to his or her subject? And how does this responsibility interact with the writer's responsibility to readers? What potential conflicts are there between the two responsibilities? These are questions profile writers invariably grapple with.

In many respects, a profile is a collaboration between the writer and the person profiled (unless, of course, the profile is based solely on other sources such as memory and research). Without the subject's cooperation, the profile will be more difficult to do—and perhaps impossible. At the same time, the subject may well have a vested interest in the profile and may, consciously or unconsciously, try to influence the outcome. Or the subject may, inadvertently or not, reveal things that if published would prove embarrassing to the person or others.

Either of these situations can pose a tricky dilemma for the writer. Profiles, after all, are meant to inform readers and offer them the writer's honest perspective—not to serve as publicity or public relations for the person profiled. If profile writers are to have an independent voice, as the ethics of journalism demands, and are to fulfill their responsibilities to readers, they must be able to make their own judgments about what is fit to print. But an important basis for these judgments is a sense of responsibility toward the subject. The writer must resist commercial pressures to sensationalize.

LOOKING AT THE GENRE: PROFILES

1. People talk about other people all the time. They tell stories about what others do and what they are like. The purposes of such stories vary, of course. They can entertain, make a point, praise or blame. The stories people tell about others can affectionately describe the idiosyncrasies of a friend or relative, warn about someone's bad temper, offer an example of a life worth living, or amount to simple gossip. In any case, people routinely sketch profiles of others in the course of everyday conversation.

   Think about the conversations you have with others—friends, relatives, co-workers, neighbors, acquaintances, strangers. In these conversations, what kinds of stories about people do you and others tell? List four or five different occasions when you or someone else told a story about another person. Write down your relationship to the person who told or listened to the story, who and what the story was about, and what you see as its main purpose.

   Observation is a key technique for researching profiles, and it can give you important insights into the oral profiles people sketch. Once you've remembered and thought about some conversations with other people, pay close attention to some conversations you are involved in or that you overhear. How often do people come up as a topic of conversation? Why do they come up, and what purposes do the stories serve? Who are the stories about, and what is the relationship of these people to those in the conversation? Are the stories focused on particular events or are they about the people in general? Do they involve much description? much analysis? Do they attempt to judge the people? After you've listened to a conversation, write down answers to these questions and add any other observations you made.

   Now work together with three or four classmates. Compare your notes, and see whether any patterns emerge. Do you, for example, see any general differences between the stories men tell and the stories women tell (and, for each, between stories told about men and stories told about women)? Can you find a system for classifying the stories—for example, by purpose or by who is telling the stories or who the stories are about? If you can classify the stories into types, can you characterize the differences between the types? In general, how would you describe the similarities and differences between the stories that come up in conversations and written profiles like those you've read?

2. Profiles inform readers about people, but they do so in a different way than does the biography, another genre of informative writing about people. To understand what distinguishes profiles, choose an encyclopedia entry on a person who interests you—a politician, scientist, artist, composer, writer, or sports figure. Such entries are essentially short biographies. Encyclopedias such as Encyclopedia Brittanica, Colliers, and World Book are available in your library in print or on-line versions.

   Compare the encyclopedia entry to the profile of Dr. Susan Love in "A Surgeon's War on Breast Cancer." Note the information that is included in—and excluded from—the two writings. Note also the arrangement of information (refer back to the analysis of the profile of Love.) How do the profile and the encyclopedia entry differ in these respects? Why do you think the respective writers have chosen the informational and organizational pattern they use? What do the differences between the two writings tell you about profiles as a genre?

3. Profile writers invariably make choices about how much emphasis to give to description and how much to interpretation. They need vivid description to bring their subject to life for readers, and they need interpretation to provide readers with a perspective on their subject. In the most successful profiles, description and interpretation complement each other and together contribute to the profile's creation of a dominant impression. Compare the way Molly O'Neill, Mike Rose, and Jon Garelick balance the need to bring their subjects to life and the need to provide commentary about their subject's significance. What are the main differences and similarities among their profiles in this regard? How are these differences and similarities related to the overall purpose of their profiles?

DESIGNING DOCUMENTS: Advertising and Publicity That Use Profiles

In the selection by Mike Rose you saw how profiles can be used to make a larger point. Advertising and publicity frequently make use of profiles. In such cases the profiles are quite definitely serving to make a larger point—they serve to promote an organization and possibly its products and to convey a message by and often about the organization. As you'll see from the three pieces included in this section, this fundamental difference in intended function significantly affects the profiles—both the information that is given about profile subjects and the way the information is expressed. Another important difference between these profiles and the others you read is that in these design plays a much more important role. Although the O'Neill selection as originally printed in the newspaper included a photo, in these selections photos are a major element and photos, graphic elements, layout, and text interact to make a point as effectively as possible.

• **Pfizer ad** Notice that the Pfizer ad is not trying to sell a product. Instead, it's trying to sell the public on the work and reputation of a leading biomedical company and thus on the need for health care legislation of a sort that would be favorable to the company. Notice also that, in terms of design, this is a two-page spread with four main elements: a photo on the left, text on the right, and, on the page with text, an opening quote and a closing logo and slogan. Think about the relationship between the photo and the text and about the relationship between the profile and the larger message.

• **Class Notables** At first glance, "Class Notables," from the alumni magazine Stanford, may appear to be largely informative—giving quick sketches of what four Stanford alumni are doing with their lives. Yet as readers read the page, they are getting not just information about these individuals but also an image of Stanford the university. Notice that two photos of different types are used—a conventional photo with borders and a photo with the text wrapping around it. This second photo is centered, and the text that wraps around it isn't just about its subject, so in a sense this photo, along with the initial heading in large type, serves to pull the four profiles together into a coherent piece that's ultimately about Stanford. As you read these profiles, think about what their individual and combined effect is and about how you might respond to the profiles if you were an alumnus reading the magazine.

• **Imar Hernandez and the Shame in Our Nation's Capital** The third piece, a New York Times advertisement paid for by the Service Employees International Union, uses the profile of Imar Hernandez to publicize the plight of janitors and to build suppport for labor law reform. Notice that, in terms of design, this ad has basically the same four elements as the Pfizer ad: a photo (this time on the right), text (this time on the left), set-off material at the top of the page over the text (with the first lie in this case also extending over the photo), and a closing element (combining a slogan, a graphic, and the organization name). As with the Pfizer ad, think about the relationship between the photo and the text and about that between the profile and the larger message. Think about the similarities and differences between the two pieces.

DISCUSSION AND ACTIVITIES

1. Re-read the Pfizer ad and then answer the following questions.
   a. Text: What is the basic message of the text? How do each of the following function to contribute to this message: the quote and first two paragraphs of the text? the third paragraph? the fourth paragraph? Why does the text end with a closing quote, instead of just ending after the fourth paragraph? What is the relationship between the opening and closing quotes? Find some words that help strengthen the message.
   b. Profile: What kind of information is given about Johnny Moore? What is a technique used to make the profile more immediate? What is the dominant impression created? How does the profile contribute to the message? Why was Johnny Moore chosen as subject of the profile?
   c. Design: Is the photo effective in capturing the reader's attention? How do the opening quote and closing logo and slogan work together?
   d. Effectiveness: What image of Pfizer does this ad project? How effective are the profile, the text of which it's a part, and the overall design in conveying this image and the intended message? Explain your answer.

Class Notables

A sampling of Class Notes from a cross section of years and places.

Ronald J. Nachman, PhD '81, (below, right) won the Arthur S. Flemming Award for his scientific achievements developing environmentally safe pesticides. He is working for the Department of Agriculture at Texas A&M, where he develops chemicals that mimic insects' natural

internal chemicals, or neuropeptides. The artificial neuropeptides disrupt insect digestion and reproduction processes, and this either kills the bugs or makes them inefficient enough to be harmless to crops. His work will reduce the harmful effects of the corn earworm, which is one of the most destructive agricultural pests in the world, as well as locusts and cockroaches. He works in collaboration with researchers in Japan, England and Sweden, and hopes to have the new pesticide available for world use in five years.

Chatty Collier Eliason, '59, has been showing horses for 17 years. Her horse, Runnin' Late, is her first world champion. Runnin' Late became the world champion amateur 3-year-old halter gelding, and the world champion open

3-year-old halter gelding at the American Quarter Horse World Championship Show in Oklahoma City, which hosted approximately 2,500 horses. Chatty has loved horses since she was a child and she rode while at Stanford. She now shows horses in 40 competitions a year around the country and also spends time fundraising for Stanford.

Amy Gillett, '92, is on a fellowship at the U.S. Embassy in Prague, where she is currently gathering information for the State Department's annual human rights report. She returned home in July after a year researching the history of gypsies. In her free time, she collects ceramic pigs and, after adding Slavic swine to her collection, may have enough to open a pig museum. She has been acquiring pigs for 10 years and has Russian, Italian and Belgian swine in her international drove.

Josh Allen, '92, (below) is making a name for himself in the St. Louis, Mo., area. After graduation, he spent 2 ½ years working for bakeries and specialty grocers in the Bay Area to gain expertise in the art of bread-making. Last year, he and his brother-in-law opened Companion Baking Company, which specializes in thick-crusted European hearth breads. The company focuses primarily on wholesale bread sales in St. Louis, but Josh hopes that their retail market will expand as their breads gain popularity.

INMAR HERNANDEZ AND THE SHAME IN OUR NATION'S CAPITAL.

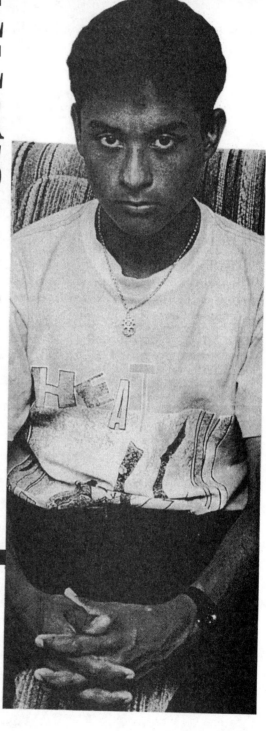

Inmar Hernandez is no ordinary 19-year-old. Since immigrating to this country five years ago, he's been working nights as an office building janitor in downtown Washington, DC to help support his family. During the day, he's been attending Wilson High School and he's graduating this year.

In June, 1992, Inmar and 11 of his co-workers were fired for trying to organize a union in two office buildings where they worked. Inmar worked in an office building owned by wealthy developer Nathan Landow at 1200 G Street. Pritchard Industries, a huge national cleaning contractor, was paying Inmar $4.80 an hour, with no sick days, vacation days, health insurance or holidays.

It took eight months for the National Labor Relations Board (NLRB) to issue a complaint alleging that Pritchard illegally fired Inmar and his co-workers. Rather than go to trial, the company offered back pay and reinstatement. But it took until late May, 1993 for the back wages to be paid. And the 12 still haven't been called back to work.

Inmar couldn't wait, so he took another job working for $5 an hour for Executive Building Maintenance at 1050 Connecticut Avenue. It's a ritzy building owned by a partnership controlled by developers Albert Abramson, Theodore Lerner and their families. Every night, after the rich and powerful of Washington finish dining at Duke Zeibert's Restaurant on the second floor, Inmar goes to work cleaning swank law offices on the fifth floor. On his list are the offices of Arent, Fox, the law firm which represents the Apartment and Office Building Association, an organization of cleaning contractors and downtown building owners which has waged a 5-year anti-union campaign against the janitors.

It's an outrageous shame in our nation's capital. And it's going on in every big city in North America.

Inmar Hernandez is one more reason why we need

LABOR LAW REFORM NOW!

JUSTICE FOR JANITORS DAY IS JUNE 15TH

SERVICE EMPLOYEES INTERNATIONAL UNION, AFL-CIO, CLC

2. Re-read the "Class Notables" selection and then answer the following questions.
   a. Profiles: What kind of information do these profiles contain? Why do you think this particular combination of people was used? What dominant impression of Stanford alumni do they give when considered together? How do these profiles differ from the others in this section? How might these differences relate to the differences in intended audience and purpose?
   b. Design: The two photographs are quite different from each other and have a different visual relationship to the text. Why do you think these two particular photos were chosen and used in this way?
   c. Effectiveness: What are the purposes of a piece like this and of alumni magazines in general? How effective do you think these profiles are in accomplishing these purposes? Explain your answer.

3. Re-read the piece from the Service Employees International Union and answer the following questions.
   a. Text: What are some specific words and phrases that help underscore the message of the selection?
   b. Profile: What kind of information is given about Inmar Hernandez? What is the dominant impression created? What function does the profile play in conveying the overall message of the piece? Compare the function of the profile here and in the Pfizer ad. Why is Hernandez more crucial here than Moore was there?
   c. Design: As mentioned, the design of this piece is similar to and yet different from that of the Pfizer ad. Compare the two designs. Hernandez is more central to the message here than Moore is to the message there. How might that difference be reflected in the design? Be sure to take into account the photos (including their placement in relation to the text) and the opening material above the text.
   d. Effectiveness: How effective are the profile, the text, and the design in conveying the intended message? Explain your answer.

4. Look through recent magazines and newspapers for other advertisements and public relations pieces that make use of profiles. Bring two or three examples to class. Work together in a group with several other students. Discuss the dominant impression that is created and the techniques that are used to create this dominant impression. Why did the business or organization want to create this dominant impression? How does the person profiled establish a public image for the group or organization? Decide which pieces are most effective—in terms of their use of the profile and their design—and why they are the most effective.

5. Compose your own piece of publicity for a particular group, organization, or cause. Depending on your teacher's directions, work individually or in a group with two or three other students to design a full-page or two-page layout that uses a profile of an individual (or individuals) to convey the desired message and image. Your purpose is to build public support for your group—to project a positive image and influence public opinion. Plan carefully so that your publicity piece will effectively accomplish this purpose. Remember that design is as important as text. When you have finished, bring the piece of publicity to class and be prepared to explain why you chose the person (persons) you did and how the profile is meant to represent the group.

GOING ON-LINE

Visiting Corporate and Non-Profit Web Sites

Most major companies, such as Microsoft, Nike, and Time-Warner, and non-profit organizations such as the Sierra Club and [the American Bar Association], now maintain and update Web sites. As more and more people surf the Web, these sites are taking on increased importance as means of publicity and public relations. Their function is not simply to sell more products or inform people about an organization's activities, but also to project a public image, using the multimedia capacities of the Web to characterize the company or organization. In this respect, Web site designers attempt to create dominant impressions, just as profile writers do. Visit the Web site of a company, organization, or group that interests you and prepare a brief report—oral, print, or electronic, depending on your teacher's directions—that describes the dominant impression the Web site seeks to create and lists several features of the site that help project this impression.

ASSIGNMENTS

WORKING TOGETHER: Analyzing celebrity profiles

For this assignment, work together in groups of three or four. Each group should pick a different magazine that regularly features profiles of stars and celebrities (e.g., People, Us, Rolling Stone, Spin, TV Guide, and Soap Opera Digest).

First, each group member should read through five or six issues of the magazine. Take notes on the following:

- What kinds of people are featured in profiles?

- How are they portrayed?

- What does the magazine seem to think is interesting and important to readers?

- How does the magazine represent success, fame, and the good life?

Next, use these notes to prepare a written or oral report that analyzes the magazine's profiles.

Finally, present oral reports or circulate written reports among all class members. As a class, consider the differences and similarities in how the various magazines treat celebrity profiles. How would you account for differences? To what extent do they point to differences in the targeted audiences of the various magazines? To what extent do similarities point to wider shared values about what it means to be a celebrity?

CALL TO WRITE: PROFILES

WRITING ASSIGNMENT

Choose a person (or a group of people) and write a profile. You should choose someone who is primarily interesting to you and whose social role, distinctive character, unusual job, or prominence in his or her field will interest readers as well. The point of this assignment is to bring that person to life in writing, so you can learn more about your subject while helping your readers to see and understand what makes your subject worth reading about. The subject you choose for your profile may teach you something about yourself; for instance, you may be able to clarify why this person or group has had a profound influence on your life and the culture around you (and this influence may be positive or negative). Likewise, you may find that a particular group of readers may have an interest at stake in learning about a subject that interests you; in this case, your call to write a profile can grow from your readers' need to know. Often profiles are based on observing and interviewing, but as the reading selections indicate, writers also produce profiles drawn from memory, as in the case of Mike Rose's "I Just Wanna Be Average," or from the public record, as in the case of the eulogy to Kurt Cobain. Here are some possibilities to help you think about whom you might profile:

- Choose someone with an interesting or unusual career or hobby—an AIDS educator, a baseball card collector, an antique dealer, a forest ranger, a web site designer.

- Choose someone whose profile will illustrate a larger social issue— a recent immigrant to the United States, a senior citizen, an environmental activist, a consumer advocate, a community organizer, a gang member. Consider submitting this profile to a paper or newsletter interested in addressing such social issues.

- Choose a local personality—a politician, writer, musician, artist, athlete, newspaper editor or columnist—or someone prominent on your own campus—a coach, administrator, distinguished teacher, well known scholar. Your community or campus newspaper might publish your profile, if you write it with your local readership in mind.

- Follow Mike Rose's example in "I Just Wanna Be Average," and compose a series of personality sketches, from memory or from interviews, that illustrates some larger point or controlling theme.

- Choose someone of public interest who has died recently and write a eulogy that makes a judgment about the meaning of that person's life.

INVENTION

FINDING A SUBJECT

Take some time to decide on the person (or persons) you want to profile. Don't limit yourself to people you know well, or whose job, hobby, or social role is familiar to you. Writing a profile offers an opportunity to learn about something new and it will allow you to bring a fresh perspective to that subject. Take some risks in compiling your list, include some people or groups that you would not contact in the course of a typical day. Likewise, take some risks in making your decision - the more you stretch, the more you can learn.

1. Make a list Make a list of people who, for one reason or another, interest you. Try to come up with a list of at least ten people. This will give you some choices. If you have trouble thinking of that many, use some memory triggers like thinking through the different periods of your life, or across the different hobbies you have had, or create a list based on the kinds of jobs your relatives hold. What have been the major turning points in your life? What kind of people impacted you during those times? If all else fails, run through each letter of the alphabet and come up with a name or group to match it.

2. Talk to others Meet with two or three other students in your class, to share the lists each of you have developed and to get some feedback and advice about which people seem to be the most promising as subjects for profiles. Knowing what you know about profiles from the readings in this chapter, which people or groups on each list seem the most promising? Ask the other students you are working with to tell you which people are most interesting to them, why, and what they would like to know about your potential subjects. Make sure you write down what they say, since their comments will help you decide on interview questions later.

3. Decide tentatively on a subject Use the feedback you have received to help you make a tentative decision about which subject you will profile. Rank your top three choices at this point, since your first choice might not be available for interviewing. In that case, you can try someone else. When you rank your choices, take your partners' reasons for being interested in one person or another into account; remember, they may have different motives and interests than you do.

4. Contact your subject Unless you are writing a eulogy or a personality sketch from memory, you need to contact your subject to arrange an interview. For many, this is the hardest part of writing a profile—making the first phone call. Explain that you're a student working on an assignment in a writing course. You'll be amazed—and reassured—by how helpful and gracious most people will be. If they don't have time, they'll tell you so, and then you can go back to your list and try your second choice. Most likely, however, you'll be able to schedule a time to meet and talk with the person. Ask the person if he or she can suggest anything you might read or research as background information before the interview to help you prepare for it.

At this point, too, it may be helpful for you to sketch out a schedule for yourself. To write this profile, you will need to allow time for several stages of both research and writing. For some guidance with managing multi-faceted projects such as this one, try following the example of the "Task Breakdown Chart" described in Chapter 3 (see page XXX).

CLARIFYING YOUR PURPOSE

Write a brief statement of purpose. This can be helpful preparation for an interview or as exploratory writing for a profile from memory or a eulogy.

EXERCISE

Take fifteen minutes to answer the following questions:
- Why are you interested in the particular person you're profiling? What is your attitude toward the person? Why do you want to profile this person?
- What do you already know about the person and his or her job, hobby, political or community activity, social role?
- What do other people think about the person you're writing about? Do you share these views? What makes your perspective on this person unique?
- What do you expect to find out by interviewing and observing the person?
- What is your purpose in profiling this particular person?

RESEARCH

Whether you're planning an interview, writing from memory, or composing a eulogy, it will help to do some background research. The nature of this research, of course, will vary depending on the person (or persons) you're profiling. Your subject may have suggested some things to read before you meet with him or her. If you're doing a eulogy of a public personality, there should be material available in your college library or on the Web.

Most likely, you will need to interview your subject. This can take time, so plan your research schedule accordingly. You will need to decide, for example, given the time available to complete this assignment, what the scope of your research will be—whether it's a single observation/ interview, an interview and follow-up, or a series of observations and interviews over a period of time.

You will also need to decide whether you plan to tape record the interview. There are considerable advantages to taping interviews. For one thing, taping frees you from the need to write during the interview, so you can devote your attention to the person you're profiling. If you plan to tape, you must, of course, ask the person's permission either when you set up the interview, or before the interview begins.

Preparing for an interview

The main point in preparing for an interview is to decide what you want to learn from your subject. One good way to do this is to write out a list of preliminary questions. The questions news reporters ask offer useful guidelines in framing these preliminary questions (these questions are sometimes known as "The 5 W's").

GUIDELINES FOR INTERVIEW QUESTIONS

Who? Ask the person you're interviewing to tell you something about his or her background, influences, training, and so on.

What? Ask the person to explain the nature of what it is he or she does. Try to elicit stories from the person you're interviewing.

Where? Ask the person about the setting in which he or she does what he or she does. What is the significance of this setting?

When? Ask the person to explain the circumstances that call on him or her to do what he or she does. When do these circumstances occur?

Why? Ask the person to explain his or her most important motivation. What form does this motivation take?

How? Ask the person to describe the processes of what she or he does. What particular techniques, procedures, or skills are involved

DURING THE INTERVIEW

It is unusual for interviews to proceed systematically through a series of questions like these. What happens more often is that interviews turn out to be fluid and freewheeling conversations. A single question such as "Tell me something about your background and how you came to do what you're doing" may be enough to generate an hour of talk. Nonetheless, preparing such questions in advance helps keep the focus on the person being interviewed by offering invitations to talk. And finally that's the point of an interview—to get your subject to explain what he or she knows. In general, interviewers should take a low profile and listen. Let the conversation take its own course and be prepared for ideas, themes, and issues to emerge that you had not anticipated. When and if it does happen, go with the line of conversation, and follow up on questions that seem interesting to you.

AFTER THE INTERVIEW

After the interview is over, make sure you give yourself time to write some notes. These notes can provide material to add vivid detail to your profile and to build a dominant impression of your subject. Follow the suggestions below to shape your post-interview notes.

GUIDELINES FOR INTERVIEW NOTES

1. Describe in as much detail as possible what the person you interviewed looks like, what he or she was wearing, how he or she moved around in the particular setting, how he or she interacted with other people on the scene, and anything else that seems striking.
2. Describe the setting in which the interview occurred, particularly if you met with the person in his or her place of work.
3. If you tape recorded the interview, transcribe the tape. Otherwise, use your notes to reconstruct dialogue. Keep vocal mannerisms intact as much as possible, and make special note of memorable phrases the interviewee might have used.
4. What was the most important thing you discovered? Try to write it in a sentence, then try to explain more about it in a paragraph.
5. What, if anything, seemed contradictory or incongruous in your encounter with the person? Jot down a quick explanation for why it seemed odd.
6. In what ways did the person confirm your preconceptions? What surprised you?
7. What larger ideas, themes, or issues were raised in the interview?

PLANNING

ESTABLISHING PERSPECTIVE FROM THE BEGINNING

When writing a profile, you will need to establish a perspective that offers your readers a point of view on the person (or persons) you're writing about. As discussed on page XX, it is this perspective that separates profile from biography. The beginning of your profile is a particularly important place to do this. The strategy you use to design an opening will depend both on your material and on the attitude you want your readers to have toward your subject. Here are some techniques for establishing perspective in a profile:

• scene setting: describe the place where you encounter your subject; give details about the physical space; describe other people who are there; explain what the people are doing; set the stage for your subject's entrance. (See opening of Molly O'Neill's "A Surgeon's War on Breast Cancer" for an example.)

• tell an anecdote: narrate an incident that involves your subject; describe how your subject acts in a revealing situation. (See opening of Jon Garelick's "Kurt Cobain 1967-94" for an example.)

- use a quotation: begin with your subject's own words; use a particularly revealing, provocative, or characteristic statement. (Notice use of quotation throughout Garelick's profile of Cobain.)

- describe your subject: use description and detail about your subject's appearance as an opening clue to the person's character. (See openings of both O'Neill's profile of Susan Love and Garelick's profile of Cobain.)

- describe a procedure: follow your subject through a characteristic routine or procedure at work; explain the purpose and technical details; use to establish your subject's expertise. (See opening of profile of Susan Love.)

- statement of controlling theme: establish perspective by stating in your own words a key theme that will be developed in the profile. (See opening of Mike Rose's "I Just Wanna Be Average" for an example.)

ARRANGING YOUR MATERIAL

You most likely have a lot of information about your subject now, so to trick is to arrange it in a way that will help you create a dominant impression of your subject. Remember that the purpose of a profile is to capture your subject at a particular moment in time and to take your readers into your subject's world. With as much information as you have gathered, this can be a daunting task. Here are some suggestions for beginning to shape that material into a text creating a dominant impression.

- Inventory the material you have to work with. Look over your notes and notice how many separate items about your subject you have. These are the building blocks of your profile, the raw material that you will put together to construct your profile. Label each item according to the kind of information it contains—physical description, biographical background, observed actions and procedures, revealing incidents or anecdotes, direct quotes, things you have read, things other people have told you, and so on.

  Writing a profile involves combining various elements (or raw materials) from a person's life and activities to create a dominant impression. It is quite likely that you will have more material than you can use in your profile, so don't worry if you can't fit everything in.

- Decide on a tentative arrangement of your material. Once you have inventoried the material you have to work with, the task is now to decide on an effective arrangement. Notice that the profiles you've read do not rely on just chronological form to present their subjects. The reason is that a strict chronological arrangement ("First, Dr. Love did this," "next, she did that") can get boring for readers and makes it difficult for writers to emphasize key points. Chronology is more appropriate for a biography that gives readers an overview of a person's life rather than a profile that seeks to create a dominant impression by capturing a moment in time.

  Molly O'Neill and Mike Rose use quite different arrangement patterns in their profiles. O'Neill uses open form to present clusters of information about Dr. Susan Love, while Rose uses claim and evidence to present a main point and then illustrate it with individual profiles, as noted in the analyses of these sections. You can find descriptions of other common arrangement techniques in Chapter 4, particularly those sections on "Analyzing" (see pages XXX).

WORKING DRAFT

By this time you have gathered a lot of material - from your interview, and from anything you might have read before or after the interview — and you have probably gotten some new insight into the person or group you are profiling. Now that you have learned something new, your challenge is to teach someone else by writing up the information into a profile. Your working draft gives you the opportunity to do that.

Right now, your task will be to shape the information you have gathered into a coherent form. The arrangement of your material will depend, of course, on your purpose in writing the profile. Do you want to use open form to create a dominant impression of your subject by presenting loosely arranged clusters of information? If so, what order will best enable you to establish a perspective for your readers? Or do you want to use your profile to illustrate a main point? If so, how can you make sure to present the main point clearly and then show how the profile or profiles give readers meaningful illustrations of the point? Look back at the statement of purpose for this assignment, and decide which organizational scheme might best help you achieve your purpose. For help thinking of other organizational forms you might use, take a look at page XXX in "XXX."

After you have arranged the information you have gathered into a coherent form, you might work through some of the suggestions below for Paragraph Development and for Beginnings and Endings. These sections offer you possibilities for revising parts of your profile before sharing it with your writing partners.

PARAGRAPH DEVELOPMENT: Comparing and Contrasting

By this time you probably have a lot of good information about the person you profiled in your interview notes, and following a pattern of development might be a good way to shape that information into your written profile. Sometimes that shaping is easier said than done; after all, there is a psychological dimension of paragraph development. Readers look, often unconsciously, for a pattern of development in each paragraph—some ordering system that weaves the sentences into a pattern of meaning. When a clearly recognizable pattern is present in a paragraph, readers can concentrate on the content of the paragraph—to think about what you are saying rather than how you are saying it. On the flip side, readers can get easily confused when the writer has not provided a recognizable pattern of development. One such pattern is comparison and contrast, in which writers draw attention to features in their subjects that are similar and dissimilar from others to help illustrate their points.

Jon Garelick, for example, tries comparing and contrasting the death of various rock stars to the death of Kurt Cobain. In the paragraph that follows, Garelick sounds like he is trying to make sense of his own reaction to the death, and he brings the readers into his mind by sharing the process of his comparison and contrast.

"Perhaps we were most shocked by our sense of shock. At the time, I couldn't imagine another rock star's death that would affect me so profoundly. Bono? Eddie Vedder? Paul Westerberg? Is it simply because I like his songs the most? That I've written most about him, "studied" him the most in my own rock-crit way? What other comparisons were there? We were more or less prepared for Frank Zappa's death. The jazz gods I worshipped - Mingus, Ellington, Dizzy Gillespie - were likewise in physical decline when they died."

Later, Garelick picks up the comparing and contrasting development pattern again.

"The only parallel that fits, and the one that Baby Boom rock crits have been throwing at Gen Xers all week, is that of John Lennon. It's a more unlikely and awkward parallel than the Boomers will allow, but there it is. Cobain himself told Fricke that Lennon was his favorite Beatle, saying with a laugh, "He was obviously disturbed." Cobain wasn't nearly as famous .... Nirvana's influence has been massive, but not on a par with the Beatles. And yet it's that same loss, that same sense of disbelief, and the shock at the violence of his passing.

There is, of course, anger as well. Lennon didn't choose his own death."

EXERCISE

If you think comparing and contrasting might work in your profile, but you can't think of a way to do it off the top of your head, try the following exercise.
- Put aside the information you have gathered on the person or people you are profiling.
- Think about a person who might be in some way similar to your subject. It might be a person who plays a similar social function, or it might be a person who just reminds you of your subject for some

other reason. Write down as many reasons for the similarities as you can think of. At the same time, you may realize more differences between them - so note those down, too.

- Think about the person or group who seems to stand for the opposite of the person or group you are profiling. List as many of the differences as you can, and in the process you might realize some similarities. Keep track of those as well, especially if they surprise you.
- Make a list of inanimate objects that you might be able to use to describe your person or group: a kitchen table, a Model T Ford, a biology textbook. As above, keep track of the features your subject as in common with that object, and where the analogy falls flat.

Although Comparing and Contrasting can be a technique that works well under certain circumstances, you may also want to be careful about the mis-use of comparisons. In the section on "Logical Fallacies" in Chapter 2, you can find a cautionary note about using "false analogies" and comparisons in ways that can be misleading. Depending on the type of profile you are writing, you might also want to consider some of the strategies offered in other chapters.

- see "Describing" (page XXX in "Letters") if you want to try more exercises to elicit more detail about your subject
- see "Narrating" (page XXX in "Memoirs") to tell a story or relate some anecdotes
- see "Defining" (page XXX in "Public Documents") to explain to your reader a new concept that is crucial to understanding something important about the subject of your profile

Once you have developed some of your paragraphs with a discernible pattern of development, you might turn your attention to different ways to begin and end your profile. Some suggestions have already been offered in this chapter on page XX, but you may find that none of those choices allow you to do what you want to do to establish the desired perspective. Below, then, is another suggestion. Additionally, if you found the comparing and contrasting exercise helpful, but you aren't sure where to use it in your profile, consider rewriting your beginning or ending to use some new insight you might have just gained.

BEGINNINGS AND ENDINGS: Framing with a Metaphorical Anecdote

On page XX, you saw a list of possibilities for establishing perspective in your profile. One of those might be working so well for you that you have decided to stick with it. On the other hand, you might want to see if a different strategy might help you achieve your purpose more effectively. There's no harm in trying different options in order to see which one works the best for you, for your reader, and for your purpose.

One possibility to consider is to begin your profile with an anecdote that doubles as a metaphor or an analogy for your person or group. You have already read about beginning your profile with an anecdote on page XX, and this strategy builds on that concept, by adding the unifying force of metaphor to the power of anecdote. Metaphors (sometimes also called analogies) draw your readers' attention to particular features of your subject; you may have noticed this if you worked through the exercise in which you compare your person to an inanimate object. They are powerful because they focus attention on some features while diverting attention away from others. They also leave a lasting impression. Molly O'Neill's profile for example, ends with a metaphor that Dr. Susan Love has created:

"'You see, the gene is like a robber in the neighborhood,' she said. 'We have the neighborhood roped off. Now all we have to do is knock on every single door.'"

Because of the metaphor of the robber in the neighborhood, readers can better visualize Love's appraisal of current breast cancer research. Metaphor, then, creates a visual interpretation in addition to a textual one; using language in this way cements a stronger image and further reinforces the points you may be making in your writing. Used selectively, metaphors can be among the most powerful tools at your disposal. They can literally help readers see something they would not have seen otherwise.

Several of the readings in this chapter begin their profiles by using metaphors interwoven with anecdotes. As already discussed, Garelick's eulogy for Kurt Cobain begins with a story from a concert, in which he describes a recurring theme of protectiveness and vulnerability amidst chaos and violence. This theme, as it turns out, runs through most of the profile. More obviously, however, Mike Rose establishes a metaphor about water early on in his anecdotes about his own educational background. The metaphor of bobbing in the water surfaces throughout the paragraph:

"Students will float to the mark you set. I and the others in the vocational classes were bobbing in pretty shallow water."

and the paragraph ends with

"But mostly the teachers had no idea of how to engage the imaginations of us kids who were scuttling along at the bottom of the pond."

If these ideas for beginnings still don't seem to work for you, try looking through the suggestions for "Beginnings and Endings" in other chapters. Choose the strategy that best helps you establish the right perspective for your profile.

- see "Using an Echo Effect to Reframe" (page XXX in "Letters") to reinforce a running theme in your profile
- see "Pointing Out Significance or Wider Consequences" (page XXX in "Memoirs") to establish the social importance of your profile
- see "Replacing a Common View with an Alternative Perspective" (page XXX in "Commentary") to shake up your readers views on your subject and catch their attention

PEER COMMENTARY

Exchange drafts with a partner. Respond in writing to these questions about your partner's draft:

- Describe what you see as the writer's purposes. Does the working draft create a dominant impression? Does it state a main point or imply one? Explain how and where the draft develops a dominant impression (and main point, if pertinent).

- Describe the working draft's arrangement. Divide the draft into sections by grouping similar paragraphs together. Explain how each section contributes to the overall impression the profile creates. Do you find the arrangement easy to follow? Does the arrangement seem to suit the writer's purposes? If there are rough spots or abrupt shifts, indicate where they are and how they affected your reading.

- Consider how effective the beginning and ending of the draft are. What suggestions would you make to strengthen the impact, increase the drama, or otherwise improve these two sections of the draft? Is there a different type of strategy the writer should use?

- Do you have other suggestions about how the writer could enhance the profile? Are there details, reported speech, descriptions, or incidents that the writer could emphasize? Are there elements you think the writer should cut?

REVISING

Use the peer commentary to do a critical reading of your draft. Are your purposes coming across clearly and emphatically? Does the draft seem to create the kind of dominant impression you intended? If you are presenting a main point, was it clear to your reader? Are there ways to enhance its presentation? Consider too how your reader has analyzed the arrangement of your profile. Notice in particular how the commentary has divided the draft into sections. Do these sections correspond to the way you wanted to arrange the profile? Are there ways to rearrange material to improve the overall effect of the profile? What did your writing partners suggest?

Once you have gotten feedback from your writing partners, you might want to turn your attention to some techniques that will make your profile easier for your readers to follow. Take a look through the categories below, and see if your writing might benefit from the use of more (and better) transitions. After that, you might experiment with some different sentence structures, and then you can check your pronoun usage just to make sure it is always clear who you are talking about throughout your profile.

CONNECTIONS AND COHERENCE: Spatial Transitions

Transitions help readers see the relationship between the sentences in a paragraph, to the relationship between two or more paragraphs. They offer signposts that help readers anticipate how what they are about into what they have just finished reading. In this chapter we will look at transitions that help readers follow the writing from place to place; these are called spatial transitions. For more on transitions, see the sections on temporal transitions, leading readers through different points in time, (page XX in "Memoirs") and logical transitions for leading readers through arguments (page XX in "Reviews").

Transitions that mark spatial relationships often appear in descriptive paragraphs that seek to locate the reader in a particular place. Below is a brief passage from Molly O'Neill's profile of Susan Love, in which O'Neill describes the accessories on Dr. Love's lab coat. Notice how the spatial transitions help you walk through a guided tour of the scene in your mind, as you follow the directions within the text: from "on the coat" to "under the necklace" to "above an earring."

"The lab coat she wore was a bulletin board of buttons. 'Keep abreast,' read one. 'Get a second opinion.' On another: 'T.G.I.F. (Thank God I'm Female).' Under the string of fat white pearls around her neck was a gold chain with an ankh, an ancient symbol of life. Above one of the gold Chanel-style earrings was a tiny labrys, the mythical double-bladed ax used by Amazons."

The following are some of the most common spatial transitions that you may use in your own writing:

near, next to, alongside, facing, adjacent, far beyond, away, off in the distance, between, through up, down, across, above, below, inside, outside.

WRITERS WORKSHOP

Richard Quitadamo wrote the following profile "A Lawyer's Crusade against Tobacco" for a course that focused on the politics of public health. Quitadamo plans on becoming a lawyer and wanted to find out more about the kind of work lawyers do in the public interest, particularly in the area of product liability. What appears here is Quitadamo's working draft, followed by his questions for a peer commentary. Read the draft, keeping in mind that it is work in progress. Then consider how you would respond to the questions Quitadamo raises in his note.

A Lawyer's Crusade against Tobacco
(working draft)

The office of the Tobacco Product Liability Project (TPLP) at Northeastern University in Boston is decorated with anti-smoking propaganda. One poster shows the damage that smoking has done to someone's lungs. The office secretary sat at her desk and typed busily, while Edward Sweda, senior attorney of the TPLP, conversed on the phone with Stanton Glantz, author of the well-known expose of the tobacco industry Cigarette Papers.

Sweda seemed fixated on one subject, the recent banning of RJ Reynolds' "Joe Camel" cartoon character from Camel cigarette advertisements. He felt it was a small victory in the ongoing war against smoking. "Look, Stanton, Joe is gone and that's great, but that really doesn't affect the foreign market. It seems the percentage of people outside the US who smoke has risen dramatically. There's got to be something we can do." They talked for a few more moments, and then Sweda hung up the phone.

Edward Sweda, a tall, slender man, with graying hair, turned in his office chair. A button on his sweater read "No Smoking." He began to discuss the history of the war on tobacco and the part he has played in it.

Sweda began his career in 1979 as a local volunteer against cigarette smoking in Massachusetts. "I hated smoking from day one. It was disgusting, and besides it can kill you." In the late 1970s, the dangers of smoking were a novel concept, and industry leaders were quick to cover up the ill effects of smoking. It was also at this time that medical professionals, political activists, and health care advocates began pushing for stronger regulation of tobacco products.

In 1980, Sweda worked in Newton, MA for regulations that would require restaurants to provide at least 15% of its seating to non-smokers. "People have to breathe, and if other people are smoking in close proximity to you, then they are infringing on your right to breathe fresh air. That's a crime. I as a non-smoker really feel strongly about this issue."

Sweda has also worked to stop free samples of cigarettes from being dispersed. "It reminded me of drugs. The first time was free, but after that, you had to pay. I figured I could stop this vicious cycle before it got a chance to start. That's why we eventually formed the TPLP, to use litigation as a tool to make the tobacco industry take responsibility for its actions."

TPLP was established in 1984, and for the following thirteen years Sweda and his associates have battled the tobacco industry. "Tobacco industry knew smoking was bad long before TPLP ever showed up. The first report of the Surgeon General on smoking in 1964 proved that cigarette smoking could have harmful effects on human health." But, Sweda continued, the only thing that the anti-smoking campaign got out of the Surgeon General's report was the Fanning Doctrine, which stated that there must be a comparable number of anti-smoking public service announcements (PSAs) to the number of cigarette advertisements. This doctrine, Sweda said, may or may not have led to the drop off of cigarette sales noticeable between 1966 and 1970.

However, on January 1, 1971, cigarette advertising was banned from TV, and along with them, the anti-smoking PSAs. "At first, I was overjoyed," Sweda said, smiling. "What a fool I was. The tobacco industry used other methods to lure potential smokers to their products, the PSAs were gone, and the levels of smoking increased nationwide. It seemed they could sidestep every regulation we imposed."

As Sweda spoke, his secretary called attention to the flashing computer screen. Sweda rose from his chair and observed the screen. "You see this? This is something I'm working on right now." Sweda was looking at the next date scheduled for hearings of the Massachusetts State Public Health Council on new proposed legislation to force the tobacco industry to disclose their secret ingredients. "What we want to do at this hearing is to make the industry sweat. They failed to block the hearing and were forced to appear. They didn't even testify on their own behalf, and I just kept talking about the list of secret ingredients and the falsified tests. You should have seen their faces."

Yet, Sweda is cautious with his optimism about the future of anti-smoking initiatives. He has seen things go wrong before. The tobacco industry has many influential lobbyists on their side, along with the political backing of tobacco state politicians. They are able to hide information and falsify reports to government officials. This makes the industry virtually untouchable at the federal level. Nonetheless, Sweda said he was more confident this time around. "Things are different in this day and age. People are more educated about the dangers of smoking. With the banning of Joe Camel and the Liggett case of 1996, we seem to be gaining ground on them. The Liggett case is probably the biggest breakthrough in our struggle because it's the first time a tobacco manufacturer cracked and admitted what we've known all along about the health hazards of smoking. And it actually resulted in a settlement."

Sweda paused, then sighed. "But there is still the problem of youth. They seem more susceptible to smoking. Maybe it's the age, maybe it's a rebellion thing, or maybe it's the advertisements. The ads seem to target youth. That's why I'm glad Joe Camel is gone."

The TPLP has been workings with the Federal Drug Administration on a game plan that focuses specifically on the youth smoking problem. The plan centers on keeping youth from smoking through education and other programs. "I hate to admit it, but it seems our best bet for beating smoking and the industry is to forget adult smokers. They've made their decisions, and it's their choice to continue smoking. Cessation programs and medical help groups exist for those who want to quit. But by focusing on youth, we are taking away the customers of the future. This is important because as the older generation of smokers fades away, the tobacco industry will be looking to recruit new smokers."

As Sweda stepped away from the computer, he said, "We'll get them, the industry, that is," and stepped to his desk, picked up the phone, and began to dial a number. This is all in a day's work for Edward Sweda and his TPLP group. They exist to promote public health and stop the growth of the tobacco industry, or as Sweda refers to them, "the merchants of death."

Quitadamo's note on his working draft

I think I do a pretty good job of setting the scene and showing Sweda at work. The guy was a great interview, and I got a lot of good quotes to use. Do these seem effective? Are they easy to understand? Do you need more information at points? Is it clear, for example, what happened in the Liggett case and why anti-smoking people consider it such a huge victory? Any suggestions in this regard would be greatly appreciated.

Another thing I'm not certain about is whether I should give more information about Sweda himself. I don't provide much background information on him or talk about his personal life. I wanted to focus on him mainly as an anti-smoking activist and felt too much biographical detail would distract from this. What do you think?

My last question involves the notorious "dominant impression" we've been talking about in class so much. Do you feel that this draft gives you a strong perspective on the person? I wasn't sure whether I should provide more commentary on my own. I want readers to see Sweda as an embattled crusader but not a fanatic. Does this come across?

WORKSHOP QUESTIONS

1. Consider Richard Quitadamo's first set of questions concerning the information in the draft. Are there places where you felt you needed more information to understand the issues? If so, indicate the passage or passages in question and explain what's not clear to you.

2. Quitadamo's second question focuses on whether he should give more background on Sweda. What is your opinion? To answer this question, take into account what Quitadamo's purpose seems to be in this profile. Would more biographical detail further his purpose or, as he worries, distract from it? Explain your response.

3. As Quitadamo notes, one mark of a successful profile is that it creates a dominant impression of the subject. Explain in your own words the impression of Sweda this draft created for you. Given what you've read here, what kind of person does he seem to be? How well does the impression you've formed match Quitadamo's goals in portraying Sweda? How could Quitadamo strengthen or enhance his portrayal?

WRITER'S INVENTORY

Write an account of how you put your profile together. Explain why you selected the person you wrote about as a subject. Then describe the interview, if you did one. Explain whether the final version of your profile confirmed or modified the initial preconceptions you had about your subject. Finally explain how writing a profile differs from other kinds of writing you have done. What demands and satisfactions are there to writing profiles?

A CLOSING NOTE

Part of the etiquette of writing profiles is to make sure the subject of the profile gets a copy. The purpose is not to get the subject's approval, for the writer will bear the final responsibility for how the writing portrays the person profiled. Still, it is common courtesy to send your subject a copy of the profile, so he or she can see the final results.

CHAPTER
EIGHT

REPORTS:
Informing and Explaining

LOOKING AT THE GENRE

Reports are a genre of writing that presents the results of research. Sometimes report writers are called on to analyze the research, draw conclusions, and make recommendations. Other times, the writer's task is simply to organize information in a useful and accessible way. Consider the following examples of various types of report writing:

- Newspapers report on recently breaking events on the national and international scene, as well as sports, weather, health, entertainment, and so on.

- Feature articles in newspapers and magazines report in greater depth on people, events, and trends. Investigative reporting brings issues to the public's attention that might otherwise go unknown.

- Physicians, psychiatrists, psychologists, and social workers write medical histories and case studies of patients and clients to record key information, provide diagnosis, and develop a plan of treatment or intervention.

- Businesses and government agencies use reports to keep track of ongoing projects, organize background information for policymakers, and recommend new directions. They also issue annual reports to stockholders and taxpayers.

- Governments and private foundations commision panels of experts to research and report on pressing issues. Public opinion polling companies survey and report on current beliefs and attitudes.

- Social, religious, political, and environmental organizations publish newsletters, leaflets, brochures, and research reports to keep their members informed and to influence public opinion.

As these examples show, report writing pervades many spheres of life. And it is likely that you have been writing reports in various subjects since elementary school. Most students are called on at one time or another to write book reports and lab reports. But you may also have reported information in other ways. For example, if you designed a poster for a science fair or a history class, you have been involved in organizing and displaying information by combining written text with graphics. Or you may have been asked to give an oral report on an influential scientist or a famous artist.

The examples listed here take place in quite different settings—from elementary school to the highest echelons of government. Nonetheless, there are characteristic features of report writing that all share. For one thing, reports are based on research. Writers have to go out, in one way or another, to gather information.

The type and range of sources writers draw on will vary, of course, depending on the situation. An eighth-grade student reporting on effects of acid rain, for example, will likely consult an encyclopedia, a textbook, and perhaps the World Wide Web. These sources, however, would be totally inadequate for a team of scientists preparing the literature review section of a report on their latest research on acid rain.

Likewise, research methods will vary. Scientists in modern research labs have access to sophisticated equipment and techniques. National panels and public opinion pollsters often have the resources to do widescale telephone surveys, individual interviews, and focus group sessions. Journalists and investigative reporters have developed contacts over the years that help them get to the heart of a story.

As you can see, the kinds of questions researchers can ask depend on the sources and methods available to them. Looking ahead to the writing assignments in this chapter, you will need to consider carefully what sources and methods are available to you as a researcher, given the practical constraints of time and resources.

A second feature that characterizes the genre of report writing concerns the writer's purpose. The point of gathering information for most reports is to organize it in ways that will inform and explain—and, depending on the situation, draw conclusions and make recommendations based on the data.

For this reason, the focus in a report tends to be placed on the subject rather than on the writer's experience and perceptions. Unlike, say, a memoir, where the reader is asked to share an important and perhaps intimate moment with the writer, report writers' relationship to their readers tends to be more formal, distanced, and impersonal. And unlike other genres, such as commentary, proposals, and reviews, in which the writer's argument is usually introduced early in a prominent position and then followed by evidence to persuade readers, in report writing the evidence normally comes first, followed by the writer's analysis, interpretation, conclusions, and perhaps recommendations. Writers often take positions in reports. But by presenting their main claims after the evidence, report writers create the impression that their conclusions have been suggested by the data itself.

This focus on the subject matter leads us to a third characteristic feature of report writing, and that concerns the writer's tone of voice. Because reports typically focus on the data, the tone of reports tends to be objective. In reports, writers strive to sound objective in the presentation of information and conclusions, not that in any realistic sense can a writer truly be objective. As you will see in the reading selections that follow, report writers are always sifting through and selecting information, according to their sense of what is notable and significant. What readers invariably get in a report is not all the information in the world on a subject but the writer's version of what is most pertinent, given the circumstances, the writer's understanding of readers' needs, and the writer's own values and beliefs.

From this perspective, the objectivity of tone in the writer's voice has to do with the credibility readers invest in the writer as a reliable, honest, and responsible source of information and analysis. If the writer's own views are featured prominently, then readers will sense they are encountering a commentary and not a report. But if the writer is successful in maintaining a focus on the subject and an objective tone, readers are likely to take the data and conclusions seriously, even as they realize that the writer has taken a strong role in shaping the presentation of the material.

The following reading selections will give you some idea of what types of writing fall under the broad category of reports. The readings begin with two news reports from the Associated Press on 30th anniversary commemoration of the Selma to Montgomery civil rights march to see how reporters use different framing devices to highlight a story. The second reading is an academic research report from the field of anthropology "Uncertainty and the Use of Magic" by Richard B. Felson and George Gmelch. The third reading "The Seven-Sided Coin" is the introduction to a report to Congress prepared by the Office of Technology Assessment that analyzes the political situation facing the nuclear power industry. The final reading is an Action Brief on youth violence published by the Michael Harrington Center for Democratic Values and Social Change.

Picture of the Kerner Commision Report

President Lyndon Johnson established the Commission on Civil Disorders (more familiarly known as the Kerner Commission after its chairman, former Illinois governor Otto Kerner) to investigate the causes and consequences of the ghetto up-risings in Watts, Chicago, Cleveland, Newark, Detroit, and forty other American cities. In 1967, issued a report whose words of warning that America was drifting "toward two societies—one black, one white—separate and unequal" have become a touchstone for discussions of race and civil rights in the United States.

REPORT

THE NATIONAL ADVISORY COMMISSION
ON CIVIL DISORDERS

MARCH 1, 1968

READINGS

"Young Blacks See Selma Anniversary as 'Ancient History,' of Little Relevance" and "A Changed Selma Recalls Historic March." Associated Press wire service. March 5, 1995 and March 6, 1995.

These two news reports appeared on the Associated Press wire service in March 1995, at the time of the 30th anniversary of the Selma to Montgomery civil rights march in 1965, led by Martin Luther King, Jr. This 54-mile march, as the news stories explain, was instrumental in passing the Voter Rights Act of 1965, a historic measure which outlawed literacy tests and other means of denying the ballot to black voters in Alabama. As you read the two news reports, you will notice that they contain a good deal of the same information, and yet the frame the event in very different terms. Framing is a device journalists use to give readers a way to make sense of the information in a news report. You can see that the titles of the two news reports frame the commemoration of 1965 march in very different ways.

Young blacks see Selma anniversary as 'ancient history,' of little relevance

SELMA, Ala. (AP) – Every day, Marcus Rush walks by the Byzantine architecture of the Brown Chapel AME Church, where thousands of people once started a 54-mile trek that would change the nation.

Every day, he passes the imposing granite monument on the church's front sidewalk immortalizing the Rev. Martin Luther King Jr., another reminder of the 1965 Selma-to-Montgomery march that inspired passage of the Voting Rights Act.

Still, amid 30th anniversary events and a commemorative march that begins at the church today, the 21-year-old who lives at a public housing project across the street wonders what all the fuss is about.

Even such a momentous episode – guaranteeing blacks access to the ballot booth in a region where they once were slaves – doesn't have much relevance three decades later to a jobless black man.

"I don't know too much about it," Rush said. "That was before my time."

As it was for 32-year-old Lee Marshall, who calls the famous march "ancient history."

"I'm just trying to make it in this world," Marshall said. "I'm just trying to survive before this world comes to an end. It's almost there with some of the things that are going on, the crime and drugs and all that."

The troubles of the day were different on March 7, 1965, as hundreds of protesters set out from the Selma church, attempting to march to the state Capitol in Montgomery for a voting rights demonstration.

Instead, they barely made it out of downtown Selma before getting mauled at the foot of the Edmund Pettus Bridge by a posse of lawmen. The unforgiving use of billy clubs and tear gas provided one of the grimmest, goriest spectacles of the civil rights movement.

Two weeks after "Bloody Sunday" horrified the nation, King and others led a second march authorized by a federal judge and protected by thousands of federal troops.

Later that year, Congress approved the law that ensured blacks would no longer be denied the right to vote through chicanery or intimidation across the South.

"Of all the things that have happened in our lifetime, this is the single most historic piece of legislation ever passed," said Joe Smitherman, a white who was mayor then. Now, drawing a modicum of black support, he's still mayor.

The Rev. Joseph Lowery, president of the Southern Christian Leadership Conference, and U.S. Rep. John Lewis, D-Ga., who suffered a blow to the head on "Bloody Sunday," will be among those participating in today's ceremonies. The commemorative march begins at the church, goes over the bridge again and culminates Saturday at the Alabama Capitol.

"This is a wonderful opportunity that has risen out of a very painful event 30 years ago," said state Sen. Hank Sanders, a black lawyer who stood with the white mayor at an anniversary event.

A changed Selma recalls historic march

■ The mayor, a former segregationist, gives the keys to the city to two men who led the city's famous civil rights march 30 years ago.

SELMA, Ala. (AP) — Led by four black members of Congress, about 2,000 marchers retraced a historic path across a bridge to mark the 30th anniversary of the "Bloody Sunday" voting rights march.

The marchers included Coretta Scott King, Martin Luther King III and Rep. John Lewis, who was beaten bloody by troopers during the first march.

Earlier, two of the men who led the original march received keys to the city from the mayor — then a segregationist, now an ally of blacks.

On March 7, 1965, white lawmen beat and gassed hundreds of marchers trying to cross Edmund Pettus Bridge. Footage of the beatings ran on national television, sparking outrage and leading to passage of the landmark Voting Rights Act, which outlawed literacy tests in many Southern states.

Two weeks later, Martin Luther King Jr. led an even bigger march all the way to the steps of the state Capitol in Montgomery.

Yesterday, a cold rain fell on marchers gathering outside the National Voting Rights Institute to walk once again across the bridge named for a Confederate general. The group also planned to make the 54-mile journey to Montgomery for a rally on Saturday; about 100 of them will walk.

"It's gratifying to see all the changes that have occurred and to see the number of black registered voters and black elected officials in the state of Alabama," said Lewis, a Georgia Democrat.

Still, there was little sense that the battle has been won.

"Once again we're having to fight for our voting rights," said the Rev. Joseph Lowery, president of the Southern Christian Leadership Conference, blasting courts that have struck down majority black congressional districts.

Lowery, Lewis, Jesse Jackson and Rep. Cynthia McKinney, D-Ga., joined in ceremonies at the Brown Chapel AME Church, where the first march also began. McKinney's district is one of those being challenged.

As the marchers passed through downtown, Lewis chatted with a couple of police escorts.

"You didn't have any blacks on the state troopers in 1965," Lewis said. "To see this integrated force here assisting in guarding us, that's gratifying."

Lewis and another leader of the original march, Hosea Williams, received keys to the city from Joe Smitherman, Selma's white segregationist mayor in 1965. He now says he was wrong and continues to hold the top government job in a city with a black majority.

ANALYSIS: Framing Events

News stories seem to be among the most straightforward forms of writing because they appear simply to report on events that have taken place. The news reporter covers a story by going to the scene and telling what he or she sees and what key figures have to say. Sometimes, as in the case of the two news stories on the 30th anniversary of the Selma to Montgomery march for voting rights, the reporter may need to fill in background information so readers can understand the full significance of the event. From this perspective, the basic purpose of news stories is to keep readers informed about current events by transmitting reliable reports of what actually happened.

From another perspective, however, news stories raise important questions about what it means to report on an event such as the anniversary of the civil rights march. As you can see from the two stories, news reporting is not just a matter of telling what has happened. The news has to be produced, put into an intelligible shape by the reporter's writing. One of the key devices reporters use to produce the news is the technique of framing events. Notice how the two news stories frame the event in very different ways—the first distancing the past from the present by portraying the Selma to Montgomery march as "ancient history" and the second emphasizing the changes that have taken place in the thirty years between the march and its commemoration. Much of the information in each story is the same. Nonetheless, readers are offered different versions of the significance of the information.

This is not to say that the reporters are being biased or unprofessional in their stories. It means rather that reports never consist solely of pure data or objective observation. The information in a report only makes sense to readers depending on how the reporter frames it.

FOR CRITICAL INQUIRY

1. Compare the titles of the two news stories. How do they frame the event for readers? How are they likely to influence the way readers understand the event?
2. Notice who is quoted in each of the news stories. How are these quotes likely to shape the way readers understand the event? What differences, if any, do you see in the use of quotes in the two stories?
3. Work in a group with two other students. Decide on a recent event that you all know something about and that interests you. (It could be a campus or local matter. It doesn't have to be a national or international story.) On your own, write a headline and opening one or two paragraphs—just enough to frame the event. Now compare your versions. How do they differ? How are they alike? How is each likely to influence readers' understanding of the event?

Richard B. Felson and George Gmelch. *"Uncertainty and the Use of Magic."*

"Uncertainty and the Use of Magic" presents research by two professors at the State University of New York at Albany, Richard B. Felson and George Gmelch. Originally published in Current Anthropology, one of the leading journals in the field, the article reports research Felson and Gmelch conducted to test Bronislaw Malinowski's famous theory that people use magic to relieve anxiety in situations of uncertainty.

Uncertainty and the Use of Magic[1]

by RICHARD B. FELSON and GEORGE GMELCH
Department of Sociology/Department of Anthropology, State University of New York at Albany, Albany, N.Y. 12222, USA. 18 I 79

Probably the most widely cited theory of magic is that of Malinowski (1948). Malinowski postulated that people resort to magic in situations of chance and uncertainty, where circumstances are not fully under human control. In what has become one of the most frequently cited examples of magic in primitive societies, he described the Trobriand Islanders' use of magic in fishing. On the open sea, where catches were uncertain and there was considerable danger, the islanders used a variety of magical practices. When fishing within the safety and plenty of the inner lagoon, they used none.

A number of other qualitative studies support the relationship between uncertainty and magic within modern, more scientifically oriented societies (e.g., Stouffer et al. 1949, Vogt 1952, MacNiece 1964, Gmelch 1978). The only previous quantitative test of this proposition, however, does not support Malinowski. Lewis (1963) found that the use of magic by American mothers with sick children depended on the mothers' knowledge of medicine and not on the uncertainty or danger of a particular illness. However, Lewis's use of length of illness as the measure of uncertainty is questionable.

According to Malinowski, people use magic to alleviate or reduce the anxiety created by conditions of uncertainty. Through the performance of the appropriate rituals, people "work off" the tensions aroused by fear. An alternative explanation would be that magic results from purely cognitive processes and represents an effort to produce favorable results. In other words, people believe that unknown forces—"good luck" and "bad luck"—play a role in the outcome of events and that these forces can be manipulated by magic.

This study examines these relationships using a sample of American and Irish college students. It considers the use of magic in six activities—gambling, athletics, exam-taking, illness, face-to-face interaction, and dangerous activities—in relation to the degree of uncertainty of each. It investigates the relationship between the use of magic and anxiety within each activity. Finally, it examines students' beliefs about the ability of magic to alleviate anxiety and produce favorable outcomes.

Questionnaires were administered to students in sociology classes in the United States (State University of New York at Albany; $N = 270$) and in the Republic of Ireland (University College, Dublin; $N = 180$). The students in the American sample were primarily urban and from middle-class and either Catholic or Jewish background. The students in the Irish sample were predominantly Catholic, of mainly middle-class background, with as many from small towns and villages as from the city. A list of concepts and the items used to measure them is presented in table 1.

Following Malinowski, we wished to compare activities known to vary in degree of uncertainty. Since it is extremely difficult to construct objective measures of uncertainty, we used independent judges—another group of sociology students ($N = 40$)—to rank the activities according to the degree of uncertainty.

TABLE 1

CONCEPTS AND QUESTIONNAIRE ITEMS USED TO MEASURE THEM

CONCEPT	QUESTIONS ASKED	CODING AND RESPONSES
Use of magic...............	Do you do anything special before or during the following activities in order to give yourself luck? (a) when you're gambling; (b) when you play in a sports contest; (c) when taking an exam; (d) before an important meeting, date, or interview; (e) in regard to something dangerous	1. Yes 0. No Missing Data: I can't answer since I don't engage in this activity
Confidence in efficacy of magic..	How certain are you that such things can bring luck?	1. Certain that they do not affect luck 2. Not at all certain 3. Somewhat certain 4. Very certain
Anxiety about activity.........	How much do you worry about the following? (a) gambling; (b) sports contests; (c) exams; (d) important meetings, dates, or interviews; (e) illness; (f) accidents	1. Not at all 2. A little 3. Very much Missing Data: I haven't engaged in this activity
Belief that magic reduces anxiety	Does it ever make you feel better when you do things to give yourself luck?	1. Yes 0. No Missing Data: I don't do things to give myself luck
Uncertainty..................	For some things it is very certain before you start how well you'll do. For other things it is pretty unpredictable and uncertain. Rank the following in terms of certainty about the outcome you would feel beforehand: when you're involved in a dangerous activity; when you're gambling; when you're ill; when you have an important meeting, date, or interview; when you play in a sports contest; when you're taking an exam	

TABLE 2

PERCENTAGE OF RESPONDENTS WHO REPORT USING MAGIC IN
ACTIVITIES VARYING IN UNCERTAINTY,
CONTROLLING FOR ANXIETY

	ANXIETY							
	U.S.A.				Ireland			
ACTIVITY	High	Medium	Low	Total	High	Medium	Low	Total
Gambling (4.5)[a]...	63	57	39	48	[b]	65	23	33
Dangerous activities (4.4)......	59	40	21	41	61	47	42	49
Exams (3.3)......	45	24	[b]	39	65	48	29	57
Sports (3.1)......	67	34	19	40	36	34	19	26
Face-to-face interaction (2.9).....	42	27	33	35	51	50	13	48
Illness (2.5).......	40	18	16	21	39	26	10	23
Correlation with uncertainty.....	.64	.92	.53	.82	.64	.78	.69	.21
Probability level...	.06	.01	.18	.02	.12	.03	.06	.34

[a] Mean uncertainty rank; a high rank indicates high uncertainty.
[b] Only three American students had low anxiety about exam-taking, and only one Irish student had high anxiety about gambling.

TABLE 3

PERCENTAGE OF USERS AND NONUSERS OF MAGIC REPORTING
VARIOUS DEGREES OF CONFIDENCE IN THE
EFFICACY OF MAGIC

	AMERICANS			IRISH		
DEGREE OF CONFIDENCE	Users (N = 183)	Nonusers (N = 81)	Total	Users (N = 126)	Nonusers (N = 43)	Total
Very certain...........	1	1	2	11	2	9
Somewhat certain......	27	12	23	31	12	26
Not at all certain......	54	46	51	33	28	31
Certain it does not bring luck................	18	41	25	25	58	34

The percentage of students who use magic for each activity and at each level of anxiety is presented in table 2. For the American sample, the correlation between mean uncertainty and mean use of magic over these six activities is quite strong, whether anxiety level is controlled or not. Respondents use more magic for uncertain activities like danger and gambling than they do for more certain activities like illness and exam-taking. For the Irish sample, the overall relationship between mean uncertainty and mean use of magic is slight. However, when anxiety level is controlled, the relationship between uncertainty and magic increases substantially.

For each activity, students who experience more anxiety are more likely to use magic. Contrary to Malinowski's hypothesis, however, the uncertainty of an activity does not have a positive relationship to the amount of anxiety experienced. In fact, this relationship is negative for both samples.

Irish students use more magic than American students in four of the six activities: exam-taking, face-to-face interactions, illness, and dangerous activities. There is also a slight tendency for Americans to use more magic in gambling and sports, although the differences between the two groups are not statistically significant. Frequency distributions for degree of confidence in the efficacy of magic for the total sample and for users and nonusers of magic are presented in table 3. The table indicates very little confidence about the efficacy of magic, even among persons who use it. On the other hand, most students who use magic indicate that it often relieves their anxiety. When asked if it ever made them feel better to use magic, 76% of the Americans and 71% of the Irish who do so answered yes.

This study supports Malinowski's basic notion that people use magic in situations of uncertainty. Students reported using more magic in activities that are relatively uncertain (e.g., gambling) and less in activities that are relatively more certain (e.g., illness). It also supports Malinowski's contention that magic is used to reduce anxiety. For a given activity, the greater the anxiety the students experience, the more magic they use. Furthermore, the students indicated that using magic reduces their anxiety. The evidence, however, does not support the notion that uncertainty results in use of magic because of the anxiety it produces. It appears instead that magic is used under conditions of uncertainty because of a belief in its ability to alter the forces of luck rather than its ability to reduce anxiety.

The fact that a significant amount of magic is used among the college students in our sample suggests that magic is not simply superstitious, irrational behavior confined to primitive peoples. Rather, magic appears to be used in various activities to produce favorable outcomes where other techniques are limited in their effectiveness. Magic is irrational, of course, if one accepts the scientific position that luck is unalterable.

Irish students reported using more magic than Americans in four of the six activities. This is not surprising, given that Ireland is a more traditional society than the United States. However, in two activities, gambling and sports, the Americans appeared to be slightly more likely to use magic than the Irish. This may be due to the fact that gambling and sports are more important and anxiety-producing for Americans.

While most students feel that magic reduces their anxiety, they do not feel as confident that it will produce favorable results. This suggests that many students are merely playing it safe. They are not sure that magic works, but they use it just in case. The cost of performing magic is small, and there is always the possibility that it may help. The lack of strong belief in the efficacy of magic may be one of the major differences between industrialized and primitive societies in the use of magic. Put simply, tribal man has faith that his magic works; modern man lacks faith but is not taking any chances.

References Cited

Gmelch, G. 1978. Baseball magic. *Human Nature* 1(8):32–39.

Lewis, L. S. 1963. Knowledge, change, certainty, and the theory of magic. *American Journal of Sociology* 69:7–12.

MacNeice, L. 1964. *Astrology*. London: Aldus Books.

Malinowski, B. 1954. *Magic, science, and religion and other essays.* New York: Anchor Books.

Stouffer, S., et al. 1949. *The American soldier*. Princeton: Princeton University Press.

Vogt, E. 1952. Water witching: An interpretation of a ritual pattern in a rural American community. *Scientific Monthly* 75:175–86.

¹ We wish to thank Marcus Felson, Sharon Gmelch, and Walter P. Zenner for their comments on an earlier draft and Don Bennett, Des McCluskey, Kevin Buckley, Debbie O'Brien, and Ruth Pasquirello for their assistance in collecting the data.

Vol. 20 · No. 3 · September 1979

Analysis: Testing a Theory

One of the key assumptions in the social and natural sciences is that knowledge must be verifiable. Let's say, for example, a molecular biology lab makes what appears to be an important discovery about the function of a particular gene. For this finding to be credible and authoritative, researchers in other labs must be able to replicate it. Otherwise, the finding will likely be treated as a fluke and have little value to researchers in the field.

The same is true of research in fields such as sociology and anthropology. "Uncertainty and the Use of Magic" offers a good example of how researchers test theories—in this case Bronislaw Malinowski's influential theory, based on his field work among the Trobiand Islanders, that magic is a means of coping with uncertainty. For such a theory to have explanatory value, it must be able to account for many instances, not just the case Malinowski analyzes. In this regard, Felson and Gmelch take Malinowski's theory to be a hypothesis that can be tested, not a proven fact.

The form of Felson and Gmelch's report follow from these purposes. Although they do not mark the sections with headings, as many scientific reports do, their report nonetheless conforms to the standard format of research reports:

Introduction. This section explains the purpose of the writers' research by defining the problem under investigation, indicating its significance, and reviewing prior research. (Sometimes a review of the literature forms a separate section.) Often the introduction forecasts the structure of the report.

Methods. This section explains how researchers went about investigating the question—the experimental techniques, materials, research methods, sample size and characteristics, and so on. (This section is increasingly de-emphasized in scientific journals: sometimes it is published in small type, located at the end of a report, or omitted altogether.)

Results. In this section, researchers summarize their results, presenting the data without commenting on its meaning or significance.

Discussion. This section explains how the data relate to the central problem posed in the introduction. It often begins with the principal finding or the strongest claim the researchers have derived from the data. The discussion points out the significance of the data and its implications. Sometimes it includes speculation about the meaning of the data—marked by terms such as perhaps and may be—and plans for future work.

Conclusion. This section provides a summary of principal findings, offering a kind of final judgment of points raised in the discussion section. It is often quite short.

FOR CRITICAL INQUIRY

1. Work together in groups of two or three. Use the outline of the main sections of a research report to divide "Uncertainty and the Uses of Magic" into sections. Compare your results to those of other groups. Work together as a whole class to decide which paragraphs comprise each section.
2. Explain how Felson and Gmelch set up the theory they plan to test in the introduction. Is there a sentence or sentences somewhere in the introduction that presents their purpose? What questions arise from their review of prior research?
3. How does Table 1 relate to the methods section? What, if anything, do you learn from it that's not in the main text? Why do you think Felson and Gmelch have included it?
4. How do Tables 2 and 3 relate to the results section? Does this visualization of data aid your understanding of their results? Why or why not?
5. What claims about the significance of their data do Felson and Gmelch make in the discussion section? Is there a sentence or sentences that presents their main claim? How does the discussion relate to the problem posed in the introduction? Do Felson and Gmelch offer speculations? If so, what data do they base these speculations on?
6. Do you think Felson and Gmelch conclude the report in an effective way? Explain your answer.

Office of Technology Assessment, U.S. Congress. "The Seven-Sided Coin."
The following selection is the introduction to a report prepared by the Office of Technology Assessment in 1984. As the report indicates, due to a number of interrelated factors, the nuclear power industry had reached an impasse in the mid-1980s, with no new nuclear plant construction planned and a decreased use of nuclear power by utility companies. As you will see, the purpose of this report is to analyze the sources of resistance to the use of nuclear power—seven constituencies with different and sometimes competing interests—in order to assess the possibility of reviving the industry.

THE NUCLEAR POWER INDUSTRY is facing a period of extreme *1* uncertainty. No nuclear plant now operating or still under active construction has been ordered since 1974, and every year since then has seen a decrease in the total utility commitment to nuclear power. By the end of this decade, almost all the projects still under construction will have been completed or canceled. Prospects for new domestic orders during the next few years are dim.

Such a bleak set of conditions has led some observers to conclude that *2* the industry has no future aside from operating the existing plants. Some conclude further that such an end is entirely appropriate because they believe that nuclear reactors will not be needed due to the low growth in demand for electricity, and that the present problems are largely a result of the industry's own mistakes.

If nuclear power were irrelevant to future energy needs, it would not *3* be of great interest to policymakers. However, several other factors must be taken into account. While electric growth has been very low over the last decade (in fact, it was negative in 1982), there is no assurance that this trend will continue. Even growth that is quite modest by historical standards would mandate new plants—that have not been ordered yet—coming online in the 1990's. Replacement of aging plants will call for still more new generating capacity. The industrial capability already exists to meet new demand with nuclear reactors even if high electric growth resumes. In addition, reactors use an abundant resource. Oil is not a realistic option for new electric-generating plants because of already high costs and vulnerability to import disruptions which are likely to increase by the end of the century. Natural gas may also be too costly or unavailable for generating large quantities of electricity.

The use of coal can and will be expanded considerably. All the plau- *4* sible growth projections considered in this study could be met entirely by coal. Such a dependence, however, would leave the Nation's electric system vulnerable to price increases and disruptions of supply. Furthermore, coal carries significant liabilities. The continued combustion of fossil fuels, especially coal, has the potential to release enough carbon dioxide to cause serious climatic changes. We do not know enough about this problem yet to say when it could happen or how severe it might be, but the possibility exists that even in the early 21st century it may become essential to reduce sharply the use of fossil fuels, especially coal. Another potentially serious problem with coal is pollution in the form of acid rain, which already is causing considerable concern. Even with the strictest current control technology, a coal plant emits large quantities of the oxides of sulfur and nitrogen that are believed to be the primary source of the problem. There are great uncertainties in our understanding of this problem also, but the potential exists for large-scale coal combustion to become unacceptable or much more expensive due to tighter restrictions on emissions.

There are other possible alternatives to coal, of course. Improving the performance of existing powerplants would make more electricity available without building new capacity. Cogeneration⁵ and improved efficiency in the use of electricity also are equivalent to adding new supply. These approaches are likely to be the biggest contributors to meeting new electric service requirements over the next few decades. Various forms of solar and geothermal energy also appear promising. Uncertainties of economics and applicability of these technologies, however, are too great to demonstrate that they will obviate the need for nuclear power over the next several decades. **5**

Therefore, there may be good national-policy reasons for wanting to see the nuclear option preserved. However, the purpose of the preceding discussion is not to show that nuclear power necessarily is vital to this Nation's well-being. It is, rather, to suggest that there are conditions under which nuclear power would be the preferred choice, and that these conditions might not be recognized before the industry has lost its ability to supply reactors efficiently and expeditiously. If the nuclear option is foreclosed, it should at least happen with foresight, not by accident or neglect. This report analyzes the technical and institutional prospects for the future of nuclear power and addresses the question of what Congress could do to revitalize the nuclear option if that should prove necessary as a national policy objective. **6**

Nuclear Disincentives

No efforts—whether by Government or the industry itself—to restore the vitality of the industry will succeed without addressing the very real problems now facing the technology. To illustrate this, consider a utility whose projections show a need for new generating capacity by the mid-1990's. In comparing coal and nuclear plants, current estimates of the cost of power over the plant's lifetime give a small advantage—perhaps 10 percent—to nuclear. Fifteen years ago, that advantage would have been decisive. Now, however, the utility managers can see difficulties at some current nuclear projects which, if repeated at a new plant, would eliminate any projected cost advantage and seriously strain the utility: **7**

• The cost projections may be inaccurate. Some plants are being finished at many times their originally estimated cost. Major portions of a plant may have to be rebuilt because of design inadequacy, sloppy workmanship, or regulatory changes. Construction leadtimes can approach 15 years, leaving the utility dangerously exposed financially. The severe cash flow shortages of the Washington Public Power Supply System are an extreme example of this problem.

• Demand growth may continue to fall below projections. A utility may commit large sums of capital to a plant only to find part way through construction that it is not needed. If the plant has to be canceled, the utility and its shareholders must absorb all the losses even though it looked like a reasonable investment at the beginning. The long construction schedules and great capital demands of nuclear plants make them especially risky in the light of such uncertainty.

• The Nuclear Regulatory Commission (NRC) continues to tighten restrictions and mandate major changes in plant designs. Although the reasons for these changes often are valid, they lead to increases in costs and schedules that are unpredictable when the plant is ordered. In addition, the paperwork and time demands on utility management are much greater burdens than for other generating options.

• Once a plant is completed, the high capital costs often lead to rate increases to utility customers, at least until the plant has been partially amortized. This can cause considerable difficulty with both the customers and the public utility commission (PUC). If rate increases are delayed to ease the shock, net payback to the utility is postponed further.

• Most of the money to pay for a plant has to be raised from the financial market, where nuclear reactors increasingly are viewed as risky investments. The huge demands for capital to pay construction costs (and the high interest costs on this capital) make unprecedented financial demands on utilities at a time when capital is costly.

• There are many opportunities for opponents of a plant to voice their concerns. Some plants have been the focus of suits over specific environmental or safety issues. In the licensing process, critics may raise a wide variety of issues to which the utility has to be prepared to respond. These responses call for a significant legal and technical effort as well as long delays, regardless of the ultimate disposition of the issue.

• Plant operation may not meet expectations. Some reactors have suffered chronic reliability problems, operating less than 50 percent of the time. Others have had to replace major components, such as steam generators, at a cost of tens of millions of dollars because of unexpectedly rapid deterioration. While there is no specific reason to think a new plant would not operate its full life expectancy without major repairs, no reactor is yet old enough to have demonstrated it. There also is the possibility of long-term shutdowns because of accidents such as Three Mile Island. Furthermore, a nuclear utility is vulnerable to shutdowns and major modifications not only from accidents at its own facility, but also from accidents at any other reactor.

• Public support for nuclear power has been slipping, largely due to concerns about safety and costs. Public concerns can manifest themselves in political opposition. Several states have held referenda banning nuclear power or restricting future construction. None has passed that would mandate shutting down operating reactors, but some have come close. Furthermore, State and local governments have considerable control over the plant through rate regulation, permitting, transportation of waste, and approval of emergency plans. If the public does not want the plant, all these levers are likely to be used against it.

Given all these uncertainties and risks, few utilities would now con- **8** sider nuclear reactors to be a reasonable choice. Moreover, the pressures arising from virtually continuous interactions with contractors, NRC, the PUCs, financial institutions, and perhaps lawsuits by opponents, make nuclear power far more burdensome to a utility than any other choice. The future of nuclear power would appear to be bleak.

Yet there is more to nuclear power than the well-publicized problems **9** affecting some reactors. In fact, many have been constructed expeditiously, and are operating with acceptable reliability. Some have enjoyed spectacular success. For instance, the McGuire unit 2 of Duke Power in North Carolina was completed in 1982 at a cost of $900/kW, less than a third of the cost of the Shoreham plant in New York. The Vermont Yankee plant operated in 1982 at 93 percent availability, one of the best records in the world for any kind of generating plant. Calvert Cliffs supplies electricity to Baltimore Gas & Electric customers at 1.7¢/kWh. Finally, safety analyses are improving steadily, and none has indicated that nuclear plants pose a level of risk to the public as high as that accepted readily from other technologies. These well-managed plants have operated safely while providing substantial economic benefits for their customers.

Such examples, however, are insufficient to counterbalance the prob- **10** lems others have encountered. Nuclear power has become entangled in a complex web of such conflicting interests and emotions that matters are at an impasse. The utility viewpoint discussed above shows that there is little advantage and a great many disadvantages to the selection of a nuclear plant when new capacity is needed. Therefore, there will be few—if any—more orders for reactors in this century without significant changes in the way the industry and the Government handle nuclear power.

The Impasse

Consider now the perspective of those Federal energy policymakers who **11** believe the nuclear option should be maintained in the national interest.

It is unlikely that the U.S. Government will heavily subsidize the purchase of reactors by utilities or that it will build and operate reactors itself. Therefore, new orders will be stimulated only by alleviating those concerns and problems that now preclude such orders. Any policy initiative that is proposed, however, is likely to be controversial, because there are at least seven parties with distinct—and often conflicting—interests:

- utilities,
- nuclear safety regulators,
- critics of nuclear power,
- the public,
- the nuclear supply industry,
- investors and the financial community, and
- State public utility commissions.

To illustrate how these interests pull in different directions for different *12* reasons, consider just one issue. Changes in plant licensing and safety regulation often are cited as necessary elements of any strategy to revitalize the option, but there is little agreement on either the type or extent of reform that should be instituted.

• Before **utilities** will make a commitment to invest several billion dollars in a nuclear plant, they want assurances that extensive modifications will not be necessary and that the regulations will remain relatively stable. Utilities contend that such regulatory changes delay construction and add greatly to costs without a clear demonstration of a significant risk to public health and safety. To the utilities, such assurances do not appear to be impossible to grant. They point out that NRC has licensed 80 plants and should know what is necessary to ensure operating safety. Therefore, they would support revisions to the regulatory process that would make it more predictable and stable.

• However, there is another side to this coin. No plant design has been analyzed exhaustively for every possible serious accident sequence, and operating experience is still too limited for all the potential problems to have been identified. Accidents at Three Mile Island and at the Browns Ferry reactor involved sequences of events that were not understood clearly enough until they occurred. If they had been, both could have been prevented easily. As the **NRC** and the industry recognize different accident sequences, backfits are needed to prevent future occurrences. Proposals to reduce NRC's ability to impose changes in accordance with its engineering judgment will be seen by safety regulators as hampering their mission of ensuring safety.

• But there is a third side to this coin. Not only do the industry and NRC see regulatory reform very differently, but **critics** of nuclear power find much to fault with both the utilities and the NRC. In particular, they feel that the NRC does not even enforce its present rules fully when such enforcement would be too costly to the industry. Furthermore, they believe that the technology has so many uncertainties that much greater margins of safety are warranted. Thus, nuclear critics strenuously oppose any changes in the NRC regulations that might limit their access to the regulatory process or constrain the implementation of potential improvements in reactor safety.

• The **public** is yet a fourth side. Public opinion polls show a long-term trend against nuclear power. The public demands that nuclear reactors pose no significant risks, is frustrated by the confusing controversy surrounding them, and is growing increasingly skeptical about any benefits from nuclear power. These conditions do not give rise to a clear mandate for regulatory reform in order to facilitate more reactor orders. Such a mandate will depend largely on improved public confidence in the management ability of utilities and their contractors, in the safety of the technology, in the effectiveness of the regulatory process, and on a perception that nuclear energy offers real benefits.

• The **nuclear supply industry's** interests are not synonymous with the utilities' and thus represent a fifth side of the coin. The utilities need to meet demand with whatever option appears least expensive. If that option is not nuclear power, something else will suffice. The supply industry, however, has a large vested interest in promoting nuclear reactors, and the careers of thousands of industry employees may hinge on policy changes to revitalize the nuclear option, including regulatory reform.

• **Investors** may be ambivalent about licensing reform. Lengthy and uncertain licensing makes nuclear power a riskier investment during construction, but any accident during operation can have the same, if not greater, effect. Insofar as more stringent licensing makes accidents less likely, it reduces the financial risk. However, investors probably will be more concerned with the near-term risks involved in getting a plant online and would be more supportive of streamlined licensing if it reduced those risks.

• As representatives of consumers' economic interest, **public utility commissions** share the investors' ambivalence, but they might give more weight to operating safety because an accident that shuts down a reactor for a prolonged period usually will mean the substitution of more expensive sources of electricity.

Thus, there are at least seven different parties in each policy debate   *13*
on nuclear power: seven sides to the coin of each issue. No doubt others
could be added, but those described above represent the major positions.
Each party is a collection of somewhat differing interests, and each will
look for different things in any policy initiative. Given such a multi-
plicity of interests, it is not surprising that the present impasse has
developed.

Figure 1 illustrates these concepts. Utilities are at the center because   *14*
they make the ultimate decision about whether to order a nuclear plant
or something else. The other parties have considerable, sometimes decisive, influence over whether a nuclear plant will be built, how much
it will cost, and how well it will work. Each of these parties has its own
agenda of conditions that must be met before it would support a decision
by a utility to order a reactor. These conditions are listed with each

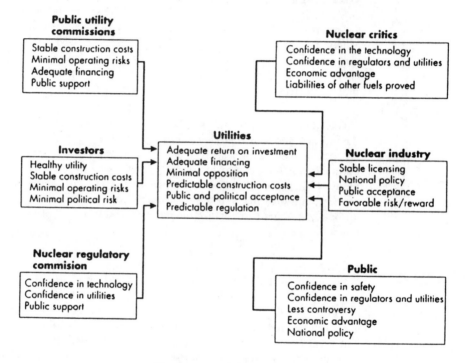

**Public utility
commissions**

Stable construction costs
Minimal operating risks
Adequate financing
Public support

Nuclear critics

Confidence in the technology
Confidence in regulators and utilities
Economic advantage
Liabilities of other fuels proved

Investors

Healthy utility
Stable construction costs
Minimal operating risks
Minimal political risk

Utilities

Adequate return on investment
Adequate financing
Minimal opposition
Predictable construction costs
Public and political acceptance
Predictable regulation

Nuclear industry

Stable licensing
National policy
Public acceptance
Favorable risk/reward

**Nuclear regulatory
commision**

Confidence in technology
Confidence in utilities
Public support

Public

Confidence in safety
Confidence in regulators and utilities
Less controversy
Economic advantage
National policy

Noncontroversial, necessary conditions

No major accidents
Reactors prove reasonably reliable
Additional generating units needed
Cost advantage for nuclear power
Convincing waste disposal program

party. Those conditions that are common to all are listed at the bottom of the figure. For instance, nuclear power must be very safe, with a very low risk of core meltdowns or major releases of radioactivity. Disputes over this point relate to the degree of safety required, the adequacy of the methodology in determining safety, the assumptions of the analyses, and the actual degree of compliance with regulations. In any case, however, existing reactors must be demonstrably safe, and future reactors probably will be held to even higher standards.

A closely related issue is reliability. A smoothly operating reactor is **15** more productive for its owners, and it also is likely to be safer than one that frequently suffers mishaps, even if those mishaps have no immediate safety consequences. Thus, it also will be considerably more reassuring to the public.

Other common criteria are that there must be a clear need for new **16** generating capacity and a significant cost advantage for nuclear power. In addition, a credible waste disposal program is a prerequisite for any more orders.

Other conditions are especially important to some groups but less **17** important to others. Some of these conditions already are met to some degree. The arrows in Figure 1 drawn to the conditions under utilities indicate the major areas that are related to the other parties.

Many of the conditions in Figure 1 are **necessary** before enough of **18** the participants in the debate will be satisfied that nuclear power is a viable energy source for the future. It is much more difficult to know how many must be met to be **sufficient**. All the groups discussed above have considerable influence over the future of nuclear power. Efforts to revive the option—whether initiated legislatively, administratively, or by industry—are unlikely to be successful if some of the interests find them unacceptable. The task of breaking the impasse therefore is formidable.

Analysis: Assessing Policy Options

This report was prepared by a committee representing a range of interest groups—the seven "parties" listed in the report and visualized in Figure 1. The participation of spokespersons from these constituencies gives the report a kind of comprehensiveness and credibility that might not have been possible if it had been written by only one person or a small group of people.

At the same time, however, as the report notes, the views of each group are "distinct—and often conflicting." And this poses a problem of how to balance and integrate the various interests and perspectives so that Congress can assess the policy options available, should it decide to revitalize the nuclear industry. Notice that the report does not make an argument about whether the nuclear industry should revived. Instead, it points out what any future policy on nuclear energy would need to take into account in order to satisfy and meet the current objections of the seven constituencies. In this regard, the report illustrates the role of analytical reports in the formation of public policy. Their function is not simply to give policymakers background information but to integrate that information into an analysis of the major factors—the political, social, economic, and technical considerations—that need to be addressed.

FOR CRITICAL ANALYSIS

1. Describe in your own words what you see as the main purpose of this report. Is there a sentence or sentences in the report that expresses this purpose?

2. Who are the seven sides of the coin noted in the title? What are their various interests? To what extent do their interests differ and conflict? What graphic devices are used to define the groups and their interests? Does the report suggest there is any common ground possible among them?

3. The tone of report is cautious, and the report explicitly declines to take a position on whether the future development of nuclear power is "vital to this Nation's well-being." How would you characterize the report's attitude toward nuclear power? What benefits does it see? What disadvantages, risks, or liabilities?

4. If the report does not take a position on constructing new nuclear power plants, does it make an argument? If so, what is the argument? How would you describe its main claim? What evidence does it offer?

5. Do you think this report was useful to Congress? Why or why not?

Michael Harrington Center for Democratic Values and Social Change. Action Brief. "Youth Violence."

The Michael Harrington Center for Democratic Values and Social Change at Queens College studies a range of social and political issues. The following Action Brief from the center focuses on the problem of youth violence. It was part of an anti-violence program the center developed with the New York State Division for Youth.

YOUTH VIOLENCE

CURRENT SITUATION IN THE UNITED STATES

Nearly 50% of all crime is committed by 5% to 7% of youth between the ages of 10-20. The juvenile arrest rate for violent crime was up 27.3% from 1980 to 1990. For whites the change was +43.8%; for blacks the change was +19.2%. Weapon law violations for juveniles increased by 62.6%. For whites it was +57.6%; for blacks it was +102.9%. Teenagers are 2.5 times more likely to be the victims of violent crime than those over 20. Black teenagers are ten times more likely to be victims; in fact, the firearm death rate for black teens is 2.8 times greater than the rate due to natural causes. The death rate of youth between the ages of 15-19 grew from 1,022 in 1984 to 1,641 in 1988. For black youth the change was from 418 in 1984 to 955 in 1988. Much of teenage violence occurs around schools. 86% of the guns taken from students are from their own homes. In New York City, for youth 15 and younger, felony assault increased from 720 in 1986 to 2,171 in 1992.

CAUSES AND SOLUTIONS

The various approaches to youth violence, other than those which could be called law and order (more police and stricter penalties), can be categorized within four models. The strength and weaknesses of any program may depend upon whether it can offer a multi-faceted, coordinated, and strategic approach.

PERSONAL: Youth violence is the product of personal background

CAUSES: Many youth turn to violence in reaction to family breakdown, neglect, and chaotic home situations. Youth who are abused as children and suffer harsh and continual physical violence are more likely to be violent. The presence of a parent with a criminal history is a factor in whether a youth will choose crime and violence. Many youth lack negotiation skills and learn to either accept or reject authority figures. Alcohol and other drugs figure in 20-25% of youth homicides.

SOLUTIONS: We should strengthen families through parenting education, provide preschool and afterschool programs for young children and adolescents. We should provide training in negotiation and conflict resolution skills, intervention in cases of adult abuse, treatment programs for violent children and youth, and treatment for alcohol and drug abuse.

CULTURAL: Youth violence is a product of a culture which encourages violence

CAUSES: Youth have become desensitized to violence through the chronic presence of violence in their communities and overexposure to media violence. Guns are readily available. Many inner-city youth have become part of a culture of despair--they see no future and want only the excitement of the moment. In some gangs, violence has become a rite of passage and a way for youth to gain power, attention, respect, and a "macho" reputation. There is an ever widening gap of distrust between youth and adults. As a result youth are not being socialized by adults, but are being left to learn about life on the streets. Persistent racism and prejudice have led to many hate crimes against people of color. The fear of violence has led people to abandon the public spaces where they used to build networks of support and information between different age groups.

SOLUTIONS: We should reduce the availability of guns, reduce media violence, build closer connections between youth and adults, encourage community policing and community patrols, support gang truces and use gangs to do constructive socializing, counteract the materialism that encourages youth to exploit others and to seek quick resolutions to problems, reclaim the public spaces, and reduce racism and prejudice.

A C T I O N

B R I E F

#1

1994

THE MICHAEL HARRINGTON CENTER FOR DEMOCRATIC VALUES AND SOCIAL CHANGE
Queens College, City University of New York, Flushing, NY 11367-1597

ECONOMIC: Youth violence is a product of socioeconomic inequality

CAUSES: Continued poverty and socioeconomic inequality have contributed to the deterioration of urban neighborhoods and the limiting of employment options for youth. The jobs that are available do not provide real opportunities for growth. For youth the major economic opportunity in urban centers is the drug trade and theft with the subsequent violent struggles for territory.

SOLUTIONS: We should provide more and better job opportunities with advancement potential for inner city youth, decriminalize drugs to undermine the high profits of the drug trade, and help stabilize and redevelop neighborhoods.

SOCIODYNAMIC: Youth violence is a reaction to institutionalized abuse

CAUSES: Violence is a reaction to institutionalized abuse of authority that youth experience at home, in schools, in the criminal justice system (police brutality, unequal arrest and sentencing), and in the employment market. Continued denial of self agency to the poor and youth creates employment for a whole host of civil servants: social workers, welfare case workers, police officers, lawyers, etc. The streets provide young people with an alternate social, cultural, and moral structure which meets a wide range of needs; e.g., from the provision of food and shelter to a system for attaining respect based on personal talent and achievement.

SOLUTIONS: We should counteract the institutionalized abuse of authority within drug enforcement, the criminal justice system, schools, and family structures, and organize youth's anti-authority energy into a force for social change.

RESOURCES

American Psychological Association, Violence and Youth: Psychology's Response, (1993), availabe from the APA, Washington, DC (202-336-5500).

E. Anderson, Street wise: Race, Class, and Change in an Urban Community (Chicago: The University of Chicago Press, 1990).

J.T. Gibbs, ed., Young Black and Male in America: An Endangered Species (Dove, Ma: Auburn House Publishing Co., 1988).

A. Reiss, Jr, and J.A. Roth, ed., Understanding and Preventing Violence (Washington, DC: National Academy Press, 1993).

N. Wamba, "Attitudes Toward Work and Schooling of a Group of Low Income Latino and African Amercian Youth in New York City," (1993), available from the Michael Harrington Center.

C. West, Race Matters (Boston: Beacon Press, 1993).

G. Witkin, "Youth and Violence," US News and World Report, April 8, 1991, 26-32.

QUESTIONS FOR GROUP ACTION

*Given the nature of schools as institutions, what can be done to prevent youth violence that has not been tried so far?

*What organizations in your community are working to resolve youth violence? What approaches are they using?

*Taking into account the different approaches, who benefits from emphasizing one approach over another? How?

*What would be a multi-faceted, realistic approach? How could young people be involved?

*On what basis would people resist or support a multi-faceted approach?

If you would like to receive future copies of ACTION BRIEF, contact The Michael Harrington Center (718-997-3070).

Analysis: Briefing

The Action Brief from the Michael Harrington Center is typical in many respects of a kind of report known as a briefing. As the name suggests, briefs are short informative reports intended to condense the best available research findings on a particular topic, issue, or problem. The purpose of briefings is often to develop programs and policies. For example, legislative aides provide briefings for Congressmen on impending legislation or project managers brief their supervisors on ongoing work.

The Action Brief on youth violence was written for policymakers, community organizers, social workers, and others concerned with juvenile crime. One of the tasks brief writers face is to provide their readers with pertinent information, analysis, and recommendations in an easily accessible form. As you can see, the Action Brief uses lots of headings to divide its materials into clearly identifiable sections. But the purpose of the Action Brief is not just to inform readers. The brief also lists solutions that respond to the various causes of youth violence. Unlike the report from the Office of Technology, which explains what policymakers need to take into account, this report makes recommendations for action.

FOR CRITICAL INQUIRY

1. Notice that opening section "Current Situation in the United States" is dense with data. How does the Action Brief use these data to establish the urgency of the problem of youth violence?
2. The largest part of the Action Brief describes four approaches to youth violence, looking first at various types of causes—personal, cultural, economic, and sociodynamic—and then at solutions that respond to the cause. Re-read each section carefully. Do the solutions listed for each cause seem to follow logically? Do the proposed solutions seem capable of dealing effectively with the cause of youth violence? Explain your answer.
3. Notice that the brief seems to reject the "law and order" approach ("more police and stricter penalties"). As you read about the four approaches, do reasons for rejecting the law and order model appear, either explicitly or implicitly? What do the reasons seem to be? Do you find them persuasive? Why or why not?
4. What does the inclusion of the final two sections, "Resources" and "Questions for Group Action," contribute to the brief?

LOOKING AT THE GENRE

1. When you want to be briefed on a subject, where do you turn? List some sources of information or analysis you have used, both in and out of school, and what your purpose was in using them. (For example, you may have used an encyclopedia to prepare a written report or read Consumer Reports to buy a car.) Compare your list to those of classmates. Pick three or four sources to analyze in some detail, choosing sources that differ from each other. Now analyze the way each source makes information or analysis available. How do interested people access the source? How does the source organize the information? What training or background knowledge, if any, do you need to use the source? Is the source considered reliable and authoritative? If so, by whom and why? Why would other people typically use the source?

2. Compare the organization of the traditional research report, as in "Uncertainty and the Use of Magic," to the organization of "The Seven-Sided Coin." To what extent are they similar? To what extent does "The Seven-Sided Coin" use a different form of organization? How would you explain the choices the authors of the report on nuclear power have made? Do you think they are effective?

3. Both "Uncertainty and the Uses of Magic" and James W. Carey's "Technology and Ideology: The Case of the Telegraph" (included in Chapter 4 "Commentary") are forms of academic writing that investigate a problem in their fields, review the literature, draw conclusions, and make claims based on evidence. And yet they are very different in organization and tone. Explain what you see as the major differences. As a reader, how would you compare your experience reading each piece? Do you find one or the other preferable in terms of organization? How do their tones differ? How did you respond?

DESIGNING DOCUMENTS: Understanding Options in Visual Display of Information

The visual display of information is becoming an increasingly important part of writing that informs and explains. Desk top publishing packages are making it easy for writers to design their own graphics, and scanners enable them to scan in illustrations and photographs from other sources.

For writers, the main point of adding graphics is changing. If graphics have traditionally been used to illustrate or add visual interest to a document that is primarily verbal, writers today are treating graphics as an important communication tool in their own right. Graphics help readers to take in information at a glance and to visualize important processes, trends, and relationships.

The visual display of information can be divided into three categories: textual, representational, and numerical.

- **Textual Graphics**   Textual graphics organize and display words, phrases, sentences, or paragraphs either within or separate from the main text. Textual graphics are generally used to review or preview key points.

You can find bulleted lists within the main text in "The Seven-Sided Coin"—the list of "nuclear disincentives" and of the seven interest groups. Figure 1 in the report is a chart, separate from the main text, that makes it easy to visualize the relations and differing interests among the three groups. Notice how arrows all point to the utilities at the center to illustrate the report's point that utilities "make the ultimate decision" about whether they will use nuclear or some other source of power.

Another common type of textual graphic is the fact box (Fig. 1). Fact boxes contain a series of statements that summarize key points in a news story, provide historical background, list key dates, or list key facts, such as population, economic, or weather information.

Time lines (Fig. 2) list events on a horizontal axis and can help readers visualize how something has developed and changed over time.

- **Representational Graphics**   Representational graphics use pictures to orient readers in time and space and to illustrate processes, relationships, and events.

As you have seen, photographs appear with the two news stories on the 30th anniversary of the Selma to Montgomery civil rights march, to help readers visualize the scene. Maps (Fig. 3) help readers visualize the location of events and, with arrows, the movement of significant actors. Diagrams such as "Anatomy of an NFL Concussion" (Fig. 4) use simplified representations, in this case of the head and brain, to help readers visualize where processes take place. Numbers and labels then show steps in the process, and arrows indicate the direction in which a concussion exerts pressure of the brain.

- **Numerical Graphics**   Numerical graphics put the primary focus on quantitative data instead of words or diagrams. Numerical graphics enable writers to analyze the data they are working with and to represent trends and relationships.

Tables are probably the simplest form of numerical graphic. They display numbers and words in rows and columns, enabling readers to see relationships at a glance. While tables have the lowest visual interest of numerical graphics, they are useful when you have large amounts of information you want to organize and display in a logical and orderly way. Tables 2 and 3 in "Uncertainty and the Use of Magic" are good examples. (Table 1 is actually a textual graphic.)

The Medical Bottom Line

SOURCE: NORML

Though largely illegal since 1937, marijuana may prove an effective alternative to more commonly prescribed drugs for some diseases. California, Arizona and Massachusetts are leading the fight to make marijuana more readily available. They aren't alone: 26 states and the District of Columbia have passed various laws and resolutions establishing therapeutic-research programs, allowing doctors to prescribe marijuana, or asking the federal government to lift the ban on medical use.

■ States with medical-marijuana laws

CONDITION	MARIJUANA TREATMENT	CONVENTIONAL TREATMENT
Cancer chemotherapy Often causes extreme nausea and vomiting	● Active ingredient THC reduces vomiting and nausea, alleviates pretreatment anxiety	● Marinol (synthetic THC): Commonly used but can cause intoxication. Pill form only, hard to swallow if you're vomiting. ● Serotonin antagonists such as Zofran (ondansetron): Can be taken intravenously but more expensive than Marinol
AIDS–related wasting Low appetite, loss of lean (muscle) mass	● Improves appetite	● Marinol: Boosts appetite, but smokable marijuana allows better dose control ● Megase (megestrol acetate): Stimulates appetite and may reduce nausea. Currently being compared to Marinol for cancer patients.
Pain and muscle spasms Associated with epilepsy and multiple sclerosis	● Reduces muscle spasms; may ease incontinence of bladder and bowel and relieve depression	● Dantrium (dantrolene sodium): Capsules or injection can relax nerves and muscles to calm spasms. Can cause liver damage. ● Lioresal (bactofen): Tablet alleviates spasticity but also causes sedation. Sudden withdrawal can cause hallucinations and seizures.
Glaucoma A progressive form of blindness due to increased pressure inside the eyeball	● When smoked, it reduces pressure within the eye. But it may also reduce blood flow to the optic nerve, exacerbating the loss of vision.	● Xalatan (latanoprost): Once-a-day eye drop. Low rate of side effects. Changes eye color in some users. ● Beta-blocker eye drops: Can cause lethargy and trigger asthma attacks ● Miotic eye drops: Allow eye to drain faster but constrict the pupil, dimming vision ● Carbonic anhydrase inhibitors: Decrease production of fluid in the eye, but can cause numbness and weight loss

Figure 1

A Growing Arsenal Against HIV

Over the past decade the FDA has approved nine drugs—six RT inhibitors and three protease inhibitors—to combat the AIDS virus. None of them is very effective by itself, but researchers are finding that certain three-drug combinations can shackle HIV for long periods.

PROTEASE INHIBITORS:

Indinavir (Crixivan) Merck & Co.

Saquinavir (Invirase) Hoffman-La Roche

Ritonavir (Norvir) Abbott Laboratories

1987 1988 1989 1990 1991 1992 1993 1994 1995 1996

AZT (Retrovir) Glaxo Wellcome

ddI (Videx) Bristol-Myers Squibb

ddC (HIVID) Hoffman-La Roche

d4T (Zerit) Bristol-Myers Squibb

3TC (Epivir) Glaxo Wellcome

Nevirapine (Viramune) Boehringer Ingelheim

Figure 2

Line graphs (Fig. 5) are often used to show variation in the quantity of something over a period of time, such as the spread of AIDS over a number of years. By charting the number of cases of AIDS on the vertical, or y, axis and the period of time on the horizontal, or x, axis, writers can establish trends.

In contrast to line graphs, which best show trends over time, bar charts (Fig. 6) enable writers to compare data and to emphasize contrasts among two or more items over time. Bar charts run along the horizontal axis, from left to right. Column charts serve the same function as bar charts but run along the vertical axis, from down to up.

Pie charts   divide the whole of something into its parts. Pie charts such as "When concussions occur in NFL games" display the individual items that make up 100% of the whole. Notice that the size of each slice is proportional to its share of the total. This helps readers see the relative weight or importance of each slice in relation to the others. And for this reason, most graphic designers agree, to ensure readability, pie charts should use five or few slices. More slices make the pie too cluttered and hard to read.

Figure 3

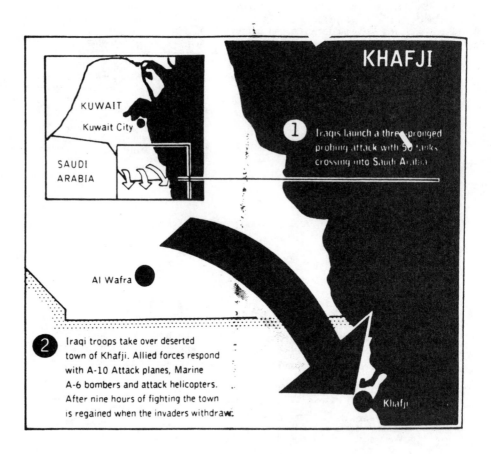

Figure 5

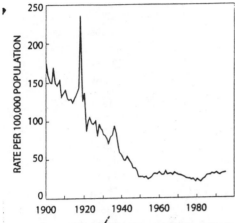

SOURCE: National Center for Health Statistics. In the graph, rates are for the death registration area, which comprised 12 states in 1900 and 48 states by 1933. Alaska was added in 1959 and Hawaii in 1960. Not adjusted for changing age composition.

Figure 6

Increasing Life Spans

We don't know what the future will be like, but experts say we will be around longer to experience it. On average, Hispanics will live the longest.

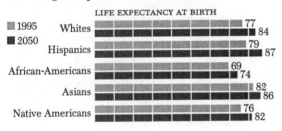

LIFE EXPECTANCY AT BIRTH

1995
2050

Whites 77 / 84
Hispanics 79 / 87
African-Americans 69 / 74
Asians 82 / 86
Native Americans 76 / 82

ETHICS OF WRITING

Establishing Trends

It was supposedly the nineteenth-century British statesman Disraeli who said, "There are lies, damn lies, and statistics," expressing a sentiment shared now by many. On one hand, most people acknowledge the important uses of statistics as a means of information gathering and a source of evidence in arguments and policy debates. And yet, at the same time, people are wary of them.

This ambivalence about statistics is not surprising because statistics can be misleading, whether intentionally or not. This is particularly true in the way writers use statistics to establish trends. All you have to do is glance at the newspaper to see how writers use statistical data to make points about what is happening and the direction things are going: The record rise in the stock market signals economic recovery and national prosperity. Growing marijuana use among young people points to a revival of the drug culture of the 1960s. The decline in highway fatalities shows an emerging consensus about the dangers of drinking and driving. The question to ask, of course, is how trustworthy such uses of statistical information are.

The current debate about teenage pregnancy is a good case in point about the ethical use of statistics. Journalists, politicians, and policymakers have claimed that an unsettling rise in teenage pregnancies has become a national problem, leading to an increase in crime, poverty, welfare dependence, school failure, destruction of family values, and so on. And they cite statistics to back up their point about this alarming trend. The line graph (Fig. 8) in the newspaper report "President to Campaign Against Teen-Age Pregnancy" (New York Times, June 10, 1994) is presented to show an increase in the "number of teenage births" over the past four decades. The fact of the matter, however, is that the number of teenagers who have children has not gone up in decades. This statistic has remained relatively constant since the 1950s. What has in fact increased is the number of "unmarried females ages 15 to 19" having children. Notice how the label on the line graph misleadingly blurs over this key distinction, seemingly equating "teen" and "unmarried" (as though people ages 15-19 don't get married.)

Moreover, nowhere in the news report, along with an accompanying line graph, is mention of the fact that the number of unmarried women in their twenties and thirties having children (like Murphy Brown on TV) has also gone up. This trend—that women in general are choosing to have children without getting married—may be just as significant as the increase in unmarried teen births, but it is suppressed, perhaps to make teen births seem more alarming.

The point here is that the responsible use of statistics must begin by taking into account all the available data. Using partial data to establish trends can only distort public debate. An ethical approach to the use of statistics in establishing trends is based as much on clarifying the issues (and the differences that divide people) as on making your point.

DISCUSSION AND ACTIVITIES

1. Look through some recent issues of magazines and newspapers to find three examples of the visual display of information to bring to class. Be prepared to explain how (or whether) your examples organize and display information in a way that makes the writer's presentation easier to understand. Take into account too whether the visual information is misleading in any respect.

2. The following situations present clusters of information that can be represented in visual form. In each case, decide whether a line graph, a bar chart, or a pie chart is the best choice to convey the information to readers. Make a sketch of your choice of visual display of information.

PROPOSALS

Trying to Curb Teen-Age Pregnancy

Elements of President Clinton's plan

WELFARE CHANGES
Require recipients to work after receiving aid for two years
Require minor mothers to live at home
Require minor mothers to seek education or training
Require mothers to identify their child's father
Try to collect more child support payments

GRANT PROGRAMS
$300 million for programs in 1,000 schools
$100 million for programs in distressed neighborhoods

BULLY PULPIT CAMPAIGN
Speeches by President Clinton and other officials
Possible nonprofit foundation to discourage teen-age pregnancy

Number of teen-age births (unmarried females ages 15 to 19)

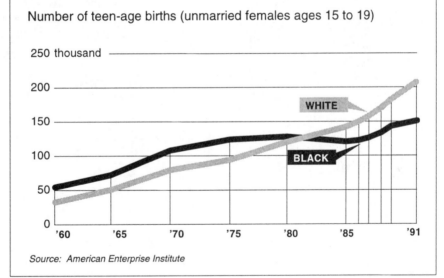

Source: American Enterprise Institute

N.Y. Times News Service

a) You are preparing the annual report for a community service organization at your college. Part of your task is to explain how the organization has spent the annual budget of $7,500 it receives from the college. Expenditures are the following: $1,500 for printing leaflets, brochures, and the quarterly newsletter; $1,000 for speakers' fees; $500 for a workshop for members; $2,500 to send five members to a national conference on community service; $1,750 for donations to local community organizations; $250 for refreshments at meetings.

b) Biology classes at your college are in high demand. No new faculty have been hired nor have any new courses been offered in the past ten years. With the rapid increase of biology majors, classes are overenrolled. In some cases, even majors can't register for the courses they need. You want to make the case that your college needs to hire more biology faculty and offer more courses. Here are the numbers of biology majors in the past ten years: 1988—125; 1989—132; 1990—114; 1991—154; 1992—158; 1993—176; 1994—212; 1995—256; 1996—301; 1997—333.

c) You are working for your college's office of alumni affairs, and you are involved in a campaign to increase alumni donations. No one has ever researched whether donations vary depending on the major of alumni. To help plan the campaign, you are asked to find out how donation differs according to the major of alumni. Here are figures on donations in 1996 by type of major: social sciences—$85,000; humanities—$67,000; business—$145,000; engineering—$98,000; sciences—$112,00; fine arts—$37,000; nursing and allied health—$54,000.

3. In a group with two or three other students, choose one of the reading selections that appear in another chapter. Design a graphic to emphasize the main point in the reading. Be prepared to explain your design.

GOING ON-LINE

The Great Chicago Fire

The Great Chicago Fire happened in 1871, virtually destroying the downtown of the city. What follows is a brief report on the fire, taken from the Encyclopedia Americana. Read this short account. Then visit the website designed by the Northwestern University professor of history Carl Smith and the artist Paul Hertz "The Great Chicago Fire and the Web of Memory" at www.chicagohs.org/fire/. Compare how the encyclopedia entry and the website present information about the fire. What do you see as the main differences? In what circumstances would the information in the encyclopedia entry be sufficient for your purposes? When would you want the more extended treatment in the website?

You will notice that the website is divided into essays, images, and archival material—with accompanying links. You can read the essays straight through or you can interrupt your reading to follow the links. Do both kinds of reading. First, simply read the screens of a particular essay. Then begin again, this time following each link as it appears. What do you see as the advantages and disadvantages in each way of navigating the website?

ASSIGNMENTS

WORKING TOGETHER: Constructing a Chronology

The following chronology appeared in a special section of the New York Times Magazine devoted to the resurgence of popular interest in jazz. Notice that it begins with the invention of the saxophone in the 1840s and continues to present, with 24 entries that note highlights and trends in the development of jazz. Use this chronology as a model to construct your own chronology of some field you are interested in. You could choose the history of photography, psychology, television situation comedies, the American automobile industry, the films of Woody Allen, major league football, social welfare policy, relations between the U.S. government and American Indian tribes, twentieth-century women painters, or molecular biology. Anything that has been around and developing over fifty years or more will work for this assignment. Assume that you are preparing the chronology for general readers who will be interested in your topic but who are not specialists.

Work together in groups of three or four. Decide on a topic you are all interested in researching. Make sure there is enough information available to you on the topic. Decide on a division of labor so that each group member will be responsible for a particular period or aspect in the history of the topic. When you are researching, keep on the lookout for key moments, whether or not they fit into the part you are responsible for.

Once you have completed the research, construct a tentative chronology with fifteen or twenty dated entries on highlights or trends. It can be helpful to get a peer reader involved at this point, to give you feedback on what is clear in the chronology and what needs more explanation. Make revisions based on this input, and depending on your teacher's directions, design graphics to accompany the text.

WRITING ASSIGNMENT

For this assignment, write a report on a subject that interests you. Your purpose is to inform readers about your subject—to analyze and explain its significance and perhaps to make recommendations. You'll need to do research, though how much you do will depend on time and your teacher's directions. Here are some ideas about how to approach this assignment.

- News report. You may want to write about a recent event in the news—whether on campus, in your local community, or on the national or international scene. As you have seen in the readings on the thirtieth anniversary of the Selma to Montgomery civil rights march, reporters not only provide informative accounts. They also shape the way readers understand events.

- Investigative reporting. Investigative reporting goes beyond simply reporting what happened to probe for the underlying causes and consequences of events. You could investigate the recent increases in employers' use of temporary contracts, the incidence of Caesarian births, proposed changes in the Social Security system, new telecommunication legislation, or the role of child labor in American-owned manufacturing abroad.

- Research report. Reports provide readers with updated information on recent developments in research. While you may not be able to do original research, as Richard B. Felson and George Gmelch do to test Malinowski's theory of magic, you can report on research on a topic that interests you—the latest developments in genetic testing, current research on whether there is life on Mars, the new spread of malaria, trends in AIDS education, research findings on bi-lingual education, or debates on whether the author of Moby-Dick Herman Melville beat his wife. In all these cases, you will be called on to find out what experts in the field think and then explain these findings to interested readers.

- Policy report. Another approach to this assignment is to take a public policy issue—affirmative action, Medicare, physician-assisted suicide, gay and lesbian marriage, the North

A JAZZOGRAPHY

FROM STORYVILLE TO LINCOLN CENTER...

A jazz progenitor: Buddy Bolden. c. 1900.

ARCHIVE PHOTOS/FRANK DRIGGS COLLECTION

c. 1840 Adolphe Sax, a Belgian, invents the saxophone.

1902 The 12-year-old Jelly Roll Morton "invents" jazz, or so he later claims. A habitué of Storyville, the red-light district of New Orleans, Morton combines ragtime, French quadrilles and the hot blues played by Buddy Bolden, the notoriously hard-living cornetist.

1917 The Dixieland Jazz Band, a white group, makes the first jazz recording, "Livery Stable Blues." It sells a million copies, launching jazz as popular music. Freddie Keppard, a black band leader, had rejected the chance to make the first jazz record — he was afraid other musicians would copy his style.

1925-1928 Take it away, Satchmo: With his Hot Fives and Hot Sevens recordings, Louis Armstrong revolutionizes the jazz form, encouraging solo improvisation over ensemble playing.

1929-1945 The swing era rises and falls. Duke Ellington, Jimmie Lunceford and Count Basie lead influential groups. Most of the big hits, though, are recorded by white band leaders like Glenn Miller, Benny Goodman and Tommy Dorsey.

c. 1935-1955: The jam session as art form: West 52d Street in Manhattan, packed with clubs, becomes the playground for Charlie Parker, Dizzy Gillespie, Miles Davis, Thelonious Monk and all their friends.

1936 Well before the rest of the country, jazz becomes integrated. At the Congress Hotel in Chicago, Lionel Hampton and Teddy Wilson sit in with Benny Goodman's ensemble. Two years later, Billie Holiday joins Artie Shaw's big band.

1939 While playing "Cherokee" during a Harlem jam session, Charlie Parker happens upon a harmonic discovery that leads to be-bop, a far more intricate style of jazz, both harmonically and rhythmically.

1943 Jazz ascends to the concert hall: The first of Duke Ellington's annual Carnegie Hall programs and the premiere of "Black, Brown and Beige," his influential long-form work about the history of American blacks.

1951 On the heels of Miles Davis's "Birth of the Cool," musicians like Chet Baker and Gerry Mulligan form the so-called cool school, turning down the volume and intensity. It happens, of course, in California.

1951 Sidney Bechet relocates to Paris, the first of many American jazz expatriates including Kenny Clarke, Arthur Taylor and Bud Powell. Racial tension was less pronounced, and European audiences were more appreciative.

1954 Jazz goes outdoors: George Wein, a pianist and singer, rewrites his jazz résumé by inviting musicians to Newport, R.I., for the first of many Jazz Festivals.

1956 A crossover dream: Ella Fitzgerald makes the first of several "Songbook" recordings for Verve, the impresario Norman Granz's new label. The Songbooks make Fitzgerald an international star.

1959 A pivotal year, with several records that expand the very possibilities of improvisation: Miles Davis's "Kind of Blue," John Coltrane's "Giant Steps," Ornette Coleman's "Shape of Jazz to Come."

1964 The avant-garde gains mainstream recognition as Thelonious Monk makes the cover of Time magazine, which

Marsalis, at 22, wins a Grammy for his "neo-bop" record "Think of One." The same night, he takes a classical Grammy for his recording of trumpet concertos.

1989-1991 Frontmen and backlash: Trying to duplicate Marsalis's commercial success, record labels snap up straight-ahead players like Roy Hargrove, Antonio Hart and Christopher Hollyday. Much grumbling ensues from those who consider these so-called Young Lions too imitative or too green.

1991 Jazz as institution: Marsalis is appointed

artistic director of the new Jazz at Lincoln Center program. Big audiences but big detractors, too, who claim that Marsalis is anti-modernist and anti-white.

1992 A new fusion trip: The British "acid jazz" group Us3, which blends hip-hop and electronic samples of jazz cuts, gets permission to raid the Blue Note archives. Meanwhile, in Brooklyn, the hip-hop group Digable Planets records "Rebirth of Slick (Cool Like Dat)," using the horn lines of James Williams's "Stretchin'." Suddenly, a new degree of jazz cool.

christens him the high priest of be-bop.

1969 Miles Davis's "Bitches Brew," a primordial jazz-rock fusion record, sells 500,000 copies, turning many rock fans on to jazz but leaving some hard-core Miles followers groaning.

1972-1977 New York's "loft jazz" scene blooms, with experimental, post-bop players performing

in lofts like Ali's Alley. Among the players on the scene are Joe Lovano and David Murray.

1979 On Jan. 5, the famously cosmic Charles Mingus dies in Cuernavaca, Mexico, at the age of 56. That same day, 56 whales beach themselves on the Mexican coast.

1984 The new generation gets a leader who looks backward: Wynton

Miles Davis, keeper of the cool, at Columbia Records studio in 19

1993 Jazzmen can be pop stars, too: Joshua Redman, the Harvard summa cum laude saxophonist, chooses jazz over Yale Law and releases two records within a year. Critics love the records and fans love Redman: in concert, young women shriek and young men pump their fists in the air.

June 1995 The Impulse record label, one of the most important in jazz history, is revived after a 21-year dormancy. It is the seventh major jazz label to be launched or relaunched in the past 10 years.

American Free Trade Agreement (NAFTA), welfare reform, and so on—and write a report for a policymaker that analyzes and explains the interests and perspectives of the various constituencies concerned with the issue. Use the Office of Technology's report to Congress "The Seven-Sided Coin" as a model.

- Action brief. This angle on the assignment asks you to research a social, political, or economic problem—it could be national or local—and to summarize the various approaches to the problem and the solutions proposed. The Action Brief from the Michael Harrington Center is a good model to follow.

INVENTION

One of the first things you need to do is identify situations which call you to write a report. In other words, what kinds of reports might grow from your involvement in local organizations, campus clubs, national interest groups, or social groups? If you donít already have an issue in mind for your report, the exercises below should help you find one that will mean something in your life. For starters, you can look through any writing inventories you may have written if you worked through Chapter 1; you can also take a look at the examples of collaboratively-written reports and recommendations described in Chapter 3 (see pages XXX).

EXERCISE

1. Make a list of your hobbies, community groups, campus interests, social organizations, and family activities. Think in particular of those that are closest to you now ñ either in college or in your hometown. Are there sports in which you participate regularly? Have you gotten involved in supporting particular political issues or candidates? Do you have a job that calls you to think about writing a report to improve your workplace conditions? Make as full a list as you can.

2. For each item in your list, consider the range of issues that might mean something to others involved in that group. If you are a weekend bicyclist, you might be interested in the status of local "Rails-to-Trails" acquisitions; likewise, if you are a member of an international group on campus, you might be interested in culling the services available for ESL students. Try to come up with at least three possible report topics for each activity or group you list.

3. Out of the full list you have generated now, note which ones seem most likely to help the members of your group in some way. Your report should be interesting for you to write, but it should also be useful to your readers. Which of the groups you have listed have a forum for distributing your report? Which would be most likely to do something with the information you present? Select those that topics that have the most interest for you and your readers.

CLARIFYING YOUR PURPOSE AND AUDIENCE

As you have seen, the basic purpose of writing a report is to inform interested readers. But to say as much doesn't really address the issue of why report writers want to inform their readers about the event, problem, situation, or concept they are treating. The issue here concerns why you—or anyone—might want to write about a particular subject in the first place.

What gives the subject an urgency or importance that makes it worth writing about? Why do readers need or want information about the subject? How is it going to help them learn something important? What is at stake for you as a writer and a person in informing your readers about your subject? Answering these questions is an important step in clarifying your own sense of what your purpose is in writing a report and what your readers need from you.

EXERCISE

Select three of the subjects you thought of in the exercise above. Ideally, you already know something about this subject, and you want to learn more. Then write for ten minutes or so in response to these questions:

1. What interests you about the subject? Why are you considering writing about it? Explain in some detail what you already know about your subject.

2. Who might be interested in reading about your subject? What are they likely to know already about it? What new information do you want to bring to them? Why do you think it is important they get this information?

3. Read over the three writings you have just done. See if this helps you to understand why you might choose one subject over the others. Which seems to you to have the clearest purpose and the most at stake for the readers?

RESEARCHING YOUR SUBJECT

Once you have decided on a subject, you will need, of course, to assess your current state of knowledge about it. Do you already have the information available that will enable you to inform your readers in a useful way? Do you need to learn more about it? If so, where can you go to get this information? Look through Part 3 of this book to find more on possible research strategies.

Earlier in this chapter, you saw that report writers often begin with research questions, and that those research questions guide where and how they research their subject. Your research questions will depend in some part on the sources and methods available to you, as well as the time constraints under which you are working. To come up with a good research question, try the following exercise.

EXERCISE

1. Take a quick survey of the resources you have available to you. Look through Part 3 to see what kinds of resources exist, and decide which ones are accessible for this project. You will probably need to spend some time in the library, and most likely you will check on the Internet for relevant information. In addition, do you need to conduct a survey? Or do you need to interview key people for additional information?

2. Next, create a timeline that you can realistically follow. You may want to put so much information in your report that it would require an entire semester to complete; obviously, that kind of report would be too ambitious right now. Instead, create a work plan in which you allot certain amounts of time to the different research components. Remember to allow time for drafting, revising, and getting responses to your report before the final version is due. Look, in particular, at the îTask Breakdown Chartî in Chapter 3 (page XXX) for a suggested format for scheduling your project.

3. Given the resources and constraints for this project, compose a series of questions that you can reasonably address with your report. Your questions might look something like this:

   • What is the current status of "Rails-to-Trails" acquisitions nationwide?
   • What actions or land acquisitions are pending locally?
   • How do such acquisitions generally take place?
   • What local action is needed to support additional acquisitions?
   • How have other communities responded?
   • What has been done in this community in the past?
   • What are the greatest obstacles to getting more land for this project?

Your project may not be able to address each one of the questions you compose, so you will want to set priorities within these questions based on the purpose of your report. Are you presenting information to enact change? Are you presenting information so your fellow members understand what is happening around them? Are you presenting information that will support the actions your group has taken in the past, given them encouragement and validation for those efforts? Your goals for the report, at this point, will determine which questions you keep, and which you will drop.

PLANNING

INTRODUCING YOUR SUBJECT

The type of introduction you write will depend in large part on the kind of report you are writing. In the case of an encyclopedia entry, for example, there is no real introduction to speak of. The writer can safely assume that the reader already has his or her reasons for looking up a particular subject, so there is normally no purpose in trying to motivate someone to read on. In other cases, however, some type of introduction is required—whether it is simply an explanation of what is to follow, a clever journalistic "hook" focusing on the human interest side of the subject, a troubling statement, or an example that makes the subject relevant to the reader's experience.

ORGANIZING YOUR INFORMATION

Organizing your report well is crucial to presenting your information in a useful and accessible way to your readers. As you have already seen in the reading selections, some reports (like the two on the Selma anniversary) use a chronological pattern to present information.

But this is not the only choice you have. Another common pattern of organization is to start with a review of the relevant research, as in "Uncertainty and the Use of Magic." As you probably noticed, the authors of that report spend the first three paragraphs summarizing research that had been done on the subject before the authors describe their own project. Once they describe their own project, however, the organization becomes somewhat chronological again (here's what our study did, here's what we found, here's what we think it means). In academic writing in particular, this is a very common organizational plan.

The report on the Nuclear Power Industry and the briefing on Youth Violence, however, use another pattern of arrangement; those writers have organized their report more by topic than by chronology.

Here is an outline of the topics presented in the Nuclear Power Industry report:

¶ 1-6:   Definition of the problem with the current state of the industry, with a call to act at the end of the 6th paragraph.

¶ 7-12:   Description of the specific problems facing the nuclear industry (from the industryís perspective), with examples.

¶ 13-16:   Description of the specific problems facing those in government who want to support the industry, with examples.

¶ 17-20: Description of other perspectives and other problems, with examples.

¶ 21-22:   Synthesis of the perspectives, with a graphic to show the connections among them.

¶ 23-26:   Wrap-up and conclusion, with implications for the future.

Whether chronological (or a modified chronological) or topical arrangement is best-suited to your report depends on the subject you are treating. Chronological arrangement makes sense for events, situations, problems, and concepts that have developed over time. In these cases, it is important to tell readers what happened and when. In other instances, topical arrangement may be more appropriate, especially when you are writing about a subject that has clusters of information you need to explain, as in the article on concussions.

EXERCISE

To help you decide whether to use chronological or topical arrangement (or some combination of the two), write a list of as many items of information you have concerning your subject. Now number the list according to the order in which the items might appear in your report. You may find that some of the information doesn't seem to fit. Don't force items into your list. You can always add them later, if needed, once you have a working draft.

WORKING DRAFT

When you write a draft of your report, follow the ordered list you have created but don't tie yourself to it in a rigid way. If you find that some information might fit better in a different position, then put it there instead. At this point, your main goal should be to get your information down on the page so you can make some decisions about what to add, what to drop, what to rearrange, what to emphasize. Remember that the most important part of writing a report is to present your information in a useful and accessible way.

PARAGRAPH DEVELOPMENT: Using Summaries

As you have seen in the readings, most reports summarize a good deal of information. This means that you will need to develop strategies for writing summaries. To get a better sense of how summaries can be used in different reports, take a look at the summaries in the two articles on the Civil Rights March. Each writer needed to offer a brief summary of the events in 1965, so each provided the necessary background information.

> The troubles of the day were different on March 7, 1965, as hundreds of protesters set out from the Selma church, attempting to march to the state Capitol in Montgomery for a voting rights demonstration.
> Instead, they barely made it out of downtown Selma before getting mauled at the foot of the Edmund Pettis Bridge by a posse of lawmen. The unforgiving use of billy clubs and tear gas provided one of the grimmest, goriest spectacles of the civil rights movement.
> — "Young Blacks See Selma Anniversary as 'Ancient History'"
> On March 7, 1965, white lawmen beat and gassed hundreds of marchers trying to cross Edmund Pettis Bridge. Footage of the beatings ran on national television, sparking outrage and leading to passage of the landmark Voting Rights Act, which outlawed literacy tests in many Southern states.
> — "A Changed Selma Recalls Historic March"

To write your own summaries, you will need to take an inventory of the information presented in the resource you are summarizing. First, gauge the most important information contained there; in other words, what absolutely has to be in your summary for it to make any sense? Next, decide which other relevant details will matter for your readers and your purpose.

For more practice with summarizing, you may want to work through the appropriate sections of Chapter 2 (see ìReading Strategiesî on pages XXX). In addition, Chapter 3 has a section on Summarizing Different Views Fairly, including instructions on Refuting, Conceding, and Negotiating (pages XXX). You might find these sections helpful at this point in your report.

If you are already comfortable writing summaries, you may want to take a look at some of the other paragraph development strategies that matter for writing reports. For example:

- see Defining (page XXX in Public Documents) to establish a common meaning for the major terminology in your report

- see Comparing and Contrasting (see page XXX in Profiles) to offer a range of perspectives on the issue in your report

- see Offering Reasons with Supporting Facts and Evidence (see page XXX in Reviews) to build your report persuasively around the information you have gathered

BEGINNINGS AND ENDINGS: Forecasting What Is to Come

One way to establish your purpose from the very beginning of your document is to start with an explicit statement about the report itself. What, precisely, should this report accomplish, for whom, and how? Just as essays sometimes begin with introductory passages informing readers how the forthcoming parts of the essay will develop the writer's train of thought, so too can a report. Notice how the writers of the Action Brief on Youth Violence begin their report by clearly stating the issue at hand. Their first paragraph explains the "Current Situation in the United States," and the second paragraph spells out what they perceive to be the "Causes and Solutions." This second paragraph serves as the forecast for the rest of the report.

"The various approaches to youth violence, other than those which could be called law and order (more police and stricter penalties), can be categorized within four models. The strength and weaknesses of any program may depend upon whether it can offer a multi-faceted, coordinated, and strategic approach."

From this point on, readers can expect the rest of the report to elaborate on this paragraph. Readers now know that each of the four models will be discussed (and, in fact, they are: "personal," "cultural," "economic," and "sociodynamic"), and that they will be evaluated based on whether they can "offer a multi-faceted, coordinated, and strategic approach." The second paragraph of the briefing, then, ably forecasts the rest of the report.

You may decide that you want to include a forecasting paragraph near the beginning of your report, when you state the purpose of the report itself. You may also decide not to state your purpose explicitly, implying your purpose through the forecasted the parts in the document. Try both patterns, and see which one works best for your report. If you can't decide, show your favorite versions to your writing partners and ask for their advice. You may also want to look at some of the Beginnings and Endings strategies presented in other chapters.

- see Pointing Out the Significance or Wider Consequences (page XXX in Memoirs) to make sure your readers understand the importance of your report

- see Using Facts, Statistics, and Background Material (page XXX in Public Documents) to begin your report with relevant and striking information, the way the Action Briefing on Youth Violence does

- see Offering a Recommendation or Solution (page XXX in Proposals) to move your conclusion upfront so your readers know what to expect from your report

PEER COMMENTARY

Exchange your working draft with a classmate and then answer these questions in writing:

1. Explain to the writer what you knew about the subject before you read the working draft, what you learned from reading it, and what (if anything) surprised you.

2. Explain to the writer whether you found the working draft easy to follow. Point to passages that are especially clear or interesting. Also point to any passages you found confusing. What questions, if any, does the draft raise in your mind that you feel are not adequately answered? Are there points in the draft where you wanted more information from the writer? If so, explain.

3. Describe how the working draft introduces the subject. How does it try to generate interest in the subject? What seems to be urgent or important about the subject? Why would readers need or want to know more about it? If you can think of other ways to motivate readers, let the writer know.

4. Remark on the tone of the report. Does it seem appropriate for the readers? If there are specific places that need revision, point them out, and suggest some alternative wording.

5. Has the writer used graphics? If so, have they been designed to help readers make sense of the information presented? How might the graphic elements be strengthened? If the writer has not used any textual graphics, can you suggest some places in the report that might be aided with some visuals.

REVISING

Use the peer commentary to do a careful critical reading of your working draft. Consider first whether the draft generates interest in the way you had hoped. Did your reader seem to understand what makes the subject important to you? If so, can you do more in a revision to emphasize this importance? If not, can you think of strategies to heighten reader interest?

Next, consider whether the draft seemed easy to follow. Finally, consider whether the draft seemed to be complete in terms of the information you present.

After you have revised your report according to the responses of your peer readers, try testing yourself on the concepts explained below. You might want to pay particular attention to the coherence devices you used or to the amount of jargon you included.

CONNECTIONS AND COHERENCE: Topical Chains

Topical chains can establish links between the sentences in a paragraph. By repeating key words and using synonyms and pronouns to refer to the main topic of a paragraph, writers can establish a topical chain that will help readers follow the paragraph's train of thought. Note, for example, the way Felson and Gmelch use selective repetition in the following paragraph to create a topical chain.

> "This study examines these relationships using a sample of American and Irish college students. It considers the use of magic in six activities—gambling, athletics, exam-taking, illness, face-to-face interaction, and dangerous activities—in relation to the degree of uncertainty of each. It investigates the relationship between the use of magic and anxiety within each activity. Finally, it examines students' beliefs about the ability of magic to alleviate anxiety and produce favorable outcomes."
> — Felson and Gmelch, "Uncertainty and the Use of Magic"

Felson and Gmelch use several techniques in this paragraph to establish a topical chain. First, they use the same sentence structure throughout the paragraph, linking "this study" in the first sentence with "it" in the second. In other words, the first sentence explains what the "it" is (their study), and the subsequent sentences explain what the "it" does (it "considers," it "investigates," and it "examines").

Next, the primary focus of the study, "magic," is repeated in each sentence. As the description of what the study will do grows more full with each sentence, the authors remind their readers in the topical chain what the main subject really is: magic.

If you would like to see more examples of topical chains functioning within topic-oriented outlines, look at the section on Analyzing in Chapter 2; in particular, read through the parts covering the Topical Outline (see page XXX). This technique might be worth trying in your report, particularly if you have a lot of information you are presenting in a relatively small amount of space. Topical chains can help your readers navigate through large amounts of text. If, however, you find that topical chains aren't the most useful coherence device for your report, take a look at some of the options presented in other chapters.

- see Temporal Transitions (see page XXX in Memoirs) to double-check your sense of chronology, particularly if your report relies on a chronological arrangement

- see Enumerative Order (see page XXX in Public Documents) to clearly signal a number of points you might be raising in your report

- see Parallelism of Ideas (see page XXX in Proposals) to assure your readers can follow your report with some consistency

You may also want to consult the section Using Jargon Appropriately in Chapter xx, especially if your subject is technical or specialized.

WRITERS WORKSHOP

The following report "Food Sources in South Providence" was written by Luis Ramirez for a field research assignment in the sociology course "Hunger in America." Ramirez's research was based on a questionnaire he administered to thirty low-income people in Providence, Rhode Island concerning how they acquire their food. Ramirez's report is preceded by a commentary he wrote when he finished his report:

LUIS RAMIREZ'S COMMENTARY

I became interested in how people use various food sources when I took a sociology course "Hunger in America." Like many people, I assumed that government programs like welfare and food stamps provided low-income people with enough to eat. I didn't realize that in fact low-income people actually rely on range of food sources beyond government programs. I was working once a week as a volunteer in the after-school program at South Providence Neighborhood Ministries (SPNM), and I decided I wanted to find out more about how low-income people served by SPNM acquire food and make ends meet. This seemed like crucial information to gather, especially considering the changes in the welfare system and government benefits just going into effect.

I didn't have much problem writing the questionnaire. I got some good advice from the TA in the sociology course. The hardest part for me was writing the report and deciding where to put the different information. I wasn't used to the report format. Most of the papers I've written in college begin with a claim and then give evidence. So it felt backwards to give results first and then discuss them.

The other thing I had to work on was the introduction. I knew the report should be concise, and so I wasn't sure how much information to put in the introduction. I knew the introduction needed to define the problem I was investigating and explain its significance, but I wasn't sure how to handle the literature review. My sociology TA was a big help when she read my working draft and explained how introductions to a report don't just tell readers what has been written about a topic. They are supposed to "create a space," in her words, for the research I had done—to show how it addresses a question that grows out of previous work.

FOOD SOURCES IN SOUTH PROVIDENCE

Luis Ramirez

Introduction

Over the next few years, access to food for many low-income individuals and families may change dramatically. "The Personal Responsibility and Work Opportunity Reconciliation Act of 1996" (PL104-193), signed into law by President Clinton on August 22, 1996, replaces "Aid to Families with Dependent Children" (AFDC) with a new program "Temporary Assistance to Needy Families" (TANF), which requires participants to work for benefits and limits the amount of time they are eligible. In addition, eligibility requirements for food stamps will be made more stringent, and individual grants will be reduced. Legal immigrants who have been in the U.S. for fewer than five years will no longer be eligible for public assistance programs such as TANF, food stamps, Supplemental Security Insurance (SSI), and Medicaid. In Rhode Island, an estimated 8,000 will lose food stamp benefits altogether, and another 30,000 will have food stamp benefits reduced from $80 to $60 a month. Another 4,000 will lose SSI benefits (Rowland, 1997).

Given these changes in the welfare system, it is crucial to understand how low-income individuals and families secure food to meet their household's dietary needs. With the implementation of the new welfare law and the elimination or restriction of public assistance programs, dependence on non-commercial food sources that low-income families use to evade hunger may increase to buffer the cuts and loss of benefits. Non-commercial food sources can be divided into four categories: 1) public assistance programs, 2) home production, 3) emergency relief, and 4) gifts (see Table 1).

A good deal of research on people's diets has focused on measuring food intake and its nutritional quality by such methods as the "twenty-four hour recall," the "food frequency" checklist, the "seven day diet record," and direct weighing and measuring of daily meals (Pelto, et al, 1980). Other researchers have attempted to develop indicators to assess hunger (Physicians Task Force on Hunger in America, 1985; Radimer, et al, 1990). These studies have been useful in providing information about general patterns of food use, diet, nutrition, and the prevalence of hunger. What these studies do not include, however, is information about how people actually acquire their food.

More recently, researchers have examined how welfare recipients and the working poor use supplemental sources of income beyond welfare benefits and wages to make ends meet (Rank and Hirschl,1995; Edin and Lein, 1997). These researchers have found that the benefits allocated from food stamps and AFDC are not enough to meet basic needs. As Rank and Hirschl write, "Even with the budgeting and stretching of resources that recipients try to do, there is simply not enough at the end of the month" (p. 243). The purpose of this study is to determine whether this is the case with low-income families in South Providence and the extent to which they depend on non-commercial food sources to provide for basic needs.

TABLE 1: Non-Commercial Food Sources

1. Public assistance	Food stamps
	AFDC
	Special Supplemental Feeding Program
	for Women, Infants, and Children (WIC)
	School breakfast and lunch programs
2. Home production	Private and community gardens
	Gathering food (nuts, berries, herbs,
	greens, etc) in public parks
	Fishing
3. Emergency food relief	Churches
	Community centers
	Food banks
4. Gifts	Familial networks
	Friends and neighbors

METHODS

A questionnaire on how people acquire their food was administered to thirty low-income individuals who use the services of South Providence Neighborhood Ministries (SPNM). SPNM is a not-for-profit community center which provides a range of services such as emergency food relief, clothing and utility assistance, English as a Second Language classes, tutoring programs, sewing lessons, public health programs, and so on. The questionnaire was administered, with the informed consent of participants, in January and February 1997.

The demographic characteristics of the study population are summarized in Table 2. Of the 30 participants, 28 (93.3%) were women and two (6.6%) were men. Twenty were Latino (66.7%), five (16.7%) African American, three (10%) Southeast Asian, and two (6.7%) African. Six (20%) worked full or part-time, while 24 (80%) were unemployed.

RESULTS

This study found that the participants draw on a number of non-commercial food sources to meet their families' dietary needs. As Table 3 illustrates, the majority participated in public assistance programs of one type or another, including AFDC (56.7%), food stamps (66.7%), WIC (50%), school lunch programs (84.2%), and school breakfast programs (78.9%).

As shown in Table 4, a number of participants fish for food (26.7%), grow food (30%), and gather food in public parks and other places (20%).

Table 5 shows the number of participants who use emergency food relief and family networks to acquire food. The vast majority of study participants use food pantries and other emergency food distribution centers (97.6%). Nineteen (65.5%) say they visit on a regular basis about once a month, and ten (34.5%) say they go sporadically. Eleven people (44%) eat at a relative's house at least once a month, and six people (24%) feed relatives at least once a month.

Table 2: Demographic Characteristics of Study Population

	Number	Percentage
Age		
younger than 18	1	3.3
18-30	6	20
31-50	18	60
51+	5	16.7
Marital Status		
Married	8	26.7
Not Married	27	73.3
Ethnicity		
Latino/ Hispanic	20	66.7
Afro-American	5	16.7
Southeast Asian	3	10
Work		
Employed	6	20
Unemployed	24	80

Table 3- Number and Percentage of Households Using Public Assistance Programs

	Number	Percentage
AFDC		
yes	17	56.7
no	13	43.3
Food Stamps		
yes	20	66.7
no	10	33.3
WIC		
yes	15	50
no	15	50
School Lunch		
yes	16	84.2
no	3	15.8
School Breakfast Program		
yes	15	78.9
no	4	21.1

Table 4-   Number and Percentage of Households Engaging in Various Forms of Home Production (Fishing for Food, Growing Food, Gathering Food)

	Number	Percentage
Fishing		
yes	8	26.7
no	22	73.3
Growing		
yes	9	30
no	24	70
Gathering		
yes	6	20
no	24	80

Table 5- Number and Percentage of Households Who Utilize Emergency Relief and Familial Networks

	Number	Percentage
Emergency Relief		
yes	29	97.6
no	1	3.3
Feed Relatives Often		
yes	6	24.0
no	19	76.0
Are Fed by Relatives Often		
yes	11	44.0
no	14	56.0

DISCUSSION

The most significant results of this study are the extent to which participants use a range of food sources to meet their basic needs. These results appear to confirm the findings of Rank and Hirschl, and Edin and Lein that neither public assistance nor low-paying jobs provide people with sufficient resources to make ends meet. My study found that benefits from AFDC and food stamps are not enough to meet a family's dietary needs. Therefore, supplemental sources, such as fishing, food production, food gathering, emergency food relief, and family food sharing are important sources of food for many low-income people.

The study results also suggest that at least some people who are eligible for public assistance do not choose it as a food option. One participant said that he does not like to use government programs and would rather use emergency food relief because the people are "nicer" and "not as condescending." It may be that food pantries are no longer temporary and infrequent means of meeting people's household food needs. Rather, people may be using food pantries as a regular strategy to feed their families, particularly at the end of the month when benefits from AFDC and food stamps run out.

Perhaps the most troubling finding is the fact that low-income people were already using many means of acquiring food, in addition to public assistance programs, before the new welfare law was implemented. These results suggest that emergency food relief sources such as food pantries may be under growing pressure when benefits from public assistance are reduced or eliminated. Familial networks are also vulnerable, as those who are currently feeding other family members lose food support through AFDC, food stamps, and SSI.

CONCLUSION

The media and politicians have pictured welfare recipients as lazy people who comfortably enjoy public assistance benefits as a substitute for work. The participants in this study present data contrary to this picture. The majority of people in the study do not rely entirely on public assistance. Rather they draw on a number of different food sources. What will happen to them as public assistance benefits are reduced or eliminated is a matter of considerable concern.

REFERENCES

Edin, K. & Lein, L. (1997). Work, welfare, and single mothers' economic survival strategies. American Sociological Review, 61, 253-266.

Pelto, G. H., Jerome, N. W., & Kandel, R. F. (1980). Methodological issues in nutritional anthropology. In N. W. Jerome, R. G. Kandel, & G. H. Pelto (Ed.), Nutritonal anthropology: Approaches to diet and culture (pp. 27-59). New York: Redgrave.

Physicians Task Force on Hunger in America (1985). Hunger in America: The growing epidemic. Boston: Harvard University School of Public Health.

Radimer, K. L., Olson, C. M., & Campbell, C. C (1990). Development of indicators to assess hunger. Journal of Nutrition, 120, 1544-48.

Rank, H. & Hirschl, R. (1995). Eating agendas. New York: Basic Books.

Rowland, C. (1997, Feb. 20). Budgets, belts getting tighter all the time. Providence Journal-Bulletin, p. 1, 5.

WORKSHOP QUESTIONS

1. The "Introduction" to Luis Ramirez's report consists of four paragraphs. Describe what you see as the function of each paragraph. Considering the four paragraphs as a section, do you think they provide the information needed to understand the purpose and significance of his research? Explain your response.

2. Is the "Results" section clear and easy to follow? Why or why not? What changes, if any, would you recommend?

3. Do the five tables help you understand the research and its results?

4. What are the major claims about his research results that Ramirez makes in the "Discussion" section? Do these claims seem to fit the data? Do they provide persuasive interpretations that point out the meaning of the data? What questions or alternative interpretations might you offer?

5. Does Ramirez's "Conclusion" seem justified in light of the research results and discussion?

WRITERS INVENTORY

Read over the report you have written and any writing you did earlier exploring what interests you about the subject, why you want to write about it, and why readers might be interested in learning about it. Write a page or two considering whether you achieved your purpose for your intended audience. Explain why or why not. Explain, too, whether your purpose changed in researching your subject and writing about it.

A CLOSING NOTE

To bring your report to final form, consider whether you want to include graphics to display information in a visual form. Is there information in your report that can be represented usefully in visual form? Is there additional information you want to add to the report that might be included in an accompanying fact box, chronology, map, diagram, or chart?

CHAPTER
NINE

COMMENTARY:
Identifying Patterns of Meaning

LOOKING AT THE GENRE

Commentary is a genre of writing that uses analysis and interpretation to find patterns of meaning in events, trends, and ideas. The purpose of commentary is not simply to report on things but to give readers a way to make sense of them.

This purpose should be clear if you think about the commentaries you've heard on radio and television and read in newspapers and magazines. For example, on television news programs, when a commentator such as Sam Donaldson or Cokie Roberts gives his or her nightly remarks, you don't see news footage on the television screen. You just see the commentator speaking directly to you. Thus, the focus has shifted away from the news itself to the commentator's analysis and interpretation of the news. Even without this visual cue, we generally don't mistake radio commentary by, say, Rush Limbaugh or Andrei Codrescu for news reports or the commentaries of newspaper columnists like Mollie Ivens or George Will for news articles.

Whether commentaries are on TV or radio or in print, we expect them to give us something to react to, to think about, and to use to make sense of contemporary experience. We have this expectation because of the feature that most clearly distinguishes the commentary from news reports and articles: commentary doesn't use the objective tone and neutral stance of reporting but instead is written from a particular perspective. Commentary takes a position and presents an interpretation that the writer hopes readers will find convincing.

The call to write commentary grows in part out of people's desire to have satisfying accounts of their experience, to identify patterns of meaning that make the world cohere for them in their daily pursuits. Commentary offers explanations of events in the news that can help readers, viewers, and listeners organize their worlds and imagine the future.

In contemporary society, in which new ideas emerge and trends and events occur at a dizzying pace, commentators play several crucial functions. For one thing, they play a labeling function, identifying current trends and giving readers labels for these trends (e.g., "Generation X," "downsizing and corporate restructuring," "the information age," "the new world order"). Second, by seeking to find patterns of meaning in events, trends, and ideas, commentators call on readers to think about the causes and consequences of what is happening in the world today (e.g. "NAFTA has led to the loss of jobs," "the drop in reading scores results from the neglect of phonics instruction"). Finally, in the process of explaining, commentators often apportion praise and blame and take a moral stance on events—whether of solidarity, indignant reaction, or ironic distance (e.g. "we should all get behind Clinton for taking on the tobacco interests," "Mike Tyson should be banned from boxing for life," "it's amusing to watch the baby-boomers of the psychedelic Sixties tell their children not to use drugs").

Because of the functions they perform, commentators help shape our sense of issues and the differences that divide people. For example, to explain the overwhelming Republican success in the 1994 Congressional elections, many can diagram the pattern of angry white male" voters as the decisive factor. Some commentators identified themselves with the views attributed to these voters: big government took much of their income in taxes, affirmative action deprived them of jobs, and that's why they justly angry. Other commentators offered an alternative view: these voters were looking for scapegoats at a time declining wages and corporate restructuring had made their lives insecure. Thus, while both sets of commentators agreed that the "angry white male" voter helped to explain the 1994 elections, they differed dramatically in the position they took toward these voters and the underlying issues. In writing their respective commentaries, they sought to persuade readers of their position. For commentary not only seeks to disclose patterns of meaning but also to shape public opinion.

These functions of commentaries largely determine the relationship between the writers of commentaries and their readers (or listeners). In analyzing and interpreting events and trends, commentators approach readers as co-thinkers, asking readers to look at the world from their perspective, whether readers ultimately agree with them or not. One of the pleasures (and aggravations) of reading commentary is that of following the commentator's line of reasoning—to see how his or her mind works to make sense of the world. For this reason, commentators tend to acquire regular readers who become familiar with the writer's views and look forward to reading what he or she will say about new issues.

Commentary is by no means limited to print and broadcast journalism, even though these may be the most familiar forms. It is also an important genre in academic and professional writing, where books and articles seek to provide persuasive explanations of issues in a particular field—whether it is the meaning of Hamlet's melancholia, the causes of slavery in the New World, the nature of human-computer interactions, the role of trade in Paleolithic economies, or the results of new AIDS therapies. In academic commentaries, the issues are often more technical and specialized than the issues commentators treat in the popular media. But in many respects, it is the same desire to go beyond the given facts—to find patterns of meaning, identify underlying causes, explain consequences—that drives academic inquiry.

Whatever the context may be, the call to write commentary grows in part out of this desire to analyze and explain what happens around us—to have satisfying accounts of our experience and to find patterns of meaning that can make the world cohere. In conversation, we routinely offer commentary on events, trends, and other people. We want to get a handle on the local scene at work, in school, in their neighborhood, and so we talk about what is going on, analyzing the motives for actions and the reasons for events. A good deal of everyday talk in fact serves as a kind of social analysis that shapes how we negotiate our relationships with others.

The reading selections in this chapter illustrate some key features of the genre of commentary. First comes a cluster of three piece published in the New York Times on the resignation of Shannon Faulkner, the first female student at The Citadel. The second reading "How To Fight the New Epidemics" by Lundy Braun begins by characterizing a recent trend—the increase in media attention to new and mysterious "killer diseases"—in order to explore assumptions in scientific and medical policymaking. The final reading is an excerpt from an academic article "Technology and Ideology: The Case of the Telegraph," in which communications professor James W. Carey explains why the scholarly neglect of the telegraph has been unfortunate.

AIDS Poster

The simple equation "Silence = Death" offers a powerful commentary on the politics of the AIDS crisis and the consequences of inaction.

COMMENTARY ON SHANNON FAULKNER'S RESIGNATION FROM THE CITADEL

"Sadness and Shame at The Citadel." New York Times. August 22, 1995.

Susan Faludi. "Shannon Faulkner's Strength in Numbers." New York Times. August 23, 1995.

Captain Erin Dowd. "Ex-Cadet's Actions Didn't Match Her Words." New York Times. August 25, 1995.

After having fought for over two years to be admitted to The Citadel, a military academy which then had a males-only policy, Shannon Faulkner resigned on August 18, 1995, at the end of her first week. As shown by the dates above, commentary on her resignation appeared on the heels of the event. This is typical of commentary that is focused on events: Writers move swiftly to have their say while the news is still current. They can assume familiarity with the event and show readers a particular way of making sense of it—of its meaning, its causes, and its larger implications. While the three pieces here represent somewhat different forms—an editorial, an op-ed piece, and a letter to the editor—all clearly belong to the genre of commentary. In reading the pieces, notice how each looks at the event from a different perspective, that is, finds a different way of making sense of it.

Sadness and Shame at The Citadel

When Shannon Faulkner took on the task of becoming the first female student at The Citadel, South Carolina's all-male military college, she also took on a broader responsibility. Like it or not, she was acting not only for herself but for all other Americans who believe that a school financed by taxpayers' money has no right to discriminate on the basis of gender.

When Ms. Faulkner, emotionally exhausted and physically depleted, dropped the banner she herself had raised, many of those rooting for her were doubtless disappointed. But she is right to hope that "next year a whole group of women will be going in" and will succeed where she failed. There are already many American women serving in the United States armed forces and performing with distinction in its service academies. West Point's top graduate this year, in fact, was Second Lieut. Rebecca E. Marier.

As many of these women warriors will attest,

Shannon Faulkner waged a more lonely battle than they did. Her "enemy," apart from tradition and sexism, was an unremittingly hostile corps of cadets whose maturity was evidenced in their behavior the day she quit. They ripped off their shirts and chanted "C-I-T-A-D-E-L," banged pipes on windowsills and shouted their joy at the school's remaining a male preserve. Whether it will stay that way is a question the Supreme Court has been asked to decide.

Ms. Faulkner surely feels sad about leaving The Citadel, but she has no reason to feel shame. More than 30 male cadets dropped out as well. In fighting as hard and long as she did, she may have opened the door for other women. It is those yahoos, those future first citizens of South Carolina and its neighbors, who shook their fists and yelled their catcalls who should feel shame. So should their commanding officers who did little to dilute their pleasure in driving a lone intruder from their turf.

Shannon Faulkner's Strength in Numbers

By Susan Faludi

LOS ANGELES
Out of all the nearly 2,000 cadets who enrolled in an all-male military academy called The Citadel this year, the only one whose name we know was the one the school didn't want: Shannon Faulkner.

This distinction seems, on its face, too obvious to mention. Of course she's famous — that she was admitted to the academy at all was a cause célèbre. But the distinction is important, because it goes to the heart of the issue. One reason the other Citadel cadets loathed Shannon Faulkner (aside from her sex) was her individuality, which affronted The Citadel's ethic. The academy purports to educate young men by making them conform. Conformity is enforced through anonymity. From the day the cadets arrive, when they are issued identical uniforms and haircuts, they become so homogeneous that, as an upperclassman explained to me, "mothers can't even tell their sons apart."

Through communal living and endless drills and rigid codes of conduct, the cadet's individuality is subordinated to the identity of the group, his strength founded in numbers and teamwork, in esprit de corps and long tradition. Going it alone, as a maverick, isn't done. "Individuals do not make it here," the commandant of cadets warned this year's freshmen on their first day. "If you want to stay an individual, every day will be a tough day."

This is what is called a military

education, and it was exactly what Shannon Faulkner wanted and could not find elsewhere in her home state of South Carolina. From the start her quest seemed hopeless: by seeking military anonymity in an all-male corps, she had to stand out. But her downfall was hastened by forces beyond The Citadel.

The largest obstacle she faced was the popular illusion that history is driven not by the actions and changing beliefs of large numbers of ordinary people, but by a few heroic giants who materialize out of no-

Can women count on solidarity only when they fail?

where to transform the landscape.

The media inflate this fairy tale by anointing a hero in every story and letting the surrounding political issues slide off their camera lenses. Paula Coughlin wasn't the only woman who said she was assaulted at Tailhook, just as Shannon Faulkner wasn't the only woman who was denied admission to The Citadel. But they were the first to raise their voices and so they were the ones the press put in the spotlight, all too often failing to illuminate the problem: male behavior that created the problem in the first place.

For the heroine of the moment, caught in the temporary spotlight of celebrity culture, it can be terribly flattering to be elevated above the masses by the mass media. But it's also dangerous to be isolated and

stranded, with so far to fall in public. Especially since, according to common consent, the entire women's movement must fall along with her.

This is the paradox that Shannon Faulkner was trying, in her way, to counter: women are only allowed the solidarity and esprit de corps of the women's movement when they are defeated. A constant refrain of Ms. Faulkner's opponents — and those of Ms. Coughlin — was that she was a stalking horse for feminism. Each of these women was accused of being a pawn of some grand and malevolent conspiracy. They weren't. They fought alone. But let them fail or prove to be only human, and the women's movement must take the hit. In an inverse of The Citadel ethic, women are condemned to fight alone and condemned to fail communally.

Solidarity is fostered in men — whole state-supported academies teach it to them — but it is suspect in women. Lately, that message has been reinforced by so-called feminist pundits, from Camille Paglia to Christina Hoff Sommers, who tell women over and over: "You can do it on your own. You don't need any help from the organized women's movement."

But once Shannon the individual stumbled, her humiliation instantly became all women's. It was a reversal Shannon Faulkner seemed achingly aware of. Standing beside her father in a pelting rain, she said in a shaky voice, "It's hard for me to leave, because ... I don't know what's going to happen with the case." A USA Today headline put the last nail in the coffin: "Even Some Feminists Fear She Hurt Cause."

Shannon Faulkner had sensed the dangers of this early on. Any journalist who followed her around — or tried to — in the last two and a half years can tell you she was not a willing heroine. With an agility and savvy remarkable in anyone, much less someone barely out of high school, she

kept reporters at arm's length and thwarted their efforts to plunder her personality, to forage through her private life for tidbits they could use to ornament their creation: Shannon Faulkner the media star.

But at the same time, she accepted the bargain: she agreed to fight alone. She was not a feminist, she said. She was "an individualist." And when a Federal judge finally ordered The Citadel to admit her to its corps of cadets, she told The New York Times that she didn't consider the ruling a victory "just for women" — only a confirmation of her belief that if you want something, you have to "go for it." She avoided the feminist label for all the usual reasons, living in the Deep South being only the most obvious. And she got lots of press points for playing the role of the lone and apolitical female ranger, with no need for a meddlesome women's movement.

But as Shannon Faulkner stood before the press last week, she shared with us her feminist epiphany, one that generally doesn't dawn on most women until much later in life: making a lone woman a star is not the same as advancing women's equality. In fact, it's counterproductive. She said, "I really hope that next year a whole group of women will be going in, because maybe it would have been different if there had been other women with me."

As I heard that remark, it occurred to me that she had received a Citadel education after all. She had grasped the only aspect of the Citadel teachings that really matters: there is strength in numbers; solidarity counts.

It's a lesson that gleeful pundits, disappointed feminists and conservative detractors of Shannon Faulkner can learn as well. "It would have been different if there had been other women with me." That's not an excuse. That's a valedictory.   ⊓

Ex-Cadet's Actions Didn't Match Her Words

To the Editor:

I am writing in response to Shannon Faulkner's failed attempt to join the cadet ranks at The Citadel (front page, Aug. 19). I applaud her effort in gaining recognition from the women's equality movement. Ms. Faulkner's drive and persistence in challenging the outdated "men only" policy at a public, federally funded institution are respectable.

I am concerned, however, that her half-hearted attempt will perpetuate the perception that women cannot achieve or exceed military standards. I am also concerned that The Citadel will be perceived as different from other academies and too difficult for the average woman.

I am a United States Army officer, and I am greatly disappointed by Ms. Faulkner's lack of preparation for the challenges of a military career. Her actions did not match her verbal public stand, so strong and unyielding.

Ms. Faulkner is visibly unfit and apparently mentally uncommitted.

She does not walk her talk.

Women can and do succeed in the military and at military institutions. The success at West Point of First Lieut. Kristen Baker and Second Lieut. Rebecca Marier are prime examples.

I have successfully worked side by side with men while carrying a load equal to more than half my body weight. I experienced combat from the front lines in Iraq and have endured the hardships common to other military veterans. I enjoy a network of female friends who jump out of planes, rappel from helicopters and meet social and physical military demands daily.

The military is designed to stress an individual both physically and mentally. It is not a game. Like many other professions, the military sets goals and standards for its officer candidates in preparation for potential experiences. Success in the military is achieved very easily: one must possess basic perseverance.

Respect is not a prerequisite; it is earned by living up to individual statements and meeting organizational standards.

Ms. Faulkner's failure is a lesson for those who attempt to achieve equality without preparing to meet the standards. Women's liberation is a necessary and productive movement. We can be physically, mentally and technically prepared to meet professional demands.

It is unfortunate that Ms. Faulkner's young shoulders bear the controversial weight of one failed attempt for women's liberation and equality. It is more unfortunate that she so quickly deprived herself of achieving a goal that could have strengthened her self-confidence and physical stamina. May women continue to challenge the admission policies at The Citadel and display the stamina and commitment to endure more than one hot day of work.   (Capt.) ERIN DOWD
Nashville, Aug. 20, 1995

ANALYSIS: Interpreting an Event from Different Perspectives

The three readings are typical in many respects of commentaries that interpret current events. Notice, for one thing, that none of the three spends much time describing the event. Instead, they use phrases, like "Shannon Faulkner's failed attempt" in the first line of Dowd's letter, that assume the event is common knowledge. The writers are able to dispense with background explanation and move quickly to presenting their main points.

Although the commentaries respond to the same event, each offers a different interpretation of Shannon Faulkner's resignation from The Citadel. Taken together, they present an interesting case study of how different writers construct the call to write in different ways. In fact, the three commentaries seem to agree fully on only one point—each comes out against The Citadel's "males only" admission policy. Aside from that point of agreement, they seem to have quite different interests in the event.

These different interests in what is at stake in the Faulkner resignation can be explained in part by the writers' backgrounds. The New York Times, as a national "establishment" newspaper, seeks in its editorials to speak on behalf of the general public interest. Susan Faludi, a feminist and author of Backlash: The Undeclared War Against American Women, is most interested in what the implications are for the woman's movement, while Captain Erin Dowd, herself an officer in the U.S. Army, seems most concerned with how the Faulkner resignation will affect other women's situation in the military.

FOR CRITICAL INQUIRY

1. What does each commentary see as the cause(s) of Shannon Faulkner's resignation from The Citadel?
2. What does each commentary see as the main lesson to be learned?
3. In one or two sentences, state what you think is the main point of each commentary. Consider how the three commentaries differ in their interpretations. How might you account for these differences?
4. How do the three commentaries seek to shape public understanding of the event? What values or attitudes does each seek to tap? How does each commentary align itself with people, ideas, or movements? Who does each commentary distance itself from?

"How To Fight the New Epidemics." Lundy Braun.

Lundy Braun does research on cervical cancer and the history of disease and teaches pathology to medical students and courses on the biological and social origins of disease to undergraduates at Brown University. "How To Fight the New Epidemics" appeared in the Providence Journal-Bulletin on May 29, 1995. Braun wrote this commentary in response to public fascination with media accounts of "killer viruses" and other epidemic diseases. But, as you will see, the issues she addresses go far beyond the often sensationalistic media coverage of infectious diseases.

How to fight the new epidemics

LUNDY BRAUN

ONE OF THE HOTTEST topics in the news these days seems to be "killer" viruses. With the outbreak of Ebola virus in Zaire and the popular accounts of epidemics of virus infection in feature films, made-for-television movies and best-selling nonfiction, the public has been captivated by the apparent power of microorganisms to sweep through towns and villages unfettered.

But hidden behind our fascination with these real and fictional epidemics is a profound feeling of betrayal, stemming from the widely held view that science had won the war against microbial infections.

The recent outbreaks have taken us by surprise, threatening our carefully nurtured sense of health and well-being. We diet, consume vitamins and exercise vigorously to ward off heart disease and cancer. But infectious diseases strike in a seemingly unpredictable pattern, leaving us feeling unprotected and vulnerable. With the re-emergence of tuberculosis as a significant public health problem in the United States, cholera in Latin America, the plague epidemic in India last year and the Ebola virus infection in Zaire, HIV infection, formerly considered an isolated occurrence confined to marginalized populations, now seems a harbinger of ever more terrifying microbial agents.

Yet, the reasons for the re-emergence of infectious diseases are not particularly mysterious. In reality, infectious diseases never were conquered, and the recent epidemics are quite predictable. For centuries, infectious diseases have been the major cause of death in the developing world. Moreover, even in the developed world, successful management relies on active disease surveillance and public health policies.

In 1966, the eminent Australian immunologist Sir MacFarlane Burnet declared, "In many ways one can think of the middle of the 20th Century as the end of one of the most important social revolutions in history, the virtual elimination of infectious disease as a significant factor in social life." Shared by most of the scientific community, this view is rooted in the rise of the germ theory in the late 19th and early 20th Centuries that associated specific microbial agents with particular diseases.

The germ theory took hold not only because of the spectacular technical achievements represented by the isolation of the microorganisms, but also because infectious disease, once seen as divine retribution for past sins, now appeared potentially controllable. The discovery of antibiotics and the development of vaccines lent further support to this notion of control. Thus, the germ theory effectively replaced disease prevention policies based on sanitary reforms, including improvement in sewage systems and better housing conditions, which were primarily responsible for the dramatic decline in the death rates from infectious disease.

The possibility of control over these great afflictions of humankind became even more appealing in the post-World War II period when a sense of endless optimism about the future was fueled by economic expansion in industrialized countries. Unfortunately, during this period, we also began to rely exclusively on science to solve the problems of disease. Throughout this century the role of the natural and social environment in the development of disease has been largely ignored by the scientific and medical communities and policy-makers.

Yet, the obstacles to management of many infectious diseases are social as well as scientific, and disease prevention policies based exclusively on science leave us ill-prepared to respond effectively to the current epidemics.

In the case of tuberculosis, we know how the bacterium is transmitted, how it causes disease and until recently, we had drugs that were relatively effective in reducing transmission and the development of disease. Despite this wealth of medical knowledge, tuberculosis continues to thrive, primarily in marginalized groups with minimal or no access to medical care. Without a concerted effort to improve access to the health care system, tuberculosis will remain a formidable challenge irrespective of the development of new drug treatments or more effective vaccines.

In the case of AIDS, basic scientific research coupled with education, public health measures and the political will to address difficult social issues are essential to managing this epidemic.

There are many other examples of microbial diseases where the failure to integrate scientific knowledge with social programs has hampered the development of sound disease prevention policies. Cervical cancer, for example, is the second most common cause of cancer-related mortality in women worldwide. Over a decade ago, sexually transmitted human papillomaviruses were linked to this cancer. Yet years later, we still know relatively little about the mechanisms by which human papillomaviruses contribute to the development of cervical cancer. To reduce the morbidity and mortality associated with this infection we need to develop more precise ways of identifying women at increased risk of progression to cancer.

An investment in basic microbiological research will be required to answer these questions. Meantime, however, we have more than sufficient scientific information to begin to educate the population most at risk of contracting the disease, namely adolescents. Again, the failure to implement such programs is fundamentally a political issue, reflecting our reluctance as a society to deal with adolescent sexuality.

Effective management of infectious diseases is achievable. Many of the agents associated with recent outbreaks are not new microbes but rather newly recognized ones that have appeared in human populations as a consequence of social disorganization and ecological disruption. To be successful, disease-prevention policies must be based on more than technical solutions. They must be firmly rooted in an ecological perspective of disease that does not separate scientific knowledge from an understanding of the influence of the natural environment on disease and a commitment to social justice.

There are no magic bullets. We will have little impact on infectious diseases without addressing the living conditions of large segments of our society and rebuilding our public health infrastructure. In the absence of such a policy, however, future outbreaks will continue to be viewed with the mixture of fascination, fear, helplessness and misdirected social policy that has characterized our response to the recent epidemics.

ANALYSIS: Identifying the Right Occasion

"How To Fight the New Epidemics" is an interesting example of a specialist turning to commentary to address a wider audience. Braun's writing for the most part grows out of her research on cervical cancer—grant proposals, reports in specialized journals, and so on. However, when new and mysterious "killer diseases" became hot topics in the news, Braun felt called on to explain the "fascination" with these epidemics and the "profound feeling of betrayal" among the public that science had not won the war against infectious diseases.

For Braun, the purpose of characterizing this public mood goes beyond simply labeling a trend in the popular mind. As her commentary unfolds, readers quickly become aware that this public mood is only the occasion for her to make a larger argument about the limits of the germ theory of disease and the failure of scientific and medical policymaking to take social conditions into account in preventing and controlling disease.

"How To Fight the New Epidemics" is a good example of how successful writers find occasions that link their own particular knowledge to what is on the public's mind. The appearance of "killer viruses" in the media gives Braun's argument about the germ theory a sense of urgency. By connecting her research into the history of disease to the present moment, Braun's commentary takes on a timeliness and relevance it might not otherwise have.

FOR CRITICAL INQUIRY

1. How would this commentary have been different had Braun not tied it to the hot news topic of "killer viruses"? Do you think readers would have less likely to read it? Would it have been less interesting in any way? Why or why not?
2. What does the popular fascination with epidemics reveal about the way we think about disease?
3. What is the central problem Braun identifies in her commentary? What does Braun see as its causes? What does she see as its consequences? What are her policy recommendations for dealing with the problem?
4. Divide the commentary into its main sections by grouping paragraphs together. What is the function of each section? What does each contribute to the commentary as a whole?
5. This commentary offers an example of a scientist pointing out the limits of science to interested readers. Why would scientists engage in this kind of commentary? Why do you think Braun has chosen to write for the general public?
6. Do you find Braun's commentary persuasive? Why or why not?

James W. Carey. "Technology and Ideology: The Case of the Telegraph."

James W. Carey is the Dean of the College of Communications at the University of Illinois and one of the leading theorists in communication studies. The following excerpt is the opening section of an article originally published in Prospects: The Annual of the American Studies Association. By opening with the observation that the telegraph has received little attention from scholarly researchers, Carey uses a typical academic strategy to introduce his commentary. As you read, notice the reasons Carey gives to explain why the telegraph is a significant topic and what we can learn by investigating it.

Analysis: Explaining Significance

One of the standard moves in academic writing is to call attention to a topic that has been neglected in a particular field of study. Carey opens the article by quickly offering some evidence to show that there has been little scholarly interest in the telegraph. According to Carey, moreover, this neglect is an unfortunate situation. By claiming as much, Carey seeks to persuade his readers that in fact there is a gap in our knowledge that needs to be filled—that something important is calling on him on him to bring the telegraph to readers' attention. In this way, Carey establishes the purpose of his writing task—to fill in a gap in our knowledge and thereby to expand our understanding of communication.

Technology and Ideology
The Case of the Telegraph

In one of the most famous paragraphs of our most famous autobiography, Henry Adams located the precise moment when "eighteenth-century troglodytic Boston" joined industrial America: "the opening of the Boston and Albany Railroad; the appearance of the first Cunard Steamers in the bay; and the telegraphic messages which carried from Baltimore to Washington the news that Henry Clay and James K. Polk were nominated for the presidency. This was May, 1844" (Adams, 1931: 5).

Adams signaled the absorption of genteel New England into industrial America by three improvements in transportation and communication. Yet for all the significance attached to the telegraph in that famous passage, it remains a product of one of the least studied technologies, certainly the least studied communications technology. The effect of the telegraph on modern life and its role as a model for future developments in communications have scarcely been explored. The first twenty-three volumes of *Technology and Culture* are virtually without reference to the telegraph. Robert L. Thompson's *Wiring a Continent*, the principal history of the telegraph, is now more than forty years old, takes the story only to 1866, and focuses almost exclusively on the formation of Western Union (Thompson, 1947).

I take the neglect of the telegraph to be unfortunate for a number of reasons. First, the telegraph was dominated by the first great industrial monopoly—Western Union, the first communications empire and the prototype of the many industrial empires that were to follow. The telegraph, in conjunction with the railroad, provided the setting in which

COMMUNICATION AS CULTURE

modern techniques for the management of complex enterprises were first worked out, though for the telegraph in what was eventually monopolistic circumstances.[1] Although the telegraph did not provide the site for the first of the titanic nineteenth-century patent struggles (that prize probably goes to Elias Howe's sewing machine) it led to one of the most significant of them in the rewriting of American law, particularly in the great "telegraph war" between Jay Gould and the Vanderbilt interests for control of the Edison patents for the quadraplex telegraph system, the innovation that Gould rightly prized as the "nerve of industry."[2]

Second, the telegraph was the first product—really the foundation—of the electrical goods industry and thus the first of the science- and engineering-based industries. David Noble's *American by Design: Science, Technology and the Rise of Corporate Capitalism* (1977) implies throughout a sharp distinction between forms of engineering, such as civil engineering, grounded in a handicraft and guild tradition, and chemical engineering and electrical engineering, which were science-based from the outset. Much that is distinctive about the telegraph, from the organization of the industry to the rhetoric that rationalized it, derives from the particular nature of the engineering it brought into being. More to the point, the telegraph was the first electrical engineering technology and therefore the first to focus on the central problem in modern engineering: the economy of a signal.[3]

Third, the telegraph brought about changes in the nature of language, of ordinary knowledge, of the very structures of awareness. Although in its early days the telegraph was used as a toy—as was the computer, which it prefigured—for playing long-distance chess, its implications for human knowledge were the subject of extended, often euphoric, and often pessimistic debate. Adams saw the telegraph as a demonic device dissipating the energy of history and displacing the Virgin with the Dynamo, whereas Thoreau saw it as an agent of trivialization. An even larger group saw the telegraph as an agency of benign improvement—spiritual, moral, economic, and political. Now that thought could travel by "the singing wire," a new form of reporting and a new form of knowledge were envisioned that would replace

TECHNOLOGY AND IDEOLOGY

traditional literature with a new and active form of scientific knowledge.

Fourth, and partly for the foregoing reasons, the telegraph was a watershed in communication, as I hope to show later. Now, it is easy to overemphasize the revolutionary consequences of the telegraph. It is not an infrequent experience to be driving along an interstate highway and to become aware that the highway is paralleled by a river, a canal, a railroad track, or telegraph and telephone wires. In that instant one may realize that each of these improvements in transportation and communications merely worked a modification on what preceded it. The telegraph twisted and altered but did not displace patterns of connection formed by natural geography: by the river and primitive foot and horse paths and later by the wooden turnpike and canal.

But the innovation of the telegraph can stand metaphorically for all the innovations that ushered in the modern phase of history and determined, even to this day, the major lines of development of American communications. The most important fact about the telegraph is at once the most obvious and innocent: It permitted for the first time the effective separation of communication from transportation. This fact was immediately recognized, but its significance has been rarely investigated. The telegraph not only allowed messages to be separated from the physical movement of objects; it also allowed communication to control physical processes actively. The early use of the telegraph in railroad signaling is an example: telegraph messages could control the physical switching of rolling stock, thereby multiplying the purposes and effectiveness of communication. The separation of communication from transportation has been exploited in most subsequent developments in communication down to computer control systems.

When the telegraph reached the West Coast eight years in advance of a transcontinental railroad, the identity of communication and transportation was ended in both fact and symbol. Before the telegraph, "communication" was used to describe transportation as well as message transmittal for the simple reason that the movement of messages was dependent

COMMUNICATION AS CULTURE

> on their being carried on foot or horseback or by rail. The telegraph, by ending the identity, allowed symbols to move independently of and faster than transportation. To put it in a slightly different way, the telegraph freed communication from the constraints of geography. The telegraph, then, not only altered the relation between communication and transportation; it also changed the fundamental ways in which communication was thought about. It provided a model for thinking about communication—a model I have called a transmission model—and displaced older religious views of communication even as the new technology was mediated through religious language. And it opened up new ways of thinking about communication within both the formal practice of theory and the practical consciousness of everyday life. In this sense the telegraph was not only a new tool of commerce but also a thing to think with, an agency for the alteration of ideas.

To make his claim persuasive, Carey knows, of course, that he needs to explain what we have missed by neglecting the telegraph. As is the case with the other commentators in this chapter, he needs to find patterns of meaning, to analyze and explain, so that the significance of the telegraph will be clear to readers. To do this, Carey offers a series of four reasons, each of which gives a different answer to the question with which Carey begins—namely, why is it unfortunate the telegraph has been neglected.

FOR CRITICAL INQUIRY

1. Why do you think Carey begins with a quote from Henry Adams? How does the quote help him set up his argument?
2. Carey marks the four reasons clearly, and he arranges them in a particular order. Why do you think he has chosen the order in which the reasons appear? Do you think the order is effective? Why or why not?
3. An effective introduction not only presents the subject and the writer's position, it should also forecast for readers what is to come in the rest of the writing. Although you do not have the complete text of Carey's article to refer to, does this introductory section give you clues about where Carey is going? Point to words, phrases, sentences, or passages that seem to forecast.
4. In the final paragraph of the opening, Carey notes that the "new technology was mediated through religious language." Later in the article, he expands on this point by looking at how people in the nineteenth century responded to the telegraph in terms of an

> ideal of universalism—the Kingdom of God and the
> Brotherhood of Man—[which] included a belief in a universal
> Human Nature. People were people—everywhere the same.
> Communication was the engine that powered this ideal. Each
> improvement in communication, by ending isolation, by
> linking people everywhere, was heralded as realizing the
> Universal Brotherhood of Universal Man.

Consider whether we still think about communication in such terms. Think particularly about the Internet and claims that have been made about its ability to link the world into a global village. Do you find such claims persuasive? Why or why not?

ETHICS OF WRITING

In Whose Interest?

Commentators often seek to persuade readers (or listeners or viewers) that their commentaries represent the best interests of the public and the common good. By speaking on behalf of the public, commentary plays a vital role in a democracy, holding accountable those in positions of power and explaining what the public's stake is in events, trends, and ideas.

Speaking in the name of the public, however, is rarely a simple matter, and it brings with it ethical responsibilities writers need to take into account. Since commentary offers explanations, it presumes, for example, to represent other people's motives. Commentators need, therefore, to avoid falling into stereotyped representations of groups of people ("single mothers on welfare have more children to get more benefits," "gay men are promiscuous," "young people today don't have a social conscience"). Such stereotypes not only characterize groups unfairly, they also turn these groups into "them" who are different from "us" and often present the interests of these groups as incompatible with the public interest.

Writers need to be aware, in other words, that speaking in the name of the public may in fact amount to speaking on behalf of some people or groups and distancing themselves from others. Writers need to examine their own assumptions about who is included in the public and try to understand how the people they write about perceive themselves and their experience.

LOOKING AT THE GENRE: COMMENTARY

1. In everyday conversations, we comment on people, events, and ideas, and trends that we have come across personally or learned about from the news. Think about a place where you routinely talk with others. It could be your workplace, the family dinner table, your dormitory, the day-care center where you pick up your child, or any place you often go.

On three or four different occasions, take notes on what people in the setting you've chosen talk about and how they comment on other people, events, trends, ideas, and so on. Write your notes as soon as possible after the conversation has ended. Use the following guidelines to take notes and to prepare a report on the role of commentary in everyday conversation:

- Describe the setting and the people involved. Explain what brings them together, what they have in common, and how they are different.

- Describe the topics that people comment on. Would you say they most often concern events, trends and ideas, or people? Explain why you think these topics come up in conversation. What makes them of interest to the people involved?

- Describe what people say about the topics.

- Describe people's interactions. Do certain people tend to introduce topics? Do people ask each other questions? Do they generally agree or disagree? When they disagree, do they tend to explore differences or to argue? Do people often reach a consensus?

- Characterize peoples' purposes in commenting on topics. To what extent is the purpose to analyze and make sense of the topics? To what extent is the purpose to persuade? What other purposes, if any, did you notice?

- Characterize the tone of the conversation—is it, for example, serious, humorous, sarcastic, emotional, cynical? Does the tone seem to vary depending on the topic?

GOING ON-LINE:

Following a Thread

You can do a similar assignment researching, analyzing, and reporting on the way people comment on topics on-line. Focus on a news group or other web site, and follow the thread of a conversation for a few days. Use the guidelines above to research and prepare your report, adjusting them as necessary. Try to characterize how commentary on-line is similar to and different from commentary in conversations and commentary in written text. Deja News searches for information about Internet newsgroups (www.dejanews.com), as does AltaVista (altavista.digital.com).

Work together in a group with two or three other students. Compare the reports from each member, noting important differences and similarities. What roles do talking with others and commenting on people, events, ideas, and trends seem to play in the particular settings group members have reported on? Use your findings to see if you as a group can form any tentative generalizations about how people use conversation to understand and manage their social lives. Finally, consider how commentary in conversation differs from written commentary.

2. Like news articles and other informative reports, commentaries are meant to inform readers about current events, trends, ideas, and so on. But, as you have seen, commentaries also go beyond informative writing to offer analysis and explanation. One of the key issues for commentary writers, then, is how to coordinate their informative and persuasive purposes. For two of the commentaries, identify where the writer's purpose seems to be largely informative and where the writer's purpose is more explicitly persuasive. What is the relationship between these informative and persuasive passages? How does the writer's persuasive purpose seem to influence the selection of factual material in the informative passages? How do the informative passages establish the credibility of the writer's analysis or interpretation? Does the writer seem to have achieved a good integration of informative and persuasive purposes? Why or why not?

3. Bring to class a commentary that interests you. The commentary can be on a topic related to that of a reading selection or on any other topic. To find it, look through the op-ed pages of newspapers (including your student newspaper) and through magazines that include editorials and commentary by columnists, critics, and feature writers (e.g., Harper's, Atlantic, Nation, Commentary, Progressive, Dissent, National Review). You don't have to agree with the commentary you choose.

Prepare a short report on the commentary. In the report, tell what event or issue is being commented on and explain why the commentary interests you. What is already known and agreed on about the topic? What particular angle or twist does the commentary give it? Describe the commentator's analysis and interpretation. Who does the writer appear to speak for or identify with? From whom, if anyone, is the writer seeking to distance himself or herself? What does the writer suggest is at stake for readers? What persuasive techniques and strategies does the writer use? How persuasive do you find the commentary?

If the reports are presented orally, as you listen to others' reports, try to identify what the commentaries have in common with one another and with the reading selections. What can you conclude about commentary as a genre?

DESIGNING DOCUMENTS: CARTOONS, COMIC STRIPS, AND POSTERS

Although this chapter focuses on written commentaries, the genre of commentary also includes cartoons and other visual forms. In fact, editorial cartoons, featured in the op-ed pages of many newspapers, are intended specifically to offer commentary. These visual forms of commentary, like their written counterparts, provide analyses and interpretations of events, ideas, and trends. Newspaper cartoons tend to focus on events, while cartoons in magazines like The New Yorker focus somewhat more on ideas and trends. Like other forms of commentary, visual forms take positions and attempt to persuade readers.

A key difference between written and visual forms of commentary lies in the heavy use that visual commentary makes of satire and other forms of humor and, in some cases, of startling effects. These can play a role in written commentary, of course, as shown, for example, by a long line of novels that offer satirical commentary—from Jonathan Swift's Gulliver's Travels to George Orwell's Animal Farm. But, given that satire typically relies on exaggerating a situation or personality in order to make a point, it's not surprising that cartoons and other visual forms use satire so often and so well—to poke fun at the rich and famous, to expose hypocrisy in public life, and to underscore the foibles of contemporary society. Gary Trudeau's Doonesbury is a good example of a comic strip that uses satire. (Satire is also characteristic of another kind of visual commentary—namely, of comic performances, such as skits on Saturday Night Live.)

Of course, these visual forms of commentary are not just visual but, rather, combine visual and text elements. The effectiveness of cartoons and other visuals often depends, in fact, on details of the drawing and of the text and on the precise way the two are integrated.

As you can see from the following examples, visual commentaries, not unlike other forms, can vary significantly in tone and in how they deal with issues. Some variation is tied to the range of visual forms possible. Consider the examples here: a cartoon; a comic strip, a visual form that, with its sequence of frames, allows a story to be told; and a poster, a form whose size can enhance the power of startling effects. The cartoon and Charles Shultz's Peanuts comic strip deal with two educational trends that have gotten a lot of attention: the skyrocketing costs of college education and the declining standards and study habits of some students. The third example is a poster designed by the Guerrilla Girls, an anonymous group of female artists and art-world professionals who wear gorilla masks and put up posters to publicize discrimination in the art world against women and minorities. In this poster, typical of their work, they have placed their trademark gorilla mask on a nude by the nineteenth-century French painter Jean-Auguste Dominique Ingres. The image is startling, and the point is driven home by the text.

Mike Peters
Dayton Daily News
Tribune Media Services

DISCUSSION AND ACTIVITIES

1. Discuss the cartoon. What exactly is the commentary? Do you find the cartoon funny? Do you find it effective as commentary? If so, what are some details of text and design that contribute to its humor and effectiveness?

2. Discuss the comic strip. To what extent do you think this comic strip offers a commentary? Do you find it effective and funny? If so, what details of text and design contribute to its humor and effectiveness? Note that there is no dialogue in the fourth frame. Why has it been included? How does it contribute to the humor? In general, what difference does it make that this is a comic strip rather than a cartoon?

3. Discuss the poster. What exactly is the commentary? How does the visual—with its superimposition of one image on another—contribute to the poster's effect? How does each element of text contribute? How is the layout—the combination of visual and text—effective? How is this kind of commentary similar to and different from that of cartoons and comic strips?

4. Pick an event or issue that has featured prominently in the news, either recently or over a period of time. Put together a group of editorial cartoons that offer commentary on the event or issue. (Good sources include Newsweek, editorial sections of newspapers like the Sunday edition of the New York Times and the Saturday edition of the Washington Post, which run cartoons from the past week drawn from various sources, and, if the issue spans a period of time, books that collect the works of particular cartoonists such as Herblock and Oliphant.)

Write an analysis of how the cartoons comment on their subject. What different positions on the event or issue do the cartoons take? Pay attention to the visual dimension, the written message, and the interaction between the two. Tell which cartoons you find particularly effective and why you think this is so.

What conclusions can you draw from your analysis? What strategies do cartoonists use in attempting to make their commentary persuasive and influence public opinion? Compared to written commentary, what are some of the advantages and disadvantages that cartoons seem to have?

5. Design your own cartoon, comic strip, or poster to comment on an event or issue. In designing this cartoon, make sure that both the visuals and the written words work to convey your position as effectively and persuasively as possible.

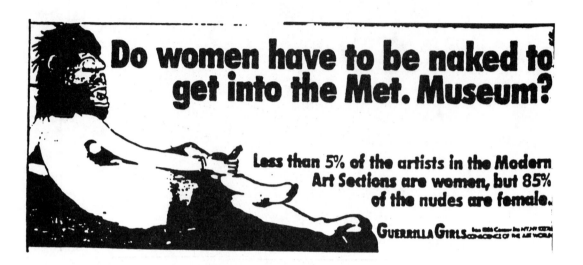

ASSIGNMENTS

WORKING TOGETHER: Assembling a Casebook

A casebook brings together writings on a topic from different perspectives. You may have used casebooks in other coursesósay, a casebook on the causes of World War I or on interpretations of The Scarlet Letter. A casebook does not itself attempt to influence readers, but rather, makes available to them key commentaries on the topic.

Work together in groups of two or three. Pick a current issue that has generated debate. It could affirmative action, bilingual education, immigration, eligibility standards for college athletes, or any other issue that has likely provoked a good deal of commentary. Assemble a casebook on the issue for high-school students.

First you'll need to do some library research—to search newspapers and magazines for commentaries written from different positions. (Don't assume there are just two sides—most controversies have many sides.) Select five or six commentaries that are representative of the various positions you found.

After rereading the commentaries you've selected, design your casebook in the following way:

- Write a brief introduction that gives readers an overview of the issue—what it is, how it began, why it is controversial—and mentions the articles you have selected.

- Include the readings. Before each reading give a headnote that tells who the writer is and briefly introduces the reading. After each reading give discussion questions to promote thinking about it. (You can use the headnotes and discussion questions in this textbook as models.)

- At the end of the casebook include several questions that pull together the various readings and make sure the students have understood the overall issue.

WRITING ASSIGNMENT

For this assignment, write a commentary that addresses a topic of interest to you. As you have noticed throughout the readings in this chapter, writing a commentary involves making an argument about an issue circulating in your culture. Commentary can also provide you with a chance to understand a curious cultural phenomenon a bit better. You may be called to write a commentary to help yourself make sense of an issue, or to bring the implications of an issue to your readersí attention. It may even arise from reading you are doing in one of your other classes in college. To help you get ideas for this assignment, consider what has called on the writers represented in this chapter's reading selections to write commentary. As you read the suggestions below, try the exercises to generate more ideas.

- **Current and historical events.** Stories that break in the news, such as Shannon Faulkner's battle with The Citadel, seem to call for swift response to coalesce readers' feelings and influence public

reaction. Here is writing at the point of opinion-making, shaping the public mood and sense of issues. You might draw on a recent event to serve as the springboard for your commentary, something current that your readers are likely to know about but where the meaning is still up for grabs.

On the flip side of the coin, you also write about the significance of a historical event from the past, as James Carey does. As you saw in his commentary about the telegraph, commentators often point out a lesson from the past, and articulate implications that would otherwise go unnoticed. You may be called to write a commentary about the significance of a historic event, an invention, a social movement, or an every day occurrence.

EXERCISE

To locate current events that might be fruitful for your commentary, find at least four different news sources (a big city newspaper, a campus newspaper, a news magazine, a TV broadcast). Within those sources, see which stories recur in all the formats ñ these are probably the stories that are the most ìpopularî right now. Make a list of the issues that show up in at least three of the sources, and mark those that seem most compelling or disturbing to you. If any of them remind you of another issue that you have felt strongly about, consider writing your commentary to make connections between the two events.

For historical events, you might look in several places for ideas. For starters, you might look through a history book, and watch for pictures or boxed anecdotes that capture your attention. If that doesnít offer you any ideas, trace through the significant social movements in your life from the time you were born, and think of specific events that were a part of that larger social movement. You might also watch movies that take place in historical times, and take note of real events that weave into the plot of the movie; if one interests you, learn more about that event for your commentary. Finally, if you are learning about an interesting historical event in another class you are taking, take the opportunity to write about it in this class as well.

- **Trends.** Labeling trends is a strategy commentators use to give readers a handle on what is taking place around them. Trends are not objective phenomena waiting to be identified, like some new species of animal. Rather they rely on the interpretive powers of commentators to name what's happening, thereby giving a series of events a distinct identity and making it available as a topic for public discussion. Lundy Braun's use of the term "killer viruses" is a good example of how trend-naming seeks to bring a public mood into sharper relief.

Writing about trends, of course, is not limited to infectious disease in contemporary America. There are plenty of other trends as well: body-piercing and tattooing, cyber-cafes, nostalgia for the 1970s, the rising use of marijuana, the growth of microbreweries, the declining crime rate, the increase of unmarried mothers in all sectors of society, corporate down-sizing and temporary contracts. You might write about the significance of a particular trend that is already well-known or you can invent a new label to characterize a trend that has not been noticed before.

EXERCISE

Although you should feel free to use any of the trends listed in the paragraph above, you can also work through some of the suggestions here to find a trend that compels you to write. To identify a trend or fad, take an inventory of the aspects of your life. This means breaking down the aspects of your life into decision-making moments, and then examine those moments to see if they fit into a larger trend. For example, when you wake up in the morning, what kinds of clothes do you put on? Are they related to any kind of a trend (like Birkenstock clogs, or a specific kind of jeans)? When you eat breakfast, what do you choose (something loaded with sugar, or something with whole wheat bran, or nothing at all)? What form of transportation do you use? Could that be part of a trend? Notice, too, the choices that people around you seem to make. By the end of the day, you should have a lengthy list of options.

• Policy issues. Commentators often address issues of public policy. In Lundy Braun's commentary, "How to Fight the New Epidemics," the main focus is on the issue of infectious disease control: Why is there suddenly so much media interest in infectious diseases? What has caused the resurgence of diseases such as tuberculosis and cholera? What public health policy will work to control infectious diseases? As you have seen, to answer these questions, Braun has analyzed the causes of diseases and the adequacy of the "germ theory" to control disease.

You might write a commentary that focuses on the origins and causes of a topic or issue that interests you. Accounting for why things happen is often the first step in explaining what should be done—to endorse, alter, or control the situation.

EXERCISE

One way to think about finding policy issues of interest to you is to identify the issues that might impact on your life—either right now or in the future. Think through your life systematically, and make a list of those communities that have an impact on your daily existence. For example, label the various parts of your identity: college student, mother of a toddler, copy-shop employee, volunteer Emergency Medical Technician, amateur photographer, weekend auto mechanic, member of a religious youth organization. Next, for each label you wrote down, think of at least three policy issues that matter to that community. As a student, for instance, you might have been affected by need-blind admissions, or particular financial aid policies and procedures. As a parent, you might have a stake in arguing for more and better child care options for your college or work community. As a copy-shop employee, you might be interested in recent copyright legislation that makes it more difficult for copy-shops to create coursepacks for classes. By the time you have gone through your list of community identities, you should have a sizable list of policy issues important to you ñ that are ripe for commentary.

• Satire and humor. As you have seen, cartoons and comic strips often use satire to bring out a public figureís real motives or the unstated logic of an event or situation. Satire and humor can be used effectively to expose the powerful, and to undermine conventional ideas.

You might write a satirical commentary that uses exaggeration to make a telling point. Or, if your instructor is agreeable, you might design and produce a poster, a cartoon, a comic strip to comment on a current event, issue, or idea. Or write and perform a comic skit with others or a monologue on your own.

EXERCISE

Humor and satire can be powerful because they grow out of a sense of outrage. Because of this connection to real anger, it may be helpful for you to find people, events, or issues that make you fighting mad. Once you have found something that irritates you to the point of distraction, you can begin to poke fun at it. Drawn caricatures are often quite mean-spirited, exaggerating the least attractive quality of the person being drawn. This, too, can grow from hostility. Humor and satire allow you to harness that hostility into a different, often more socially acceptable, format.

Other times, however, humorists just see the silliness in something quite mundane. Or they begin by imitating somebody they notice. If you don't have a sense of rage over a particular issue, person, or event, cast about to think of times you've just poked fun at something that seems absurd to you. Reconstruct conversations you've had with friends and family, either recently or in the past, and find the sources of humor in those conversations. These moments can form the basis of your commentary; after selecting a defining moment growing out of humor, you can write more seriously about its implications.

- Responses to readings. Another strategy to find issues for your position paper is to respond to one of the reading selections in this book, or something you have read recently in another course. You can frame your commentary by agreeing or disagreeing with another writer. Or you can use that writer's presentation of an issue as a jumping-off point to develop your own perspective and position. Here are some possible topics drawn from readings in other chapters of this textbook:

- Read Mark Patinkin's column "Commit a Crime, Suffer the Consequences" (page XXX in ì?ⁿì) and develop your own position on what the controversy over the caning of William Fay means.

- Read Mike Rose's essay "I Just Wanna Be Average" (page XXX in Profiles) and write a commentary on whether you think high schools should track students.

- Read the essay by Nicola Clark "How to Draft a National Service Plan" (page XXX in Proposals) and write on why you think young people should or should not be required to perform community service.

If you want more specific advice with responding to readings, look through Chapter 2, Reading and Writing: The Critical Connection, particularly the sections on Responding (see pages XXX) and Evaluating (see pages XXX).

INVENTION

You have already begun a list of informal commentary that you run into on a daily basis, and you have probably generated a substantial list of possibilities from the exercises above. If it helps generate even more ideas, look at any Writing Inventories you may have written in Chapter 1 (especially those on pages XXX). In the next several sections, you will narrow your options and begin working in depth on one commentary. This next stage of invention requires distinguishing the topic of your writing (what people already know), and the issue you are bringing up (what you want to say about the topic).

NAMING YOUR TOPIC

As you have seen in the reading selections, commentary offers perspectives after the fact—after events have been reported in news stories, personalities have emerged in the media, or ideas, styles, fads, and moods are floating around in the public consciousness. The point of commentary is to offer ideas and perspectives to explain the significance of what has happened in the past and what is going on in the present.

Shannon Faulkner's struggle to enter The Citadel, the capital punishment debate, or the new epidemics are topics because they refer to things your readers are likely to have read about in the news or observed in their personal experience—events, situations, trends, ideas, conflicts, or debates that people are talking about.

Topics are forms of knowledge, the facts and information that have acquired public recognition and that you can assume your readers will recognize and be familiar with. Topics have names—whether those of individuals (Shannon Faulkner, O.J. Simpson), historical and political events (slavery, the Vietnam War, Reagan's presidency), social and cultural trends (increase in two-career families, body-piercing, animal rights advocacy), or concepts (natural selection, Einstein's theory of relativity, the germ theory of disease). You can look up a topic and find information on it in the library. Your topic is the source of your commentary, the information whose significance you want to explore.

EXERCISE

State the topic you are considering writing about in the form of a noun phrase (the Protestant Reformation, conversation patterns between men and women, the Oklahoma City bombing). To explore the topic, respond to the following questions in writing:

- What do you know about the topic? How do you know what you know about it? What is the source of your knowledge? List as many sources as you can. Which, if any, of these sources are available to you? Which might it be helpful to locate and re-read?

- What do you think other people know about the topic? Is it widely known or is it likely to be of interest to a more limited readership? How are other people likely to have learned about the topic? Through newspapers, television news, personal experience?

- Are there conflicting views or a range of opinion on the topic? If so, how would you describe the conflict or difference of opinion? Are there readily distinguishable sides involved? If so, do you tend to have allegiances to one rather than the other? Explain how you align yourself to the topic and to what others have said about it.

IDENTIFYING THE ISSUE

An issue refers to how the writer focuses attention on what he or she thinks is important about the topic. This is where the function of commentary comes in. Commentators establish issues to explain some meaningful aspect of the topic according to their own perspective. For a breakdown of the types of issues, and a discussion of their implications, see relevant sections in Chapter 3, particularly Analyzing Issues (page XXX) and Types of Claims (page XXX).

Notice in the following chart how the same topic can generate a number of different issues.

Topic: The Shannon Faulkner case		
Source: the media		
Issues:	New York Times	Susan Faludi	Capt. Erin Dowd
	gender equity	gender equity	gender equity
	immaturity of cadet behavior	popular illusions about heroes and celebrities	Faulkner's lack of preparation

Notice there is some overlap in the three selections. Each writer announces early on where he or she stands on the central controversy in Shannon Faulkner's two and one half year struggle to gain admission—the issue of gender equity in the military. All three make it clear that they support an end to discrimination at men-only military academies and women's right to attend The Citadel. As you can see, however, while the writers all share a similar position on the issue of gender equity, they go on to introduce and explore very different issues concerning the Shannon Faulkner case.

After you have identified the issue that most interests you within the topic, you can begin to explain the particular urgency of your issue. Why should your readers be concerned and interested? Why is the issue being raised in the first place? (Or, if you're writing about an issue that has not received attention, why has the issue been ignored and why do you want to raise it?)

EXERCISE

1. Locate three readings (from newspapers, magazines, journals, or books) on the topic you are planning to write about. Use the chart above as a model to name the topic, indicate the source, and identify the issues others have written about.

2. List as many other issues as you can. You don't have to agree with the sense of the issue or be interested in writing about it just yet. The point at this stage is to get as wide a picture

as possible of available issues. For now, just brainstorm for all the issues you can; you will pare the list down to the most interesting ones later.

3. Circle the three or four issues that are most interesting to you. Consider what, if anything, they have in common with one another. Do they overlap in any way? How do they differ? Does one bring to light something that the others donít? If you notice that a connection between the issues you circled, that connection may well be worth writing about in your commentary.

4. Decide tentatively on one issue to write about. What would you say about the issue in a commentary? How would your commentary bring you into alliance with some people and positions but not with others?

5. Think about the implications of your commentary. If people were persuaded by your position, what would happen? How would this be an improvement over the present condition of things? If your readers your commentary seriously, what would you hope to achieve? Is there something you would like them to do?

6. Consider the position of people who differ with you. What are the key points of difference? What objections might people have to your commentary? Are any valid? Are there any points of agreement or common values? How can you use these in your commentary? What differences do you feel need to be addressed in your statement? For more guidance on anticipating and working with different points of view, see portions of Chapter 5, especially those on Differing Views (pages XXX) and Negotiating Differences (pages XXX).

PLANNING

FRAMING THE ISSUE

Like the frame of a painting, the frame of a commentary goes on the outside, to give it boundaries and a focus of attention. Commentaries typically open by framing an issue—defining it, explaining its relevance to readers, and using it to set up the writer's position. Framing the issue, then, has two main purposes.

First, framing the issue focuses readers' attention on a particular aspect of the topic. It establishes a perspective for readers to see significant features of a topic they already know something about. Framing the issue often begins with the familiar and then seeks to add a new or different angle or way of analyzing and explaining what is known.

Second, framing the issue sets the writer up to present the main point of his or her commentary. Depending on how the writer frames the issue, he or she will enter into one or another relationship to the topic and what other people have said about it.

There are many techniques commentary writers use to frame issues. Here are a few:

- Describe an event or an existing situation. The point is to establish what is known in order to set the writer up to explain what new perspective he or she is going to bring to the issue. The amount of detail will depend on how familiar you think your readers will be with your topic.

- Describe the sides to a controversy, conflict, or debate. On issues where people differ or find themselves on opposing sides, commentary writers often sketch briefly what the different views are in order to explain what they believe is at stake in these differences. By analyzing and evaluating the sides that already exist, you can set yourself up to present your own perspective and to show how it allies you with some people and positions but not with others.

- Explain the causes or origins of an issue. Giving readers accounts of how something got started raises underlying issues of cause and effect: Why does something occur in the first place? What causes things to happen over a period of time? What are the results? Who is affected? Who is responsible? By explaining the causes or origins of an issue, you can set yourself up to show readers how something came to have the shape and importance it does.

- Explain how you became aware of the issue. Writers draw on what they have read, observed, or experienced that brought a particular issue to their attention—how something hit home for them. This technique can help set writers up to explain an event, a situation, a conflict, a debate by showing why and on what terms the writer is invested in the issue.

- Explain points and principles you share in common with readers. Writers will often join together with others on certain shared points or principles. By affirming common values and attitudes, you can gain consideration for your views, and this can help set you up to introduce ideas which may not fit readily with others' thinking.

- Use examples or personal anecdote. Begin with an example or anecdote that illustrates the issue you are writing about. More importantly, then, draw explicit connections between the example or anecdote and the larger issue. Is the example or anecdote representative of the situation your position addresses (or is it an exception)? Make this clear in your framing of the commentary.

DESIGNING AN ENDING

Endings apply the final frame to the writer's position. They give the writer the chance to have the last word, to leave readers with a closing sense of the issue and the writer's stand. Here are some ways writers design endings:

- Point out the consequences of your position. What would happen if your position were taken up? How would that improve the current situation?

- Reaffirm shared values and beliefs. What common values and beliefs does your commentary draw on? How does your position express these values and beliefs?

- Make recommendations. What would your commentary look like if it were carried through in practice? What concrete proposals does it lead to?

- Call on readers to take action. What steps can readers take, assuming they agree with the writer? What changes in thinking, in personal habits, or in public policy follow from your commentary?

EMPHASIZING THE MAIN POINT

Notice in the reading selections how commentary writers explicitly or implicitly identify lessons to be learned from the events, trends, ideas, and debates they are writing about. Readers of commentary expect the writer to make a clear point. Readers assume that the point of reading a commentary is not primarily to be informed about an issue but to consider what the writer has to say about it. For this reason, it is important that the writer's main point can be easily found.

Here are some questions to take into account as you design your commentary—to make sure your main point has the emphasis it needs:

- Does the way the introduction frames the issues effectively forecast your main point and the direction of your commentary?

- Is the main point located at an effective place in the commentary? How much background or context is necessary for your main point to take on significance? When it does appear, is the main point stated as clearly as possible?

- Are details, facts, and other information about the topic clearly related to your main point? If you are using examples, is it clear what point or points the examples are intended to illustrate?

- Do your explanations develop the main point of the commentary or do they raise other issues? If they do, is this intended on your part, or are you starting to jump from issue to issue? Can you point out the connection between issues so readers will be able to follow your line of thought.

- Does the ending offer a satisfying sense of closure? Will readers find it easy to see how they arrived at your final point? Does the ending help to emphasize the main point or lesson of the commentary?

THE WORKING DRAFT

Write a page or two as quickly as you can. Imagine that you are simply doing some exploratory writing for yourself and that no one will necessarily see what you have written. Just write off the top of your head without worrying about organization or sentence structure ñ as if you are warming up to write the ìrealî draft. Use this writing as a discovery draft to clarify your own perspective on the issue you are writing about, to explore your own sympathies, and to understand on whose behalf you want to speak and with whom you differ. Use this draft to produce a working draft of your commentary.

PARAGRAPH DEVELOPMENT: Using Reasons to Explain

Because commentaries often seek to explain what is happening and why, they typically use reasons as one way to establish the focus of a paragraph. Notice in the following sequence of paragraphs, how Laurie Ouellette offers reasons to explain why "young women have shunned feminism."

Given all this, what can explain why so many young women have shunned feminism? In her survey of young women, *Feminist Fatale: Voices from the Twentysomething Generation Explore the Future of the Women's Movement*, Paul Kamen found that media-fueled stereotypes of feminists as "man-bashers" and "radical extremists" were behind the fact that many young women don't identify with the women's movement.

But these are not the only reasons. Kamen also points to the lack of young feminist role models as an important factor. The failure of a major feminist organization such as NOW to reach out to a wider spectrum of women, including young women, must be acknowledged as a part of this problem. While individual chapters do have young feminist committees and sometimes officers, they and the national office are led and staffed primarily by older women, and consequently often fail to reflect the interests and needs of a complex generation of young women.

Yet another reason young women have turned away from feminism may lie within its history. If the young women who have gained the most from feminism — that is, white, middle-class women who took advantage of increased accessibility to higher education and professional employment — have been reluctant to associate themselves with feminism, it is hardly surprising that most economically disadvantaged women and women of color, who have seen fewer of those gains, have not been eager to embrace feminism either. The women's movement of the seventies has been called an upper-middle-class white women's movement, and to a large degree I believe that is true. More than a few young feminists — many influenced by feminists of color such as Flo Kennedy, Audre Lorde, and bell hooks — have realized that feminism must also acknowledge issues of race and class to reach out to those women whose concerns have been overlooked by the women's movement of the past. Indeed, numerous statistics, including a poll by the *New York Times*, have noted that young African-American women are more likely than white women to acknowledge many of the concerns conducive to a feminist agenda, including a need for job training and equal earning power outside the professional sector. But for them, feminism has not provided the only answer. Only by making issues of class and race a priority can feminism hope to influence the lives of the millions of women for whom the daily struggle to survive, not feminist activism, is a priority. Will ours be the first generation of feminists to give priority to fighting cuts in Aid to Families with Dependent Children, establishing the right to national health care, day care, and parental leave, and bringing to the forefront other issues pertinent to the daily struggle of many women's lives? If there is to be a third wave of feminism, they must.

We can diagram the pattern of development in the three paragraphs.

¶1   Reason: media stereotypes of feminists
     Supporting examples: ìman-bashers,î ìradical extremistsî
¶2   Reason: lack of young feminist role models
     Supporting fact: NOW local chapters and national office staffed largely by older women
¶3   Reason: the history of feminism
     Supporting fact: womenís movement is white and upper-middle-class
     Supporting testimony: Flo Kennedy, Audre Lorde, bell hooks note women of color's concerns have been overlooked
     Supporting statistic: New York Times poll notes young African American women's concerns with feminist issues but not feminist movement

As you can see, Ouellette understands that the reasons she offers do not speak for themselves. Each must be supported by one form of evidence or another.

BEGINNINGS AND ENDINGS: Replacing a Common View with an Alternative Perspective

You have already written at least one version of a frame you can use to set up your commentary. Take a look at that beginning now, and see if you like the way it is working. Then, look at the way you end your commentary. Does it tie in somehow with the beginning? If not, you might consider using the technique of replacing a common view with an alternative perspective. This can work either at the beginning of the commentary, to establish your frame, or at the end, to reinforce the main point you are making about your issue.

In her piece on Shannon Faulkner, Susan Faludi offers a good example of how writers conclude their writing by starting with a common view they know their readers will recognize quite readily, whether or not they agree with the view, and then offering her own take on it. Faludi replaces the common view (that Shannon Faulkner was a failure) with an alternative that concludes Faludiís argument (that Faulkner learned, and we can learn with her, that collective action means more than individual, isolated attempts at change). Faludi, in other words, turns this into a success story.

> It's a lesson that gleeful pundits, disappointed feminists and conservative detractors of Shannon Faulkner can learn as well. "It would have been different if there had been other women with me." That's not an excuse. That's a valedictory.
> — Susan Faludi, "Shannon Faulkner's Strength in Numbers"

If this strategy doesn't work for you, look through other chapters for more ideas. For example, you can:

* see Using an Echo Effect to Reframe (page XXX in Letters) to knit your beginning and ending together more tightly

* see Pointing Out the Significance or Wider Consequences (page XXX in Memoirs) to make sure your approach to your issue comes through clearly

* see Setting Up with a Metaphorical Anecdote (page XXX in Profiles) to frame your commentary using a representative story

PEER COMMENTARY

Exchange working drafts and respond in writing to these questions about your partner's draft:

1. Identify the topic of the draft. How does the writer frame the main issue? Point to a phrase or sentence. Where did you become aware of what the writer has to say about the issue? Point to a phrase or sentence where you first got the writer's point. If you can't point to

particular phrases or sentences, what answers does the writer seem to imply to these questions?

2. Who is likely to agree with the writer's commentary? What beliefs and values does the commentary appeal to? Does the commentary seem to choose sides? If so, who else is on the writer's side? Who is excluded?

3. Do you share the writer's perspective on the issue? If so, does the writer make the most effective case in presenting that perspective? Can you offer suggestions about ways to improve it? If you don't share the writer's perspective, explain why. Describe your own perspective.

REVISING

Read the remarks you get on your working draft. Use them as a check to make sure you've framed the issue clearly and your main point is easily identifiable. If you sense that your message is not coming across clearly to readers, you probably need to work on framing the issue and emphasizing your main point. You may well need to revise the opening parts of your draft so readers can feel confident they know what it at issue, and what your perspective is.

Once you have revised your working draft based on the response from your writing partner, go through your text again and check for connections and coherence.

CONNECTIONS AND COHERENCE: Linking Evidence to Claims

If you state your position clearly somewhere near the beginning of your statement, then the sections that follow should show readers how the evidence being presented links back to and supports the your claim. Notice in James Carey's "Technology and Ideology: The Case of the Telegraph" how he makes such explicit links between his claim and the evidence he offers to support it:

Claim (in ¶ 2 and 3): "Yet for all the significance attached to the telegraph in that famous passage, it remains a product of one of the least studied technologies. . . . I take the neglect of the telegraph to be unfortunate for a number of reasons."

3: First, the telegraph was dominated by the first great industrial monopoly . . .

4: Second, the telegraph was the first product ñ really the foundation ñ of the electrical goods industry . . .

5: Third, the telegraph brought about changes in the nature of language . . .

¶ 6: Fourth . . . the telegraph was a watershed in communication . . .

7: (summary of preceding sections): But the innovation of the telegraph can stand metaphorically for all the innovations that ushered in the modern phase of history . . .

As you can see from this example, Carey sets up his main point early in his commentary, then builds on it in each paragraph that follows. He signals the connections with the first sentence in each paragraph, many of which enumerate the point (for more on marking transitions with enumerative order, see page XXX in Public Documents). These transitions function to link each new point back to his initial proposition: that the telegraph is worthy of more critical attention than it has received. After listing his four main points, Carey provides additional paragraphs which emphasize the larger implications of his subject.

In addition to linking each of your paragraphs to your proposition, as the example from Carey illustrates, you might also want to consider other kinds of transitions that help signal where you want your readers to make important shifts with you. Specific devices are listed in Taking a Position: Crafting a Rhetorical Stance in Chapter 3 (pages XXX). Beyond that, you might also:

- see Temporal Transitions (page XXX in Memoirs) to indicate when time sequences are shifting

- see Enumerative Order (see page XXX in Public Documents) to emphasize distinctive subpoints you are making

- see Logical Transitions (page XXX in Reviews) to make firm links between parts of your argument

WRITERS WORKSHOP

Rachel Smith wrote the following commentary "Socially Acceptable Discrimination" as an assignment in her first-year writing course. It is followed by an interview with the writer.

Rachel Smith
12-9-95
WA # 5

Socially Acceptable Discrimination?

I looked up at the billboard as we drove home from church one Sunday and saw the advertisement for the newest Steve Martin movie Leap of Faith. Martin stood in the center of the board, arms raised above him, his suitcoat gaudy and sparkling. His face was tilted upwards. A slight smile on his lips, his eyes were squinted. His stance suggested religious worship. Lights shown down from behind him, and the words LEAP OF FAITH were pasted on the board over his head. At first glance, the picture looked sincere; here was a man worshipping God. However, when I noticed the overdone clothes and the pious look on his face, I knew that this was not a picture of a man praising his God. This was an advertisement for a movie whose sole purpose was to make a "hilarious" comedy out of the life of a television evangelist. Later, when I saw the preview trailers for Leap of Faith on television, I saw Steve Martin pushing fat, sweating women to the floor in a cheap imitation of what sometimes happens at real evangelical tent meetings. He had this look of intense pleasure on his face, his body language wide and over-the-top, almost as if he was getting a sexual kick out of what he was doing. The character was described as being "a born-again, Spirit-filled, holy-rollin' Christian," and often spouted "Well, Peraaaise God!" This movie is only one example of the way that born-again Christians are portrayed in the media. America's most popular image of a born-again Christian is a narrow-minded, Bible-waving, bigot who doesn't know how to have fun.

Now, don't get me wrong; I'm not saying that we don't sometimes wave our Bibles around. There are people who call themselves born-again Christians who find it absolutely imperative that they shove their beliefs down everyone's throat, "waving their Bible" all the while. They chain themselves to abortion-clinic doors and support the madmen who shoot the doctors that perform abortions. There are people in every group, whether it is feminists, African-

Americans, those of Middle Eastern descent, or teenagers, who are the "black sheep," so to speak, of the group. They are the radicals and therefore are sensational. They get the publicity and portray their group as being as radical and unbalanced as they are. Not all African-Americans harbour deep, hateful grudges against whites. Actually, a large majority of them don't. Often, in movies, they are portrayed in the stereotype that they all hate whites, as in Malcolm X. This portrayal is the most sensational, and therefore the most newsworthy. Why hasn't anyone made a major, widely-released movie about the life of Martin Luther King, Jr.? Because he didn't have a checkered past, his life wasn't filled with violence and anger (on his part, at least), and he preached a message of forgiveness. Those things aren't sensational. They aren't as newsworthy as the radical, insane things that the media prefers to focus on.

Because of the media's attraction to the sensational, often groups are represented erroneously. What's sensational about the rest of the born-again Christians? They don't attack doctors and plant explosives in office buildings. They don't all go around condemning everyone they meet to hell. They live just like everyone else. Granted, they don't frequent too many bars and brothels, they tend to spend more time in church than most Americans, and they live, very strictly, by the Bible. Because of this last point, many believe that Christians don't have any fun. That is one of the main reasons movies like Leap of Faith were made. The media says that underneath that "good" image, Christians are probably really warped human beings, following some long-dead cult that says the world will come to an end pretty soon, so all the rest of us had better join up or we'll be in lots of trouble. Leap of Faith just gives people a laugh and helps relieve them of the little suspicion that those crazy, born-again Christians just might have something. When a prominent televangelist is exposed, the media jumps into the fray and triumphantly holds up the tattered pieces, flaunting the fall of someone supposed to be "good." This concentration on the negative side of Christianity lends itself to making the public see born-again Christians as completely unbalanced, non-rational, bigoted people. We are portrayed in only the worst ways.

My intent in writing on this subject is not to whine about injustice and the liberal media, but to bring out the other side of the issue. To put it plainly, every special interest group in America has gained a lot of publicity for fighting discrimination, except for the born-again Christians. Politically correct speech is the newest fad; everyone is careful about what they say. More movies are being released that center on the lives of homosexuals, there is a rise in the frequency of African-American sitcoms, Greenday gets news coverage every time they try to sue a lumber company, and whenever there is a story on abortion, a majority of the personal interviews come from the Pro-choice side. In all this "political correctness," born-again Christians are invariably left out by the media because the beliefs that we hold do *not* embrace all the personal preferences that people have. We live by a definite standard of right and wrong, and because people do not want to be told that something they are doing is wrong, they invent their own morality: situation ethics. Born-again Christians do not fit into that jelly-mold of American society. When a movie like Leap Of Faith came out, the only protests against such discrimination were in Christian magazines and books. We fight the currents, and yes, we do make people uncomfortable sometimes, but why is discrimination against us more culturally acceptable?

INTERVIEW WITH RACHEL SMITH

Q: What prompted you to write "Socially Acceptable Discrimination"?

A: I have felt for a long time that people unfairly judge born-again Christians like myself. If you go by the newspapers, born-agains are narrow-minded bigots, madmen who kill abortion doctors, or hypocrites like Jim Bakker. I know this isn't the real story, but it seemed that these stereotypes of born-agains are just something I had to live with. That I couldn't really do anything about it. Then I saw the Steve Martin movie Leap of Faith, and I began to think that this might give me an occasion to try to correct perceptions.

Q: How did you decide to focus on the particular issues you explore in "Socially Acceptable Discrimination"?

A: I knew I wanted to change the way people perceive born-again Christians but I also knew I couldn't just say, "Hey, you've got it all wrong. That's not the way we really are." I'd be asking people to accept my personal experience, and I was pretty sure this wasn't going to work. So I thought that if I focused on how the media portrayed born-again Christians and tied this to the idea that the media loves to sensationalize things that I might get a different response from readers. I figured most people think the media is sensationalistic and that by using this as a kind of common ground with readers, I could introduce my own point of view in a way that might get a hearing.

Q: What conflicts, if any, did you experience writing this commentary?

A: It's hard because movies like Leap of Faith and all the media coverage of crazed evangelicals really gets me angry. I know it's a false picture and totally unfair to me and other born-agains, who are just normal people who happen to believe in God and want to follow the Bible. I wanted to make this point, but I also knew that if I let my anger come out too strongly that I was going to lose readers—or maybe even confirm their impression that we're all nuts. So I definitely experienced this conflict of wanting to be loyal to other believers and to get their real story out and, at the same time, knowing that I had to write in a reasonable tone. That's where the Steve Martin movie and the idea of media sensationalism were so helpful to me. By analyzing them (instead of screaming at people, which is what I felt like doing), I think I got some critical distance and could still be true to what I wanted to say.

WORKSHOP QUESTIONS

1. As Rachel Smith notes in the interview, her main purpose is to "correct perceptions" of born-again Christians. What was your attitude toward born-again Christians before you read "Socially Acceptable Discrimination"? How did this attitude influence your response to her commentary? Did reading her commentary confirm, modify, change, or otherwise affect the attitude you began with? Explain what happened and why. How successful is Smith in achieving her purpose?
2. Smith says that she realized she couldn't persuade people solely on the basis of her personal experience as a born-again Christian. Instead, she focuses on how the media portrays born-agains. Evaluate this strategy. To what extent does it offer the common ground with readers that she hopes to find?
3. Smith notes a conflict between her loyalty to other believers and her desire to reach out to her readers. One way this conflict manifests itself is in the tension between the anger she feels about being portrayed unfairly and the need she acknowledges to maintain a reasonable tone in her writing. How well do you think she handles this tension? Do you find her tone to be reasonable? Are there passages where her anger comes across? If so, what is the effect? Does it, as Smith fears, confirm impressions that born-agains are "all nuts"? Or does the anger seem to be legitimate?

WRITERS INVENTORY

Use the questions in the interview with Rachel Smith to interview someone who has recently written a commentary. It could be classmate but also consider interviewing columnists in your student or local newspaper. The questions are these:

1. What prompted you to write the commentary?
2. How did you decide to establish the focus of the piece?
3. What conflicts, if any, did you experience when you wrote it?

A CLOSING NOTE

As you have seen throughout this chapter, commentary involves writers in speaking on be-half of others. Re-read the commentary you've written to see how the perspective you offer in your commentary allies you with some people and divides you from others. Use the information you get to make sure you are comfortable with the way your commentary establishes your relation-ship to others and whether there are passages you want to revise.

CHAPTER
TEN

PROPOSALS:
Formulating and Solving Problems

LOOKING AT THE GENRE

Proposals put forth plans of action and seek to persuade readers that these plans should be implemented. Like commentary, proposals involve analyzing issues, taking a position, and making an argument. However, proposals go beyond commentaries by recommending a course of action, oftentimes a solution to a problem that has been identified as needing attention. Like commentaries, proposals use arguments to influence readers' beliefs, but they do so with the aim of advancing a new program or policy.

This difference between commentaries and proposals is not an absolute one but a matter of emphasis. After all, the positions writers take in commentaries have consequences. Whether writers make it explicit+ or not, their positions imply certain policies, courses of action, and ways of living. But proposals emphasize this dimension of making policy, devising courses of action, and negotiating the demands of everyday life. The focus of attention shifts from the statement and explanation of the writer's position to what we ought to do about it. Thus, in proposals, writer's positions have a practical or applied dimension in that they involve identifying problems and offering solutions.

Making proposals, of course, is a familiar everyday activity that people perform routinely, often without being conscious that they are engaging in a fairly predictable pattern—defining a problem, surveying alternatives, and choosing a course of action. Let's say you're making a plan for Saturday night—whether with your family or with your friends—and you have a limited budget. The problem here is to propose something that others will enjoy but that still fits within your finances.

You survey the possibilities, immediately ruling out a first-run movie or dinner in an expensive restaurant. You realize you could go out for pizza and still have enough money left for a second-run theater or a movie playing on campus. Or you could eat at a Chinese or Mexican restaurant and then rent a movie for your family to watch at home or go with your friends to the campus coffee house, which is featuring a local band with no door charge.

To persuade your family or your friends to go along with your proposal, you need first of all to make sure it really solves the problem (that's why you ruled out the expensive dinner and first-run movie). In addition, you'll want to make sure that you've considered all possible alternatives (maybe there's a free concert at your church or you can get into a basketball game on campus with your student ID) and that you've anticipated possible objections (what if one of your children doesn't like Chinese food or one of your friends had it just last night?). As you can see, this real-life example illustrates several features proposals must have to be effective. You need to persuade others that the solution proposed is possible—that budgetary and other constraints have been taken into account—and that it is a good one—that it considers alternatives and anticipates objections.

People in many walks of life do this kind of problem-solving when they write proposals. One common type of proposal is the grant proposal, in which writers request funding to support a project. For example, scientists define research problems in their field and write a proposal to the National Science Foundation or some other potential sponsor, in which they explain why the line of investigation they intend to pursue promises to yield significant findings. Bids for contracts by, say, engineering firms are proposals explaining how the firms would solve a manufacturing company's problem of solid waste disposal or improve the efficiency of assembly-line production.

Many proposals involve problems and solutions in matters of public policy. For example, private foundations and government agencies commission bodies of experts to study a problem in their field—education, the environment, civil rights, international trade, labor relations, and so on—and to issue a report with proposals for change. By the same token, citizens' organizations and advocacy groups of all sorts—from neighborhood and church associations to local preservationist and environmental groups to national organizations such as Greenpeace, National Organization of Women (NOW), and National Rifle Association (NRA)—also study problems, consider alternatives, and make recommendations to appropriate government bodies. Their proposals seek to gain public support and influence government policy.

Let's look at a situation that might call for a written proposal, in order to explore the main features shared by these different kinds of proposals. A local community group thinks that a vacant lot the city owns could be converted into a neighborhood park. The group knows that

Endorsement resolution. Recycling Initiative Campaign.

This petition circulated by the Recycling Initiative   a problem and endorses a proposed solution.
Campaign, like many other proposals, formulates

29 Temple Place, Boston, MA 02111-1305 (617) 292-4824

ENDORSEMENT RESOLUTION

WHEREAS, packaging comprises one-third of all solid waste by weight (one-half by volume);

WHEREAS, the increased use of recycled content is critical to the success of recycling because it creates the necessary market demand for materials collected through local recycling programs;

WHEREAS, consumers are increasingly interested in using their purchasing power to help the environment, but lack the information to make informed environmental purchasing decisions;

BE IT THEREFORE RESOLVED THAT the signator (s) endorses An Act Regulating Consumer Information Labeling (H. 1715) which would require that packaging display a consumer information label stating what percent of the package is recycled material.

AND BE IT FURTHER RESOLVED THAT the signator (s) strongly urge other individuals and organizations to endorse "The Recycled Content Labeling Bill".

ORGANIZATION_____

CONTACT NAME_____TITLE_____

ADDRESS_____

CITY, STATE, ZIP_____

PHONE (H)/(W)_____

SIGNATURE_____DATE_____

PLEASE RETURN THIS FORM TO THE RECYCLING INITIATIVE CAMPAIGN 29 TEMPLE PLACE, BOSTON MA 02111 (617)292-4824

knows that there's strong support for local parks and recreation among city residents and municipal officials. But the group also knows that the city's resources are limited so that any proposal involving spending would need ample justification—to show that the proposed park would solve a problem of some urgency and consequence. For example, the group might show that compared to other areas of the city the neighborhood lacks recreational facilities. Or, if the lot has given rise to other problems—if, for example, it is becoming a site for drug-dealing or vandalism—the group might argue that a park could simultaneously solve those problems. For a proposal to be persuasive, it would require a clear and convincing statement of the problem and of the general goals and specific objectives being proposed.

In its proposal, the group would need to show that the solution proposed is capable of having the intended effects. If the group claims that drug dealing is part of the problem, then its proposal needs to explain exactly how turning the lot into a park can in fact solve the problem and get rid of the dealers. But this isn't enough. The group would also need to show that the solution deals with the problem in the best, most appropriate way. Perhaps drug dealing could be dealt with more cheaply and effectively through increased police surveillance. Perhaps the lot is too small to serve all age groups, and the neighborhood and city would be better off expanding a park in an adjoining neighborhood. The group also needs to explain how the park is a suitable solution, given the alternatives available and the needs and values of the people affected. A proposal that is both capable of solving the problem and suitable for doing so is said to be feasible. To have a chance of being implemented, a proposal needs to establish that it passes the feasibility test—that its solution will have the intended effects and that it fits the situation.

Proposals often require research. The community group proposing the park could strengthen its case considerably, for example, by showing that the proposed park fits the needs of the neighborhood, given the age and interests of its residents. This information could be obtained by surveying households, as could specifics about the kinds of recreational facilities to include in the park. And by comparing the parks in their neighborhood to those elsewhere in the city, the group could argue that their neighborhood needs to be brought up to the city standard.

Depending on the situation, proposal writers may be called on to present certain information in a certain order. Funding agencies often have particular guidelines that writers need to follow, and companies often have standard forms for preparing proposals. More generally, proposals tend to have a structure that reflects their two basic elements: statement of a problem and proposal of a solution.

Proposals need to convince readers—to fund a project, to implement a solution, to change a policy. Proposals are a form of persuasive writing, and clear statements of problems and solutions, demonstrations of feasibility, documentation through research, and careful organization can all help make a proposal persuasive to readers.

The reading selections offer a number of examples of the various situations that call on people to write proposals. The first selection "And Everything Nice" is an excerpt from a grant proposal written by the film maker Julie Gustafson to request funding for a one-hour documentary. The next two selections concern public policy, in this case recent proposals for national service. Although they address the same topic, "National Service?: Yes, for the Sake of Renewal" by Christopher Dodd and "How to Draft a National Service Plan" by Nicola Clark, are in fact very different kinds of proposals. The final selection "Making Single Motherhood Normal" by Iris Marion Young challenges conventional wisdom and shows how proposals can redefine a problem.

AND EVERTHING NICE.

Proposal submitted to the National Endowment for the Humanities.

Julie Gustafson.

Julie Gustafson is a documentary film maker. Her documentary on the abortion controversy *Cast the First Stone* was shown on PBS. The following is an excerpt from a grant proposal she submitted to the National Endowment for the Humanities to plan a documentary film on "the formation of identity and sexuality in a diverse group of teenage girls from New Orleans." The proposal was funded, and additional support from the Ford Foundation and the Mott Foundation enabled Gustafson to complete filming. The project is currently being edited. The reading selection consists of three sections from the proposal: "Introduction," "Project Rationale," and "Feasibility and Nature of Relationship with Proposed Subjects." The proposal in its entirety is much longer and also includes an overview of the film's contents, an explanation of how Gustafson's and her project advisors' have the credentials to make the film, and a budget.

INTRODUCTION

> "You can't get pregnant the first time."
> "You can't get pregnant if you don't enjoy it."
> "You can't get pregnant standing up. You can't
> get pregnant if you drink ice water, because
> you're reproductive system will be frozen."
> "I don't know a virgin anymore."
>
> Girls, Ages 13-17, 1993

AND EVERYTHING NICE is a documentary about sexuality and identity among teenage girls. A one-hour video work, it will focus on the moral reasoning and pivotal life choices of four or five junior and senior high school girls, all from New Orleans. The work takes place along a streetcar line (now converted to bus) that ends, just as it did in Tennessee William play, at DESIRE, the world's largest housing project. The line, and the documentary, cover a cross-section of New Orleans neighborhoods, from wealthy, to middle class, to working poor. None of the girls in the documentary know each other, but their lives are unified both geographically and metaphorically.

Produced by videomaker Julie Gustafson, in collaboration with

humanities scholars from the disciplines of cultural
anthropology, philosophy and social history, AND EVERYTHING NICE
will probe beneath headlines about "the epidemic of teen sexual
activity and pregnancy." The work will focus on the moral
reasoning and maturational processes of five young women. It
will make visible to viewers the ways in which the decisions of
these young women, often taken to be private, are frequently
linked to larger factors: socioeconomic status, race, ethnicity,
and ultimately, their hopes for the future. Finally, the
documentary will make clear the striking ways in which girls from
diverse backgrounds share the experience of being young and being
female in a rapidly changing social and cultural landscape.

Both the analytic framework and dramatic structure of AND
EVERYTHING NICE will provide viewers with an opportunity to
confront the words and points of view of the young people whose
lives and choices are at the heart of the controversy. It will
also invite audiences to observe the context in which teenage
girls make their decisions, and the consequences which follow out
of them. Finally, the work will highlight for audiences the
conflicting values and perspectives on sexuality and morality of
parents, teachers, religious leaders, media experts and other
important adults in the girls lives.

Julie Gustafson has more than twenty years of experience
producing documentaries about American family and culture,
particularly at points where the ethical and social problems
facing people intersect with public and private life. Her widely
distributed works have dealt with sensitive subjects: birth,
death, marriage and intimacy, the problems of caring for aging
parents, teenage suicide, and the abortion controversy. She also
has a long history of collaboration with humanities scholars, and
her work has a congruence with humanities methods and subject
matter that makes her an ideal producer to attempt this subject.

Gustafson will observe both ethnographic concerns and her own
long-standing practice of working closely with subjects, by
inviting the teenagers who are her subjects to actively
participate in the process of exploring and representing the
issues confronting them around sexuality, moral reflection and
identity. At times, she will give cameras to the girls so that
in the final program, 'video diaries' shot by them can be
interwoven with the material she shoots. She will also involve
the girls to participate in important stages of editing and
presenting the tape to the public.

Finally, there will be a reflexive element in the documentary.
The project team plans to periodically document its work
processes, as videomaker Julie Gustafson and the location
scholars do field work with teenage girls or community members,
or, as they work on framing and editing the documentary. Lightly
woven through the hour, this footage will let audiences know
something about how the makers arrived at the images they chose,
as well as to help them understand the analytic framework of the
project.

PROJECT RATIONALE

"There are 14 million teenagers in America,
7 million are having sex- Of the 3 million who get   pregnant
every year, approximately 1.5 million are having
abortions, and 1.5 million are having babies."

In 1955, the statistics above would have been inconceivable;
today, they are ruefully accepted facts. Studies indicate that
nearly 40% of 14 year olds, and 72% of 17 year olds in the United
States have had sexual intercourse. The percentage rise in
sexual activity for girls is particularly dramatic.

There are many reasons for these changes, including a popular
culture obsessed with sexuality, and the fact that girls reach
puberty much earlier than they did fifty years ago. Today, while
the age of first marriage is steadily rising, the age of first
intercourse is falling. Either through choice, persuasion, or
force, more and more girls are having sex, some as early as age
ten or eleven.

Everywhere, concerned adults are sounding the alarm, fearing such
consequences of early sexual activity as emotional disturbance,
unplanned pregnancies, and AIDS. While most attention is fixed
on unwed teenage mothers as the 'big problem' (particularly poor,
African-American girls), the reality is that a very high
percentage of teenage girls are having sex and risking pregnancy.
Regardless of ethnicity, it is the economically disadvantaged who
are becoming unwed teen mothers. Having sex does not sort out by
class, having babies does.

Moreover, half of the teenagers who have one child, will have a
second child within a year. According to researchers, these
girls view motherhood as one of the few palatable choices they
have. They are, as project advisor Kristin Luker points out,
"making reasoned choices - attempting to maximize options in a
society that offers uneducated or economically disadvantaged
women limited alternatives."

At the same time, despite their greater resources, more affluent girls are faced with very difficult choice as well. Like their less well-off counterparts, they are inundated with messages from advertising and the popular culture 'to be sexy.' And, while having access to birth control and abortion is the marker of middle class teenagers, many experience great emotional and practical difficulty in choosing whether to have sex or not, in using contraception, or if they do become pregnant in deciding what to do. These girls are at risk for a different set of problems, among them a high rate of eating disorders, alcohol and drug problems, sexual abuse and other identity disturbances.

The sexual, gender, and work revolutions of the last three decades have had a particularly potent impact on teenage girls. Advances in reproductive technology, changing definitions of what it means to be female, as well as work force changes, represent an exhilarating but confusing challenge. The messages that young women today receive about standards of moral behavior and gender role models from parents teacher, religion and the media are multiple and often conflicting. While they see and hear much about changing roles of women in society, some of it is decidedly mixed, such as the 'double burden' on working women who shoulder most family obligations along with their jobs, as well as evidence that if things go badly in parenting or marriage, that they may be abandoned by men to bear the brunt of long term financial and custodial care of children - alone.

Additionally, teenage girls witness that though increasing numbers of women are laboring alongside men in the work world, most still make 52 cents on the dollar to a man's wage. Violence against women is still high. The striking growth in divorce and the number of single women, who can't find adequate partners or who choose to raise children on their own, prompts even feminists to ask, "Is this what the sexual revolution is about?" As Project Advisor Martha Ward has commented, "all girls today are struggling with a play and a script they didn't write, on a stage of someone else's making."

While the girls we select for the project will come from a wide variety of social classes and ethnic backgrounds, their life experiences and choices will be linked by the powerful forces of gender and age. In fact, never again will gender be a more important and determining factor than in these years.
As female adolescents they share anxieties over relationships with boys, (boys, boys), social status, physical appearance and problems within their families.

Whether from privileged families or poorer families, each of our subjects is likely to face normal anxieties about growing up, separating from parents, and earning a living. They are also increasingly likely to face some serious worries and even physical or emotional danger caused by their own early sexual activity, by family problems like divorce, sexual abuse,

eating disorders, alcoholism or drug addiction. Finally either
they or a close friend faces serious possibilities of early death
through suicide, drunk driving, and if they are poor, and African
American, as a result of violent crime.

In addition, each child is subject to the tumultuous and
confusing physiological changes of adolescence. As every
generation of girls enters physical adolescence it is as though
it is happening for the first time. For the most part, schools,
parents, tv and other institutions down play the changes. Unlike
boys their age adolescent girls do not for the most part become
sexually active in pursuit of physical fulfillment. Instead they
are seeking a way to attract boys, keep their attention, and gain
social standing among their peers.

Each of the girls we select is likely to inhabit two worlds a
public world of school, family or community world, and a deeply
private inner world in which the child struggles alone or with
peers to make sense of their existence. From the rich worlds
of letter, diaries, songs of teenagers collected from kids, one
of our scholars reports that the world of 13 -14 year old girls
is rich one, rarely penetrated. It can be a lonely world.

AND EVERYTHING NICE aims to make this complex drama visible. It
will provide a framework which allows the young women we focus on
to reflect on the complicated dynamics which propel them into
pivotal decisions. We will not attempt to tie these complex
cultural phenomena into a single cohesive thesis. Nor will our
selection or ordering of visual events attempt to persuade
viewers of the rightness or wrongness of any point of view.
Instead, we hope to show that values and choices are based on a
complex interplay of many factors and circumstances. And, that
these values and complex circumstantial factors, are expressed in
a particularly compelling way, in the thoughts, words and deeds
of young women struggling to shape their moral and social
identities.

FEASIBILITY AND NATURE OF RELATIONSHIP WITH PROPOSED SUBJECTS

[Gustafson's]

~~Her~~ production method is based on an unusual amount of collaboration with her subjects. She spends a great deal of time in their homes and communities, getting to know them, and videotaping with them, as they face critical moments of decision, change and crisis. Her subjects are always involved in the editing process.

Though the project takes on a highly sensitive topic, and one which is sure to present some difficulties in finding and working with subjects, the project team believes strongly in its approach. Gustafson's previous experience in using a highly collaborative production method, along with the field experiences and contacts of Ward, Luker and Young- make us feel that we will be successful in earning the trust and involvement of both the teenagers and the adults needed to accomplish our goals.

We plan to focus only on teens and families who express a strong interest in the project, we will get releases and over shoot to safe-guard against participant drop-out. Also, giving the girls their own cameras not only empowers and validates their voices, but also encourages their continued interest and participation. Because the girls are not just subjects, but actual participants, there is a higher level of comfort and openness with being taped.

We believe that the fact that most teenagers attach a critical importance to issues of their own sexuality, identity and moral development, will encourage a diverse and interesting group of young people to participate.

ANALYSIS: Rationale and Feasibility

The structure of Julie Gustafson's proposal to the National Endowment for the Humanities is fairly typical of grant proposals. As you can see, the Introduction and Project Rationale sections explain the need for the proposed project, while the Feasibility section explains how Gustafson is capable of carrying it out.

While the Introduction does describe in a general way what the film will show (a fuller discussion appears in a later section), it also makes an implicit argument for the film. It explains how the film will "probe beneath headlines about 'the epidemic of teen sexual activity and pregnancy'" and provide an opportunity for viewers to "confront the words and points of view of the young people whose lives and choices are at the heart of the controversy." In other words, the Introduction both informs those who will read the proposal about what the film maker wants to do and suggests that there is something significant "beneath the headlines" that the film will bring to light.

The Project Rationale section makes explicit what there is to learn by probing "beneath the headlines." According to the proposal, public attention has been focused too narrowly on poor and unwed African American teenage mothers, while in reality the issue of teenage sexuality is a much wider one that affects all classes. This section seeks to establish the need for the film by explaining the complicated context in which young women struggle to shape their "moral and social identities." The Feasibility section, then, shows how the film maker is capable of making this struggle visible by working closely with her subjects.

FOR CRITICAL INQUIRY

1. Notice that Julie Gustafson begins the Introduction with a series of quotes from teenage girls, ages 13-17. Why do you think she has chosen to do so? How do the quotes tie in to the approach Gustafson proposes to take in her film? How do they support her explanation of the need for the film?

2. Although the section in which Gustafson presents her own and her co-workers' credentials, she manages to incorporate some reference to credentials in these sections. Where does she do this? Why? Do you think this is an effective choice on her part? Why or why not?

3. How does Gustafson define the problem her film will address in the Project Rationale section? Does this definition of the problem establish the timeliness and importance of the film? Do you think Gustafson has achieved a good match between the problem stated and the proposed film project? Why or why not?

4. Describe what you see as the function of the section Feasibility and Nature of Relationship to Proposed Subjects. What does it contribute to the proposal? Do you find it persuasive? Why or why not?

Christopher Dodd. "National Service? Yes, for the Sake of Renewal." Providence Journal-Bulletin. January 12, 1993.

The following selection was written by Christopher Dodd, Democratic senator from Connecticut, and appeared in the op-ed pages of the Providence Journal-Bulletin in January 1993, shortly after President Bill Clinton was elected to his first term in office. During his campaign, Clinton had proposed that voluntary community service programs for young people be established to address pressing social problems and help volunteers repay student loans. In this selection, Dodd supports Clinton's proposal by arguing that it will successfully address the problems. As you read the selection, notice the strategies Dodd uses to persuade readers of the feasibility of the solution.

National service: Yes or no?
Yes, for the sake of renewal

CHRISTOPHER DODD

TWELVE YEARS ago, Americans were asked a question that framed the view of many toward their government. Ronald Reagan asked, "Are you better off today than you were four years ago?" — an essential question for the "Me Generation." It measured the achievements of government, indeed of society, in terms of each individual. The size of a house, account balance or salary became a yard stick for the well-being of society as a whole.

John Kennedy asked Americans a different question, "Ask not what your country can do for you. Ask what you can do for your country." President-elect Clinton is asking Americans today to redefine their relationship with government and society in terms of others as well as in terms of themselves.

Clinton proposes to build on successful models and develop a national program adapted to today's needs. Many are unfortunately all too familiar. Poverty, homelessness, unemployment, illiteracy, drugs, and hopelessness remain the realities of everyday life for too many Americans. Our natural resources and infrastructure are in need of renewal.

We must as a society renew our commitment to meet these critical needs and, as Clinton has proposed, revitalize our efforts with a new corps of talented volunteers. The concept of community service did not begin or end with John Kennedy. In fact, it has played an important role in our history. Since the Revolution, young Americans have been asked to make the greatest sacrifice of all and serve in the armed forces.

In the 1930s, Franklin D. Roosevelt, faced with an 25 percent unemployment rate, created the Civilian Conversation Corps to hire young men left jobless by the Depression. Within six months of its implementation, over a quarter of a million men were working in conservation projects and receiving special training.

In the 1960s, Kennedy enabled America's youth to serve their country abroad through the Peace Corps. And in the 1970s, under the leadership of Richard Nixon, the ACTION agency was established to coordinate existing volunteer programs that address the needs of the community, like VISTA (Volunteers in Service to America) and the Older Americans Volunteer Programs.

Most recently, we saw the enactment of President Bush's Points of Light Foundation, which rewards acts of service and encourages volunteerism.

The Clinton plan would motivate a new generation of volunteers by linking student loan forgiveness to community service. Students and families hardpressed by rising tuitions would have access to student loans directly from the federal government. They would have the option of repaying these loans with community service or through an income-contingent repayment plan managed by the IRS.

While the Clinton plan involves new spending, it saves dollars lost to defaults and payments to banks in the current system; these expenditures cost the government nearly $4 billion each year.

Some argue that, even with these savings, the cost of Clinton's community service will be too high. Any fair analysis, however, must weigh the benefits of a program as well as the costs — a more educated and well-trained citizenry, reduced poverty, a cleaner environment and improved infrastructure. One must also consider the costs of inaction.

Others argue that in setting up a new program we will create a new bureaucracy. In confronting the challenge of the structure of a new community service program, we are fortunate to have a multitude of public, private and community programs from which we can build a network.

In addition, there are numerous government programs that can be consolidated. There is no need, as many suggest, to reinvent the wheel; we have programs of proven effectiveness in place. They are simply in need of federal leadership and a renewed commitment.

If we do not take steps today to embrace creative, constructive ideas to address the problems of many of our communities, then our nation will soon find itself unable to compete, with declining wages and increasing hopelessness.

President-elect Bill Clinton offers an alternative — a thoughtful program providing young Americans with the opportunity to better the lives of others as well as their own.

GOING ON-LINE

Requests for Proposals

Major funding sources such as the National Science Foundation (www.nsf.org), the National Endowment for the Humanities (www.neh.org.), and the National Endowment for the Arts (www.nea.org) maintain web sites that include information on the research projects, artistic work, and educational programs they sponsor. Typi-cally these agencies issue requests for proposals (often referred to as RFPs) that describe the kinds of activites they will fund. Visit one of the sites to find out about the kinds of proposals they invite. What information does the site offer about guide-lines for writing proposals and the criteria used in evaluating proposals? What opportunities does the funding agency offer to undergraduates?

ANALYSIS: Endorsing a Proposal

Christopher Dodd's editorial "National Service?: Yes, For the Sake of Renewal" endorses President Bill Clinton's proposal for a volunteer community service program. As you can see, the proposal is still in the early stages of development, and Dodd's purpose is to generate public support for the basic concept. For this reason, Dodd does not provide a detailed description of the problem and proposed solution. Instead, he concentrates on persuading readers of the feasibility of the proposal.

As discussed in the chapter introduction, to be feasible, a proposal must be both capable of solving a problem and suitable to the circumstances, given the cost of the proposal and the values of those affected. Dodd is aware that for some people the cost of Clinton's community service plan may not be acceptable. Notice how Dodd anticipates these objections by arguing that benefits as well as costs must be taken into account. Dodd tries to overcome possible resistance to the cost of Clinton's plan by emphasizing how community service has many precedents in American history and is in keeping with traditional American values, endorsed by Democrats and Republicans alike.

FOR CRITICAL INQUIRY

1. Christopher Dodd uses the opening paragraphs to juxtapose the question raised by Reagan in 1980 with that raised by Kennedy two decades earlier. With respect to these two contrasting views of the individual and society, where does Dodd position Clinton and his proposal? How might this opening help Dodd appeal to a range of readers? What does it define as the larger issue at stake?

2. Dodd devotes a large part of the selection to precedents for Clinton's plan for voluntary community service. What examples does he use and why does he use these particular examples? How do you think these examples are meant to contribute to Dodd's argument? Do you find them effective? Why or why not?

3. The word ìrenewalî appears not only in the title but also at several points in the text. Find some of these mentions of renewing and renewal. How does the word help tie together the immediate problems the proposal is meant to address and the larger, more general problem Dodd sees?

4. What function do paragraphs 9-12 play? Summarize the objections Dodd anticipates and his responses. Do you think these are the main objections readers are likely to have? Do you find Doddís responses persuasive? Why or why not?

5. How do the last two paragraphs serve as a conclusion to the proposal?

6. How effective do you find the proposal in general? Has Dodd convinced you that national service is a feasible proposal? Why or why not?

NICOLA CLARK. "HOW TO DRAFT A NATIONAL SERVICE PLAN." WALL STREET JOURNAL. MAY 18, 1993.

Nicola Clark's editorial "How to Draft a National Service Plan" appeared in the Wall Street Journal in May 1993, when President Clinton's voluntary community service plan was receiving a good deal of national attention. Her proposal—to use the draft to provide young people as low-cost community service workers, as a number of European countries do—contrasts sharply with the voluntary plan that Dodd endorses. As you read, notice how Clark asks whether the use of the draft is really feasible, given American values and beliefs.

How to Draft a National Service Plan

By NICOLA CLARK

President Clinton is winding up a week-long promotional tour of his economic plan. Among what he has advertised as interdependent proposals is his plan for a national service corps—an idea pollsters have found to be extremely popular with the MTV generation. More than 4,000 twentysomethings have already besieged the White House with letters volunteering to join a modest pilot corps of 1,000. These eager souls would be put to work as teachers, day-care, health and environmental workers in return for college tuition benefits. The idea is to increase the corps to 25,000 by next year and work up to 150,000 by 1997. And the latest estimates place the cost of this "domestic Peace Corps" at about $9.5 billion.

That price tag is steep compared with that of Mr. Clinton's favorite model country, Germany. In Germany, 135,000 national servants each year work in hospitals, nursing homes, kindergartens, and other public and nonprofit agencies for the bargain-basement cost to taxpayers of just over $3 billion a year. How do they do it? It's an old idea called the draft.

The U.S., Canada, Japan and Britain are the only major industrial countries without a draft. Of the countries that do draft, more than three-fourths have a national service alternative for conscientious objectors. But while petitioners for national service in most countries are subject to an intensive appeal process to prove their moral or religious objections to military service, this has not been the case in Germany since 1985. With its more lenient policy, Germany has been able to entice 40% of draftable males into its national service corps as an alternative to the military.

Germans have become hugely dependent upon their army of conscripted national servants. *Zivildienstleistende,* or "Zivis," as they are called, are age 18 to 28. They serve for 15 months—three months longer than soldiers—and the government pays them a conscript's wage that starts at about $8.50 a day. Room and board, if a Zivi needs it, are paid by the employing institution. These national service conscripts can be found working in the homes of Germany's elderly and handicapped, or in hospital examination rooms measuring patients' temperatures and blood pressure. They assist the Red Cross during disasters and kindergarten teachers in their classrooms, and even count geese in the marshes near the Baltic coast.

According to a recent study by the German army's Social Science Institute, every Zivi hired in place of a civilian saves an average of $21,000 annually. And nowhere is this cheap labor pool more intensively used than in Germany's health-care sector: More than half the Zivis are employed in health-care-related jobs, and a full 30% work in German hospitals—saving $1 billion annually.

Low-paid conscripted national servants are the only way governments can afford to make good on the generous welfare promises they have made to voters without burying their nations in debt.

This may sound like a drop in the bucket for a nearly $2 trillion economy, but the Germans clearly recognize the important role national servants play in keeping their system afloat: "In its more than 30 years of existence," explained Minister of Women and Youth Angela Merkel in 1991, "[the national service] has become an important and fully legitimized component of our social reality."

In an article this February headlined "The Welfare State Cannot Do Without Zivis," the popular weekly news magazine Der Spiegel described Germany—the highest labor-cost country in the world—as a "low-wage country" when it comes to social services. As enormous reunification costs are compounded by a deepening recession, the German government is looking for all the cheap help it can get.

Just last year, Ms. Merkel's ministry, which administers the national service program, began an active campaign to encourage German "hospitals, nursing homes, facilities for the handicapped and also ... organizations that are particularly active in environmental protection to investigate if perhaps the number of positions [for Zivis] could be increased."

Currently 94% of all petitioners for national service are accepted. This partly reflects the need to absorb conscripts from the new eastern states; but it is clear that many private German "help" organizations recognize the boon of national service as well. For example, Cologne-based Malteser-Hilfedienst, an ecumenical humanitarian aid organization, employs 3,571 Zivis while its regular staff numbers only 1,951. A quarter of the German Red Cross is staffed by national servants.

Germany is not alone in its use of conscripted labor in the service of politically popular but budget-busting government programs. The Danes, for example, dispatch their national servants as civilian public works laborers and foresters. French and Portuguese Zivis are funneled to various humanitarian organizations or are sent to do development work in their former colonies. And in 1992, anticipating the effects of a rapidly aging population on their health system, doctors in Switzerland actually proposed supplementing the newly introduced Swiss national service with a corps devoted to providing low-cost ambulatory care for the elderly. Poles already can choose between joining such a 24-month "health-care service" alternative to armed service or an environmental conservation corps.

Mr. Clinton has inundated Americans with proposals for expanded government programs in public works, environmental conservation, child care, health care, community policing—many of which are the kinds of things that are done by extremely low-paid conscripted national servants in other advanced industrialized countries. Why? Because it's the only way these governments can afford to make good on the generous welfare promises they have made to voters without burying their nations in debt. European societies years ago decided, for better or worse, that they were willing to cash in some of the citizenry's freedom of choice for the luxury of welfare largesse for all.

Americans, on the other hand, have time and again refused to make such trade-offs. And yet the only way President Clinton's myriad social programs could produce measurable results would be if citizens were prepared not only to fund them with higher taxes but perhaps also to accept something as extreme—and unpopular—as a draft.

What a truly radical idea for Mr. Clinton and the Rock-the-Vote crowd.

ANALYSIS: Challenging a Proposal

Nicola Clark describes President Clinton's proposal for voluntary service and immediately raises an objection about its feasibility. According to Clark, its estimated cost of $9.5 billion is simply too expensive for the proposal to be acceptable. She contrasts Clinton's proposal with national service in Germany, a program whose far lower costs are made possible by Germany's use of the draft. Clark then goes on to describe the German system and the important role it plays in Germany.

At first glance, then, Clark appears to be arguing that Clinton's proposal is not feasible in terms of its financial cost and presenting an alternative that would be financial feasible. Feasibility, however, involves more than just financial considerations. As you have seen in Christopher Dodd's endorsement of Clinton's voluntary service plan, to be feasible, a proposal must be in keeping with the values and beliefs of those it would affect. In her concluding paragraphs, Clark points out that Americans, in contrast to Europeans, have not been "willing to cash in the citizenry's freedom of choice for the luxury of welfare largesse for all." In Clark's view, to have a real effect, Clinton's social programs would require citizens not only to pay higher taxes but "perhaps also to accept something as extreme—and unpopular—as a draft."

Thus, Clark's real point becomes clear: she is challenging not only the feasibility of Clinton's proposal but also the feasibility of the German model in an American context. In this sense, her proposal of a national service program with acceptable financial cost was essentially a "straw man"—proposed in order to be rejected.

FOR CRITICAL INQUIRY

1. As you have seen, Clark goes into considerable detail explaining how the German system of national service works—only to call its feasibility into question at the end. What do you see as the purpose of Clark's "straw man" strategy? What is she arguing against? What, if anything, is she arguing for?

2. Clark ends her discussion of the German system by saying, "European societies years ago decided, for better or worse, that they were willing to cash in some of the citizenry's freedom of choice for the luxury of welfare largesse for all." Consider the word choices Clark makes in this sentence. What attitudes toward social programs do they reveal? How do these attitudes shape the overall argument Clark makes?

3. How do you think Christopher Dodd would respond to Clark? What might he say, given Clark's objections, to defend Clinton's voluntary service proposal? What do you think he might say about the German model of national service?

4. Do you think that the way Clark has chosen to make her argument is effective? Why or why not?

Iris Marion Young. "Making Single Motherhood Normal." Dissent. Winter 1994.

Iris Marion Young is a leading feminist philosopher who teaches at the University of Pittsburgh. Her book Justice and the Politics of Difference (1990) is an award-winning study. The following essay, whose position is clearly indicated in the title, responds to the growing trend of policymakers across the political spectrum to blame social ills such as poverty, drug abuse, and crime on the breakdown of the traditional American family. Young seeks to counter such views by redefining the problem and proposing solutions accordingly.

Iris Marion Young

MAKING SINGLE MOTHERHOOD NORMAL

When Dan Quayle denounced Murphy Brown for having a baby without a husband in May 1992, most liberals and leftists recognized it for the ploy it was: a Republican attempt to win an election by an irrational appeal to "tradition" and "order." To their credit, American voters did not take the bait. The Clinton campaign successfully turned the family values rhetoric against the GOP by pointing to George Bush's veto of the Family and Medical Leave Act and by linking family well-being to economic prosperity.

Nonetheless, family values rhetoric has survived the election. Particularly disturbing is the fact that the refrain has been joined by people who, by most measures, should be called liberals, but who can accept only the two-parent heterosexual family. Communitarians are leading the liberal chorus denouncing divorce and single motherhood. In *The Spirit of Community*, Amitai Etzioni calls for social measures to privilege two-parent families and encourage parents to take care of young children at home. Etzioni is joined by political theorist William Galston—currently White House adviser on domestic policy—in supporting policies that will make divorce more difficult. Jean Bethke Elshtain is another example of a social liberal—that is, someone who believes in state regulation of business, redistributive economic policies, religious toleration and broad principles of free speech—who argues that not all kinds of families should be considered equal from the point of view of social policy or moral education. William Julius Wilson, another academic who has been close to Democratic party policy makers, considers out-of-wedlock birth to be a symptom of social pathology and promotes marriage as one solution to problems of urban black poverty.

Although those using family values rhetoric rarely mention gays and lesbians, this celebration of stable marriage is hardly good news for gay and lesbian efforts to win legitimacy for their lives and relationships. But I am concerned here with the implications of family values rhetoric for another despised and discriminated-against group: single mothers. Celebrating marriage brings a renewed stigmatization of these women, and makes them scapegoats/for social ills of which they are often the most serious victims. The only antidote to this injustice is for public policy to regard single mothers as normal, and to give them the social supports they need to overcome disadvantage.

Most people have forgotten another explicit aim of Dan Quayle's appeal to family values: to "explain" the disorders in Los Angeles in May 1992. Unmarried women with children lie at the source of the "lawless social anarchy" that sends youths into the streets with torches and guns. Their "welfare ethos" impedes individual efforts to move ahead in society.

Liberal family values rhetoric also finds the "breakdown" of "the family" to be a primary cause of all our social ills. "It is not an exaggeration," says Barbara Dafoe Whitehead in the *Atlantic* (April 1993) "to characterize [family disruption] as a central cause of many of our most vexing social problems, including poverty, crime, and declining school performance." Etzioni lays our worst social problems at the door of self-indulgent divorced or never-married parents. "Gang warfare in the streets, massive drug abuse, a poorly committed workforce, and a strong sense of entitlement and a weak sense of responsibility are, to a large extent, the product of poor parenting." Similarly, Galston attributes fearsome social consequences to divorce and single parenthood.

"The consequences of family failure affect society at large. We all pay for systems of welfare, criminal justice, and incarceration, as well as for physical and mental disability; we are all made poorer by the inability or unwillingness of young adults to become contributing members of society; we all suffer if our society is unsafe and divided."

Reductionism in the physical sciences has faced such devastating criticism that few serious physicists would endorse a theory that traced a one-way causal relationship between the behavior of a particular sort of atom and, say, an earthquake. Real-world physical phenomena are understood to have many mutually conditioning forces. Yet here we have otherwise subtle and intelligent people putting forward the most absurd social reductionism. In this simplistic model of society, the family is the most basic unit, the first cause that is itself uncaused. Through that magical process called socialization, families cause the attitudes, dispositions, and capacities of individual children who in turn as adults cause political and economic institutions to work or not work.

The great and dangerous fallacy in this imagery, of course, is its implicit assumption that non-familial social processes do not cause family conditions. How do single-mother families "cause" poverty, for example? Any sensible look at some of these families shows us that poverty is a cause of their difficulties and failures. Doesn't it make sense to trace some of the conflicts that motivate divorce to the structure of work or to the lack of work? And what about all the causal influences on families and children over which parents have very little control—peer groups, dilapidated and understaffed schools, consumer culture, television and movie imagery, lack of investment in neighborhoods, cutbacks in public services? Families unprotected by wide networks of supportive institutions and economic resources are bound to suffer. Ignoring the myriad social conditions that affect families only enables the government and the public to escape responsibility for investing in the ghettos, building new houses and schools, and creating the millions of decent jobs that we need to restore millions of people to dignity.

Family-values reductionism scapegoats parents, and especially single parents, and proposes a low-cost answer to crime, poverty, and unemployment: get married and stay married.

Whitehead, Galston, Etzioni, and others claim that there is enough impressive evidence that divorce harms children emotionally to justify policies that discourage parents from divorcing. A closer look at the data, however, yields a much more ambiguous picture. One meta-analysis of ninety-two studies of the effects of divorce on American children, for example, finds statistically insignificant differences between children of divorced parents and children from intact families in various measures of well-being.[1] Many studies of children of divorce fail to compare them to children from "intact" families, or fail to rule out predivorce conditions as causes. A ten-year longitudinal study released in Australia last June found that conflict between parents—whether divorced or not—is a frequent cause of emotional distress in children. This stress is mitigated, however, if the child has a close supportive relationship with at least one of the parents.[2] Results also suggest that Australia's stronger welfare state and less adversarial divorce process may partly account for differences with U.S. findings.

Thus the evidence that divorce produces lasting damage to children is ambiguous at best, and I do not see how the ambiguities can be definitively resolved one way or the other. Complex and multiple social causation makes it naive to think we can conclusively test for a clear causal relationship between divorce and children's well-being. Without such certainty, however, it is wrong to suggest that the liberty of adults in their personal lives should be restricted. Galston and Etzioni endorse proposals that would impose a waiting period between the time a couple applied for divorce and the beginning of divorce proceedings. Divorce today already often drags on in prolonged acrimony. Children would likely benefit more from making it easier and less adversarial.

Although many Americans agree with me about divorce, they also agree with Quayle, Wilson, Galston, and others that single motherhood is undesirable for children, a deviant social condition that policy ought to try to correct. Etzioni claims that children of single parents receive less parental supervision and support than do children in two-parent families. It is certainly plausible that parenting is easier and more effective if two or more adults discuss the children's needs and provide different kinds of interactions for them. It does not follow, however, that the second adult must be a live-in husband. Some studies have found that the addition of any adult to a single-mother household, whether a relative, lover, or friend, tends to offset the tendency of single parents to relinquish decision making too early.[3] Stephanie Coontz suggests that fine-tuned research on single-parent families would probably find that they are better for children in some respects and worse in others. For example, although adults in single-parent families spend less time supervising homework, single parents are less likely to pressure their children into social conformity and more likely to praise good grades.[4]

Much less controversial is the claim that children in single-parent families are more often poor than those in two-parent families. One should be careful not to correlate poverty with single-parenthood, however; according to Coontz, a greater part of the increase in family poverty since 1979 has occurred in families with both spouses present, with only 38 percent concentrated in single-parent families. As many as 50 percent of single-parent families are likely to be poor, which is a shocking fact, but intact two-parent families are also increasingly likely to be poor, especially if the parents are in their twenties or younger.[5]

It is harder to raise children alone than with at least one other adult, and the stresses of doing so can take their toll on children. I do not question that children in families that depend primarily on a woman's wage-earning ability are often disadvantaged. I do question the conclusion that getting single mothers married is the answer to childhood disadvantage.

Conservatives have always stated a preference for two-parent families. Having liberals join this chorus is disturbing because it makes such preference much more mainstream, thus legitimizing discrimination against single mothers. Single mothers commonly experience credit and employment discrimination. Discrimination against single mothers in renting apartments was legal until 1988, and continues to be routine in most cities. In a study of housing fairness in Pittsburgh in which I participated, most people questioned said that rental housing discrimination is normal in the area. Single mothers and their children also face biases in schools.[6]

There is no hope that discrimination of this sort will ever end unless public discourse and government policy recognize that female-headed families are a viable, normal, and permanent family form, rather than something broken and deviant that policy should eradicate. Around one-third of families in the United States are headed by a woman alone; this proportion is about the same world-wide. The single-mother family is not going to fade away. Many women raise children alone because their husbands left them or because lack of access to contraception and abortion forced them to bear unwanted children. But many women are single mothers by choice. Women increasingly initiate divorces, and many single mothers report being happier after divorce and uninterested in remarriage, even when they are poorer.

Women who give birth out of wedlock, moreover, often have chosen to do so. Discussion of the "problem" of "illegitimate" births commonly assumes the image of the irresponsible and uneducated teenager (of color) as the unwed mother. When citing statistics about rising rates of out-of-wedlock birth, journalists and scholars rarely break them down by the mother's age, occupation, and so on. Although the majority of these births continue to be to young mothers, a rising proportion are to mid-life women with steady jobs who choose to have children. Women persist in such choices despite the fact that they are stigmatized and sometimes punished for them.

In a world where it can be argued that there are already too many people, it may sometimes be wrong for people to have babies. The planned birth of a third child in a stable two-parent family may be morally questionable from this point of view. But principles of equality and reproductive freedom must hold that there is nothing *more* wrong with a woman in her thirties with a stable job and income having a baby than with a similar married couple.

If teen pregnancy is a social problem, this is not because the mothers are unmarried, but because they are young. They are inexperienced in the ways of the world and lack the skills necessary to get a job to support their children; once they become parents, their opportunities to develop those skills usually decrease. But these remain problems even when the women marry the young men with whom they have conceived children. Young inexperienced men today are just as ill prepared for parenting and just as unlikely to find decent jobs.

Although many young unmarried women who bear children do so because they are effectively denied access to abortions, many of these mothers want their babies. Today the prospects for meaningful work and a decent income appear dim to many youth, and especially to poor youth. Having a baby can give a young woman's life meaning, earn her respectful attention, make her feel grown up, and give her an excuse to exit the "wild" teenager scene that has begun to make her uncomfortable. Constructing an education and employment system that took girls as seriously as boys, that trained girls and boys for meaningful and available work would be a far more effective antidote to teen birth than reprimanding, stigmatizing, and punishing these girls.

Just as we should examine the assumption that something is wrong with a mid-life woman having a child without a husband, so we ought to ask a more radical question: just what *in principle* is *more* wrong in a young woman's bearing a child without a husband than in an older woman's doing so? When making their reproductive decisions, everyone ought to ask whether there are too many people in the world. Beyond that, I submit that we should affirm an unmarried young woman's right to bear a child as much as any other person's right.

There is reason to think that much of the world, including the United States, has plural childbearing cultures. Recently I heard a radio interview with an eighteen-year-old African-American woman in Washington, D.C. who had recently given birth to her second child. She affirmed wanting both children, and said that she planned to have no more. She lives in a subsidized apartment and participates in a job training program as a condition for receiving AFDC. She resisted the interviewer's suggestion that there was something morally wrong or at least unfortunate with her choices and her life. She does not like being poor, and does not like having uncertain child care arrangements when she is away from her children. But she believes that in ten years, with hard work, social support, and good luck, she will have a community college degree and a decent job doing something she likes, as does her mother, now thirty-four.

There is nothing in principle wrong with such a pattern of having children first and getting education and job training later. Indeed, millions of white professional women currently in their fifties followed a similar pattern. Most of them, of course, were supported by husbands, and not state subsidy, when they stayed home to take care of their young children. Our racism, sexism, and classism are only thinly concealed when we praise stay-at-home mothers who are married, white, and middle class, and propose a limit of two years on welfare to unmarried, mostly non-white, and poor women who do the same thing. From a moral point of view, is there an important difference between the two kinds of dependence? If there is any serious commitment to equality in the United States, it must include an equal respect for people's reproductive choices. In order for children to have equal opportunities, moreover, equal respect for parents, and especially mothers, requires state policies that give greater support to some than others.

If we assume that there is nothing morally wrong with single-mother families, but that they are often disadvantaged by lack of child care and by economic discrimination and social stigma, then what follows for public policy? Some of the answers to this question are obvious, some not so obvious, but in the current climate promoting a stingy and punitive welfare state, all bear discussion. I will close by sketching a few proposals.

1. *There is nothing in principle any more wrong with a teenage woman's choice to have a child than with anyone else's.* Still, there is something wrong with a society that gives her few alternatives to a mothering vocation and little opportunity for meaningful job training. If we want to reduce the number of teenage women who want to have babies, then education and employment policies have to take girls and women much more seriously.

2. *Whether poor mothers are single because they are divorced or because they never married, it is wrong for a society to allow mothers to raise children in poverty and then tell them that it's their fault when their children have deprived lives.* Only if the economy offered women decent-paying jobs, moreover, would forcing welfare women to get jobs lift them out of poverty. Of course, with good job opportunities most of them would not need to be forced off welfare. But job training and employment programs for girls and women must be based on the assumption that a large proportion of them will support children alone. Needless to say, there is a need for massive increases in state support for child care if these women are to hold jobs. Public policy should, however, also acknowledge that taking care of children at home is work, and then support this work with unstigmatized subsidy where necessary to give children a decent life.

3. *The programs of schools, colleges, and vocational and professional training institutions ought to accommodate a plurality of women's life plans, combining childbearing and child-rearing with other activities.* They should not assume that there is a single appropriate time to bear and rear children. No woman should be disadvantaged in her education and employment opportunities because she has children at age fifteen, twenty-five, thirty-five, or forty-five (for the most part, education and job structures are currently such that each of these ages is the "wrong time").

4. *Public policy should take positive steps to dispel the assumption that the two-parent heterosexual nuclear family is normal and all other family forms deviant.* For example, the state should assist single-parent support systems, such as the "mothers' houses" in some European countries that provide spaces for shared child minding and cooking while at the same time preserving family privacy.

5. *Some people might object that my call for recognizing single motherhood as normal lets men off the hook when it comes to children.* Too many men are running out on pregnant women and on the mothers of their children with whom they have lived. They are free to seek adventure, sleep around, or start new families, while single mothers languish in poverty with their children. This objection voices a very important concern, but there are ways to address it other than forcing men to get or stay married to the mothers of their children.

First, the state should force men who are not poor themselves to pay child support for children they have recognized as theirs. I see nothing wrong with attaching paychecks and bank accounts to promote this end. But the objection above requires more than child support. Relating to children is a good thing in itself. Citizens who love and are committed to some particular children are more apt than others to think of the world in the long term, and to see it from the perspective of the more vulnerable people. Assuming that around one-third of households will continue to be headed by women alone, men should be encouraged to involve themselves in close relationships with children, not necessarily their biological offspring.

6. *More broadly, the American public must cease assuming that support and care for children are the responsibility of their parents' alone, and that parents who require social support have somehow failed.* Most parents require social support, some more than others. According to Coontz, for a good part of American history this fact was assumed. I am not invoking a Platonic vision of communal childrearing; children need particular significant others. But non-parents ought to take substantial economic and social responsibility for the welfare of children.

After health care, Clinton's next big reform effort is likely to be aimed at welfare. Condemning single mothers will legitimate harsh welfare reforms that will make the lives of some of them harder. The left should press instead for the sorts of principles and policies that treat single mothers as equal citizens. □

Notes

[1] P.R. Amato and B. Keith, "Parental divorce and the well-being of children: a meta-analysis," *Psychological Bulletin* 110, (1), 1991, pp. 26–46.

[2] Rosemary Dunlop and Alisa Burns, "The Sleeper Effect—Myth or Reality?—Findings from a ten-year study of the effects of parental divorce at adolescence." Presented at the Fourth Australian Family Research Conference, Manly, New South Wales, February 1993.

[3] Nan Marie Astone and Sara McLanahan, "Family Structure and High School Completion: The Role of Parental Practices," Institute for Research on Poverty Discussion Paper no. 905-9; Madison, WI, 1989.

[4] Stephanie Coontz, *The Way We Never Were* (Basic Books, 1992).

[5] Coontz, op. cit., pp. 259–60.

[6] In the work cited above, Astone and McLanahan found that teachers treated children differently if they believed that they came from "broken" homes.

ANALYSIS: Redefining a Problem

Iris Marion Young's article "Making Single Motherhood Normal" is a response to the current trend of blaming a wide variety of social problems on the breakdown of the traditional two-parent family and to label single mothers as deviant and abnormal. For Young the call to write comes not so much from conservative attacks on single motherhood, divorce, and out-of-wedlock births—conservative appeals to "family values" are business as usual—as from the fact that liberals also are beginning to espouse such views. For this reason, Young wants to address a specific audience of readers, especially those who may have some influence on Democratic party policymakers and on President Clinton's welfare reform plans. Significantly, Young published her article in Dissent, a magazine read by liberals and leftists. Young is not trying to talk conservatives out of their "family values." Rather she is challenging liberals to examine the reasoning that has led many of them to blame social ills on single mothers.

Young wants to convince her readers that the problem has been stated wrongly—and therefore needs to be redefined. By seeking to show that single-motherhood neither causes the social problems blamed on it nor is morally wrong, Young challenges conventional wisdom and proposing an alternative way of thinking that takes single-motherhood to be normal. The six proposals that close the article show what the consequences of such a change in thinking would be for public policy.

FOR CRITICAL INQUIRY

1. Notice that Young's article is divided into five sections. The opening section explains the call to write and formulates the problem she considers in the rest of the essay. In which sentences in this section does Young summarize the problem and her position? How does she establish a sense of urgency about the problem?

2. In the second section of the article, Young analyzes the "reductionism" in her opponents' interpretation of single motherhood. Explain what Young means by "reductionism" and how she uses the term to critique others' views. How does this critique enable her to develop her position? Why do you think she applies this critique first to divorce and, only then, in the next section to the desirability of single-motherhood?

3. In the third section on which points does Young concede and on which does she refuse to concede? In this section, she also expands her initial discussion of why stigmatizing single mothers is a problem. What evidence does she offer for this claim?

4. In the fourth section, Young presents explicitly the enabling assumption in her argument. What is this assumption? What kinds of backing does she provide for the assumption? Do you find the enabling assumption and its backing persuasive? Why or why not?

5. The final sections presents the implications of Young's argument in the form of six proposals. According to Young, what would happen if these proposals to change public policy were put into effect? Do you think they are capable of making the changes she intends? Do you find them suitable to the situation? That is, do you find her proposal to be a feasible one? Why or why not?

LOOKING AT THE GENRE: PROPOSALS

1. In the course of our daily lives we are constantly making proposals. Analyze one such proposal by describing an instance in which you encountered a situation, defined it as a problem, and proposed a solution. Explain the steps you followed to define the problem, consider alternatives, anticipate objections, and formulate a feasible solution—even though you probably did not experience the problem-solving you engaged in as a series of steps. Looking back on this experience, what do you think made your solution successful or unsuccessful? Were there any unforeseen consequences?

ETHICS OF WRITING

Problems and Conflicts

Turning the situations that confront us in everyday life and in public affairs into problems is a powerful way of making reality more manageable. Once you have something defined as a problem, after all, it then becomes possible to think in terms of a solution. From this, however, it follows that problems don't just exist, waiting for solutions, but rather, take shape according to the way people define them. Consider the controversy over abortion. Some people define the problem in terms of the fetusís right to life. Others define it in terms of the woman's right to control her own body. Depending on how the problem is defined, particular solutions seem moreóor lessólogical than others. And, of course, a proposal aims to do precisely that: define a problem in a way that makes a particular solution appear logical.

Yet, as the abortion controversy makes quite clear, underlying many definitions of problems are real conflicts about values and beliefs. That is, genuine differences in belief lead to very different statements of the problem and, thus, to different proposed solutions.

Formulating a problem invariably means taking a position in relation to what others think and believe—aligning yourself with particular values and beliefs and distancing yourself from others. If you assume that you can simply define a problem in an objective fashion, you might well wind up ignoring the underlying conflicts in the situation and the interpretations and needs of others. Such ethical issues arise with other genres, but they become especially important with proposals, because proposals are focused on action and in many cases influence decisions about the use of limited resources.

---

2. Pick two of the reading selections in this chapter and assess them in terms of the solutions proposed. You can assess each separately or you can compare the two. Include among your criteria as many of the following as possible: the apparent importance of the problem, the clarity of goals and objectives, the fit between the problem as stated and the solution proposed, the solutionís capability to solve the problem, and the solutionís suitability in terms of likely costs, superiority over alternative solutions, and fit with the needs and values of those who would be affected.

3. Pick two of the reading selections in this chapter and assess them in terms of their likely effectiveness in persuading readers. In making your assessment, consider the following questions: Who appears to be the intended audience? What attitudes and beliefs related to the proposal might these readers have? Are these emphasized in some way? Is background that is likely to be necessary provided? What kind of relationship does the writer seek to enter into with the audience? Is the tone that is adopted appropriate? What objections might readers have and has the author taken these into account? What kind of effect does the writer seem to be seeking to have? How well is it achieved? How would you account for differences and similarities in the writers' approach to readers? Which do you find more effective and why?

4. Find a proposal in a newspaper or magazine and bring it to class. Summarize the proposal and explain what features make it a proposal. Briefly analyze its effectiveness in terms of some of the factors mentioned in questions 2 and 3.

DESIGNING DOCUMENTS: Literature from Advocacy Group Campaigns

Advocacy groups, concerning themselves with a single issue or with a range of issues, have long been an important part of the American scene. And advocacy groups have a long history of mounting public campaigns that publicize urgent problems and present solutions. At the heart of these campaigns are written appeals, which are in effect another form of proposals, stating the problems as the groups see them and offering solutions.

The PIRGs Campaign to Ban Dioxin

The Problem:

Dioxin is one of the most toxic substances known to humans. Recent studies by the Environmental Protection Agency (EPA) reaffirm the link between dioxin and cancer, and also highlight dioxin's potential non-cancer health effects, such as birth defects, learning disabilities, decreased fertility, and reduced sperm counts.

> "Human exposure to dioxin may pose a number of significant health risks, including the stunting of fetal growth and suppression of the immune and hormone systems."
>
> Environmental Protection Agency in May 1994

Dioxin is created when chlorine is exposed to high temperatures. The major sources of dioxin include paper mills, which use chlorine in the bleaching process, solvents, polyvinyl chloride (PVC) plastics, and incinerators, which produce dioxin when they burn chlorine-containing products like PVC plastics.

In September 1994, the EPA released a "draft" of its three year dioxin reassessment. The EPA is now accepting public comments and holding hearings around the country until January 13, 1995 while considering action to address the dioxin threat.

Other Facts About Dioxin:

• Dioxin is the contaminant in "Agent Orange" that Vietnam veterans argue is linked to their high rates of cancer, birth defects, and other serious health problems.

• Dioxin released into the air by incinerators falls on our land and water, is consumed by fish, cows, and other animals, and works its way up the food chain.

• Dioxin can be passed to fetuses in the womb, and babies through breast milk.

• Children may have 4 to 12% of their lifetime contamination from dioxin in their bodies by their first birthdays, according to EPA estimates.

• More than 90% of human intake of dioxin is through food, particularly animal and dairy products, according to EPA estimates.

• Two states have issued health advisories warning pregnant women, nursing mothers, and women of child-bearing age not to eat parts of lobsters due to dioxin contamination.

The State PIRGs
218 D Street SE, Washington D.C. 20003

The Solution:

The production of dioxin can be virtually eliminated simply by substituting manufacturing and cleaning methods that do not use chlorine, and by stopping waste incineration. Alternative methods already exist for the major industrial uses of chlorine products and processes linked to dioxin formation. To address the dangers dioxin poses to our health we must:

- Phase out the use of chlorine in the manufacture of solvents and PVC plastics.
- Ban within five years the use of chlorine in the manufacture of paper.
- Phase out the incineration of municipal, medical or hazardous wastes, and ban the start-up of new incinerators, or expansion of existing incinerators.
- Require reporting for dioxin under the Toxic Release Inventory.

The Opposition:

The major producers and users of products that generate dioxin, including the chemical, pulp and paper, and incinerator industries, argue that the scientific evidence is inconclusive and that it is premature to regulate. Dow Chemical, Dupont, International Paper, Georgia Pacific, and trade associations such as the Chlorine Chemistry Council of the Chemical Manufacturers Association, and American Forest and Paper Products, are pressuring both the EPA and Congress to stall or take inadequate action to address this serious health problem.

How You Can Help:

The state PIRGs, working with the Sierra Club, Greenpeace, Environmental Defense Fund, the American Public Health Association and other groups, are pushing the EPA to propose phasing out dioxin-producing chemicals. The EPA is accepting written comments from the public on its dioxin study and proposals until January 13, 1995. Please write to EPA Administrator Carol Browner expressing your concern about dioxin and your support for chemical phase-outs.

Sample Letter

The Honorable Carol Browner
U.S. Environmental Protection Agency
401 M Street SW
Washington, DC 20460

Dear Administrator Browner:

I am writing to express my concern about the threat dioxin poses to the health of both humans and wildlife. As announced by EPA in September 1994, dioxin has been linked to cancer as well as numerous health effects such as birth defects, learning disabilities, and decreased fertility.

I urge the EPA to act swiftly to: phase out the use of chlorine in the manufacturing of solvents and PVC plastics, ban within five years the use of chlorine in paper manufacturing, ban the start-up or expansion of incinerators, and phase out the incineration of municipal, medical, and hazardous waste. We must also require publicly-accessible reporting for dioxin under the national TRI database.

Half measures won't do. Please take a firm stand: do not "compromise" our health and environment due to pressure from the incinerator, paper, and chemical industries.

I look forward to hearing from you on this critical matter. Please place my letter in the official file of public comments.

Sincerely,
(your name and address)

HERE ARE SEVEN REASONS WHY YOU SHOULD SUPPORT
A MORATORIUM ON IMMIGRATION

1 WE'RE FULL NOW. We are living through the greatest sustained wave of immigration in American history. Why? The Census Bureau says that current immigration trends will increase our population to nearly 400 million by 2050 and 70 percent of the increase will be due to immigration. That's 130 million more people than are here today.

2 THE SYSTEM'S OVERLOADED. There are nearly four million people waiting in line to enter. The latest wave of new citizen naturalizations will generate millions more new relative petitions. System overload has caused the immigration enforcement arm of the Federal government to nearly collapse while too many people enter too fast, and backlogs grow exponentially. We need a break.

3 WE NEED TIME TO ASSIMILATE. Throughout American history, the country has had sustained periods of low or negligible immigration. These periodic lulls enabled the country to absorb and assimilate those who had come before. Remember how the turn-of-the-century immigrant ghettos of our large northern cities melted away into the American mainstream during the low-immigration years leading up to 1965? We need another sustained lull now.

4 A DECLINING STANDARD OF LIVING. Immigration trends are troubling. Immigrants today are less skilled, less educated, and more likely to use welfare (1990 Census). Recent studies show that immigrants are far more likely than citizens to be on welfare, live in poverty, get the Earned Income Tax Credit, be in prison, work without health insurance, and live in overcrowded housing conditions. New data from the General Accounting Office reveal that immigrants are now using federal welfare programs like SSI and AFDC at skyrocketing rates.

5 LABOR MARKET. Immigrants are entering the country without regard to our changing labor needs. This means an increased supply of low skilled labor and heightened competition in many labor sectors; the resulting wage depression is increasing the gap between rich and poor in the highest immigrant-receiving communities.

6 THE PEOPLE WANT AN IMMIGRATION MORATORIUM. Polls show an overwhelming majority of the American people want a lot less immigration or even an immigration moratorium. (Roper Poll, May 1992; Latino National Political Survey, December 1992). These are persistent results over time. Most of the people cannot be wrong all the time!

7 THE SYSTEM'S BROKEN. The current system breeds lawlessness. Thousands of illegal immigrants enter the country every day—two to three million a year. Fake documents are easily obtained, providing access to welfare and benefits meant for citizens and legal residents.

Think about it.

We're FAIR (Federation for American Immigration Reform): a national, public educational organization working to stop illegal immigration and limit legal immigration. It's time for you to get involved. Make a difference in America's future.

For more information call: 800-395-0890

Like advertisements for products and services, these appeals must capture readers' attention, and, whereas advertisements are offering readers something, these appeals are asking readers to contribute their time and money. Proposals are geared to action, and with advocacy group appeals, readers are very much being called on to act. So document design is an important element of this campaign literature: the design must make readers look at the message and must help make the message effective.

The importance of design is reflected in the two examples of advocacy group campaign literature included here. The first is from the Public Interest Research Group (PIRG), a multi-issue consumer and citizen group. The second is from the Federation for American Immigration Reform (FAIR), an organization formed around the single issue of immigration.

- **The PIRG Campaign to Ban Dioxin** The PIRG flyer was sent out to supporters and contributors as part of the group's campaign to ban dioxin. The text has a basic problem-solution structure, in that it analyzes the problem of dioxin and then proposes a solution, and it ends by calling on readers to take action. As you read the flyer, notice how its design underscores the problem-solution structure of the text and otherwise contributes to the flyer's effectiveness.

- **A Moratorium on Immigration. Federation for American Immigration Reform (FAIR)** The FAIR advertisement was published in the National Review, a conservative journal of opinion. Notice here that the solution proposed comes first—in the title of the ad—and the problem definition follows—in the list of seven reasons. Like the PIRG flyer, the ad calls on readers to do something to do—in this case, enroll in FAIR. Again, as you read the appeal, notice the contribution of design.

DISCUSSION AND ACTIVITIES

1. Compare the two pieces of campaign literature with regard to content and design. First, summarize the content of each—the problem stated, the solution proposed, and the action readers are called on to take. Describe the design of each—the elements into which the text is divided and any special features (bullet points, lists, boxes, heads) that are used.
   Next, characterize differences between the two pieces. Which of these differences, if any, might relate to differences in form, intended audience, and purpose? (One piece is a flyer sent out to supporters asking them to take action for a particular reason—the EPA hearings on dioxin—the other is single-page ad that is trying to attract new supporters).
   Finally, assess the two pieces, keeping intended audience and purpose in mind. How well supported and persuasive do you find their statement of the problem and the proposed solution? How effective do you find the design in drawing the reader's attention, making the text readable, and supporting the message of the text? Overall, do you think one of the pieces would be more effective than the other in getting readers to respond? Explain why.

2. Bring to class an example of campaign literature—an advertisement, flyer, poster, or other appeal—from a public interest group. Working together in groups of four, analyze each of the examples. What problem do they define, what solution do they propose, and what do they call on readers to do? How effective is the text? How effective is the design? What contributes to the effectiveness of the text and design? Does the design work to support the text?
   Present to the class or analyze in a written report the examples your group finds most and least effective from the standpoint of text and design. Explain your assessments.

3. Analyze an advertisement for a product or service in a newspaper, magazine, letter, or flyer. The analysis should be of both text and design, based on questions such as those in listed in 2. Or, if you have a VCR available, you can tape an advertisement on television and analyze it. Present the advertisement and your analysis to the class.

ASSIGNMENTS

WORKING TOGETHER: Advocacy Group Proposals

Advocacy groups do a wide range of writing that falls into the genre of proposals. Such writing includes campaign literature— advertisements in newspapers and magazines and on radio and television, flyers, letters of appeal, and posters and bumper stickers

—articles in the opinion pages of newspapers, petitions, and of course grant proposals.

Work together in a group of three or four to write two pieces of different types. Choose an issue that could interest an advocacy group—whether a campus or other local issue (drinking on campus, increased tuition, etc.) or a broader issue that group members are fairly familiar with (gun control, health insurance, literacy, etc.). What is a key problem connected with the issue? What might be a feasible solution to the problem? As a group, come to a consensus about a problem and feasible solution.

Once you have defined the problem you want to address, think about which of the types of writing listed above might be most relevant for dealing with the problem and choose two types. What will the specific purpose of each piece be? Who is the likely audience for each piece and how can you most effectively address this audience? For example, what do you want your supporters to do and how might you appeal to those who are undecided about or even oppose your proposal?

As general model of the various types of writing, you can use any of the selections in this chapter or pieces that have been brought in to class. Keep in mind the criteria for effective proposals, and also try to use design as effectively as possible.

When you are finished, write an introduction to the project, explaining the problem you defined and the solution you proposed, why you chose the types of writing you chose, how audience and purpose were reflected in what you wrote, and what you did to make the pieces effective.

CALL TO WRITE: PROPOSALS

WRITING ASSIGNMENT

For this assignment, write a proposal that formulates a problem, considers the alternatives, and offers a solution for a particular group.

You will need to think of an existing situation that calls for attention, whether it is on campus or at the local, national, or international level. Something may be wrong that needs to be changed or corrected. Something may be lacking that needs to be added. Something worthwhile may not be working properly and therefore needs to be improved. Or it may be that a situation needs to be redefined in order to find new approaches and solutions.

In any case, your proposal should be directed at changing something for somebody. You may want to direct your proposal at those who are in a position to enact change; you may also want to write a proposal to a group offering suggestions for how they can best help themselves. In other words, the audience you choose for your proposal will help determine the kinds of actions you can expect as a result of your call to write.

You may also find yourself in a situation in which your proposal needs to be written collaboratively, with the support and active participation of other writers. If this is the case, be sure to read the relevant sections in Chapter x, particularly those on writing proposals collaboratively (see pages XXX). Here are some more specific possibilities:

- Proposals for new or improved services: proposals to government agencies, professional associations, educational institutions, and private foundations to provide new or improved services—in health care, education, recreation, and so on. The student proposal "For a Campus Coffee House" (page XX) is a good example of such a proposal for a college campus. You might write a proposal based on a situation you see on campus—to improve residential life, food service, social climate, advising, academic programs, and so on. Or you may want to write a proposal for new or improved services in your local community or at the state or federal level.

- Public policy proposals: these range from editorials in newspapers and journals of opinion to actual legislation that proposes to do things such as change immigration laws, recognize gay and lesbian relationships, require a balanced budget, devise a national health care plan, and so on. The two editorials on national service, by Christopher Dodd and Nicola Clark, offer examples of short public policy proposals that seek to influence public opinion and create a favorable political climate for the writer's plan.

   Often, public policy proposals enter a debate that is already ongoing, where a problem has been identified and various proposals are vying for influence. For example, you could write a proposal about an environmental issue, such as a PIRG campaign to ban dioxin or an editorial proposing changes in U.S. foreign policy or domestic programs. You could make proposals about the education system or about sports, immigration, the national parks, or public entertainment.

- Proposals on customs and habits: personal advice columnists such as Ann Landers and Dear Abby make their living proposing attitudes and courses of action in everyday life (don't feel guilty, express your feelings, see a counselor, talk to a priest or minister, consult a doctor, change your job). Proposals about manners and morals are frequent topics of journalists and essayists offer "tips" on dealing with the complexities of daily living. Consider writing a proposal about contemporary relations between the sexes, family matters, or life at work.

INVENTION

To think more systematically about proposals you might be called to write, try working through the following exercises. Your proposal may well grow out of a situation you are currently in, or it may stem from an experience you have had in the recent past.

1. Start by taking an inventory of the issues around you that might call for a solution. As you could tell from the readings, there is a wide range of possibilities open to you. Begin by thinking small and local. Make a list of those positions in which you have the most power to enact change. Are you an officer of any groups, clubs, or organizations? Are you in any classes where the teacher allows the students to carry a lot of responsibility? Are you a leader or captain on a team? If so, write down each of the examples where you find yourself speaking from a position of authority. Then think through the issues that confront those groups, and keep track of them as possibilities.

2. Next, identify those positions you hold where you would be listened to as a fellow member, rather than as a leader. What other groups are you a part of? What are the issues that circulate in each of those groups? Do any of those issues call you to try to propose a solution (even if you haven't thought of one yet)? If so, write them down as good possibilities.

3. Now that you have thought about the options that might be closer to home, you can broaden your thinking to national and international issues. Which do you identify as real problems? Which do you care enough about to spend time thinking of, and proposing a solution to? What kind of a power position are you in when you talk about these types of issues? Who might listen to you? What is the best forum for getting people to hear your proposal?

4. Once you have created your lists of possibilities, narrow it down to the three options you think are most promising. Begin with the ones you care most about, or those that have the potential to make your life (or that of someone you know) markedly better. Then, try the next set of exercises on formulating a problem, assessing alternatives, and matching problems and solutions with your top three choices. After you have thought about your potential proposal from all those directions, you should be able to tell which one will make the best proposal.

5. Decide tentatively on the audience for your proposal. To whom can you write to realistically make changes happen? To whom do you have realistic access? With whom do you have credibility? Is there a specific person, or governing body, who is in a position to enact the changes you will present? Create a list of at least three possible audiences, and consider the implications each audience holds for the successful implementation of your proposal. Notice how your definition of the problem may change depending on your audience. Do these shifts in definition hold any consequence for your, or for those you are trying to help?

FORMULATING THE PROBLEM

As you have seen, problems don't just come in pre-packaged form, calling on us to solve them. Problems first have to be defined. By formulating problems, writers take situations that already exist and point out what aspects call for urgent attention and action. In this sense, problem formulation is always in part an interpretation—a way of establishing the relevance of a problem to readers. This is a powerful move, since as a writer you are taking a group of people, and defining them (and their problems) in a particular way. As a proposal writer, you establish criteria for deciding what is good and normal, and what is bad and in need of some sort of repair. There are, of course, many ways to define problems, so part of your job is to do so responsibly and ethically. If you are interested in more guidance on defining concepts, see page XXX in Public Documents.

Illegal drugs offers a good example of how problems can be defined in a number of ways. If you asked most Americans about the problems that currently beset American society, it is quite likely that many of them would name "drugs" as one of the most pressing problems. But what exactly is the problem with "drugs"? There is little question that millions of Americans use illegal drugs and that there is a flourishing criminal drug trade. To say as much, however, only describes an existing situation. It gives you an issue in the broadest sense, namely what, if anything, should we do about illegal drugs? But to propose solutions to the issue will require writers to define more precisely what they see as the problem raised by "drugs."

Depending on the writer's perspective, the problem can vary considerably and lead to very different proposals. For example, some would say that the problem with drugs is that illegal drug trade results in police corruption and powerful underworld drug cartels. Others would argue that drugs are causing social decay and destroying the moral fiber of a generation of American young people. Still others would hold that Americans and drug laws haven't distinguished adequately between recreational drugs like marijuana and addictive drugs like heroin and cocaine. Notice on the following chart how different problem formulation leads to different proposals. Notice, too, how each solution growing from the problem formulation will impact a different community:

Issue:	Illegal drug use		
Problem:	Underworld drug trade	Social decay	Need for redefinition
Proposed Solution:	Step up war against major drug dealers	Education, jobs programs.	Decriminalize marijuana
	Cut off drugs at point of distribution.	Eliminate conditions of drug use, such as poverty and hopelessness.	Make legal distinctions that recognize differences between kinds of drugs (recreational v. addictive).

Use the chart as a guide to analyze an existing situation by breaking it down into a number of problems. It's unlikely that you will be able to address in one proposal all the aspects of the situation that you identify as problems. In fact, you may find that the proposed solutions suggested by the various problems are contradictory or mutually exclusive. The idea at this point is to see how many different problems you can formulate so that you will be able to decide which seems most pressing or important to you.

1. Begin by considering the current situation. In a short phrase (such as "illegal drug use") describe the main topic as you see it.
2. Now consider what problems this topic raises. What's wrong? What's lacking? What, if anything, could be redefined? In short phrases, state a number of problems that you see in the current situation.
3. Next, consider what proposed solutions seem to emerge from the problems as you have defined them. What are people currently doing? How effective are current solutions? What have people proposed to add to, change, or redefine the situation?
4. Finally, go back to the first two steps and re-consider the way you are defining the problem itself. Why did you choose this particular tack? What others are possibilities? How does your definition of the problem position those people it most concerns? How else might they be positioned, using a different definition? Who are you hoping to represent? Once you have answered these questions, you might want to revise your responses to the first three parts of this exercise.

ASSESSING ALTERNATIVES

Once you have identified a number of possible solutions to the problems you've defined, you can then assess relative strengths and weaknesses of proposals. One way to do this is to test the feasibility of proposed solutions—their capability and suitability to solve problems. Again this can be done by using a chart:

Problem:	What policy on international drug trade should the government follow?	
Proposed Solution:	Legalize drug trade under state control	Step up the war against international drug trade
Capability:	Unknown. Costs and benefits uncertain. require considerable U.S. administration. What about possible black market?	Could reduce amount of Would illegal drugs to enter the However, very costly to have widespread effect. What about domestic trade?
Suitability:	Politically unpopular. Voters would interpret as a state endorsement of drug use.	Foreign policy implications need to be carefully considered.

Construct your own chart that assesses the feasibility of solutions.

1. State the problem in the form of a question.
2. List two or more potential solutions to the problem. Even if you do not support or endorse one or more of the solutions, thinking through its feasibility can help you develop the benefits of your solution and explain why it is preferable to other approaches.
3. Spend some time figuring out what the criteria might be for a good solution. This means making a list of the qualities a good solution might have. What are the requirements for a good solution? What are other characteristics that are desirable? And what qualities would be like icing on the cake, nice but not absolutely necessary. Test your tentative solutions against your lists of criteria.

4. Consider whether each proposed solution is in fact capable of solving the problem as it has been stated. Evaluating the capability of a proposed solution, as is the case on the chart above, may not lead to a yes or no answer. Rather, it may lead to further questions that need to be addressed, in this case about the expense and possible consequences of the proposal.

5. Consider the suitability of the proposed solutions. Here you are likely to uncover conflicts of values and interests. In the case of the two proposals listed above, one (legalizing the drug trade) conflicts with many Americans' values, while the other (stepping up the war against the international drug trade) raises potential conflicts of interest with American foreign policy objectives, particularly in regard to countries that export illegal drugs. Uncovering such conflicts can help you clarify what readers you can most effectively appeal to for support and what values and attitudes you might emphasize as a basis of support.

6. Check the validity of your reasoning. At this point, it might be helpful to run through the list of potential logical fallacies covered in Chapter 2 (see pages XXX). Once you are sure you have not mistakenly stepped into any of the fallacies listed there, you can feel confident that your proposal is on solid footing.

PLANNING

MATCHING PROBLEMS AND SOLUTIONS

Perhaps the most important feature of a persuasive proposal is the match between the problem as the writer defines it and the solution as the writer describes it. Unless the two fit together in a logical and compelling way, readers are unlikely to have confidence in the proposal.

Proposal writers often link solutions to problems in two ways—in terms of long-term overall goals and in terms of objectives that specify the outcome of the proposal. In the case of Christopher Dodd's proposal for national service, for example, the overall goal is a renewal of the spirit of community service and volunteering, while the specific objective is to motivate a new generation of volunteers by linking the repayment of student loans to community service.

Objectives normally tell who is going to do what, when they are going to do it, what the projected results will be, and (in some instances) how the results will be measured. A proposal for grant funding from a homeless shelter, for example, might state the following objective: the Oak Street Shelter Agency (who) proposes to increase the number of employed clients (what) during the next 18 months (when) by 15 percent (results) as noted in the Department of Social Welfare Homeless Survey Report (measurement).

As you design your proposal, consider how you can effectively present your goals and objectives. Your goals will give readers a sense of your values and offer common ground as the basis for the reader's support, while your objectives will help convince readers you have a concrete plan of action that can succeed.

DEVELOPING A WORKING OUTLINE

The outline of a proposal generally follows a predictable order: statement of the problem, goals and objectives, description of the solution, an explanation of the reasons for the solution, and an ending.

A working outline of Christopher Dodd's proposal "National Service?: Yes, for the Sake of Renewal" might look something like this:

- Statement of the problem contrasts two attitudes toward government, Reagan's v. Kennedy's points out need to redefine relationship with government and renew commitment to meet social needs

- Goals and objectives states the goal is to renew our commitment to meet the social needs mentioned above

- Description of the solutionm proposes national community service of volunteers cites his-

torical precedents
Roosevelt's Civilian Conservation Corps (1930s)
Kennedy's Peace Corps (1960s)
Nixon's ACTION agency (1970s)
Bush's Points of Light Foundation (1980s)

describes implementation: how community service could be used to repay student loans

• Explanation of reason concedes new spending but points out other savingsdeals with counterargumentscost of program: must be seen in terms of overall benefits new government bureaucracy: draw on existing public, private, and community programs, consolidate programs lists consequences of failing to act: declining competitiveness and wages, hopelessness

• Ending restates proposal and its advantages

GUIDELINES FOR A WORKING OUTLINE

1. Statement of the problem. You will need to decide how readily readers will recognize the problem and how much agreement already exists about how to solve it. (In some instances, such as the proposal "For a Campus Coffee House" below, a large part of the writer's work is to establish that a problem does in fact exist and needs to be addressed.) Your first task is to establish the relevance of the problem to your intended audience. Who does the problem affect? What makes it urgent? What will happen if the problem is not addressed?
2. Description of the solution. Since effective proposals present both general goals that appeal to shared values and attitudes and specific objectives that the proposal will accomplish, you need to state the goals you have identified. Then, you should state clearly how and why your proposed solution will work. Describe the solution and the steps needed to implement it. You will need to decide on the level of detail required to give readers the necessary information to evaluate your proposal.
3. Explanation of reasons. You will need to identify the best reasons in support of your proposal. You will also need to consider what alternatives are currently available and how much you need to address them. Finally, you need to think about what counterarguments are likely to arise and how much you need to deal with them.
4. Ending. Some proposals have short endings that reinforce the main point. Others, such as the advertisements commonly found in magazines and newspapers, end by calling on readers to do something.

WORKING DRAFT

Use the working outline you have developed to write a draft of your proposal. While you are writing, you may want to work through some of the paragraph development ideas suggested below, and you might be interested in trying a variety of ways to begin and end your proposal.

PARAGRAPH DEVELOPMENT: Moving from Old Information to New Information

One technique you can use to develop your paragraphs with some consistency is to use old information to in order to establish the basis for new information. When you follow this sentence arrangement, you create links between points already covered, and the points you have yet to make. Notice in the following paragraph from a proposal by FAIR (the Federation for American Immigration Reform) how each sentence introduces a new item of information. When readers assimilate the new information, they effectively convert it into old information that can then serve as the basis for more new information. In this way, when writers carefully introduce new information in the context of old information, they can guide their readers to build up complex patterns of meaning.

WE NEED TIME TO ASSIMILATE. Throughout American history, the country has sustained periods of low or negligible immigration. These periodic lulls enabled the country to absorb and assimilate those who had come before. Remember how the turn-of-the-century immigrant ghettos of our large northern cities melted away into the American mainstream during the low-immigration years leading up to 1965? We need another sustained lull now.

Here is a schematic way of representing this paragraph:

Old information . . . . New information
S1 there is a historical precedent . . . . the country has immigration   lulls

S2 immigration lulls . . . . allow time to assimilate

S3 assimilation time . . . . allows the immigrants to move from poverty to the mainstream

S4 we need to allow that to happen again now

You may want to try this paragraph development strategy in your own writing. Or you may want to try some alternative strategies, as explained in other chapters. For example, you might:

- see Using Summaries (page XXX in Reports) to work with substantial amounts of outside information

- see Defining (page XXX in Public Documents) to further clarify the goals and objectives of your proposal

- see Offering Reasons with Supporting Facts and Evidence (page XXX in Reviews) to establish your proposal on solid argumentative ground

BEGINNINGS AND ENDINGS: Offering a Solution or Recommendation

In some cases, writers sense that they need to do more at the end of an essay than explain what the consequences or wider implications of their proposition might be. They feel the need to explain what action needs to be taken by readers who find their way of thinking persuasive. In a proposal, readers expect some sort of recommendation or solution to the problem that the writer has carefully established.

Recommendations and solutions can vary in their format and their sense of urgency. In the readings throughout this chapter, you saw a wide range of solutions, and a variety of methods for posing them. Some are incorporated into the body of the text.

> And yet the only way President Clinton's myriad social programs could produce measurable results would be if citizens were prepared not only to fund them with higher taxes but perhaps also to accept something as extreme— and unpopular—as a draft.
> — Nicola Clark, "How to Draft a National Service Plan"

Others are set off in a separate section, as in the case of the call to act that ends the PIRG statement about dioxin.

> How You Can Help: The state PIRGs, working with the Sierra Club, Greenpeace, Environmental Defense Fund, the American Public Health Association and other groups, are pushing the EPA to propose phasing out dioxin-producing chemicals. The EPA is accepting written comments from the public on its dioxin study and proposals until January 13, 1995. Please write to EPA Administrator Carol Browner expressing your concern about dioxin and your support for chemical phase-outs.
> — "The PIRG Campaign to Ban Dioxin"

Still others list their recommendation by enumerating them, as in the case of Iris Marion Young. You can see here that Young sets up her list of proposals with a short paragraph explaining what she is about to do.

> If we assume there is nothing morally wrong with single-mother families, but that they are often disadvantaged by lack of child care by economic discrimination and social stigma, then what follows for public policy? Some of the answers are obvious, some are not so obvious, but in the current climate promoting a stingy and punitive welfare state, all bear discussion. I will close by sketching a few proposals[.]
>
> — Iris Marion Young, "Making Single Motherhood Normal"

You can decide for yourself which strategies works better for you, given the overall tone of your proposal, your purpose, and the position of power from which you are writing. If none of these beginning and ending strategies work well for you (if, for example, you want to place your solutions throughout the body of your text rather than at the end), consider some of the beginning and ending ideas discussed in other chapters. For example, see:

- see Using an Echo Effect to Reframe (page XXX in Letters) to follow through a theme that unifies your proposal

- see Using Facts, Statistics, and Background Information (page XXX in Public Documents) to establish that the problem you are discussing is a serious one.

- see Setting Up with a Metaphorical Anecdote (page XXX in Profiles) to frame your proposal with an image that will resonate with your readers

PEER COMMENTARY

Once you have written a draft proposal, exchange drafts with a classmate. If you are working in a group, exchange drafts between groups. Write a commentary to the draft, using the following guidelines.

1. How does the proposal establish the need for something to be done—by defining a problem, describing a situation, using an example, providing facts and background information? Is the need for action convincing? Who is likely to recognize and want to address the main issue of the proposal? Who might feel excluded? Is there any way to include more potential supporters?

2. Identify where the proposal first appears in the draft. Is it clear and easy to find? Put the proposal in your own words. If you cannot readily paraphrase it, explain why. What is the objective of the proposal? Is it clear who is going to do what, when, how much, and (if appropriate) how the results will be evaluated? Do you think the proposal will have the results intended? Why or why not? What other results might occur?

3. What reasons are offered on behalf of the proposal? Do you find these reasons persuasive? Why or why not? Are these the best reasons available? What other reasons might the writers use?

4. Does the solution appear to be feasible? Why or why not? Does the writer need to include more information to make the proposal seem more feasible? What would it take to convince you this proposal would work?

5. Does the proposal seem to be addressed to an appropriate audience? Can the audience do anything to support the actions suggested in the proposal? If not, can you suggest a more appropriate audience? If so, does the way the proposal is written seem suitable for that audience? Point to specific places in the text that need revision. What kinds of changes would make the proposal work better for the audience?

REVISING

Now that you have received feedback on your proposal from other writers, you can revise those points you feel are necessary. In the section that follows, you will find advice on revising for coherence.

CONNECTIONS AND COHERENCE: PARALLELISM OF IDEAS

One way to assure coherence in your proposal is to make sure that the ideas you are presented are parallel. This means that they are equal in some way, either because they use a similar grammatical pattern to introduce each one, or because they are set off in your text in the same way. You can still have hierarchies within those ideas (many writers will put the most important points either first or last), but the treatment of the ideas remains roughly the same. This kind of parallelism allows readers to easily follow your movement from idea to idea, or from solution to solution. The key to parallelism, as you will see, is selective repetition. Many of the readings in this chapter use this technique of parallelism of ideas. Consider, for example, this paragraph from the proposal for "And Everything Nice."

Produced by videomaker Julie Gustafson, in collaboration with humanities scholars from the disciplines of cultural anthropology, philosophy, and social history, "And Everything Nice" will probe beneath headlines about "the epidemic of teen sexual activity and pregnancy." The work will focus on the moral reasoning and maturational processes of five young women. It will make visible to viewers the ways in which the decisions of these young women, often taken to be private, are frequently linked to larger factors: socioeconomic status, race, ethnicity, and ultimately, their hopes for the future. Finally, the documentary will make clear the striking ways in which girls from diverse backgrounds share the experience of being young and being female in a rapidly changing social and cultural landscape.

This one paragraph shows parallelism of ideas. Notice how most of the sentences follow a similar pattern:

[noun describing the project] will [verb] [attribute 1,
    attribute 2, attribute 3].

This could have been a rather dense paragraph, with so much information that it would be difficult to read, but the repetition of that sentence structure makes it easy for the reader to make meaning out of the words.

Parallelism can also work on a much smaller level, with individual sentences. If you are interested in learning more about it, take a look at page XXX in Letters. On the other hand, if parallelism is a concept you already have well in hand, you might consider working through some of the coherence devices described in other chapters:

- see Temporal Transitions (page XXX in Memoirs) to establish a clear time line within your proposal

- see Enumerative Order (page XXX in Public Documents) to arrange your points with numbering strategies

- see Linking the Parts to the Proposition (page XXX in Commentary) to show the connections between the problem and your suggested solutions.

WRITERS WORKSHOP

A group of three students wrote the following "Proposal for a Campus Coffee House" in response to an assignment in a business writing class that called on students to produce a collaboratively written proposal to deal with a campus problem. Their commentary on the decisions they made formulating problems and solutions and designing the format appears after the proposal.

Proposal for a Campus Coffee House

To meet the problem of excessive drinking on campus, we propose that a coffee house, open on Friday and Saturday nights with live entertainment, be established in the auxiliary dining room in Morgan Commons and operated by the Student Management Club to provide an alcohol-free alternative to undergraduate social life.

The Problem: Drinking on Campus. A recent study by the Student Health Center indicates high levels of drinking by undergraduates on campus (Martinez & Johnson, 1998). Both legal and underage students drink frequently (Fig. 1). They also increasingly engage in unhealthy "binge drinking" to the point of unconsciousness. The number of students admitted to the student infirmary for excessive drinking has increased 50% in the past four years (Fig. 2). These patterns of drinking conform to those observed in a recent national study (Dollenmayer, 1998). Like many other colleges and universities, Warehouse State is faced with a serious student drinking problem (Weiss, 1997).

Currently there are few alternatives for students seeking an alcohol-free social life. Campus social life is dominated by the fraternities, whose parties make alcohol easily available to minors. Off campus, local bars that feature live bands are popular with students, and underage students have little difficulty obtaining and using fake IDs.

The Solution: Campus Coffee House. The Student Management Club proposes to operate a campus coffee house with live entertainment on Friday and Saturday nights in order to provide an alcohol-free social environment on campus for 200 students (capacity of auxiliary dining room in Morgan Commons when set up cabaret-style).

Such a campus coffee house would have a number of benefits. It would serve as a public endorsement of alcohol-free social life, enhance student culture by providing low-cost alcohol-free entertainment on campus, and support current ongoing alcohol abuse treatment and prevention programs. The Student Counseling Center currently counsels students with drinking problems and has recently instituted a promising peer counselor program to educate students about the risks of drinking. Such programs, however, will be limited and largely reactive unless there are alcohol-free alternatives to social life on campus.

Organizational capability. The Student Management Club has the experience and expertise needed to run the proposed coffee house. Since 1991, it has successfully run a coffee counter in Adams Union, open five days a week from 8 to 3:30. Management majors are interested in expanding their work into the areas of arts programming and publicity.

Budget. The proposed campus coffee house will require initial funding of $1250 to begin operations. See cost breakdown in Table 1 Initial Expenditure. We believe, however, that such expenditures are one-time only and that the campus coffee house should become self-supporting. See projected budget in Table 2.

Table 1: Initial expenditures.

Supplies (mugs, plates, spoons, forks, paper products, etc)	$ 750
Coffee, tea, milk, pastries	250
Publicity	250
Total	$1,250

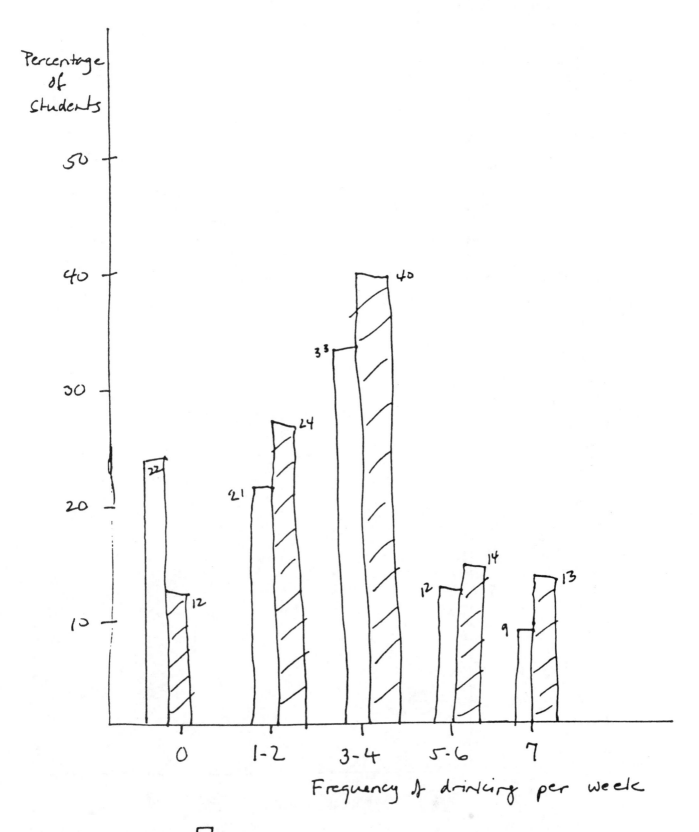

Percentage of students

50

40 40

30 33

24

22

21

20

14 13

12 12

10 9

0   1-2   3-4   5-6   7

Frequency of drinking per week

underage

legal

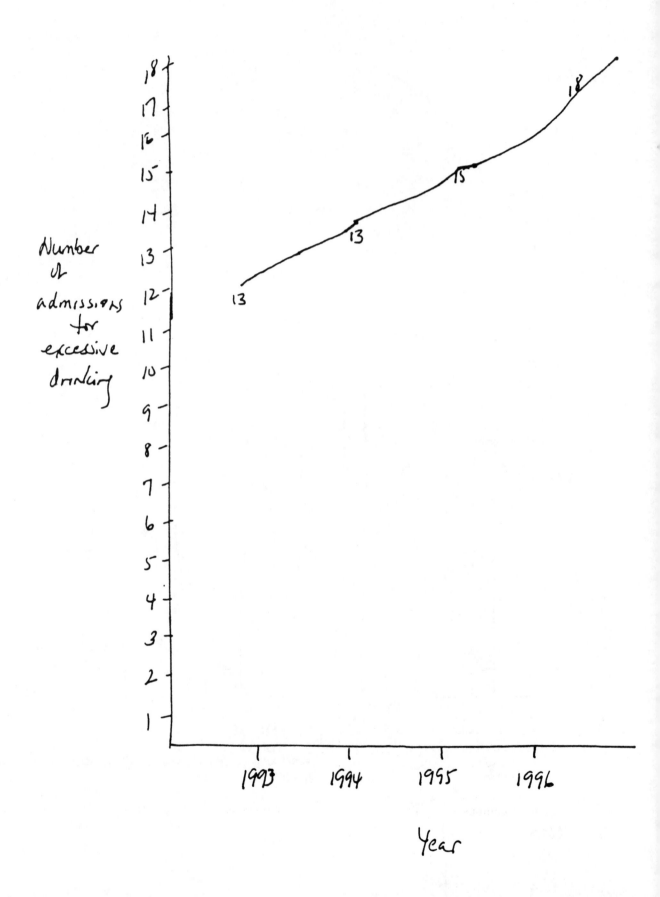

Table 2: **Projected budget**

Per evening of operation

Income	Expenses	
(estimated) $400	Entertainment (band or singer)	$100.00
	Staff (2 persons, 5 hrs each @ $5.35)	53.50
	Supplies	75.00
	Food	100.00
	Publicity	25.00
	Total	$353.50

References

Dollenmayer, L.C. (1998). "Patterns of Alcohol Use among American College Students." *Journal of the American Medical Association*, 275 (16), 223-229.

Martinez, M., & Johnson, R. (1998). "Alcohol Use and Campus Social Life." Student Health Center, Warehouse State University.

Weiss, I. (1997, December 2). "Drinking Deaths Prompt Concern on Campus." *New York Times*, p. 1, 7.

COMMENTARY

What follow are excerpts from a group meeting, which the participants taped. Here are some passages from the transcript where the three group members, Kathy, Andrea, and Bruce talk about why they got involved in the coffee house project and how they went about writing the proposal.

Kathy: One of the things that has been interesting about working in this group is that the members come to it from different perspectives. Andrea and I see the coffee house more as a crusade against drinking, which we've watched do a lot of damage to some people we know. So that's a pretty big motivation to get involved, to provide alternatives. Bruce, I think, is into it more out of his interest in folk music and running coffee houses.

Bruce. Yeah, I mean I do support the idea of having alcohol-free alternative places for students to go. That makes sense to me. But, I agree, definitely. My main thing is arts programming and administration, that whole business. If I can, that's what I want to do when I graduate.

******

Bruce: Some of that came up when we were trying to think of reasons for the coffee house, and I was into how it would help promote the arts on campus. We ended up not using that stuff.

Andrea: Right, but I think Kathy and I became more aware of how we had to make sure the proposal didn't sound moralistic. Remember at first we defined the problem as "drinking on campus" and only later changed it to "excessive drinking." We wanted the proposal to sound positive— that a coffee house would enhance student life.

Bruce: Exactly. We didn't want it to sound like punishment. And you're right, the proposal doesn't really come out against drinking as the problem but against excessive drinking, binge drinking. I mean alcohol is legal for people over twenty-one. Besides it's unrealistic to think a campus coffee house or anything else for that matter is going to end drinking on campus.

****

Andrea: Another thing I felt we tried to do in the proposal was link the coffee house concept to other campus anti-drinking programs. I thought we did a pretty good job of listing benefits in the solution section.

WORKSHOP QUESTIONS

1. As you have seen, one of the marks of a successful proposal is that the proposed solution matches the problem as it is defined. Consider the fit between problem and solution in this proposal. How is the problem defined? What evidence is offered to indicate the scope and seriousness of the problem? Does the problem seem to be a genuine one that needs attention? How well does the solution address the problem? Does it seem to offer an effective approach to excessive drinking on campus? Are there other important factors the writers have not taken into account?

2. The writers, as you may have noticed, are reasonably concerned that their proposal doesn't sound moralistic, even though Kathy and Andrea were intially interested in the idea because of their strong feelings about drinking. Do you think they have been successful in presenting their proposal as a "positive" step to "enhance student life"? If so, what is it about the proposal that creates this impression? If not, why?

3. Imagine that you are on a campus committee that reviews proposals and decides which ones to support. There are more worthy proposals than there are funds available so you will have to make some hard decisions. The proposal for a campus coffee house is one of the finalists, and the committee plans to meet each group of proposers before making its decision. Draw up a list of questions you would ask Kathy, Andrea, and Bruce to help you make a decision.

WRITERS INVENTORY

If you did a group proposal, hold a meeting when you have finished to look back and evaluate the experience of working together.

- Explore the reasons each member was drawn to the problem the proposal addresses. To what extent do these reasons overlap? How are they distinct from each other? How did they combine in the group? What influence did this have on writing the proposal?

- Describe how the group went about writing the proposal. What parts went smoothly? What problems, if any, did the group have? How did individual members and the group deal with problems in the writing?

If you wrote an individual proposal, ask similar questions: What called you to the problem you address? What made it important or urgent? How did you go about writing the proposal? What was easy about it? What problems, if any, did you have? How did you deal with these problems?

A CLOSING NOTE

The real test of a proposal, of course, is whether it works on its intended audience—whether readers will support the goals and objectives of the proposal and do what they can to implement it. For this reason, if you want to find out how effective your proposal is, you need to send it out. Your instructor and classmates can offer useful advice in the context of a writing classroom, but you are likely to get a very different and potentially interesting response by sending your proposal to the group, agency, or institution who can actually implement it.

CHAPTER
ELEVEN

REVIEWS:
Evaluating Works and Performances

LOOKING AT THE GENRE

Reviews are a genre of writing people turn to when they are called on to make evaluations. Of course, reviewers normally describe and analyze whatever they are reviewing—whether a movie, a CD, an employee's performance, or a government program. Still, as readers are aware, reviewers provide this background information and analysis as evidence for the evaluation they are making. In some cases, reviewers also offer recommendations ("Avoid this slasher unless you like to be entertained with pointless blood and gore" or "Develop quality control measures to monitor the new manufacturing process"). But what is invariably present is the evaluation itself. As Siskel and Ebert's movie reviews demonstrate quite literally, reviewers are in the business of saying thumbs up or thumbs down.

Reviews take place informally all the time in everyday life. Part of daily conversation is talking about what people need, what they have seen and done, and what kinds of judgments they make about their experience. It's not unusual to ask: What kind of lawnmower should I buy? Is the psychology course you're taking any good? Is the latest Spike Lee movie worth seeing? Do you like your new car? Where's a good place to get a cheap meal?

At times, the informal judgments that result from such questions can spark extended debate. Sports fans, for example, can argue endlessly about everything from who was the best quarterback of the 1990s to which team is going to win the game on Saturday. In these debates, individuals not only make claims—"Babe Ruth was the greatest baseball player of all time." They must also be able to state the criteria these claims are based on—"No one else has been able to hit the way Babe Ruth did." And, if necessary, they have to justify these criteria. After all, someone might respond that Willie Mays was the greatest because he was the best all-round player. Then the first person would have to justify using hitting as the main criterion. Making evaluations based on justified criteria is at the heart of these informal reviews—and of their formal, written counterparts as well.

Perhaps the most familiar written reviews are newspaper and magazine reviews of the arts—reviews of books, music, film, art, architecture, television, and dance. Newspapers and magazines also feature other kinds of reviews. For example, Consumer Reports reviews a broad range of products, and specialized magazines like Runner's World or Wired routinely assess the particular products their readers are interested in. Most newspapers review local restaurants and have a travel section that reviews tourist attractions and vacation spots, often with tips on what to see and do and where to stay. As these examples suggest, readers use reviews in a variety of ways—to get information, to get advice from experts, and to compare their judgments to the reviewer's.

The workplace also uses reviews. Annual reviews that evaluate employee performance and productivity are standard features in both the private and public sector, often determining salaries and promotions. And it's not just individuals that are assessed. Organizations periodically bring in consultants to review programs and procedures and to make recommendations about how they should operate.

At the center of all these reviews are the criteria used to make evaluations. The criteria on which a movie might be evaluated, for example, include the performance of the actors, the plot and its pacing, the effectiveness of the direction and camera work, and so on. The criteria on which Consumer Reports bases its evaluation of a car include the car's features, fuel efficiency, and repair record (see the sample in "Designing Documents: Rating Systems").

The criteria reviewers use may be explicit or implicit. Consumer Reports, for example, uses explicit criteria based on quantitative data. Readers can find them listed and explained on the page. Often, however, the criteria are far less explicit. In movie reviews, it is frequently the case that readers must figure out the criteria from the critic's discussion and analysis of the film.

The way readers respond to a review and whether they find its evaluation persuasive will depend to a large extent on whether they believe the criteria used are justifiable. Car reviews in Consumer Reports, for example, are likely to persuade readers who accept repair records and gas mileage as the most important considerations in buying a car. For readers who are more interested in style, luxury, and comfort in buying a car, these criteria may not be the most compelling.

Readers, of course, may agree with the criteria used and yet not agree with the assessments. This sometimes happens when readers disagree with the way the criteria are applied. For example, a film critic and readers might share the belief that the performance of the leading actress is crucial to the success of a film but disagree nonetheless about the performance of a particular actress in a particular movie. Similarly, a sports fan might agree with Thomas George's assessment that Superbowl XXXII between Green Bay and Denver was a matchup of size versus quickness but not predict, as George does, that Green Bay will prevail on the basis of "physical, brute, exacting" play. In fact, if you had used the same criteria to predict a Denver victory based on the quickness of the Bronco's offensive line and how it dominated the larger Packer defense, you would have been correct.

MATCHUP: SUPERBOWL XXXII

Matchup: Super Bowl XXXI
By Timothy W. Smith

Patriots 13-5

Packers 15-3

KEY STATS:
The Packers have the No. 1 scoring offense and the No. 1 scoring defense in the N.F.L. In the last two playoff games, the Patriots' defense held Pittsburgh's Jerome Bettis and Jacksonville's Natrone Means to 43 yards each.

COMMENTS:
The Packers were one of the most powerful, and dangerous teams in the league this year. Quarterback Brett Favre led the league in touchdown passes for the second consecutive season and has the kind of elusiveness that drives teams crazy. He'll be tough to stop. The big question for New England is whether Drew Bledsoe will be able to raise his game to a championship level, because the Packers' defensive game plan is geared toward stopping running back Curtis Martin. Defensive, offense and special teams – the Packers are the complete package. Despite having the best game-day coach in the business in Bill Parcells, the Patriots won't be able to stop the Packers.

PREDICTION   Green Bay Packers 34, New England Patriots 23

In other cases of evaluation, however, people differ not because they apply shared criteria in different ways but because their criteria of evaluation differ altogether. This is why professional reviewers and critics get into such heated debates about the quality of a book, a movie, a musical performance, or a television show. Take the ongoing debate over daytime talk shows, for example. Some critics see Oprah, Sally Jesse Raphael, Jennie Jones, and Geraldo as offering little more than sensationalism. Others hold that these talk shows raise important issues and give ordinary people a chance to be heard in a medium dominated by celebrities and experts. Clearly these critics are using different criteria to evaluate these talk shows and are making different assumptions about the role of television and the mass media in contemporary culture. In a heterogeneous society like our own, it is virtually inevitable that people's evaluations—whether in politics, the arts, or other areas—and the criteria and assumptions that underlie them will differ considerably.

The reading selections in this chapter offer some examples of how reviewers seek to establish justifiable criteria as the basis for their evaluations and of how reviewers' judgments can differ. The first two readings are reviews of the film Evita, starring Madonna and directed by Alan Parker. As you will see, the two reviews, by Peter Keough in the Boston Phoenix and Anthony Lake in the New Yorker, make assessments that are in some ways very similar and yet in other ways very different. In the next selection, excerpted from "Report and Recommendations Concerning the Handling of Incidents Such As the Branch Davidian Standoff in Waco, Texas," Alan A. Stone reviews the FBI's handling of the 1993 incident and arrives at an assessment that differs from that reached by the Justice Department in its official review. The final selection is a book review. Well-known novelist Stephen King reviews Louisa May Alcott's rediscovered suspense novel A Long Fatal Love Chase. As you read these reviews, focus on the evaluations made and the criteria on which they are based.

TWO MOVIE REVIEWS

Peter Keough. "Goon Squad: Evita Bludgeons, but Seduces." Boston Phoenix. January 13, 1997.

Anthony Lane. "Immaterial Girls." New Yorker. January 6, 1997.

These two reviews of Alan Parker's film adaptation of Andrew Lloyd Webber's rock opera Evita offer an interesting case study of how reviewers agree and differ—and why. As you may know, Evita recounts the story of Eva Peron (played by Madonna in the film), her marriage to Argentine president Juan Peron, and her rise to prominence and power in the 1940s and early 1950s. Worshipped by some Argentineans, vilified by others, Eva Peron was glamorous and controversial óan ideal subject for a Hollywood film extravaganza.

As you will see, the reviewers agree the film is indeed a lavish and stunning production. They differ, however, in their judgments about the quality of the film in general and Madonna's performance in particular. Peter Keough is a regular reviewer for the Boston Phoenix, while Anthony Lane often writes the New Yorkerís "Current Cinema" feature, of which this review is a part. As you read, notice the criteria each reviewer uses and the judgments he makes.

Goon squad

Evita bludgeons, but seduces

BY PETER KEOUGH Alan Parker's *Evita* exhilarates, enraptures, and exhausts. After two-and-a-half hours you feel as beaten down by musical

and cinematic excess as the film's poor proles are by the batons of their oppressors. Somehow Parker has managed an unsettling and intriguing fusion of dark hipness and tony schmaltz — a kind of meeting of his own *The Wall* with *Showboat*, or perhaps *The Pirates of Penzance*. It's an almost opaque onslaught of relentless music and dark, daunting imagery that is made endurable, even moving, by the incandescent performances of the leads.

Yes. Madonna can act — at least when she's singing, which in *Evita* she's doing all the time. As Eva Duarte Perón, the illegitimate daughter of a peasant woman from the Pampas who became one of the most powerful women in the world through a combination of innocence, seductiveness, ruthlessness, genius, and charisma, Madonna reprises most of the personae of her 15-year career in a format similar to the medium most kind to her talents: MTV. Parker serves his first lady well. He cuts and patches her performances together in brisk montages, shot with dramatic camerawork in semi-surreal settings.

It's not insignificant that Madonna's biggest scenes are addressed to large audiences: the show-stopping "Don't Cry for Me" number, for example, is stunningly delivered before thousands of adorers from the balcony of the Casa Rosanda, the Argentine presidential palace from which Eva Perón announced her own retirement from political life. What's surprising is that her best scenes are intimate duets like "Another Suitcase in Another Hall," a poignant, winsome exploration of pathos, defilement, and resolution sung by a young, struggling Eva forced into prostitution with a series of drab johns. And "You Must Love Me," her climactic duet with her husband, Argentine president Juan Perón (Jonathan Pryce), is an aching farewell that dispels the illusion of a romance-of-convenience to reveal the inescapable love and tragedy beneath.

Pryce is astonishing in this number, as he is throughout. No vocalist, he holds his own with Madonna thanks to nuance, timing, and a great actor's meticulous technique. Even more impressive is Antonio Banderas as Ché, the tale's cynical, impassioned narrator and commentator. Emerging as a face from the crowd in the opening spectacle of Evita's funeral, he relates with rueful disdain and reluctant affection her humble origins and meteoric ascent. When the story focuses on her rise from bruised innocence to the top of Buenos Aires society through Machiavellian sexual maneuverings, *Evita* takes on the corrupt pizzazz of Bob Fosse's *Cabaret*, with Banderas an earthier, sexually unambiguous Joel Grey.

When Eva finally meets and seduces Perón, however, the film becomes entangled in the complexities and brute realities of its politics. Whereas in *Cabaret* the rise of Nazism lurked in the background, chilling the foreground gaiety but never joining in with it, the bloody street battles and savage oppression of the Perón years are all part of the show here. When ranks of showering soldiers start singing about military coups, it's hard not to think of "Springtime for Hitler" in Mel Brooks's *The Producers*.

★★★
EVITA

Directed by Alan Parker. Written by Alan Parker and Oliver Stone, based on the musical play with lyrics by Tim Rice and music by Andrew Lloyd Webber. With Madonna, Antonio Banderas, Jonathan Pryce, Jimmy Nail, Victoria Sus, Julian Littman, Olga Merediz, and Laura Pallas. A Hollywood Pictures release. At the Cheri.

It undercuts the subject's gravity, needless to say, and the boisterous montage that Parker makes of Argentine history leaves it impossible to understand what Juan and Evita stood for or who they were, other than a glorified whore-with-a-heart-of-gold who died young and her enigmatic, sinister sugar daddy. The secret to old musicals was that the singing and dancing emerged from a stylized realism in order to transport us to another, magical realm. In *Evita*, we're in that magical realm from beginning to end; there are no moments of silence or clarity to allow reflection. The nightmare of history is not confronted, and so the dream of artistic transcendence is never realized.

There are moments when it is approached, however. In "Waltz for Eva and Ché," Banderas and Madonna dance a dark, hallucinatory *pas de deux* that touches on the failed grandeur of their mutual ideals and passions. It is a splendid, still moment in Parker's furious whirligig of a musical, and one wishes there were more. Despite her plea not to be cried for, this *Evita* could use a few more tears. ∎

IMMATERIAL GIRLS

Evita Perón and Isabel Archer make the scene.

BY ANTHONY LANE

THE movie "Evita" is hardly a movie at all. In the experienced hands of the director Alan Parker, it is far more than a film version of a stage show, but what we should really be doing is watching this stuff on MTV. It's the biggest, loudest, most expensive music video ever made.

The story goes as follows: Eva Duarte (Madonna) grows up poor in provincial Argentina, hooks up with a guitar-strumming jerk (Jimmy Nail), goes to Buenos Aires, hooks up with further jerks, lands a big fish named Colonel Juan Perón (Jonathan Pryce), prods him along the march to power, becomes a power in her own right, wins acclaim and reverence as the First Lady of her nation, suffers, dies, and ascends into Heaven. One can imagine countless political, social, and sexual complications that could usefully embellish the tale, but "Evita," for all its sound and fury, is content to remain uncomplicated. It is in the business of mythmaking, and however hard it tries to promote argument about its heroine along the way, it begs us finally to adopt the same attitude toward her that we see in the rained-upon faces of the citizens who pray outside the palace while she fades. How can a modern movie arrive at something so close to beatification? Maybe because it gets there via kitsch.

Parker is not to blame; he has done more with the basic material than anyone could have expected. But, oh dear, the material. Apart from a mortifying school trip to "Jesus Christ Superstar," I have never been to an Andrew Lloyd Webber show; in that respect, at least, life has been good to me. Is there any form more bastard than rock opera?

When Eva's passing is announced near the start of the film, we get an instant storm of grief from those onscreen, plus a thrashing jam of guitar runs, suggesting nothing so much as the encore to a Led Zeppelin concert circa 1973. Lloyd Webber lights on the occasional sweet melody, but the sheer smothering bombast of his orchestrations soon foams over it. Then there's the stuff in between the songs, the sung conversations that I hesitate to dignify with the name of recitative. This is where Tim Rice, the lyricist, comes into his own—where his cotton-candy vaporings and sticky clusters of syllables lodge in the craws of the stars. "When you act," Juan croons to Eva at their first meeting, "you take us away from the squalor of the real world." Some of us can't wait to get back.

The real world has been deposed and exiled from this picture. You catch more humanity from two minutes' worth of back-street joshing in Parker's previous music-laden movie, "The Commitments," than from the whole thunderous expanse of "Evita." Bodies of soldiers lie in neat rows beside a road; riots and putsches rise and fall like hemlines. The film boasts no more than three and a half main characters, while the working classes for whom Eva Perón is said to have given her life—and who were certainly agog at what that life had become—are abandoned as an abstraction, or egged on to form parading patterns. When Madonna hands them cash and blows them kisses, she doesn't look like a philanthropic saint who bleeds for her compatriots; she looks like, well, Madonna signing albums on tour.

LARA TOMLIN

The role of Eva Perón is ideal for Madonna, of course, since it seldom requires her to deliver her lines in normal human speech, which was never her forte. She has deepened her singing tone to cope with all the big, vibrating numbers, although I for one rather miss that old pop cheerfulness, not to mention the slutty slouch that came so naturally to her in "Desperately Seeking Susan." Her eye makeup and bone-white skin are right on target, and she has mastered the celebrated Evita wave, which involves crooking the elbow at sixty degrees and swivelling the palm toward her head, as if she were trying to unscrew the light bulb inside an invisible lampshade. Beyond that, she doesn't so much act as pose, which is more her scene anyway, and seems closer to the weird self-invention practiced by the unknowable Miss Duarte. The hour of Eva's death, at which she croaks a few last platitudes to her beloved Juan, is not remotely affecting, largely because we have no handle on the private existence of this woman, let alone on her immortal soul, which has long ago been bartered for the love of the mob.

Pryce's Perón is wonderfully nimble and quiet, with a touch of dry rot in his heart; he pounces on others' weakness and struggles to veil his own. But the movie tends to treat him, as it does Eva, as a living effigy, and the only person here who quickens the blood is Antonio Banderas. He enjoys himself immensely as Che, our official guide to the narrative, who sidles through almost every scene in the appropriate costume, from white tie and tails to peasant chic, singing very hard at the camera. Although Banderas doesn't have a wide range of expressions, most of them are matadorial and all of them are sexy, and he fights to resist not merely the Evita legend but the pomp of the film itself.

Needless to say, it's a losing battle; by the end, he is tangoing with Eva and lining up to kiss her coffin. He caves in, just like the rest of us: "Evita" is fiercely efficient at manhandling our emotions, and Parker, together with his editor, Gerry Hambling, rises to an astounding swiftness and punch in some of the montages. But you can feel the rattle of images chaining you in; just as the Peronist cause slid toward Fascistic methods of persuasion and suppression, so there are times during this bullying and undeniably entertaining picture when you simply lie down and let it swagger all over you. It comes as no surprise to learn that Parker wrote the screenplay with Oliver Stone; I was hoping for some groovy, conspiratorial proof that Perón was alive and well and living in Vietnam. But, hey, you can't have everything.

ANALYSIS: Different but Overlapping Assessments

Peter Keough's "Goon Squad" and Anthony Lane's "Immaterial Girls" illustrate the basic function of movie reviews: to provide readers with a quick, well-argued, and readable evaluation of a movie. As you can see, these reviews do not attempt to tell readers whether or not they should see Evita. Reviewers are rarely that prescriptive, and they are quite aware that different readers have different tastes and interests. (After all, Lane's very criticism of Evita as "the biggest, loudest, most expensive music video ever made" could lead some readers to want to see it.) Instead, reviewers focus on issues of artistic quality, offering evaluations and the criteria they used to arrive at them. They approach their readers as serious viewers and seek to engage them in a consideration of the merits and flaws of a film.

Interestingly, these two reviewers see many of the same merits and flaws—the film is stunning and captivating but is excessive and in some ways flat—and yet Keough's review is largely positive whereas Lane's is largely negative. Thus, for example, both make the point that the movie is MTV-like, but Keough makes it in the context of saying that Madonna's role suits her, whereas Lane makes it to say that Evita is just the "biggest, loudest, most expensive music video ever made."

The criteria that the two reviewers use to make these evaluations also overlap to a great extent. They include the main criteria readers expect to see used: the quality of the performances overall, the quality of each lead's performance, the treatment of the subject, the impact on the viewer. Note that at the heart of each review is a different comparison to something outside the film: Keogh compares the film to old musicals, saying that it doesn't work as well because its fantasy world isn't initially grounded in reality, as theirs were. Lane compares the film to its source, Andrew Lloyd Webber's rock opera, and finds the basic adherence to that material to be the main problem underlying the film.

FOR CRITICAL INQUIRY

1. Notice how the opening paragraph of each review establishes the writer's basic evaluation of Evita. For each review, find particular words and phrases that make this evaluation clear and then write a sentence or two summarizing the evaluation.
2. Both writers use comparisons to other films to make points about the film they're reviewing—something done quite often in reviews. List the comparisons in each review, and for each review briefly explain what points the reviewer is using these films to make. What role do the comparisons used in each play in the overall judgment of the film offered in the review?
3. Reviews of a film about a historical figure inevitably include some discussion of how well the film captures what happened. This is a criterion on which the two reviewers make similar assessments. Summarize the assessments they make, and explain how these assessments fit with the overall reviews.
4. In many ways, the reviewers' evaluations of Madonna's performance are the best illustration of how the assessments overlap but are ultimately very different. How would you characterize each of their evaluations of her performance? How would you account for the differences in these evaluations?
5. In the case of the male leads, the evaluations are more similar and yet are clearly influenced by the overall context of the review. Find the relevant paragraphs and explain how these evaluations are similar and different.
6. What is your response as a movie-goer to each of these reviews? Would you want to see the movie if you read Keough's review? If you read Lane's review? Explain what in the reviews might influence your decision to see or not see the movie.

Alan A. Stone. From "Report and Recommendations Concerning the Handling of Incidents Such As the Branch Davidian Standoff in Waco, Texas."

Alan A. Stone, a professor of law and psychiatry at Harvard University, was one of ten outside experts selected by the Deputy Attorney General to review the FBI's handling of the siege on the Branch Davidian compound in Waco, Texas, in 1993. As you may remember, the standoff between David Koresh's followers and federal agents ended in a shootout and fire that resulted in the deaths of twelve adults and twenty-five children. Stone's review was to be published in a Justice Department report consisting of three parts: a "factual investigation" carried out by the Justice Department; an evaluation of the FBI's handling of the incident by Edward Dennis, a former assistant attorney general; and the reviews by the outside experts. However, the report was released without Stone's review. Dennis concluded that the FBI "exhibited extraordinary restraint and handled this crisis with great professionalism.î As you will see, Stone disagrees with this conclusion. Pay particular attention to how and why Stone disagrees.

In creating its report, the Justice Department sifted through a mountain of information. This evidence overwhelmingly proves that David Koresh and the Branch Davidians set the fire and killed themselves in the conflagration at Waco, which fulfilled their apocalyptic prophecy. My report does not question that conclusion; instead, my concern is whether the FBI strategy pursued at Waco in some way contributed to the tragedy that resulted in the death of twenty-five innocent children along with many adults. The department's factual investigation and the [Edward] Dennis evaluation seem to agree with the FBI commander on the ground, who is convinced that nothing the FBI could have done would have changed the outcome. That is not my impression.

On the evening of February 28 and the morning of March 1, the FBI replaced the Bureau of Alcohol, Tobacco, and Firearms [ATF] at the Branch Davidian compound. There had been casualties on both sides during the ATF's attempted "dynamic entry." David Koresh, the leader of the Branch Davidians, had been shot through the hip, and the situation was in flux.

During the first phase of the FBI's engagement at Waco, a period of a few days, the agents on the ground at the compound proceeded with a strategy of conciliatory negotiation, which had the approval and understanding of the entire chain of command. In the view of the negotiating team, considerable progress was made—for example, some adults and children came out of the compound—but David Koresh and the Branch Davidians made many promises to the negotiators that they then did not keep. Pushed by the tactical leader, the FBI's commander on the ground began to allow tactical pressures to be placed on the compound in addition to negotiation, e.g., turning off the electricity, so that those in the compound would be as cold as the agents outside during the twenty-degree night. This tactical pressure was applied over the objections of the FBI's own experts in negotiation and behavioral science, who specifically advised against it. These experts warned the FBI command about the potentially fatal consequences of using such measures.

By March 21, the FBI was concentrating on tactical pressure alone: first, by using all-out psycho-physiological warfare intended to stress and intimidate the Branch Davidians; and second, by "tightening the noose" with a circle of armored vehicles. The FBI considered these efforts a success because no shots were fired at them by the Branch Davidians.

This changing negotiation strategy at the compound from (1) conciliatory negotiating to (2) negotiation and tactical pressure and then to (3) tactical pressure alone evolved over the objections of the FBI's own experts. When the fourth and ultimate strategy, the insertion of C.S. gas [tear gas] into the compound, was presented to Attorney General Janet Reno, the FBI had abandoned any serious effort to reach a negotiated solution and was well along in its strategy of all-out tactical pressure, thereby leaving little choice as to how to end the Waco standoff. By the time the attorney general made her decision, the noose was closed and, as one agent told me, the FBI believed they had "three options—gas, gas, and gas."

There is, to my mind, unequivocal evidence that the Branch Davidians set the compound on fire themselves and ended their lives on David Koresh's order. However, I am now convinced that the FBI's noose-tightening tactics may well have precipitated Koresh's decision to commit himself and his followers to this course of mass suicide.

There is a wealth of criminology, behavioral-science, and psychiatric literature on the subject of murder followed by suicide that indicates that these behaviors and the mental states that motivate them have very important and complicated links. Even more important is what has been called the "gamble with death." For example, inner-city youths often provoke a shoot-out, "gambling" with death by provoking police into killing them. In the case of the Branch Davidians, there was direct empirical evidence supporting the assumption that those at the compound, because of their own unconventional beliefs, were in the "gamble with death" mode. The evidence for this was their response to the

ATF's misguided assault. The ATF claims gunfire came from forty different locations. If true, this means that at least forty Branch Davidians were willing to shoot at federal agents and kill or be killed as martyr-suicide victims defending their "faith." The FBI's behavioral-science unit realized that Koresh and his followers were in a desperate kill-or-be-killed mode. They were also well aware of the significance and meaning of the Branch Davidians' apocalyptic faith. They understood that David Koresh interpreted law-enforcement attacks as related to the prophesied apocalyptic ending. The idea that people with those beliefs, expecting the apocalypse, would submit to tactical pressure is a conclusion that flies in the face of their behavior during the ATF raid.

In deciding to move to a show-of-force tactical strategy, the FBI made the critical assumption that David Koresh and the Branch Davidians, like ordinary persons, would respond to pressure in the form of a closing circle of armed vehicles by concluding that survival was in their self-interest and surrendering. This ill-fated assumption runs contrary to all of the relevant behavioral-science and psychiatric literature as well as the understanding that it offered of David Koresh and the Branch Davidians.

The ATF investigation report [issued in September] states that the so-called dynamic entry turned into what is described as being "ambushed." As I tried to get a sense of the state of mind and behavior of the people in the compound, the idea that the Branch Davidians' actions were considered an "ambush" troubled me. If they were militants determined to ambush and kill as many ATF agents as possible, it seemed to me that given their firepower, the devastation would have been even worse. They apparently did not maximize the number of ATF agents killed. This comports with all of the state-of-mind evidence and suggests that the Branch Davidians were neither depressed, suicidal people nor determined, cold-blooded killers; rather, they were desperate religious fanatics expecting an apocalyptic ending, in which they were destined to

die defending their sacred ground and destined to achieve salvation.

The psychology of such behavior—together with its religious significance for the Branch Davidians—was mistakenly evaluated, if not simply ignored, by those responsible for the FBI strategy of "tightening the noose." The overwhelming show of force was not working in the way the tacticians suppose. It did not provoke the Branch Davidians to surrender, but it may have provoked David Koresh to order the mass suicide.

Throughout the [Justice Department's] official factual investigation, there are references to the failure of communication between the tactical and negotiation arms of the FBI. The commander on the ground has said that the official investigation and evaluation exaggerate the extent and significance of that failure. I disagree. Consider the memo of March 5, from Special Agents Peter Smerick and Mark Young, on the subject "Negotiation Strategy and Considerations." Agents Smerick and Young were not Monday-morning quarterbacks, as we panelists are; they were members of the FBI team on the field of play. The agents emphasized that the strategy of negotiations coupled with ever-increasing tactical pressure was inapplicable. They wrote, "This strategy, if carried to excess, could eventually be counterproductive and could result in loss of life." The agents were also fully aware that Koresh's followers believed in his teachings and would "die for his cause."

What went wrong at Waco was not that the FBI lacked expertise in behavioral science or in the understanding of unconventional religious groups. Rather, the commander on the ground and others committed to tactical-aggressive, traditional law-enforcement practices disregarded those experts and tried to assert control and demonstrate to Koresh that they were in charge. There is nothing surprising or esoteric in this explanation, nor does it arise only from the clear wisdom of hindsight. The FBI's own experts recognized and predicted in memoranda that there was the risk that the active, aggressive law-enforcement mentality of the FBI—the so-called action imperative—would prevail in the face of frustration and delay. They warned that, in these circumstances, there might be tragic consequences from the FBI's "action imperative." They were correct.

ANALYSIS: Supporting an Evaluation with Analysis

Alan A. Stone's review of the FBI's handling of the crisis at Waco is interesting for several reasons. First, it's a good example of a common type of review: a review in which an outside evaluator assesses the performance of an organization's personnel. Second, in this case, the review concerned an incident that had captured the nation's attention and had ended in a tragedy that stirred some people's anger at the government—in other words, a controversial, highly charged incident. Third, reviewers' evaluations conflicted. Specifically, the evaluation in this review conflicted with official evaluations, and the review was evidently suppressed.

Stone does not dispute the basic facts established by the Justice Department's investigation. He notes the investigation had ìsifted through a mountain of informationî that overwhelmingly proved that David Koresh and his followers "set the fire and killed themselves in the conflagration at Waco." Rather, he disagrees with the evaluation that the FBI did not contribute to the tragedy. His own evaluation is that the FBI's handling of the crisis, far from not being a factor, actually made the final outcome inevitable. Stone backs up this evaluation with background information and analysis: He describes the events, going back to the period when the ATF was still involved and tracing the evolution of the FBI's strategy once it took over. He also draws on both a "wealth of criminology, behavioral-science, and psychiatric literature" and memos written by FBI agents at the time of the incident.

FOR CRITICAL INQUIRY

1. Stone's review is divided into three sections, each of which has a somewhat different function in the review as a whole. Look back at each section, summarize its content, and identify what it does.
2. Three major elements of the background information and analysis leading to Stone's evaluation are the chronology of events at Waco, relevant literature from a range of fields, and FBI internal communications. Explain how Stone uses these three elements together to arrive at and support his evaluation. Why is each of these elements needed?
3. In his analysis Stone gives a particularly prominent role to the "gamble with death" concept. Why is this concept so important to his overall evaluation?
4. What are some of the criteria that Stone evidently uses to assess the FBI's performance at Waco? Do you agree with these criteria? Why or why not?
5. Recommendations often follow from evaluations of performance. What recommendations for FBI conduct in future situations does Stone's evaluation suggest?
6. The section written by former assistant attorney general Edward Dennis concluded that the FBI "exhibited extraordinary restraint and handled this crisis with great professionalism." This assessment is dramatically different from Stone's. Having read Stone's review, what kind of analysis do you think Dennis's very different evaluation could have been based on?

Stephen King. "Blood and Thunder in Concord." Review of A Long Fatal Love Chase by Louisa May Alcott. New York Times Book Review. September 10, 1995.

Stephen King is the author of best-selling horror and suspense fiction including The Shining, Carrie, and Children of the Corn. Louisa May Alcott was a nineteenth-century writer, best known for Little Women. Her thriller A Long Fatal Love Chase was completed but never published during her lifetime. Its publication in 1995 not only added to the body of her work available but also offered critics and reviewers a new opportunity to assess this body of work. As you read the selection, note how King evaluates both the book and the body of work.

By Stephen King

HOW much has the suspense novel — subgenre "woman stalked/woman in peril" — changed over the last 130 years or so? Well, consider: during the summer of 1992 I wrote a novel in which a woman named Rose leaves her violent, mentally unstable husband and flees to another city. Here she is taken in at a women's shelter and begins to build a new life. She also meets a much gentler man who falls in love with her. While all this is going on, her obsessed husband is hard at work, tracking her down.

In 1866, Louisa May Alcott wrote A Long Fatal Love Chase," a novel in which a woman named Rose leaves her violent, mentally unstable husband and flees to another city. Here she is taken in at a women's shelter (a convent, in the Alcott version) and begins to build a new life. This life includes a much gentler man who falls in love with her. (That he happens to be a priest was only one of the problems Alcott had with the subject matter of her book.) While all this is going on, her obsessed husband is hard at work, tracking her down.

There are, of course, many differences between these two books, but the similarities are striking. So are the ironies. One is that, although written 125 years later, mine was published first, and in an edition of almost two million copies. It was reviewed respectfully (if not always favorably). Louisa May Alcott's version of Rose on the run, on the other hand, wasn't published at all. "I like horrible books if they have power," remarks a character in "Love Chase." It was not, apparently, a feeling shared by anyone at Roberts Brothers, Alcott's Boston publishers.

Alcott was the chief breadwinner of her family. Her father, Bronson, was a respected but impecunious New England transcendentalist who had "no gift for money making," according to Alcott's journal. As a result, her novel's rejection hurt for reasons beyond the obvious ones of injured pride and bruised ego: the Alcotts flat-out needed the money the book was written to provide. Alcott revised it ruthlessly, taking out as many of the naughty bits as she could and toning down what remained, but the book's central plot device — that Rosamond for a year lives as wife to a man to whom she is not married — was impervious to all revisions.

In her introduction to the omnibus edition of Alcott's shorter thrillers, "Louisa May Alcott Unmasked: Collected Thrillers" (Northeastern University, cloth, $55; paper, $24.95), Madeleine B. Stern draws on the distinction feminist critics have made between Alcott's daylight reality and midnight fantasies. Alcott's long-suppressed suspense novel proves that even this most commercial-minded of writers, whose pseudonymous work was only discovered and identified through her detailed (obsessional, some might say) financial ledgers, was essentially powerless before her extraordinary imagination: not its mistress, at least in her younger years, but its servant. The book is a wonderful entertainment (Ms. Stern calls Alcott's short stories fast and good reads, which is equally true of "Love Chase"), and it tends to confirm Alcott's position as the country's most articulate 19th-century feminist. But the novel, edited by Kent Bicknell, the headmaster of a New Hampshire day school and an Alcott collector who acquired and then edited the manuscript to restore it to its original, more sensational form, offers something perhaps even more valuable: a

fascinating look into a divided mind that was both attracted to themes of violence and sexuality and ashamed by its own interest.

"A Long Fatal Love Chase" was the last and longest of what Elaine Showalter, in "Alternative Alcott" — a 1988 collection of Louisa May Alcott's essays, journalism and fiction that makes an ideal guide to her midnight fantasies — calls her sensation stories. It begins with the fair Rosamond, bored with her cold-hearted grandfather and her isolated existence, uttering blasphemy in jest: "I often feel as if I'd gladly sell my soul to Satan for a year of freedom." On the very heels of this declaration comes Phillip Tempest, accompanied by peals of thunder and a tree-demolishing bolt of lightning. He wins the right to court Rosamond ("my little Rose," he calls her) by playing cards with Gramps, a gentleman who appears in dire need of Gamblers Anonymous. Tempest is reti-

cent about his past; he is magnetic and moody by turns, in the best Heathcliff tradition. He's also a liar, but Rose is too fascinated — and too sexually attracted, Alcott hints — to care.

In a sequence worthy of Poe, Tempest lures a frail old man named Willoughby to a grisly death by cholera, first wearing down Willoughby's resistance in a dank monastery crypt and then finishing the job at a pestilential funeral service. This effort to keep Rose from learning of her "husband's" checkered past eventually comes to naught, of course. Rose discovers that the merry Greek boy who serves as Phillip's valet is actually his son, and that Phillip is still married to the boy's mother. She discovers, in short, that she isn't a wife but a mistress. Hardly a shocking plot twist to a reading public that has been exposed to the culinary peculiarities of Hannibal Lecter, I suppose, but in the Victorian hothouse that was post-Civil War American literature, it was enough to sink Alcott's brave but rather too frank romance. Frank Leslie's Chimney Corner and his Illustrated Newspaper, where Alcott published such stories as "Perilous Play" ("Heaven bless hashish, if its dreams end like this!" is that tale's provocative concluding line), might have published it, but Roberts Brothers wanted nothing to do with it.

WHEN Rose discovers the true nature of her position, she flees at once. Phillip Tempest, a modern villain in mid-19th-century dress ("I seem a brute, but it is my love which drives me to such harsh measures," he moans), has no intention of being balked by his beloved, however, and the love chase begins. It's a suspenseful and thoroughly charming story, a strange but not unpalatable crossing of the Brothers Grimm and V. C. Andrews. It ends on a darker note than any modern editor would be comfortable with, I suspect, but one in chilling harmony with any contemporary newspaper's front-page story of domestic abuse escalating into madness and murder. Dying by his own hand, Phillip gathers Rose's sodden corpse in his arms and voices the novel's creepy last line: "Mine first — mine last — mine even in the grave!" This is quite a distance from the sunny sensibilities and high moral tone of "Little Women."

"A Long Fatal Love Chase" is not the best of Alcott's sensation stories; that is probably "Behind a Mask," which can be found in several of the incarnations of Alcott's love-suspense stories to be offered by Ms. Stern, who has reshuffled Alcott's tales with a relentlessness that is a little dismaying. In addition to "Modern Magic," the forthcoming Modern Library edition of Alcott's short fiction, and "Louisa May Alcott Unmasked," she has parlayed Alcott's stories into at least three other collections, including two being reissued this year: "Behind a Mask: The Unknown Thrillers of Louisa May Alcott" (Morrow, $23) and "The Lost Stories of Louisa May Alcott" (Citadel, paper, $10.95), co-edited with Daniel Shealy.

•   •   •

How good are these rediscovered tales, which are more frequently referred to in the context of feminism than of literature? "Behind a Mask" is very good indeed, a brilliant and mordantly funny take on a woman's ability to twist men around the ends of her delicate fingers. The story's success can be measured by our ambivalent feelings about Jean Muir. One applauds her nerve, sympathizes with the desperateness of her situation, but is ultimately glad she found someone else's family upon which to sharpen her claws. "A Long Fatal Love Chase" is nearly as good. Like the short stories in "Modern Magic," it is a fast and good read, but it is also textured in a way the short stories are not — Alcott even tries to give Phillip some depth, although she mostly fails. Best of all in the novel is the character of Rose, a spunky and courageous young woman who never loses her optimism or moral compass. Trying to con the depth of her love, Phillip asks what she would do if she discovered him to be base and false in every way. Would she die as heroines in books do, "tender slaves as they are"?

"No," Rose replies in decisive tones that will resonate for every modern woman who reads this novel, "live and forget you."

Is "Love Chase" or any of the "sensation stories" as good as "Little Women"? I think not. Alcott's publisher (and Alcott herself) considered "Little Women" to be a boring book, and both were surprised when it took off like a rocket, finally conveying upon its author the financial stability she had been looking for her whole life. The first rule of successful fiction, now as in 1866, when Louisa May Alcott wrote "A Long Fatal Love Chase," is "write what you know." And in "Little Women," Alcott did. There is a scene in that book where Amy, the youngest of the March girls, plays dress-up in her aunt's attic. She strolls back and forth, all got up in flounces and crinolines, twirling a parasol over her head, while Aunt March's scraggy old parrot clatters along the boards beside her, cawing, "Ain't we fine? Get along, you fright! Hold your tongue! Kiss me, my dear!" It's as funny as anything Mark Twain ever wrote, mostly because it rings true to the ear and heart, and there is nothing to match it in any of Alcott's pulsing and often purple tales of romantic suspense.

The stories in "Modern Magic" are stories Agatha Christie would undoubtedly have loved if she had known of them; they are very like her own. Yes, they are fun, and yes, they are fast and good reads, but most of them also feel hurried (after Sybil's long and harrowing madhouse stay in "A Whisper in the Dark," an experiment explodes, killing the evil madhouse keeper, and setting our heroine free in a disappointingly perfunctory manner); the plots often break hideously. In "Love Chase," Rose keeps meeting old friends long after our patience with such happy coincidences is exhausted, and in one case (it is the novel's one lapse into unintended hilarity), Rose finds a convenient suicide victim and trades identities, thus managing to evade Phillip's unwelcome attentions for a chapter or two.

THESE flaws are common to the works of all writers in a rush — writers who need to pay the grocery bill as well as answer the urgings of the muse — but in Alcott's case there was something more. She appears to have been a deeply conventional woman who completely accepted her own Marmee's belief that a woman should be self-sacrificing and totally, uncritically supportive of the men in her life. But buried within the creative part of her conventional nature (and perhaps fueled by her own father's disregard of public opinion) was an alien lode of wildness. These stories mine that lode. The woman who wrote, in "Little Women," that "the quiet man sitting among his books was still the head of the family, the household conscience, anchor, and comforter" was also the woman who wrote "What fools men are!" and created the terrifying Phillip Tempest, who tells Rose, when he has finally decided to doff his own mask: "I am master here, my will is law, and disobedience I punish without mercy."

But if there were two Louisa May Alcotts, in the end the daylight version was probably the more real of the two —if, that is, one equates the dominant traits of a personality with "reality." The key to the dichotomy can probably be found in "Little Women," where the priggish and unintentionally repulsive Professor Bhaer lectures Jo March on her sensational tales in The Spread Eagle and The Weekly Volcano. "I would more rather give my boys gunpowder to play with than this bad trash," he says, and Jo herself is forced to agree. They are trash, she says of her stories. "I can't read this stuff in sober earnest without being horribly ashamed of it." And then she thinks, as surely Alcott herself must have on more than one occasion: "I almost wish I hadn't any conscience, it's so inconvenient." These reflections are followed by what is surely the most horrible sentence in "Little Women," the one that finishes "and Jo corked up her inkstand.

So did Louisa, at least when it came to penny-dreadful fiction, following "A Long Fatal Love Chase." She supported her family with sensational tales for 10 years, from 1857 to 1867, then simply stopped. Fortunately for her readers, she had work left to do that would satisfy both them and her repressive moral sense, which made her as contemptuous of those who read her thrillers as she was of herself for writing them, and made some of the moralizing in her later works so tedious. Worst of all, she may have thought, was how much she enjoyed what she was doing. She claimed it was a matter of sheer practicality ("blood and thunder" stories are "easier to 'compoze' & are better paid than moral tales"). To some extent that may have been true, but practicality alone cannot explain the final five or six chapters of "A Long Fatal Love Chase," in which the narrator seems on fire with excitement, delirious with the joy of creation.

In "Little Women," Alcott wrote of Jo March: "Every few weeks she would shut herself up in her room, put on her scribbling suit, and 'fall into a vortex,' as she expressed it ... her family, during these periods, kept their distance, merely popping in their heads semi-occasionally to ask, with interest, 'Does genius burn, Jo?' " Genius burned for Louisa May Alcott following "A Long Fatal Love Chase," brightly but never again with such primitive and joyful heat. One wonders what kind of writer she might have been had she been able to cast the malignantly conventional spirit of Professor Bhaer from her, and to take her thrillers as seriously as her feminist editors and elucidators do today.   □

ANALYSIS: Evaluating a Body of Work

Stephen King begins his review by classifying Louisa May Alcott's book—as a suspense novel of the subgenre "woman stalked/woman in peril"—and listing some strikingly similarities between its plot and that of his own work *Rose Madder*. In this way, he simultaneously introduces the subject of his review, intrigues his readers, and identifies himself as a fellow writer of love-suspense fiction, someone well equipped to have insights into the book.

In a review of this length, King has the space to stretch out—and he uses it to enlarge the scope of what he is doing. Although he devotes ample discussion to *A Long Fatal Love Chase*, describing its plot in some detail, he isn't just evaluating this novel. Rather, he evaluates it in the context of Alcott and her other writings—the other ìsensation storiesî and, especially, the very different *Little Women*. What's more, he uses his evaluation of the novel in this context to arrive at a fuller understanding of Alcott as a person and a writer. King judges *Little Women* to be the better novel but finds in *A Long Fatal Love Chase* a certain "joy of creation." He provides an explanation for this by drawing on the distinction some recent critics have made between Alcott's daytime reality and midnight fantasies and by finding a key piece of evidence in a scene in *Little Women*.

FOR CRITICAL INQUIRY

1. Before you read this review, had you heard of Stephen King, read any of his novels or short stories, or seen movies based on his books? If so, how did this knowledge influence the way you read and responded to his evaluation of Louisa May Alcott as a writer?

2. In the course of the review, King makes a series of comparisons. The most important of these are the comparisons of *A Long Fatal Love Chase* to Alcott's short suspense stories like "Behind a Mask" and to her well-known novel, *Little Women*. What criteria does King use to make these comparisons? What functions do these different comparisons serve?

3. What role does the extended summary of the plot of *A Long Fatal Love Chase* play within the review?

4. King includes considerable background on Alcott's life, and this, too, is important to the evaluation he makes of the novel and of her work in general. Explain how this background is important to these evaluations. Notice that the background is given at various points in the review, rather in all in one place. Mark the relevant passages. Why might King have presented it in this way?

5. Summarize Kingís assessment of *A Long Fatal Love Chase* and Alcott's work in general. Summarize his analysis of how the dichotomy in Louisa May Alcott—the two Louisa May Alcotts—helps explain the strengths and the flaws of *A Long Fatal Love Chase*.

LOOKING AT THE GENRE: REVIEWS

1. Use the following questions to look at how you and the people around you make informal reviews and use othersí reviews, both formal and informal. Write for ten or fifteen minutes in response to the questions.

   • How do you find out about movies, CDs, television shows, live music, books and magazines, restaurants, plays, dance performances, concerts, Web sites, and so on? How do you know whether you want to see *Evita*, read a certain Stephen King book, go to a local club, attend a particular concert, etc.? That is, what factors make you decide you want to do something (or not do something)?

   • Do you read (or listen to) formal reviews? If so, of what kinds of things? Where do the reviews appear? To what extent and in what ways are you influenced by them? What use do you make of them?

   • How often do you hear and make use of informal, word-of-mouth reviews? From whom—

ETHICS OF WRITING

Reviewing as a Partisan Activity

Reviewers are by no means neutral observers. On the contrary, they are in the business of being partisans. Whatever field of human activity their review concerns, they support some performances and find fault with others. Not only are reviewers incapable of being neutral, but they are also incapable of being objective. After all, even the more quantitative and objective reviews, such as the product ratings in Consumer Reports, require that criteria for evaluation be chosen and weighted.

Reviewers have a clear responsibility to their readers. For example, the purpose of Consumer Reports is to provide reliable information to consumers, who are often overwhelmed by manufacturers' claims. The magazine therefore has the responsibility to use the best information and criteria available so readers can make informed decisions. In more subjective reviews, like movie and book reviews, while reviewersí personal tastes can play more of a role, the responsibility to accurately present information to readers remains.

Reviewers have a responsibility to their readers because something of consequence is at stake: A consumer wants to spend money on the best available product; an employer wants to know which workers to promote; a business or government agency needs to know what changes in system are needed.

For precisely this same reason, reviewers have a responsibility to those whose products and performances are being reviewed. Even if unfair, negative reviews can kill a play or cost an employee his or her job.

As you begin considering what kind of review you might write, these issues of partisanship and responsibility will inevitably arise. On whose behalf will you be writing? What are the potential consequences of the evaluations you will make? What responsibilities does this bring to you as a reviewer?

---

family, friends, co-workersódo you usually hear these reviews? About what kinds of things are these reviews? How do they usually occur in conversation? How do they influence you and what use do you make of them?

- If reviews—whether formal or informal—conflict, how do you resolve such conflicts?
- When do you give reviews? What are some of the main criteria you use in your reviews?
- Think about a particularly striking instance of a discussion you had in which people's evaluations differed. What was being reviewed? What did people say? Why did their evaluations differ? Did they seem to be using the same criteria but applying them differently or using different criteria? How did the discussion end? Did anyone modify their views?

After looking over what youíve written, get together with two or three other students and take turns describing your experiences evaluating arts and entertainment. Be sure to talk about your use of formal and word-of-mouth reviews, about the reviews you give, and about conflicting evaluations. Then compare what group members have said. What are some of the similarities and differences in the ways people give and use reviews?

2. In each of the four reading selections, information is presented and used in the evaluation that is being made. Reviewers always face the question of how much and what kind of information to incorporate. They must also, of course, decide where to incorporate this information (e.g., whether to give it at the beginning or throughout). Pick any two of the reading selections. Compare them in terms of how much and what kind of information they include and how they integrate it into the review. How are they similar and different in these respects and what might account for the differences? In each case, what role does such information play in establishing the grounds for the evaluation? In view of this role and of the needs of intended readers, do you feel each reviewís use of information is appropriate?

3. Reviews can have a broad range of subjects, as exemplified by the reviews included here. Look over one of the movie reviews and the other two reviews. What are some of the differences among these reviews related to their different subject matters and purposes? What are some of their basic similarities as reviews?

4. One of Stephen King's purposes in his review of A Long, Fatal Chase is to offer a literary profile of Louisa May Alcott—to understand her as a writer. In accomplishing this purpose, King uses one of the techniques typical of profile writing: He creates a dominant impression of Alcott. Find phrases and passages where King characterizes Alcott. Compare King's review to one of the profiles in Chapter 9. How does each go about creating a dominant impression? Are the techniques used more similar or different? Do any of the differences seem to relate to the differences between the genres? What role does each writer's characterization of the subject seem intended to play in the piece of writing? In what ways, if any, does the characterization in the review seem to serve a more evaluative function?

DESIGNING DOCUMENTS: RATING SYSTEMS

Rating systems of many kinds—from Siskel and Ebert's thumbs-up or thumbs-down to the weekly rankings in the college football polls—are a common, and often largely visual, form of review. They may themselves be part of a review or may stand on their own. The three examples here illustrate some of the standard features that rating systems use.

Car Rating. Consumer Reports

Consumer Reports is used by many for its comparative product evaluations, such as the guide to current compact cars included here. Notice that the table summarizes a wide variety of quantitative and qualitative data.

Film Strips. Boston Phoenix.

The four (or five) star rating system is widely used in reviewing movies, musical recordings, television programs, and other performances. The Boston Phoenix uses this system in both its regular reviews of films and its ìfilm strips,î summary reviews of recent releases arranged alphabetically as a guide to movie-goers. Think about how this star rating system interacts with the written evaluation.

Conventional Wisdom Watch. Newsweek.

Conventional Wisdom Watch is a weekly feature in Newsweek. It looks at how certain people, institutions, and companies in the weekís news have done from a public relations standpoint. Notice that this three-way rating system is accompanied by a minimum of text, with the feature depending on the reader's familiarity with the news to make its points.

DISCUSSION AND ACTIVITIES

1. Using the information in the table and the text that precedes it, list the criteria that Consumer Reports uses to rank vehicles (where a criterion includes more specific subcriteria, include these in a parentheses following the criterion). Can you think of anything you would add to these criteria? Based on the text, which criteria seem more objective and which seem more subjective? Do you agree with the basis on which recommendations are made?

2. Look now at the design of the Consumer Reports table. What elements of the design do you find help make the table easier to read and use? What is the effect of the single pair of vertical lines within the box? One element that could perhaps be reworked for greater clarity is the reliability symbols. What problem do these symbols have? Can you develop a set of symbols that would avoid this problem?

Overall Ratings *Within types, listed in order of overall score*

Key no.	Brand and model	Discs	Price	Overall score (0 – 100, P F G VG E)	Performance — Problem Discs	Locate Speed	Taping Ease	Convenience
	SINGLE-DISC MODELS							
1	Onkyo DX-7210	1	$180	▬▬▬▬▬	●	◐	●	◐
2	Technics SL-PG450	1	150	▬▬▬▬▬	◐	●	●	◐
3	Yamaha CDX-490	1	240	▬▬▬▬▬	◐	●	●	◐
4	JVC XL-V282BK	1	170	▬▬▬▬	◐	●	●	○
5	Sony CDP-XE500	1	160	▬▬▬▬	◐	●	●	○
	CAROUSEL MODELS							
6	Technics SL-PD987	5	225	▬▬▬▬	●	●	○	◐
7	Kenwood DP-R4080	5	200	▬▬▬▬	◐	◐	◐	○
8	Yamaha CDC-655	5	280	▬▬▬	◐	◐	●	○
9	Sony CDP-CE405	5	190	▬▬▬	○	◐	●	◐
10	Onkyo DX-C330	6	275	▬▬▬	◐	◐	◖	○
11	Denon DCM-260	5	270	▬▬▬	◐	◐	◖	○
12	RCA RP-8055	5	105	▬▬	○	○	◖	◐
	MAGAZINE MODELS							
13	Optimus (Radio Shack) CD-7300	6	240	▬▬▬	○	◐	○	○
14	JVC XL-M318BK	6+1	225	▬▬▬	●	○	◖	○
	CD JUKEBOXES							
15	Kenwood DP-J2070	100	450	▬▬▬	●	○	○	○
16	JVC XL-MC302	100+1	775*	▬▬▬	●	○	◖	○
17	Technics SL-MC700	110+1	390	▬▬▬	◐	○	◖	○
18	Sony CDP-CX153	100	440	▬▬	○	◐	◖	○
19	Pioneer PD-F605	25	200	▬▬▬	○	○	◐	◖
20	Sony CDP-CX200	200	345	▬▬	○	◐	◖	○

3. The film strip is a one-paragraph summary of Keough's longer review, "Goon Squad." Compare the summary with the full version to see which ideas were included and which were omitted. Does the summary retain more of the evaluation or more of the description? Why do you think this is so?

4. If you had read the film strip without knowing the rating, would you have anticipated three stars or some other rating? Explain, citing specific language in the review. Stars are also included in the full review. Do you think the visual impact of the stars is the same in both versions? In general, how much importance would you give to the number of stars a film gets as opposed to the rest of a review? To what extent would star ratings influence your decision about whether to see a film?

5. What do the symbols used in the Conventional Wisdom Watch mean? Explain how the visual arrangement of material within this table is effective. Why are the symbols crucial to the table?

6. Explain how the design and the tone in each of these three reviews is in keeping with the purpose of the review.

7. Design your own system to rate a certain type of product, art, performance, or anything else you're familiar enough with to know how to rate. You can design a detailed system as in Consumer Reports, a star system as in the film strips, or arrows as in the Conventional Wisdom Watch. Or you can create your own system, using icons, numbers, letters, or anything else that works to convey the information. After you design your rating system, write a short explanation of how it is to be used and justification of why it is appropriate for what it is meant to rate.

GOING ON-LINE

Fan Talk

Reviews play an especially important role in fan culture. Fans are, after all, not your average viewers or listeners. They are hard-core, committed followers of a particular movie, television series, performer, or team—devotees of, say, Star Trek, As the World Turns, Metallica, or the Chicago Bulls. They read fan magazines, go to fan conventions, and correspond by letter and the Internet. You may know fans or be one yourself.

One way to get a sense of how fans talk is to check out an electronic mail discussion. You can find interest groups on Star Wars, The Simpsons, Twin Peaks, soap operas, daytime talk shows, most professional sports teams, and much, much more. Pick a discussion group that's on someone or something you are familiar with and for a few days follow what people are writing. Pay particular attention to the kinds of evaluations that participants make and to how they justify them. Compare these evaluations to the kinds you are likely to find in professionally written reviews. What appear to be the main differences and similarities? How would you explain the differences?

ASSIGNMENTS

WORKING TOGETHER: Course Review

Your assignment is to work together as a class to review your writing course. The review will require planning questions and methods, conducting research, compiling and analyzing the information obtained, and finally, evaluating the course based on this information. Here is a basic procedure, which you may want to modify, depending on the size of your class and the scope of your review:

1. Work together in groups of five or six. Think about what criteria you want to use to evaluate the course. What is important in a writing course: interesting readings, lively discussions, group activities, engaging and varied writing assignments, the teacher's presentations and instructions, classroom atmosphere, and/or the results obtained—in terms of improvement in writing, preparation for writing in other classes or at work, and/or changed attitudes toward writing and a greater understanding of its usefulness? These are, of course, only some criteria you might use. Make a list of as many specific questions as you can think of that would give you information related to the criteria you want to use to evaluate the course. Once you have a list, decide which questions seem the most important and useful. Write a final list of questions, and make enough copies of the list for everyone in class.

2. Meet together as a whole class. Have each group present its questions. Try as a class to synthesize the questions into a master list that everyone can agree to. If there are questions on a lot of different areas, you might have to make a joint decision to eliminate some areas and focus on others. Or you may decide to assign separate groups to the various areas.

3. With your questions in mind, decide how you will go about getting your answers—what forms of research you want to use. You could, for example, use any combination of the following: surveys, written evaluations, interviews, discussion groups, video or audio recording of a class, or outside observers. Decide which methods would be practical as well as most useful for getting the information you need.

4. At this point, you should separate again into groups, with each group responsible for a particular research method and/or a particular area of inquiry. Make sure that everyone has a role in the research process. Each group should make final decisions about the specifics of how it will conduct its research.

5. In groups, conduct the research and compile the results of your research. The way you compile results will, of course, depend on the method of gathering information you used. For example, surveys can be tallied, whereas videos would have to be analyzed in terms of the issues you had decided to look at.

6. The final steps are to analyze and interpret the results of your research and prepare a final evaluation based on this analysis. You can begin by having the groups that conducted the research give reports to the class. These reports should include tentative conclusions and judgments drawn from the data. The class can discuss each report, agreeing or disagreeing with these conclusions and judgments. The reports and discussion can then be the basis of a written course review. A group can be given the responsibility of writing the review or different groups can write sections, but the entire class should read and approve the final course review.

CALL TO WRITE: REVIEWS

WRITING ASSIGNMENT

For this assignment, write a review. Pick something to review that you know well or that you find interesting and would like to learn more about. You will write this review for a particular group of readers, so you might target a particular publication, such as a student or local newspaper or one of the national magazines you are familiar with. This will help you anticipate what your readers already know, what they value, and what criteria they accept as a basis of evaluation. If it is appropriate, design your own rating system or borrow one from a newspaper or magazine.

The subject of your review can be drawn from many spheres of life. Here are some common types of reviews:

- Live performances. Go to a musical concert, a play, a club with live music. Keep track of what you hear and see, and write it up in a review.

- Media. Television programs, radio shows, movies, and musical recordings are all possible subjects for reviews. Or you could create your own best-of-the-year list. Or you could rank the all-time movies, rock bands, or Beatles recordings.

- World Wide Web sites. As the Internet grows more crowded, people can use more help finding which sites are worth visiting, and which are not. Gather an assortment of related Web sites and write a comparative review of them. Or just focus on one site, and review it in depth. If the site has an email address for contacting the designer or the Webmaster, consider sending a copy of your review to that person.

- Exhibitions. Local museums, on and off campus, may be featuring special art, historical, or scientific exhibitions. Write a review of one and submit it to a local paper.

- Books. You could review a bestseller, a recent book in an academic field that interests you, a controversial book such as The Bell Curve, a book that is particularly popular with college students, or an older book that invites a revisit.

- Sports. Write a preview of an upcoming season in a college or professional sport. Like the arts, sports lends itself to all-time great lists, whether the greatest Superbowl to be played or the best baseball players of the past twenty-five years.

- Leisure and entertainment. Write a restaurant review, a guide to entertainment on campus, or an evaluation of backpacking routes you have taken. Visit historical places, local parks, or parts of a city and write an evaluation of what they have to offer.

- Education. Write a review of a course you have taken, a textbook, or a program you have been involved in (such as an orientation for first-year students or a summer program).

- Letters of recommendation. You may be in a position to write somebody you know a letter of recommendation. Such letters, in fact, are reviews of the person you are recommending (they are, by nature, generally positive reviews). If you have a friend applying to colleges, or to organizations which require recommendations, you can consider the writing you do for that person for this assignment. Likewise, if you have worked with somebody who is searching for a job, consider writing that person a recommendation that he or she can take to interviews.

- Politics and the public sphere. You could write a review of a particular elected official, candidate for office, proposed law, or ongoing program.

INVENTION

EXPLORING YOUR TOPIC

To get started thinking about your topic and how you might approach it in a review, it can help to assess what you already know and what further information you need.

EXERCISE

Write about your topic, using the following points of departure. Write what you know and don't worry if your response is incomplete or you have little or no information. The following questions can help you determine whether you need to do further research.

- Describe your subject. Tell as much as you know about it. If it's a book or movie, identify the genre (for example, coming of age novel, action adventure movie, biography, or political analysis) and write a brief summary. If it's a musical performance or recording, identify the style (for example, classical, modern jazz, urban blues, heavy metal, or country and western), the musicians and instruments, and the tunes or scores they play.

- State your current feelings and opinions. Do you like or dislike what you are reviewing? Everything or just aspects? Do you think it is a good, average, mediocre, or poor example of its kind? Have you always had the same feelings and opinions or have your views changed? Are there similar works you prefer? If so, why? Are there similar works you think are inferior to your subject? If so, why?
- Give background information. What do you know about the author of the book, the director of the film, the composer or musical leader? What other works do you know beside the one you are reviewing? How is this work like or different from the author's or director's or composer's other works? What do you know about the history of the genre or style of the work? What other examples can you think of?
- List what others have written. Do you know of reviews or articles on your subject? Are there books on it? What have other people said? Do the critics and reviewers seem to agree or are there debates, differences, or controversies? If so, what's at stake?
- Describe your readers. Who is likely to be interested in your subject? Why? What values and attitudes are they likely to hold? How knowledgeable are your readers likely to be about your subject and other subjects of similar type? What kinds of judgments have they made in the past? What are they likely to think about your opinion? Do you think they will agree or disagree, be surprised, shocked, amused, or angry? At this point, you might want to look carefully at the readers that tend to read the publication you are hoping to submit your review to. What kinds of reviews have appeared there before? What kinds of values do the readers of that publication seem to have?

ESTABLISHING CRITERIA OF EVALUATION

Criteria are the standards critics and reviewers use to justify their evaluations. Criteria will vary, depending on what you are reviewing and who your audience is. For example, the criteria you would use to judge suitable movies for eight-year-olds will quite likely differ in at least some important respects from the criteria you would use for college students or other adults. You might recommend the Disney version of *Pocahontas* or *The Secret Garden* for an eight-year-old but rule out Pulp Fiction, even though it won an Academy Award and received generally enthusiastic reviews.

To put it another way, one of your criteria in this example would be age-appropriateness. Applying this criterion of evaluation might lead to assertions such as these:

I think children (not to mention most adults) will enjoy Pocahontas because it has great animation, wonderful music, and most of all a memorable heroine who is intelligent and independent.
or
Quentin Tarantino may indeed put sex and violence to good cinematic use in Pulp Fiction, but it's not a movie for children or the squeamish.

Notice in this case that the assertions are based on the same criterion, namely age-appropriateness. Readers who accept this criterion are likely to agree or at least to give your assertions a sympathetic reading.

As a review writer, then, part of your job is to identify the criteria that makes for the most appropriate and compelling review. If you are looking at a movie, you may not be concerned about age-appropriateness; in this case, that criterion is irrelevant. You, as the writer, need to decide which criteria will matter; you also need to identify the criteria to your readers so they know whether or not to accept your evaluation. In the case of satirical movie critic Joe Bob Briggs, he has decided to give movies high marks for violence, swearing, partial nudity, and massive explosions. In his reviews, he makes sure his readers understand these are the qualities he prizes.

EXERCISE

To identify criteria that may help you in your evaluation, respond to the following questions.

1. What kinds of qualities do you look for in a good example of the type of item you are reviewing? List at least seven or eight qualities. Rank that list from most to least important.
2. What qualities seem to be acceptable to most people? What qualities seem to be the most attractive? Again, list as many qualities as you can, and rank them in order of importance.
3. What makes a particularly bad example? When you write this list, donít simply write the opposite of the ìgoodî qualities listed above. Instead, think of several specific bad examples, and try to identify what made them really stand out as inferior. List these and rank them.
4. Ask others about their most and least desirable criteria. You may want to do an informal survey of the types of people who read the publication you are writing for.
5. By the time you have completed these questions, you should have a full list of possible criteria. Now you can select those that you feel are the most appropriate to your project, and those that mean the most to you and your readers. Keep that list handy, as you will need to explain it in your review when you write your working draft.

Simply sharing criteria, however, does not assure that people will come to the same conclusion. People may draw differing conclusions from the same criteria. Or they might not share the same criteria at all. Both possibilities are evident in the two reviews of Evita. Notice how Keough and Lane apply the same criteria to differing ends or use criteria not shared by the other reviewer:

Criteria	Keough	Lane
Quality of performances		
Overall	"incandescent"	——-
Madonna	"Yes, Madonna can act"	"she doesn't so much act as pose"
Jonathan Pryce	"astonishing"	"wonderfully nimble"

Antonio Banderas	"even more impressive"	"quickens the blood"
Quality of the original musical stage show	——-	"Is there any form more bastard than rock opera?" "smothering bombast" "cotton-candy vaporings'"
Depiction of Argentine history, the rise of Peron	"impossible to understand" "nightmare of history is not confronted"	"Real world has been deposed" Workers are "abandoned as an abstraction"
Integration of singing and dancing with the drama	Inferior to the "stylized realism" of the old musicals	——-
Overall impact	"exhilarates, enraptures, and exhausts"	"bullying and undeniably entertaining"

At this point you can make some decisions about the criteria you have selected for your own assignment. Remember, you will need to justify your criteria to your readers, so make sure you have fully evaluated their appropriateness.

EXERCISE

1. Write down a series of assertions you want to make about what you are reviewing. Use this form of sentence: "I really liked X because Y" or "What made X a great movie is Y.'

2. Analyze the assertions. What criteria are you applying in each instance? Do you think readers are likely to accept these criteria as reasonable ones? Why or why not?

3. How might people apply the same criteria but come up with a different evaluation? Are there criteria of evaluation people might use that differ from those you use? How would these criteria influence a reviewer's evaluation?

4. How does the forum in which your review will appear determine the criteria? In other words, does New Yorker seem to have one set of criteria for its reviews, while The Boston Phoenix has another? If you need to, read through the two reviews of Evita again to respond to this question.

Criteria of evaluation in a review can also be described as the enabling assumptions by which reviewers link their claim (the movie was good, bad, disappointing, sensationalistic, etc.) to the available evidence (the movie itself). To justify their criteria, reviewers offer backing. For more explanation of these terms, see Making an Argument in Chapter 3.

PLANNING

CONSIDERING THE RELATION BETWEEN DESCRIPTION AND EVALUATION

One issue reviewers face is how much they need to describe what they are reviewing. How much detail should you give? Should you summarize the plot of the movie or book? If so, where and in what detail? Do you need to tell readers what kind of music a band is playing or what type of television show you are reviewing? How can you best combine such description with your evaluation?

Answers to these questions will depend in part on what the reviewer assumes readers are likely to know about the topic. Their level of familarity will shape how much the reviewer feels called on to explain by way of background information and description.

These are very real considerations. At the same time, however, it is important to see description and evaluation not as separate writing strategies that require separate space in a review but as strategies that are related to each other.

Stephen King's review of Louisa May Alcott's A Long Fatal Love Chase offers a good example of a skillful integration of description and evaluation. As you have seen, King devotes considerable space to recounting the plot of the novel, as well as to presenting details about Alcott's life. But notice this is not simple plot summary with the aim of informing readers about a work of literature, though of course King's summary does indeed inform readers. Nor is his inclusion of details meant solely to provide biographical information. King's point rather is to use description of the plot and biographical information as evidence to support the evaluations he is making of Alcott's novel and of her standing as a writer.

USING COMPARISONS

Comparison is a good strategy to put what you are reviewing in perspective by seeing how it stacks up to something similar. Notice in King's review the prominent role comparison plays in its structure and organization.

Comparison	Function in the Review
Compares the plot of A Long Fatal Love Chase to plot of King's novel.	Establishes a working definition of the genre and subgenre.
Compares A Long Fatal Love Chase to "Behind a Mask."	Establishes a criteria of judgment, namely Alcott's ability to shock and challenge convention.
Compares A Long Fatal Love Chase to Little Women.	Establishes another criteria of judgment, namely writers write best when they write about what they know.
Compares Alcott's "sensation stories" to Agatha Christie.	Ranks Alcott along with recognized master of the genre.
Returns to comparison of Little Women and "sensation stories." her writing,	Explores Alcott's own contradictory feelings about her "daylight realities" and her "midnight fantasies."

WORKING DRAFT

Use the writing you have already done to get started. Consider how your opening can make your evaluation clear to readers. Reviewers do not necessarily point out the criteria of judgment they are using. Nonetheless, to engage your readers, you need to make sure the criteria is easy to identify, even if it is only implied. Consider too how you can weave description and other background information into your review. Are there comparisons worth making?

PARAGRAPH DEVELOPMENT: Supporting with Facts or Evidence

Once you state your evaluation, readers expect to find out why you have made that particular assertion. Giving reasons will help readers follow your train of thought (and call on you to clarify why you formulated your stance in the first place). In turn, reasons require their own kind of support, just as they provide support for your general position. One of the best kinds of support you can provide for your reasons takes the form of facts and evidence. Facts can be statistical data you have gathered or read, or they can be statements that your readers can easily check up on, if they want to. Other kinds of evidence include statements from experts, anecdotes from your own experience, and observations you can back up with specific examples.

Alan Stone provides plenty of evidence throughout his review of the Waco standoff in order to disprove the FBI's assertion that they handled the situation well. In fact, Stone's entire recommendation report is organized by the pieces of evidence he presents. If it seems appropriate for your review, try this as an organizational strategy.

Factual and documentary evidence is not the only kind of evidence you can use to support your evaluations, however. In the two Evita reviews, both writers use ample evidence from the movie itself. Note how both reviewers describe specific scenes from the movie to illustrate the points they are making:

> It's not insignificant that Madonna's biggest scenes are addressed to large audiences: the show-stopping "Donít Cry for Me Argentina" number, for example, is stunningly delivered before thousands of adorers from the balcony of the Casa Rosanda, the Argentine presidential palace from which Eva Peron announced her own retirement from political life.
> — Peter Keough, "Goon Squad"

and

> When Madonna hands them cash and blows them kisses, she doesnít look like a philanthropic saint who bleeds for her compatriots; she looks like, well, Madonna signing albums on tour.
> — Anthony Lane, "Immaterial Girls"

You will probably want to make sure that your most important assertions are backed up with evidence of one sort or another. If you would like more information about working with types of evidence, see the section on Evaluating the Writerís Evidence in Chapter (pages XXX), and the box on Questions to Ask about Evidence in Chapter 3 (page XXX). On the other hand, if you feel you have already done a thorough job of providing evidence where it is needed, you it might be helpful to look at some more paragraph development ideas in other chapters. For example, you might try:

- see Describing (page XXX in Letters) to increase the amount of sensory information you give your readers

- see Using Summaries (page XXX in Reports) to work on the proper amount of description to assure your readers have enough information to agree with your evaluation

- see Evaluating Claims and Evidence (page XXX in Commentary) to compare your evaluation with that of another writer

BEGINNINGS AND ENDINGS: Establishing and Justifying Criteria

You have already spent a good bit of time in this assignment thinking about your criteria for evaluating the subject of your review. Now you can put this effort to good use by including it as part of the introduction to your review. As you noticed with the auto ratings from Consumer Reports, some reviews put their criteria upfront; in fact, with the kinds rating systems for which Consumer Reports is known, the criteria are the most important pieces of information the writer can offer. In the explanation at the top of the rating chart, the writer makes clear how the evaluations were reached:

To earn our recommendation—marked by a — a model has to perform well in our tests and must have been at least average in reliability.

You, too, can let your readers know how and why you reached your conclusions by telling them your criteria at the beginning of the review. If you feel you have already expressed your criteria clearly at other points in the review, and you want to try other techniques for your introduction, look at some of the options described in other chapters.

- see Setting up with a Metaphorical Anecdote (page XXX in Profiles) to establish a guiding theme for your review

- see Replacing a Common View with an Alternative Perspective (page XXX in Commentary) to set up your review against mainstream opinion

- see Offering a Recommendation or Solution (page XXX in Proposals) to show readers what you expect of them after they read your review

PEER COMMENTARY

Exchange the working draft of your review with a classmate. Respond to these questions in writing:

1. Is the subject defined clearly? Does the review give the reader enough details and background information to understand the reviewer's evaluation? Are there things you wanted to know that the writer left out? Are there things the writer mentions but that you would like to know more about?
2. Does the reviewer's evaluation come across clearly? As you read the draft, where did you become aware of the reviewer's evaluation? Point to the sentence or passage. Do you understand what the reviewer's criteria are? Do they need to be stated more clearly? Are they reasonable criteria? Are there other criteria you think the writer should take into account?
3. Does the review seem balanced? How does the reviewer combine description and evaluation? Does the reviewer talk about good and bad points, positive and negative aspects? Is the tone appropriate?
4. Does the reviewer use comparisons? If so, where and for what purposes?
5. What suggestions would you make to strengthen the review?

REVISING

Use the peer responses to re-read your working draft. Consider again whether your evaluation is clear and easy to understand or whether you are hedging in one way or another. Remember that in writing reviews balance means attending to both good and bad points, positive and negative features. It does not mean being objective or neutral. To make an evaluation you have to commit yourself. You can't stay out of controversy by listing the good and the bad. Rather you need to explain how, given the good and the bad, you have made a judgment based on criteria. After responding to the advice from your peers, work through the following section to fine-tune your review.

CONNECTIONS AND COHERENCE: Logical Transitions

These transitions help readers understand how the ideas in a paragraph are related to each other. Notice in the following paragraph how Alan Stone uses a variety of transitions to guide the reader through a fairly complicated train of thought. He begins with some enumerated points, then moves to cause-and-effect by the end of the paragraph.

This changing negotiation strategy at the compound from (1) conciliatory negotiating to (2) negotiation and tactical pressure and then to (3) tactical pressure alone evolved over the objections of the FBI's own experts. When the fourth and ultimate strategy, the insertion of C.S. gas [tear gas] into the compound, was presented to Attorney General Janet Reno, the FBI had abandoned any serious effort to reach a negotiated solution and was well along in its strategy of all-out tactical pressure, thereby leaving little choice as to how to end the Waco stand-off. By the time the attorney general made her decision, the noose was closed and, as one agent told me, the FBI believed they had "three options—gas, gas, and gas."
— Alan A. Stone, "How the FBI Helped Fuel the Waco Fire"

Here is a list of some of the most commonly used transitions and the functions they perform:

To set up an illustration or example: for example, for instance, specifically, namely, in particular.

To identify items in a series: first, second, third . . . etc, next, then, furthermore, moreover, in addition, also, in the first place, for one thing . . . for another thing, as well as, along with.

To emphasize a conclusion or result: therefore, consequently, accordingly, as a result, thus, so, finally, in conclusion, to sum up.

To introduce an alternative or contrary idea or point of view: but, however, on the other hand, in contrast, nevertheless, instead.

If you feel comfortable with the logical transitions you have used in your review, you might want to learn about some different types of coherence devices. Look, for example, at the following sections:

- see Temporal Transitions (page XXX in Memoirs) to help keep track of a timeline for the review

- see Enumerative Order (page XXX in Public Documents) to organize any number of points you may be making

- see Parallelism of Ideas (page XXX in Proposals) to follow a set pattern that helps readers follow the flow of your reasons

WRITERS WORKSHOP

The following is a working draft of a review of Donna Gaines' book Teenage Wasteland, written for a sociology course on youth culture. The assignment was to draft a four-page review that evaluated the book, exchange for peer commentary, and revise. The writer, Denise Sega, had a number of concerns she wanted her partner to address on the peer commentary. Here's the note she wrote:

I'm worried that I spend too much time summarizing the book and not enough explaining my evaluation of it. What do you think? Do I say too much about the author and the book's contents? Is my evaluation clear to you? Do you think I give enough explanation of why I liked the book so much? Any other suggestions are also appreciated. Thanks.

As you read, keep in mind what Denise asked her partner. When you finish reading the working draft, consider how you would respond.

More Than Just Burnouts

Denise Sega
(Working Draft)

Donna Gaines. Teenage Wasteland: Suburbia's Dead End Kids. New York: Harper, 1991.
    Youth culture. Teenagers have devised many different ways of growing up. From jocks and preps to neo-Beatnicks and hip-hop kids, most high schools contain a range of distinctive social groupings. In Teenage Wasteland, Donna Gaines looks at a group "burnouts" and heavy metal teens in suburban New Jersey, the "dead end" working-class kids who are alienated from school and community. The opening paragraphs explains the situation that led Gaines to write this book:

> When I heard about the suicide pact it grabbed me in the
> solar plexus. I looked at the pictures of the kids and their
> friends. I read what reporters said. I was sitting in my
> garden apartment looking out on Long Island's Jericho
> Turnpike thinking maybe this is how the world ends, with the
> last generation bowing out first.
> In Bergenfield, New Jersey, on the morning of March 11,
> 1987, the bodies of four teenagers were discovered inside a
> 1977 Chevrolet Camaro. The car, which belonged to Thomas
> Olton, was parked in an unused garage in the Foster Village
> garden apartment complex, behnd the Foster Village Shopping
> Center. Two sisters, Lisa and Cheryl Burress, and their
> friends, Thomas Rizzo and Thomas Olton, had died of carbon
> monoxide poisoning. (3)

The remainder of the introduction reveals the rationale and research plan for Gaine's investigation of the suicides. What began as an assignment for the Village Voice, for which Gaines writes regularly, her investigation eventually became her doctoral work as well as the book in review.
    Besides providing more details about the instigating event, the Bergenfield suicide pact, the introductory pages also provide autobiographical details about the author which are essential to understanding Gaines' devotion to her task, as well as her informed frame of reference. Gaines, too, in many ways, was a "burnout." She describes her growing up years and habits. She explains that "like many of [her] peers, [she] spent a lot of [her] adulthood recovering from a personal history of substance abuse, family trauma, school failure, and arrests" (4). To put this life behind her, Gaines turned to social work, first as a "big sister" with junior high students in Brooklyn and then as a helper on a suicide prevention hotline. After becoming a New York State certified social worker, Gaines worked in the special adoptions and youth services divisions and as a street worker providing services for troubled teens. Eventually moved into research and program evaluation and finally returned to school to complete her doctorate in sociology.
    In the introduction, Gaines also explains the need for the book. Initially, she was reluctant to write about suicidal teens because she felt that "if I couldn't help them, I didn't want to bother them" (6). She did not like the idea of turning vulnerable people like the Bergenfield teens into "research subjects" by getting them to trust her with their secrets. Despite these qualms, however, she did decide to go to Bergenfield and ultimately spent two years hanging out with the "burnouts" and "dropouts" of suburban New Jersey, talking to them about heavy metal music, Satanism, work, school, the future, and many other things. Gaines was angry because these teens had been classified by adults as "losers" and never allowed to tell their side of the story. The press had explained the suicides as the result of the individual problems of troubled teens and failed to see, as Gaines does so clearly in her book, how the suicides "symbolized a tragic defeat for young people" (6) and a wider pattern of alienation.
    Teenage Wasteland reveals the sense of sadness among the teens in Bergenfield. "By nineteen," Gaines writes, "you've hit the brick wall and you really need something. Because there is nothing

to do here and there is nowhere to go" (78). Young people hanging out seems to annoy and even frighten adults. Nevertheless, for these teens, there does not seem to be anything else to do. According to Gaines, they have been neglected by society for so long, experienced so much lack of care in so many ways, that they see no alternatives. They see no hope for anything better.

The only "ticket out" these teens see is to be like Jon Bon Jovi or Keith Richards. The chances of becoming a rock star, of course, is one in a million. The dream breaks down, the kids realize their limitations, and they feel they have run out of choices for the future. There seem to be no alternatives to their bleak situations:

> At the bottom are kids with poor basic skills, short
> attention spans, limited emotional investment in the future.
> Also poor housing, poor nutrition, bad schooling, bad lives.
> And in their bad jobs they will face careers of unsatisfying
> part-time work, low pay, no benefits, and no opportunity for
> advancement.
> There are the few possibilities offered by a relative—a
> coveted place in a union, a chance to join a small family
> business in a service trade, a spot in a small shop. In my
> neighborhood, kids dream of making a good score on the cop
> tests, working up from hostess to waitress. Most hang out in
> limbo hoping to get called for a job in the sheriff's
> department, or the parks, or sanitation. They're on all the
> lists, although they know the odds for getting called are slim.
> The lists are frozen, the screening process is endless. (155)

According to Gaines, these are "America's invisible classes," the "unseen and unheard . . . legions of young people who now serve the baby boom and others, in fancy eateries, video stores, and supermarkets" (157). Given this situation, it is no surprise that Bergenfield's teens turn to Satanism and heavy metal to give them a sense of power and a refuge in a world over which they feel they have no control. There are no good jobs, and the social programs for these teens only label them as "troubled" or "deviant" or "burnouts" and do not work.

One truly fascinating part of the book involves Gaines' etymology of the term "burnout." Besides providing at least twenty-five synonyms for the term, she also explains its evolution. Furthermore, she differentiates between "burnouts" and "dirtbags"—a subtle yet significant distinction. Her discussion of how these terms reflect teens feeling "powerless, useless, and ineffectual" is, in itself, powerful, useful, and effectual in helping readers understand the deep sense of alienation afflicting the "teenage wasteland."

In conclusion, I believe this is an important book that should b read by anyone interested in finding out more about the "gritty underside of white teen life in the suburbs" (cover notes). Compared to the sensationalistic stories in the press that blame teenage suicide on drugs or heavy metal, Donna Gaines has taken the time to listen—and to hear what the kids have to say.

WORKSHOP QUESTIONS

1. In her note to her partner, Denise Sega raises a number of issues about her working draft. One of these concerns the amounts of description and evaluation that appear in the draft. She seems worried that she spends too much time summarizing the book and talking about the author and not enough on evaluation. How would you respond to this concern on the part of the writer? What suggestions would you offer the writer?

2. It is obvious that Sega admires Teenage Wasteland, but she raises the question of whether the criteria of evaluation she uses come across clearly enough. Re-read the draft and mark those passages that make an evaluation or imply one. What seem to be the criteria Sega uses in each case? If the criteria are not stated explicitly, express in your own words what they seem to be. What advice would you give Sega about presenting her criteria of evalu-

ation more explicitly?

3. In the third paragraph, Sega compares the treatment of the Bergenfield suicide pact by the press to Gaines's treatment in Teenage Wasteland. What is the point of this comparison? Do you think Sega could do more with it? If so, how could the comparison be extended and strengthened? Do other comparisons appear in the draft? If so, are they effective or could they use more work? Are there other comparisons you can think of that Sega might use?

WRITERS INVENTORY

The assignments throughout the chapter have put you in the role of a reviewer and looked at how you might evaluate a performance, a program, a policy. For your portfolio, shift focus to discuss how you have been reviewed by others—by teachers in school, supervisors at work, judges at performances, and peer commentators in your writing course.

First, give a little background on your experiences being evaluated in and out of school. What were the circumstances of the evaluations? Why were you being evaluated? What criteria were used? What was your response to the evaluations? Do you consider these experiences to have been helpful to you? Explain why or why not.

Second, use this background to reconstruct your attitude toward evaluation when you entered your writing course. Has your attitude changed? Why or why not? What has been the effect on you as a writer, a student, and a person of receiving reviews from both your teacher and your peers? What differences, if any, do you see between teachers' and peers' evaluation? What suggestions would you offer for improving the process of evaluation in your writing course?

A CLOSING NOTE

Reviews, of course, are made to be read by the public, by the readers, viewers, listeners, concert-goers, diners, tourists, and fans who care about arts and entertainment. By the same token, reviews of educational programs and government actions and policies are meant to be read by the people in charge. Consider publishing your review or sending it to the appropriate officials. Student newspapers often publish reviews, as well as predictions about sporting events. Electronic mail discussion groups are another possible outlet.

PART THREE

WRITERS AT WORK

I N T R O D U C T I O N :
MANAGING WRITING TASKS

D ifferent writing tasks demand different ways of working. Let's look at writers at work in three different situations to see how they respond to the call to write:

- A first-year college student receives an e-mail message from a friend at another college. She decides to respond immediately and without stopping to plan writes a long e-mail message. First she talks about how funny her political science teacher was today in class and sends along a joke he told. Then, after pausing briefly, she launches into a discussion of two mutual friends from high school she saw over the weekend. This makes her think about Christmas vacation coming up, and she asks her friend when she is coming home and whether they can plan a get-together of all four friends. Then she stops, re-reads what she has written, deletes something she said about one of the friends as too gossipy, adds a short note that she just saw a really scary movie, and sends the e-mail message. Two days later her friend sends a message with details about getting together over Christmas vacation.

- A local newspaper is planning a special supplement to mark the beginning of the baseball season, and the sports editor asks a free-lance writer (and baseball fan) to contribute a 1,000 word essay. They talk in a general way about the focus of the essay—something to evoke nostalgia for the traditions of America's national pastime. Based on this discussion, the writer goes to work. He sketches a series of notes on a pad and then begins drafting by hand a personal account of going to Wrigley Field with his dad to see the Chicago Cubs play in the days before the ballpark had lights. He enters the draft on his computer, making a number of changes along the way. Discussion with a close friend who has read the draft, however, makes it clear that the piece of writing is really a memoir that concentrates on the writer's relationship with his father and is not appropriate for the baseball supplement. Nonetheless a section of the draft discussing changes in baseball gives him an idea—to compare the old-fashioned joys of going to the ballpark to see the hometown team with the new era of free agency, million-dollar salaries, sports complexes, and luxury boxes. He writes another draft, focusing this time on how greedy owners, high ticket prices, and players with no team loyalties are ruining the game. When the writer's friend reads this draft, he notices that the tone is wrong—too angry, too much a scathing criticism of the game. But both he and the writer also notice that the strongest passages are those where the writer describes ballparks from a fan's point of view (something he has carried over from the first version). So he decides to write a commentary on how baseball stadiums have changed over the years—from the old-fashioned parks such as Wrigley Field to the suburban multipurpose sports complexes such as the Oakland Coliseum and now back to baseball-only stadiums such as Baltimore's Camden Yards which embody a nostalgia for tradition. This focus seems to give the writer the critical distance he needs to adjust his tone and emphasis to the occasion. He writes a new draft in a day, only to realize he needs some information on the Houston Astrodome. After looking up and incorporating the new material, he spends two days tinkering with sentences and passages, revising on hard copy by hand. He enters the final changes, prints and proof reads the essay, and sends it to the editor.

- The marketing manager of a regional drug store chain is asked to prepare a report on the results of the company's decision to add a small grocery and dairy section to its stores. From experience, she has a fairly clear idea of the information and the form of writing her readers expect. Her first step is to create a document on her computer by outlining the main sections of her report. Then she assembles relevant information—the original plan for the grocery and dairy section, sales figures, financial statements, and advertising reports—and spends an hour with the head of marketing research discussing the results of a recent customer survey. As she reads these materials, she marks information and written passages to incorporate into her report. She spends the better part of a day filling in her outline, moving figures, tables, graphs, and passages from other documents into sections of her report. She makes sure adequate summaries, transitions, and explanations hold the parts together. Finally, she returns to the introduction, which had been left a sketchy few sentences, and drafts a full version. The next day, she reads the report carefully, changes the order of two sentences, re-writes a few others, and corrects some typos. Then she proof-reads, checks the figures and tables, adds a title page, and submits the document.

As these examples show, writers manage their writing tasks in very different ways. Sometimes, they spend lots of time planning, as the marketing manager does. In other cases, the writing comes out spontaneously, as it does for the e-mail writer. Sometimes, the purpose and focus of the writing emerge gradually, as you can see in the free-lance writer's experience, and the writer spends a great deal of time revising. In other cases, less revision is needed.

These differences in managing the writing task can be traced in part to the different genres the three writers are using. For the first writer, the openness and informality of the personal letter or e-mail allows her to link observations and anecdotes together loosely, without worrying about transitions or logical connections. In the case of the marketing manager, the predictable form of the business report provides her with a scaffolding to organize her material. For the free-lance writer, however, genre poses a problem he needs to solve in order to complete the writing task, and one of his key decisions is to shift from memoir to commentary.

You can see from these examples too that writers use feedback and discussion with others in different ways. The e-mail writer, for example, is responding to a friend's message and in turn her friend sends a reply. Their personal correspondence is likely to continue this way as long as they are friends. In the case of the free-lance writer and the marketing manager, however, consulting with others does more than maintain personal relationships. The free-lance writer's friend has provided careful readings and important feedback that shaped the writer's revisions. For the marketing manager, discussion with a colleague provided useful information for her report.

Finally, these examples show how writers use the tools of writing in different ways. Some writers draft at the keyboard, while others prefer to write with pen in hand. Some revise directly on the screen, while others like to work on hard copy. And as the case of the marketing manager show, new writing technologies enable writers to move material easily from one document to another.

The following two chapters explain how you can work with others—on your own writing projects and on collaboratively written ones. The third chapter in this part concerns the tools writers use, especially the new writing technologies. But before we turn to these matters, let's take a little closer look at how people manage writing tasks and the habits they develop as writers.

Elements of Writing Tasks

No two writers compose the same way, and an individual may work in different ways on different writing tasks. Nonetheless, there are predictable elements in a writing project that can be listed. As you can see, these elements appear in the writing assignments in Part 2:

- Invention. Developing an approach to the topic and to readers, assessing purpose, doing research, choosing the appropriate genre.

- Planning. Designing the arrangement of material, finding an appropriate pattern of organization.

- Drafting. Creating a working draft, getting ideas down on paper.

- Peer commentary. Getting feedback from others, seeing the working draft through a reader's eyes.

- Revising. Re-reading a working draft, clarifying purpose and organization, connecting the parts.

- Manuscript preparation. Document design, editing, proofreading.

Listing the elements of writing like this may suggest they are a series of steps you can follow. If you look at writers at work, however, you'll see that they may well manage these elements in quite different ways. Some writers like to start drafting before they develop a clear plan, while others would not think of drafting without a carefully developed outline.

Nor are the elements necessarily separate from each other. Some people revise as they draft, working carefully over each section before going on to the next, while others write quickly and then think about needed revisions. Nor do writers spend the same amount of time on each of the elements. Depending on the writing task and the person's own writing habits, writers learn how to manage the elements in ways that work for them.

Writing can be exhilirating, but it can be aggravating too. You can probably think of times writing seemed to pour out, leading you to previously unsuspected ideas and precisely the right way of saying things. On the other hand, you may have had moments when you couldn't begin a writing task or got stuck in the middle. The way to get to the source of such difficulties is to think about how you are managing the elements of your writing task. Are you spending your time doing what needs to be done to get the writing task completed? Should you be revising and editing passages that you may eventually discard? Is this keeping you from figuring out how (or whether) the passage connects to other points? If you see your draft diverge from your outline, should you follow it or go back and revise your plan? When you're stuck in the middle of a draft, do you need to turn to invention—to read more or talk to others?

Answers to these questions will vary, of course, depending on the writing task and your own habits as a writer. The point is that experienced writers learn to ask such questions in order to set their bearings, especially when the writing is not going well, to see where they stand in putting a piece of writing together and what they need to do next.

WRITING INVENTORY: Analyzing How You Managed a Writing Task

Think of a writing task you completed recently, in school or out of school. Analyze how you managed the task. To do this, consider the following questions:

1. What called on you to write? Describe how you defined the writing task. How did you establish your purpose? What did your exploration of the topic involve? How did you imagine your readers and the relationship you wanted to establish with them? What genre did you choose? Did you talk to others about your ideas?
2. Explain how you planned the writing. How much planning did you do, when, and what form did it take?
3. Describe how you drafted. When did you begin? How much invention and planning did you do before you started drafting?
4. Describe what feedback, if any, you got to your draft. What was the effect of this feedback?
5. What kinds of revision did you make? When did you revise— during drafting, after you had a complete working draft, at various points?
6. What final form did the writing take? Were any considerations of document design involved? Did you edit and proofread the final version?

Now look back over your answers to these questions. What conclusions can you draw about you managed the elements of the writing process in this instance? What, if anything, would you do differently if had the task to do over?

Writing Habits

We've all got our idiosyncracies, and writers are no exception, especially when it comes to writing. Most experienced writers have well-developed habits concerning their writing. In fact, often these habits are so developed that they take on a ritualized character, much the way athletes have pre-game rituals and superstitions.

It's not surprising that writers develop their own habits. Writing can be hard work, and writer's habits are a way of handling the difficulties and emotional stress of writing. To be productive, writers need to be in the right frame of mind, and their writing habits can help writers prepare themselves mentally to face their writing task and to pace themselves over its duration. In this sense, individual writing habits are part of the way writers manage the writing process.

- Time and place. Some writers like to get up early in the morning to write, while others prefer late-night writing sessions. Some writers need total quiet and solitude, while others prefer public places or music in the background.

- Technology. Some writers have special pens they use and particular kinds of lined paper, while others always compose on an old typewriter and still others on a computer equipped with the latest word-processing program.

- Pre-writing habits. Some writers find they are most productive if they write after they have run or swum or worked out in the gym. Some writers need to straighten up their desk or work environment as preparation to write. Some play computer games or read for awhile before they write. Others even need to put on certain clothes—to dress in a particular way to take on the role of the writer.

- Pacing the task. Some writers like to write for as long as they can, until they're exhausted or have reached an impasse. Others will write for a predetermined amount of time and then stop no matter where they are. Still others will stop only at a point where they know exactly what they want to say next, so that getting started again will be easy. And some writers play with fire: they wait until the last minute, with a deadline bearing down on them, to start writing.

- Breaks. For writers, a break is an opportunity to relax and unwind or to gain some distance and mull over a problem in the writing. Some writers like to take long walks, whether in the city or the country. Others go to the movies or watch television. Still others do household chores or gardening. In any case, it's important to see breaks as part of the writing process, not a retreat from it.

WRITING INVENTORY: Describing Your Writing Habits

Describe your writing habits. At what time of day do you like to write? Where do you like to write? What tools of writing best suit you? What pre-writing habits, if any, do you follow? How do you pace yourself? When do you take breaks and what do you do for breaks? Which of your habits are most useful to you? Which, if any, would you consider changing?

CHAPTER
TWELVE

WORKING TOGETHER:
Individual Writing Projects

If you asked people to describe a writer at work, it is likely they would describe a lonely figure at a desk, surrounded by books and manuscripts, facing the terrors of the blank page or computer screen, sustained by endless cups of coffee. The image of the writer as an individual struggling in isolation to produce works of writing is deeply engrained in the popular consciousness.

Now it's true that writers often spend a good deal of time working independently. But this does not necessarily mean that they are working in isolation. In fact, writing often involves considerable social interaction. Consider, for example, these two scenarios:

- A group of poets known as the Olney Street Collective have been meeting monthly for over twenty years in Providence, Rhode Island. Members of the group come from many walks of life—teaching, law, public relations, journalism, and business. None of them is a famous poet, but all have published in small literary magazines. They write in their spare time, when they have the chance, and sometimes they go through long stretches without writing at all. The group's membership has changed over the years, as people moved away or lost interest. But the group itself has kept going because it seems to fill a need for people who write poetry to get together and read their poems. The meetings are informal. There's lots of talk about poetry, movies, life, jobs, people's children or lovers or spouses but little criticism or discussion of the poems the members read. People come to read their poems and listen to others read.

- A history professor is preparing an article based on her research on the role of women in the anti-Vietnam War movement and its connection to the emergence of contemporary feminism. She has already interviewed many women who played key roles in both the anti-war and women's liberation movements, and she has discussed these issues at length with students in a history seminar. She presented some of her research at a conference of American historians and received responses, questions, and counter-interpretations from her co-panelists and from members of the audience. She has also spent a good deal of time talking about her research with a trusted colleague in the history department.

These two scenarios only begin to suggest the range of social interactions that surround and sustain acts of writing. For the poets, the monthly meetings of their poetry group serve as a support system and an occasion to get together with like-minded people to share their writing. Accordingly, the history professor's work has benefited from the women she interviewed, the presentation at the conference, and informal discussion with her colleague. In each case, individuals draw on common interests and professional connections with others to foster their writing. At the same time, while they depend in crucial respects on these interactions, the poets and the history professor are working as individual authors to produce their own writing, taking full responsibility for it and receiving the credit.

As you will see in the next chapter, there are other writing situations in which people work together to produce collaboratively written projects. In this chapter, you'll see how writers and readers can work together on individual writing projects.

WORKING TOGETHER ON INDIVIDUAL WRITING PROJECTS

Analyzing writing assignments with classmates, talking with others about ideas for a paper, reading and responding to working drafts, offering suggestions for editing—these are some of the ways that writers and readers can work together on individual writing projects. The writing assignments in Part Two include suggestions for collaborating at various steps in the writing task and directions for peer commentary. Teachers in other classes may also ask you to comment on another student's work-in-progress. For these reasons, it's worth taking a moment to look at some of the benefits of working together on individual writing assignments.

The main premise behind working together on individual writing assignments is the old idea that two (or more) heads are better than one. By interacting with others, writers can draw on a wider range of experience, knowledge, and problem-solving strategies. Feedback from readers brings new perspectives to an issue or problem, so that writers can consider alternatives that might not otherwise have occurred to them and develop ways to negotiate their differences with others.

Besides, working together can be fun and rewarding in its own right. There's something about people working together that seems to create energy and increase everyone's involvement in the work.

Working with other students on individual writing projects can help you in your role as a writer who gets feedback and suggestions and as a reader who is learning to read carefully and make helpful comments.

- For you as a writer, getting feedback from others helps overcome the sense of isolation writers often experience working alone by exploring how your work in progress communicates to readers. In this way, collaboration with others can help you discover your purpose, clarify your focus, and understand your readers' need for precise language and coherent organization.

- For you as a reader, providing feedback at various stages in the writing process enables you to see how other writers shape their ideas and manage their work in progress. In this way, collaboration involves readers in the messy and creative work of planning and drafting, helps them learn to read carefully and critically, and promotes a sense of tactful response to others' work.

To see how writers and readers can work together effectively on individual writing projects, in the rest of this chapter we'll follow a student Krista Gugliemetti working on a paper for a mass communication course. This case study can help you understand the various points in the writing process that people can work together, what use writers can make of response from readers, and where the writer needs to work independently.

WRITING INVENTORY: Reflecting on Collaboration

Have you been involved in writing workshops where you worked with other students on individual writing assignments? What types of interaction took place? Did you discuss ideas for papers with classmates? Did you exchange drafts and respond to other students' writing? Describe your experiences. What has it been like for you to get response to your writing from other students? What has it been like for you to respond to other students' work? What do you see as the difference between a teacher's and a fellow student's response to your writing?

CASE STUDY OF A WRITING ASSIGNMENT

In the following case study, you will see how writers and readers can collaborate at various stages of an individual work in progress. The type of collaboration most appropriate will depend in part on knowing where you are in the process of managing your writing project and getting feedback that is responsive to the actual progress of your work. As you will see, collaboration begins with discussion of ideas and approaches before any drafting takes place. At later stages, once the writer has produced a working draft, readers may provide written commentary.

INVENTION

You don't need to wait until you have a working draft to collaborate with others on your writing. Experienced writers often find they want—and need—to talk to others before they begin writing. Talking with others helps writers to think more concretely about their audience and purpose and to brainstorm ideas about their topic. Here are some ways you can work with others at early stages in a writing project.

- **Assessing your purpose** It can be difficult to get started on a writing project if you are uncertain about the call to write and the kind of writing task it presents. You may not be clear, for example, about what an assignment in one of your courses is calling on you to do. If you feel shaky about the purpose of a writing assignment, other students in the class probably do too. Of course, you could talk to the teacher, but you may also want to collaborate with classmates to clarify the purpose of the assignment and develop an approach to it.

Here is the writing assignment given to students in Introduction to Mass Communication. This is the assignment Krista Gugliemetti responded to in the case study we'll be following in this chapter. Read the assignment. Then work together with classmates to determine what it seems to call on students to do.

Writing Assignment

Introduction to Mass Communication

Much as visual representations from the past idealized families huddled around the fireplace for warmth and comfort, we now have idealized pictures of families gathered together in front of the television set. (See the accompanying illustration.) Media critics have raised questions about what such viewing time actually means for the contemporary family. Does it represent an important moment of family togetherness, or a means of avoiding really encountering each other, or something else? Draw on your family's viewing habits to write a short (2 page, 500 work) essay that explains the role television plays in the contemporary family. You will need to describe how your family uses television viewing, but your essay should also analyze what such viewing practices tell us about the role of television in the contemporary family.

EXERCISE

Work together with two or three classmates to analyze this writing assignment and to determine what it is calling on students in the Introduction to Mass Communication course to do. The following guidelines can be used for virtually any writing assignment. For this exercise, of course, since you are not actually a student in the mass communication class, you won't have all the information available to Krista and her classmates. Nonetheless, you can make some informed guesses by picking up important cues from the assignment.

Guidelines for Analyzing Writing Assignments

- Look for key words in the assignment—"describe," "summarize," "explain," "analyze," "evaluate critically," and so on. Discuss what these terms might mean in relation to the material you're being asked to write about and to the goals and focus of the course.

- Consider what information you need to do the assignment successfully. Where can you get this information? Does the assignment call for additional research or is it based on class readings and discussion? Are there things you know or have learned in other classes that might prove useful?

- Look for any special directions the assignment provides about the form of writing. Does it call for a specific genre (a report, proposal, review, and so on)? Does it call for documentation? Consider the length assigned. What is possible to do well within these limits?

After your group has answered these questions, compare your response to those of other groups. What advice, at this point, would you give Krista as she begins the assignment?

- **Understanding readers** Another difficulty getting started on a writing task may be the writers' uncertainty about what will interest their readers. Sometimes writers feel that if they have thought of something, everyone else must have too. Underestimating the importance of their own ideas, they feel reluctant to express them. One way to test out your ideas is to discuss them with other people. This way you can not only reassure yourself that your ideas are valid but you can also begin to formulate a plan for approaching your readers.

Talking out the ideas you have for a paper is one of the best ways to understand your readers. Here are some guidelines for doing this, followed by a transcript of Krista's discussion with her roomate Tamika.

Guidelines for Understanding Your Readers

- Find a willing listener, describe your writing task, and then tell your listener what you are thinking of writing about and what you are thinking of saying about it.

- Ask what your listener already knows about your subject, what he or she would like to know about it, and whether he or she has ideas or information you could use in your writing.

TRANSCRIPT OF KRISTA'S DISCUSSION WITH TAMIKA

K: I've got to write this paper for my mass comm course on families and television viewing. We're supposed to use our own family to explain what television means in terms of family life.

T: Sounds cool. In my lit class all we write about is John Milton and Alexander Pope. At least you've met these people. So what are you going to say?

K: Well, that's the problem. As you know, my family is a disaster. But I don't want to lay on all this dysfunctional stuff. I thought I could maybe say something about how families use television to avoid really relating to each other. That's sure what happens in my family. But I'm worried this is too obvious. What do you think? Does that sound interesting?

T: Oh yeah. People these days are definitely using TV as a means of avoidance. You're supposed to be all happy together, only nobody talks to each other because some TV show is going on.

K: Why is that?

T: In my opinion, people care more about what happens to those idiots on Melrose Place than their own selves.

K: You really think so? I mean, do you think I can do something here? My teacher has to like it, you know.

T: That goes without saying. Just think up some reasons why people like TV more than they like real life. That's the point. You go, girl. You got your main idea.

K: I hope so. Thanks, Tamika. I better get to work.

T: Yeah, but how about cleaning your side of the room first?

- **Exploring the topic** At a certain point, writers need to get some ideas down on paper, even if the writing is of a preliminary sort. One way to start is to do exploratory writing, in which you're tentatively working out the focus and direction of your paper. If you want someone to look at your exploratory writing, you can use the guidelines below. Make sure that the person who reads your writing understands it is an initial attempt to discover what you want to say.

Guidelines for Responding to Exploratory Writing

- Ask your reader to circle or underline key phrases and interesting ideas, whether or not they seem to be the main point of the writing.

- Ask your reader to tell you if there seem to be, implied or lurking just off the page, ideas that you could develop.

After thinking about her conversation with Tamika, Krista decided to do some exploratory writing. Below is the writing and the response from her friend Eric.

KRISTA'S EXPLORATORY WRITING

When I was a kid, I dreaded Friday nights. I would be up in my room happily reading a book when I would be summoned by my father to come down and watch TV with the rest of the family. There was no escape. This was supposed to be "quality time"—one of the few moments in the week the family got together. Only we weren't really together. How can you be, sitting silently in front of a TV set? It was pitiful, watching some family in a sit com on TV instead of being a family. All we succeeded in doing was to substitute a fictional family for the real one—us.

ERIC'S RESPONSE

To me, the most interesting point here is the one about how people substitute fictional TV families for real ones. I think you could use this as the basis for your essay. I sense a lot of anger at your family, and I think you need to be careful with this. As I understand it, your assignment is an analytical one, not just a personal essay about your family. Maybe you could look more into why people want to watch TV families. What are the reasons? If you could develop some ideas about why TV families are preferable to real ones, you could explain why and how your family used TV families to create this sense of false togetherness.

PLANNING

Using discussions with others about their ideas for a writing project, writers need to develop a plan for their writing. The key issue at this point is how to arrange their material so that they highlight the main point and provide supporting evidence.

After Krista talked to Tamika and got response to her exploratory writing from Eric, she mulled over the results. She knew it was time to use this information to plan her essay. Tamika and Eric helped her see that she needed to write an analytical essay that made a central claim and backed it up with evidence. A personal essay that focused on her feelings about her family was not the kind of writing called for by the assignment.

At this point, she worked by herself, developing her main idea and arranging reasons to support it. She sketched the following brief outline so that she could begin drafting.

KRISTA'S BRIEF OUTLINE

Introduction
   Begin with an anecdote about my family
      getting called down on Friday night to watch TV with the family.
   Generalize this experience
      Claim: the only quality family time left is spent in front of TV

Body
>   Give reasons why this is so
>   It's easy
>   Actors are doing the work of being a family for us
>   For TV's fictional families, everything works out

Ending
>   How to deal with this problem?
>   Turn off the TV and talk to your family

DRAFTING

Any plan a writer develops needs to be tested by writing a working draft. Outlines, sketches, or other preliminary planning can only tell you so much. To see where your ideas are going, you must commit them to paper.

After she sketched a brief outline, the next step for Krista was to write a working draft. As you can see, she used ideas and suggestions from Tamika and Eric. But, as is the case in individual writing projects, she worked independently to write the draft. Here is what she came up with.

Krista's Working Draft

It's 8:00 on a Monday night, and I am sitting at home in my bedroom peacefully reading a novel. Suddenly, the dreaded call comes, "Kris, you been in that room for two hours. Come on out here and be with the family for awhile. Cosby is going to start in five minutes. Don't you want to watch it with us?" Well, actually no. I was content with my book. But Dad and the family saw these hours in front of the television as quality, and I was expected to participate. What I constantly wondered every Monday was why? When did sitting in front of the tube become family time?

Unfortunately, my family is not the exception but the rule. People are able to remember it is Monday and at 5:00 they can watch the heartwarming merger of blended families on Full House. Yet, without a calendar, they have a difficult time remembering that this particular Monday is their stepmother's or stepfather's birthday and they should get a card or gift on the way home from work or school. They can tell you that the hot couple is headed for divorce on Melrose Place more easily than they can see the status of their own marriage. People may not have noticed, but the only quality family time left is that shared on the TV. The family has left the living room and has gone to live in the TV set in the form of fictional families living fictional lives that the real people would be living if they weren't watching TV.

So what happened? When did fiction become stronger than reality? And is there a way out? I propose the theory that it happened because it was easy. It takes no effort to sit and stare at the TV. It takes work to relate to your family. Now, that is what we pay actors for: to do that work for us, to relate to their families in the ways that we no longer can. On TV, blended families always work out, drug addicts are always treated, and no one is ever hurt permanently. It's easy. Just follow the script and everything will be fine. After all, if you're watching TV, you won't fight (except over who has the remote). If you don't fight, no one can get hurt and everyone will be happy. Let the TV characters fight. They always make up on the half hour. What could be simpler?

The solution? That's simpler and more obvious than the problem. If the TV is taking over your life, unplug it. Instead of watching TV dads, watch your own. Ask him questions, find out how his day went. Read those books when you want to escape the family. This way, when you come back, your family won't be under the illusion you were with them, and you may have learned something from your reading you can share with them. One night per week, just unplug the box and have real quality time. That's all it will take. Soon, it will become like a popular series. How did mom's big promotion interview at work go? Tune in next week for the answer. And soon will come the realization that you don't have to wait. You can ask her tomorrow. And more easily than you watched TV your whole life, you have become a family again.

PEER COMMENTARY

Once writers have a working draft down on paper, they need to figure out what kinds of revisions seem called for. Clearly, feedback from readers can be useful at this point. To get the most useful kind of feedback to your own working drafts, make sure your readers know they're looking at a work-in-progress and not a final draft.

There are different kinds of commentary you can get from readers at this point. Your readers can

---

ETHICS OF COLLABORATION:

Responsibilities of Writers and

Readers

Productive collaboration depends in large part on the quality of the relationship established between writers and readers. Each has responsibilities toward the other to make sure that open and meaningful communication can take place.

Writers, for example, need to provide their readers with legible working drafts, preferably typed and double-spaced, with any hand-written additions or deletions easy to follow. For readers to respond appropriately, writers should let them know how far along the working draft is—whether it's an early attempt to get ideas down on paper or a full draft based on a working plan. Most important, writers need to keep an open mind and avoid defensiveness when they read peer commentaries or discuss their work with readers. The main responsibility of writers is to understand what their readers are saying and what in their working draft has prompted the reader's response.

By the same token, the main responsibility of readers is to offer the writer an honest account of their experience reading the writer's work. To do this, readers need to understand that they are not playing the role of a teacher (with the authority to instruct, correct, and evaluate that goes along with it) but rather are acting as peers and colleagues. Readers may worry their comments will hurt the writer's feelings or that they are not qualified to provide useful feedback. These feelings are understandable, but it's just as important to understand that empty praise ("Great ideas, your paper really flowed") and vague comments ("Maybe give more examples") don't really help the writer or convey much information about the writer's work. To be a responsible reader, you

don't have to be an expert. Instead, you need to give a clear and accurate explanation of how and why you responded to the writer's work ("I see how you set up the main point in the opening paragraph but it wasn't really clear to me how the ideas in the second paragraph are connected to it").

Finally, writers and readers need to understand their responsibilities when they disagree. Disagreements can take various forms. For example, writers and readers may disagree about the organization of a paper. The writer, say, may believe the introduction or one of the key reasons is particularly effective, but the reader may fail to see the point, feel confused, or just plain disagree. Clearly, their responsibility is to negotiate their differences. They need to keep talking, not so much to decide who is right and who is wrong but rather to understand why they differ and how the working draft might produce such different readings.

The same is true when writers and readers disagree about ideas and arguments. Such disagreements can at times feel dangerous because people's beliefs about important and controversial cultural, social, and political issues can be deeply held—and genuine conflict may be unavoidable. In such instances, it is the reader's responsibility to explain why he or she disagrees with the writer's views without turning points of difference into an attack on the writer. In turn, it is the writer's responsibility to hear what the reader has to say and engage in negotiation. Their joint goal is to make their differences—the conflict of ideas and beliefs—into a productive encounter. The point is not to win the argument or convince the other person (though that may occur) but rather to identify the assumptions that divide them and to consider whether there is any common ground that might connect them.

- describe the function of the paragraphs in your draft,

- analyze the organization of the essay, and

- evaluate the argument.

Each kind of commentary provides different information to help you plan revisions. Sometimes you'll want just one kind of commentary; other times you'll want more than one.

The following sections describe the different kinds of feedback, explain their purposes, and provide guidelines. After each, you'll find an example of the type of peer commentary, in response to Krista's working draft.

- **Describe the function of paragraphs** A good first step in getting feedback on a working draft is to ask readers to describe the function of each paragraph. This type of commentary asks your reader to suspend judgment for a moment and instead to analyze what function each paragraph in your working draft performs—how the paragraphs support the main point and how they are connected to each other. In this way, a reader can give you a blueprint of what you have written. This can help you see how (or whether) the parts fit together. You can use this information to decide how well your paragraphs play the roles you intended for them (or whether they perform some other function). This can also be a good basis for the following two types of commentary, in which readers analyze the organization and evaluate the ideas of a working draft.

Guidelines for Describing the Function of Paragraphs

- What is the writer's main point? Identify the sentence or sentences in the working draft that express the main point. If you don't find such a sentence, write your own version of what you think the main point is.

- Write a statement about each paragraph that explains what function it performs and how it fits into the organization of the working draft. Use words that describe function, such as "describes," "explains," "gives reasons," "proposes," "compares," and so on.

SAMPLE DESCRIPTION OF KRISTA'S DRAFT

Main point: The "only family quality time left is that shared on the TV." Families have substituted fictional for real life.
¶ 1: Tells a story about her family that introduces the main problem.
   Asks a series of questions.
¶ 2: Generalizes from her family's experience to point out they
aren't exceptions.
   Gives two further examples of the problem.
   Explains how families have substituted fictional for real life.
¶ 3: Raises a question about why the problem has developed.
   Offers a theory to explain the problem.

¶ 4: Proposes a solution and describes the outcome.

- **Analyze organization** Sometimes in the struggle to get your ideas down on paper you may lose perspective on how effectively you've organized them. For this reason, it can be helpful to ask someone else to analyze how you've organized and presented your main idea and the supporting evidence.

Again, ask readers to put aside their personal responses to your ideas. Explain that you want them instead to focus on the organization of what you have written. If they have already described the function of paragraphs in the draft, they can use this description as the basis of their analysis. Tell them, in any case, to consider the following questions:

Guidelines for Analyzing Organization

- What is the main point of the draft? Is it clear and easy to find? Does the introduction help readers anticipate where the draft will be going?

- Do the paragraphs that follow develop the main point? Or do they seem to develop some other point? Is it easy to tell how the paragraphs relate to the main point? Or do they need to be connected more explicitly to it?

- Is each of the paragraphs well focused? Or do some of them seem to have several ideas contending for the reader's attention? If a paragraph needs more focus, how could this be achieved?

- Within the supporting paragraphs, are there points that seem to need more development? Are there points that don't belong at all?

- Is the ending or conclusion effective? Does it provide a sense of closure?

Sample Analysis of the Organization of Krista's Draft

I like the opening story because I can see what you are getting at. But I wasn't totally clear on the main point for awhile. At first, it seemed like it was just about your family. Then in ¶ 2 you broadened things to include American families in general. I think you could use a clinching statement at the end of the first ¶ that says what your main point is. The questions left me up in the air.

In ¶ 2, you give two examples that illustrate the problem. I think you could put these in the introduction to show what the problem looks like beyond your family. Then you could expand the final part of ¶ 2 that explains how we're substituting fictional for real families. That's a great point because it analyzes the problem instead of just describing it. The last sentence is long and hard to follow.

¶ 3 explains why people have substituted fictional for real families. I like the theory you propose, but I think you should emphasize the point that on TV everything works out and the characters in the shows do the work for us. This seems like the main idea in the ¶ more than TV took over because it was easy.

Finally, your solution in ¶ 4 makes sense. I wonder whether escaping the family by reading takes away from your main point.

- **Evaluate the argument**

    While the first two kinds of commentary ask readers to set aside their evaluation of your ideas, sometimes you'll really want to know what they think. This is especially likely if you're making an argument or dealing with a controversial topic. For this kind of peer commentary in particular, you'll find it helpful to have more than one reader and to discuss with each reader the comments he or she makes. In this way, you'll have the opportunity to see how your ideas relate to other points of view and to understand the enabling assumptions you and others bring to the issue. This can help you make decisions about how to clarify your own position and handle differing views as you revise.

    If your readers have described the function of paragraphs and analyzed the organization of your working draft, they can use these as a basis to evaluate the argument. In any case, your readers should begin by analyzing the parts of your argument before they evaluate it.

Guidelines for Evaluating the Argument

- Analyze the parts of the argument. What is the claim or main point of the working draft? What supporting evidence is provided? What enabling assumptions connect the evidence to the claim? (For more on claims, evidence, and enabling assumptions, see Chapter 3, pp.   .)

- Do you agree with the essay's main point? Do you accept the essay's assumptions? Explain why.

- If you disagree with the essay's main point or do not accept one or more of the essay's assumptions, what position would you take on the issue yourself? How would you support your position? What assumptions would you make? How would you refute the main point of the essay? What alternate perspectives does the draft need to take into account?

- If you agree with the essay's position, explain why. Do you think the essay makes the best possible argument supporting it? How would you strengthen it? What would you change, add, or omit? Why?

- Discuss the responses with your readers. If you disagree, the idea is not to argue about who is right but to keep talking to understand why your positions differ and what assumptions might have led you to take differing positions.

Sample Evaluations of the Argument in Krista's Draft

Commentary 1

Krista, your main claim seems to be at the end of the second paragraph where you say that the only quality family time is watching TV, and you support this idea by talking about how families have substituted fictional families for real families. The evidence you give is that it's easier that way—the actors do the work for us and everything works out fine. The assumption that connects the evidence to your main claim seems to be that families can't deal with reality any more and so they need a fictional substitute.

I can see what you mean, in that TV shows always have happy endings and wrap up everything in an hour or half hour. But I think there can also be times TV contributes to family life. For example, in my family, watching football together is a big deal, and I have lots of good memories of sitting with my father, grandfather, and brothers watching the 49ers. Maybe this was just a male-bonding ritual but everybody talked and shared. I'm not sure but I feel you're a little too negative.

Commentary 2

[Analysis of the parts of the argument is similar to Response 1.]

I agree totally with your analysis of so-called quality time in front of the tube. What you say is exactly true of my family, and I'm sick of it. My suggestion here is that the evidence you give to back up your main point doesn't seem developed enough. It's all jammed in paragraph 3. To me, the point is not that watching TV is easy but that TV does the work for us in these packaged hour segments. I think that idea would come out more clearly if you developed it more.

The only other thing is the final paragraph. For this kind of assignment, I'm not sure your teacher wants personal advice at the end. Maybe there's some way you could make the ending more analytical by pointing out larger problems or consequences.

REVISING

Writing isn't a precise science with right and wrong answers, and neither is talking about written work in progress. When others comment on your writing, each person will have his or her own response, insights, and suggestions. At times you'll get differing suggestions about what to do with your working draft, as is the case with the two commentaries on Krista's working draft. This doesn't necessarily mean that one reader has seen the true problem in your writing and the other has missed it altogether. By telling you the effect your writing has on each of them, both readers are giving you some information to work with.

The point is to understand why readers have responded to your writing as they did. Try to imagine their point of view and what in your writing might have prompted their response. Peer commentary doesn't provide writers with a set of directions they can carry out mechanically. Rather, writers such as Krista must analyze and interpret their reader's responses.

Notice in Krista's revisions of her working draft how she uses ideas from the two commentaries to plan a revision. First, we present two paragraphs from the working draft with Krista's annotated plans for revision. This is followed by the final draft.

It's 8:00 on a Monday night, and I am sitting at home in my bedroom peacefully reading a novel. Suddenly, the dreaded call comes, "Kris, you been in that room for two hours. Come on out here and be with the family for awhile. Cosby is going to start in five minutes. Don't you want to watch it with us?" Well, actually no. I was content with my book. But Dad and the family saw these hours in front of the television as quality, and I was expected to participate. What I constantly wondered every Monday was why? When did sitting in front of the tube become family time?

cut [margin annotation]

Combine #1 & 2 [margin annotation]

Unfortunately, my family is not the exception but the rule. People are able to remember it is Monday and at 5:00 they can watch the heartwarming merger of blended families on Full House. Yet, without a calendar, they have a difficult time remembering that this particular Monday is their stepmother's or stepfather's birthday and they should get a card or gift on the way home from work or school. They can tell you that the hot couple is headed for divorce on Melrose Place more easily than they can see the status of their own marriage. People may not have noticed, but the only quality family time left is that shared on the TV. In families like mine, television viewing too often means evading each other by replacing real families with fictional ones. ~~The family has left the living room and has gone to live in the TV set in the form of fictional families living fictional lives that the real people would be living if they weren't watching TV.~~

Use it as example [margin annotation]

Add concession that TV can be quality time [margin annotation]

-- Turn next ¶ into 2 ¶s: 1) how TV families do the work for no, 2) how TV families always solve their problems

-- Change ending: explain results instead of giving advice

Krista Gugliemetti
Introduction to Mass Communication
October 2, 1998

Family Life and Television

It's 8:00 on a Monday night, and I am sitting at home in my bedroom peacefully reading a novel. Suddenly, the dreaded call comes, "Kris, you been in that room for two hours. Come on out here and be with the family for awhile. Cosby is going to start in five minutes. Don't you want to watch it with us?" This predictable Monday night call from my Dad reveals one of the ways families use television viewing. It is supposed to be "quality" time, where real families gather together to watch fictional families in sit coms like Cosby. Now it may be true that in some families people actually interact while they are watching television, discussing the meaning of recent news or sharing in the victory or defeat of their favorite team. But in families like mine, television viewing too often means evading each other by replacing real families with fictional ones.

When my family watches television together, what we share is not the experience of actual family members but episodes in the fictional lives of television families. One of the effects of watching these television families is that we use the actors and actresses to do our work for us. The fictional families offer televison viewers vicarious experiences that can substitute for real experience. People, for example, remember it is Thursday and at 5:00 they can watch the heartwarming merger of the blended family Full House. Yet, without a calendar, they have a difficult time remembering that this particular Monday is their stepmother's or stepfather's birthday and they should get a card or gift on the way home from work or school. Television viewers can tell you that the hot couple is headed for divorce on Melrose Place more easily than they can see the status of their own marriage. People may not have noticed, but fiction has become stronger than reality.

Perhaps the greatest attraction to fictional television families is that, unlike real families, they can solve their problems in hour or half hour segments. On TV, blended families always work out, drug addicts are always treated, and no one is ever hurt permanently. It's easy. Just follow the script and everything will be fine. After all, if you're watching TV, you won't fight (except over who has the remote). If you don't fight, no one can get hurt and everyone will be happy. So we let the TV characters do our fighting for us because they always make up on the half hour.

In my family, watching televison families work things out doesn't bring us closer together. Instead of being shared quality time, our experience as television viewers brings about a sense of failure and demoralization. Even though no one says so, we all know we'll never measure up to the television families. Our lives are messier, and our problems seem to persist no matter how much we watch Cosby.

FINAL TOUCHES

Writers collaborate with others throughout the writing process, and that includes working on the final touches. Copy-editors routinely edit the manuscripts of even the most famous writers, making suggestions about words, phrases, sentences, or passages that might be unclear, awkward, or grammatically incorrect. Then, proofreaders carefully review the final draft for any misspellings, missing words, typos, or other flaws.

In school writing, teachers sometimes consider such collaborative work editing and proofreading as unwarranted assistance from other students. If your teacher permits it, collaboration can be quite useful in applying the final touches to your work.

• **Directions for editing** Ask the person editing your manuscript to look for any words, phrases, sentences, or passages that need to be changed. You can do this one of two ways: The person can simply underline or circle problems, write a brief note of explanation in the margin when necessary, and let you make the changes. Or the person can go ahead and make tentative changes for you to consider. Your teacher will let you know which method to follow.

Kristal,
"you" seems
too informal
for an
academic
paper.
:)

Sample Editing
¶ 3

It's easy. Just follow the script and everything will be fine. After all, if you're watching TV, you won't fight (except over who has the remote). If you don't fight, no one can get hurt and everyone will be happy. So we let the TV characters do our fighting for us because they always make up on the half hour.

- **Directions for proofreading** This is simple. The person proofreading your final copy can underline or circle grammatical errors, usage problems, typos, and misspellings and let you make the final corrections. Or the person can supply the corrections. Again, it's up to your teacher which method to follow.

TALKING TO TEACHERS

Much of what has been said here about how writers and readers can collaborate also applies to talking about your writing with teachers. There may be times, for example, when you have trouble figuring out a writing assignment. You may be confused about the suggestions you've received on peer commentaries, or you may not fully understand the comments a teacher has written on a paper. In situations such as these, you might request a conference with your teacher.

Talking about writing with teachers can be most productive if you prepare ahead of time. If you want to discuss a writing assignment, re-read the directions carefully and prepare questions about what isn't clear to you about the assignment. If you want to talk about the feedback you've gotten on peer commentaries, re-read the commentaries and bring them with you to the conference. If you want to talk about a paper that has already been graded, make sure you read it over carefully, paying particular attention to the teacher's comments.

In any case, have realistic expectations about what can happen in the conference. Don't expect your teacher to change your grade or to give you a formula for completing the assignment. The point of the conference is for you to understand what your teacher is looking for in a piece of writing.

GOING TO THE WRITING CENTER

One of the best places to talk about writing is a writing center, where you can meet and discuss your writing with people who are interested in the writing process and in how students develop as writers. Find out if your college has a writing center. It will be listed in the campus directory, and your writing teacher will know about its hours and procedures.

Sometimes students think only those with serious writing problems go to the writing center, but this is not the case. Students of all abilities can benefit from talking to writing tutors. Whether the people who staff the writing center at your college are undergraduates, graduate students, or professional tutors, they are experienced writers who like to talk about writing.

If your campus has a writing center, make an appointment to interview one of the tutors. Ask what kinds of services the center provides and what insights into college writing the tutor can offer. Even better, take a writing assignment you're working on or a paper that's already been graded to serve as the basis for a conversation with the tutor.

WRITING INVENTORY: Analyzing a Writing Project

Collaborating on an individual writing project, as you have seen in this chapter, involves alternating between working together (by getting feedback from others) and working alone (making sense of the feedback and using it to plan, draft, and revise). Consider a writing project you have completed recently that included feedback and commentary from others. Explain how working with others influenced the direction of your writing and the final form your writing took. How did you make use of the feedback and commentary you received? If you disagreed with what others said or felt confused by or uncertain about their responses, what did you do?

CHAPTER
THIRTEEN

WORKING TOGETHER:
Collaborative Writing Projects

Working on collaborative writing projects differs in important respects from working with others on individual writing projects. In the case of your own writing projects, the final result belongs to you. You are accountable for it, and you get the bulk of the credit, even though the writing reflects the input of others. Collaborative writing, on the other hand, aims for a collective outcome, produced jointly by a team of people, with shared responsibility for the results.

Here are examples of how people in various settings work together in collaborative writing projects.

- A group of nineteen automotive engineers is designing a prototype for a new car model. The engineers are divided into a number of working groups—engine design, emissions control, aerodynamics and body design, suspension, electrical system, interior design and safety features—with a project manager to coordinate the various groups. They meet regularly to discuss ongoing design plans and to ensure that each group's work fits with the other groups'. At these meetings, the leader of each working group reports orally and submits written progress reports to the project manager. As the work nears its completion, each group drafts a section of what will be the final report, to take to the company's executives for approval to build an actual prototype. The project manager edits the various sections and writes an introduction and an executive summary, so that the end result is a single, coherent document.

- Homeowners from a neighborhood meet to form a citizens' group opposing a plan to build a gambling casino nearby. Theirs is a quiet residential area, and they want to keep it that way. The streets are safe, there is little traffic, and their children can play outside. They know they're in for a tough fight, especially since the real estate firms and developers who are pushing the plan have political clout. They decide to write a petititon to take door to door to show widespread opposition to the casino. The group works together composing the petition, with many people suggesting the appeal and wording they should use. When everyone is satisfied with the petition, one group member volunteers to format it on her computer and make copies for all to circulate.

- A group of three students is working together on a research project in an environmental studies course. Their task is to create a map of the sidewalk shade trees the city has planted and maintained in the downtown area over the years and to make recommendations about where new trees should be planted. After they have surveyed the downtown, sketched a preliminary map, and made tentative decisions about where new trees should go, they decide that one group member should write a working draft of their findings. Once the draft is finished, the group meets to consider what revisions are needed to produce a final report. The writer of the working draft makes these changes, while the other two members create the map.

As you can see, when individuals are working together on collaborative writing projects, they will manage the writing task in various ways, depending on the nature of the task and the decisions the group makes. Sometimes, as in the case of the automotive engineers, individuals will each write separate sections which are then compiled into a single document and edited for uniformity of style. Or, as in the case of the neighborhood citizens group, they may work together so closely in planning, drafting, and revising a document that it becomes impossible to distinguish one person's work from another's. In still other cases, such as that of the student group in the environmental studies course, the group will work together planning and doing research, one individual will do the drafting, and then the group will work together again to plan revisions.

There isn't a single best way to work on collaborative writing projects. Experienced writers learn when it makes sense to produce a collaboratively written document and which writing strategy the situation seems to call for.

Collaborative writing tasks are often those that are complex, with many separate parts (such as the design work of the automotive engineers) or that require extensive time and effort (such as the group research project in the environmental studies course). But in other cases, collaboration is appropriate because the writing that results is meant to speak for a group of people rather than an individual (as in the case of the neighborhood citizens group).

While these examples of collaborative writing projects differ in many respects, each of them reveals one of the most important benefits of working together—namely that the final written product is based on the collective judgment of a group of people. When a group works well together, the resulting energy and involvement can lead to writing that goes beyond what anyone in the group could have produced alone.

Successful collaborative writing depends on organization, meetings, and constant communication. This chapter looks at how groups can produce effective collaborative writing. The first section offers some general guidelines about working in groups. The second section considers how groups can manage a collaborative writing project from start to finish. The final section presents further writing suggestions for groups.

WORKING TOGETHER: What Makes Groups Work?

Form a group with three or four other students. Each student describes an experience in which he or she worked together with other people. The experience can be positive or negative, and it need not involve writing. After everyone has described an experience, try to reach a consensus, even if you agree to disagree, about what makes group work successful or unsuccessful.

GUIDELINES FOR COLLABORATING IN GROUPS

Any group of people working together on a project will face certain issues, and a group collaborating on a writing project is no exception. The following guidelines are meant to keep a group running smoothly and to forestall some common problems.

- **Recognize that group members need to get acquainted and that groups take time to form**

  People entering new groups sometimes make snap judgments without getting to know the other people or giving the group time to form and develop. Initial impressions are rarely reliable indicators of how a group will be. Like individuals, groups have life histories, and one of the most awkward and difficult moments is getting started. Group members may be nervous, defensive, or overly assertive. It takes some time for people to get to know one another and to develop a sense of connectedness to the group.

- **Clarify group purposes and individual roles**

  Much of people's initial discomfort and anxiety has to do with their uncertainty about what the purpose of the group is and what their role in the group will be. Group members need to define their collective task and develop a plan to do it. This way, members will know what to expect and how the group will operate.

- **Recognize that members bring different styles to the group**

  As you have seen in the Introduction to Part 3, individual styles of composing can vary considerably. The same is true of individuals' styles of working in groups. For example, individuals differ in the way they approach problems. Some people like to spend a lot of time formulating problems, exploring the complexities, contradictions, and nuances of a situation. Others want to define problems quickly and then spend their time figuring out how to solve them. By the same token, people have different styles of interacting in groups. Some people like to develop their ideas by talking, while others prefer to decide what they think before speaking. So successful groups learn to incorporate the strengths of all these styles, making sure that even the most reticent members participate.

- **Recognize that you may not play the same role in every group**

  In some instances, you may be the group leader, but in other instances the role you'll need to play is that of the mediator, helping members negotiate their differences, or the critic, questioning the others' ideas, or the time keeper, prompting the group to stick to deadlines. You may play different roles in the same group from meeting to meeting or even within a meeting. For a group to be successful, members must be willing and able to respond flexibly to the work at hand.

- **Monitor group progress and reassess goals and procedures**

    It's helpful to step back periodically to take stock of what has been accomplished and what remains to be done. Groups also need to look at their own internal workings, to see if the procedures they have set up are effective and if everyone is participating.

- **Quickly address problems in group dynamics**

    Problems arise in group work. Some members may dominate and talk too much. Others may withdraw and not contribute. Still others may fail to carry out assigned tasks. If a group avoids confronting these problems, the problems will only get worse. Remember, the point of raising a problem is not to blame individuals but to promote an understanding about what's expected of each person and what the group can do to encourage everyone's participation.

- **Encourage differences of opinion**

    One of the things that makes groups productive is the different perspectives individual members bring to group work. In fact, groups of like-minded people who share basic assumptions often are not as creative as groups where there are differences among members. At the same time, group members may feel that there are ideas or feelings they can't bring up in the group because to do so would threaten group harmony. This feeling is understandable. Sometimes it's difficult to take a position that diverges from what other members of the group think and believe. But groups are not forms of social organization to enforce conformity. They are working bodies that need to consider all the available options and points of view. For this reason, groups need to encourage the discussion of differences and to look at conflicting viewpoints.

HOW TO WORK TOGETHER ON COLLABORATIVE WRITING PROJECTS

Because collaborative writing differs from individual writing, it is worth looking at each step involved in working on a joint project.

ORGANIZING THE GROUP

One of the keys to collaborative writing is to get off to a good start. You'll need to decide on the size of the group, its composition, and what to do at your first meeting.

- **Group Size**

For many collaborative writing projects in college classes, a group of three or four is often the best size. Smaller size—only two students—doesn't offer the group as many resources, and anything larger than four can create problems in managing the work with so many involved.

Of course, there can be exceptions. For example, your teacher may decide to do a collaborative project involving the entire class—say, developing a home page for the class or a web site devoted to a particular topic with everyone's participation.

- **Group Composition**

Some teachers like to put groups together themselves. Others like to give students input into the group they will be in. If the teacher is going to put the groups together, it's can be a good idea to ask each student if there is someone in class he or she particularly wants to work with or particularly wants to avoid working with. It can help too to take schedules into account and match students who have common times they can meet.

- **The First Meeting**

The first meeting should focus on the basics:

1. Exchange phone numbers, e-mail addresses, campus box numbers, and the best times to reach group members.
2. If possible, establish a listserv of group members on the campus network.
3. Identify best times for meetings.
4. Agree on some basic procedures for running meetings. For example, do you want to have a group coordinator lead meetings? If so, will one person serve throughout the project or will you rotate that position? How do you plan to keep records of meetings? Will you have a recorder for the project or rotate? How long will each meeting last? Who is responsible for developing the agenda?

- **Division of Labor or Integrated Team?**

Some groups approach collaborative projects by developing a division of labor that assigns particular tasks to group members who complete them individually and then bring the results back to the group. This has been the traditional model for collaborative work in business, industry, and government. It is an efficient method of work, especially when groups are composed of highly skilled members. Its limitations are that weak group members can affect the quality of the overall work and that group members may lose sight of the overall project because they are so caught up in their own specialized work.

More recently, groups have begun to explore a more integrated approach in which group members all work together through each stage of the project. An integrated team approach involves members more fully in the work and helps them maintain an overall view of the project's goals and progress. But it also takes more time—more time must be devoted to meetings and, often, devoted to developing good working relations among members.

These two models of group work are not mutually exclusive. In fact many groups function along integrated team lines when they are planning and reviewing work but also farm out particular tasks to individuals or sub-groups. The point is you need to discuss and develop some basic guidelines on group functioning.

ORGANIZING THE PROJECT: The Proposal

The first task is to decide what the project is and what its goals are. One of the best ways to do this is to write a proposal. Your teacher is the logical audience for your proposal. If you are doing a project with an on- or off-campus group, they should receive your proposal as well.

Proposals should include:

- **A statement of purpose**

Define the topic or issue you are working on. Explain why it is important or significant. What have others said about it? State what you plan to do and explain why.

- **A description of methods**

Explain how you plan to go about the project. What research will you need to do? How will you do it?

- **A plan for managing the work**

Explain what roles group members will play and what skills they bring to the task.

- **A task breakdown chart**

A task breakdown (or Gantt) chart shows the tasks involved and their scheduling. Such as chart is especially useful for planning collaborative projects because it shows how tasks relate to each other.

TASK BREAKDOWN CHART

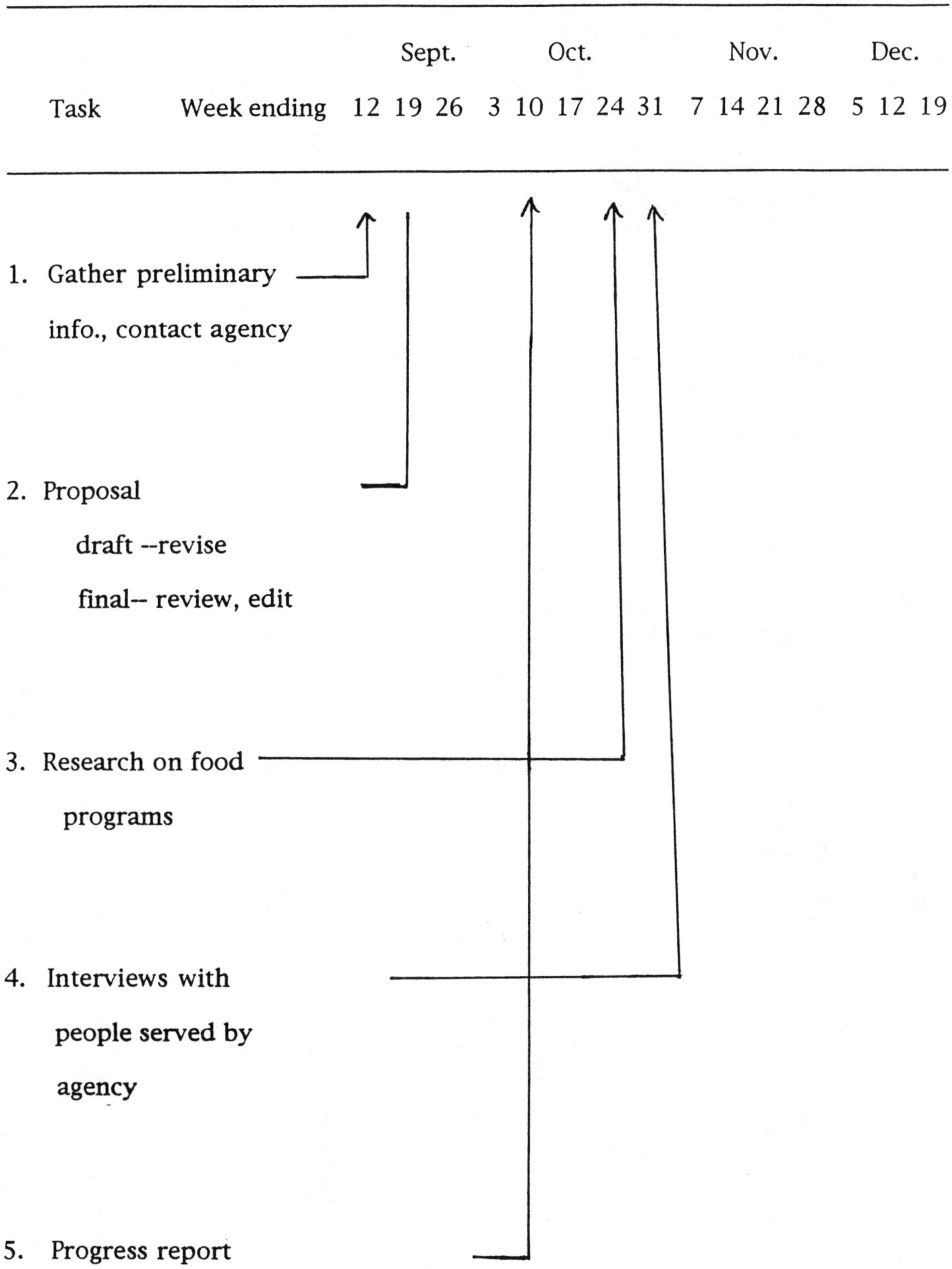

Task	Week ending	Sept.			Oct.					Nov.				Dec.		
		12	19	26	3	10	17	24	31	7	14	21	28	5	12	19

1. Gather preliminary

   info., contact agency

2. Proposal

   draft --revise

   final-- review, edit

3. Research on food

   programs

4. Interviews with

   people served by

   agency

5. Progress report

		Sept.			Oct.				Nov.			Dec.		
Task	Week ending	12	19	26	3	10	17	24	31	7	14	21	28	5	12	19

6. Brochure design

   get photos

   graphics

7. Write text

8. Progress report

9. Print brochure

   take to agency

   feedback

   revision

10. Final version

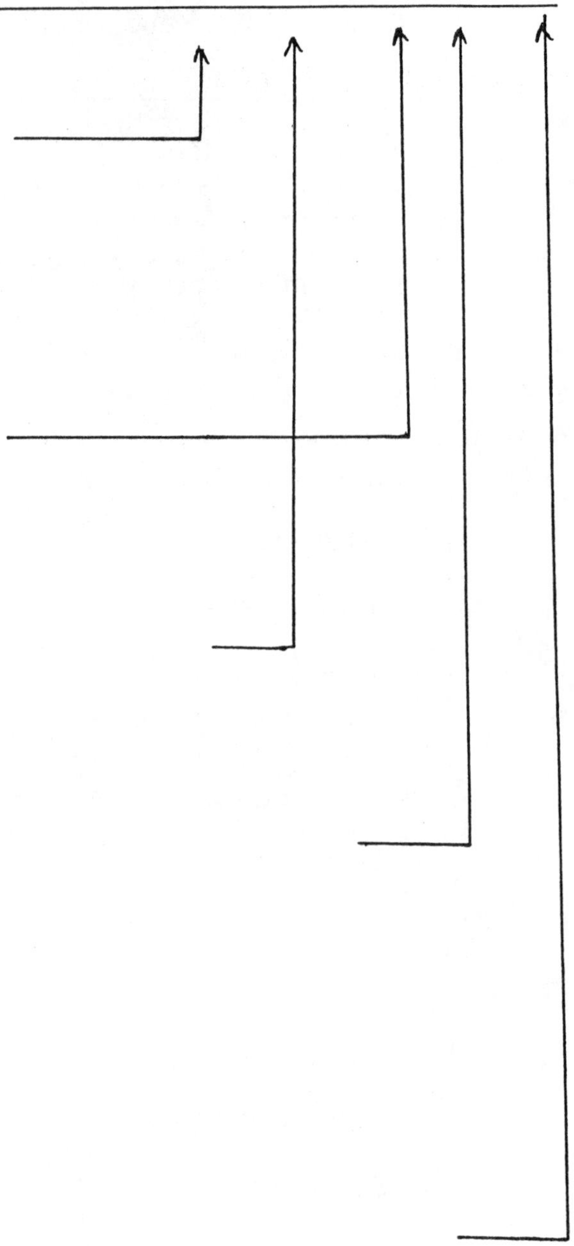

STAYING ON TRACK

Once the group is up and running, it will need to figure out how to stay on track—how to keep the work moving ahead and deal effectively with problems as they arise.

Using the calendar on your task breakdown chart is one way to stay oriented. Two other ways are to run productive meetings and write interim progress reports.

PRODUCTIVE MEETINGS

Group meetings are productive when they get work done, address issues and conflicts, and keep group members accountable. Although failing to meet can cause group members to feel disconnected, meeting when there is no reason to meet can be just as demoralizing. For meetings to be productive, there must be a real agenda and work that needs to be done. One way to set an agenda is to agree at the end of each meeting what will be accomplished before the next meeting and by whom. That way the agenda grows out of the progress of the project, and group members are kept accountable. If problems in group functioning come up, they need to be addressed immediately, in the next meeting.

PROGRESS REPORTS

Progress reports are another way to enhance the group members' accountability—both to each other and to their teacher. They serve to chart the development of a project at regular intervals. You will want to include one or two progress reports on your task breakdown chart. These reports should follow completion of major parts of the project. Include in your reports the following:

- Tasks completed: describe with details what you have done.

- Tasks in progress: be specific about what you are doing and give completion dates.

- Tasks scheduled: describe briefly tasks you haven't yet started, including any not originally on the task breakdown chart.

- Issues, problems, obstacles: explain how these emerged and how your group is dealing with them.

In some cases, teachers may ask groups for oral as well as written progress reports. This is a good way for everyone in class to see what the other groups are doing.

CONFIDENTIAL SELF-EVALUATION

In addition to group progress reports, some teachers also like to ask students individually to assess how their group has been functioning and what their role in it has been. These self-evaluations are confidential and directed only to the teacher. They can be useful in helping the teacher anticipate when groups are having difficulties or personality problems. They are also useful to individual students because they offer an occasion to reflect on the experience of group work and what it means to them as writers, learners, and persons.

DRAFTING, REVISING, AND EDITING

One thing that often surprises students working in groups for the first time is that they have already started to draft their document—from the moment they began to put their proposal together.

For many writing tasks, the final document will draw on and expand what is in the proposal—explaining why the issue or problem is important, what others have said about it, what the group has learned about it, and what recommendations the group has to make.

But whatever the writing task happens to be, groups need to make decisions about how to handle drafting, revising, and editing collaboratively written documents. Here are some possible approaches. Your group will need to decide which best suits your purposes.

- The group plans and outlines the document together. Members draft individual sections. The group compiles the sections and revises together.

- The group plans and outlines the document together. One person writes a draft. The group revises together.

- The group plans and outlines the document together. Members draft individual sections. One person compiles the sections and revises the document.

With any of these approaches, a final editing needs to be done, by an individual or by the group. However you decide to organize drafting, revising, and editing, make sure everyone contributes to the final document. The draft does not become final until everyone has signed off on it.

Collaborative drafting and revising can raise sensitive issues about individual group members' writing styles and abilities. Some people can be protective of their writing and defensive when it is criticized or revised. Be aware of this. If you think other group members either are trying to impose their own style or are feeling beat up on, bring these matters to everyone's attention and try to sort them out before you continue on the writing task.

GIVING CREDIT

Some teachers ask collaborative writing groups to preface their final document with an acknowledgments page that explains who should get credit for what in the overall project. You should also acknowledge ayone outside your group who helped you on the project.

FINAL PRESENTATION

The final presentation of a collaborative project takes place when the document reaches its intended destination—whether the teacher's desk, the World Wide Web, a politician or government official's office, or a community organization. You may want to schedule an oral presentation to go along with the delivery of the document.

ETHICS OF WRITING

Giving credit and taking responsibility

One of a writer's ethical obligations is to acknowledge collaborators. How this is done varies. In the case of single-authored works, writers will often acknowledge their debt to people who helped with ideas and discussion and who read and commented on drafts. If you look at the preface or acknowledgments of nonfiction books, you'll see that writers typically thank friends, colleagues, editors, and family for their input and support. They will then also take responsibility, noting that they alone are responsible for the views expressed and for any errors.

In collaborative writing, all coauthors should get credit and take responsibility. This is not always as simple as it sounds. People participate to different extents, and sometimes it can be difficult to determine just who should be included among the coauthors. A number of ethical controversies have arisen, especially in the area of science research. For example, many have argued that Rosalind Franklin's contributions entitled her to be a coauthor with James Watson and Francis Crick on their Nobel Prize-winning work on the structure of DNA but that she was excluded because she was a woman.

ON-LINE COLLABORATION

The new electronic communication technologies have created new ways for groups to work together, even when their members are far apart. It's no longer necessary to meet face-to-face to have the kind of exchange that gives a joint project energy and creativity. With the nearly instantaneous transmission of documents, commentary, and conversation, collaborators can now stay in touch, confer, argue, and refine their ideas with an immediacy that was unimaginable in the past.

Of course, group members don't need to be half-way around the world from each other to take advantage of the new technologies. Here are some good ways to use these new technologies in collaborative writing projects.

- **Stay in touch with group members**

  Ongoing communication among group members is one of the keys to successful group work. Setting up a listserv on e-mail can help members to stay in touch in and out of class.

- **Consult with people everywhere**

  Through e-mail, newsgroups, and web sites your group can contact a wide range of people who are knowledgeable about your topic—to ask questions, get information, and try out ideas. On-line communication can be much quicker and simpler than letters or phone calls.

- **Share working drafts**

  To put together a successful collaboratively written document, coauthors need easy access to the working drafts. Drafts can be shared in ways that range from downloading files on e-mail to state-of-the-art hypertext authoring systems.

- **Conference on drafts**

  On-line conferences make it easy for all group members to have input on drafts. New methods include "real time" synchronous conferences facilitated by networking software.

IDENTIFYING THE CALL TO WRITE: Types of Projects

When is the call to write best answered by collaborative writing? As already indicated, collaborative writing is most appropriate for complex projects, for example, projects that require developing an initial proposal, doing research of various kinds, analyzing the results of this research, designing a document, and producing text and graphics. The amount and variety of work needed for such projects is better handled by a group than by one person working alone. Partly for this reason, collaborative writing is also especially appropriate to projects that involve significant community issues and require working closely with one or more community groups.

Below you'll find listings of possible topics for collaborative writing projects. The topics are organized by genre, or writing type (see Part 2 for discussions of genres). These projects re intended to be more than simply multiauthor versions of conventional research papers. They are intended to be the sorts of projects collaborative writing is most conducive to—projects in which the call to write grows out of the needs of people in our society and out of issues that touch of people's lives.

How these topics are used is up to you and your teacher. You may want to use them, or similar topics that you think of, as the basis for an actual project that you undertake this term. Or you might just read them to get a better sense of how to identify a call to write that can be answered collaboratively. For in collaborative writing, as in any writing, the first step is to identify a call to write.

REPORTS AND RECOMMENDATIONS

To do this type of project, a group identifies an issue that is controversial or that needs to be raised, researches the issue (for example, at the library and through surveys and interviews), prepares a report, and makes recommendations.

Local Issues

- Should the city or town impose a curfew on those under 18?

- Should a state permit gambling casinos?

- What kind of property tax reform is called for?

- How adequate are local services, such as shelters for the homeless and for battered women, food and nutrition programs, and adult literacy and English as a Second Language classes? (You might want to look at just one of these categories.)

School Issues

- What kind of bilingual program, if any, hould the local school system have?

- Should the schools have a dress code?

- What kind of sex education is appropriate at each level?

- Should the schools dismantle tracking and replace it with multi-ability classrooms?

Campus Issues

- How can the campus food service be improved?

- What steps should be taken to deal with underage and excessive drinking?

- Should fraternities and sororities be abolished?

- How can students' first-year experience be improved?

PROPOSALS FOR GRANT FUNDING

Working with a community, student, or other organization, the group identifies a need the organization has, locates and contacts possible funding sources, develops a budget, and writes and submits a grant proposal on behalf of the organization.

Community Organizations

- Proposal to fund a photography class for adolescents at a community center

- Proposal to fund a midnight basketball league

- Proposal to fund a community garden using vacant lots owned by the city

- Proposal to fund job preparation workshops for recent immigrants

Student Organizations

- Proposal to fund a speaker's series

- Proposal to fund a film series

- Proposal to fund AIDS awareness workshops and counseling

- Proposal to fund community service projects

INFORMATIVE WRITING

Working with a community organization, social service agency, health care facility, or other organization, the group researches a topic and designs and produces one or more pieces of informative writing.

Community Organizations

- Brochure on domestic violence and what battered women can do

- Leaflet on how to compost

- Series of bilingual flyers on furniture and clothing banks, and on adult literacy, English as a Second Language, and GED classes

- Poster advertising the services of a local community center

Social Service Agencies

- Brochure on how recent immigrants can qualify for green cards, permanent resident, and citizenship status

- Brochure on the availability of food programs

- Bilingual flyers on emergency heat and rent programs

- Poster on child care options

Health Care Facilities

- Posters advertising immunization programs

- Brochure on sexually transmitted diseases

- Flyers advertising programs on alcohol abuse

- Brochures on risks of and ways of dealing with radon, asbesto, lead, and/or other substances that may occur in the home

OTHER POSSIBILITIES

The possibilities are broad—both for the content of the writing and for its form. Here are several more suggestions:

- Prepare a briefing on a current issue (such as NAFTA, corporate downsizing, tax reform proposals, U.S. Cuban policy) for a politician, government official, or legislative body.

- Develop a multimedia educational exhibit on a current topic (e.g., gene therapy, the aftermath of the breakup of the Soviet Union, new directions in telecommunications) for a junior high class.

- Design a museum exhibit with captions and a leaflet.

- Design a guide to your campus and local community for first-year students.

- Design a web site on a topic or issue you are interested in.

- Develop a MOO environment with opportunities for role playing.

WRITING INVENTORY: Analyzing Collaborative Writing

Consider a collaborative writing task you have completed. Explain why the particular situation seemed to call for a collaboratively written document instead of an individually written one. How did your group go about organizing and managing the writing task? What role or roles did you play in the group? What problems or issues did you confront and how did you handle them? What was the result of the group's work? From your own perspective, what do you see as the main differences between collaborative and individual writing? What do you see as the benefits and limits of each?

CHAPTER
FOURTEEN

THE WRITER'S TOOLS:

Word Processing and Electronic Communication

We are living in a transitional time. Personal computers, word processing, document design programs, and desk top publishing have changed the way writers produce printed texts. Increased access to the Internet and the World Wide Web—the so-called "information superhighway"—though distributed mainly among privileged groups in the wealthy nations, has made the term "cyberspace" a household word and in some cases appears to be on the verge of replacing printed texts with electronic communication.

For many writers, these are changes that need to be reckoned with. If writers once composed their manuscripts long-hand, only gradually replacing quill and ink first with fountain pens and then with ball-point pens, writers have now abandoned their typewriters as composing has become a matter of word processing. For some writers, computers simply offer a better way to do the same old work. For others, however, the new technologies have changed the way they imagine writing.

Researchers, for example, no longer go to the card catalogue in the library but now search a library's holdings on-line and browse the Internet. For many people, the rapid transmission of an e-mail or fax message seems vastly preferable to the slower "snail mail." Both corporate executives and environmentalists talk enthusiastically about the benefits of the "paperless" office. Desktop publishing enables writers to do the kind of work that was once the business of graphic designers in print shops. The Internet and World Wide Web provide interactive public forums that make possible a kind of participation and feedback that is difficult to achieve with printed texts. And hypertext and multi-media present new ways of designing documents that organize data, create links to other sources, and incorporate sound, graphics, and video.

For these reasons, it is fair to assume that writing increasingly will involve some familiarity with word processing and the new forms of electronic communication. Of course, individuals have different reactions to the new writing technologies. Some are intimidated, while others are enthusiatic users. You may have considerable knowledge and experience, or you may have little or none.

Whatever the case may be, a point to keep in mind is that the new writing technologies are tools for you to use, just as skilled craftspeople use the tools of their trade. The more you know about them, the more effectively you'll be able to use them. And the more you learn about these new technologies, the more you'll understand their impact on contemporary life—and the ongoing debates about regulating the Internet, access to information, and intellectual property rights.

The writing classroom can be an ideal setting in which to investigate and experiment with the new forms of electronic communication. Throughout this textbook are opportunities to go on-line and explore the Internet and the World Wide Web. But even if the new technologies are not a focus of your course, you might want to learn more by going to your campus computer center and by talking to students who have knowledge and experience.

In this chapter, we look first at how writers use word processing and then at how they use the new forms of electronic communication.

WORD PROCESSING

There can be little question that word processing has some very real benefits for writers. Time permitting, writers can now revise extensively without having to re-type an entire document. They can add, delete, and shift material with ease.

Some word processing programs offer split-screens or windows so that writers can look at two files or two sections of text at the same time. This enables them to have notes or other material available on the screen as they are composing. Other programs are designed so teachers or peer readers can write running comments in the margin to give the writer feedback and suggestions.

In addition, most word processing programs make available spell checkers, which compare each word in a text to an on-line dictionary; various kinds of style checkers, which can locate passive constructions, wordy phrases, and cliches and can indicate the number of words in a text, average sentence length, and readability level; and an on-line thesaurus, which lists alternative word choices.

Another benefit of word processing is that it can make collaborative writing easier, as writers can transmit files electronically. This can help you to work more effectively with other students on group writing projects, especially when group members have conflicting schedules. And it enables people from different locations to work together without having to send manuscripts through the mail.

As you have already seen, writers vary in the way they incorporate word processing into their writing process. Some writers do all their work on the screen—planning, drafting, revising, and editing. Others, however, find that the size of the computer screen doesn't allow them to view enough text, and so they like to work on hard copy where they can more easily shuffle pages back and forth.

Whatever use you decide to make of word processing, you might find the following suggestions to be helpful:

- **Label and organize your computer files** It's amazing how often even the most experienced writers can't find a particular document they've worked on. "I know it's somewhere in there," people say, "but I just don't remember which file I put it in." To avoid the time-consuming task of having to open and scroll through file after file, develop your own system of labeling and organizing your files. Make sure the names you give to individual files will call to mind what you have in them. "Notes 1" or "Writing 2" isn't a good name because it doesn't tell you enough. "Ozone pollution.notes" and "Greenhouse effect.draft 2" are much better. Depending on the word processing program you use, you may be limited to the number of letters you can use for file names, so develop a system accordingly.

  In addition, many word processing programs allow writers to organize their files in folders. You might, for example, set up separate folders for each of your courses or use one folder for all the files you've produced for a research project. You could have another file for personal correspondence or club activities. The point is to develop a system that works for you. And it makes sense to review your files and folders periodically, to throw out files you no longer want and to reorganize if necessary.

- **Save your work frequently** One great fear many writers have is that the computer will "eat" their documents—that a power failure, technical glitch, or wrong command will cause their writing to disappear. This is a realistic fear, and the best way to deal with it is to save your work frequently. Don't wait until the end of a work session to save. Saving every fifteen minutes or so is a sensible practice. Some word processing programs have a function you can set to come on the screen at regular intervals and ask whether you want to save.

- **Back up your work** Computers basically have three options for saving files. You can store them on hard drive, on a disk, or over a network to a file server. The best practice is to store files in two different places. This gives you an added measure of protection should something malfunction in your computer, your disk get damaged, or the network or file server go down. The one qualification here concerns the storage size of your hard drive. It may be too small to contain all the files you have. A crowded hard drive too can slow down your computer's response time. In these cases, back up your work on a second disk. If your file has graphics, sound, or video, it will probably not fit on a disk. Large files need to be stored on the hard drive, on a file server, or on other removable storage media, such as a zip disk or magneto-optical disk.

- **Make a hard copy of work you want to protect** As a final protective measure, make hard copies of your work, if possible. If you are concerned about wasting paper, there are some ways to minimize the amount of paper you use when you make hard copies. You might, for example, print back up copies single-spaced instead of double, thereby reducing the amount of paper you use by half. Or, you can obtain paper that has already been used and print on the blank side.

- **Develop revision strategies** Since word processing makes it so easy to change written text, there is the danger of losing material. Once you delete a sentence, paragraph, or passage, it's gone, and if you decide later that you want to use material you have deleted, then you've got a problem. One way to deal with this, besides making hard copies of each draft, is to create a sequence of drafts on the computer. When you begin a revision session, simply create a new file to work in. You can do this in a number of ways, depending on your word processing program. If you have a "save as" function, use it to create a new file. Or you can mark your original file and use the "copy" function to transfer it into a new file. Either method allows you to keep the original in one file and have a new one to work on. Make sure, of course, that you label the files accurately so you know which draft is which.

- **Learn and use your tools** Part of learning to use a word processing program is discovering what the program can do for you as a writer. Spend some time exploring the program you're using to see what it enables you to do. Use the spell checker (but remember it can't decide whether the word you want is "their" or "there," "its" or "it's," or "affect" or "effect"). If your program has a style checker, see what information it can provide you about sentence length, readability level, and so on. Use your on-line thesaurus as you would a print version: to consider word choices.

ELECTRONIC COMMUNICATION

The Internet has changed the way people with access to this new medium of reading and writing communicate. Once you're on-line, some of the things you can do are

- stay in touch with others via email

- gather information for personal purposes
- conduct research for academic projects
- participate in discussion with like-minded people on issues that concern you
- explore the art of Web site design
- entertain yourself
- shop

In this section, we look at some of the most common uses of the Internet.

- **E-mail** If you've been using e-mail, you already know its benefits. If you haven't, it's probably time to learn (assuming you have access to the Internet). E-mail (short for electronic mail) sends messages through the Internet, allowing people to communicate almost instantaneously with other network users, whether they are at the same college or halfway around the world. Such on-line correspondence is rapidly replacing the traditional letter for many personal and public purposes.

Most people who use e-mail regularly have a mail-reader software program that makes it easy to read and compose e-mail and to organize and store messages. Your campus computer center can tell you how to establish an account so that you can use e-mail and what mail readers are available.

The style of writing used in e-mail is often quite informal compared to printed texts, with writers abbreviating more and worrying less about grammar and spelling. People like to chat on e-mail, and users have developed emoticons to signify tone of voice and abbreviations (see Fig. 1). Some personalize their e-mail messages with a distinctive signature line (see Fig. 2). A good rule of thumb for using e-mail is to remember what your purpose is and who your reader will be. If you are asking your instructor to clarify

:-)	smile	IMHO	in my humble opinion
:-(	frown	VBG	very big grin
;-)	wink	LOL	laughing out loud
;-	Ptongue sticking out	TTL	talk to you later
8 -)	googly eyes	BRB	be right back

Fig. 1 Common email emoticons and abbreviations

Dolores Fuentes Phone: (602) 965-2676
Box 143
Arizona State University
Tempe, AZ 85287

"When other races have given up their tongue we've kept ours."
—Gloria Anzaldua

Fig. 2 Personalized signature line

a writing assignment or interviewing an expert on a research project be business-like and to the point. With friends, of course, you can write more informally.

Most mail-reader programs enable you to respond directly to all or part of a message by reproducing the original on the screen marked with >. Notice how the following exchange incorporates the reader's response into the text of the writer's original message. The first writer begins with her ideas for a group project, and the reader/
second writer offers commentary and suggestions.

>I've been thinking about our group project on
>document design and maybe we should do a poster or
>brochure on AIDS.

I'd rather do a brochure because we can use my Pagemaker program and scan in illustrations if we need to. I'm not so sure about how to make a high quality poster.

>We could pitch it to high school kids and explain risky
>behaviors and prevention methods like using condoms.

OK, good idea. One thing we'll need to decide is whether the brochure is pitched to girls, boys, or both. The approach would probably differ some, depending.

>And we could make a prototype and get some feedback
>from high school kids before we do the final version.

Right! I can ask my sister to get some kids from her school together. I'm sure they'd help us with a pilot version.

• Listserv discussions

A listserv turns any number of e-mail addresses into a mailing list and sends copies of posted messages to everyone on the list. Listservs consist of people who are interested in a particular topic and want to share information and participate in ongoing discussions with others. Individuals generally subscribe to listservs because they are serious about the topic and have chosen for personal or professional reasons to keep up on current issues. For this reason, listservs offer a good way to become knowledgeable about a topic and to learn how people who are serious and committed think about it.

You can find thousands of listservs on a wide range of topics by going to "http://tile.net/lists" on the World Wide Web. Notice how the keyword "basketball" identified five listservs on the topic (Fig. 3) and how the reference to "Big 10 Women's Basketball" (Fig. 4) gives information on how to join the listserv. If you subscribe, you'll receive all the messages sent to the group, and any messages you send to the listserv address will in turn be sent to everyone on the list.

Figure 4

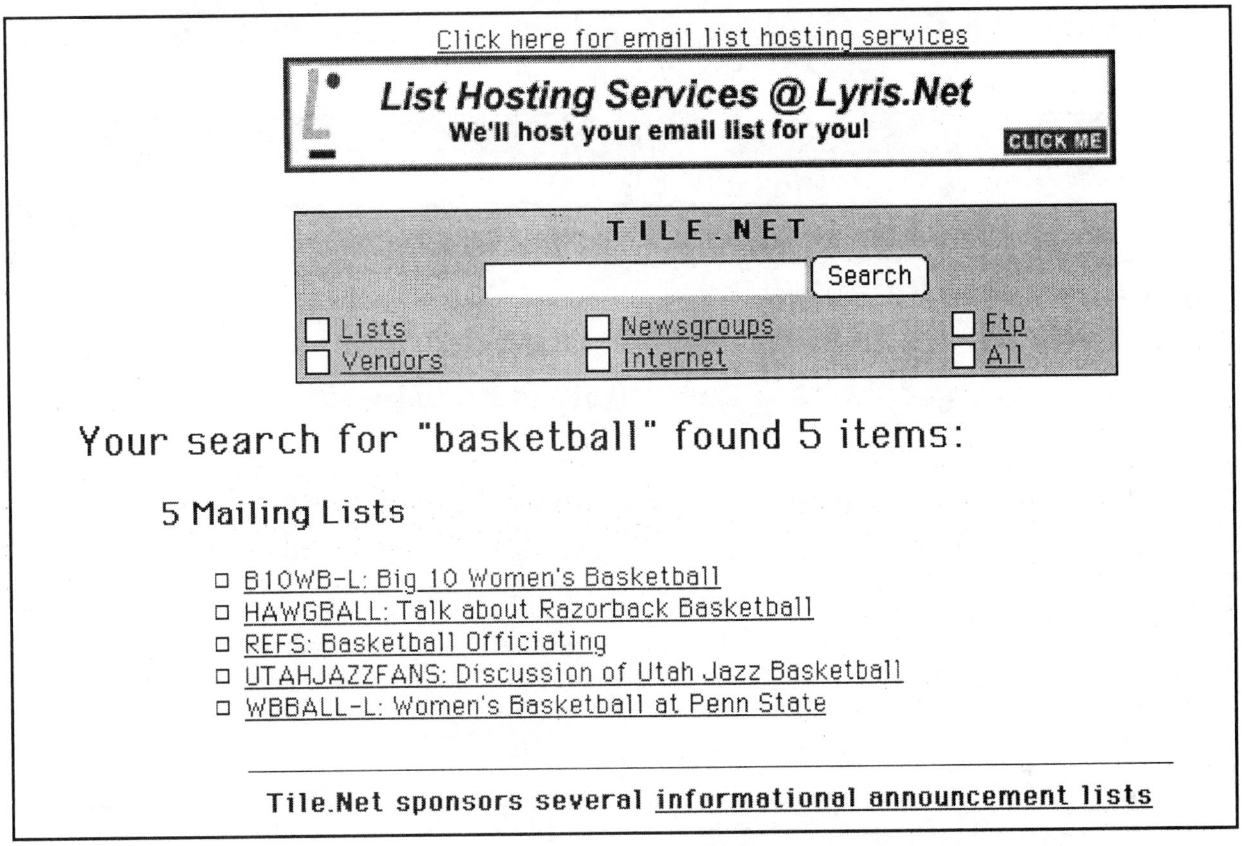

Click here for email list hosting services

List Hosting Services @ Lyris.Net
We'll host your email list for you!
`CLICK ME`

T I L E . N E T

[   ] [Search]

☐ Lists   ☐ Newsgroups   ☐ Ftp
☐ Vendors ☐ Internet   ☐ All

Your search for "basketball" found 5 items:

5 Mailing Lists

☐ B10WB-L: Big 10 Women's Basketball
☐ HAWGBALL: Talk about Razorback Basketball
☐ REFS: Basketball Officiating
☐ UTAHJAZZFANS: Discussion of Utah Jazz Basketball
☐ WBBALL-L: Women's Basketball at Penn State

Tile.Net sponsors several informational announcement lists

Figure 4

TILE.NET/LISTS

Lists　　Newsgroups
Vendors　　Internet

Get a Joke a Day for free! Click: join@jokeaday.com

The Reference to Internet Discussion Lists

B10WB-L	
Big 10 Women's Basketball	
Country:	**U S**
Site:	**Pennsylvania State University**
Computerized administrator:	**listserv@lists.psu.edu**
Human administrator:	**b10wb-l-request@lists.psu.edu**
You can join this group by sending the message "***sub B10WB-L your name*** " to **listserv@lists.psu.edu**	

Disclaimer: Trademarks for the companies, products and services listed here are held by their respective trademark owners. This page is part of an independent directory of publicly available information. Tile.Net and Walter Shelby Group, Ltd. have no affiliation with any of these companies, their products or services.

Return to tile.net/lists/　　**Return to tile.net**

Information about advertising on tile.net
Copyright © 1995-1998 Walter Shelby Group Ltd. All rights reserved worldwide.

Tile.Net sponsors several informational announcement lists

Please visit our sponsors:
Lyris: revolutionary email list server
PostMaster Direct: targeted opt-in email marketing
MailShield: protect your Mail server from spam.

Although the style of writing on listservs can vary dramatically, the tone of listserv discussion is often thoughtful and reasonable, even when users disagree. Listserv members generally expect informed, up-to-date contributions to the ongoing discussion, requests for information, and well-considered questions for list members to think about. Users learn to recognize "threads," which consist of a posting and a series of replies on the same topic, often using the same subject heading. Such threads can offer interesting examples of argument and counterargument, with users maintaining or modifying their positions in light of what others have said.

Because listserv participants tend to be knowledgeable about their topic, you need to learn about a listserv's purposes and the focus of its discussions before posting a message. You can get important background information if a listserv provides frequently asked questions (FAQs). When you do post a message, make sure you clearly identify your purpose—to comment on a thread of discussion, ask a question, propose an answer or solution, and so on.

their positions in light of what others have said.

Notice in the following exchange, taken from a listserv set up in an introduction to literature course, how the first writer identifies her purpose and how the second posting responds in a thoughtful yet probing manner:

> To: listserv_intro.lit@wpi.edu
> From: melanie@wpi.edu

We've been trying to decide whether Willie Loman [in Arthur Miller's play Death of a Salesman] is really a tragic hero—and I'm more confused than ever. Can someone help me out? Willie doesn't exactly fit Aristotle's definition that tragedy needs a noble protagonist (Willie is a "low man"), a moment of recognition (I'm not sure this happens in the play), and a reversal (which definitely does) that evokes pity and fear in the audience. I do pity Willie, but sometimes I think he's more pathetic than tragic. At the same time, I do feel some fear anybody could end up like Willie.

> To: listserv_intro.lit@wpi.edu
> From: armando@wpi.edu

I have the same problem with Death of a Salesman that Melanie talks about. My thinking right now is that Arthur Miller is trying to update Aristotle's definition of tragedy by writing what he calls a tragedy of the common man—common person :-) and raise questions about the tragic consequences of staking everything on being "well liked." In Modern Tragedy, Raymond Williams talks about tragedy of ordinary people and that seems right for Miller.

- **Usenet newsgroups**

  Usenet newsgroups are Internet sites where news from the Associated Press and Reuters wire services, articles, personal postings, and other types of information and argument are made available to users. Often called electronic bulletin boards, a newsgroup is usually devoted to a particular topic of interest and can be useful in providing leads for researchers and in organizing ongoing discussions.

  Thousands of newsgroups exist, devoted to virtually any topic you can think of—politics, the environment, health, sports, popular culture, and so on. Some groups are moderated—that is, a moderator decides what postings will appear—but many are unmoderated and open to anyone.

  You can find newsgroups by going to "http://tile.net/news" on the World Wide Web. One of the tricks to locating newsgroups is using effective keywords in your search. Notice, for example, how "international relations" only turned up one newsgroup (Fig. 5) but "Irish immigration" turned up sixteen (Fig. 6). You need to be persistent and experiment with different combinations of words. Fig. 7 shows the detailed information Tile.Net makes available about a newsgroup.

Figure 5

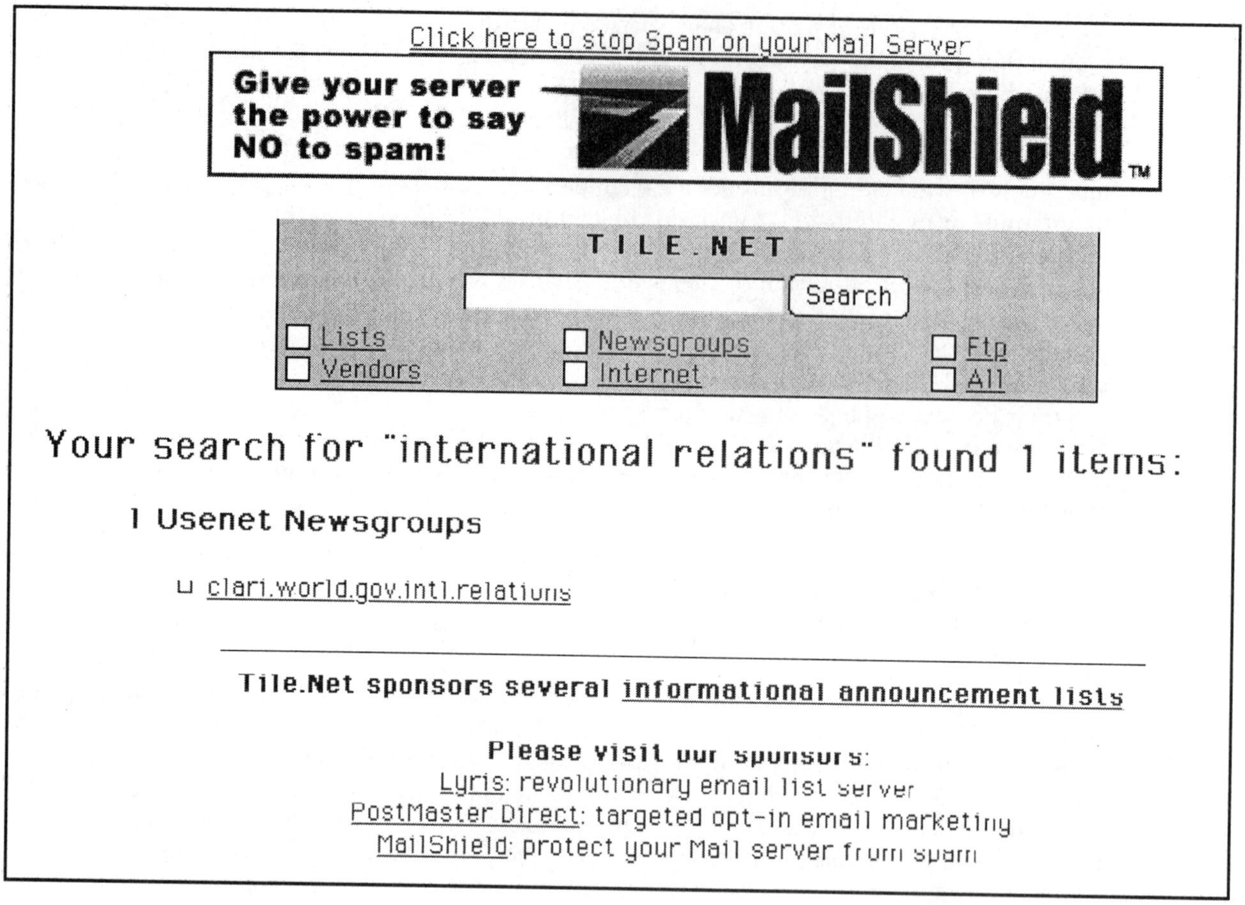
Click here to stop Spam on your Mail Server
Give your server the power to say NO to spam!
MailShield™
TILE.NET
Search
Lists
Vendors
Newsgroups
Internet
Ftp
All
Your search for "international relations" found 1 items:
1 Usenet Newsgroups
clari.world.gov.intl.relations
Tile.Net sponsors several informational announcement lists
Please visit our sponsors:
Lyris: revolutionary email list server
PostMaster Direct: targeted opt-in email marketing
MailShield: protect your Mail server from spam

Figure 6

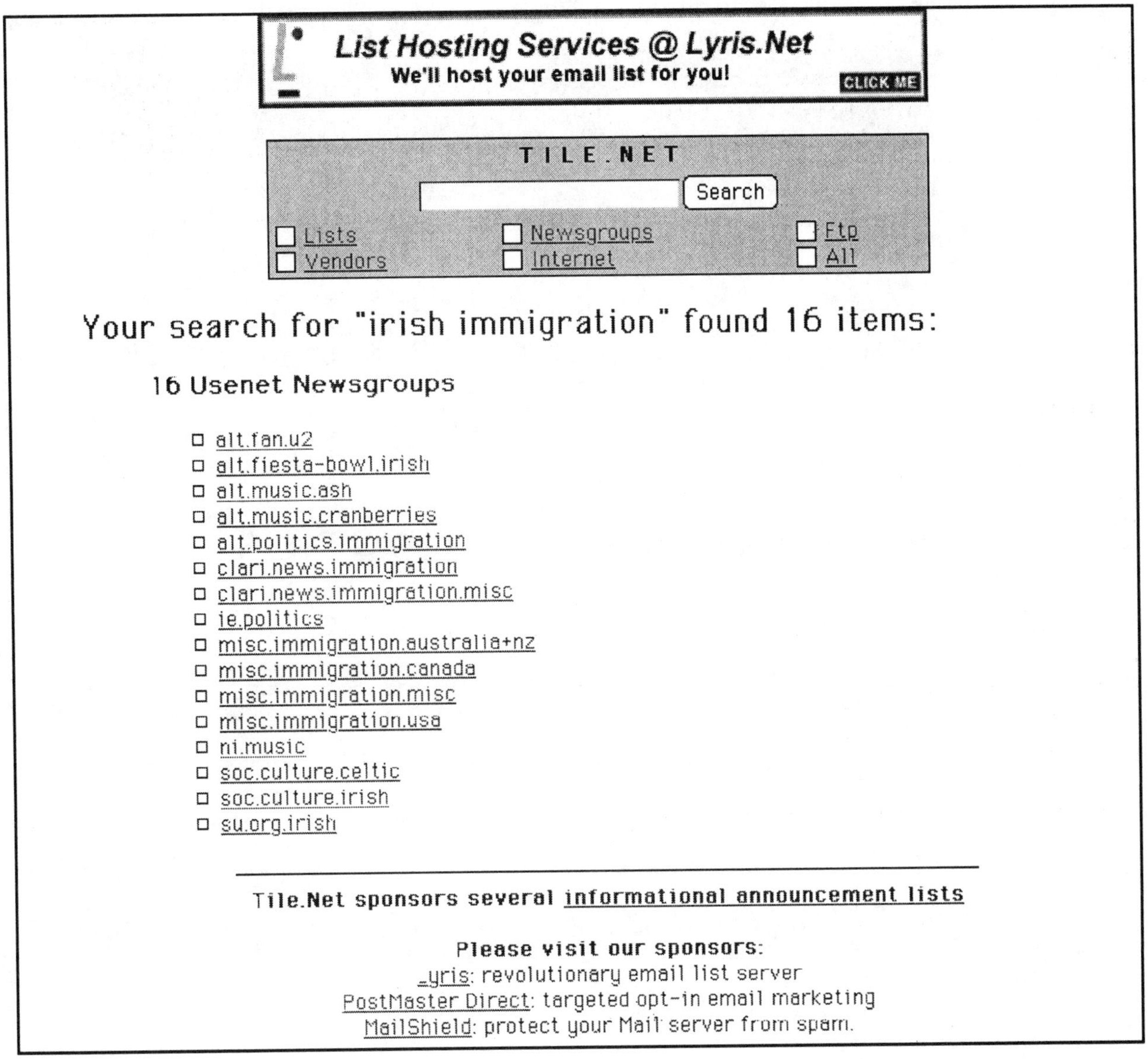

List Hosting Services @ Lyris.Net
We'll host your email list for you!
`CLICK ME`

T I L E . N E T

`[            ]` `Search`

☐ Lists   ☐ Newsgroups   ☐ Ftp
☐ Vendors   ☐ Internet   ☐ All

Your search for "irish immigration" found 16 items:

16 Usenet Newsgroups

☐ alt.fan.u2
☐ alt.fiesta-bowl.irish
☐ alt.music.ash
☐ alt.music.cranberries
☐ alt.politics.immigration
☐ clari.news.immigration
☐ clari.news.immigration.misc
☐ ie.politics
☐ misc.immigration.australia+nz
☐ misc.immigration.canada
☐ misc.immigration.misc
☐ misc.immigration.usa
☐ ni.music
☐ soc.culture.celtic
☐ soc.culture.irish
☐ su.org.irish

Tile.Net sponsors several informational announcement lists

Please visit our sponsors:
Lyris: revolutionary email list server
PostMaster Direct: targeted opt-in email marketing
MailShield: protect your Mail server from spam.

Figure 7

EVERYTHING YOU NEED TO KNOW ABOUT THE INTERNET! click here

Browsers | **Chat** | **Email** | **ISPs**

TILE.NET/NEWS

Lists
Vendors

Newsgroups
Internet

Ftp
All

Get a Joke a Day for free! Click: join@jokeaday.com

The Complete Reference to Usenet Newsgroups

soc.culture.irish

Ireland and Irish culture.

To go to this newsgroup, click: **soc.culture.irish**

Statistics:

Actual readers of this group: 5300
Average number of messages per day: 115
Kilobytes per day: 227k
Percentage of Internet sites who receive this group: 32%
Crossposting: 8%

The following documents are available:

Irish FAQ: Basics [1 10]
Irish FAQ: Cuisine (Recipes) [7 10]
Irish FAQ: Glossary [10 10]
Irish FAQ: History [5 10]
Irish FAQ: Introduction [0 10]
Irish FAQ: Irish Names [9 10]
Irish FAQ: Miscellaneous [8 10]
Irish FAQ: Politics [4 10]
Irish FAQ: The Famine [6 10]
Irish FAQ: The Irish Language [3 10]
Irish FAQ: Tourism and the Web [2 10]

MIT's RTFM server archives most USENET frequently asked questions.

Search for related topics using Lycos:

soc culture irish

This is the list of Frequently Asked Questions of
soc.culture.irish with answers. Send corrections, suggestions,
additions, and other feedback to <irish-faq@salmon.muc.de>

The Famine

1) Why is it important?
2) Why is it controversial?
3) What happened?
4) Why did so many people die?
5) Was the Famine genocide?
6) Any references?
7) Where can I find other points of view?

Subject: 1) Why is it important?

   More Irish died in the Famine of 1845 to 1849 than in any war
   before or since. The best estimates (based on census data
   from 1841 and 1851, as well as other figures) are that around
   one million people died, or one out of every nine inhabitants.
   About one and a half million emigrated in the decade after 1845
   (the peak was in 1851, when a quarter of a million people left
   the island). The population continued to decline in Ireland
   through emigration until well into the second half of this century
   (it nearly halved between 1840 and 1910). Many say that the
   west of the country never recovered.

   The Famine hit one of the richest kingdoms of western Europe in
   a time of peace. There have been food shortages since and even
   starvation, but western Europe has not seen a large scale famine
   since.

Subject: 2) Why is it controversial?

   Most of the controversy is over the question of blame. Those who
   look for a simple answer usually settle on one of two targets:
   the British government of the time or the Irish themselves.
   The government is accused of genocide and even of instigating an
   "Irish holocaust". The Irish are accused of marrying too early
   and having too many children, making a Malthusian catastrophe
   inevitable.

   However the Famine is too complicated to allow a simple
   apportionment of blame. There were a number of social and
   political forces at work, not to mention the seed of the calamity,
   the potato blight that robbed people of their food.

ETHICS OF WRITING

IN CYBERSPACE

Because on-line writing offers writers the possibility of anonymity, where writers can use a nickname instead of their real name, writers may feel that their messages are detached from them personally and that they are not accountable in the same way they would be if they signed their messages. This has led to an unfortunate tendency to use the Internet for personal rants and "flame wars," and the kinds of sexist, racist, and homophobic messages you can find in cyberspace are distressing. People sometimes say they are "only joking" or showing how ridiculous hate speech is. But they are not taking into account the effect on other people.

Some people simply use newsgroups to gather information or keep abreast of current discussions on a particular topic or issue. If you want to experience the interactive character of the Internet first hand, consider posting to a newsgroup on a topic that is important to you. Remember, though, that unlike listservs where people subscribe, newsgroups are wide-open and the tone of discussion can get quite heated. In most newsgroups, for example, newcomers (or "newbies") are expected to "lurk" for awhile, consulting FAQs (see Fig. 8), reading current postings, and learning the issues and concerns of participants. If you post a message too soon, you may well get "flamed" for your efforts.

Also keep in mind that you need to read what appears on the Internet with special care. Newspapers, national magazines, scholarly journals, and books from commercial and university presses use a number of filtering procedures—professional training, peer review, editing, fact checking, and so on—that guarantees the legitimacy and reliability of these print sources. Information and opinion on the Internet, on the other hand, can come from anywhere. Part of the excitement of the Internet is that it is not regulated, but this means you need to evaluate carefully what you read. It can be particularly helpful to compare newsgroup comments to conventional sources and to consider users' personal investments in the issues, especially when their remarks are heated, passionate, questionable, or extreme.

• World Wide Web

Surfing the web is fast becoming a major pastime—and there are good reasons for this. When you visit a particular web site, you may well find it includes sound, graphics, video, and text—all in one document. Moreover, a web site is likely to provide you with links to other sites.

With e-mail, listserv discussions, and newsgroups (as well as print literacy), people normally read in a linear way, following the sequence of the message, the posting, or the printed text from start to finish. On the web, however, there is no one way to move through a document because it is multi-layered and offers various opportunities for readers to click on highlighted words, phrases, or images to activate links to other documents. The technology of the web enables users to move fluidly from one chunk of information or node to another.

For this reason, building web pages can be an interesting writing task because it involves not only composing text but also creating links for readers to follow. Web building uses a scripting language called Hypertext Markup Language (HTML), which enables writers to construct links and connect files with sound, video, graphics, and text.

Notice how the home page in James Crawford's award-winning web site "Language Policy Web Site and Emporium" (Fig. 9) explains who he is and the purpose of the web site. By clicking on underlined words and phrase, you can access links to other nodes in Crawford's web site as wells as to other web sites. For example, if you clicked on "English Only movement," you'd get this node (Fig. 10), which contains not only Crawford's analysis of the movement but also links to the home pages of a wide range of organizations that have taken positions on English Only. At this point, you would have to decide where to go next. As you can see, there are many paths available.

Figure 9

James Crawford's

Language Policy Web Site & Emporium

Welcome.

I am an independent writer and lecturer - formerly the Washington editor of *Education Week* - who specializes in the politics of language. Since 1985, I have been reporting on the English Only movement, English Plus, bilingual education, efforts to save endangered languages, and language rights in the U.S.A.

This site is designed to

- encourage discussion of language policy issues,
- publish updates on current developments,
- report on pending language legislation,
- flush out canards about bilingualism,
- track the continuing struggle against Proposition 227, NEW California's anti-bilingual education initiative, approved on June 2,
- highlight links to other sources of information, and - to be totally candid -
- promote my publications.

Back to Language Policy

Issues in U.S. Language Policy

The English Only Movement

Among special-interest lobbies, the English Only movement stands out. It's easy to understand the origins of the Tobacco Institute or the Peanut Advisory Council or the Valve Manufacturers Association. But how does a language acquire a multimillion-dollar advocacy group? *Cui bono?* Who seeks to benefit by pushing the idea of English as the official language? Certainly not the National Council of Teachers of English or the Teachers of English to Speakers of Other Languages or the Linguistic Society of America – these organizations strongly oppose English Only measures.

U.S. English and English First, two national groups spearheading this legislation, started small in the mid-1980s. Drawing support mainly from direct-mail contributions, they have grown steadily in budgets, staffs, and influence. H.R. 123, the leading "Language of Government" bill in the 104th Congress, boasted nearly 200 cosponsors. Public support has exceeded 85 percent in some opinion polls. English Only is no longer a fringe movement.

Who are these people and what do they want?

A. Citizens who want to preserve our common language and avoid ethnic strife
B. Bigots seeking to roll back civil rights advances for language-minority groups
C. Conservatives hoping to impose a sense of national unity and civic responsibility
D. Liberals who fear that bilingual education and bilingual voting discourage assimilation
E. Nativists trying to fan animosity toward

immigrants and build support for tighter
quotas

F. Euro-ethnics who resent "unfair
   advantages" enjoyed by Hispanics and
   Asians today
G. Politicians attempting to exploit a national
   mood of isolationism and xenophobia
H. Racists who equate multiculturalism and
   ethnic separatism
I. Americans who feel threatened by
   diversity, among other unsetting changes
J. All of the above

A good case could be made for "all of the above."
You be the judge. I have elaborated my own
analysis in "Hispanophobia," a chapter from my
book Hold Your Tongue. For differing views,
you may want to visit the home pages of U.S.
English and English First.

Links

Others taking positions on English Only
legislation include:

- American Civil Liberties Union
- Center for Equal Opportunity
- House Republican Policy Committee
- Joint National Committee for
  Languages
- Linguistic Society of America
- Mexican American Legal Defense and
  Educational Fund
- National Council of Teachers of
  English
- National Education Association
- Teachers of English to Speakers of
  Other Languages

• **"Real time" communication** There now exist technologies that allow users to engage in "real time" or nearly instantaneous communication with other users. Unlike e-mail, listservs, or newsgroups, which are called asynchronous because they involve a lapse of time between messages, synchronous technologies create virtual spaces where users can interact in a way that more nearly resembles face-to-face conversation. All the participants can "speak" at the same time, instead of waiting to send and receive individual messages, and real-time communication has the uninterrupted flow of people talking back and forth.

One example is the computer-networked classroom that makes real-time interaction possible through special software. Another is the Internet Relay Chat (IRC), which provides Internet channels for real-time discussion groups organized, like Usenet newsgroups, by topics of mutual interest. A third type adds text-based virtual environments to real-time interaction. Originally designed for role-playing games like Dungeons and Dragons, technologies such as Multi User Domains (MUDs) and MUD Object Oriented (MOOs) enable users to move around and interact with objects in a virtual environment— which could represent anything from a university to the Globe Theater in Shakespeare's London to a post-apocalyptic nightmare fantasy. In MUDs and MOOs, users often construct an alternative identity for themselves, at times changing their gender or race.

One of the most striking features about real-time communication is the way it differs from traditional classroom discussion, where students raise their hands and wait to be called on, or the conversations of everyday life, where people normally take turns speaking. Real-time communication can sometimes feel chaotic and unstructured, with users writing the first thing that pops into their minds. But it can also encourage people who are reluctant to talk in groups to have their say. You may want to explore some of these virtual spaces to see the kinds of interactions that take place.

Here is an example of a real-time class discussion in a networked classroom comparing an article in Ladies' Home Journal "How to Keep Your Man Monogamous" to Arlie Russell Hochschild's book Managed Heart, in which she argues that women become "emotional managers" of others' feelings due to their lack of power and authority. Consider how the use of nicknames affects what individuals say. And remember this is a real-time discussion, with each message appearing on the screen in rapid succession:

Adam Heart: What should we say?

yeah boy: what's up butthead?

arm pit: isn't this so fun. let's not talk about the reading!!!

INDIANA JONES: Monogamy is a thing of the past.

Laverne: What does the article support, yeah boy?

Cherri Champagne: Monogamy sucks.

Biff: Like, it's the same, dude.

joe: butthead?

GARFIELD: Yes, I think it does support it.

Mighty Mouse: Cherri Champagne, How about STD's?

yeah boy: someone reply to the article.

King Kong Bundy: Ich weiss es nichts.

joe: monogamy is not a thing of the past i mean how can you sleep with a zillion different people with all the creepy crawlies out there?

Cherri Champagne: What are STD's?

Laverne: O.k. LJH article supports Hochschild or whatever her name is.

—from Lester Faigley, Fragments of Rationality, p. 193

WORKING TOGETHER: New Writing Technologies

1. Spend fifteen minutes or so writing individual responses to these questions:
   - Do you normally use a word processor? What experience, if any, have you had with e-mail, listservs, newsgroups, the World Wide Web, and "real-time" communication? If you have used these technologies, what purposes do they serve for you?
   - How would you describe your attitude toward the new writing technologies and the new forms of electronic communication?
   - What would you like to learn about the new writing technologies? If you are just beginning, what skills would you like to acquire? If you already have some experience, how would you like to enhance your skills? What are some realistic goals you might set for yourself? If you do have some knowledge of these writing tools, would you be willing to share it with other students? What do you know that you could teach others?
2. Once you have completed the individual responses, meet in a group with three or four other students. Take turns explaining what you have written. You can read some or all of your response or you can just summarize it orally. Divide the time so that everyone has an equal opportunity to speak. If you know a lot about computers, the Internet, and the Web, explain what you know and what purposes the new writing tools have served for you. If you are inexperienced, don't feel defensive or intimidated by others' knowledge. The point of this discussion is to find what knowledge and experience are available within your class, what goals individual students have for themselves, and how students might draw on each other's expertise to meet their goals.
3. Once you have discussed your responses, decide on one person to report to the whole class. In the report, give a brief summary of what people already know, what their goals are, and who might be willing to help other students. Without attributing attitudes to specific students, characterize the range of attitudes that were expressed in the group.

PART
FOUR

GUIDE TO RESEARCH

PART
FOUR

INTRODUCTION:
DOING RESEARCH

People do research in one form or another all the time, perhaps without even being aware of it. You may associate research with the kinds of formal research projects assigned in school, but research takes place in virtually every sphere of life.

- If you need to buy a birthday present for your mother, you may well ask other family members for suggestions. Many students do considerable research deciding which colleges they are going to apply to. People who want to buy a new car often consult Consumer Reports and talk to friends about the best deal. If you are planning a vacation, you might look at travel guides in your local bookstore or library.

- Many types of research take place in the workplace-marketing research, product development, productivity studies, and so on. People in business need to research current trends in the market, state and federal regulations, and tax codes. The professions, such as law and medicine, are defined in many respects by the kind of research practitioners in these fields do to deal with clients' legal situations or diagnose patients' conditions and recommend treatment.

- Public opinion polling has become a common feature of politics and journalism, a way to keep track of the public mood and people's attitudes about the issues of the day. Public advocacy groups often conduct their own research on questions that matter to them-whether the impact of mining on national lands, the effect of NAFTA on American jobs, drunk driving, or impending changes in the welfare law.

- Research, of course, is a familiar part of academic life, for students and faculty alike. You may recall some of the research assignments you encountered in elementary and high school-term papers, book reports, science fair projects, history posters, oral presentations-and you will almost certainly do research in your college courses. Faculty do research when they prepare for their classes or plan new ones. The saying "publish or perish" reveals the importance of research in the professional careers of faculty. Their work is defined in part by the research of their academic discipline and the expectation to participate in the creation of new knowledge in their field.

As you can see, not all research enters into the written record. Sometimes, research is just a matter of getting some information to make a decision or take an action. In other cases, such as a teacher's lecture notes or a memo to co-workers, research leads to writing but not to formal publication. But in many instances, research is intended for a wider readership-a journalist's investigative reporting on child labor in American-owned factories abroad, a study of global warming by a panel of scientists, an article in a history journal presenting a new interpretation of American attitudes toward immigration, a recent book by a team of sociologists on the causes and consequences of homelessness in San Francisco.

RESEARCH TECHNIQUES

These various examples reveal that research not only takes many different forms. It also involves different research techniques. Some research deals largely with written records-previous work published on the subject, historical archives, old newspapers and magazines, government documents, unpublished manuscripts, letters, and personal journals or diaries. Much of this material can be found in college libraries, but some researchers travel around the world to visit special collections, local historical societies, or families and individuals with important documents.

In other cases, research projects require field research. Marketing researchers, for example, use focus groups, telephone interviews, and surveys to accumulate data. A journalist working on child labor may well visit plants around the world and talk to company executives and experts on labor relations. A wildlife biologist is likely to spend considerable time in the field, observing the behavior of birds or animals.

In still other cases, researchers conduct experiments in laboratories. Molecular biologists, for example, use highly sophisticated techniques and equipment to study the function of genes. Psychologists routinely use laboratory conditions to study how people solve particular kinds of tasks or respond to sex and violence in the media.

SCALE OF RESEARCH

The scale of research will also vary, often depending on the amount of time and the resources a researcher has available. The team of sociologists studying homelessness, for example, decided to concentrate their research on one city, San Francisco, instead of trying to investigate homelessness everywhere in the U.S. or in the world. This is not doubt a wise decision, for whatever the researchers may lose in the scope of their research they are likely to make up for in the amount of detail and the depth of analysis they can achieve by focusing on a single location.

The historian investigating American attitudes toward immigration faces a similar situation. To offer a persuasive interpretation of American attitudes from the colonial period to the present is a massive undertaking that would undoubtedly take years to complete, and the results would require a book-length (or even multi-volume) treatment. For these reasons, the historian decides to focus his research on a particular time frame, 1880-1920, which is widely recognized as an important period in immigration history, when millions of immigrants came to the U.S. from southern and eastern Europe. As a necessary background, he will want to understand American attitudes in earlier periods, as well as attitudes toward the "new" immigration from Southeast Asia, India and Pakistan, Korea, the Caribbean, and Central and Latin America of recent years. But by concentrating on the period 1880-1920, the historian has set a manageable research task that can realistically lead to an article offering a new interpretation.

NEED TO KNOW

As you have seen, the forms, techniques, and scale of research may vary widely. Nonetheless, there is one thing all the examples of research have in common. They are all motivated by the need to know. In each case, something is calling on a person or a group of people to do research-to get the information needed, to investigate a problem, to provide a new way of seeing things. To put it another way, research begins when people have questions they need or want to answer: what kind of computer should I buy, how are consumers likely to respond to a new product or service, what does the public think about Clinton's second term in office, what causes breast cancer, why did Lyndon Johnson escalate the war in Vietnam?

Researchers in different fields of study, of course, have different ways of asking questions and different ways of answering them. Take the AIDS epidemic, for example. Scientific researchers have been asking questions about the nature and behavior of the human immunodeficiency virus (HIV) and about the kinds of treatment that can alter the course of infection. Psychologists and sociologists, in contrast, have studied the effect of AIDS on the identities of HIV-negative gay men and the benefits and drawbacks of needle-exchange programs. Economists, on the other hand, have calculated the financial impact of AIDS on medical institutions, health insurance companies, government programs, and employers.

Researchers, as you can see, do not just think of a topic and start to investigate it. They turn the general topic of AIDS into specific questions that concern people in their field of study. This gives them an angle on the problem and a way of starting their research. In many cases, you can discover what led a researcher to ask a particular question of set of questions by looking at the preface or introduction to book-length research studies.

Notice how the following passage from the introduction to Paul Starr's Pulitzer Prize-winning work The Social Transformation of American Medicine explains the questions he has in mind and what he believes the significance of these questions to be at the time he finished the book in 1982.

THE SOCIAL TRANSFORMATION OF AMERICAN MEDICINE.

PAUL STARR

PREFACE

sections

I HAVE DIVIDED this history into two [books] to emphasize two long movements in the development of American medicine: first, the rise of professional sovereignty; and second, the transformation of medicine into an industry and the growing, though still unsettled, role of corporations and the state. Within this framework I explore a variety of specific questions, such as:

why Americans, who were wary of medical authority in the early and mid-nineteenth century, became devoted to it in the twentieth;

how American doctors, who were bitterly divided and financially insecure in the nineteenth century, became a united and prosperous profession in the twentieth;

why hospitals, medical schools, clinics, and other organizations assumed distinctive institutional forms in the United States;

why hospitals became the central institutions in medical care;

why public health did not;

why there is no national health insurance in the United States;

why Blue Cross and commercial indemnity insurance, rather than other types of health plans, dominated the private insurance market;

why the federal government in recent years shifted from policies that encouraged growth without changes in the organization of medical care to policies that encouraged reorganization to control growth;

why physicians long escaped from the control of the modern corporation, but are now witnessing and indeed taking part in the creation of corporate health care systems.

This last question became more salient while this book was in progress. When I began work in 1974, it was widely thought that medical schools, planners, and administrators were emerging as the chief counterweight to private physicians. Government seemed to be assuming a

x   Preface

major, perhaps dominant role in the organization of medical care. Decisions that had formerly been private and professional were becoming public and political. Eight years later this is no longer clearly the direction of change, but neither is the status quo ante being restored. Private corporations are gaining a more powerful position in American medicine; if leading members of the Reagan administration have their way, the future may well belong to corporate medicine. However, the origins of this development precede the current administration; the force behind it is more powerful than the changing fashions in Washington. Precisely because of what is now taking place, it has become more necessary to understand medicine as a business as well as a cultural phenomenon—and perhaps most important, to understand the relation between the two.

The following excerpts from the "Introduction" Donna Gaines's Teenage Wasteland offer a more extended and personal account of why she decided to do research on the suicide pact of four working-class teenagers in Bergenfield, New Jersey. Gaines's research is interesting because it began, as you will see, as you will see, as an assignment from her editor at The Village Voice then turned into the basis of her doctoral thesis in sociology at the State University of New York at Stony Brook, and finally was published as a book directed to a general readership, not just an academic audience.

As you read, notice how Gaines explains her motivation for doing research, what questions she is asking, and how these questions shape the kind of research she did.

"Introduction." Teenage Wasteland

Danna Gaines

When I heard about the suicide pact it grabbed me in the solar plexus. I looked at the pictures of the kids and their friends. I read what the reporters said. I was sitting in my garden apartment looking out on Long Island's Jericho Turnpike thinking maybe this is how the world ends, with the last generation bowing out first.

In Bergenfield, New Jersey, on the morning of March 11, 1987, the bodies of four teenagers were discovered inside a 1977 rust-colored Chevrolet Camaro. The car, which belonged to Thomas Olton, was parked in an unused garage in the Foster Village garden apartment complex, behind the Foster Village Shopping Center. Two sisters, Lisa and Cheryl Burress, and their friends, Thomas Rizzo and Thomas Olton, had died of carbon monoxide poisoning.

Lisa was sixteen, Cheryl was seventeen, and the boys were nineteen—they were suburban teens, turnpike kids like the ones in the town I live in. And thinking about them made me remember how it felt being a teenager too. I was horrified that it had come to this. I believed I understood why they did it, although it wasn't a feeling I could have put into words.

You could tell from the newspapers that they were rock and roll kids. The police had found a cassette tape cover of AC/DC's *If You Want Blood, You've Got It* near the bodies. Their friends were described as kids who listened to thrash metal, had shaggy haircuts, wore lots of black and leather. "Dropouts," "druggies," the papers called them. Teenage suburban rockers whose lives revolved around their favorite bands and their friends. Youths who barely got by in school and at home and who did not impress authority figures in any remarkable way. ~~Except as fuck-ups.~~

● ● ●

A week or two after the suicide pact, *The Village Voice* assigned me to go to Bergenfield. Now this was not a story I would've volunteered for. Usually I write about things I enjoy: computers, guns, pornography, tattoos, rock and roll, cars. I don't like the idea of "research subjects" or getting vulnerable people to trust me with their secrets so I can go back and tell about them. Generally, I prefer leaving people alone.

But one day my editor at the *Voice* called to ask if I wanted to go to Bergenfield. She knew my background—that I knew suburbia, that I could talk to kids. By now I fully embraced the sociologist's ethical commitment to the "rights of the researched," and the social worker's vow of client confidentiality. As far as suicidal teenagers were concerned, I felt that if I couldn't help them, I didn't want to bother them.

But I was really pissed off at what I kept reading. How people in Bergenfield openly referred to the four kids as "troubled losers." Even after they were dead, nobody cut them any slack. "Burnouts," "druggies," "dropouts." Something was wrong. So I took the opportunity.

From the beginning, I believed that the Bergenfield suicides symbolized a tragic defeat for young people. Something was happening in the larger society that was not yet comprehended. Scholars spoke ominously of "the postmodern condition," "societal upheaval," "decay," "anomie." Meanwhile, American kids kept losing ground, showing all the symptoms of societal neglect. Many were left to fend for themselves, often with little success. The news got worse. Teenage suicides continued, and still nobody seemed to be getting the point.

Now, in trying to understand this event, I might have continued working within the established discourse on teenage suicide. I might have carried on the tradition of obscuring the bigger picture, psychologizing the Bergenfield suicide pact, interviewing the parents of the four youths, hounding their friends for the gory details. I might have spent my time probing school records, tracking down their teachers and shrinks for insights, focusing on their personal histories and intimate relationships. I might have searched out the individual motivations behind the words left in the note written and signed by each youth on the brown paper bag found with their bodies on March 11. But I did not.

Because the suicide pact was a *collective act*, it warrants a social explanation—a portrait of the "burnouts" in Bergenfield as actors within a particular social landscape.

For a long time now, the discourse of teenage suicide has been dominated by atomizing psychological and medical models. And so the larger picture of American youth as members of a distinctive generation with a unique collective biography, emerging at a particular moment in history, has been lost.

The starting-off point for this book, then, is a teenage suicide pact in an "upper-poor" white ethnic suburb in northern New Jersey. But, of course, the story did not begin and will not end in Bergenfield.

Yes, there were specific sociocultural patterns operating in Bergenfield through which a teenage suicide pact became objectively

possible. Yes, there were particular conditions which influenced how the town reacted to the event. Yes, there were reasons—that unique constellation of circumstances congealed in the lives of the four youths in the years, weeks, and days prior to March 11—that made suicide seem like their best alternative.

Given the four youths' personal histories, their losses, their failures, their shattered dreams, the motivation to die in this way seems transparent. Yet, after the suicide pact, in towns across the country, on television and in the press, people asked, "Why did they do it?" But I went to Bergenfield with other questions.

This was a suicide pact that involved close friends who were by no accounts obsessed, star-crossed lovers. What would make four people want to die together? Why would they ask, in their collective suicide note, to be waked and buried together? Were they part of a suicide cult?

If not, what was the nature of the *social* bond that tied them so closely? What could be so intimately binding that in the early morning hours of March 11 not one of them could stop, step back from the pact they had made to say, "Wait, I can't do this"? Who were these kids that everybody called "burnouts"?

"Greasers," "hoods," "beats," "freaks," "hippies," "punks." From the 1950s onward, these groups have signified young people's refusal to cooperate. In the social order of the American high school, teens are expected to do what they are told—make the grade, win the prize, play the game. Kids who refuse have always found something else to do. Sometimes it kills them; sometimes it sets them free.

In the eighties, as before, high school kids at the top were the "preps," "jocks," or "brains," depending on the region. In white suburban high schools in towns like Bergenfield, the "burnouts" are often the kids near the bottom—academically, economically, and socially.

To outsiders, they look tough, scruffy, poor, wild. Uninvolved in and unimpressed by convention, they create an alternative world, a retreat, a refuge. Some burnouts are proud; they "wave their freak flags high." They call themselves burnouts to flaunt their break with the existing order, as a form of resistance, a statement of refusal.

But the meaning changes when "burnout" is hurled by an out-

sider. Then it hurts. It's an insult. Everyone knows you don't call somebody a burnout to their face unless you are looking for a fight. At that point, the word becomes synonymous with "troubled loser," "druggie"—all the things the press and some residents of the town called the four kids who died together in Tommy Olton's Camaro.

How did kids in Bergenfield *become* "burnouts," I wondered. At what point were they identified as outcasts? Was this a labeling process or one of self-selection? What kinds of lives did they have? What resources were available for them? What choices did they have? What ties did these kids have to the world outside Bergenfield? Where did their particular subculture come from? Why in the 1980s, the Reagan years, in white, suburban America?

What were their hopes and fears? What did heavy metal, Satan, suicide, and long hair mean to them? Who were their heroes, their gods? What saved them and what betrayed them in the long, cold night?

And what was this "something evil in the air" that people spoke about? Were the kids in Bergenfield "possessed"? Was the suicide pact an act of cowardice by four "losers," or the final refuge of kids helplessly and hopelessly trapped? How different was Bergenfield from other towns?

Could kids be labeled to death? How much power did these labels have? I wanted to meet other kids in Bergenfield who were identified as "burnouts" to find out what it felt like to carry these labels. I wanted to understand the existential situation they operated in—not simply as hapless losers, helpless victims, or tragic martyrs, but also as *historical actors* determined in their choices, resistant, defiant.

Because the suicide pact in Bergenfield seemed to be a symptom of something larger, a metaphor for something more universal, I moved on from there to other towns. For almost two years I spent my time reading thrash magazines, seeing shows, and hanging out with "burnouts" and "dirtbags" as well as kids who slip through such labels.

* * *

From the beginning, I decided I didn't want to dwell too much on the negatives. I wanted to understand how alienated kids survived, as well as how they were defeated. How did they maintain their humanity against what I now felt were impossible odds? I wondered. What keeps young people together when the world they are told to trust no longer seems to work? What motivates them to be decent human beings when nobody seems to respect them or take them seriously?

CHAPTER
FIFTEEN

RESEARCH PROJECTS:
USING PRINT AND ELECTRONIC SOURCES

The way people do research is changing. For most college research projects, the library is still likely to be your main source of information, so you can count on spending a large part of your research time reading and evaluating what you find in books and articles from newspapers, magazines, and academic journals (although your topic and research questions may also lead you to conduct field research—which is treated in the next chapter).

What has changed is that a good deal of the information you'll need for a research project is now available online or on CD-ROMs—everything from the library's catalog and subject headings to indexes, bibliographies, and other electronic databases. In addition, there is a world of information in cyberspace you can access over the Internet, material that ranges from serious scholarly discussion to wildly opinionated debates of questionable value. When anyone can start a discussion group or put up a Web site, you'll find useful electronic sources of information created and maintained by individuals, museums, advocacy groups, and government agencies—and some that are just plain crackpot. For these reasons, doing research today is a matter of knowing your way around both print and electronic sources and understanding the difference between sources that are credible and those that aren't.

This chapter covers a number of helpful sources you'll find in your library and on the Internet. Before you plunge into the library or cyberspace, however, it's worth looking first at how to organize your research project so that you can make best use of the sources you turn up. We begin with an overview of the research process. Then we follow the research process step by step to show how you can find, read, and evaluate print and electronic sources.

OVERVIEW OF THE RESEARCH PROCESS

As you saw in the Introduction, research typically begins when people need to know something and they have important questions to answer. Now it is only fair to say that in college the call to do research most often comes from teachers, in the form of a research assignment. Most faculty believe that an important part of a college education is learning how to pose a meaningful problem to investigate, research and evaluate what others have said about it, and form your own judgment. The following overview of the research process identifies the main steps to respond to this call to write and lists the tasks involved at each point:

1. Getting Started. Analyze the research assignment. Do preliminary research to get an overview of your topic. Start to focus your reading to develop a research question. Evaluate your research question and revise or modify, if necessary. Write a proposal to clarify the purpose of your research.
2. Finding Sources. Use your library's card catalog, indexes, bibliographies, and other databases to identify print and electronic sources. Browse sites on the Internet. Keep a working bibliography.
3. Reading and Evaluating Sources. Take notes. Photocopy sources. Assess the relevance and credibility of the sources. Look for assumptions and biases. Keep an open mind. Be prepared to revise or modify your own thinking in light of what you've read.
4. Planning and Drafting. Reread your notes and photocopies. Develop a working outline of your paper. Start drafting. Reread sources and find additional information as needed. Revise or modify your outline, if necessary.

This chapter looks in more detail at each of these steps in the research process.

GETTING STARTED

Research depends in part on knowing what you are looking for. This will depend, of course, on the research assignment. In some cases, the assignment will provide specific directions, but in others, it will be open-ended. If you have questions about what the assignment is calling on you to do, make sure you consult with your instructor.

Let's say you are taking a course on American popular music, and your teacher assigns an open-ended research paper. The topic is yours to determine, and you decide you want to write something about rock 'n' roll as a cultural phenomenon. Good start. The problem, however, is that such a broad topic is not likely to give you much direction in your research. The first step in organizing a research project, then, is to develop a focused question to guide your investigation.

Preliminary Research

Sometimes you may know right away what you want to research —what, for example, was the public reaction to Elvis Presley in the mid-1950s, how did folksinging traditions influence the development of rock in the 1960s, or what does the emergence of punk in the late 1970s tell us about American culture at that time? In other cases, especially when the topic you're researching is new to you, you'll need to do some preliminary research to develop a research question. The following sources offer good places to start:

- World Wide Web. Web sites sometimes offer helpful starting places for research projects. See Finding a Research Path for an example of how a student used the Web to do preliminary research and develop a research question.

- Encyclopedias. You can find an overview of many topics in general encyclopedias. It can also be helpful to consult specialized encyclopedias that cover a particular field of study and often include bibliographies for each entry. See the list of encyclopedias that follows.

- Recent book. Skim a recent book on your topic, looking in particular at its introduction to see how the writer describes the issues the book addresses. Notice too what the book seems to cover by reading the table of contents. And don't forget to see whether it has a bibliography.

- Recent article. Find a recent article in a scholarly journal or a popular magazine on your topic. Read the article, noticing what question or questions the writer poses and (in the case of academic articles) what sources are listed in the references.

- Classmates, librarians, teaching assistants, faculty members. Talk to other people who know something about your topic and the current questions people are asking about it. They can help you understand what the issues are and what sources you might look for.

Your preliminary research should give you some ideas about the way others have approached the topic you're interested in, the kinds of questions they raise, and the differences of opinion and interpretation that divide them. This research should also help you identify other books and articles on the subject that you may want to consult.

BOXENCYCLOPEDIAS

GENERAL

Collier's Encyclopedia, 24 vols.
Encyclopedia Americana, 30 vols. plus yearbooks
Grolier Multimedia Encyclopedia (CD-ROM)
Microsoft Encarta (CD-ROM, includes 24 vol. Funk and Wagnalls New
Encyclopedia)
The New Encyclopedia Britannica, 32 vols.
World Book Encyclopedia, 22 vols. plus yearbooks

SPECIALIZED (by field)

Art, Film, Television
Encyclopedia of World Architecture
Encyclopedia of World Art
International Encyclopedia of Film
International Encyclopedia of Television
International Television Almanac
Economics and Business
Encyclopedia of Advertising
Encyclopedia of American Economic History
Encyclopedia of Banking and Finance
Encyclopedia of Management
Handbook of Modern Marketing
McGraw-Hill Dictionary of Modern Economics

Education

Encylopedia of Education
Foreign Relations
Encyclopedia of American Foreign Policy
Encyclopedia of the Third World

History

An Encyclopedia of World History
Cambridge Ancient History
Cambridge History of China
Dictionary of American History
Encyclopedia of Latin-American History
Harvard Guide to American History
New Cambridge Modern History

Literature

Cambridge Guide to English Literature
Encyclopedia of World Literature in the 20th Century

Funk and Wagnall's Standard Dictionary of Folklore, Mythology, and
Legend
McGraw-Hill Encyclopedia of World Drama
Oxford Companion to American Literature

Music

Dance Encyclopedia
Encyclopedia of Pop, Rock, and Soul
New Grove Dictionary of American Music
New Grove Dictionary of Music and Musicians

Religion and Philosophy

Dictionary of the History of Ideas
Encyclopedia of Philosophy
Encyclopedia of Religion
Encyclopedia of Bioethics
New Standard Jewish Encyclopedia
Oxford Dictionary of the Christian Church

Science and Technology

Encyclopedia of Biological Sciences
Encyclopedia of Chemistry
Encyclopedia of Computer Science and Technology
Encyclopedia of Oceanography
Encyclopaedic Dictionary of Physics
Introduction to the History of Science
McGraw-Hill Dictionary of Earth Sciences
McGraw Hill Encyclopedia of Science and Technology
The Software Toolworks Multimedia Encyclopedia
Van Nostrand's Scientific Encyclopedia

Social Sciences

Dictionary of Anthropology
Encyclopedia of American Political History
Encyclopedia of Crime and Justice
Encyclopedia of Educational Research
Encyclopedia of Psychology
International Encyclopedia of the Social Sciences
Literature of Geography
Literature of Political Science
New Dictionary of the Social Sciences

Women's Studies

Women's Studies Encyclopedia

FINDING A RESEARCH PATH:

World Wide Web

Here is Amira Patel's account of how she got started on a research project in her American immigration history course using the Web:

I was assigned a ten-page research paper on any aspect of immigration. I wasn't sure what I wanted to write about—maybe something on attitudes toward immigrants—so I decided to check out the Web and see if I could get some ideas for the paper.

First, I selected Infoseek as a search engine and entered the keyword "immigration." I got 56,518 pages so I felt a little overwhelmed. I decided to try "anti-immigration" and got a more manageable number, 218. Unfortunately, Infoseek couldn't process my request because the system was flooded with other requests.

Therefore, I decided to switch to Yahoo! Yahoo! can be good because it lets you match a keyword like "immigration" to categories. I first chose "Arts: Humanities: History: U.S. History: Immigration" and got four hits. I browsed each quickly. "Immigration in the Gilded Age and Progressive Era" brought up the issue of nativism and anti-immigration sentiment in the early 20th century, but I wasn't really sure I wanted to research that historical period.

Then I tried "Government Law: Immigration" and clicked on a link to the National Immigration Forum. I checked out the page "Immigration Facts" and then clicked on another link "Issue Brief: Cycles of Nativism in U.S. History." I read through it and became interested in the "English Only" movement. I got curious about why so many people think English should be the official language and why they feel that way right now, when there are so many new immigrants from Asia and Latin America coming into the United States.

Now that I had narrowed my search down to "English Only," I stayed with Yahoo! and typed in "English Only." The first site I got, "Language Policy Research Center," is about languages in Israel and was not helpful to my search. I tried a second site, James Crawford's "Language Policy Web Site and Emporium," and found a ton of information on the history of the English Only movement and English Only legislation. It also gives links to other web sites so that I could read what supporters of English Only, such as the advocacy group U.S. English, had to say about the issue.

By this point, I felt confident I had found a good topic in "English Only" and enough bibliographical sources to get started in the library. I decided I wanted to do research to explain why the English Only movement has emerged in recent years.

Full Coverage:US News:Immigration

News Stories:

- Study Indicates INS Naturalized Thousands of Ineligible Applicants - Washington Post (02/10/98)

- INS Proposing Citizenship Test Overhaul - Washington Post (02/09/98)

- U.S. Congressman Introduces Anti-Torture Bill - Reuters (02/05/98)

- Guatemalan Refugees Rally for Permanent Residency - LatinoLink (01/30/98)

- Immigration Advocates to Seek Softening of Laws - Washington Post (01/30/98)

- Immigrant pensioners cheating on health-tax payments - Jerusalem Post (01/28/98)

- Guatemalans Heading for Washington - LatinoLink (01/27/98)

- Report: Immigration agents now outnumber those in FBI - CNN (01/26/98)

- EU plans illegal immigrant measures - BBC (01/07/98)

- INS Given High Marks In Naturalization Audit - Washington Post (12/17/97)

more...

Related Web Sites

- Will the New Immigration Law Require Me to Leave the US? - questions and answers, by a U.S. immigration attorney.

- Future Immigrants or Illegal Aliens? - explanation of Section 245(i) of the Immigration and Nationality Act, set to expire Tuesday.

- Stop the Separation of Families - "Section 245(i) is set to expire September 30 and could lead to the separation of thousands of children and spouses from their family members." From the NNIRR.

- U.S. Immigration Law, Regulations and Procedures - many links to resources.

- Bharati Mukherjee: American Dreamer - "I am an American, not an Asian-American. My rejection of hyphenation has been called race treachery, but it is really a demand that America deliver the promises of its dream to all its citizens equally." From Mother Jones.

- American Immigration Center Citizenship Page

News Sources

Yahoo! News Search: Immigration

Wash Post/AP Search

Audio

Oct 14: New Immigration Rules

Yahoo! Categories

Immigration

U.S. Immigration Information

Video

CNN Report on Immigration

Internet

INS: Immigration

- <u>FAQ - U.S. Immigration</u>

- <u>House Leadership Action on Section 245(i) Subverts Laws Against Illegal Immigration</u> - press release.

- <u>National Immigration Forum (NIF)</u> - defends legal immigration, fights anti-immigrant prejudice, and preserves the American tradition of diversity.

- <u>Immigration Still a Plus for California Economy But Benefits Are Eroding</u> - from the RAND Institute.

<u>more...</u>

Search News Headlines

<u>options</u>

IMMIGRATION FACTS

The following pages cover a variety of immigration-related issues in an accessible format for your convenience.

The A,B,Cs of U.S. Immigration

Immigration Chronology

Facts on Refugees and Asylees

Facts on Employment-Based Immigration

Facts on Family-Sponsored Immigration

Facts on Immigrants and Public Benefits

Facts on Naturalization

Facts on Other INS Categories

Immigrants in the News

Issue Brief: Cycles of Nativism in U.S. History

Learning English - Some Basic Facts on Immigrants and Acquisition of tl Language

National Academy of Science Study Confirms Benefits of Immigration

GOLDEN DOOR   CURRENT ISSUES   IMMIGRATION FACTS   RACE/ETHNIC RELATIONS   HOME   SEARCH THIS SITE   DISCUSSION FORUM   NIF RESOURCES

IMMIGRATION FACTS

Issue Brief:
Cycles of Nativism
in U.S. History

Our progress in degeneracy appears to me to be pretty rapid. As a nation, we began by declaring that "all men are created equal." We now practically read it "all men are created equal, except Negroes." When the Know-Nothings get control, it will read "all men are created equal, except Negroes, and foreigners, and Catholics." When it comes to this I should prefer emigrating to some county where they make no pretence of loving liberty - to Russia, for instance, where despotism can be take pure, and without the base alloy of hypocrisy.

Abraham Lincoln

As a nation of immigrants, the United States has also been a nation of we have offered, in Tom Paine's words, "an asylum for the persecuted and religious liberty" from all parts of the world. At other times Ameri the persecuting—passing discriminatory laws against the foreign-born fundamental rights, assaulting them with mob violence, even lynching welcomed immigrants in periods of expansion and optimism, reviled t stagnation and cynicism. Our attitudes have depended primarily on dor economics, secondarily on the volume and characteristics of the newc American nativism has had less to do with "them" than us.

Friction is inevitable when cultures collide. All too often, immigrants a misunderstanding and intolerance. But ethnocentrism has flared into na ethnic prejudice has produced significant anti-immigrant movements— in U.S. history. Fear and loathing of foreigners reach such levels wher problems become so intractable that some people seek scapegoats. Typ periods feature a political or economic crisis, combined with a loss of f institutions and a sense that the national community is gravely fracturec yearning for social homogeneity that needs an internal enemy to sustain "alien." Nativists' targets have reflected America's basic divisions: clas and, to a lesser extent, language and culture. Yet each anti-immigrant c dynamics.

Alien and Sedition Acts. Few immigrants arrived in the nation among them were European radicals who caused great alarm among the Federalists. Worried that excessive democracy posed a threat to propert the Adams administration regarded politically active immigrants as subv mention partisan adversaries—most were aligned with Jefferson's Democratic-Republican clubs. In 1798, Congress passed the Alien and giving the President arbitrary powers to exclude or deport foreigners de and to prosecute anyone who criticized the government (used mainly to immigrant editors and pamphleteers). A new Naturalization Act sought t immigrants' electoral clout by extending the waiting period for citizensh

Protestant Crusade. Immigration grew sharply in the 1830s-40s increasingly Roman Catholic, with the arrival of large waves of Irish an Simultaneously a Protestant revival flourished in a climate of economic c insecurity. Evangelists demonized Catholics as "Papists" who followed leaders, imported crime and disease, stole native jobs, and practiced mo A barrage of such agitation led Protestant workingmen to burn the Ursul near Boston and to riot in several cities—30 were killed and hundreds in Philadelphia in 1844. By the mid-1850s the nativist American Party (a.k "Know-Nothings") won six governorships and controlled legislatures in Massachusetts, New Hampshire, Connecticut, Rhode Island, Pennsylva Maryland, Kentucky, and California. They enacted numerous laws to ha penalize immigrants (as well as newly annexed Mexicans), including the tests for voting, which were designed to disfranchise the Irish in particul the "un-American" foreigner served as a diversion for those unwilling to America's own irreconcilable difference—slavery versus abolition—whi nativists themselves. As sectional conflict sharpened, Know-Nothingism 1860, the party had virtually collapsed.

#3
(Add hvnd:) B Diagram of a Research Path

Here is a visualization of Amira's research path. Notice that, typical of most
Web searches, it is a wandering one, with some dead ends as well as important
leads.

In to seek

    ↳ "immigration" -- 56,518 pages

    ↳ "anti-immigration" -- 218 pages

          ↳ system couldn't process request....

Yahoo!

    ↳ "Immigration in the Gilded Age and Progressive Era"

        ↳ not sure....

    ↳ " National Immigration Forum"

        ↳ "Immigration Facts"

            ↳ " Issue Brief: Cycles 2 Nativism"

                ↳ English Only

                    ↳ " Language Policy Research
                          Center"↳ not relevant....

                  ↳ "Language Policy Web Site +
                      Emporium"

                        ↳ " English Only movement
                          ↳ FOCUS!

("Language Policy Web Site + Emporium" and "English Only
Movement" appear in Chapter 14.)

USING SEARCH ENGINES

The search engines that are readily available through Web browsers like Netscape may search different sites, so if you don't find what you are looking for with one, try another.

The key to using search engines is finding the right keyword or combination of keywords for your purposes. As you have seen, when Amira used "immigration" as a keyword on Infoseek, she got over 50,000 hits, clearly an unmanageable number. But when she shifted to "anti-immigration," she got 218. And as you can see in the account of her search, switching from the broad topic "immigration" to the more limited one "English Only" helped make her search more focused and more productive.

Another way to focus a search is to combine keywords with operators (AND, OR, NOT, quotation marks, etc.). For example, if you type the two words—death penalty—you will be inundated with sources because your search will find documents that contain either of the words entered. (One search engine found 15,819, most of which had nothing to do with the death penalty.) However, if you put quotation marks around the words—"death penalty"—you turn it into one phrase and set up a more focused search. Furthermore, if you combine the phrase "death penalty" with another keyword, such as "abolish" or the phrase "supreme court," you can focus your search considerably. By using "death penalty" AND abolish

a search turned up 21 hits, most or all of which are likely to be relevant.

Popular search engines include the following:

AltaVista   http://altavista.digital.com
Searches more than 30 million pages on the Web and Usenet newsgroups.

Elnet's   Galaxy
http://galaxy.einet.net/galaxy.html
An indexed directory of selected information on the World Wide Web sorted by subject area.

Excite   http://www.excite.com
Provides weekly updates of Web site reviews, as well as current news and newsgroups.

Infoseek http://guide.infoseek.com
Searches Web pages and Usenet newsgroups, offers news and reviews from newspapers and magazines; permits users to post search questions.

Lycoshttp://www.lycos.com
A comprehensive search engine of Web sites, offers quick searches of a limited number of sites and in-depth searches of its entire collection.

Magellan   http://www.mckinley.com
Includes reviews of selected sites and categories to narrow searches.

Yahoo! http://www.yahoo.com
Enables users to link keywords to categories.

DEVELOPING A RESEARCH QUESTION

Once you've done some preliminary research, use the following questions to refine your own sense of the research question you want to investigate:

1. What questions, issues, and problems appear repeatedly? Why do people seem to think they are important?
2. Are there arguments, debates, or controversies that appear in what you've read? What positions have others taken? What seems to be at stake in these arguments? Do you find yourself siding with some people and disagreeing with others?
3. Is there some aspect of your topic that people don't seem to pay much attention to? Why do you think this is so? Are they neglecting questions or issues that could provide a good focus for research?
4. Given what you've read so far, what are the most interesting questions, issues, arguments, controversies for you? What, in your view, makes them important?

EVALUATING A RESEARCH QUESTION

Let's say, for example, that your preliminary research for a course on the history of postwar America has led you from the general topic "Race in America" to the more specific topic "Asian Americans" to the research question "Do media portrayals of Asian Americans perpetuate social stereotypes?" This sounds like a good starting point, but it's worth pausing for a moment to make sure. Here are some questions that can help you evaluate your research question:

1. Are you genuinely interested in the question? (Research is work and takes time, so you want to be sure you are committed enough to sustain your efforts.)
2. Is the question an important one that will have significance for others? Does the question pose a significant problem, investigate a controversy, or participate in an ongoing debate? (You'll be making the results of your research public, so you need to make sure others will find it meaningful. It doesn't make sense, for example, to research the question "Was Captain Cook the first European to travel to Australia?" because the answer is already accepted as established fact.)
3. Is your research question limited enough to handle in the amount of time you have available and in the length of the paper you've been assigned? (Plenty of good research questions may be too big to treat effectively, given constraints of time and space.)
4. Are there enough sources available to find the information you need to answer your research question? (If not, you need to revise, modify, or abandon your research question.)

Writing a Proposal

Some teachers ask students to write a proposal that defines the purpose of their research, explains its significance, and indicates their research plan. Even if your teacher does not require a proposal, writing one can be a useful exercise to help you clarify your purpose. To say that you want to investigate a particular question is only the beginning. You will also need to decide how you plan to handle the information you turn up in your research. Your purpose and the stance you take toward your readers and the material can vary considerably. Here are some typical purposes of researchers:

- To provide an overview of the current thinking of experts. In this case, your purpose is largely an informative one, to report on what experts in the field think about an important issue. You might, for example, explain the current views of experts on the extinction of dinosaurs or report the latest results of drug treatment of HIV-positive people.

- To review the arguments in a controversy. Again, your purpose is largely informative, to explain to readers what positions people have taken in a current debate. You might, for example, explain current debates in literary studies between those who believe there is an established canon of masterpieces all students should read and those who believe the traditional canon excludes women, minority, working-class, and Third World writers. Or you could report on the current legal controversy prompted by the prosecution of pregnant women for doing harm to their fetuses by drinking or taking drugs.

- To answer an important question or solve a problem. In this case, your purpose is not simply to report on what is known but to put forward your own analysis and interpretation. You might, for example, explain why there has been a resurgence of tuberculosis or what the consequences of deregulation in the telecommunications industry have been.

- To position your own interpretation in relation to what others have said. In this case, your purpose is similar in many respects to that of answering an important question. The key difference is that instead of simply using what others have written as evidence for your interpretation, you also explain how your analysis or interpretation relates to the views of others—how and why it differs, how and why it shares common ground. You might, for example, position your own interpretation of Madonna as a cultural symbol in relation to others' interpretations of her. Or you might explain how your analysis of Martin Luther King's "I Have a Dream" speech differs from and is similar to the analyses of others.

- To take a stand in a controversy. Here your purpose is not simply to report and analyze but also to persuade. In this case, you have an argument to make. You might claim, for example, that there should (or should not) be mandatory testing for the HIV virus. Or you could argue that the U.S. should (or should not) adopt more stringent limits on commercial fishing in the North Atlantic.

SAMPLE RESEARCH PROPOSAL

Here is an example of what a research proposal might look like. Notice how it does three things: 1) explains the purpose of the research, 2) indicates its significance, and 3) sketches briefly the research plan:

My plan is to research the question "Do media portrayals of Asian Americans perpetuate social stereotypes?" Given what I've read so far, my basic purpose will be to show that this is an important question and to provide some answers. I haven't found any major differences of opinion or interpretation, so I don't foresee any major controversies I'll need to talk about. I will need to explain how the media portrays Asian Americans and define what a social stereotype is and the effects it has. From what I've read, it seems the media pictures Asian Americans as good at math and science, hardworking, serious, and eager to assimilate. As I see it, the problem here is that this picture lumps all Asian Americans together and overlooks significant differences between Chinese, Japanese, Koreans, and Southeast Asians. The "all work, no play" stereotype also ignores the poverty and gang life in certain Asian American communities. I plan to do more reading. I've got plenty of sources that look good. And I'll probably watch some recent movies, such as Joy Luck Club and Wedding Banquet.

FINDING SOURCES

Once you have established a direction for your research project, the next step is to do in-depth research. By this point, you have probably turned up a number of promising sources through your preliminary research. This section provides information on keeping a working bibliography and how you can find further sources.

Keeping a Working Bibliography

A working bibliography is just what it says: a list of the sources you plan to work with on your research project. A working bibliography can save you a lot of time and aggravation by serving two important purposes: 1) it enables you to keep track of the sources you want to consult, and 2) when you're finishing your paper, it makes it easy for you to prepare your Works Cited or References page (without having to make last-minute trips to the library to get bibliographical information).

Include in your working bibliography more sources than you expect to use in the final paper. Some of the sources may be unavailable at your library, and others may not be useful to your purposes. If you've done a good job of research, you won't use all the sources you've found.

Researchers have different styles of keeping working bibliographies. You can use 3 x 5 cards, with a new note card for each entry. This enables you to put your entries in order by topics when you're doing research and alphabetically when you're preparing your paper. Or you might prefer to use a computer. Many word processing, spread sheet, and data base programs allow you to sort entries and print out lists, which can be added to as you go along and turned into the final Works Cited or Reference page when you've finished.

The working bibliography should contain the information that you need to find the source and the information you'll need for your Works Cited or Reference page.

Books

Call number
Author(s), editor(s), translator(s)
Title and subtitle
City of publication, name of publisher, and date of publication

Articles

Author(s)
Title and subtitle of article
Periodical name
Volume and issue number (if periodical uses them)
Date
Page numbers

Electronic Information

Name of source
Date you accessed information
Name of sender, if e-mail
Electronic address

THE LIBRARY CATALOG

Your college library is likely to be your main source for books and periodicals. A library catalog lists the library's holdings by author, title, periodical, and subject. Libraries have traditionally used card catalogs, and researchers shuttled from drawer to draw to find the information they were looking for. Today, most libraries have replaced the unwieldy card catalog by putting their catalogs on line.

As you can see from the following screen introducing users to the online catalog at the University of South Florida, you can search by author, title, periodical, subject, or keyword. Your library's catalog may differ from the one shown here. Check with your reference librarian for information on how to use it.

UNIV OF SOUTH FLORIDA

University of South Florida Catalog
(Copyright 1985, State University System of Florida)
Type command WITH   To search by: Examples:
search term:

A=	Authors	a=twain mark
T=	All titles	t=tom sawyer
TJ=	Journal/magazine/newspaper titles	tj=newsweek
S=	General subject headings	s=ecology
SM=	Medical subject headings	sm=myocardia
CL=	Library of Congress call numbers	cl=qh546.3
K=	Keywords	k=solar energy

or WITHOUT search term:
K to get Keyword input screen
EXS to enter a complex keyword search
Search statements are made up of a letter representing the type of search desired, followed by = (equals sign) and the search term(s).
Example: A=SHAKESPEAREFind all authors with the last name SHAKESPEARE

To do a subject heading search, you can save time by first consulting the Library of Congress Subject Headings (LCSH), a reference source that lists the standard subject headings used in catalogs and indexes.

FINDING A RESEARCH PATH:

The Library Catalog

Let's return to Amira Patel's research on the English Only movement. Here is her account of how she used the library catalog.

I already had the titles of some books from browsing the Web, but I wanted to do a systematic search of the university library.

First, I tried "English-only movement" as a subject heading and got the titles of two books. When I looked up one of the book titles in the online catalog, I noticed that the entry listed a number of other subjects: "Language policy—United States," "English language—Political aspects—

United States," and "English language—social aspects—United States."

So next, I tried each of the three subject headings. The best one by far was "Language policy—United States." It turned up seventeen references.

Finally, I decided to take a little different approach and do a keyword search using "immigration and language." This gave me a list of eleven other books. Not all of these are relevant, but a number look like they might give me a useful perspective on language policy issues like English Only.

I printed out all the searches and started to look for individual books. Then I headed for the stacks.

As you can see from the following entry for the book Nativism reborn?: the official English only movement and the American states, online catalogs provide a good deal of information about the library's holdings. In addition, some online catalogs allow users to browse the shelf where the book is located, to see other related titles.

Indiana University Libraries

INDYCAT

Subject Search Request: Nativism reborn? : the official English language movement and the

LONG VIEW

| Help | New Subject Search | Return to Title List | Search Menu |

Author Tatalovich, Raymond.

Title Nativism reborn? : the official English language movement and the American states / Raymond Tatalovich.

Published Lexington, Ky. : University Press of Kentucky, 1995.

Description xiii, 319 p. ; 23 cm.   *Number of pages, whether illustrated, size*

Notes Includes bibliographical references and index.   *Information on content*

Subjects Language policy--United States.

English language--Political aspects--United States   *Related Library of Congress*
English language--Social aspects--United States.   *subject headings*
English-only movement

ISBN 0813119189 (acid-free)   *Book number useful for locating or purchasing*

Location IUPUI UNIV LIB

Call Number P119.32.U6 T38 1995

Status ~~Item missing~~ *Checked in*

| Help | New Subject Search | Return to Title List | Search Menu |

Indiana University Libraries

INDYCAT

Subject Search Request: Language policy--United States.
Search Results: 17 results
TITLE LIST
    Select item and click on location code for call number and available copies.

| Browse List | New Subject Search | Search Menu |

English Language Empowerment Act of 1996 : report together with m   1996
    Held by: [I-IUPUI UL]

English-only question : an official language for Americans? /   1990
    Held by: [I-IUPUI UL]

English--our official language? /   1994
    Held by: [I-IUPUI UL] [Columbus]

Ethnicity and language /   1987
    Held by: [I-IUPUI UL]

Hearing on English as a common language : hearing before the Subc   1996
    Held by: [I-IUPUI UL]

Hearing on English as the common language : hearing before the Su   1996
    Held by: [I-IUPUI UL]

Hold your tongue : bilingualism and the politics of English only   1992
    Held by: [I-IUPUI UL]

Language loyalties : a source book on the official English contro   1992
    Held by: [I-IUPUI UL]

Languages in America : a pluralist view /   1996

Latino language and education : communication and the dream defer   1995
    Held by: [I-IUPUI UL]

Nativism reborn? : the official English language movement and the   1995
    Held by: [I-IUPUI UL]

Official English, English only : more than meets the eye /   1988
    Held by: [I-IUPUI UL]

Only English? : law and language policy in the United States /   1990
    Held by: [I-IUPUI UL]

Perspectives on official English : the campaign for English as th   1990
    Held by: [I-IUPUI UL]

S. 356--Language of Government Act of 1995 : hearings before the   1996
    Held by: [I-IUPUI UL]

Voting Rights Act Language Assistance Amendments of 1992 : hearin   1993

Voting Rights Act Language Assistance Amendments of 1992 report t   1992

BIBLIOGRAPHIES

Bibliographies list books and articles published on particular subjects. One place to look for bibliographies, of course, is in the books and articles you're already using in your research. Web sites, especially those maintained for academic purposes, often include bibliographies. You may notice that some books and articles appear frequently in bibliographies, Works Cited, or References. If so, the book or article listed is probably an important one and therefore worth looking at.

You can also find book-length bibliographies devoted to specific topics or fields of study, usually in the reference section of the library. Some bibliographies are annotated, including brief descriptions of the entries and sometimes evaluations. Make sure you consult an up-to-date bibliography. The Bibliographic Index is published every year, providing a master list of bibliographies from that year. Check back over several years to see what is available that might be relevant to your research.

Here are some standard bibliographies in a number of academic fields:

Annual Bibliography of English Language and Literature
Film Research: A Critical Bibliography with Annotations and Essays
Foreign Affairs Bibliography
International Bibliography of the Social Sciences
MLA International Bibliography of Books and Articles on Modern
　Languages and Literatures
References Sources in English and American Literature: An
　Annotated Bibliography

PERIODICAL INDEXES

For many research projects, the most up-to-date sources available on a topic appear in periodicals—newspapers, magazines, academic journals, and professional publications. You can locate articles in periodicals by consulting an index—whether in a traditional print version or online.

Indexes can treat a general range of subjects and current affairs, The Readers' Guide to Periodical Literature, for example, indexes articles in popular magazines by author, title, and subject. Here is what Amira Patel found under the heading "English language" from the 1995 volume.

ENGLISH LANGUAGE
　　See also
　　Booksellers and bookselling—English language literature
　　English as a second language
　　Sex discrimination in language
The comeback of English. D. Seligman. il *Fortune* v131 p141
　Ap 3 '95
One nation, one language? [English-only movement; cover story] S. Headden. il map *U.S. News & World Report* v119
　p38–42 S 25 '95
Open letter [G.O.P. must respond to court decision striking
　down Arizona's English-only law] *National Review* v47
　p14+ N 6 '95
Se habla. ingles [debate over English as the national language]
　W. F. Buckley. *National Review* v47 p70–1 O 9 '95
Speaking in tongues [opinions of S. Reinhardt and A. Kozinski in court decision striking down Arizona's English-only
　law] H. Johnson. il *National Review* v47 p28–30 N 6 '95
　　　Accents
Let's talk southern [C. O. Hadley teaches southern accent to
　actors] C. Griffith-Roberts. il por *Southern Living* v30 p82
　F '95

The following list includes some of the most frequently used indexes. Many are also available in online or CD-ROM versions, sometimes under a different title. (See the next section on Electronic Databases.)

GENERAL

Readers' Guide to Periodical Literature

New York Times Index

Wall Street Journal Index

Washington Post Index

Editorials on File

Facts on File

Access: The Supplementary Index to Periodicals

Alternative Press Index

Left Index

Chicano Index

Index to Black Periodicals

Business Periodical Index

Biography Index

General Academic Index

SPECIALIZED (by field)

Education

Current Index to Journals in Education

Education Index

Humanities

America: History and Life

Art Index

Historical Abstracts

Humanities Index

Music Index

Philosopher's Index

Religion Index One: Periodicals

Science and Technology

Applied Science and Technology Index

Biological and Agricultural Index

Engineering Index

General Science Index

Index Medicus

Physics Abstracts

Science Abstracts

Social Sciences

American Statistics Index

Index to Legal Periodicals

PAIS (Public Affairs Information Service) International in Print

Psychological Abstracts

Social Sciences Index

ELECTRONIC DATABASES

As already noted, many of the indexes listed above are available in online or CD-ROM versions. Like online catalogs, electronic databases have several advantages over their printed counterparts. To begin with, they can be updated more frequently than the print sources, allowing you to find more current information. Also, instead of searching indexes volume by volume to get information on your topic from different years, you can search the entire index at once—or you can limit your search to certain years. Finally, many databases provide abstracts or full-text articles online.

Some data bases can also help you locate sources. They'll tell you whether the sources are in your library or in a library that participates with yours in an interlibrary loan program. Some data bases will also provide copies of articles by mail or e-mail, usually for a fee.

Check with your reference librarian about what electronic databases are available at your college library.

FINDING A RESEARCH PATH:

Electronic Databases

Let's follow Amira Patel again, as she checks out electronic databases in her college library.

I felt that I had pretty much identified the books I needed for my research, but I had very few articles on language policy in the United States or the English Only movement. So I decided to try doing a computer search. I had never done this before so I asked a librarian to show me what to do. She gave me a list of the indexes in the social sciences available online and explained that I could search more than one at a time.

The most promising database seemed to be Sociofile but I also included Criminal Justice Abstracts, PAIS International, and Social Work Abstracts in the search. As usual the big thing was finding the right keywords. First I tried "immigration" and "language" and got 323 references. I took a look at the first few and realized I needed more focus. So I decided to use "Language policy—United States" as keywords. It worked when I was searching the library catalog, and it worked again. I got 30 references—many of which are relevant. And I also got abstracts of each article.

```
WinSPIRS 2.0

Usage is subject to the terms and conditions of the subscription and License Agreement and the
applicable Copyright and intellectual property protection as dictated by the appropriate laws of
your country and/or International Convention.

  No.      Records    Request
    1        20442     LANGUAGE
    2       137013     POLICY
    3       257170     THE
    4       173538     UNITED
    5       186668     STATES
*   6           30     LANGUAGE POLICY AND THE UNITED STATES

Record 1 of 30 - PAIS International 1972-1/98
AN:  91-0301338
TI:  The "official English" movement and the symbolic politics of language in the United States.
AU:  Citrin,-Jack
SO:  Western-Political-Quarterly; 43:535-59 S 1990
PY:  1990
NT:  Analyzes the role of feelings of national identity in the debate over language policy.
DE:  United-States-Languages; United-States-Nationalism; Bilingualism-United-States
LA:  E; English
IS:  0043-4078
SF:  bibl(s) table(s)
PT:  P; Periodical
```

Record 2 of 30 - Social Work Abstracts 1977-9/97
AN: 21739
TI: Effects of the English-only movement on bilingual education.
AU: Edwards-R-L; Curiel-H
AD: Mandel School of Applied Social Sciences, Case Western Reserve Univ., Cleveland, OH 44106
SO: Social-Work-in-Education. 12(1): 53-66, Oct. 1989.
PY: 1989
HC: 26(1), 1990, No. 306
AB: In recent years, we have witnessed in this country the emergence of a new social movement,
     called the English-only movement, that advocates the adoption of legislation making English
     the official language of our land. This movement focuses much of its attention on efforts to
     eliminate bilingual education. A study provides an overview of the evolution of the
     English-only movement in the United States, with particular attention paid to the
     relationship between that movement and bilingual education. The history of official U.S.
     involvement with language policy is reviewed, and the potential impact of the legislative
     agenda of English-only proponents is considered.
DE: Bilingual-programs; Education-
CC: 3230 Education-Schools

Record 3 of 30 - sociofile 1/74-12/97
TI: The Hispanophobia of the Official English Movement in the United States; La hispanofobia del
     movimiento "Ingles oficial" en los Estados Unidos por la oficializacion del ingles
AU: Zentella,-Ana-Celia; Sepulveda,-Sandra
IN: City U New York, NY 10021
JN: Alteridades; 1995, 5, 10, 55-65.
IS: 0188-7017
CO: ALTEFL
NT: Translated from English by Sandra Sepulveda.
DT: aja Abstract-of-Journal-Article
LA: Spanish
CP: Mexico
PY: 1995
AB: Recent attempts in the US to introduce various laws on state & federal levels sanctioning
     exclusive use of English in public communication & efforts to amend the country's
     constitution by recognizing English as the only official language of the land are
     interpreted as hispanophobic, discriminatory, & racist. The social & political causes are
     sought, & the arguments behind these initiatives are refuted. After some episodes of
     linguistic intolerance are related, results of a questionnaire conducted in 1988 & 1994 (N =
     417 & 320, respectively) are reported. Informants of different ethnic origins were asked
     their opinions regarding the bilingualism of 911 operators, bilingual ballots, education, &
     advertising & official status of English. Changes between 1988 & 1994 are discussed, &
     ethnic origin is identified as the dominant variable affecting attitudes. Adapted from the
     source document. (Copyright 1997, Sociological Abstracts, Inc., all rights reserved.)
DE: *Language-Policy (D445500); *Nativism- (D550200); *Bilingualism- (D079500); *Hispanic-
     Americans (D360600); *Racism- (D690000); *Xenophobia- (D935200); *Whites- (D919800); *Social-
     Attitudes (D780300); *English-Language (D261600)

Government Publications

The United States government publishes massive amounts of information annually, largely through
the Government Printing Office (GPO). Some of the most commonly used publications are these:

Congressional Quarterly Almanac. Published annually, includes overview of legislation
and policy, as well as important speeches an debates and some analysis.

Congressional Quarterly Weekly Report. Weekly news updates on legislative and
executive actions, includes overviews of policy debates.

Statistical Abstract of the United States. Annual report of the Bureau of the Census,
includes a range of social, economic, and political statistics, with tables, graphs, charts, and
references to other sources.

Many government documents are now available online:

"Keeping America Informed." The home page of the GPO, provides online access to many publications.   http://www.gpo.gov/

Library of Congress. Offers access to an enormous range of government and library resources.
          http://lcweb.loc.gov

"Thomas: Legislative Information on the Internet." Developed by the Library of Congress,
includes databases on Congress, current bills, public laws, committee information, online version
of the Congressional Record, and historical documents.   http://thomas.loc.gov/

FINDING A RESEARCH PATH:

Using Government Documents

Here is Amira's account of how she found government documents relevant to her research.

As I got deeper into my research, I realized that the English Only movement emerged as immigration to the United States increased after the immigration law changed in 1965. I wanted to get some statistics on the patterns of immigration—where people came from, how many new immigrants there are, where they settled. I remembered that one of the Web sites I had browsed when I was getting started included a link to the U.S. Immigration and Naturalization Service (INS) home page, so I decided to check it out. I found it contained lots of the information I was looking for.

| Home | Where is? | Text Only | | INS |

United States Immigration & Naturalization Servic

- INS home
- INS forms
- law & regulations
- public affairs
- statistics
- employer information
- what's new?
- inside INS
- other government sites

Immigration and Naturalization Statistics

Welcome to the INS Statistics page. This page provides comprehensive annual immigration statistics from 1994-1996, as well as state estimates of the United States' illegal alien resident and foreign-born populations. Also, be sure to check out the updated Immigration Fact Sheet. Test your knowledge by checking out the overview of the legislative history of immigration to the United States in the Statistical Yearbook.

- Annual Statistical Reports
  - Immigration to the United States in Fiscal Year 1996
  - Immigration to the United States in Fiscal Year 1995
  - Immigration to the United States in Fiscal Year 1994
- Illegal Alien Resident Population
- State Population Estimates of Legal Permanent Residents and Aliens Eligible to Apply for Naturalization
- INS Statistical Publications
- Immigration Fact Sheet
- Immigration and Naturalization Legislation from Statistical Yearbook
- Glossary from Statistical Yearbook
- U.S. Census Bureau: The Foreign-Born Population

Last Modified 11/25/1997

Other Internet Sources

Browsing the Web has become, without a doubt, the most popular way of searching for information on the Internet. There are, however, a number of other ways to access information in cyberspace. Here are brief descriptions:

Telnet. Telnet is an application that allows you to log on to a remote computer, called a host computer, and access its services and information. Many libraries, for example, allow Telnet access to their catalogs, so that you can browse the holdings of, say, the New York Public Library or the Harvard University library without leaving your computer terminal at home. Telnet also enables you to use FTP and gopher to locate and download information from host computers anywhere in the world.

File Transfer Protocol (FTP). File transfer protocol (FTP) is a communication tool that can connect you to a file server and copy files directly to your computer. Like telnet, FTP enables you to log on to a host computer. In addition, it also allows you to transfer information from the host to your computer, provided that you have been granted access. Many libraries and other information sources have publicly accessible host computers you can log on to by entering "anonymous" or "guest" or pressing Enter.

Gopher. Gopher is one of the earliest protocols for searching the Internet. Gopher programs can simplify searchs by allowing users to browse by topic (instead of file name). Since Gopherspace links computers all over the world, navigating through all the directories to find files would be impossible if it weren't for the gopher search protocols—such as Veronica, Jughead, and Archie—which use keywords and allow you to limit your search using operators.

E-mail, Listservs, and Newsgroups. You may also find it helpful to read listservs or newsgroups on the topic you're researching and to post queries. You might also consider e-mailing questions to someone knowledgeable about your topic.

"Real Time" Communication. Internet Relay Chat (IRC), MUDs, and MOOs enable users to communicate instantaneously. Some Web sites include chat rooms where "real time" conversations take place, and some e-mail programs offer "real time" talk sessions. These are often used for social purposes, but depending on availability and your own interest, you may find "real time" conversation a viable option in contacting other Internet users concerning your research project.

FINDING A RESEARCH PATH:

Posting a Query

Amira decided she would check out listservs to see if there were ongoing discussions of language policy and English only. One of the librarians showed her how to find locate online discussion groups. Under the heading "languages and linguistics," Amira found a number of listservs, including Multi-L, maintained by the International Association of Applied Linguistics and devoted to "the exchange of information, news, and opinion about all aspects of minority language education."

Amira wrote a brief query, explaining her research project and requesting suggestions.

Friends: I am an undergraduate doing research on the emergence of the English Only movement. One of the central claims of English Only supporters is that the U.S. needs an official language because many recent immigrants, especially Spanish speakers, resist learning English. Do you know of any studies that investigate the acquisition of English by immigrants? Any suggestions would be appreciated. A quick response would help me a lot. Thanks in advance.

Within a few days, Amira received six messages with information on recent studies of English acquisition, as well as notes of encouragement and further reading suggestions.

READING AND EVALUATING SOURCES

How you read depends on your purpose and where you are in the research process. As you have seen, preliminary research involves reading to develop a research question. At such early stages in your research, you may well be doing a good deal of skimming, just to get a sense of what the issues are.

Once you've decided on a research question and located sources, you can get down to the work of reading with a direction in mind. At this stage, you are probably reading to gather information and to understand what others have said about the question you're investigating.

As you read, you also need to start thinking about how you can use your sources in your research paper. It can helpful to see the reading you do as part of planning your paper. Here are some of the ways researchers typically use source material in shaping their research reports:

- To provide background information on the question

- To review previous research on the question

- To explain existing differences of analysis and interpretation of the question

- To offer supporting evidence for your position

- To present counterevidence that calls your position into question

—evidence you'll need to account for

- To present opposing positions you'll need to respond to

TAKING NOTES

The way you take notes will depend on what you are reading and what use you might make of it. For example, if it's fairly early in your research, you may not be sure a particular source will be useful. In such cases, you can just write a short summary, noting what kinds of information the reading contains. Later on, you can go back and take fuller notes if it makes sense to do so.

For readings that provide background information, record the pertinent facts and data. In other cases, especially when you're reading about previous research or existing differences of interpretation, your notes should be more extensive. If your purpose is to answer an important question or solve a problem, you may want to indicate in your notes how the evidence you've turned up provides support for your interpretation or analysis. If you're planning to explain how your views relate to others' views or to argue a position where there are opposing views, make sure you summarize fully and fairly what others have said.

Perhaps the most important point to make about taking notes is that they need to be complete and accurate. You can avoid the last-minute hassle of running back to the library to check a fact or statistic by making sure you record it accurately in the first place. The same is true for quotes. Make sure you copy the writer's words exactly and that you put in quotation marks so you'll know where the quote begins and ends. And don't forget to note the number of the page on which the quote appears.

People use different methods of taking notes. Some like note cards because you can arrange them according to the sections of your paper. Others worry note cards will get lost and prefer to use spiral notebooks where you can keep all your notes in one place. Still others like to make photocopies to underline and annotate—and then quote or cite directly. Finally, researchers are increasingly using computers to record and store notes. Computer programs can save you time by allowing you to search your notes for keywords and phrases and to cut and paste quotes.

FINDING A RESEARCH PATH:

Taking Notes

Here are the notes Amira Patel took on an article she found in the National Review. Notice how she is careful first to record information and quotes fully and accurately from the article. Then she follows up with her own notes about how she might use this source and what further questions it raises for her research.

O'Beirne, Kate. "English as the Official Language of the U.S. and Bilingual Education." National Review 1 July 1996: 21.

Cites a number of opinion polls:

- In a 1996 Gallup poll, 82% favored making English the official language.
- A 1993 poll by the Tarrance Group found 78% of registered voters favored official-English laws, and over 60% favored it strongly.
- A 1993 poll by the San Francisco Chronicle found that 90% of Filipino, 78% of Chinese, and nearly 70% of Hispanic immigrants in California favored official English.

Gives details on the Republican Party position on official English and bilingual education, ballots, and health care. Argues that given popular support for official English and opposition to bilingualism, Republican should take a stronger line.

Key quote:

"We must stop the practice of multilingual education as a means of instilling ethnic pride, or as a therapy for low self-esteem, or out of elitist guilt over a culture build on the traditions of the West." Bob Dole, in a speech to the American Legion.

Notes:

Check San Francisco Chronicle poll. I may need to explain such high support of official English among immigrant groups. My guess is it's a sign of the desire to assimilate and could be used to argue that official English is unnecessary.

English Only and bilingual education is caught up to some extent in party politics. But I'm not sure this helps explain it.

Quote from Dole may be useful in defining the English Only position.

EVALUATING SOURCES

Evaluating sources is treated in detail in "Evaluating" in Chapter 2 and "Questions to Ask About Evidence" in Chapter 3. The following questions distill the main considerations you should take into account. Consult the relevant sections in the two chapters for a fuller discussion.

1. Does the source provide information that is relevant to your research question? Don't include a source just because it has interesting information or gives you another item for your Works Cited page.
2. Is the source up-to-date? Or, if it's an older source, is it acknowledged as important by recent writers in the field? After all, intellectual figures such as Darwin, Marx, Freud, and Max Weber are still important.
3. What credibility does the writer have? Is he or she recognized as an authority in the field?
4. What is the writer's point of view? What are his or her political or social allegiances? How do these allegiances influence what you have read?
5. Is the publication in which the source appears or the press that published it one of good reputation? What is its editorial slant?

Keeping an Open Mind

One of the main purposes of doing research is to learn new things and encounter new perspectives. It's helpful to imagine research not just as a matter of looking things up but of making new acquaintances and listening to what they have to say.

Research involves you in an ongoing conversation, and as in any conversation in which you participate, other speakers may well influence what you think and believe. Stay open to these influences. Don't let yourself get boxed in trying to prove something when the weight of the evidence runs against you. Be flexible. It's not unusual that researchers modify their initial ideas in light of what they find in their research. On the other hand, don't be bullied into abandoning your views. Just because someone you've read is an expert in the field doesn't necessarily mean that you should agree with his or her views or that you can't come up with persuasive alternatives.

A good way to keep an open mind during the process of research is to use exploratory writing periodically to reflect on what you've been reading. You might, for example, respond to the following questions to think about your research:

1. Given what you've read so far, what sources have made the strongest impression on you, whether you agree with them or not?
2. How have these and other sources influenced your thinking? Do you see your research question in the same way you did when you started researching? What changes, if any, have occurred?
3. What new questions or perspectives have you encountered? How do you plan to deal with them?

(See "Exploratory Writing" in Chapter 2.)

PLANNING AND DRAFTING

There's always more to read, and it may seem that the research process could continue indefinitely. In certain respects, of course, this is true. Individuals have devoted their lives to research and never really reached the end of what they could learn. That's why deadlines are so useful—to remind us we need to emerge from the research process and start writing.

An important point here is that you need to make sure you're not using research to procrastinate and avoid writing. As already mentioned, when you're reading and evaluating your sources, you should also be making tentative plans about how to use these materials in your paper. Moreover, you can begin drafting well before you end your research. In fact, many researchers find that drafting helps them refine the focus of their research and directs them to issues they need to investigate further. To put it another way, you don't have to stop your research when you begin writing. But you do have to begin writing.

FINDING A RESEARCH PATH:

Sketching an Outline

Once her research got into high gear, Amira Patel decided to sketch an outline of her paper. She realized that this was only a tentative plan, but it helped her see what kind of information and analysis she needed.

Set up the issue of English Only

background information on states with English Only laws

public opinion polls

emergence of U.S. English and English First

present basic positions and arguments of English Only

State purpose of paper: to explain the emergence of English

Only movement as "hispanophobia" resulting from new

patterns of immigration and cultural anxiety

Historical background

relation of language policy and nativism/Americanization

Anti-Irish literacy requirements for voting (1850s)

American Protective Association's campaign vs. German-

language instruction in parochial schools (1880s)

U.S. Bureau of Americanization (early 1900s)

1965 Immigration Reform Act

ended racial quotas

"new immigration"

demographic shifts—increase in Latino population

Analysis of English Only movement

familiar sources of nativism

economic stagnation (California)

widening gap between rich and poor

distrust of public institutions

breakdown of community

"hispanophobia" in California and the Southwest historical roots

present manifestations

explain focus on language as symbol of imagined lost community

CHAPTER
SIXTEEN

FIELD RESEARCH

Not all research is conducted in the library, of course. In fact, the library may be just a starting point, providing you with an overview of your topic and the background information you need in order to undertake field research. Field research includes making observations, conducting interviews, using questionnaires, attending performances, and watching the media. In fact, researchers often combine two or more of these methods in a research project.

Researchers turn to these methods of inquiry when they have questions that can't be addressed solely on the basis of print or electronic sources. Here are some research questions that call for field work:

- to determine whether a shopping mall in the area should enforce a curfew for teenagers, you could observe the mall on weekend nights to see what danger or nuisance, if any, teenagers pose

- to compare the personal experiences of Vietnam veterans to historians' accounts of the war, a student in an American history course decides to locate and interview five vets

- to find out how much the undergraduates at their college drink each week, a group of students design and administer an anonymous questionnaire

- to write a paper in a literature course on the popularity of Poetry Slams, it would make sense to attend a number of performances

- to research the plots of soap operas, the role of the audience in daytime talk TV, or the films of Martin Scorsese, you would no doubt spend a good deal of time watching footage

As you can see from these examples, the kind of field research you do and how extensive it will be depends on the questions with which you begin, as well as the amount of time you have. Field research can be time consuming, but it can also give you information and insights that you could not get any other way.

In this chapter, we'll look at how researchers work in the field and three common methods they use—observation, interviews, and questionnaires. Then we'll look briefly at how to use performances, museums, and the media for research.

OBSERVATIONS

Observation has an important advantage over other research methods: it gives you direct access to people's behaviors. Let's say you've done some background research on how men and women interact in conversations and want to test some of the findings in the published literature. You might decide, for example, to see whether students at your college follow the pattern described by Deborah Tannen in You Just Don't Understand that men interrupt more during conversations and are less likely to use questions to elicit comments from others. Interviewing or surveying wouldn't give you very reliable information, because even if people were willing to be honest about how they behave in conversations, it's not likely that they could be accurate. In contrast, by going to the school dining hall over a period of several days, you could observe what men and women in fact do when they talk and what conversational patterns emerge.

The Process of Observation

Here are some basic considerations to take into account when you're making observations.
Planning.
These questions can help guide your planning:

- Why does the line of research you're pursuing seem to call for observation? What research question or questions are you addressing?

- How exactly can observations help you answer your research question?

- What kinds of observations would be most useful? Who and what do you want to observe? What are the best times and places for these observations? How many observations should you do?

- What should your observations focus on? What exactly do you want to record in your field notes? What method or methods will you use to record your observations? You may need to request permission to observe, as well as permission to use any recording devices.

Conducting Observations

When you arrive at the place you're observing, look for a vantage point where you will be able to see what's going on and yet won't be obtrusive. Consider whether you want to move periodically from one spot to another—to get a number of different perspective on the activity or place you're observing. Make sure any equipment you've brought—camera or tape recorder—is ready to use.

Researchers typically develop their own system of taking field notes. Nonetheless, a few suggestions may be helpful. Begin by writing down the basic facts—the date, time, and place. Keep your notes on one side of the page. Depending on your research questions, here are some things to consider:

- The setting. Describe the overall size, shape, and layout of the place. You may want to sketch it or draw a diagram. Note details—both what they are and how they are arranged. Pay attention to sounds and smells, as well as what you can see.

- The people. Note the number of people. What are they doing? Describe their activities, movement, and behavior. What are they wearing? Note ages, race, nationality, and gender of the people. How do they seem to relate to each other? Record overheard conversation in quotation marks.

- Your response. As you observe, note anything that is surprising, puzzling, or unusual. Note also your own feelings and reactions, as well as any new ideas or questions that arise.

ANALYZING YOUR NOTES

After you've finished your observation, read through your notes carefully and, if you want, type them up, adding related points that you remember. Then make sure you analyze your notes from the standpoint of your research questions:

- What patterns emerge from your notes? What do your main findings seem to be? What, if anything, surprised you?

- What research questions do your notes address? What issues remain to be addressed?

- Do your observations confirm what you have read? How would you explain any discrepancies?

- What should your next step be? Should you go back to the library? Should you conduct further observations? If further observations are needed, what form should they take?

FIELD WORK PRACTICE

After getting their permission, observe the dinner-time conversation and interaction of your family or a group of friends, taking notes of your observations. When you are finished, read through your notes, considering what they reveal about the patterns of interaction you observed. Then answer the following questions:

- Do you think your presence as an observer had an effect on what people said and did?

- How difficult is it to observe and keep notes? What, if anything, could you do to make the process easier?

- What did you expect would happen during the dinner? How did these assumptions influence your observations? Were some things you observed unexpected? Do you think your assumptions caused you to miss anything? Were there certain things you chose not to include in your notes? Why?

- What tentative conclusions do you think are legitimate to draw from your observations?

WORKING TOGETHER: Evaluating Documentaries

Many documentary films and television shows are based on observation. These include National Geographic shows on animals in the wild, investigative reporting on 60 Minutes, 20/20, and other news programs, and films such as Frederick Wiseman's acclaimed documentaries (Titicut Follies, High School, and others), Don't Look Back (on Bob Dylan), Hoop Dreams, and Streetwise. Locate a documentary television show or film that makes use of information obtained through observation. Work with two or three other students. Watch the documentary. Then see if you can reach a consensus on these questions, even if the only consensus is to agree to disagree:

- What kinds of information were obtained through observation? What procedures did the film or video-maker use? What does the film or video-maker's relationship to the subject of the documentary seem to be?

- Describe what you see as the purpose of the documentary. How do the filmed observations relate to these purposes? What is their effect on you as a viewer?

- Evaluate the selection of observations presented in the documentary. Why do you think the film or video-maker chose what is shown in the documentary? What, if anything, seems to be left out? Do you think the film or video-maker has made reasonable decisions concerning selection? Explain why or why not.

INTERVIEWS

As you can see in Chapter 7 "Profiles," interviews are often an essential part of capturing the personality and opinions of the person being profiled. Interviews, of course, are not limited to profiles. They have a range of uses. Here are three common situations in which researchers can make good use of interviews:

- Interviews with experts. Interviewing an expert on anorexia, the 1930s jazz scene in Kansas City, the current status of the cod fishing industry, or virtually any topic you're researching can provide you with up-to-date information and analysis, as well as a deepened understanding of the issues involved in these topics—and in this way make a significant contribution to a research project. In cases such as these, interviewing an expert offers a source of information that supplements print or electronic sources.

- Interviews with key participants. Interviews can do more than just supplement your research. In some cases, interviewing takes on a central role in a research project, especially in research on contemporary issues where it makes sense to talk to the people involved. Suppose you are planning to research the role of public libraries in relation to recent immigrants. You would certainly want to see what's been written about the topic, but you could also interview librarians in neighborhood branches who work with, say, Russian Jews, Southeast Asians, Haitians, and Latinos. In turn these interviews could lead to further interviews with recent immigrants, as well as community organizations, to get their perspective on what libraries are doing and might do. The research paper you write will quite likely feature the information you've gathered from these interviews in a prominent way, as the main source of data, with print and electronic sources providing background and context for your research.

- Oral histories. Interviews with people who participated in significant historical events can provide a useful focus for research. You might, for example, interview a trade unionist who participated in a significant strike to understand the event from the perspective of a rank and file worker. Or you might interview someone who was involved in the founding of Young Americans for Freedom to understand the origins of the New Right on college campuses in the early 1960s. Or you could interview your grandmother about her experience migrating from Oklahoma to California in the 1930s to understand the Dust Bowl and Great Depression. Interviews such as these are often called oral histories because they are the spoken accounts of important historical moments based on people's memories of their lived experience. For this type of research, you need, of course, to look at what historians have said—both to generate questions before the interview and to relate the oral history to professional accounts after the interview, as part of the written presentation of your research.

As you can see, the type of interviewing you do depends largely on the kind of research question you're raising and the sources it leads you to.

The Interview Process

Planning

The following considerations can help you get started planning interviews. You can use these considerations to write a proposal that explains how the interviews fit into your research design (see "Writing Proposals for Field Research").

- Background research. The first step, as in any research, is to get an overview and basic information about your topic. At this point, you are likely to be formulating questions to guide your research. Consider how interviewing can help you answer these questions. What do you hope to find out?

- Choosing interview subjects. The nature of your research question should suggest appropriate subjects to interview. Does it make sense to interview an expert on the topic? Or does your research seem to call for interviews with a number of people involved in the issue you're investigating? Are the subjects you're considering likely to provide the information you're looking for?

- Preparing interview questions. Use the notes from your background research to prepare interview questions. Interviewers normally use open-ended questions to get their subjects talking. Phrasing questions in such a way that the natural answer is a "yes" or "no" generally leads to a dead end. How open-ended, of course, depends on your research question and your subject. If you are interviewing an expert on your topic, your questions should be precise and seek specific information ("Estimates vary on the number of cod in the North Atlantic. Can you give me your view?"). For oral histories, on the other hand, questions often begin at a more general level ("Tell me what it was like growing up in Oklahoma") but move to the more specific ("Do you recall when and why your family decided to migrate to California?"). When you have come up with a list of questions, organize them so that one question leads logically to the next.

- Considering the types of interviews. In-person, face-to-face interviews are probably the best-known type of interview, but there are alternatives you may want or need to consider. The following box summarizes four possibilities, their advantages and disadvantages.

FOUR TYPES OF INTERVIEWS

- In-Person. In-person interviews have some significant advantages over other types. Often, when answering your question, the person you are interviewing may take the conversation in a new direction. Although at times this means you'll need to politely guide the conversation back to your topic, sometimes the new direction is one that you hadn't thought of and would like to explore. At other times you may realize that your questions aren't working and that, to get the information you need, you'll have to revise and supplement them on the spur of the moment. But often in-person interviews take on a life of their own—the person you are interviewing starts talking and all you have to do is sit back and listen.

Some researchers prefer to take hand-written notes during in-person interviews. Doing so, however, poses certain difficulties. Responses to your questions may be long, and you may not be able to write fast enough. And devoting all your attention to note-taking makes it harder to think about what the person is saying and guide the interview by choosing the next question or formulating a new one. For these reasons, many researchers use tape recorders. But be flexible about using a tape recorder. Most people don't mind, and the tape recorder will simply fade into the background. But some people are bothered by them and might not be as open as they would be if you took notes. If you feel the disadvantages of taping are outweighing the advantages, be prepared to change methods.

- Telephone Interviews. Telephone interviews are similar to in-person interviews. Like in-person interviews, telephone interviews enable you to be flexible in your questioning. For some people, telephone interviews can feel a bit more difficult to manage because rapport may not emerge as easily as in an in-person interview. For others, though, a telephone interview can feel liberating, as they don't have to deal with the added variables of the interview setting.

A speaker phone is useful if you've been given permission to record the conversation. Even if you haven't, a speaker phone makes it easier for you to take notes.

- Mail and E-Mail Interviews. Sometimes you might prefer or have to conduct your interview by mail or e-mail. You might, for example, want to interview someone who isn't willing or able to schedule an in-person or telephone interview but who has no objection to answering questions you send. One advantage of mail or e-mail interviews is that they provide you with a written record. Unlike in-person or phone interviews, there's nothing that needs to be transcribed or that could be forgotten. On the other hand, a disadvantage is that it may be difficult to follow up on interesting ideas or to clarify points. Phrasing and organization of questions are especially crucial in mail or e-mail interviews because you can't adjust your line of questioning as you can in an in-person or telephone interview.

If possible, use e-mail rather than traditional mail. With e-mail the process is considerably quicker. Moreover, with e-mail you can easily quote and respond to messages, so that there is some conversational give and take.

- On-Line Interviews. Interviews can also be conducted on line. Real-time synchronous communication sites, such as IRCs (Internet Relay Chat), MUDs (Multi-User Dimensions), and MOOs (MUD, Object Oriented), allow computer users from around the world to "talk" to each other in writing in real time (for more information on IRCs, MUDs, and MOOs, see Chapter 14). On-line interviews can be especially useful if you're researching a topic related to cyberspace. For example, if you're writing about Internet censorship or the growing commercialization of the Web, you'll find many people who are knowledgeable about this issue on line (though, for balance, you'd also want to get off-line views as well).

Like mail and e-mail interviews, on-line interviews can help simplify note taking by recording the conversations. Make sure, however, that you are familiar with the technology necessary to record the interview—you don't want to lose all of your hard work.

Setting Up the Interview

Whether the person you plan to interview is a stranger or a friend or relative, you'll need to set up an interview. Generally this means writing a letter or making a telephone call, both to ask for permission and to set a time (or a deadline in the case of an interview by mail). Introduce yourself and your purpose. Be honest about what you are doing—many busy people are happy to help students with assignments. However, be prepared to be turned down. Sometimes busy people are just that—busy. If someone seems too busy to meet with you in person, try asking whether you could interview them by telephone, mail, or e-mail—or whether they know someone else you could interview. Above all, be polite. Be sure to schedule the interview far enough in advance of the due date of your research project to allow you to follow up with more questions if necessary or with further research if the interview leads to areas you had not previously considered. For in-person or telephone interviews that you want to record, ask at this point for permission to record. And, if it's appropriate, ask the person you're interviewing if there is anything you should read before the interview.

Conducting an In-Person or Telephone Interview

For in-person and telephone interviews, the interview itself is a crucial moment in your research. To get an in-person interview off on the right foot, arrive promptly. Make sure that you dress appropriately and that you bring your questions, tape recorder (if you have permission to record the interview), a pad and pens, and any other materials that you might need. For telephone interviews, make sure you call at the time agreed upon.

Because in-person and telephone interviews are really conversations, the results you get will depend in part on your flexibility as a listener and a questioner. The person you're interviewing will be looking to you for guidance, and it is quite likely that you'll be faced with choices during the interview. Let's say you are interviewing someone about why she attends your college and she says, "I came because they've got a really good computer science program, I got a good financial aid package, and I didn't want to go very far from home. You know what I mean?"—then pauses, looking at you for direction. You've got a choice to make about which thread to follow—the student's academic interests, her financial situation, or her desire to stay near home.

Right After the Interview

Especially with in-person and telephone interviews, plan time immediately afterward to review the results of the interview and to make further notes. Transcribe your tape if you recorded the interview or print out hard copies of e-mail or on-line interviews. Make sure that you've noted direct quotations and that you've written down pertinent information about the interview (such as the time, date, and location).

Analyzing the Transcript

Material from an interview can be used in many different ways in a research project. It can be central to the final report or provide supplementary quotes and statistics. The ideas you had ahead of time about how you would use the interview might be changed by the interview or by other aspects of your research process. To help you understand what use to make of the interview, write responses to these questions:

- What are the most important things you learned? List what seem to be the main points.

- What, if anything, surprised you? Why?

- What does the interview contribute to your understanding of your research question? How does the information relate to what you've already learned about your topic? If information, opinion, or point of view differ, how would you account for this?

- What questions does the interview raise for further research? What sources does it suggest you use?

A FINAL NOTE ON INTERVIEWS

Make sure you thank people you interview. (A note or e-mail message is a nice touch.) And, when you've finished your paper, send them a copy along with a letter or e-mail thanking them again.

FIELD WORK PRACTICE

Work with a partner. Interview your partner about why he or she decided to attend your college. Before the interview, think about the questions you want to ask, how you want to conduct the interview—in person, by telephone, on-line, or via e-mail—and how you want to keep track of what's said. Write a paragraph or two about the interview experience. What sorts of questions were the most effective? Did any ideas and topics come up that you had not expected? What decisions did you make during the interview about threads to follow in the conversation? What, if any, were the advantages and disadvantages of the interview method you chose? What problems, if any, did you experience in recording information.

Compare your response to the interview process with those of classmates. What generalizations can you as a class draw about interviewing?

WORKING TOGETHER: Evaluating an Interview

Work in a group with two or three other students. Locate a print or televised interview. If it's in print, make sure it follows a question and answer format. (Weekly news magazines such as Time and Newsweek frequently feature question and answer interviews.) If it's televised, make sure it's an extended interview, such as those on Oprah or the Larry King Show, and not just a sound bite. Read or watch the interview. Then respond to these questions:

- Why do you think the person interviewed was chosen? What makes the interview significant to readers or viewers?

- Consider the interviewer's questioning strategy. What does he or she seem to want to find out? Do the questions seem well-designed to provide this information? Do they seem to follow a logical order?

- What decisions does the interviewer seem to make during the course of the interview? What threads does the interviewer pursue along the way? Are there threads the interviewer seems to ignore?

- How does the person interviewed respond? Are there some questions he or she seems more willing to talk about? Does the subject seem to dodge others? What does the interviewer do in such a case?

- Do you think the interview is successful one? If so, on what terms and for whom—the interviewer, the person interviewed, or both? If the interview seems less than a success, why do you think this is so and who is at fault—the interviewer or the person interviewed?

QUESTIONNAIRES

Questionnaires are similar in many ways to interviews, except that they obtain responses from a sizeable group of people rather than from just a limited number. Questionnaires can target a particular group of people, to find out, for example, why students at your college have chosen to major in bio-medical engineering or the reasons employees at a particular company do or don't participate in community service activities. Or questionnaires can survey the beliefs and opinions of the "general public," as is the case with those conducted by political pollsters and market researchers on everything from people's sexual habits to their religious beliefs to their product preferences.

While interview questions are generally open ended, questionnaires tend to use multiple choice, yes/no, and other "closed" sorts of questions. In a sense, they sacrifice the depth of an interview for the breadth of data provided by a survey.

Deciding whether you should design and distribute a questionnaire depends largely on what you're trying to find out. If, for example, you've read some research on the television viewing habits of college students and want to find out if students at your school fit the patterns described, it makes sense to survey students about their habits rather than interview three or four students. The results you get are liable to give you a more accurate picture.

THE PROCESS OF DESIGNING AND CONDUCTING A SURVEY

If a questionnaire seems appropriate to your research project, you'll need to decide whom you will survey, prepare a questionnaire, conduct your survey, and then compile and analyze the results. It can help to write a proposal that explains why a survey is an appropriate strategy for your research project (see "Writing Proposals for Field Research").

BACKGROUND

The process for designing a survey is similar in certain respects to that for interviews. Namely, you'll begin by researching your topic, to get an overview and background information. Then you need to determine whether a survey is the most appropriate method to address your research question. Does it make sense to gather information on the opinions and habits of a number of people instead of talking to a few in depth or doing other forms of research? At this point, before you expend the time and effort it takes to design and conduct a survey, make sure that a questionnaire is likely to provide you with the information you're seeking.

SELECTING PARTICIPANTS

To be sure that they can generalize from the results of their surveys, professional researchers try to obtain responses from a sample of people that is representative of the population they're investigating. If, for example, you're surveying students who major in bio-engineering or employees of a company, it should be easy enough to send questionnaires to all of them. In other cases, however, you may need to choose people within the population at random for inclusion in the survey.

For example, if you're studying the opinions that students in the first-year writing program have of the program, you could get a random sample by surveying every tenth person on the class lists. But even in this case, make sure that your responses are representative of the actual population in these classes and reflect their demographic composition. You may need to modify the distribution of your survey to guarantee it reaches a representative sample of men, women, blacks, whites, Latinos, Asians, and so on.

If your results are to be meaningful, you'll also need to include enough participants in your survey to give it credibility. Keep in mind that, regardless of how you conduct your survey, not everyone will participate. In fact, as pollsters are well aware, it's generally necessary to survey many more people than you can expect to receive responses from. Often as few as 10 percent of the questionnaires mailed out will be returned. A good rule of thumb is to aim for 40 percent and, if you don't get it the first time, to do multiple distributions.

When you write up your findings, any generalizations based on your survey should be limited to the population that your survey was representative of (you could not, for example, make generalizations about American voters as a whole based on a survey of students at your college). Be sure that you discuss any potentially relevant information on survey participants, such as information on age, gender, occupation, and so on.

DESIGNING THE QUESTIONNAIRE

The results of your survey will depend to a large extent on your questionnaire. Here are some considerations to take into account in designing a questionnaire:

- Include a short introduction that explains the purpose of the survey and what you will do with the results. Point out that survey participants' opinions are important. Ask survey participants to complete the survey and estimate the time it will take.

- Make sure the questions you ask can are focused on the information you need for your research. There is a temptation in designing questionnaire to ask all sorts of things you're curious about. The results can be interesting, to be sure, but asking more questions than you actually need can reduce your response rate. In general, keep the survey brief in order to maximize returns.

- Design the questionnaire so it is easy to read. Make the visual design suggest it won't take long to fill out. Don't crowd questions together to save space. And leave plenty of space for open questions, reminding survey respondents they can write on the back.

- At the end of the survey, write a thank you and explain where or to whom the survey should be returned.

TYPES OF QUESTIONS

Questions can take the form of checklists, yes/no questions, multiple choice questions, ranking scales, and open questions. Each type works somewhat differently. Usually you will want to combine the types to give you the particular information you need. You will also need to consider the most effective and logical order to present the questions on the survey. Surveys typically begin with the least complicated or most general questions in the beginning and the open-ended questions at the end.

When you're writing questions, avoid "leading" questions that prompt the respondent to give the answer you'd like to get. For example, instead of asking, "Do you agree that it is important for college freshman to learn to write well?" (which reveals the researcher's bias), you could ask, "What do you think are the most important skills for college freshmen to learn?"

ETHICS OF RESEARCH: Loaded Questions

Public opinion polls are a fixture in American politics. Most political candidates, the two major political parties, and many other political organizations and advocacy groups use opinion polls to understand the public's mood and to shape policy. In fact, at times, political polls can go beyond simply providing information to play an active role in the formation of public policy. In political debates, the results of opinion polls are often used to buttress the position of one side or the other. Because opinion polls have become such an important part of political life, there is the temptation to use them in a partisan way.

Take, for example, a poll conducted by advocates of casino gambling in Rhode Island to determine the degree of public support. The main question in poll—"Would you approve a casino if it would reduce your property taxes and improve education?"—was clearly a loaded one because it stacks the deck with casino proponents' arguments. As political pollster Darrell West noted, the "corollary question from an anti-gambling perspective" might read, "Would you support a casino if you thought it would raise crime rates and increase the level of gambling addiction?"

Not surprisingly, a majority of people polled favored casino gambling when the question was framed in terms of casino revenues reducing taxes and improving education. However, when the question was posed in an unbiased way—"Do you favor or oppose the construction of a gambling casino?"—the results were quite different. Fifty-three percent opposed the casino, 42 percent supported it, and 5 percent had no opinion.

Also, avoid writing questions that ask for more than one response. For example, instead of asking "Should personal development and academic success be goals of the first-year writing course?" separate "personal development" and "academic success" into separate items.

Here are examples of the most common types of questions designed for a research project investigating whether the political attitudes and involvement of students at the researcher's college supported or refuted claims in the published literature that students today are generally apathetic when it comes to politics.

- **Checklist.**

    Which of these political activities have you participated in? Please check all that apply.

    _____voted in national election

    _____voted in state or local election

    _____campaigned for candidate

    _____worked for a political party

    _____attended a political rally or demonstration

    _____belonged to a political organization or advocacy group

    _____other (specify): _____

- **Yes/No Questions**

    Are you a registered voter?

    _____Yes

    _____No

- **Multiple Choice Questions**

    How would you describe your political views?

    _____left-wing

    _____liberal

    _____moderate

    _____conservative

    _____right-wing

    _____none of the above/don't know

- **Ranking Scales**

    Please rank the following items according to their importance as national priorities. (Use 1 for the highest priority, 7 for the lowest.)

    _____Strengthening the economy

    _____Reducing crime

    _____Balancing the budget

    _____Improving education

    _____Improving the health-care system

    _____Improving race relations

    _____Reducing poverty

- **Lickert Scale** Lickert scale questionnaire items gauge the degree of agreement with particular statements of opinion. Researchers typically design a sequence of such items.

    Please indicate the degree to whick you agree or disagree with the following statements. Enter the number that best expresses your view on each item.

    1 — Strongly agree

    2 — Agree

    3 — Not Sure

    4 — Disagree

    5 — Strongly Disagree

___ It is important to be well-informed about current political
events.

___ There's no point in getting involved in politics because individuals can have little influence.

___ Voting in elections is a responsibility not just a right.

___ The political system is controlled by politicians and lobbyists.

• **Open Questions** Open questions call for brief responses. Such questions are more time-consuming and difficult to tabulate, but they can often yield information that other types of questions will not.

What, if anything, has motivated you to be interested in political affairs?

_____

_____

_____

What, if anything, has posed obstacles to your being interested in political affairs?

_____

_____

_____

After you've prepared your questionnaire, try it out on a few people. Do their answers tell you what you wanted to know? Based on these answers, have you covered all the issues and have you phrased your questions well? If you see any problems, revise your questionnaire. Now is the time to get it right—before you administer it to a lot of people.

CONDUCTING THE SURVEY

Your questionnaire can be distributed in various ways—including in person, by mail, by telephone, or on line through listservs, newsgroups, or Web sites. Your choice of how to conduct the survey will depend on your choice of a sample population, on your deadline, and on your resources (mail surveys, for example, can be quite expensive because you'll need to provide stamped self-addressed envelops).

COMPILING, PRESENTING, AND ANALYZING RESULTS

Compiling results amounts to tallying up the answers to each question. This is a fairly straight-forward procedure for closed questions such as checklist, yes/no, multiple choice, and ranking and Lickert scale items. For open questions, you might write down key words or phrases that emerge in the responses and tally the number of times these (or similar) words or phrases occur. Keep a list of answers that seem of special interest, to use in your research report as quotes.

Researchers present the results of closed questions as percentages in the text of their reports. In addition, you may want to design tables or other visual displays of your results to complement the written report. (See "Understanding Options in the Visual Display of Information." pp. .)

Remember that your results do not speak for themselves. You need to analyze and explain their significance to your research project. The following questions can help you begin such an analysis:

- What patterns emerge from response to individual questions? What patterns emerge from responses across questions?

- How would you explain these patterns? Try to think of two or more explanations, even if they appear to be contradictory or mutually exclusive.

- What is the significance of these explanations for your research? If the explanations seem contradictory, can you think of ways to reconcile them? If not, on what grounds would you choose one or the other?

- What tentative claims might you make based on your analysis of the results? How would you justify such claims?

WORKING TOGETHER: Questionnaire Design

Work together in a group of three or four. Your task is to design a pilot questionnaire that surveys student opinion about some aspect of the academic program or student services at your college. You could focus on, say, advising, orientation for new students, required first-year courses, tutoring, or anything else that interests you. Begin by listing the kind of information that you want to get from the survey. Then write 5-10 questions that seem likely to give you this information. Test your questionnaire by administering it to 10-15 classmates. Once you've gotten their responses, evaluate your questionnaire:

- Did you get the information you were looking for?

- Is each of the questions worded in such a way that it provides the information you anticipated?

- Should you word any of the questions differently to obtain the information you're seeking? Should you delete any of the questions or add new ones? Explain your answer.

Compare your group's experience to that of other groups. What conclusions can you draw about questionnaire design?

PERFORMANCES, MUSEUMS, AND THE MEDIA

Attending performances such as lectures, seminars, readings, plays, and concerts; visiting museums; and watching films, videos, and television or listening to the radio and recorded music can all be important forms of research. Depending on the nature of your research, these activities can provide information and perspectives to supplement your work with print and electronic sources. Or they can be the main focus of your research. This section briefly explains what performances, museums, and the media offer researchers.

Performances

Your college may sponsor lectures, readings, or seminars that bring noted speakers to campus. Attending such events can provide you with information that you couldn't find elsewhere—and with the opportunity to question the speaker. In addition, college or local theaters and music and dance companies may stage plays and concerts related to your research. Attending such live performances can deepen your understanding, say, of a Shakespeare play, a Verdi opera, or a style of jazz, folk, or popular music—and offer a useful supplement to reading about the topic or listening to recordings. In all these instances, taking notes is probably the most appropriate research strategy.

On the other hand, performances may themselves provide the focus for your research. You might, for example, want to research what takes place at a Metallica concert or a poetry reading in a local bookstore. In cases such as these, you'll likely draw on observation and perhaps interviews, as well as reading pertinent sources or listening to recordings.

Museums

Visiting art, science, natural history, and history museums can provide you with a wealth of information to enhance your research. Depending on your topic, you can see in person paintings, sculpture, or photographs pertinent to your research, artifacts and displays from a historical period you're investigating, or scientific exhibits. Some museums, as well as historical societies, have special collections and archives that offer research sources unavailable elsewhere. Again, note taking is probably the research strategy you'll use.

Museums can also be the focus of a research project. Museum studies is a relatively new field that is interested in who visits museums, why, and what they do. By reading some of the literature in this field, you can frame questions to answer with field research methods—observation, interviews, and questionnaires.

Media

As you're probably aware, documentary films, television and radio programs, and music and spoken word recordings can be good sources of information to add to the print and electronic sources you're using. Research in such cases is likely to be a matter of taking notes.

At the same time, films, television, radio, or recorded music can also be valuable sources to study the media and mass communication. For example, if you want to investigate the issue of violence in children's television shows, as part of your research you may want to watch a variety of children's programs to count the incidences of violence and identify the types of violence depicted. Or you could analyze television commercials to see how men and women are depicted and what, if any, gender stereotypes are perpetuated. In this type of research, it can be quite helpful to tape television or radio programs so that you can return to them in the course of your inquiry.

WORKING TOGETHER: Media Research

Working together with two or three classmates, think of three research questions that investigate some aspect of the media—film, television, radio, or music. What sources would you use to answer each question? What information would they offer? How easy or difficult would it be to gain access to these sources? After you've answered these questions, evaluate the original three research questions. Are they all equally feasible or does one or more seem to offer a better option for research? Explain your answer.

PART
FIVE

PRESENTING YOUR WORK

PART FIVE

INTRODUCTION:

COMMUNICATING WITH YOUR READERS

The struggle to get your ideas on paper may make manuscript preparation and document design seem like an afterthought, something you attend to after the real work of drafting is done. Finishing a writing task, however, involves more than just printing out what you've written. Written texts, after all, do not transmit thoughts directly from the writer's mind to the reader's. Like other forms of communication (the telephone, radio, television, or film), writing uses particular media such as the printed page and the computer screen to record and transmit messages. Looked at this way, manuscript preparation and document design become central to the activity of writing: they call attention to the material form and visual appearance writing takes on to present your ideas to readers.

There are three main reasons to learn more about manuscript preparation and document design:

- To make a favorable impression on your readers. Reader's first impression of your writing is likely to be influenced by its visual appearance. A sloppy manuscript, a research paper that doesn't use the proper conventions of citation, or a lab report that fails to present the standard pattern of organization will raise doubts in readers' minds about the credibility of the person that prepared it. Obviously, this can undermine the rhetorical effectiveness of the writing, no matter how interesting or insightful the contents may be. To put it another way, manuscript preparation and document design are means of establishing the writer's ethos—of presenting the writer as a credible and authoritative person. (For more on ethos, see "Rhetorical Stance" in Chapter 5.)

- To enhance readability. One of the marks of effective writing is that readers find it easy to follow. When they don't have to struggle reading the written text, they can concentrate on what the writer is trying to say. And this will make it more likely your readers will give your ideas a fair hearing. As you've seen throughout this book, writers strive in various ways to emphasize main points and connect them to supporting evidence. There are a number of visual resources writers can draw on that cue readers to the important information and line of reasoning in a written text—everything from paragraph breaks to bulleted lists to section headings to graphic display of facts and data. Learning how to use these visual resources is an important way to enhance the readability of your writing.

- To assist you in planning and drafting. Thinking of writing not just as getting ideas down on paper but as designing the visual appearance of a manuscript or document can, in many writing tasks, actually help you plan and draft. Many of genres you've studied in this book use standard forms or variations of them—fundraising letters, certain public documents, various types of reports, proposals for grant funding. Each of these genres—as well as memos, resumes, newsletters, flyers, and brochures—have a typical "look" on the page. The "look" of the page not only enables readers to identify easily what they are reading. The visual appearance of these forms of writing also provide a kind of scaffolding that can help writers organize their material. (Memos, resumes, flyers, newsletters, brochuresm and Web sites are treated below in Chapter 18 "Document Design.")

As you have seen, there have already been discussions of the visual appearance of written texts at various points in this book—particularly in the treatment of some of the genres and the "Designing Documents" sections in Part 2. In the following chapters, you'll find more information on how to prepare manuscripts and design documents. Chapte 17 explains how to present the results of research in two standard formats, based on the guidelines of the Modern Language Association (MLA) and the American Psychological Association (APA). Chapter 18 "Document Design" treats the design and layout of a number of familiar documents—essays, letters, memos, resumes, flyers, newsletters, brochures, and Web sites. Chapter 19 "Essay Exams" offers suggestions about how you can most effective present your work when you are writing under pressure. Chapter 20 "Writing Portfolions" shows how you can design a portfolio of writing that presents and comments on the work you have done in your writing course.

CHAPTER
SEVENTEEN

RESEARCH PAPERS:
USING MLA, APA, AND COS STYLE

s a college student, you are likely to be called on in some of your courses to do research and present the results in written form. The research papers you're asked to write may be short ones that rely on only a few sources or longer term papers based on much more extensive research. In either case, your task as a writer is to present your research by integrating the sources of information, analysis, and argument you've found into a paper of your own design. This chapter explains how to integrate your research materials and how to cite your sources appropriately.

Most documentation systems use in-text citations with a list of works cited at the end of a paper. There are two main styles of citation in academic research:

- Modern Language Association (MLA) style, which uses an author + page number system common to the arts and humanities, and

- American Psychological Association (APA) style, which uses an author + year system common to social and natural sciences.

Check with your instructor if you're not certain about which style to use or whether you should use another system. In addition, the Columbia Online System (COS) offers guidelines for citing online sources.

This chapter presents information on how to integrate your source material into a research paper and on the basic features of MLA, APA, and COS style.

USING SOURCES IN ACADEMIC WRITING

Academic writing does more than simply present the results of research. More important, it shows how the writer's research grows out of issues and problems in a particular field of study and explains the significance of the research to this ongoing discussion. Integrating and citing sources in a research paper lets your readers know how your work fits into a larger conversation.

Students sometimes think that using sources weakens their writing—that readers will think the important ideas in a paper come from others instead of from them. In college, however, readers expect writers to use and cite sources. Readers want to understand what others have said about the issue you've researched, who has influenced your thinking, and how you stand in relation to the analyses, interpretations, and arguments others have offered.

In this sense, using and acknowledging sources is not just a way of avoiding plagiarism. It's also a way of providing your readers with the grounds to understand and evaluate the research you've done and the significance you claim for it. And the system of citation you use—whether MLA or APA style—enables your readers to consult your sources for further information.

In Part 2, you'll find examples of both MLA and APA style citation.

MLA	APA
James W. Carey. "Technology and Ideology." (Chapter 11)	Richard B. Felson and George Gmelch. "Uncertainty and the Use of Magic." (Chapter 10)
Iris Marion Young. "Making Single Motherhood Normal." (Chapter 12)	Luis Ramirez. "Food Sources in South Providence." (Chapter 10)
Denise Sega. "More Than Just Burnouts." (Chapter 13)	"Proposal for a Campus Coffee House." (Chapter 12)

INTEGRATING SOURCES

The three basic methods of integrating sources into a research paper are paraphrasing, summarizing, and quoting. Each method has its own distinct function:

- Paraphrasing. Paraphrase means to restate in your own words. A paraphrase is typically the same length as the original. It's normally used when you want to present in your own words all the information in a passage. Because paraphrase reproduces in your words the details in the original, it is usually used for brief passages that you want to explain thoroughly.

- Summarizing. Summarizing means to select main ideas from the original and to present them in your own words. Unlike a paraphrase, which is approximately the same length as the original, a summary condenses the material. Depending on your purposes, you can summarize all or a portion of the source that is pertinent to your research. (If you do summarize selectively, make sure you don't distort the meaning of the original.) Summaries can range from a sentence to a paragraph or more in length, depending on the amount of detail you need. Summaries are typically used to define a problem, explain a controversy, support an interpretation, present and refute an opposing view.

- Quoting. Quoting means duplicating the exact words as they appear in the original. In general you should use direct quotes sparingly. Quotes are best suited when you want to capture something in the tone of the original that you'd lose by paraphrasing or when a direct quote from a respected expert will lend authority to your writing. Short quotes, even a key phrase, taken from the original and worked into a sentence of you own contstruction, are often more effective than a longer quote.

SAMPLE PARAPHRASE AND SUMMARY

The following passage is from Alan M. Kraut's chapter "Plagues and Prejudice: Nativism's Construction of Disease in Nineteenth- and Twentieth-Century New York City" that appears in Hives of Sickness: Public Health and Epidemics in New York City. It's fairly representative of the kinds of sources you're likely to be working with.

Original:

As early as the 1830s, Irish immigrants who lived in rundown shanties and tenements along New York's rivers were being blamed for importing the cholera epidemic (from which they suffered disproportionately). Fear of cholera, especially after the epidemic of 1832, stimulated public demand for inspection of emigrants prior to departure. Soon, those who left from western European ports began to receive an exam from a physician employed by the country of departure, lest shiploads of emigrants be annihilated by cholera during the voyage.

from Alan M. Kraut, "Plagues and Prejudice," p. 67

Paraphrase:

According to Alan M. Kraut, during the 1830s, there was widespread concern about the danger of cholera being brought to the U.S. by immigrants. Prime suspects were Irish immigrants, who lived in substandard housing near the rivers of New York City and suffered a high rate of cholera. Following the cholera epidemic of 1832, public pressure mounted to examine emigrants before they left Europe. In order to prevent devastating outbreaks of disease onboard the ships, physicians hired by the European countries inspected departing passengers (67).

Summary:

During the 1830s, in Alan M. Kraut's view, the fear that immigrants were bringing cholera with them to the U.S. led to health inspections of departing passengers in the European ports (67).

CITING THE AUTHOR

Citing the author at the beginning of a paraphrase, summary, or quote and including an in-text citation at the end enables you to mark clearly the presentation of material from your sources so that readers can distinguish it easily from your own ideas. Notice both the paraphrase and summary presented here introduce the information and ideas by attributing them to the author, public health historian Alan M. Kraut. Phrases such as "according to Kraut," "in Kraut's view," "Kraut claims," "Kraut points out," and so on serve as identifying tags. The citation that appears in parenthesis—(67)—shows readers where the paraphrase or summary ends and provides the page number in the original for readers who want to find the passage. These examples use MLA style.

ETHICS OF CITATION: AVOIDING PLAGIARISM

Plagiarism takes place when writers take the words or ideas of someone else and pass them off as their own. It means not giving credit to others by failing to acknowledge them properly.

Sometimes plagiarism is an ethical lapse that amounts to stealing and cheating—for example, when students buy research papers, turn in work that someone else has done for them, or copy passages out of books or articles to present as their own. Often, however, plagiarism is unintentional, resulting from a misunderstanding of how to use and cite sources properly.

For example, a person may know that direct quotes must be cited but fail to acknowledge summaries and paraphrases of research sources. Keep in mind that it's not only the use of exact words that must be cited but also sources of information and ideas. In other cases, sloppy notetaking can lead to plagiarism when a researcher fails to enclose all of the words from the original source in quotation marks. Notice how the following paraphrase of the passage from "Plagues and Prejudice" fails to put in quotes words that appear in the original. The plagiarized phrases are underlined:

PLAGIARIZED PARAPHRASE:

According to Alan M. Kraut, during the 1830s, there was widespread concern about the danger of cholera being brought to the U.S. by immigrants. Prime suspects were Irish immigrants, who lived in rundown shanties and tenements along New York's rivers and who suffered a high rate of cholera. Following the cholera epidemic of 1832, public pressure mounted to examine emigrants before they left Europe. Physicians hired by the European countries inspected departing passengers, lest shiploads of emigrants be annihilated by cholera during the voyage (67).

WORKING WITH QUOTES

There are two types of quotes you need to know about—long quotes and short quotes. Short quotes are inserted into your own sentences and identified by quotation marks. Long quotes are set off from the rest of the text in block form and don't use quotation marks (except for any quotes that may appear in the original). MLA style identifies long quotes as any passage more than four lines in length, while APA style considers any passage more than forty words to be a long quote. This section provides information about how to set up short and long quotes.

Long quotes

For long quotes, indent one inch (or ten spaces) from the left margin if you are using MLA style or a half inch (or five spaces) from the left margin if you are using APA style and double space the passage. Using this block form tells readers the material is quoted directly from the original so you don't need quotation marks. The page citation goes in parentheses two spaces after the punctuation at the end of the quote. This example uses MLA style—ten spaces to form the block. For single paragraphs or portions, do not indent the first line. If you quote two or more paragraphs, indent five spaces at the beginning of each paragraph.

Make sure you introduce block quotes. The usual punctuation is a colon.

Public health historian Alan M. Kraut explains how Americans have long viewed immigrants as carriers of disease:

As early as the 1830s, Irish immigrants who lived in rundown
shanties and tenements along New York's rivers were being
blamed for importing the cholera epidemic (from which they
suffered disproportionately). Fear of cholera, especially after
the epidemic of 1832, stimulated public demand for inspection
of emigrants prior to departure. Soon, those who left from
western European ports began to receive an exam from a
physician employed by the country of departure, lest
shiploads of emigrants be annihilated by cholera during the
voyage. (67)

Short quotes

You can incorporate short quotes into sentences in a number of places. Notice how citing the
author appears at the beginning, in the middle, and at the end of the following sentences. The citation style used is MLA.

- **Beginning** According to Alan M. Kraut, "Fear of cholera, especially after the epidemic of 1832,
stimulated public demand for inspection of emigrants prior to departure" (67).

- **Middle** "As early as the 1830s," Alan M. Kraut notes, "Irish immigrants who lived in rundown
shanties and tenements along New York's rivers were being blamed for importing the cholera epidemic" (67).

- **End** "Fear of cholera, especially after the epidemic of 1832, stimulated public demand for inspection of emigrants prior to departure," Alan M. Kraut claims (67).

PHRASES AND CLAUSES

In the examples presented so far, the quoted materials form complete sentences. In other
cases, you may want to integrate words, phrases, or clauses from the original into your own sentence:

Alan M. Kraut explains how the growing fear that immigrants were bringing cholera to the U.S.
"stimulated public demand for inspection of emigrants prior to departure" from Europe (67).

Fitting quotes to your sentences

Under certain circumstances, you may modify the material you're quoting. The two basic
techniques for modifying the original passage are ellipses and brackets. You use ellipses to omit
something in the original and brackets to add or change something. Here are examples of typical
uses of each.

- Ellipses. Ellipses are a set of three periods with a space before and after each (. . .). Use ellipses when you want to omit part of the original passage.
  "As early as the 1830s," Alan M. Kraut notes, "Irish immigrants . . . were being blamed for importing the cholera epidemic" (67).
  When you quote single words or phrases, you don't need to use ellipses because readers can
see you're quoting only part of a passage. Notice the example above under "Phrases and clauses"
doesn't use ellipses.
  If the material you're omitting occurs between sentences, add a fourth period to mark the end
of the first sentence.
  Alan M. Kraut notes similarities between the official response to cholera, polio, and tuberculosis in the nineteenth and early twentieth century and to AIDS in the 1990s:
  In the early 1990s, the federal government continued to pursue institutional means of epidemic control to stop AIDS at the border, a means that stigmatizes immigrants of all nationalities

. . . . As in earlier crises, the federal government had sought to use exclusion to control the epidemic; immigrants were subjected to mandatory testing for no clear epidemiological reason other than foreign birth. (83)

• **Brackets.** Brackets are used to make small changes in the original passage so that it fits grammatically into your sentences.

According to Alan M. Kraut, the federal government's use of mandatory AIDS testing repeats a pattern that can be found in earlier public health crises, "stigmatiz[ing] immigrants of all nationalities" (83).

Brackets can also be used to change capitalization and add clarifying material.

Original:

Wealthy New York City merchants and uptown landowners, who in the early 1850s proposed the creation of Central Park, hoped to create a refined setting for their own socializing. But seeking to establish the public value of their project, they also invoked the language of the English sanitary reformers and claimed the park would improve the health and morals of the city's working people. (Kraut 57)

Use of brackets:

Alan M. Kraut shows how the proposal to create Central Park drew on themes from the public health movement. "[S]eeking to establish the public value of their project, they [wealthy New York City merchants and uptown landowners] also invoked the language of the English sanitary reformers and claimed the park would improve the health and morals of the city's working people" (57).

• **Quotes within quotes** The passage you want to quote may at times contain quoted material. If the passage is long enough to use block form, then keep the quotation marks as they are in the original. If, however, you are going to incorporate a quote that includes a quote into your own sentence, then change the double quotation marks in the original (") into single marks (').

Original:

Against this backdrop of economic depression, the physician and city inspector John Griscom launched a new phase of sanitary reform in his 1842 report when he singled out "the crowded conditions, with insufficient ventilation" of dwellings as "first among the most serious causes of disordered public health" (Kraut 54).

Quotes within a quote:

Alan M. Kraut claims that "John Griscom launched a new phase of sanitary reform in his 1842 report when he singled out 'the crowded conditions, with insufficient ventilation' of dwellings as 'first among the most serious causes of disordered public health' " (54).

IN-TEXT CITATIONS

Documenting your sources is a crucial aspect of presenting your work in a research paper. A reliable rule of thumb is that you should cite the source of any information, analysis, interpretation, or argument that is not common knowledge (e.g. William Shakespeare was a British playwrite in Elizabethan England, the earth travels around the sun, Darwin formulated the theory of natural selection).

Until recently researchers generally used footnotes or endnotes to cite the work of others. Today, however, the two main styles of citation—MLA and APA—use parenthetical citations instead. Information about the source is included in the text and keyed to a list of works cited at the end of the paper. The information called for by MLA and APA in the parenthetical citation differs somewhat. MLA uses author and page, while APA uses author, year, and page.

The following list shows how MLA and APA styles set up parenthetical citations for many types of sources. For further information, ask your teacher or consult MLA Handbook for Writers of Research Papers (4th ed., 1995) and Publication Manual of the American Psychological Association (4th ed., 1994).

- **Sources with one author**

In many instances, you'll be citing the author in the sentence that uses source material.

MLA

According to Daniel J. Czitrom, following the Civil War, there appeared the "first rush of literature on the pathology of mass communication, with which we are so familiar today" (19).

Note that you do not repeat the author's name when you give the page number at the end of the quote.

APA

According to Daniel J. Czitrom (1982), following the Civil War, there appeared the "first rush of literature on the pathology of mass communication, with which we are so familiar today" (p. 19).

Note that in APA style the date of publication appears immediately after the author's name. If you don't cite the author, then use these forms:

MLA

Following the Civil War, there appeared the "first rush of literature on the pathology of mass communication, with which we are so familiar today" (Czitrom 19).

MLA style notes the author and the page number, with no punctuation in between or "p." before the page.

APA

Following the Civil War, there appeared the "first rush of literature on the pathology of mass communication, with which we are so familiar today" (Czitrom, 1982, p. 19).

APA style includes the author's name, the date of publication, and the page number, with commas in between and "p." before the page number.

Notice that for both MLA and APA style the final period comes after the citation. If you have used two or more sources by the same author:

MLA

Following the Civil War, there appeared the "first rush of literature on the pathology of mass communication, with which we are so familiar today" (Czitrom, Media 19).

When you have more than one source by an author, MLA style uses the author's name, a shortened version of the title (the full title is Media and the American Mind: From Morse to McLuhan), and page number.

APA

Following the Civil War, there appeared the "first rush of literature on the pathology of mass communication, with which we are so familiar today"

(Czitrom, 1982, p. 19).

APA style remains the same because the work is already noted by the year. However, if you are citing in APA style more than one work published by an author in the same year, add a letter to the date (1982a, 1982b) and key these to your references at the end of the paper. For example, if you cited a second work Czitrom published in 1982, the first work would be cited as:

(Czitrom, 1982a, p. 19)

and the second would look like this:

(Czitrom, 1982b, p. 43)

- **Sources with multiple authors**

  MLA and APA use different systems to cite sources having more than one author.

MLA

If the work has two or three authors, cite all:

Despite the claims made for it, literacy "is not in itself a panacea for social inequity" (Lunsford, Moglen, and Slevin 2).

If the work has more than three authors, use the first author's name followed by "et al."

What we know of Indian cultures prior to 1700 has mostly been gleaned from the evidence of various artifacts, such as pottery, weapons, and stories passed down from generation to generation (Lauter et al. 5).

APA

If the source you are citing has two authors, include both last names in the reference, separated by an ampersand (&).

An infusion of IT (Information Technology) will result in a "net employment reduction for the institution" (Massey & Zemsky, 1995, p. 245).

For sources with three to five authors, list all of the authors' last names the first time you cite the source, separating each name by a comma and putting an ampersand before the final name.

Despite the claims made for it, literacy "is not in itself a panacea for social inequity" (Lunsford, Moglen, & Slevin, 1990, p. 2).

For subsequent citations, include simply the last name of the first author followed by "et al." If sources have six or more authors, use the last name of the first author and "et al." in every citation:

Despite the claims made for it, literacy "is not in itself a panacea for social inequity" (Lunsford et al, 1990, p. 2).

- **Works with no author listed**

  If no author is listed on the work, both MLA and APA use a shortened version of the title.

MLA

A recent study found that men who frequent prostitutes or have many sexual partners may increase their wives' risk of cervical cancer ("Man's Sex Life" 15).

APA

A recent study found that men who frequent prostitutes or have many sexual partners may increase their wives' risk of cervical cancer ("Man's Sex Life," 1996, p. 15).

The work cited is a shortened version of the article "Man's Sex Life and Cancer in Wife Linked" that appeared in the New York Times with no author listed.

- **Citing a quotation from a secondary source**

Whenever possible, you should cite the source where a quotation appears originally. There may be times, however, when you need to cite a quotation within someone else's work. You can do so by using "qtd. in" (MLA) or "cited in" (APA). In the following two examples, the writer is quoting the blues musician Son House from an interview that appeared originally in Pete Welding's book The Living Blues. Unable to locate Welding's book, the writer cites the interview as it is quoted in Greil Marcus's book Mystery Train.

MLA

"He sold his soul to the devil to get to play like that," House told blues historian Pete Welding (qtd. in Marcus 32).

APA

"He sold his soul to the devil to get to play like that," House told blues historian Pete Welding (cited. in Marcus 32).

WORKS CITED (MLA) AND REFERENCES (APA)

Every source that appears in the text should be included in a list at the end of your paper. Don't include works that you read but did not cite. MLA calls the list "Works Cited," while APA uses "References." Both systems alphabetize by author's last name or the first word in the title of a work with no author.

BOOKS

Here is the basic format for MLA and APA. Notice how they differ.

MLA

Gardner, Howard. Multiple Intelligence: The Theory in Practice.
New York: Basic, 1993.

MLA style uses the complete first name of the author, capitalizes throughout the title, lists the date at the end of the citation, and indents the second line five spaces.

APA

Gardner, H. 1993. Multiple intelligence: The theory in practice.
New York: Basic.

APA style abbreviates the author's first name, lists the date right after the author's name, capitalizes only the first word in the title and after a colon, and indents the second line three spaces.

Both systems double space throughout.

Notice in the examples that the place of publication is well-known. In these cases, don't add the state. In other instances, where the place of publication is not well known, do add the state:

Thousand Oaks, CA: Sage

For university presses, use the "UP" abbreviation:

Boston: Northeastern UP

- **Two listings by one author**

    MLA

    Gardner, Howard. Extraordinary Minds: Portraits of Exceptional
    Individuals andan Examination of Our Extraordinariness. New
    York: Basic, 1997.

    — . Multiple Intelligence: The Theory in Practice. New York: Basic, 1993.

    When you're listing two or more works by the same author, use alphabetical order according to title. For the second title, type three hyphens and a period for the author.

    APA

    Gardner, H. (1993). Multiple intelligence: The theory in practice.
      New York: Basic.
    Gardner, H. (1997). Extraordinary minds: Portraits of exceptional
      individuals and an examination of our extraordinariness. New
      York: Basic.
    Gould, S. J. (1977a). Ontogeny and phylogeny. Cambridge: Belknap.
    Gould, S. J. (1977b). Sociobiology: The art of storytelling. New
      Scientist, 80, 530-533.

    APA style uses chronological order to list works. When an author has more than one work published in the same year, list them in alphabetical order and add lower case letters to the year—1977a, 1977b.

- **Books with multiple authors**

    MLA

    For two or three authors, list them in the order they appear. Invert only the first author's name.
    Current, Richard Nelson, and Marcia Ewing Current. Loie Fuller,
    Goddess of Light. Boston: Northeastern UP, 1997.

    If there are more than three authors, you may list them all or list only the first author followed by "et al."
    Anderson, Daniel, Bret Benjamin, Christopher Busiel, and Bill
    Parades-Holt. Teaching On-Line: Internet Research, Conversation,
    and Composition. New York: HarperCollins, 1996.
    or
    Anderson, Daniel, et al. Teaching On-Line: Internet Research,
    Conversation, and Composition. New York: HarperCollins, 1996.

APA

For works with two to six authors, list the authors in the order in which they appear on the title page, using last name and initials. Use an ampersand before the last author's name.

Anderson, D., Benjamin, B., Busiel, C. & Parades-Holt, B. (1996)

Teaching on-line: Internet research, conversation, and composition.

New York: HarperCollins.

For more than six authors, give the first author's name followed by "et al."

Hare, A. et al. (1994). Small group research: A handbook. Norwood,

NJ: Ablex.

- **Books by a corporate author or organization**

  If no individual is named as author, give the name of the corporate or organizational author as it appears on the title page.

  MLA

  NOW Legal Defense and Educational Fund. Facts on Reproductive Rights: A Resource Manual. New York: The Fund, 1989.

  APA

  NOW Legal Defense and Educational Fund. (1989). Facts on reproductive rights: A resource manual. New York: The Fund.

- **Books by an anonymous author.**

  If no author is listed or the author is anonymous, begin with the title of the publication.

  MLA

  Primary Colors: A Novel of Politics. New York: Random, 1996.

  APA

  Primary colors: A novel of politics. (1996). New York: Random.

- **An edition of an original work**

  MLA

  Melville, Herman. Moby-Dick. 1851. Ed. Alfred Kazin. Boston: Houghton Mifflin, 1956.

  APA

  Melville, H. (1956). Moby-Dick. (A. Kazin, Ed.). Boston: Houghton Mifflin. (Original work published 1851)\

- **An introduction, preface, foreword, or afterword**

  MLA

  Kazin, Alfred. Introduction. Moby-Dick. By Herman Melville. Ed. Alfred Kazin. Boston: Houghton Mifflin, 1956. v-xiv.

  APA

  Kazin, A. (1956). Introduction. In H. Melville, Moby-Dick. (A. Kazin, Ed.). (pp. v-xiv). Boston: Houghton Mifflin.

- **Edited collections**

  MLA

  Grumet, Robert S., ed. Northeastern Indian Lives. Amherst, MA: U of Massachusetts P, 1996.

  APA

  Grumet, R S. (Ed.) (1996) Northeastern Indian lives. Amherst, MA: U of Massachusetts P.

- **Works in collections and anthologies**

  MLA

  Ochs, Donovan J. "Cicero's Rhetorical Theory." A Synoptic History of Classical Rhetoric. Ed. James J. Murphy. Davis, CA: Hermagoras, 1983. 90-150.
  Fitzgerald, F. Scott. "Bernice Bobs Her Hair." The Short Stories of F. Scott Fitzgerald: A New Collection. Ed. Matthew J. Bruccoli. New York: Scribner, 1989. 25-47.

  APA

  Ochs, D. J. (1983). Cicero's rhetorical theory. In J. J. Murphy (Ed.), A synoptic history of classical rhetoric (pp. 90-150). Davis, CA: Hermagoras.
  Fitzgerald, F. (1989). "Bernice Bobs Her Hair." In Matthew J. Bruccoli (Ed.), The short stories of F. Scott Fitzgerald: A new collection (pp. 25-47). New York: Scribner.

- **Translations**

  MLA

  Sartre, Jean Paul. The Age of Reason. Trans. Eric Sutton. New York: Bantam, 1959.

  APA

  Sartre, J. P. (1959). The age of reason. (E. Sutton, Trans.). New York: Bantam.

- **Book in a later edition**

  MLA

  Woloch, Nancy. Women and the American Experience. 2nd ed. New York: McGraw, 1994.

  APA

  Woloch, N. (1994). Women and the American experience (2nd ed). New York: McGraw.

- **Dictionary entries and encyclopedia articles**

  MLA

  "Freeze-etching." Merriam-Webster's Collegiate Dictionary. 10th ed. 1996.
  "Australia." The Concise Columbia Encyclopedia. 3rd ed. 1994.
  Jolliffe, David A. "Genre." Encyclopedia of Rhetoric and Composition. Ed. Theresa Enos. New York: Garland, 1996.

For familiar reference works such as *Merriam-Webster's Collegiate Dictionary* and *The Concise Columbia Encyclopedia*, you can omit listing the editors and publication information. For less familiar or more specialized sources, however, you should include all the information. Page numbers are not needed as long as the work is arranged alphabetically.

APA

Freeze-etching." (1996) Merriam-Webster's collegiate dictionary
   (10th ed.). Springfield, MA: Merriam Webster.

Australia. (1994). The concise Columbia encyclopedia (3rd ed.).
   New York: Columbia UP.

Jolliffe, D. A. (1996). "Genre." In Theresa Enos (Ed.), Encyclopedia of
   rhetoric and composition. New York: Garland.

• **Government documents**

MLA

United States. Department of Commerce, International Trade
Administration. A Guide to Financing Exports. Washington:
GPO, 1985.

APA

United States. Department of Commerce, International Trade
   Administration. (1985)   A guide to financing exports. (Monthly
   Catalog No. 85024488). Washington, DC: U.S. Government Printing
   Office.

APA includes the catalogue number of the publication.

• **Unpublished doctoral dissertations**

MLA

Herzong, Mary Lucinda. "Living and Dying: Accommodating AIDS
into Autobiography (Immune Deficiency)." Diss. U of California, 1995.

APA

Herzong, M. L. (1995). Living and dying: Accommodating AIDS
   into autobiography (immune deficiency)." Unpublished doctoral
   dissertation. University of California, Berkeley, CA.

ARTICLES IN PERIODICALS

Here are examples of the basic MLA and APA formats for listing articles that appear in periodicals such as scholarly journals, magazines, and newspapers.

MLA

Eldred, Janet Carey. "The Technology of Voice." College Composition
and Communication 48 (1997): 334-47.

MLA style uses the author's full name, marks article titles by using quotation marks and capitalization, and shortens the number of the last page (334-47).

APA

Eldred, J. C. (1997). The technology of voice. College Composition

and Communication, 48, 334-347.

APA style uses abbreviations for first and middle names, and the date follows the author's name. APA does not use either either quotation marks or capitalization for articles (except for the first word of the title). In APA style the name of the journal, the volume number (48), and the comma that follows it are all underlined. APA style includes full page numbers (334-347).

- **Scholarly journals with continuous pagination**
  Notice in the examples that the only number given is the volume number—48. This is because the journal paginates continuously from issue to issue over the course of the volume. In such cases, simply list the volume number in the appropriate place. You don't need to include the issue number.

- **Scholarly journals that page each issue separately**
  If every issue of the journal begins with page one, include the issue number along with the volume number.

MLA

Ebert, Theresa. "Writing in the Political: Resistance (Post)

modernism." Legal Studies Forum 15.4 (1991): 291-303.

APA

Ebert, T. (1991). Writing in the political: Resistance (post)

modernism." Legal Studies Forum, 15(4), 291-303.

- **Magazine articles**
  The first two examples show how to list magazines that appear monthly or bi-monthly and weekly or bi-weekly. The third example is an article without an author listed.

MLA

Wahl, K.U. "Chinese Wind-Driven Kite Flutes." Experimental Musical

Instruments Sept. 1997: 26-30.

Pollitt, Katha. "The Other L Word." Nation 8 Sept. 1997: 10.

"Pleas from Prison." Newsweek 24 Nov. 1997: 44.

APA

Wahl, K.U. (1997, September). Chinese wind-driven kite flutes.

Experimental Musical Instruments, pp. 26-30.

Pollitt, K. (1997, September 8). The other l word. Nation, p. 10.

Pleas from prison. (1997, November 24). Newsweek, p. 44.

- **Newspaper articles**

MLA

Morrow, David J. "Attention Disorder Is Found in Growing Number of

Adults." New York Times 2 Sept. 1997: A1.

"AMA Plans Seal of Approval for Physicians." Providence Journal-

Bulletin 19 November 1997: A5.

APA

Morrow, D. J. (1997, September 2). Attention disorder is found in growing number of adults." New York Times, p. A1.

AMA plans seal of approval for physicians. (1997, November 19). Providence Journal-Bulletin, p. A5.

- **Editorial**

  MLA

  "The Bludgeoning of Taiwan." Editorial. New York Times 8 Mar. 1996: A30.

  APA

  The bludgeoning of Taiwan. (1996, March 8). [Editorial]. New York Times, p. A30.

- **Review**

  MLA

  Ewald, Paul W. "Pedigree of a Retrovirus." Rev. of Viral Sex: The Nature of AIDS, by Jaap Goudsmit. Natural History June 1997: 8-9.

  APA

  Ewald, P. W. (1997, June). Pedigree of a retrovirus. [Review of the book Viral Sex: The Nature of AIDS]. Natural History, pp. 8-9.

If there is no author listed for the review, begin with the title of the review. If there is no title, use "Rev. of + title" for MLA format and "[Review of the book + title"] for APA. Alphabetize under the title of the book being reviewed.

- **Letter to the editor**

  MLA

  Daniels, John. Letter. New York Times 8 March 1996: A30.

  APA

  Daniels, J. (1996, March 8). [Letter to the editor]. New York Times, p. A30.

MISCELLANEOUS SOURCES

- **Films and videocassettes**

  MLA

  Citizen Kane. By Orson Welles. Dir. Orson Welles. RKO, 1941.
  Star Wars. Dir. George Lucas. Perf. Mark Hamill, Harrison Ford, Carrie Fisher, and Alec Guiness. Videocassette. CBS Fox, 1992.

  APA

  Welles, O. (Writer and Director). (1941). Citizen Kane. Hollywood: RKO.
  Lucas, G. (Director). (1992). Star wars. [Videocassette]. Hollywood: CBS Fox.

The amount of information to include about films and videocassettes depends on how you have used the source. In addition to title and director, you may cite the writer and performers as well.

- **Television and radio programs**

  MLA

  "Tuskegee Experiment." Nova. WGBH, Boston. 4 April 1995.

  APA

  Tuskegee experiment. (1995, April 4). Nova. Boston: WGBH.

- **Records, tapes, and CDs**

  MLA

  Ellington, Duke. The Far East Suite. Bluebird, 1995.

  Springsteen, Bruce. "Youngstown." The Ghost of Tom Joad. Columbia, 1995.

  Verdi, Giuseppe. La Traviata. London Symphony Orchestra. Cond.
  Carlo Rizzi. Teldec, 1992.

  APA

  Ellington, Duke. (Composer). (1995). The Far East Suite. New York:
  Bluebird.

  Springsteen, B. (Singer and Composer). (1995). Youngstown. The
  Ghost of Tom Joad. New York: Columbia.

  Verdi, G. (Composer). (1992). La Traviata. [With C. Rizzi conducting
  the London Symphony Orchestra]. New York: Teldec.

- **Interviews**

  MLA

  Haraway, Donna. "Writing, Literacy, and Technology: Toward a
  Cyborg Literature." By Gary A. Olson. Women Writing Culture.
  Ed. Gary A. Olson and Elaine Hirsch. Albany: SUNY, 1995. 45-
  77.

  Kenny, Maurice. Personal interview. 27 April 1997.

  MLA cites interviews by listing the person being interviewed first and then the interviewer.

  APA

  Olson, G. A. (1995). Writing, literacy, and technology: Toward a
  cyborg literature." [Interview with Donna Haraway]. In G. A. Olson
  & E. Hirsch (Eds.), Women writing culture (pp. 45-77). Albany: SUNY.

APA style lists the name of the interviewer first and then puts information on the interview in brackets . APA style does not list unpublished interviews in references but cites them only in parenthetical citations in the text: (M. Kenny, personal inteview, April 27, 1997).

- **Lecture or speech**

    MLA

    Kern, David. "Recent Trends in Occupational Medicine." Memorial
     Hospital, Pawtucket, RI. 2 Oct. 1997.

    APA

    Kern, D. (1997, October 2). Recent trends in occupational medicine.
     Memorial Hospital, Pawtucket, RI.

ONLINE AND ELECTRONIC SOURCES

The dramatic increase of information available through the Internet is changing the way people do research—and simultaneously raises the problem for researchers of how to cite such online sources as Web sites, email, listservs, newsgroups, and electronic books and periodicals. In this section we look at the guidelines provided by the MLA, the APA, and Columbia Online Systems (COS).

Modern Language Association

The MLA Style Manual and Guide to Scholarly Publishing, 2nd edition (1998) has expanded and updated MLA formats for citing online sources. The models presented in this section follow these recent guidelines (which replace the formats in the 1995 MLA Handbook).

For online sources, MLA style includes much of the same information you use for print sources, such as author and title, but also calls for two special items of information:

Dates. Online sources can change quickly, so you need to give the date when the source you consulted was posted online (located with publication information) and the date you accessed the source (near the end of the entry, just before the electronic address).

Electronic address. In order that readers can access online sources, give each source's exact and complete electronic address. Note in the examples that MLA style uses angle brackets (< >) to enclose the address. If you have to break up an address at the end of a line, make the break only where a slash (/) appears.

- **Web sites**
    Scholarly projects and databases
    History of "Race" in Science, Medicine, and Technology. Ed. Evelynn
    Hammonds and Michelle Murphy. 2 Feb. 1998. Massachusetts Institute of
    Technology. 5 May 1998. <http://www.mit.edu/his.race.html >.

    For citing an entire project or database, provide title and name of any editor; date of publication; sponsoring organization or institution; date you consulted the source; and electronic address. If there is a version number (such as Vers. 2.4), include it after the editor's name and before the publication date.

    If you are citing a short work (such as an article or poem) published as part of the project, begin with author's name and title. Then follow the model, with the specific electronic address for the work:
    Muniz, Hector. "Comment on the American Anthropological Association's
    Official Statement on Race." History of "Race" in Science, Medicine, and
    Technology. Ed. Evelynn Hammonds and Michelle Murphy. 2 Feb. 1998.
    Massachusetts Institute of Technology. 5 May 1998. <http://www.mit.edu/
    his.race/muniz.html >.

    Personal, professional, and organizational sites
    James Crawford. Language Policy Web Site & Emporium. 8 Feb. 1998.

<http://ourworld.compuserve.com/hompages/JWCRAWFORD >.
Home Page. U.S. English Only. 8 Feb. 1998. <http://www.us-english.org >.
Stone, Eric J. "What Would the Founding Fathers Think About Official
English?" Home Page. 30 Dec. 1997. U.S. English Only. 8 Feb. 1998. <http://
www.us-english.org/stone.html>.
"Bilingual Education: A Tool for Equal Opportunity." Home Page. 12 Jan.
1998. Northern California Coalition for Immigrant Rights. 8 Feb. 1998.
<http://www.progway.org/nccir.html>.

Cite personal or professional web sites by listing author, title underlined, date you consulted
it, and electronic address. If a web site does not have a title, as in the second example, describe
it as "home page" without quotation marks or underlining. The third and fourth examples show
how to cite specific works from organizational web sites.

- **E-mail, listservs, and newsgroups**
  Fox, Tom. E-mail to the author. 25 Feb. 1996.
  Braun, Lundy. "Re: Myth of Killer Viruses." E-mail to the author. 4 May
  1998.

For e-mail, list author, the title (if there is one) from the e-mail's subject heading, a description
of transmission, and the date.
  Marshall, Richard. "The Political Economy of Cancer Research." 21 Apr.
  1997. Online posting. H-NET List on the History of Science, Medicine, and
  Technology. 28 Sept. 1997. <H-SCI-MED-TECH@H-NET.MSU.EDU>.

For listservs and other subscription-based discussion groups, give author's name, title from
subject heading, date of posting, "online posting" without quotation marks, the name of the list,
the date you consulted it, and the electronic address. If the posting has an identifying number,
list it immediately after the list's name—e.g. Global Economy Discussion List 22365.
  Murphy, Christian. "Irish FAQ: The Famine." 5 Apr. 1998. Online posting. 1
  May 1998. <news:soc.culture.irish /Irish_FAQ_The_Famine>.

For Usenet newsgroups, which are not subscription-based, follow the procedure for listservs.
In the angle brackets at the end, list "news" before group's name.

- **Synchronous communication (MUD, MOO, etc.)**
  Bronson, Emilie. MediaMOO Symposium: Museums as Virtual Worlds. 2 Feb.
  1998. MediaMOO. 8 Mar. 1998. <http://www.mit.edu/fac/Bronson/
  MediaMOO/amvw-symposium-98.html>.

List name of speaker, description of the event, date of the event, the forum, date you consulted
the source, and electronic address.

- **On-line books**
  Ginsburg, Allen. Howl and Other Poems. San Francisco: City Lights, 1956. 14
  Sept. 1998. <http://php.indiana.edu/~avigdor/poetry/ginsburg.html>.

For an online book, list author, title, information on original print version, date you consulted
the source, and electronic address. If the book is published for the first time online, use the date
of electronic publication instead of print publication.

If the book has an editor or translator, follow this model:
Hawthorne, Nathaniel. The Scarlet Letter. Ed. H. Bruce Franklin.
New York: Viking, 1963. 10 Feb. 1998. <http://www.etext.virginia.edu/
hawthorne/scarletl.html>.

- **An article in an on-line periodical**

  Article in a scholarly journal:

  Warren, William. "Allergies and Spatio-Temporal Disorders." Modern Psychology 6.3 (1997): 15 pars. 13 Nov. 1998. <http://www..liasu.edu/modpsy/warren6(3).html>.

  Use same information as for scholarly articles in print. If the journal does not number pages in sequence, list number of paragraphs (as in example), pages, or other numbered sections. Include date you consulted the source and the electronic address.

  Article in a magazine

  Rimington, Eleanor. "Court Case Challenges Microsoft." WinNews Electronic Newsletter 8 Mar. 1998: 1+. 15 May 1998. <http://www.winnews.com/yr1998/mar/rimington_8768.html>.

  Use same information as for print articles, with any page, paragraph, or section numbers, date you consulted source, and electronic address.

  Article in a newspaper

  Morrow, David J. "Attention Disorder Is Found in Growing Number of Adults." New York Times on the Web 2 Sept. 1997: A1. 15 Oct. 1997. <http://www.nytimes.com/sciencetimes/02.09.html>.

  Use same information as for print articles, with any page, paragraph, or section numbers, date you consulted the source, and electronic address.

- **CD-ROM**

  Zieger, Herman E. "Aldehyde." The Software Toolworks Multimedia Encyclopedia. Vers. 1.5. Software Toolworks. CD-ROM. Boston: Grolier, 1992.

  Cite sources on CD-ROM, diskette, or magnetic tape much as you would print sources. Add the vendor (Software Toolworkds in this example) if there is one in addition to the publisher and the medium ("CD-ROM," "Diskette," or "Magnetic Tape").

  If the source is a periodical, include usual information for print sources, plus the title of the CD-ROm, the medium, the vendor (or distributor), and the date of electronic publication.

  Morrow, David J. "Attention Disorder Is Found in Growing Number of Adults." New York Times 2 Sept. 1997: A1. New York Times Ondisc. CD-ROM. UMI-Proquest. June 1998.

  American Psychological Association

  The most recent Publication Manual of the American Psychological Association available at the time of writing was the 4th edition, published in 1994. It provides guidelines for citing a number of online sources, using the following basic information: the name of the author or authors, date of publication, title of work (such as book or article in periodical), the electronic or online medium, and an availability statement that provides enough information to retrieve the source.

- **Online book**

  Patel, R., & Shah, N. (1997). Language policy in postcolonial India [On-line]. Available: Internet: Gopher AskERIC/Digests

  Note that no punctuation follows the path of retrieval.

- **Online article**

  Montgomery, S. (1998). Recent trends in addiction support groups. Journal of Chemical Dependency Treatment [On-line] 2 (1). Available: DIALOG File: Journal of Chemical Dependency

Morrow, D. J. (1997, September 2). Attention disorder is found in
growing number of adults. New York Times [On-line]. Available: Internet: Nexis

- **On-line abstract**
  Morrow, David J. (1997, September 2). Attention disorder is found in growing
  number of adults [On-line]. New York Times, p. A1. Abstract from: Lexis/
  Nexis/CURNWS

- **CD-ROM abstract**
  Montgomery, S. (1998). Recent trends in addiction support groups. Journal of
  Chemical Dependency Treatment, 2, 76-83. Abstract from: SilverPlatter File:
  PsycLIT   Item: 67-54980

- **CD-ROM**
  Zieger, H. (1992). Aldehyde. in The Software Toolworks multimedia
  encyclopedia (Vers. 1.5) [CD-ROM]. Software Toolworks. Boston: Grolier.

- **E-mail, listservs, and newsgroups**
  APA style treats online sources such as e-mail, listservs, and newsgroups as non-retrievable
  sources similar to personal interviews. Cite such sources in the text but do not list them on the
  References page. For example:
  Medical historians have challenged Elaine Showalter's view of chronic fatigue syndrome
  (Lundy Braun, Re: Myth of killer viruses. E -mail to the author, February 25, 1996).

COS GUIDELINES FOR INTERNET SOURCES

Columbia Online System has developed guidelines for citing a number of Internet sources in
MLA and APA style. Consult with your teacher if you are not certain what format to use. And keep
in mind that the Internet is in a constant state of flux and that specific forms of citation may
change as the sites themselves do.

The basic COS format
Author's Last Name, First Name. "Title of Work." Title of Complete
Work version, edition, or date of work. Protocol and address or
path. (Date of visit).

- **World Wide Web Sites**

  MLA

  Poole, Jason. "On Borrowed Ground: Free African-American Life in

  Charlestown, South Carolina 1810-61." Essays in History 36

  (1994). http://www.lib.virginia.edu/journals/EH/EH36/poole.

  html (10 Mar. 1996).

  APA

  Poole, J. (1994). On borrowed ground: Free African-American life in

  Charlestown, South Carolina 1810-61. Essays in History 36 .
  http://www.lib.virginia.edu/journals/EH/EH36/poole.html
  (10 March 1996).

- **FTP (File Transfer Protocol) Sites**

  MLA

  Goodkind, Daniel. "Estimates of Averted Chinese Births 1971-1990:

Comparisons of Fertility Decline, Family Planning Policy and Development in Six Confucian Societies." Ftp coombs.anu.edu.au/coombsarchives/demography/demog-wk-paper-38-abstr.txt (1 Sept. 1997.

APA

Goodkind, D. Estimates of averted Chinese births 1971-1990: Comparisons of fertility decline, family planning policy and development in six Confucian societies. Ftp coombs.anu.edu.au/coombsarchives/demography/demog-wk-paper-38-abstr.txt (1 September 1997.

- **Telnet sites**

  MLA

  "Help." Internet Public Library. telnet ipl.org:8888, help (1 Sept. 1997).

  APA

  Help. Internet Public Library. telnet ipl.org:8888, help (1 September 1997).

- **Gopher sites**

  MLA

  Fanderclai, Thomas, and Greg Siering. "The Netoric Project." gopher daedalus.com/Alliance for Computers & Writing/NETORIC/netoric. guide (13 Jan. 1996).

  APA

  Fanderclai, T., & G. Siering. The Netoric project. gopher daedalus.com/Alliance for Computers & Writing/NETORIC/netoric. guide (13 January 1996).

- **Synchronous Communications (MOOs, MUDs, IRC, etc.)**

  MLA

  Cross, James. "Netoric's Tuesday Cafe: Why Use MUDs in the Writing Classroom?" MediaMOO. telnet purple-crayon.media.mit.edu 8888, @go Tuesday (27 Feb. 1997).

  APA

  Cross, J. (27 February 1997). Netoric's Tuesday cafe: Why use MUDs in the writing classroom? MediaMOO. telnet purple-crayon. media. mit.edu 8888, @go Tuesday

SAMPLE MLA AND APA RESEARCH PAPERS

The following two research papers are good examples of MLA and APA styles. Brion Keagle's "Blues Song and Devil's Music" (MLA format) was written for a term paper assignment in an African-American literature and culture course. Jenny Chen's "Defining Disease: The Case of Chronic Fatigue Syndrome" (APA format) was written in response to a research assignment in a science writing course.

Before we present the papers, it may be useful to note manuscript preparation features common to MLA and APA and features that are distinct.

CHECKLIST OF MANUSCRIPT PREPARATION FOR MLA AND APA STYLE RESEARCH PAPERS

Features common to both MLA and APA style:

- Manuscript should be double-spaced, including block quotations and "Works Cited" and "References" pages.

- Format a one inch margin all around, top and bottom, left and right.

- Indent five spaces to begin a paragraph.

- Number pages consecutively, including "Works Cited" and "References" pages.

Special features called for by MLA style:

- Unless your teacher tells you to, do not include a separate cover sheet. Type the following information, double-spaced, at the top left corner of the manuscript, in this order: your name, your professor's name, course number, and date. Double-space and center the title of your paper. Follow conventional rules of capitalizing words in a title. Don't use boldface, underline, all capitals, or showy fonts. Double-space and begin the text.

- Page numbers are located in the upper right corner, flush with the right margin, one-half inch from the top of the page. Precede the page number with your last name. Begin the text one inch from the top.

- Your bibliography should be a separate page, titled "Works Cited." Center it one inch from the top, without quotes, underline, boldface, italics, etc. Include in the Works Cited only those works you have cited in the text of the paper. It is not a comprehensive bibliography. You may have used other works which are not cited.

SPECIAL FEATURES CALLED FOR BY APA STYLE:

- APA format does use a separate cover page. Locate your paper's title, centered, approximately one-third from the top of the page. Type the title double-spaced if it has more than one line. Follow usual capitalization conventions. Don't use all caps, boldface, quotes, or italics. Double-space and type your name centered. Double-space again and type the course number, and then following another double-space, type the date.

- On the page immediately following the cover sheet, include a 100-150 word Abstract that summarizes the contents of your paper.

- Begin the text on the third page. Don't repeat the title. Number all the pages, beginning with the cover sheet as page one and the Abstract as page two. Type a running head (shortened version of the title) before the page number.

- APA style research papers are much more likely than MLA style papers to use section headings. Some research papers will use the conventional headings—Introduction, Methods, Results, and Discussion—but others will use headings based on the content of the paper. Notice the section headings Jenny Chen uses in her paper.

- Your bibliography or "References" should begin on a separate page, following the text. Center "References" one inch from the top, without underlining, quotes, boldface, or all caps.

Brion Keagle

Dr. Trimbur

English 1XX

2 May 199X

BLUES SONGS AND THE DEVIL'S MUSIC

In the 1930s, Son House and Charlie Patton were names to remember in the Mississippi Delta. Two of the most popular blues singers on the circuit, they did not have the time or interest to show a newcomer named Robert Johnson the ropes. Trying unsuccessfully to hang out with the older, more accomplished musicians, Johnson could not play the guitar to save his life and was often an object of ridicule. Eventually he disappeared and was promptly forgotten. Two years later, however, he appeared again, still looking to be heard. His elders tried to put him off, but he persisted. Finally, they let him play during a break and left him alone with the tables and chairs. Outside, taking the air, House and others heard a loud, devastating music of a purity and brilliance beyond anything in the memory of the Mississippi Delta. "He sold his soul to the devil to get to play like that," House told blues historian Pete Welding (qtd. in Marcus 32).

Thus was born the legend of Robert Johnson. He had sold his soul to the devil to play the blues. As Jon Spencer puts it, "The ambitious, daring, or desperate individual who wanted to learn the so-called 'black art' of playing the blues was believed to have gone to the crossroads at midnight where and when he 'took up' his instrument from the devil" (27). Opinion is divided on whether Johnson actually did sell his soul to the devil. There are, on one hand, the "bluesmen who knew [Johnson] and believed he made a pact with the devil" and, on the other, the "folklorists who don't" (Finn 210). In the minds of Johnson's contemporaries one thing was certain: no one could get so good so fast without some kind of supernatural intervention.

The compositions that resulted from the supposed deal were so intricately woven and suffused with the dark, the satanic, the evil, and the terrible as to be almost supernatural themselves. As music critic Greil Marcus says, "There were demons in his songs—blues that walked like a man, the devil, or the two in league with each other" (24). The terror in Johnson's "Cross Road Blues" can be seen, for example, on a literal level, as part of a "tragic" song about a "homeless man adrift on the highways of America" (Yurchenco 452), trying to flag a ride as the sun goes down. For a lone black man in the 1930s, the crossroads could be a dangerous place. But, as Robert Palmer says, Johnson is not afraid simply of the white sheriff or passing rednecks. The terror in "Cross Road Blues" is also "metaphysical" (126). In the first verse, Johnson sings, "Went down to the crossroads, fell down on my knees / Asked the Lord above, have mercy, save poor Bob if you please" (Johnson).

To say that Johnson's blues are haunted is to understate the sense of evil pursuing him. In "Hellhound on My Trail," Johnson seems to feel the devil closing in on him, perhaps to exact his part of the bargain:

I got to keep moving
Blues falling down like hail
Ummmm
Blues falling down like hail
And the days keep on worrying me
There's a hellhound on my trail.

It could be, as Julio Finn argues, that when Johnson went away for two years, he was initiated into a voodoo cult by a Root Doctor deep in the bayous of the Mississippi Delta (215). Whether an actual initiation is the source of Johnson's legendary deal with the devil, the story of Robert Johnson reveals a deep-seated association of the blues with evil. In the words of blues singer Rosa Lee Hill, "The blues . . . is for the bad man and the church songs for the Lord" (qtd in Mitchell 66). The elder of a church congregation warned an aging blues singer: "You better quit singing them blues. You ain't too old for the devil to get you" (qtd. in Mitchell 133).

Clearly there is a profound mistrust of the blues where the fate of one's soul is concerned. For many, the word "blues" has a negative, ungodly connotation, while gospel, first cousin to the blues, is considered righteous, pious, and acceptable in the eyes of God. In Blues People, Leroi Jones (Amiri Baraka), says that with "the legal end of slavery, there was now proposed . . . a much fuller life outside the church. There came to be more and more backsliders and more of the devil's music was heard" (40). To understand how the blues and gospel polarized as forms of musical and cultural expression, we need to examine both African and American culture and the process of acculturation that translated African values and beliefs to life in North America.

Musically speaking, blues and gospel share the same components. Most of the musical elements have their antecedents in West African tradition. Key ingredients are the use of polyrhythms (generally with the off beat emphasized), "blue notes" (rising emotions are associated with a falling pitch), and a variety of vocal techniques to color the melody and give it identity and expressiveness (Barlow 4). Good musicians use their instruments as they would their voices, to emulate the sounds of human speech. Notes are bent or flattened, and special attention is paid to volume. Ending the description here, however, would be to neglect the most crucial, elemental aspect of both the blues and gospel, the component which avid listeners never fail to discern and the property which makes or breaks performers depending on how they use it and how much of it they possess. This most prominent aspect of the blues and gospel is called soul. If one were to mention it in the right circles, an entire dancehall or church full of people would comprehend it instantly but remain almost entirely unable to define it.

The term "soul" is such an elusive one that it rarely appears in the index of books on African American music. As a musical label, soul music refers to the Motown and Memphis sounds of the 1960s. But the term has been in use much longer, as the gospel singer Mahalia Jackson explains:

> What some people call the "blues singing feeling" is expressed by the Church of God in Christ. Songs like "The Lord Followed Me" became so emotional . . . [they] almost led to panic. But the blues was here before they called it the blues. This kind of song came after spirituals. The old folk prayed to God because they were in an oppressed condition. While in slavery they got a different kind of blues. Take these later songs like "Summertime," it's the same as "Sometimes I Feel Like a Motherless Child" . . . which had the blue note in it. The basic thing is soul feeling. The same in blues as in spirituals. And also with gospel music. It is soul music. (qtd. in Ricks 139)

Soul, as the British writer Clive Anderson puts it, "is made by black Americans and elevates 'feeling' above all else. . . . Soul assumes a shared experience, a relationship with the listener . . . where the singer confirms and works out the feelings of the audience. In this sense it remains sacramental" (qtd. in Guralnick, Sweet Soul 3). Soul, in other words, means empathy, solidarity, and what Richard Wright called an "other worldly yearning" (128) for a better time and an end to oppression. Rooted in the spirituals of slavery, soul is a spiritual and emotional force that binds performer and audience together in the blues and gospel alike.

From a musical standpoint, there are more similarities than differences between blues and gospel. Both embrace the concept of soul and a technical vocabulary of blue notes, dynamic vocal displays, polyrhythms, semitones, and bent or slurred notes. Nonetheless, despite the common property of soul, the blues are marked as secular and gospel as sacred. According to Charles Keil, a "transgressing" bluesman must give up his evil ways once and for all to answer the call of the church. "The transition," Keil says, "from blues role to preacher role is unidirectional" (Urban Blues 148). For most of the history of the blues and gospel, the line between the two has been a fixed one. One was in the blues camp or the gospel camp. For this reason, when Guitar Slim recorded the eight bar ballad "Feelin' Sad" in 1952, his use of heart wrenching gospel cries and moans over horn and piano accompaniment was viewed as blasphemous and disrespectful. The idea of "unadulterated backcountry gospel with secular lyrics" was, as Robert Palmer notes, a matter of "using the Lord's music to do the Devil's work" (248). Similarly, "Ray Charles's transformation of dignified gospel standards into cries of secular ecstasy came in for a good deal of criticism at first, mostly from the pulpit" (Guralnick 2).

The schism between blues and gospel, secular and sacred music in the African American tradition, evolved out of the lived experience of the Africans brought to North America as slaves. African values held by the

earliest slaves had to be adapted to fit into a Christian culture, while traditional folkloristic and religious figures had to assume new guises in order to survive in the New World. For our purposes, the transformation of Legba, the Yoruban trickster, is particularly illuminating.

Jon Spencer suggests that of all the African trickster-gods, Legba "best personified the blues . . . . He is both malevolent and benevolent, disruptive and reconciliatory, profane and sacred, and yet the predominant attitude toward him is affection rather than fear" (11). Legba intervenes between humans and the gods. He is the guardian who opens the door for other supernatural powers. He is considered the only entirely unpredictable god in the Yoruban pantheon. Thriving on chaos and confusion, he is not summonable by the ordinary means used to call on the other gods. Instead, he is encountered at the crossroads in his role as the "ultimate master of potentiality" with the power "to make all things happen" (Thompson 18).

In the figure of Legba, there is no separation of good and evil, the sacred and the secular. Legba stands for the integration of all the contradictory forces of life. According to Julio Finn, it is not the devil Robert Johnson encountered at the crossroads but Legba the trickster who meets him at midnight, tunes his guitar, and gives him the power of the blues song (215-217). The story of Robert Johnson selling his soul to the devil comes from a reinterpretation of the Legba figure that turns him from Yoruban trickster to Christian devil. The life forces that coexist in the African Legba polarize into good and evil under the pressure of Christianity. In the Christian faith, God represents all that is good, Satan is the ultimate agent of evil, and there remains no room in between for a trickster deity like Legba.

The Yoruban trickster turns from a unification of opposites into a polarized figure—with the emphasis on his evil and frightful side. Similarly, African American music polarized as well. As a polytheistic people oriented themselves to the monotheistic world of Christianity, good and evil separated. The concurrent development of gospel and blues is a direct result of this process. From their common sources in slave songs, gospel became the African American's devotional music, while the blues became the sinful counterpart. There was no middle ground.

This theme of polarization is readily apparent in the relation of the preacher to the bluesman. It has often been said that the two roles are similar. "As professions," Keil says, "blues singing and preaching seem to be closely linked in both the rural or small town settings and in the urban ghettos" (Urban Blues 143). Both employ the same call and response pattern of performance. The difference is that in gospel praise is directed toward God. In blues, the acclaim is for the benefit of the performer. For this reason, no one can be a bluesman and preacher simultaneously. The social roles are mutual exclusive. There are many instances of bluesmen becoming preachers, or preachers backsliding into the blues. But there are virtually no examples of individuals serving both masters at the same time. In his youth, blues singer Big Bill Broonzy alternated back and forth between roles and was told categorically by his father to stop "straddling the fence" (Keil, Urban Blues 145).

The separation of the sacred and secular is also evident in the comparison of the church and the juke joint. Charles Keil refers to a "Saturday night and Sunday morning pattern" of African American weekends (Urban Blues 164). Saturday night was often spent at the juke joint where blues musicians provided the entertainment by engaging the audience in such participatory actions as hand clapping, dance, and call and response rituals where the bluesman asks "Did you ever love a woman who didn't love you?" Sunday morning was occupied in a similar way. In church the hand clapping, dance, and call and response pattern are just as apparent, only the preacher asks "Have you got good religion?"

Bluesmen like Robert Johnson and Peetie Wheatstraw used this polarization of the sacred and the secular to their advantage in constructing an image for themselves. As Keil says, "In most things connected with the blues, there is a pattern of African American culture and at the same time there is a commercial aspect to it in terms of what will sell. The aura sold records" (personal interview). As Finn notes, the fact that bluesmen vouched for the credibility of Robert Johnson's deal with the devil is in part a marketing strategy that "adds to the charm of this blues life—and it sells records" (210).

The history of the blues is filled with musicians playing with names and personas, inventing a reputation for themselves. Peetie Wheatstraw, the self-proclaimed "High Sheriff from Hell," is a classic example. Robert Johnson bought the image. Tommy Johnson may have invented it. He advised his fellow bluesmen: "you take your guitar and go to . . . where a crossroad is. . . . . A big black man will walk up there and take your guitar, and he'll tune it. And then he'll play a piece and hand it back to you. That's the way I learned to play anything I want" (qtd. in Guralnick, Searching). These men knew the appeal of the transgressive side of human nature and the power that the "devil's music" seems to hold. They knew that the power of the crossroads, black cat bones, and conjuring were more immediate and tangible than any promise Heaven could make.

Paul Oliver says the blues are the songs of people who have turned their back on religion. There is certainly some truth to this statement, but it relies too much on the polarization of sacred and secular traced in this paper. In many respects, the notion of the blues as a gift from Legba, the black man at the crossroads, is not a turn away from religion as much as it is a turn back to an older religion, an African one without the severe polarization of good and evil, god and devil, heaven and earth of Christianity. As Jon Spencer notes, the reason some blues musicians might have sold their souls to the devil is that they "were seemingly not that frightened of him" (31). If not a source of "good," in the dualistic Christian sense, the devil was more like a conjure man than a satanic anti-Christ, a source of power in this world.

Works Cited

Finn, Julio. The Bluesman: The Musical Heritage of Black Men and Women in the Americas. New York: Interlink, 1992.

Guralnick, Peter. Searching for Robert Johnson. New York: Harper and Row, 1982. 14 Oct. 1998. <http://www.the bluehighway.com/tbh1.html>.

—— . Sweet Soul Music: Rhythm and Blues and the Southern Dream of Freedom. New York: Harper and Row, 1986.

Johnson, Robert. Robert Johnson: King of the Delta Blues Singers. Columbia, PCT 1654, 1985.

Jones, Leroi (Amiri Baraka). Blues People. New York: Morrow, 1963.

Keil, Charles. Personal interview. 15 April 1997.

——— . Urban Blues. Chicago: U of Chicago P, 1969.

Marcus, Greil. Mystery Train. New York: Dutton, 1975.

Mitchell, George. Blow My Blues Away. Baton Rouge, LA: Louisiana State UP, 1971.

Oliver, Paul. Blues Fell This Morning: Meaning in the Blues, 2nd ed. Cambridge: Cambridge UP, 1990.

Palmer, Robert. Deep Blues. New York: Viking, 1981.

Ricks, George Robinson. Some Aspects of the Religious Music of the United States Negro: An Ethnomusicological Study with Special Emphasis on the Gospel Tradition. New York: Arno, 1977.

Spencer, Jon Michael. Blues and Evil. Knoxville: U of Tennessee P, 1993.

Thompson, Robert Farris. Flash of the Spirit. New York: Vintage, 1983.

Wright, Richard. 12 Million Black Voices: A Folk History of the Negro in the United States. New York: Viking, 1941.

Yurchenco, Henrietta. "'Blues Fallin' Down like Hail': Recorded Blues, 1920s-1940s." American Music 13.4 (1995): 448-69.

DEFINING DISEASE:
THE CASE OF CHRONIC FATIGUE SYNDROME
Jenny Chen
English 123
November 20, 19XX

ABSTRACT

The current controversy about whether chronic fatigue syndrome (CFS) is an illness with an organic basis or an imaginary condition poses important questions about how the medical profession defines disease and contains important consequences for treatment. CFS affects predominantly white, middle-class women. Literary critic Elaine Showalter has recently argued that CFS is a contemporary version of nineteenth-century neurasthenia or nervous exhaustion and should be treated by psycho-therapy. Others argue that treating CFS as a psychological disorder stigmatizes CFS patients and causes conflicts between patients and doctors. Recently some physicians have proposed that the biomedical model of disease is too rigid and that the medical profession and the public need to understand how the physical and psychological operate simultaneously in patients' illness.

The publication of Elaine Showalter's Hystories: Hysterical Epidemics and Modern Media (1997) has intensified the debate over chronic fatigue syndrome (CFS) and how it should be defined as a medical condition. According to a recent report (Reyes et al., 1997), CFS has been recognized since the early 1980s as an illness whose cause is unknown and for which no diagnostic tests have been developed. CFS patients are predominantly white middle-class women. The "illness is diagnosed primarily on the basis of symptoms and signs reported by the patient and exclusion of other possible causes of prolonged, debilitating fatigue" (Reyes et al., p. 2).

In Showalter's view, CFS is a psychogenic condition, a modern day form of nineteenth-century neurasthenia or nervous exhaustion. For Showalter, CFS has no physical basis but results from repressed and unarticulated psychological conflicts that manifest themselves in such flu-like symptoms as sore throat, tired and achy feeling, low-grade fever, and swollen lymph nodes. The appropriate treatment is psychotherapy.

One of the things that makes Showalter's book so controversial is that she groups CFS, as well as gulf war syndrome and multiple personality syndrome, with other contemporary "hysterical epidemics" such as alien abductions, satanic ritual abuse, and recovered memory. In Showalter's account, people "learn" the symptoms of these disorders from the media, telecommunications, and e-mail: "Infectious epidemics of hysteria spread by stories circulated through self-help books, articles in newspapers and magazines, TV talk shows and series, films, the Internet, and even literary criticism" (p. 5). For her critics, however, lumping illnesses such as CFS and gulf war syndrome together with UFOs and satanic cults trivializes real suffering. By defining "illness as a story instead of a physical condition (with the CFS sufferer acting out, say, the narrative of the bored and frustrated housewife), Showalter diverts our attention from real suffering" (Marcie Richardson, Re: Showalter as medical historian, E-mail to the author, April 15, 1997).

The controversy over Showalter's new book is not just an academic one. CFS presents an interesting and important case study of how medical conditions are categorized and how they acquire legitimacy. Skepticism concerning CFS is not limited to literary critics such as Showalter. It is also widespread within the medical profession. Whether CFS is an illness with an organic basis or an imaginary condition is a question that carries important implications for treatment. Should CFS be treated by a physician or a psychiatrist? Answers to this question depend on assumptions about how illness is defined.

BACKGROUND ON CFS

Chronic fatigue syndrome began to draw national attention in the early 1980s. In 1984, the outbreak of a mysterious illness in Incline Village, a small town of 6,000 inhabitants near Lake Tahoe, manifested a number of symptoms subsequently associated with CFS—dizziness, sore throats, headaches, diarrhea, shortness of breath, rapid heartbeat, and overall weakness. Within a year, there were over one hundred cases reported, and the Center for Disease Control (CDC) sent a team to investigate. CDC officials concluded that the Epstein-Barr virus, suspected at the time of being the source of chronic fatigue symptoms, could not be established as the cause of the mysterious illness (Johnson, 1996, pp. 33-51).

The Lake Tahoe outbreak is emblematic in many respects of the state of knowledge about CFS. For one thing, many of the patients were affluent young professionals, and their condition became known in the media in the 1980s as "Yuppie Flu." At the time, some physicians believed the cause of fatigue might be stress or overwork.

Second, physicians and researchers noted that patient conditions included immunological and neurological dysfunction. Nonetheless, no causal agent could be established. Lake Tahoe patients were no more likely than the general population to show evidence of infection with Epstein-Barr virus, and subsequent studies have eliminated Epstein-Barr as a candidate (Reyes, et al., 1997, p. 2). Other studies have eliminated a host of chemicals, bacteria, and viruses as suspected causes (Showalter, 1997, p. 125). At present, the etiology of CFS is unknown. The condition remains elusive to researchers.

Third, while there is no established cause, there are nonetheless a cluster of symptoms that seem to be associated. The persistence of these symptoms led CDC in 1988 to classify chronic fatigue as a syndrome and publish a case definition of CFS. According to CDC guidelines, the diagnosis of CFS depends on two major criteria, namely the exclusion of other clinical conditions (such as cancer, AIDS, or multiple sclerosis) and the persistence of symptoms over a period of six months or more. Then patients must show at least six of the following eleven symptoms: mild fever, sore throat, painful lymph nodes, muscle aches, excessive fatigue after normal activity, headaches, joint pain, impaired mental functioning (forgetfulness, excessive irritability, confusion, inability to concentrate, and so on), sleep disorders, and rapid onset of symptoms.

To put it in other words, the CDC classification of chronic fatigue as a syndrome establishes CFS as a medical condition that can be diagnosed as a cause of illness. CFS does not have the status of disease. Instead, it is considered to be a syndrome, or cluster of associated symptoms whose causes are unknown.

A recent report from CDC (Reyes, et al., 1997) summarizes a good deal of available information about the demographics of CFS. It confirms earlier studies that set the mean age of CFS patients at the time of onset at 30 years. It notes that the reported prevalence of CFS ranges from 3.8 to 9.6 cases per 100,000. And it indicates that the vast majority of CFS patients are white (96%) and female (85%), with median household income of $40,000.

DEFINING ILLNESS

As Simon Wessely (1994) says, "Worrying about whether or not CFS exists . . . is hardly the issue. It exists in the real world . . . . What lies behind CFS is neither a virus, nor psychiatry, but our idea of what constitutes a real illness, what doesn't, and what we do to make something real" (p. 29). Although Showalter argues that people should not be ashamed of hysteria, there is nonetheless a strong stigma attached to imaginary illnesses. As Arthur Kleinman and Stephen Straus (1993) write, "In much of biomedicine, only a tangible or laboratory abnormality justifies the imprimatur of a 'real' disease" (p. 3).

Often if the organic cause of an illness is not known, the illness is dismissed as a "real" disease and the sufferer is not entitled to sympathy from doctors or society. Charles Rosenburg (1992) says that "[f]or many Americans, the meaning of disease is the mechanism that defines it" (p. 312). For patients with cancer, tuberculosis, multiple sclerosis, and other diseases with established etiologies, an identity and a social role are available to patients based on diagnosis by the medical profession. Naming a patient's disease in effect gives him or her "permission" to be sick and offers validation to the patient's complaints.

Such diagnosis, as Hans Selye writes, can have direct benefit to the patient: "It is well-established that the mere fact of knowing what hurts you has an inherent curative value" (cited in Berne, 1995, p. 53). Rosenburg makes a similar point when he says that even "a bad prognosis can be better than no prognosis at all; even a dangerous disease, if it is made familiar and understandable, can be emotionally more manageable than a mysterious and unpredictable one" (p. 310).

Moreover, there are very real legal and financial consequences to the diagnosis of disease. Health benefits from insurance companies normally cover only those medical conditions that are considered to be legitimate and well established. Similarly eligibility for disability benefits and other social services is based on medical diagnosis. Employers' policies concerning medical leave, job responsibilities, special accomodations, and so on likewise depend on definitions of illness and disease.

DEFINING AND TREATING CFS

The popular press and medical journals discuss CFS in very different terms. According to a study of all the articles published in the British scientific, medical, and popular press between 1980 and 1994, only 31% of articles in medical journals believed the cause of CFS to be organic rather than psychological, while 69% of the articles in newspapers and magazines held to an organic explanation for the illness (MacLean & Wessely, 1994). This division between journalism and biomedicine is a troubling one because it points to divisions between patients and physicians concerning the origins and treatment of CFS.

In newspapers and magazines, CFS is often portrayed as a mystery disease which has yet to be conquered by modern medicine. The idea that the cause of CFS is out there to be found is reassuring to CFS patients, in part because it tells the familiar story of the march of scientific progress and its victories over disease. In this sense, CFS patients have their own stake in desiring that the causes of CFS are organic. Such a view of causation, where a pathogenic agent causes a pathological effect, is the basis for a potential cure in store—the magic bullet that can knock out the illness.

An organic cause of the illness not only makes CFS more treatable. It would also lift feelings of guilt and stigma from patients and clear them of charges of laziness, malingering, depression, and deceit. As David Bell (1995) writes, "Patients are angry and frustrated, interpreting the debate over emotions as trivializations of their illness and as the explanation for why so little is done for them" (p. 53). In many of the magazine articles, especially in personal accounts of CFS, patients express deep and abiding anger that physicians routinely describe their illness as psychological in origin. Part of the conflict between patients and doctors stems from the fact that defining CFS as a psychological syndrome, as most physicians do, appears to disqualify the patient's experience as a proper illness and portray it as a moral failing instead.

The most sympathetic physicians, on the other hand, respond that patients and the public at large need to recognize that psychological illness is just as real as illness that has a somatic basis. Anthony Komaroff (1994) says that CFS "may become a paradigmatic illness that leads us away from being trapped in the rigidity of the conventional biomedical model and leads us toward a fuller understanding of suffering" (52). Komaroff's sentiments are important ones, and there seems in principle to be growing agreement, in the words of the British Royal College of Physicians, Psychiatrists, and General Practitioners, that "CFS cannot be considered either 'physical' or 'psychological'—both need to be considered simultaneously to understand the syndrome" (cited in Brody, 1996, p. C14).

Nonetheless, the paradigm shift that Komaroff talks about has yet to take place, and the world of medicine continues to hold to a traditional biomedical model of illness in which patients with organic illness are treated by physicians and patients with psychological problems are treated by psychiatrists. So the basic problem of legitimate and illegitimate illness remains, marked by the presence or absence of organic causes. Perhaps the best solution, as Kleinman (1993) suggests, is to have physicians, not psychiatrists, treat CFS patients. "One can affirm the illness experience," he says, "without affirming the attribution for it; in other words, we can work within a 'somatic' language and do all the interventions . . . from the psychosocial side, but in such a way to spare patients the . . . delegitimization of their experience" (p. 329).

References

Bell, D.S. (1995). The doctor's guide to chronic fatigue syndrome. Boston: Addison-Wesley.

Berne, K.H. (1995). Running on empty: A complete guide to chronic fatigue syndrome. Alameda, CA: Hunter House.

Brody, J.E. (1996, October 9). Battling an elusive foe: Fatigue syndrome. New York Times, p. C14.

Johnson, H. (1996). Osler's web. New York: Crown.

Kleinman, A. (1993). CFS and the illness narrative. In A. Kleinman & S. Straus (Eds.), Chronic fatigue syndrome (pp. 318-332). London: Wiley.

Kleinman, A., & Straus, S. (1993). Introduction. In A. Kleinman & S. Straus (Eds.), Chronic fatigue syndrome (pp. 3-25). London: Wiley.

Komaroff, A.K. (1994). Clinical presentation and evaluation of fatigue in CFS. In S. Straus (Ed.), Chronic fatigue syndrome (pp. 47-64). New York: Marcel Dekker.

MacLean, G., & & Wessely, S. (1994). Professional and popular views of chronic fatigue syndrome. British Medical Journal, 308, 773-786.

Reyes, M. et al. (1997, February 21). Surveillance for chronic fatigue syndrome: Four U.S. cities, September 1989 through August 1993. Morbidity and Mortality Weekly Report, 46 (SS-2), 1-13.

Rosenburg, C. (1992). Explaining epidemics and other studies in the history of medicine. New York: Cambridge UP.

Showalter, E. (1997). Hystories: Hysterical epidemics and modern media. New York: Columbia UP.

Wessely, S. (1994). The history of chronic fatigue syndrome. In S. Straus (Ed.), Chronic fatigue syndrome (pp. 11-34). New York: Marcel Dekker.

CHAPTER
EIGHTEEN

DOCUMENT DESIGN

D ocument design concerns the visual dimension of written communication. The look of a page sends a message to readers. In many instances, written documents have a characteristic visual appearance that enables readers to identify immediately the genre of writing and the kind of communication the writing contains.

The purpose of this chapter is to present some of the basic principles involved in document design and to explain how you can design effective documents of your own.

SOME BASIC GUIDELINES FOR DOCUMENT DESIGN

To imagine that you are not only writing something but that you are also designing how it will look on the page means that your writing is going to be read by others. Whether the writing is a paper for a college course, a memo at work, or a brochure for a community service project, the design of the document has to do with how the writing will be delivered to others—to teachers, to supervisors and co-workers, or to people in the community. Document design involves packaging your message so that it will have the kind of influence on your readers that you intend.

This chapter covers some of the techniques writers use to design effective documents. Document design depends a good deal on the situation that calls on you to write, who your readers are, and the material you are treating. Nonetheless, there a few generalizations that can be made about document design. The following three guidelines offer rules of thumb that hold for virtually any kind of document.

- Readability: The design of a document should make it as easy as possible for the reader to process. Word processing, desktop publishing, and laser printers have opened up the range of design features available. The task is to choose those features that work to enhance the readability of the document you are designing.

- Appropriateness: The design of a document should be appropriate to the occasion. The task is to choose those design features that best fit the situation, the message, and the audience.

- Persuasiveness: The design of a document will inevitably influence readers' reception of it, whether they are aware or not of how they respond to the visual appearance. The task is to choose those design features that will enhance the overall effect of the document.

Keeping these basic guidelines in mind, we will look in the following sections at standard page designs used for college papers, letters, memos, and resumes, as well as the use of headings and type. Then we'll see some of the options word processing and desktop publishing make available to enhance the design of the page. Finally, we'll look at how you can design effective layouts for flyers, newsletters, brochures, and Web pages.

SOME STANDARD PAGE DESIGNS

Page design is a matter of preparing your document so it is readable and appropriate to your purposes. As you will see, college papers, letters, memos, and resumes have conventional design features that make them immediately recognizable. The following points about document preparation apply to all:

- Use good quality white, 20-pound weight, 8 1/2 x 11" paper. If your printer uses continuous sheets, separate the pages and remove the feeder strips.

- Make sure your document appears letter-quality. Use a dark ribbon. If possible, use a laser, ink-jet, or other type of printer that can produce letter-quality results. If you wish, you can use a dot matrix printer for drafts—but not for final documents.

- Use 10 or 12 point type size. (A point is 1/72".) Use a standard typeface, such as New York, Bookman, or Times. (See discussion below of serif and sans serif typefaces.)

- In general, avoid fancy fonts, icons, or anything that seems cute or gimmicky. Your page should have a formal, serious look.

- In most cases, avoid using all-caps, italics, or boldface in extended sections of text. Use these features sparingly, to emphasize single words and phrases or to document sources.

- Make sure you proofread carefully. For most college papers, you can make final corrections on the manuscript neatly in ink. If there are more than one or two on a page, you should re-type it. For business or other formal letters, memos, and resumes, re-type.

COLLEGE PAPERS

Some instructors will give you specific directions about how to format your work (e.g. a lab report, a case study, a field research report). Research papers in MLA and APA format are covered in Chapters 14 and 15. Otherwise, for most college papers, you can follow these guidelines:

- Give your paper a title. This is a key design feature that announces your topic and your approach to it. Center your title at the top of the first page. Some teachers ask for title pages. Others don't. Check with your instructor. In either case, include the following information: your name, course number, instructor's name, and date. See examples below (Fig. 1 and Fig. 2).

- Use one inch margins all around—in part to enhance readability by avoiding a sense of crowding on the page and in part to provide space for comments and annotation.

- Double space papers, align them on the left with ragged right margins, and indent five spaces for new paragraphs.

- Make sure you include page numbers, top right.

- Staple the paper in the top left corner.

Figure 1

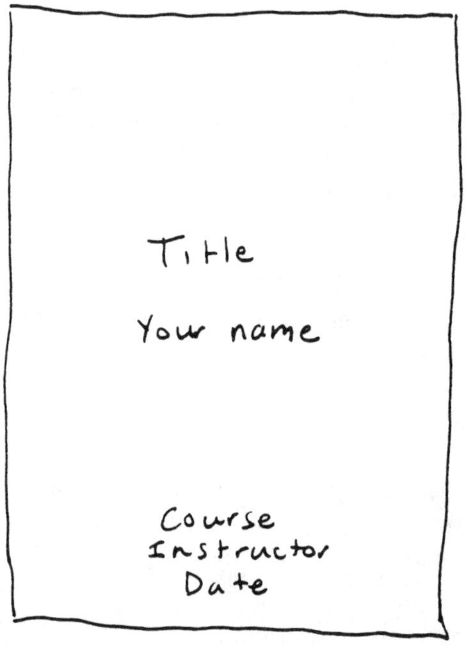

Figure 2

LETTERS

For business and other types of letters (such as those to editors, public officials, college administrators, faculty, and so on), use the standard business letter form. This way your letter will have a serious, formal appearance. (If you're uncertain how formal to be, it's probably best to be formal.) Make sure you know the person's correct title for the inside address.

Use one inch margins all around. Single space paragraphs, and double space between paragraphs. If you're using letterhead stationery that includes the return address, align all the sections on the left margin (Fig. 3). (Some people like to design their own letter head on the word processor.) If you're typing in your return address, use the modified block form (Fig. 4).

Figure 3

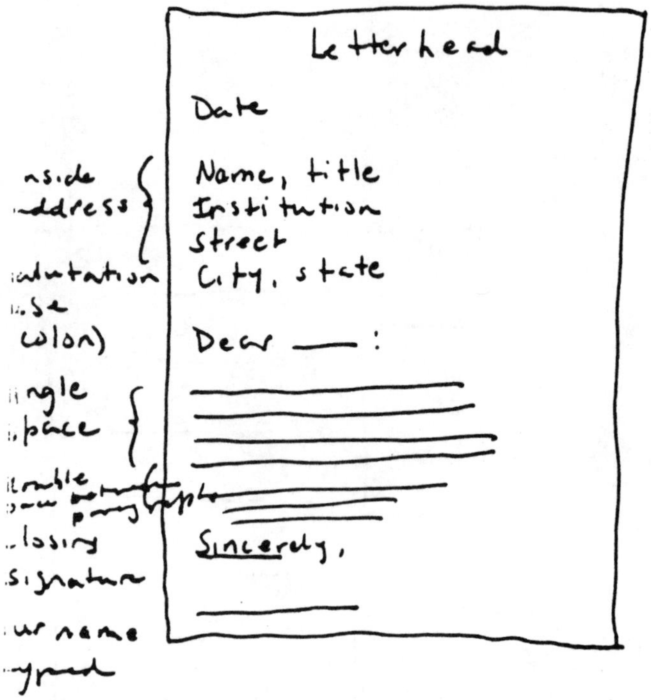

Figure 4

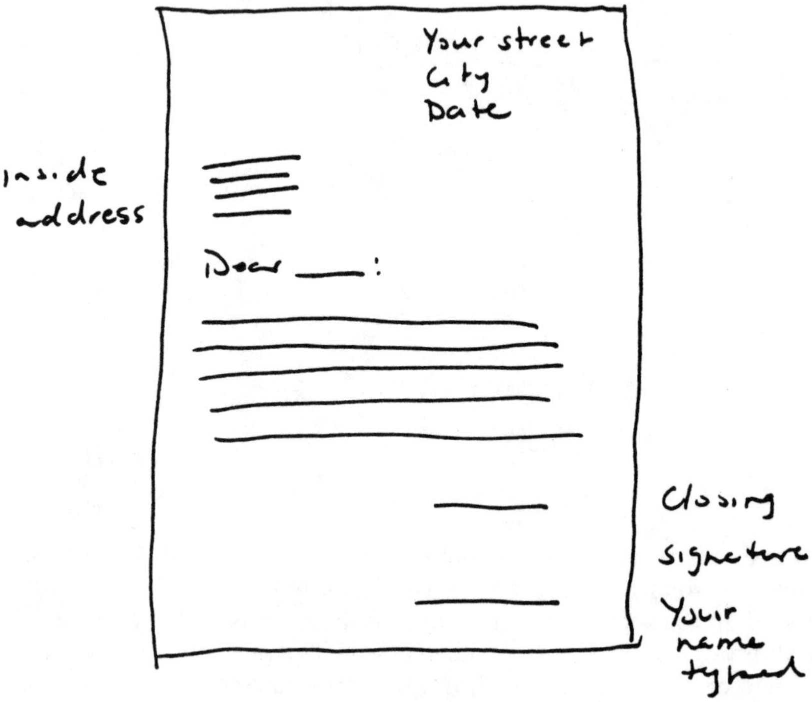

MEMOS

Memos are normally brief communications within organizations to report information, make requests, or recommend actions. Sometimes they are distributed widely. Other times, they go to just one person. They're designed to be read quickly.

Notice how the recipient, author, date, and subject are listed at the top of the memo (Fig. 5). "cc:" indicates other people who will receive the memo. Again use one inch margins all around, single space paragraphs, and double space between.

Figure 5

RESUMES

Designing resumes is really an exercise in presenting yourself by highlighting key information about your education, work experience, and accomplishments for prospective employers. Resumes need to be brief so readers read them quickly and pick out relevant material. Notice in the example how the headings (education, experience, and so on) and bulleted parallel phrases emphasize important information and make the resume easy to read quickly.

Martha Smith
143 Oakland Avenue
Philadelphia, PA 19122
(215) 865-3308

Education:

Junior - English major, with journalism minor - Temple University
Expected graduation date - May 1999

Experience:

Journalism internship - Philadelphia Inquirer
May 1998 - December 1998 (15 hrs. per week)

- Covered and wrote by-lined articles on school board meetings
- Researched sex education K-12 for special report
- Assisted editor in preparing special education supplement

Public Relations Assistant - Trinity Repertory Theater, Camden, NJ
May 1997 - September 1997

- Wrote advertising copy and designed promotional brochures
- Conducted focus groups
- Prepared instructional materials for Theater in the Schools

Writing Center Tutor - Temple University
September 1996 - May 1999

- Tutored students on wide range of writing assignments
- Taught grammar, editing, and revising
- Worked with international students
- Trained new tutors

Entertainment Editor - Temple Daily News
September 1997 - May 1998

- Planned and assigned music, art, drama, and film reviews
- Edited reviews
- Led staff meetings

Special Abilities/ Courses:

- Computer literacy - Macintosh, Windows
- Desktop publishing - Pagemaker, Adobe, Photoshop
- Written and spoken fluency in Spanish, reading ability in French
- Feature Writing, Graphic Design, Editing, Photojournalism

Achievements/ Activities:

- Dean's list (every semester)
- Member of Sigma Tau Delta, International English Honor Society
- Secretary of Amnesty International, Temple University chapter
- Varsity crosscountry and indoor and outdoor track

References:

Available upon request

WORKING TOGETHER: Designing Resumes

Design your own resume, using the headings in the sample resume —education, experience, special abilities/course, achievements/ activities—or some variation that enables you to present yourself effectively. You might also use bullets. Work together with two or three other students. Exchange resumes and answer these questions:

1. Is the resume easy to read quickly? Is the information easy to understand? Was there anything you didn't understand?
2. Do the headings organize information in a logical way? Do they present information in a logical and effective order?
3. Is there enough detail? Too much?
4. Is the visual appearance effective?

After answering these questions, discuss the design features of an effective resume. Compare your results to those of other groups.

USING HEADINGS

Headings have a number of functions in document design. First, headings make longer documents seem more inviting to read. They break up the density of written text by organizing information in more manageable chunks. Second, by marking sections, headings give readers a way to survey an entire document and get an overall sense of what the document contains and how it is organized. Finally, headings enable readers to use written documents in more efficient ways. Instead of having to read or skim through unmarked passages, readers can use headings to identify the parts of a document that are relevant to their purposes.

Settting up headings

Setting up headings in a document amounts to devising a logical and consistent system of presentation.

Headings should be easy to find. If they are buried in the text, they can't perform their function very well. One common way of emphasizing headings is to use boldface, underlining, italics, or capital letters.

To use headings effectively, you need to develop a system that indicates to readers the various sections' relative level of importance. The basic principle is that the more prominently displayed a heading is, the greater relative importance it has.

Here is a schematic look at the levels writers typically use. Remember that you won't necessarily be using all these levels in a document. The number of levels will depend on the organization of the document and what most enhances readability.

The first level

(Often reserved for the title alone.)

The second level

(When title alone is first level, use this level for major headings.)

The third level.

This heading is followed on the same line by text. (Use for minor headings.)

The fourth level.

Indented and followed by text. (Use for less important minor headings.)

You can overdo headings. Excessive use makes the page look too busy—and may make it hard for readers to see which headings are more important than others. In college papers, for example, major headings are probably sufficient.

How to write headings

Headings should be brief and informative. In general, use phrases instead of complete sentences. (See below for two exceptions, in cases when writers use questions or imperative sentences.) Avoid witty or clever headings. They do not always convey information clearly to readers. Be consistent and use parallel phrases as much as possible throughout the document.

The most common styles of headings are -ing phrases, noun phrases, questions, and imperative sentences.

- -ing phrases. Because phrases that begin with -ing verb forms imply action, they are a good choice for documents that explain how to do something (like a manual or set of directions) or that concentrate on solving problems. Here are some examples.

from a computer manual:
Getting started
Taking a closer look
Unpacking your computer
Putting it all together
Starting up the computer

from a report on global warming:
Defining global warning
Understanding the causes
Calculating the effects
Designing a response
Planning for the future

- Noun phrases. Noun phrases can be quite useful in documents that cover a variety of topics. Scientific papers typically use noun phrases to mark sections—introduction, literature review, materials and methods, results, discussion. Here are the section headings that might appear in a case study of a corporation's productivity program:

Characteristics of the Corporation
Productivity Planning of the Corporation
Obstacles to Productivity Planning
A Plan for Future Productivity Growth

- Questions. Questions offer another option for headings. They tend to elicit reader interest and involvement as well as mark the content of a section. Take for example the following headings from a brochure on sexually transmitted diseases (STDs):

What Is an STD?

How Are STD's Transmitted?

Can STD's Be Treated?

How Can You Prevent STD's?

- Imperative sentences. Imperative sentences are best suited for giving advice or directions about how to do something. Here are some headings that might appear in a booklet on how to finance a college education:

Plan Early
Start Saving a Little Each Month
Invest in Tax-Free Bonds

Explore Scholarships
Apply for Financial Aid
Consider Taking Out a Student Loan

DOCUMENT DESIGN ACTIVITY

Examine a chapter in one of your textbooks to see how it uses headings and sub-headings. How does it chunk information in sections? What design features does it use to display headings? How does it phrase headings? Do the headings make the chapter more readable? Explain your answer.

WORKING WITH TYPE

Type refers to standardized forms of letters and characters. Until quite recently, it was largely graphic designers in printing companies who knew about the various styles of type and determined which ones to use for a particular document. In the age of the personal computer, this has changed dramatically. Now writers have access to hundreds of type fonts and can change their size and underline, italicize, or make them boldface with the click of a mouse.

The vast range of possibilities now available, however, can be overwhelming. Writers need to understand what their options are using type and what kinds of effect their design decisions are likely to have on readers.

TYPE AND WHITE SPACE

In document design, white space is not simply the empty places on a page where no writing or illustrations appear. White space plays an active role in setting off type, adding to visual interest, and breaking up the monotony of solid text. As you have seen in the section on headings, the surrounding white space makes headings more or less prominent. Here are two reductions of the page you just read. Notice how the absence of white space makes the page dense and forbidding in the first reduction:

DOCUMENT DESIGN ACTIVITY Examine a chapter in one of your textbooks to see how it uses headings and sub-headings. How does it chunk information in sections? What design features does it use to display headings? How does it phrase headings? Do the headings make the chapter more readable? Explain your answer. WORKING WITH TYPE Type refers to standardized forms of letters and characters. Until quite recently, it was largely graphic designers in printing companies who knew about the various styles of type and determined which ones to use for a particular document. In the age of the personal computer, this has changed dramatically. Now writers have access to hundreds of type fonts and can change their size and underline, italicize, or make them boldface with the click of a mouse.The vast range of possibilities now available, however, can be overwhelming. Writers need to understand what their options are using type and what kinds of effect their design decisions are likely to have on readers.Combining type and white space to enhance readability In document design, white space is not simply the empty places on a page where no writing or illustrations appear. White space plays an active role in framing text, adding to visual interest, and breaking up the monotony of solid type. As you have seen in the section on headings, the surrounding white space makes headings

And how you can at least find your way around in the second reduction:

DOCUMENT DESIGN ACTIVITY

Examine a chapter in one of your textbooks to see how it uses headings and sub-headings. How does it chunk information in sections? What design features does it use to display headings? How does it phrase headings? Do the headings make the chapter more readable? Explain your answer.

WORKING WITH TYPE

Type refers to standardized forms of letters and characters. Until quite recently, it was largely graphic designers in printing companies who knew about the various styles of type and determined which ones to use for a particular document. In the age of the personal computer, this has changed dramatically. Now writers have access to hundreds of type fonts and can change their size and underline, italicize, or make them boldface with the click of a mouse.

The vast range of possibilities now available, however, can be overwhelming. Writers need to understand what their options are using type and what kinds of effect their design decisions are likely to have on readers.

Combining type and white space to enhance readability

In document design, white space is not simply the empty places on a page where no writing or illustrations appear. White space plays an active role in framing text, adding to visual interest, and breaking up the monotony of solid type. As you have seen in the section on headings, the surrounding white space makes headings more or less prominent. Here are two visualizations of the page you

When you encounter a page that looks like the first version, one of two things is likely to be true: there is a need to get as much information as possible on each page (as in many reference books), or someone doesn't really want to make the information accessible (notice the fine print in advertisements, credit card statements, contracts, etc.).

Assuming you aren't trying to hide anything, here are some guidelines about making type readable:

- Indent paragraphs and use white space to emphasize paragraph divisions. Notice in the second reduction how white space enables readers to identify paragraphs easily and to treat each as a separate unit of meaning. White space contributes to the openness of the page by breaking up large expanses of type.

- Use upper and lower case letters. In general, the combination of upper and lower case letters is easier to read than all upper case. This is because upper case (or capital) letters are uniform in size, making them more difficult to recognize than lower case letters. The combination of upper and lower case uses more white space and therefore produces more visual variety. Notice the difference between these two paragraphs:

USE UPPER AND LOWER CASE LETTERS. IN GENERAL, THE COMBINATION IS EASIER TO READ THAN ALL UPPER CASE. THIS IS BECAUSE UPPER CASE (OR CAPITAL) LETTERS ARE UNIFORM IN SIZE, MAKING THEM MORE DIFFICULT TO RECOGNIZE THAN LOWER CASE LETTERS, WHERE THERE IS MORE WHITE SPACE AND THEREFORE MORE VISUAL VARIETY. NOTICE THE DIFFERENCE:

Use upper and lower case letters. In general, the combination is easier to read than all upper case. This is because upper case (or capital) letters are uniform in size, making them more difficult to recognize than lower case letters, where there is more white space and therefore more visual variety. Notice the difference:

- Use leading appropriately. Leading is the typographer's term for the white space that appears above and below a line of type. Leading is what makes a printed page look more or less "gray." The grayer the page, the denser the type and the harder to read. The basic guideline is that you need more leading, or space above and below type, when lines of print are long, less when they're short.

Compare the readability of these two paragraphs:

Long lines of type are easier to read when they have more leading. This is particularly true if the type itself is small. Compare the readability of these two passages of 9 point type. This passage is single-spaced. The extra leading in the second passage helps direct reader's eyes, so they don't skip a line or return to the one they've just read.

Long lines of type are easier to read when they have more leading. This is particularly true if the type itself is small. Compare the readability of these two passages of 9 point type. This passage is a space and a half. The extra leading in the second passage helps direct reader's eyes, so they don't skip a line or return to the one they've just read.

Notice the difference between Column A and Column B:

Column A

For shorter lines, as in

newsletters and other

documents with columns, use

less leading. If there's too

much white space, reader's

eyes can drift when they leave

one line and look for the start

of the next.

Column B

For shorter lines, as in
newsletters and other
documents with columns, use
less leading. If there's too
much white space, reader's
eyes can drift when they leave
one line and look for the start
of the next.

On other hand, headlines are easier to read when the leading is tighter, integrating the words into one visual block. Notice the difference:

Entertaining Satan:
Witchcraft and the Culture
of Early New England

Entertaining Satan:
Witchcraft and the Culture
of Early New England

• **Use alignment appropriately.** In general, use flush-left/ragged right alignment for lines of type. This way all lines start in the same place at the left margin, and readers' eyes can return easily to the same spot when they finish reading a line. Ragged-right alignment creates an open, informal feeling by providing variable amounts of white space at the end of a line. This variability enables readers to see the difference between the lines, making it easier for them to move from line to line and thereby avoid inadvertantly skipping a line.

Type that is justified (or aligned uniformly on the right margin) normally creates a darker, denser-looking page. Justified type can often be more difficult to read because more words are hyphenated and gaps can appear between words. Notice the difference in the two columns:

flush left/justified right:

Type is easier to read if it is aligned along the left margin. This way all lines start in the same place, and readers' eyes can return easily to the same spot when they finish reading a line. On the other hand, type that is justified (or aligned on the right margin is often more difficult to read. This is . . . .

flush left/ragged right:

Type is easier to read if it is aligned along the left margin. This way all lines start in the same place, and readers' eyes can return easily to the same spot when they finish reading a line. On the other hand, type that is justified (or aligned on the right margin is often more difficult to read. This is . . . .

In some cases, of course, you'll want to use centering—for titles or to give a formal tone to a document such as an invitation or official announcement.

TYPEFACE

Typeface refers to the design of letters, numbers, and other characters. There are thousands available. The visual appearance of typeface contributes to the personality or character of your document. Part of working with type is choosing the typeface that creates the right image and thereby sends the appropriate message to your readers.

• Serif and sans serif typefaces. Typefaces are normally divided into two groups—serif and sans serif. Serif typefaces include horizontal lines—or serifs—added to the major strokes of a letter or character (such as a number). Sans serif typefaces, by contrast, do not have serifs. Notice the difference:

Serif	Sans serif
New York	Geneva
Palatino	Espy Sans
Times	Monaco
Courier	Helvetica

The typical use and stylistic impact of the typefaces vary considerably. Serif typeface is more traditional, conservative, and formal in its appearance. By contrast, sans serif offers a more contemporary, progressive, and informal look. Accordingly, serif is often used for longer pieces of writing, such as novels and textbooks. It is also the best bet for college papers. The horizontal lines make serif easier to read, especially in dense passages, because they guide the reader's eyes from left to right across the page. On the other hand, technical writers often use sans serif for user's manuals and other documents because it evokes a more modern, "high tech" look.

Typeface also differs in weight—or the thickness of the letters. A heavier, blacker type will darken your page, making your message appear more serious and substantial. A lighter type will show more white space and create a more spacious, informal mood. With "bold," "italic," and "underline" functions on a word processor, you can make further alterations.

Heavier type   **New York bold**

Lighter type   Helvetica

- Display or decorative typefaces. Display or decorative typefaces offer many options for creating the look you want in newsletter nameplates, organizational logos, invitations, posters, signs, advertisements, and other documents. Display typefaces can project the mood and image that's appropriate for an organization or occasion. The trick, of course, is finding the style that's right—that conveys the message you want to readers.

Notice the different images display type creates for Jetstream Printers. This type projects a sleek and contemporary look:

Jetstream

This type, however, is probably too staid and conservative, more appropriate, say, for a bank, stock brockerage company, or law firm:

JETSTREAM

On the other hand, this type is too light-hearted and informal. It's better suited for a restaurant or fashion boutique:

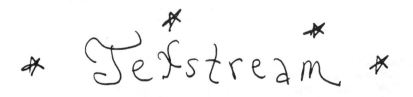

By the same token, notice how the "alternative" style of type in the following announcement doesn't match the occasion.

The Office of the President
at
Worcester Polytechnic Institute
invites you

Reception and Banquet
in honor
of
Retiring Professor of Mechanical Engineering
Aldous Smiley

If you received such an invitation, you might well feel, perhaps without fully realizing why, that something is off—the delivery or packaging of the message doesn't fit the occasion. On the other hand, if the typeface had been more formal, you probably would not have even noticed it. Appropriate type sometimes does its work by not calling attention to itself.

- Mixing typeface. In some cases, combining different typeface can enhance document design. Newsletters, for example, often use sans serif type for headlines and serif for text. Make sure, however, that combinations of typeface project a consistent image and that the styles used are compatible. Notice the sense of chaos mixed styles can create:

The Office of the President

of

Worcester Polytechnic Institutes

invites you

Reception and Banquet

in honor

of

Retiring Professor of Mechanical Engineering
Aldous Smiley

WORKING TOGETHER: Designing a Logo

Logos use graphics, typeface, or a combination of the two to create an immediately recognizable image or identity for a company, an organization, or an institution. The logo of IBM, for example, (Fig. 6) created by the noted graphic designer Paul Rand, uses bold, square capital serif letters to give the company a powerful and conservative image. On the other hand, April Greiman's logo for the clothing and gift store Vertigo (Fig. 7) projects a playful, contemporary, "new wave" look. Sometimes designers hit the wrong note, as is the case with the original Apple Computer logo (Fig. 8)—which was replaced by Apple's now well-known apple logo.

Figure 6

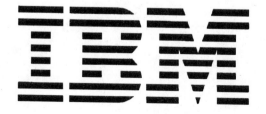

Figure 7

Figure 8

Work with two or three other students.

- First, consider Apple's original logo. In terms of readability, appropriateness, and persuasiveness, what do you see as the strengths and weaknesses in the original design? Do you think designers created an effective alternative in the current logo? Explain your answer.

- Second, imagine you have been commissioned to create a logo for a company, organization, or institution . What image and identity will you want to project? What graphics, typeface, or combination could you use to create this identity? Sketch one or more logos. Explain your design decisions.

ENHANCING PAGE DESIGN

The following section describes a number of options word processing and desktop publishing make available to enhance the visual appearance of page design.

Most of the document design features discussed so far in this chapter and many discussed below are included in standard word processing programs. Some word processing programs also offer built-in drawing and statistical graphic packages, libraries of clip art, and layout systems. Many have import features that enable you to bring in graphics and clip art from other programs.

There are, of course, further possibilities to explore. You can add more typefaces and clip art to your word processing program. Illustration programs enable you to draw free hand pictures and manipulate clip art and images imported through a scanner. Layout or page design programs allow you to work on the full-size page and are especially useful for documents such as newsletters and brochures. The expense and ease of operation of these further possibilities vary considerably. You'll have to decide what kind of document design tools make sense for you.

Here are basic suggestions about page design that you can follow with many word processing programs:

- Use borders to draw attention to the "live area" on the page—where text, display type, and graphics appear. Borders draw readers' eyes to the text and graphics on a page. Borders can be tangible lines that frame the page or they can be assumed, creating the illusion of a frame. The basic tangible border is a line surrounding the page (Fig. 9). On some occasions, decorative borders are appropriate. Assumed borders are created by the edges of columns, boxes, and graphics (Fig. 10).
- Use rules to emphasize or frame elements on the page. Rules are horizontal or vertical lines that separate items on a page. Notice how horizontal rules draw attention to headings and vertical rules separate the columns of type (Fig. 11).

Figure 9

Figure 10

Figure 11

- Use infographics to display information and break up the density of the page. Infographics are useful means of organizing and displaying information. The most familiar types are treated in Chapter "Understanding Options in the Visual Display of Information." Infographics can also enhance the appearance of a page. Notice the difference between the two pages (Fig. 12 and Fig. 13). Each contains the same information but the use of a line graph and column chart in Fig. 13 makes the information easy to understand in a glance, as well as the making the page more inviting to read.

Figure 12

```
the average late riser, this product will revolutionize his or her
sleeping habits.

CURRENT SNOOZE ALARM SALES

As stated previously, we believe that a high number of present users of
snooze alarm technology will want to own TardiSnooz.  Current sales of
snooze alarms have never been higher, as the figures below show:

YEAR        # UNITS SOLD      $ RETAIL

1965            1,100        $    12,000
1970           65,000           430,000
1975          220,000         2,800,000
1980          673,000         5,900,000
1985        1,220,000        11,670,000

A corresponding trend of employee tardiness has become evident,
particularly in the last ten years.  In fact, some researchers believe
that snooze alarms have indeed played a large part in causing employee
tardiness.  According to Real Life Information in Palo Alto, California,
"Snooze alarm technology is largely responsible for the dramatic rise in
employee tardiness and late calls.  Further, the admonishment thrust upon
the average employee, compounded by the guilt, feelings of inadequacy and
consequent resentment, creates an unresolved authority-figure conflict,
resulting in sharply decreased productivity....One solution to this
problem is a mechanism whereby the employee can at least call in late
with a feeling of efficiency and accomplishment, instead of languishing
in commuter-frustrated dissonance on his or her way to work."

Clearly, the above findings indicate the need for added features to
snooze technology.  This, coupled with the fall in wholesale modem chip
prices, could make TardiSnooz our sale item of the decade.

PROJECTED TARDISNOOZ SALES

Based on a 1,000-piece consumer survey mailed last month (see attached
data), we found consumers receptive, and indeed eager, to pay the
slightly higher price that TardiSnooz would command.  Below are projected
sales figures, based on our survey:

PROJECTED TARDISNOOZ SALES

YEAR        # UNITS PROJECTED        $ RETAIL

1990           34,000             $    430,000
1991           81,000                  970,000
1992          239,000 (Break-
                        even)        2,400,000
1993          310,000                3,700,000
1994          228,000 (Recession
                        Projected)   2,200,000
1995          426,000                4,450,000

When you examine the above figures, and consider that all we have to do
is add a $.93 modem chip to our present alarms, the conclusion is
inescapable to all but the most ardent critics that our company should
```

Figure 13

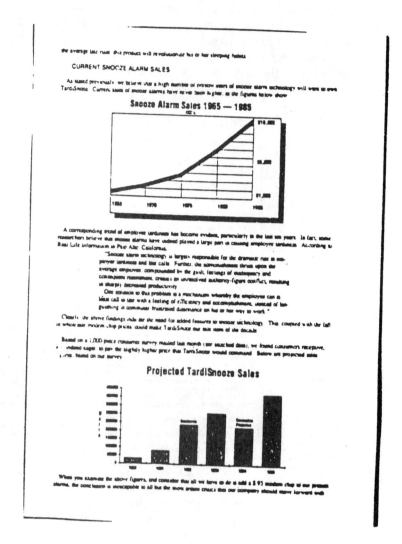

- Use sidebars, displayed lists, and pull quotes to create emphasis and visual variety. Because they are prominently displayed on a page, these design features are often the first things a reader notices and thereby serve as a "teaser," to prompt readers to read the entire text. Often the type differs from the main text—using either a different typeface or a different size.

Sidebars contain information which supplements the main text, such as lists, examples, quotes, or, as in Fig. 14, a menu for a Web site. Often sidebars appear in a box. As their name implies, sidebars run alongside a section of text. Sidebars can also be used in newsletters or organizational letterhead to list table of contents, activities, or board of directior.

Displayed lists can be incorporated into virtually any document by using bullets to separate and highlight the items. This textbook, for example, frequently uses displayed lists. Or they can appear in a separate box (Fig 15). Like sidebars, displayed lists enable writers to condense and display pertinent information in a way that draws special attention to it.

Pull quotes (Fig. 16) feature quotations from the main text. Like sidebars and displayed lists, they enhance the visual appeal of a page by breaking up the density of text.

Figure 14

THOMAS — Legislative Information on the Internet

QUICK SEARCH TEXT OF BILLS 105th CONGRESS:

Search by Bill Number:

Ex: s 435, H.R. 842

OR
Search by Word/Phrase:

Ex: *line item veto, tax reform*

| Search | Clear |

105th Congress:
House Directories
Senate Directories

Congressional Internet Services:
House - Senate
Library of Congress

GPO - GAO - CBO
AOC - OTA - More

Library of Congress Web Links:
Legislative
Executive
Judicial
State/Local

■ CONGRESS NOW

Congress in the News
House and Senate: Floor Activities
House: Latest Floor Actions - Floor Activities This Week
National Bipartisan Commission on the Future of Medicare

■ BILLS

Bill Summary & Status: 105th (1997-98)
Previous Congresses (1973 - 1996)

Bill Text:
105th (1997-98) - 104th (1995-96) - 103rd (1993-94) - 102nd (1991-93) - 101st (1989-90)

House Roll Call Votes [Help]: 105th - 2nd (1998) - 105th - 1st (1997)
Previous Congresses (1990 - 1996)

Senate Roll Call Votes [Help]: 105th - 2nd (1998) - 105th - 1st (1997)
Previous Congresses (1989 - 1996)

Public Laws By Law Number: 105th (1997-98)
Previous Congresses (1973 - 1996)

Major Legislation: [Definition]
105th: By topic - By popular/short title - By bill number/type - Enacted into law
104th: By topic - By popular/short title - By bill number/type - Enacted into law

■ CONGRESSIONAL RECORD

Congressional Record Text: Most Recent Issue
105th (1997-98) - 104th (1995-96) - 103rd (1993-94) - 102 (1991-92) - 101st (1989-90)

Congressional Record Index:
105th - 2nd (1998) - 105th - 1st (1997) - 104th - 2nd (1996) - 104th - 1st (1995) - 103rd - 2nd (1994)

Résumés of Congressional Activity:
105th - 1st (1997) - Previous Congresses (1969 - 1996)

Annals of Congress (Precursor of the *Congressional Record*) [About]
1st Congress (1789-1791) - 2nd Congress (1791-1793)

■ COMMITTEE INFORMATION

Committee Reports: Congress: 105th (1997-98) - 104th (1995-96)

Committee Home Pages: House - Senate

House Committees: Today's Schedule - Schedules and Oversight Plans - Selected Hearing Transcripts

■ THE LEGISLATIVE PROCESS

How Our Laws Are Made (by Charles Johnson, House Parliamentarian)

Enactment of a Law (By Robert Dove, Senate

Figure 15

Lights, Camera, Dollars!

The list of the most expensive movies ever made includes hits, bombs and—in the top slot—an eight-hour Soviet epic.

YEAR	MOVIE	COST IN MILLIONS ORIGINAL	1997$
1967	War and Peace	$100	$482
1997	Titanic	200	200
1963	Cleopatra	37	195
1995	Waterworld	175	185
1997	Speed 2: Cruise Control	160	160
1994	True Lies	105	114
1962	Mutiny on the Bounty	21	112
1996	Space Jam	105	108
1996	Eraser	100	103
1997	Batman & Robin	100	100

Figure 16

BOB HERBERT

The Success Taboo

Somehow over the past two or three decades a lot of black kids absorbed the message that academic achievement was something to be shunned. Excellence in sports or the various entertainment fields was one thing, a good thing, but high marks and academic honors were something else. Academic achievement, according to this mind-bogglingly destructive way of thinking, was a white thing, and thus in some sense contemptible. The tragic result has been that in many schools across the country black kids who apply themselves to their studies are often ridiculed and at times ostracized.

A black teacher in the Bronx told me in a despairing tone that she has male students who would rather be paraded in handcuffs before television cameras than be caught reading a book. I've had many students tell me in interviews that they are afraid to raise their hands in the classroom because they don't want to repeat the experience of being laughed at for giving the correct answer.

A black 17-year-old girl who worked part time at a mall in Marietta, Ga., was taunted recently by high school classmates who showed up at her job to express their resentment at the high marks she was getting.

Now, and not a moment too soon, comes Hugh Price, president of the National Urban League, with an ambitious first step toward turning this madness around.

"We haven't surrounded our young people with enough opportunities to excel academically and to be recognized for excelling," said Mr. Price. "We haven't had the rituals in our own community that reward young people for doing well."

The Urban League has drawn together 20 national black organizations, including the Congress of National Black Churches, for what it calls the Campaign for African-American Achievement. The idea is to improve the academic standing of black youngsters by encouraging and rewarding excellence in the classroom, and by improving the quality of the education that is offered to black youngsters in the public schools.

A statement announcing the campaign said: "We have to reverse the increasing gap in academic achievement between African-American and other children. We have to increase the low rates of enrollment of African-American youngsters in college preparatory courses and attack the inequitable allocation of resources for public education."

There is an urgency in Mr. Price's manner as he talks about this effort. He and his colleagues recognize that black men and women will have to be substantially better prepared educationally if they are to survive economically as we move into the 21st century. Employers, as Mr. Price noted, "expect much more in the way of academic preparation than ever before." And affirmative action, however one feels about it, is almost certain to continue its fade from the scene.

The achievement campaign will try in a variety of ways to generate en-

When black students excel.

thusiasm among students and parents for the hard work that is necessary to succeed academically. This will not be easy in environments that are plagued by poverty, broken families, drug abuse, violence and the widespread notion that what is taught in the classroom is not relevant to the lives of the students.

The campaign will establish an honor society, called the National Achievers Society, to focus attention on black youngsters who excel academically. The first induction ceremony, to be presided over by Gen. Colin Powell, will be held next spring.

September has been designated Achievement Month by the campaign. The plan is to have Urban League affiliates, black churches and other organizations conduct a month-long series of high-profile events each year celebrating the efforts of black youngsters who are doing well in school.

Meanwhile, leaders of the campaign are working with professional organizations and universities around the country to determine where improvements in the public schools need to be made and what specific kinds of academic help are needed for underachieving students.

This is not a perfect plan. Much of it will be modified and some of it will fail. But it does send the crucial message that academic achievement is as important for black people as anyone else. It's a message that somehow has escaped the consciousness of too many black children.   □

LAYOUT

Layout is a matter of integrating the design features you've been reading about—headings, type, borders, rules, infographics, sidebars, displayed lists, and pull quotes—in order to create an attractive, readable page that is appropriate for conveying your message. Document designers often think of the page as a frame within which design features can be arranged to produce the intended effect on readers. Here are some basic suggestions about layout:

- Page layout should create a unified, balanced look without distracting "holes" or white space. Borders (whether tangible or assumed) frame the page, creating the space in which the design features of the document should combine to give the page a unified, balanced look. "Holes" are trapped white space that can undermine page layout. Notice in Fig. 17 the layout creates "holes" between the headline and graphic in the left column and between the article and headline in the right column. This page could be tightened and unified by increasing the size of headline type and enlarging the visual.

A variation of trapped white space occurs when text starts at different distances from the top of the page (Fig. 18). This creates a "jumping horizon"—a disconcerting up-and-down effect that disunifies the page.

Figure 17

Figure 18

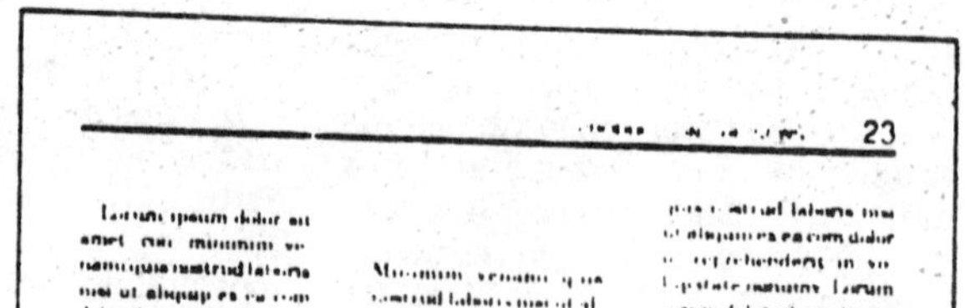

- Page layout should create appropriate breathing space around design features. To avoid a claustrophobic sense of crowding, design features such as graphics and columns of type need to be framed so that they stand out. In Fig. 19, notice the layout allows insufficient white space to frame the box in the left column, and the columns of type themselves are crowded next to each other and squeezed against the edge of the page.

Figure 19

- Avoid tombstoning. Tombstoning is the effect created when design features such as graphics or headings are located adjacent to each other on a multi-column page. When this happens, they compete for the reader's visual attention, and their overall impact is diminished (Fig. 20).

Figure 20

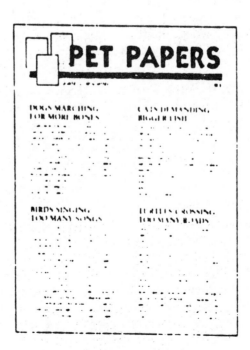

- Plan runarounds carefully. Runarounds are lines of type that wrap around an illustration or capital letter. Runarounds are a good way to link text and graphics together and to give an attractive look to the page.

Runarounds can cause problems if not planned carefully. Notice in Fig. 21 that the outline of the runaround text is too choppy and that too much white space is trapped to the right of the illustration. The best solution in this case is to put the illustration in a box.

trud laboris nisi ut aliquip.
Lorum ipsum dolor sit amet.
con: minimim venami quis nos.
trud laboris nisi ut aliquip
com dolor. In reprehender-
it in volupatate nonumy.
Lorum ipsum dolor sit amet.
con: minimim venami quis sin
nostrud laboris nisi ut aliqui
ea com dolor in reprehe-
nderit in volupatate
Lorum ipsum dolor sit
amet. con: minimin
venami quis nostrud laboris nisi
ut aliquip ex ea com dolor. Lorum ipsum dolor

DOCUMENT DESIGN PROJECTS

The following section looks at some of the considerations writers typically take into account when they design and produce documents such as flyers, newsletters, brochures, and Web home pages.

Preliminary considerations

Like other writing tasks, document design projects begin with a call to write—the felt need to send a message from an individual, group, or organization to prospective readers. Developing the design of a particular document will depend on answering questions such as these:

- What is the occasion that calls on you to design a document? What kind of document is most appropriate given the circumstances (a flyer, leaflet, letter, brochure, etc.)? What is its purpose? Whose interests are involved? What is your relationship to the people who want the document produced and to those who will read it? What image should the document project?

- Who are your readers? What use will they make of the document? What do you want them to do after they have read the document? What tone and style are likely to be effective?

- What information will you be working with? How much of the document will be written text? What graphics do you have to use? How many sections do you foresee? In what order will they appear? Will you be doing all the writing? Some? Who else is involved?

- What technology do you have to work with? What does it enable you to do? What constraints does it put on the document?

- Are there any financial or time constraints you need to be aware of? Who will pay for the printing? When does the document need to be finished? Is this a realistic time frame?

By answering these questions, you can begin to make some basic decisions about the layout and other design features of your document. In particular, you will need to decide on the materials you will use in the document—whether you can use color, what type and color of ink, what type and color of paper, whether you plan to scan in illustrations or photos, what clip art if any you plan to use.

By answering these questions, you can begin to make some basic decisions about the layout and other design features of your document. In particular, you will need to decide on the materials you will use in the document—whether you can use color, what type and color of ink, what type and color of paper, whether you plan to scan in illustrations or photos, what clip art if any you plan to use.

WORKING SKETCHES

The next step is to sketch a preliminary layout for the document. At this point, document designers often sketch a number of different arrangements. Such working sketches can help you identify potential problems you may face.

The working sketches for a newsletter and brochure might look the ones here (Fig. 22 and Fig. 23). Notice how each sketch uses a frame within which the page components are arranged. In both instances, the document designer is working with columns and sketching where headlines, headings, boxes, and so on will go. For brochures, you'll need to pay attention to how the panels will work when the brochure is folded (Fig. 24).

Figure 22

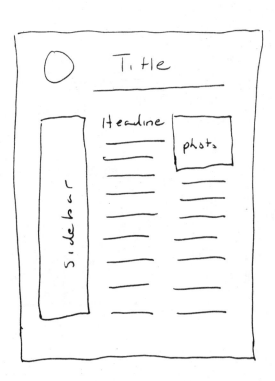

Figure 23

Figure 24

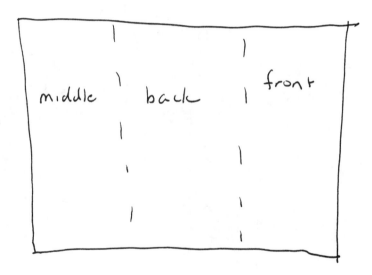

FROM SKETCH TO DOCUMENT: SOME EXAMPLES

The following sections contain examples of four types of common documents—flyers, newsletters, brochures, and Web pages.

Flyers

Flyers are really small posters that can be passed out or posted on bulletin boards. They may announce upcoming meetings, events, and performances; advertise sales and other limited-time promotions; or urge people to do something. To be effective, flyers need to convey all the pertinent information in a glance. To do so, successful flyers usually include:

- Large headlines.
- A minimum of text in the body.
- Attention-getting visuals and/or design features.

Figure 25

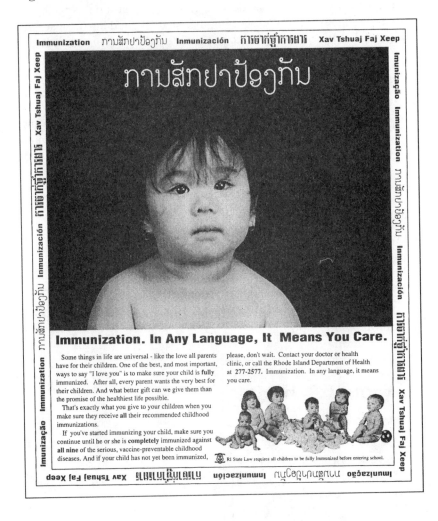

This flyer was designed by the Rhode Island Department of Health to urge parents to immunize their children. The headline is the word "immunization" in Khmer, the national language of Cambodia. Notice how the word in its English, Khmer, Lao, Hmong, Spanish, and Portuguese versions creates a strong border to frame the flyer. The flyer uses an attention-getting photo and concise text.

(Also see the "Consumer Alert" flyer in Chapter 1, p. .)

Newsletters

Newsletters are used by companies and organizations to communicate within the group and to the public. They run from a single page to eight pages or so, depending on their purpose and frequency. In many respects, they are like newspapers or little magazines. Key elements to a successful newsletter include

- A distinctive nameplate and logo that identifies the newsletter.

- Clear identification of the sponsoring organization.

- Volume and/or issue number and date.

- A table of contents—on front or back cover.

- Consistent design that maintains the identity of the newsletter from one issue to the next.

- Use of design features such as sidebars, boxes, pull quotes, photos, and illustrations to break up the text and add visual interest.

The San Miguel School

1996 Winter Newsletter—Issue #13

Board of Directors

Robert McMahon—Chair
Deputy Superintendent of Parks

Edward Handy—Vice Chair
Senior Vice-President
Citizens Bank

Oliver H.L. Bennett
Vice-President, Fleet Bank

Marcia Carpenter
Carpenter Realty

Mark Chute
Businessman

Bernadette Coletta
Businesswoman

Edward DeFalco, Esq.

Bro. Brendan Gerrity, FSC
Executive Director, Ocean Tides

Bro. Lawrence Goyette, FSC
Principal, The San Miguel School

William Greene
Director of Retail Brokerage
Hayes & Sherry Realtors

Miguel Luna
Family AIDS Center for
Treatment and Support

Bro. Michael McKenery, FSC
Provincial
De La Salle Christian Brothers

Evette McCray
Assistant Vice-President
Hospital Trust

Bro. Edmond Precourt, FSC
Assistant Provincial
De La Salle Christian Brothers

John Quigley, Esq.

Frank Sullivan, Account Executive
Chemical Residential Mortgage

Sheila Wilhelm, Parent

Students Speak Out on San Miguel

It doesn't take long to get a response when you ask a group of San Miguel students what's different about their school. "It's smaller." "You get more attention."

"Everyone's nicer" "You get rewarded for doing well." "You get to be the Miguel Man of the Week!"

When pressed to be more specific each boy has his own story. "We do community service here. I wouldn't have known about old people, you know. I just wouldn't have paid attention. But now I do." "We've learned to pick up the trash around the neighborhood. Before I wouldn't have noticed, but now I hate trash."

A different attitude is evident here.

"Man, there used to be lots of fights at my old school. We don't do that here. Here there's someone to help when you get angry and so we talk it out." Asked what they felt when they came from public school, there is consensus. "It was weird, man, there was just this little circle of kids. We weren't used to that. We had to get to know each other and learn to get along. But once you got used to it, it was much better."

One flour-bedecked boy

had been making cakes with other community service participants for McAuley House, a local house of hospitality and soup kitchen. Asked if they were frosted, he replied, "We got silver balls, frosting, jimmies, everything!"

It's evident the boys love their school and respond to their environment. They proudly displayed pictures of the new courtyard and back entrance and spoke enthusiastically about the football field they had drawn. Everyone's love and passion for the school was evident. They are fully appreciating their time here.

As one parent has said, "The *praise* the children receive here for the small things is wonderful."

by Jean Cavanaugh

- **Brochure**

Companies and organizations use brochures for promotional and informational purposes. Brochures usually include three or four panels. The brochure The National Language Policy is a good example of a four panel informational brochure that explains the Conference on College Composition and Communication's official position on English Only legislation (see Chapter 8, pp.).

Here are some considerations to take into account when you're designing a brochure:

- Make the purpose of the brochure easy to identify. The front cover headline should cue readers to the subject and purpose.

- The brochure should be easy to use. The outside panels—front, back, and middle—are often designed to be read separately. The inside panels should be designed as a continuous space.

- Make sure the brochure has all the information readers need—name, address, and phone of organizations; maps to get to a store, museum, or historic district; bibliography; steps readers can take; answers to frequently asked questions; basic facts.

Can you make a difference in the life of a child?

Consider Foster Care

Rhode Island's Children are Everyone's Responsibility

Rhode Island Department of Children, Youth & Families
610 Mt. Pleasant Avenue
Providence, RI 02908
1-800-922-3737

DCYF Foster Care Program

Rhode Island Foster Care Facts

Of the 3000 children in DCYF care who can not live with their families, approximately 1000 live with non-relative foster families.

Of these 1000 children:

50% are five years of age or under
30% are 6 to 12 years of age
11% are 13 to 16 years old
9% are 17 & older

52% are Caucasian
26% are African American
14% are Hispanic
1% are Asian

50% are girls
50% are boys

Approximately 140 children are placed in foster care for the first time each month.

Foster families are needed to care for children on a short term, long term, respite and emergency care basis. Foster families from minority ethnic backgrounds are especially needed.

Why are foster parents needed?

Foster parents are needed to provide temporary care for children when they are unable to remain in their own homes.

How long does a child stay with a foster family?

A child's stay with a foster family may be temporary and last for only 1 or 2 days, or it may be long term and last for 1 or 2 years.

Who are the children who need foster families?

The children who need foster homes are of all ages and ethnic backgrounds. These children have been separated from their parents and many of them have been abused and neglected. They range from drug exposed infants to teen moms; all of them are in crisis and need to be placed in safe, nurturing, and culturally sensitive foster homes.

What about their parents?

Foster children maintain relationships with their parents through planned visitation. All visits between foster children and their parents are arranged and coordinated by the child's social worker.

"Fostering has been a wonderful experience. If I were to list the things I have done with my life that I am most proud of, it would be being a foster parent..." "P.L., former DCYF foster parent

Does the family need a certain income to be considered as a foster parent?

No minimum income is required but a family must have sufficient income to support its own members before it can be licensed as a foster home.

What are some of the other requirements?

You must be at least 21 years old, physically able to care for a child, and have a home that can pass a fire inspection. You may own or rent your home. You may be married or single. Your history must be free of child abuse and neglect charges and serious police charges. If any of your children have been involved with DCYF, you may not be considered for foster care.

How do you become a foster parent?

To become a foster parent, you need to be licensed by DCYF. Before you can be licensed you need to complete an application, have a home study and fire inspection done, and attend a six week pre-service training course.

Are foster parents reimbursed for the care they provide?

DCYF reimburses its foster parents $63 and $77 dollars a week depending upon the age of the child. For children with special needs, the reimbursement rate may be higher.

What kind of help or support can you expect after you become a foster parent?

Services include support groups for foster parents, a mentor program for newly licensed foster parents, a help line for questions and support, and membership in the Rhode Island Foster Parents Association. Ongoing training is offered by DCYF, as well as the services of the foster child's social worker.

Who do I call for more information?

DCYF Foster Care Program   277-4742
                            1-800-922-3737
            TDD   457-5336

Urban League of Rhode Island
Minority Recruitment Program   351-5000

R.I. Foster Parents Association   738-9915

- **Web pages**

Web sites expand dramatically the design options available to you, enabling the use of multimedia features such as graphics, video, and sound. Web sites also present a different way of thinking about and using documents. Instead of organizing information in a linear way, from start to finish, web sites provide links within the document and to external web sites so that readers can decide on their own path.

Depending on your interest and technical skill, you can draw on the multimedia capabilities of the Web or you can keep it simple. Here are some of the basic considerations web site designers take into account when constructing home pages:

- A home page should give an overview of the web site—identifying the purpose of the site, summarizing the information it contains, and providing directions to navigate the site.

- Even though web sites offer multimedia design features, written text is still their key element. Use clearly identified concise units of text. Remember it's harder to read text on the screen than on the page. Provide links for readers to get more details.

- Graphics, video, and sound are exciting features of web site design—but they also take more time to download than text does. For this reason, use these features carefully. If it takes too long to download, readers may get impatient and leave your site. And remember that some people browse the Web with their graphics capacity turned off. Make sure your message will come across in text.

- Use headings, frames, and rules to break up the page.

- Make links easy to find and easy to use. Links can send readers to other nodes (or pages) in your web site. Or they can be external, sending them to other sites. Links can be words or icons. You'll need to decide if there is an order you want readers to follow or if they can browse as they wish. External links are valuable because they connect your readers to other sources, but remember you can also lose them that way. Make sure the purpose of any external links is clear.

- Web sites are interactive. Provide feedback forms so readers can respond to your site.

NATIONAL BREAST CANCER COALITION

« a grassroots advocacy effort »

Welcome to the National Breast Cancer Coalition Web Site!

What's New:

- The National Breast Cancer Coalition Fund will host its first <u>Workshop For The Media, Understanding Breast Cancer Research And Policy</u>, on Tuesday, September 30, 1997 in New York City.

- NBCC culminates <u>Campaign 2.6</u> by delivering nearly 2.7 million signatures for $2.6 billion for breast cancer research to the U.S. Capitol during our 1997 <u>Advocacy Training Conference</u>.

About NBCC:
The National Breast Cancer Coalition is a grassroots advocacy effort in the fight against breast cancer. In 1991, the Coalition was formed with one mission, to eradicate breast cancer through *action* and *advocacy*.

Our Web site will help you join the fight against breast cancer. Here you'll find information about our <u>goals and accomplishments</u>, <u>how to become a member</u>, our <u>legislative agenda and political campaign</u>, and our current programs, including <u>Project LEAD</u> and our <u>Clinical Trials Project</u>.

How can this Web site further our cause and improve action and advocacy on-line? Use our <u>feedback form</u> to send us your comments.

The National Breast Cancer Coalition
1707 L Street, NW, Suite 1060
Washington, D.C. 20036
(202) 296-7477 *voice*
(202) 265-6854 *fax*

© 1996 The National Breast Cancer Coalition.
Last Modified: May, 1997 by the webmaster at CALIBRE Systems, Inc.

Visitors since
Friday, August 15, 1997
05972

CHAPTER
NINETEEN

ESSAY EXAMS

Essay examinations are certainly among the most challenging writing situations you face in college. The reason is pretty straightforward. Whether the exam consists of identification items, short answer questions, full length essays, or a combination, you have to write under pressure. First, there is the pressure to finish all the parts of an exam within the alloted time. Then, there is the pressure of writing on demand, when someone else—namely, your instructor—chooses the topics and asks the questions. There is also the pressure of writing for evaluation, to demonstrate to your instructor that you understand the course material and can work with it in meaningful ways. And finally, there is the pressure of writing without having available the usual resources, such as notes, textbooks, articles, a dictionary, and so on—a pressure that calls on you to write from recall.

As many students can attest (and many teachers remember from their days as students), these pressures can be anxiety provoking. Small wonder. After all, something real is on the line, you can't know in advance exactly what will appear on the exam, and you have to produce on the spot, often by juggling multiple parts of a test. At the same time, writing under pressure can push you to new insights and unforeseen connections—when the course material seems to jell in ways you had not quite imagined. Exams indeed call on you to perform for a grade, but successful students realize that exams can also be important learning experiences, in which you clarify for yourself the main themes and key concepts in a course. In fact, grades often depend on this kind of clarification, as it takes place in response to the questions on an exam.

The writing task you face on essay exams can be stated quite simply: you need to produce a good first draft in the time you're given. To do this, you'll need to develop an overall approach to writing essay exams. Developing a systematic strategy is your best bet to deal with the pressures of an essay exam and to maximize your performance. In the following sections, we'll look at the four basic steps of successful exam writing:

- Preparing for essay exams

- Analyzing the format and questions of an exam

- Planning an answer

- Writing the essay exam.

PREPARING FOR ESSAY EXAMS

Your preparation for an essay exam should begin at the very start of the course. Going to class, taking good notes, keeping up with the readings, doing the assignments, and participating in discussion sections are all ways to prepare for exams—and generally more successful than cramming at the last minute. But this is no doubt advice you've heard before. Assuming that you're keeping up, the real question is how you can get the most out of studying the material in the course.

Students sometimes equate studying with simply memorizing bodies of information. Now certainly, in some courses, where the exams consist of multiple choice, true/false, matching, and fill-in-the-blank items, test taking may rely heavily on the recall of memorized information. Make sure you understand how you will be tested. It's perfectly reasonable to ask your instructor, a teaching assistant, or a student who has already taken the course about the types of exams you can expect so that you can plan your study accordingly.

In courses with essay exams, you'll need to recall information but largely to show what you can do with it: how you can relate facts, details, examples, terms, and so on to the main themes and key concepts of the course. In such courses, instructors are not likely to hold you responsible for every item of information covered in the class. Instead, they want to see whether you can identify the central issues of the course and explain how information fits together in meaningful patterns. The danger of relying exclusively on memorization in these courses is that it can cause you to stuff your head full of separate items of information and fail to see the big picture.

In this sense, preparing for essay exams amounts to finding the big picture—the main ideas, terminology, controversies, explanations, and conceptual frameworks in a course. You can do this in part by paying attention to chapter headings, summaries, and highlighted terms in your textbook and in part by noticing what your instructor emphasizes in lectures, writes on the board, or includes in review sheets distributed before exams. Teachers and textbooks alike will often mark key points: "The two most important criticisms of sociobiology are . . . " or "the three main factors that led to the construction of the Ringstrasse in 19th century Vienna are . . . ."

Pay attention to how the material in the course is divided. If it is organized chronologically, look for distinct periods (such as Reconstruction or the Great Depression) and the emergence of artistic, intellectual, and political trends (such as the Harlem Renaissance, Freudian psychoanalysis, or McCarthyism). If the course is organized thematically, look for connections between readings and the central themes. If the course presents an introduction to a broad field of study, keep track of the topics that form the separate sections. You may want to meet regularly with a small study group of classmates to review course material and discuss the most important themes and concepts.

As exams approach, you (and your study group) can prepare by trying to anticipate questions your instructor might ask and what an effective answer might be. Remember that an essay exam is likely to call on you to work with the course material—not just to recall information but to analyze key themes, explain their signficance, make an interpretation, defend a position, criticize a theory, or recommend a path of action.

WORKING TOGETHER: Preparing for Exams

Work together with two or three other students. Read a chapter from a textbook in a course one or more of you are taking. As a group, identify key ideas, terms, concepts, theories, controversies, and so on in the chapter. Write two essay questions based on the chapter. Present the questions to your class, explaining why you think they capture central issues in the chapter.

ANALYZING EXAMS

You can save yourself a lot of problems by paying close attention to the overall format of the exam and by reading each question carefully.

SURVEYING THE FORMAT

Before you start writing answers to exam questions, take time to survey the format of the exam. Notice how many questions there are, how many points each one carries, and any directions about how long an answer should be (or how much space the exam allots to it).

Use this information to divide your time, so that you'll be able to answer each question. Careful time management can keep you from running out of time.

As you survey the exam, make some tentative decisions about which questions to answer when choices are offered and the order you will follow. You don't have to take the exam from start to finish. Students often find they do their best when they begin with the questions that seem the easiest to them. That way you can build some confidence before tackling questions you find more difficult. But if you do decide to answer questions out of their order, make sure you don't inadvertently skip a question altogether.

ANALYZING EXAM QUESTIONS

Analyzing exam questions is really a matter of recognizing the type of question and then clarifying what the question is calling on you to do.

The three most common types of questions that call for written answers are identification items (often called ID's), short answer questions, and essays. They differ in the length of writing called for and in the points they carry. Usually you can tell the type of question at a glance, according to its format, the directions it gives, and the amount of space provided for an answer.

GUIDELINES FOR ANALYZING EXAM QUESTIONS

The following guidelines can help you analyze any exam question that calls for a written answer.

- Look for key terms in the exam questions. Some key terms—such as "describe," "summarize," "explain," "analyze," and "evaluate"—provide directions. Other key terms are topics from course material. Take, for example, the exam question, "Describe the Monroe Doctrine and give two examples when it was used." The key term "Monroe Doctrine" refers to a topic from lectures and reading, while "describe" and "give two examples" provide directions. Putting directions and topics together will help you understand the purpose of the question and clarify how you should treat course material in your answer.

- Notice whether the question has more than one part. If so, make sure you understand what each part calls on you to do. The question on the Monroe Doctrine, for example, contains two parts—first to describe it and then to give two examples.

- Consider what information you need to answer the question. Draw on course material from lectures, readings, and discussions.

- How many points does the question carry? How much time do you have to answer it? How much space is provided on the exam? Use these questions to determine the amount of time you can spend on your answer and how long it should be.

- **Identification items (ID's)**

    Identification items normally call for short statements that identify or define material from the course. You'll frequently get a series of items, and usually each item will carry only a few points.
    Sample ID items (from Media and Mass Communication):
    Define each term in a sentence or two. (2 points each)
    A. cognitive dissonance
    B. agenda-setting
    C. technological determinism
    D. hot and cool media
    E. gate-keepers
ID items such as these call on you to define course topics clearly and concisely. Most often, you'll have only a few minutes to spend on each item. For example,
    A. cognitive dissonance
Cognitive dissonance is a state of psychological discomfort that occurs when information a person receives is inconsistent with the person's already-held attitudes.

- **Short answer questions**

    Short answer questions call for answers that can range from a sentence or two to a mini-essay. Typically short answers are a paragraph or two in length. Depending on the question, you'll have anywhere from a few minutes to ten minutes or so to write your answer.
    Sample short answer questions (from General Chemistry):

    Answer each question in a sentence or two. (5 points each)
    1. Contrast mass and weight.
    2. Define the word molecule.
    3. Explain the relationships among the number of protons, neutrons, and electrons in an atom.
    4. Compare physical processes with chemical processes.
    5. Describe how a percent yield is calculated for a chemical reaction.

Note that a key term in each question—"contrast," "define," "explain," "compare," and "describe"—gives directions about what to do with course topics such as "mass," "weight," "molecule," and so on.

Sample short answer questions (from Early American History):

Write a paragraph or two on each of the following items. Define the term and explain why it is significant. (10 points each)
1. The Glorious Revolution
2. The Middle Passage
3. Virgin Soil Epidemics

Note that the key terms in this question call first for the recall of information ("define") about a particular course topic and second for an elaboration of its significance ("explain"). For example,

1. The Glorious Revolution

In 1688, James II baptized his first son a Catholic, thereby perpetuating a Catholic monarchy in England. Fed up with James' arbitrary rule, parliamentary leaders responded by inviting James' Protestant daughter Mary and her husband William of Orange to take over as king and queen. James fled to France, and this bloodless change in the monarchy became known as the Glorious Revolution.

The Glorious Revolution had significant effects on the colonies. Colonists in Boston arrested the royal governor Sir Edward Andros and restored the colonial assembly he had tried to abolish. The Bill of Rights and Toleration Act passed by parliament in 1689 limited the power of rulers and guaranteed a degree of religious freedom. More important, the Glorious Revolution set a precedent for revolution against the king. John Locke's defense of the Glorious Revolution, Two Treatises on Government (1690), profoundly influenced political thinking in the colonies by arguing that when rulers violated the people's natural rights, they had the right to overthrow their government.

- **Essay questions**

Essay questions are usually alloted more time and more points on an exam than ID items and short answer questions. You'll have more time to plan and write your response. Typically essay questions will give you anywhere from 20 minutes to an hour.

As is true of ID items and short answer questions, the secret to writing effective essay exams is recognizing what the question calls on you to do. The following box presents some of the most common writing tasks you'll encounter on essay exams.

WORKING TOGETHER: Analyzing Essay Questions

Working with two or three classmates, analyze the essay questions listed above. What are the key terms given—directions and topics? What information would you need to answer the question successfully? What does each question call on students to do in their answers?

PLANNING YOUR ANSWER

How you plan your answer depends largely on the type of question and the time and points alloted to it. Answering ID items, for example, should take you just a few seconds to recall the key information you need. For short answer questions that call for a paragraph or two, you may want to underline key terms or write down a few quick notes to help you organize your answer. (Note in the sample short answer above on the Glorious Revolution how the writer uses a key term in the directions to focus each of the two paragraphs: first she "defines" the event and then "explains" why it was significant to the American colonies.)

SOME COMMON ESSAY EXAM QUESTIONS

- **Summarize main ideas.** Asks you to recall main ideas and present them clearly and accurately. Example from an anthropology course:

  In their article "The Consequences of Literacy," Ian Watt and Jack Goody trace changes that occur with the rise of literacy. What do they see as the main differences between oral and literate cultures. In their view, what are the main consequences of literacy?

- **Explain significance.** Asks you to explain the importance of course material by giving reasons and examples. Example from a history of science course:

  Watson and Crick's discovery in 1953 of the double helical structure of DNA ushered in the "molecular revolution." What exactly did they discover? Explain the significance of their discovery to the field of biology. Give examples to illustrate the "molecular revolution" they initiated.

- **Apply concepts.** Ask you to apply concepts to works studied in the course or to your own experience. Example from an African American literature course:

  The theme of "passing" as white appears in a number of important African American novels. Analyze the theme of "passing" in at least three of the following novels we've read: Frances E.W. Harper's Iola Leroy, James P. Johnson's Autobiography of an Ex-Coloured Man, Jessie Faucett's Plum Bun, Nella Larsen's Passing. What do you see as the main differences and similarities in the treatment of this theme?

  Example from a sociology course:

  Define Erving Goffman's notion of "underlife" behavior. Explain how and why it takes place and in what contexts. Use the notion of "underlife" to explain behavior you have observed or read about.

- **Discuss a quotation.** Asks you to comment on a quotation you are seeing for the first time. Often written by your instructor, these quotations will typically raise a controversial point to discuss. Example from an American history course:

  "The coming of the Civil War and the failures of Reconstruction have been seen by historians and others as failures of morality. This is wrong. The problems were actually political. Smarter politicians could have resolved these problems easily." How would you respond to this argument?

- **Compare and contrast.** Asks you to analyze differences and similarities between two works or ideas. Example from a Latin American literature course:

  Julia Alvarez's How the Garcia Girls Lost Their Accents and Cristina Garcia's Dreaming in Cuban both treat issues of immigration and acculturation. Compare and contrast the two novels' exploration of cultural identity and change.

- **Analyze causes.** Asks you to explain why and how something happened. Example from a film course:

  Explain the emergence of film noir in Hollywood films of the 1940s and 1950s. What values, beliefs, and ideologies of the time do these films embody?

  Example from a Russian history course:

  What factors led to Stalin's consolidation of control in the Soviet Union?

- **Evaluate.** Asks you to make a judgment about the strengths and weaknesses of one or more works or concepts. Example from a mass communication course:

  Evaluate the debate between Walter Lippmann in The Phantom Public and John Dewey in The Public and Its Problems. Explain the respective positions each thinker takes on the role of the public in political life. What do you see as the strengths and weaknesses of their arguments? Where do you stand in the debate?

- **Propose a course of action.** Asks you to analyze a problem and propose your own solution. Example from an education course:

Briefly summarize the arguments for and against bilingual education. Then explain what you think should be done. Be specific in describing the kinds of programs you think can be successful.

- Synthesize a number of sources. Asks you to develop a coherent framework to pull together ideas and information from a number of sources. Example from a management course:

You have read case studies of managerial strategies in a number of major coompanies—IBM, Nike, Harley Davidson, Apple, and General Motors. Based on these readings, explain what you see as the major challenges currently facing management. Use information from the case studies to illustrate your points.

- Creative questions. Occasionally instructors will ask students to take on the identity of a historical or literary character, to write dialogue, or to do other types of creative responses. Example from a colonial Latin American history course:

The year is 1808, and Spanish Americans are reeling from the news that Napoleon has invaded Spain and deposed the king. Two creoles meet in a tavern, and their conversation soon turns to the political future of the colonies. Create a dialogue in which one argues for independence while the other urges continued loyalty to Spain.

Full-length essays, of course, will require more planning time. In fact, it's not unusual to spend a quarter of the time alloted planning an answer. Here are some guidelines for planning:

- Read the question carefully, noting key terms to clarify what your purpose should be. What kind of answer is the question calling for? What is the topic of the question? Are you being asked simply to define, describe, or summarize? To what extent are you asked to analyze, interpret, evaluate, or argue according to your own understanding of the material?

- See if the question offers any organizational cues. If the question has multiple parts, consider whether these parts offer a possible scheme to arrange your answer. Often the parts consist of questions that lead logically from one to another.

- Write a brief outline of key points. Begin with the main point—the response that answers the main question being asked. Then decide how to arrange supporting reasons, details, and examples.

- Before you start writing, double check your outline to make sure it answers what the question asks—not what you want it to say.

Notice how the brief outline below uses the essay question to organize an answer.

Essay Question

You have read arguments for and against legislation to make English the official language in the United States. Write an essay that explains why this has become such a controversial issue. What is at stake for each side in the debate? Explain your own position, citing evidence to support it.

Brief Outline

Main point: Demographic changes in the U.S. and the "new immigration" from Latin America and Asis have called national identity into question.

Pro: Desire for national unity Anxiety about immigration Belief that "old immigrants" (1890-1920) assimiliated and learned English quickly

Con: U.S. as nation of immigrants Value of many languages in global economy Belief in multiculturalism

My position: Against English Only legislation For increased language classes for recent immigrants

WRITING A GOOD ANSWER

Writing a good answer on an essay exam amounts to producing a good first draft. You can make additions and corrections, but you won't have the time to do throrough revisions. Here are some suggestions to help you write an effective answer:

- Essay exams don't need introductions to set up the main point. State the main answer to the question in the opening paragraph. One good strategy is to use the question (or main question when there is a series) as the basis of your opening sentence. Answer the question as clearly as you can. First impressions on essay exams count. Your opening paragraph should encapsulate the main line of your thinking and forecast what's to come.

- Provide supporting evidence, reasons, details, and examples in the paragraphs that follow. Draw on material from lectures and readings, but don't pad with extraneous material. You don't need to show off how much you can recall. Instead, you need to show how you can relate supporting evidence to your main answer.

- Highlight your understanding of the course material. Demonstrate how you can work with the information, ideas, and themes in the course. Make sure, however, that you're not just presenting personal opinions for their own sake. Link your insights, evaluations, and proposals to the course material.

- Write an ending, even if you're running out of time. A sentence or two can tie together main points at the end.

- Make additions neatly. New ideas may occur to you as you're writing, and you should incorporate them if they fit into the main line of your thinking. You can add a sentence or two by writing neatly in the margins and using an arrow to show where they go in your answer.

- Write legibly and proofread when you've finished. You can make corrections by crossing and replacing words and phrases. Do so as neatly as you can. A messy exam is hard to read and creates a negative impression.

- Watch the clock. If you're running out of time or need to go on to another question, it's best to list points from outline. This way you can show where your essay is going, even if you can't finish it.

SAMPLE ESSAY ANSWERS

The following two essays were written in a colonial Latin American history course in response to this question:

"Latin America's ruling elites maintained their position largely through ideological domination. Witness their ability to make patriarchy an unchallenged social assumption. Aside from such exceptional figures as Sor Juana, women at every level of society readily accepted their inferior status, along with the rigid gender conventions that called for female passivity, obedience, and sexual modesty." Discuss.

As you can see, the essay question is a quotation that takes a position on issues in the course, along with the direction "discuss." The key term "discuss" doesn't seem to provide a lot of guidance, but experienced students know that "discuss" really calls on them to offer their own interpretation of the quotation, along with reasons and supporting evidence from readings and lecture.

The first essay is annotated. You can use the second one to sharpen your own sense of an effective essay answer.

Answer A:

Although Latin American elites frequently used a policy of coercion to govern indigenous and African populations, they also used consent to maintain their position in colonial society through ideological domination. Colonial society was based on a hierarchical system of authority and dependence, in which the ruling elite established strong ties with the ruled through a shared ideology. Patriarchy, the social assumption that men were responsible for controlling the lives of women, was central to this shared ideology.

The colonial elite based its political and moral authority on the patriarchal ideology of men's superiority, masculinity, and honor and women's inferiority, modesty, and submission. Dignified men acquired their authority by controlling and protecting their dependents—women, servants, workers, and slaves. Women, on the other hand, were socialized to be modest and obedient and were regarded as dangerous and likely to succumb to temptations, instincts, and desires unless controlled by fathers and husbands.

From father to husband, men had power over a women's sexuality. Marriage was used by fathers to improve their status and make alliances with other families. Little consideration was given to a woman's own preferences. Once married, a woman was subordinate to her husband. The crime of rape, for example, was seen not as a crime against the woman but rather an assault on the honor of her father or husband. In cases of rape, fathers or husbands would publicly profess their shame, humiliation, and lack of honor for failing to protect a daughter or wife.

There were certain groups that posed exceptions to this gender ideology of male control and female dependence. Heiresses, nuns, and widows negotiated a certain amount of autonomy in specific circumstances. For example, the Condessa de Santiago inherited a fortune and became a powerful economic and political force—until she married and her power ended. Nuns such as Sor Juana found a limited space for self-expression in the convent, as demonstrated by the numerous literary works produced by nuns. Widows were the largest group of autonomous women. By law, dowries reverted to widows when their husbands died. However, women without husbands, especially widows, were suspected of immoral acts. The legend of La Florona, the "weeping widow," illustrates how autonomous women were seen as uncontrolled and threatening.

In the lower classes, there was a significant gap between the theory and practice of patriarchal ideology. Plebeian women were in the public sphere much more than elite women not because of their greater autonomy but because of financial necessity. The labor these women did as vendors, seamstresses, and domestic servants was hardly empowering, and they were often subjected to verbal, physical, and sexual abuse. In this way, they still adhered to the system of patriarchy and remained the dependents of their male employers.

For men, masculinity, honor, and social superiority were achieved by controlling dependents. By accepting such a patriarchal ideology, male plebeians, servants, and slaves were constantly reminded of their own position as dependents, with little economic or political authority over their lives. Lower-class and slave men could not exercise the type of patriarchal control and protect their women as the upper classes did. But because the lower classes believed in patriarchal control, they in effect consented to the moral and political leadership of the upper classes.

Morality, dignity, and honor, thus, were identified with the ruling elite in colonial society. This gender ideology reinforced the power of the ruling elite as both women and plebeian men consented to its patriarchal assumptions.

Answer B:

Depending on the circumstances, the ruling elite in colonial Latin America used force or consent to govern. For example, they routinely used military power against the Indian population and to suppress slave revolts. In addition, the Inquisition in Latin America used physical force, including torture to eliminate dissent.

Ideological domination was an important tool of the ruling elite, and patriarchy became one of the unchallenged social assumptions that reinforced the authority of the upper classes. The view was widely held by members of colonial society that men were the natural rulers and that women should be controlled by men. Men were considered authoritative, while women were supposed to be obedient.

Thus women in colonial society were excluded from both economic and political power. Excluded from the priesthood, higher education, and the professions, women were forced to remain in the home. This dependence reinforced male authority and kept women powerless and unable to challenge dominant social assumptions. Because women were the socializers of the family, they transferred this gender ideology to their children and thereby further reproduced the system.

If a woman misbehaved, she would dishonor her father or husband and her household. A stain on a woman's reputation tainted the reputation of her entire family. It was therefore a man's responsibility to control a woman and protect her against herself and keep her in the domestic sphere. Fathers decided the person a woman would marry or if she should become a nun. An unmarried women in the presence of unmarried men was always accompanied by a chaperone to guard her virtue. Husbands controlled their wives and protected them. By engraining women with the dominant ideology of patriarchy, the elite were able to rule without opposition.

This gender ideology, however, did not transfer completely to the lower classes in colonial society because in order to be proper, women had to come from wealthy families. Single lower-class women often worked before they married, and this was considered threatening to their morals. Still, plebeian women did view males as authority figures. Once they married, they were subordinated to their husbands and restricted to the home. Women were considered devious and threatening and therefore needed to be protected and controlled by male authority.

Lower-class men, however, never achieved total patriarchal power and were in no position to challenge authority figures or social assumptions. While they accepted the rigid gender conventions of the dominant ideology, plebeian men remained dependents in relation to the upper classes. Due to their servile and economically insecure position in society, plebeian could not fully protect their women, which was one of the prerequisites of full manhood as colonial society understood it.

Nuns, heiresses, and widows were able in limited ways to evade patriarchal control. Except for priests, men were basically excluded from convents, and so to some extent the nuns could organize their own affairs. Heiresses might achieve a measure of autonomy by inheriting money, and widows received their dowries if their husbands died.

Overall, though, the gender ideology of patriarchy in colonial Latin America was very unfair to women in general and was used to keep lower-class men in their place.

WORKING TOGETHER: Analyzing an Essay Answer

In a group with two or three other students, follow these steps:

- Look again at the Essay Question that appears at the beginning of this section. What exactly does it call on students to do? Clarify for yourselves what seems to be the main writing task facing students who are taking this exam in colonial Latin American history?

- Read the first essay answer and annotations. How well do you think it handles the writing task?

- Read and analyze the second essay answer. Given your sense of what the writing task calls for and how well the first essay answer handles the task, what do you see as the strengths and weaknesses of the second answer? Be specific. What particular features of the essay work well or not so well?

Annotations to Answer A

¶ 1:Connects key terms in essay question—"consent," "ideological domination," and "patriarchy"—to establish main focus of the answer.

¶ 2: Explains key term—"patriarchal ideology."

¶ 3: Illustrates key term with details and an example.

¶ 4: Notes exception to the quotation. Gives examples of exceptions.

¶ 5: Analyzes role of patriarchal ideology among plebeian women.

¶ 6: Analyzes role of patriarchal ideology among plebeian men.

¶ 7: Ending ties key terms together.

CHAPTER
TWENTY

WRITING PORTFOLIOS

Portfolios are often used by painters, graphic designers, architects, photographers, and other visual artists to present their work to teachers, prospective clients, museum officials, gallery owners, fellowship selection committees, and so on. Portfolios enable artists to select a representative sample of their best work and to display it in an organized form. The same is true for writing portfolios. In a writing portfolio, students choose a sample of their work to present as the culminating project of a writing class.

Writing portfolios offer students a number of benefits. Portfolios allow students to decide on the writing they want to present to the teacher for evaluation. Students typically select from among their various writing assignments, to revise a limited number for their portfolios. In this way, students can show teachers how they have handled different kinds of writing tasks. Portfolios also provide students with the opportunity to reflect on how they have developed as writers and to explain what the writing they've done means to them as students, learners, and persons.

Writing portfolios have benefits for teachers too. A portfolio provides teachers with a range of writing to evaluate instead of single papers. One of the premises of writing portfolios is that teachers can make fairer and more accurate appraisals of student writing if they can read various types of writing, written for various purposes, in various forms, for various audiences.

How portfolios are graded varies. In some writing programs, portfolios are evaluated by one or more other teachers who do blind readings—that is, students' names are removed. In other cases, portfolios are submitted to and graded by the student's teacher. The weight assigned to the portfolio grade varies too. If your teacher asks you to prepare a portfolio, he or she will tell you how much it counts toward your final grade.

WHAT SHOULD YOU INCLUDE IN A PORTFOLIO?

To put together a final portfolio, you will need to include samples of various kinds of writing. Your teacher will give you further directions. Some teachers are quite specific about what to include, while others will offer students more room to plan the contents of their portfolios.

Amount of Writing to Include

Part of designing a portfolio is making decisions about what best represents you as a writer. If you include most of the writing you've done, you defeat the purpose. Many teachers ask for only four or five pieces of writing. Others ask for more or leave the number open to student choice.

Type of Writing to Include

Designing a portfolio asks you to select not only a limited number but also a range of writing that represents the different types you've done. If you include only personal narratives or informative writing or argumentative essays, you won't give readers enough sense of this range, and your portfolio will seem too one-dimensional. Your teacher may tell you exactly what types to include or you may have more room to decide.

SOME OPTIONS FOR A WRITING PORTFOLIO

Here are some types of writing often included in portfolios:

A REFLECTIVE LETTER

Almost all writing portfolios begin with a letter of reflection that introduces you and your portfolio. The purpose of such a letter is to persuade your instructor (or any other readers) that you have accomplished the goals of the course.

A reflective letter might discuss the choices you have made in designing your portfolio, explain your development as a writer and the role of writing in your life, evaluate strengths and weaknesses in your writing, and discuss your experience as a writer and a person in your writing class. The letter should provide readers with a sense of who you are. And it might also indicate where you see yourself going next to develop your writing.

The writing you have done in response to the "Literacy Narrative" assignment in Chapter 1 and the "Writing Inventories" throughout the book can provide you with material for your reflective letter.

SAMPLE REFLECTIVE LETTER

Jennifer Principe

Dear Professor Trimbur:

Writing has always been an important form of expression for me. I have always had a hard time expressing myself verbally, and I feel that writing gives me a control over my words that I can't find anywhere else. Writing has almost become a form of medication for me, an objective ear always willing to listen. For as long as I can remember, I have kept a journal that I write in whenever there is something I want to straighten out in my life. My journal is one of the best ways I know to explore my thoughts and decide on a course of action to take. Writing forces me to slow down and really consider how I feel about something. It also creates a permanent record that I can go back to at any time.

Although I enjoy and rely on this sort of informal writing, I have felt for a long time that the formal writing I do in my courses could use improvement, and English 101 has definitely helped me to grow as a formal writer. In high school, my English teachers told me I had good ideas but that my writing was wordy and unfocused. I understood what they were saying, but unfortunately they never explained what I should do about my problem. This made writing a very frustrating experience for me.

In English 101, I think the most important thing I learned is that when I start writing I usually don't have a definite idea of where I am going. What I have found through the writing assignments and the peer commentaries is that my main ideas are often unclear at first, but as I get to the end of a draft they become much clearer. As I write more, I begin to focus on an idea and my essay begins to make more sense. In many cases, I could take ideas from the end of a draft and bring them up to my introduction to give me focus.

The writing sample included in my portfolio were chosen with several criteria in mind. First, I chose writing that I had strong personal feelings about because when I believe in a topic my writing tends to be more passionate and heartfelt, and thus more effective. For this reason, the writing samples that are included in this portfolio are strongly rooted in my personal beliefs. Second, I chose different kinds of writing so readers could see how I approached various writing assignments.

I chose to include the peer commentary I wrote for Joe Scherpa. I don't think this was necessarily the best commentary I did, but I was particularly happy about Joe's reaction to it. A week or so after I completed the commentary, Joe told that my commentary helped him do a complete revision on that assignment. He seemed grateful for my suggestions and happy with the revised version of his work. Although I realize that my commentary was not the sole motivation for his revisions, I was happy to see that he felt it had made a difference in his writing.

In conclusion, I feel this class has been quite beneficial in my growth as a writer. I got lots of practice in different kinds of writing. I'm planning to major in chemical engineering, and I know that writing will be an important part of my upcoming career, as well as in my personal life. For my career, writing will be a tool that I will often need to get my point across. I feel that I need to work on knowing when to put personal opinions into my writing and when I should be more objective. Sometimes I get carried away by my feelings about a topic. This class has helped me to understand different writing situations, and I think I am now better able to see when the personal side is appropriate and when it's not.

Revised Writing Assignments

Portfolios usually include revised writing assignments. This gives you the opportunity to review the work you have done over the course of a term and to decide which writings you want to bring to final form and which best represent your abilities. It's a good idea to select a range of purposes and a range of genres. Your teacher will tell you how many to include.

A CASE STUDY

Some teachers ask students to include a case study of one of the writing assignments—with working draft, peer commentary, and the final version, as well as your own explanation of how you worked on the piece of writing. Case studies look in detail at how you planned, drafted, and revised one particular piece of writing. Case studies offer you the opportunity to analyze the choices you made. Be specific by examining how you drafted and revised a key passage or two.

SAMPLE CASE STUDY

Matt Axt

Introduction

I decided to present my essay "Citizens X" as a case study because it is the paper I revised the most and the one I got the most helpful peer commentary on. I have included the working draft of the essay, the two peer commentaries I received, and the final draft.

The two peer commentaries made me realize a couple of things about my first draft. Both seemed to agree that my position wasn't as clear as it should be and that the ideas in paragraph three didn't connect to my main idea very well. I agreed with this right away. I thought the draft had a good opening and was going along fine until the end of paragraph two. At that point, I lost interest in what I was doing. Maybe I just lost track of what I wanted to do. Anyway, paragraph three is basically filled up with a bunch of ideas that I don't really think explain my generation but that other people often bring out. It started to dawn on me that if I wanted to use these ideas I'd need to make sure readers didn't see them as mine.

The other main consideration I had to deal with comes up in the second peer commentary. This was written by a kid I'm pretty good friends with, and at first I was a little irritated about him trying to tell me what I think. And I had no idea what he meant about not being so nice. I thought we were supposed to use a reasonable tone. I put this one away and tried to forget about the paper for a day or two.

When I re-read the draft and the feedback after two days, I started to agree with my friend that I needed to work on how I stated my position but that there was also a bigger problem concerning what the purpose of the essay was. When I wrote the working draft, I thought I was simply explaining why my generation is so apathetic—that it had to do with our childhood and current social problems. After thinking about it more, however, I realized I really wanted to defend my generation—not to claim a lot of us aren't apathetic, burned out, and cynical about politics but to say that the apathy isn't exclusively our fault and that the media shouldn't blame us. I particularly liked what my friend said about how the media is run by a bunch of baby boomers trying to blame us for their own failures. So my friend gave me a little more heart to get back to the draft and say what was really on my mind. This can be seen in the way I revised my main point at the end of paragraph one, changing the sentence "I believe the conditions and attitudes present during our childhood have caused this 'decline'" to the much more forceful "We're taking the blame for the failures of previous generations."

WORKING DRAFT

Citizens X

I'm a member of Generation X, and believe me, it's not that much fun. The generation I belong to has been under fire for the last few years. As the media and journalists portray us, we're disinterested in politics, obsessed by personal success, and stressed out by everyday life. In the United States, young people are supposed to be the hope of the future, but if you read the popular press, you might well conclude that there is no future. No generation in the recent past has been as vilified as my generation has. We're pictured as a generation in decline, an ominous sign of the bankruptcy of the American Dream. But what has caused the so-called decline of youth over the past twenty years or so? I believe the conditions and attitudes present during our childhood have caused this "decline."

The political atmosphere of the late sixties and early seventies has caused an apathetic attitude toward politics. The resignation of President Richard Nixon, following the Watergate scandal, seems to exemplify politics for people my age. The illegal activities committed by the head of state caused negative attitudes to develop toward politics and politicians. Growing up in the shadow of Watergate, people my age developed a distrust in politics. As a result, the youth of today have much less interest in government and politics than young people had in the past. My generation was preceded by the Movement and the furor of Vietnam War protests. The energy that the youth of the Vietnam War era invested in changing the political system was phenomenal. Following this period of political activism should come a lull, and I believe we are it.

Social problems such as the AIDS epidemic, drug abuse, homelessness and poverty, and the decline of America as an economic power are contributing factors to the decline of youth. Faced with a terrible disease like AIDS, young people have realized that we are not invincible. Drugs offer an escape from reality, but only intensify the condescending attitude of our elders. How can one have an optimistic attitude toward the future when our economy has slowed down, our national debt has skyrocketed, and the baby boomers already have all the good jobs? Growing up with these problems has caused pessimism and fear about the future.

PEER COMMENTARY #1

Matt,

I think you've got a great idea for an essay here. Your opening paragraph sets out the issues well, but I wasn't altogether sure what position you're taking. At first, I thought you were going to explain why and how "conditions and attitudes present during our childhood has caused this 'decline.'" But as I read on, I wasn't sure. I think my uncertainty has to do with how the reasons you give in paragraphs two and three are connected to the position you state in the last sentence of paragraph one.

The first reason—that political scandals such as Watergate has caused cynicism—is pretty clear, but toward the end of the paragraph, when you talk about the Movement of the sixties, you make it sound like it's a natural progression to go from an activist generation to a disinterested or passive one.

The third paragraph opens with a bunch of social problems. I agree they're all problems that affect us, but they're not from our childhood. They're all happening right now, so to raise them doesn't really seem to support the position you've stated in your opening.

Basically I agree with a lot of what you're saying. My problem with the essay so far has to do with how the third paragraph connects to your position. It seems you're just throwing in a lot of ideas and then the essay just seems to run out of steam and stop. I'm not sure what to suggest. Somehow you need to connect the two paragraphs to your position statement more clearly and then give a stronger ending.

I think this draft positions readers in a confusing way. At first it seems you're going to defend our generation against charges that we're apathetic, materialistic, and stressed out. But then it seems that you agree that there has been a decline. So I couldn't really figure out whether your position was one of defending us against the media or explaining why we're in "decline." Plus, I'm not sure what you mean by decline.

PEER COMMENTARY #2

Dear Matt,

Your essay starts out by saying that you "believe the conditions and attitudes present during our childhood have caused this 'decline.'" OK, paragraph two sort of explains how that has happened, but I don't exactly see how all the social problems in the third paragraph give reasons.

I'm going out on a limb here (we're pretty good friends) and read between the lines. If you want my opinion (here it comes), you're not really saying what I sense is your real position. I think you want to defend our generation to some extent by saying hey, it may be true that we appear to be apathetic in comparison to other generations, like anti-war activists during the Vietnam War, but that it's not our fault. We didn't make this mess. We inherited it, and the media (mostly burned out baby-boomers, by the way) are trying to blame us. They're the ones who can't face reality. We're the nightmare they created—apathetic voidoids with pierced body parts and tattoos.

So my advice is don't be so nice. You seem to want to finesse it, and maybe your real feelings aren't coming out as strongly as they could.

FINAL DRAFT

Citizens X

I'm a member of Generation X, perhaps the most vilified generation in recent American history. My generation has been under fire for the last five years or so. As the media and journalists portray us, we're apathetic about politics, obsessed by personal success, and stressed out by everyday life. In the United States, young people are supposed to be the hope of the future, but if you read the popular press, you might well think the future is a nightmare of body-pierced, tattooed young people hooked on drugs, MTV, and Beverly Hills 90210. We're pictured as a generation in decline, an ominous sign of the bankruptcy of the American Dream. And in many ways, we like to act the part. We're the busters, the slackers, the affectless voidoid generation. But beneath this pose is a real problem that has not been fully addressed by either the media images or youth culture styles. Why has this generation been so vilified? We're taking the blame for the failures of previous generations.

The media would like to represent my generation as a symbol of everything that has gone wrong in America over the past twenty years. We're presented as the product of divorce, broken homes, and single parents. Even if our parents stayed married—and statistically speaking, about half of them did—they both went to work, leaving us alone at home, latch-key kids raised by afternoon television. In the face of a declining economy, a skyrocketing national debt, downsizing, and layoffs, the media has labeled us materialistic and careerist, when in fact the baby-boomers have already bagged all the good jobs. Compared to the political activists in the civil rights, anti-war, and feminist movements of the sixties and early seventies, our generation is portrayed as passive, apathetic, cynical—without a galvanizing issue to give it a cause and a sense of mission.

These portrayals of my generation are not altogether wrong. They each help describe what the older generation seems to see as the particularly disturbing mood of young people today. But they don't go very toward explaining this mood. People forget that the shaping political experiences of my generation begin with Watergate and the resignation of President Richard Nixon, with scandal and illegal activities in high places. Growing up in the shadow of Watergate, people my age developed a distrust in politics and politicians, and nothing has come along on the political scene to give us much hope for an attitude adjustment. Despite our support for Bill Clinton, the country's first MTV presidential candidate, his presidency seems bogged down, ineffective, and wavering on issues like gays in the military and universal health care.

Apathy does indeed run deep through my generation. If anything, it's become a dominant style. Acting cool, distanced, and nonchalant is all part of the image. But to blame us for this apathy is another matter. While we may fail the political activism test when we're compared to the protesters and organizers of the sixties and early seventies, the comparison itself is self-serving because it fails to ask what the activists accomplished. It's precisely this generation of baby boomers who are now running the country and shaping public opinion. Blaming young people my age for the country's current social problems is a convenient way to evade responsibility for the world they have built but don't like the looks of.

PEER COMMENTARY

If you have written peer commentaries, you may want to include a representative one, prefaced with an explanation of what you learned through the peer commentaries and what it was like for you to do them.

SAMPLE INTRODUCTION TO PEER COMMENTARY

Margaret King

At first, it was difficult to criticize a classmate's work for fear of being too harsh and possibly offending them. But as the term progressed, it became easier because I learned what to look for and how to make helpful suggestions. I realized that as a writer I wanted my classmates to give me honest feedback and that the best peer commentaries I got didn't try to judge my working draft but to give me suggestions about what to do with it. I tried to apply these ideas to the peer commentaries I wrote. I think the peer commentaries gave me insight as a writer and helped me to learn to read more critically and make choices in the revision process.

SAMPLES OF EXPLORATORY WRITING

If you have done exploratory writing, you could include a few samples that, for whatever reason, you like the most. Write an introduction that explains what it was like for you to do exploratory , what you learned, how this kind of writing differs other writing assignments, the benefits you see, and so on.

SAMPLE INTRODUCTION TO EXPLORATORY WRITING

John Hogan

Exploratory writing was one of my favorite things in this course. When doing this type of writing, I felt free to say what I wanted, any way I wanted. All of this freedom allowed me to put down on paper exactly what I was thinking. Usually when writing a more formal paper, I find that as I am writing I spend too much time making sure everything is structurally and grammatically correct. Many times I lose sight of some of my new ideas, as I try to perfect the previous ones. Here, there was no pattern or structure that had to be followed. When doing exploratory writing I simply wrote and did not worry about grammar, spelling, unity, or coherence.

COMMENTARY ON COLLABORATIVE WRITING

If you were involved in a collaborative writing project, you might write a short commentary about your experience. What role did you play in the group's work? How does collaborative writing differ from individual writing? What is gained? What, if anything, is lost? Explain your thoughts and feelings about your involvement in producing a group-written project.

SAMPLE COMMENTARY ON COLLABORATIVE WRITING

David Sanchez

To me, group projects have both good and bad points. Luckily, however, I believe the good points outweigh the bad points. In my opinion, the worst part about doing a group project is setting up meetings. With an abundant amount of other work, finding a time that everyone can meet sometimes becomes difficult. In addition, when the group finally meets, you usually end up talking about other things and basically just hanging out. It seems that for every hour or so of a meeting, only about thirty minutes of work is done.

On a good note, however, the actual project usually produces an interesting result. By having more than one person work on a project, especially a written one, a better result will usually come out. Each person adds a different view and also finds mistakes others have missed. As we have seen through our writing assignments, no one can write a perfect paper the first time. Through each peer commentary, many possible areas of improvement come to light and therefore a better final paper. The same is true of writing a paper with other people.

An additional drawback to writing a group paper, however, is that since it is written by more than one person, more than one idea is conveyed. Yes, as I said before, this is good in a way, but it also makes it harder to write a creative paper. Each person ends up having to modify their view in order to go along with everyone else.

Another bad thing, which can arise from some group projects, occurs when one or more people in the group do not do their parts. When this happens, the other people in the group end up doing too much work and get frustrated. I was happy to find that both John and Joe were willing to do the work. We first met a couple of times to decide on a topic for the project and to begin work. Next we all contributed to the collection of data for the survey. We then divided the paper into three sections, and each wrote one. Finally we had a meeting in order to bring the three parts together and to write an introduction and a conclusion.

Overall, I enjoyed doing the group project with John and Joe. Prior to doing it, I had not known either of them very well. Through this project, I can say that I have become friends with both of them. We all worked together quite well and produced a project I was happy with.

MISCELLANEOUS

Depending on your teacher's directions, you may include a miscellany of writing done in or out of class—letters, notes, e-mail, newsgroup dialogue, poetry, fiction, posters, leaflets, flyers, and so on. Introduce these writings and explain what called on you to write them and how they differ from the other writing in your portfolio.

ON-LINE PORTFOLIOS

People usually think of portfolios as a sequence of printed documents that readers go through from start to finish. If your teacher agrees, you could design an on-line portfolio on the web. You would need, of course, to include all the required components of a print portfolio. A challenging part of designing such an on-line portfolio is making it easy for readers to understand how the parts are linked together.

PART
SIX

GUIDE TO EDITING

INTRODUCTION:
WHY WRITERS EDIT

When the mention of editing comes up in a writing course, the first thing students often think of is grammar and English teachers marking sentence errors in red ink. The very notion of editing seems to shift attention from how writers compose persuasive pieces of writing to the system of rules and regulations called grammar and usage.

Now there can be no doubt that writers must learn to edit their work according to the prevailing standards of grammar and usage. But the reason is not simply to avoid grammatical errors, misspellings, and poor style—as if writing were a matter of abiding by the law. There are two further reasons for editing that are important to understand.

One is that the correctness of writing influences readers. Readers invariably form judgments about writing depending on how well writers handle the conventions of standard English usage. For better or worse, sentence errors, punctuation mistakes, misspelled words, and stylistic lapses can distract readers and undermine a writer's credibility.

A second reason is that sentences are basic units of meaning that express relationships among ideas. Writers edit not just to make sure their sentences are grammatically correct but also to clarify what they are trying to say.

For these reasons, experienced writers think of editing as more than just avoiding errors. Editing involves working with sentences to make a piece of writing persuasive to readers. In this regard, to think of sentences simply as grammatical problems—to be identified, marked, and corrected—can get in the way of seeing how important sentences are to the effects a piece of writing will have on readers.

In the following chapter, we will be looking at how writers work with sentences. The chapter is divided into four parts:

- First, we consider some of the basic strategies writers use in composing sentences.

- Second, we present editing techniques to enhance the clarity, emphasis, and variety in sentences.

- Third, we review ten common sentence problems, along with editing strategies to correct them.

- Fourth, we look at some typical editing issues that arise for second language writers.

CHAPTER
TWENTY ONE

WORKING WITH SENTENCES

Asentence, as everybody knows, is supposed to express a complete thought. To do this, a sentence needs to have a subject and a predicate. Otherwise, the sentence is incomplete. Fair enough. Readers are likely to be puzzled by the following writing:

> Left England and came to North America in hope of reforming the Church of England.

> Unlike the settlers at Plymouth, the Puritans of the Massachusetts Bay Colony.

The first sentence lacks a subject (who left England and came to North America?), while the second lacks a predicate (what did the Puritans do?). When you put them together, however, the combination makes good sense:

> Unlike the settlers at Plymouth, the Puritans of the Massachusetts Bay Colony left England and came to North America in hope of reforming the Church of England.

The point here is that the sentence now expresses a complete thought because it expresses a relationship among the elements in the sentence by linking the subject ("the Puritans") to the predicate ("left England and came to the North America"). The sentence now says who did what, and it also explains unlike what other group and for what purpose. When writers compose sentences, they are looking to express such relationships in order to establish patterns of meaning.

The following section looks at some of the options writers have to weave sentences into these patterns. Next we present strategies writers use to edit for clarity, emphasis, and variety. Then we review ten common editing problems. Finally, we consider some of the editing issues of special concern to second language writers of English.

COMPOSING SENTENCES

Here are a series of statements that appear in a passage taken from Alan M. Kraut's "Plagues and Prejudice," a chapter on American attitudes toward immigrants and disease that appears in the book Hives of Sickness: Public Health and Epidemics in New York City.

> Shipmasters sought to maximize profits. They crammed into their holds as many immigrants as possible. Shipboard illness was quite common. Mortality was common too. Typhus ravaged tightly packed passengers to the New World. So did diarrhea.

Now obviously there is something wrong with the way this passage reads. Not only is it choppy, it also fails to link the key elements to each other so readers can see what their relationship is. Here's how Kraut wrote the passage. Notice how he combines elements together to form a pattern of meaning:

> Because shipmasters sought to maximize profits by cramming their holds as many immigrant as possible, shipboard illness and mortality was quite common. Typhus and diarrhea ravaged tightly packed passengers to the New World.

COORDINATION AND SUBORDINATION

The techniques Kraut uses to form a pattern of meaning are coordination and subordination.

- Coordination links two or more similar elements in a way that emphasizes their relatively equal weight in a sentence. Notice how the following sentences can be combined by coordination:

No one showed up for the concert.

The band put on their uniforms.

They picked up their instruments.

The band played the opening tune right on time.

No one showed up for the concert, but the band put on their uniforms, picked up their instruments, and played the opening tune right on time.

or

No one showed up for the concert; nonetheless, the band put on their uniforms, picked up their instruments, and played the opening tune right on time.

Notice how much easier it is now for readers to grasp the relationships among the actions described in the original sentences. The first clause ("no one showed up") is balanced in relationship to the second clause about the band, with each receiving relatively equal weight and thereby relatively equal attention on the reader's part. Further, by combining the predicates "put on," "picked up," and "played," the sentence now makes it easier for readers to see how they form a series of continuous actions.

• Subordination links elements in ways that emphasize how some elements in a sentence modify, qualify, or comment on the main clause. Here's a version that uses subordination instead of coordination to combine elements:

Even though no one showed up for the concert, the band put on their uniforms, picked up their instruments, and played the opening tune right on time.

Here the use of subordination focuses readers' attention more emphatically on the band, and the fact that no one showed up is now represented as the circumstances in which the band acted.

Or you could change the emphasis altogether:

Since they had already put on their uniforms and picked up their instruments, the band played the opening tune right on time, even though no one showed up to hear them.

Writers use coordination and subordination in passages of writing to avoid the monotony of simple sentences and to guide the reader to the relationships and points of emphasis that are important to the writer's meaning.

WORKING TOGETHER: Using Coordination and Subordination

The following is a passage taken from an American history textbook but rewritten to eliminate coordination and subordination as much as possible. Notice how choppy the passage is. Your task is to revise the passage by using coordination and subordination to combine elements so that the sentences better express key relationships and points of emphasis. Follow these steps:

• First, do a revision of the passage on your own.

• Next, work with two or three other students. Compare the revisions. Where do they differ? At this point, don't argue about better or worse versions. Instead, consider each group member's reasons for the revisions he or she has made.

• Once you have gone through the whole passage this way, go back to the beginning and working together as a group, see if you can agree on a revision.

- Compare the revision your group has done to the revisions of other groups. Again, locate differences and consider the reasons why groups have revised in different ways. Then see if the groups can agree on one revised version.

"The 1988 Election" by George B. Tindall and David B. Shi

The Republican convention took place in New Orleans in August. The Republicans nominated George Bush. He was Reagan's two-time vice-president. Bush had a rocky start in the primaries. He had easily cast aside his rivals in the primaries. He was Reagan's hand-picked heir. Bush claimed credit for the administration's successes. He was like all dutiful vice-presidents. He also faced the challenge of defining and asserting his own political agenda. Bush was a veteran government official. He served as a Texas congressman. He served as envoy to China. He served as ambassador to the U.N. He headed the C.I.A. He projected none of Reagan's charisma, charm, or rhetorical skills. Cartoonist caricatured him. He was a patrician vice-president. He was the son of a rich Connecticut senator. He was schooled at Andover and Yale. Cartoonists caricatured him as a well-heeled "wimp." One Democrat described him as a man born "with a silver foot in his mouth." Early polls showed Dukakis with a surprisingly wide lead.

MODIFICATION

Subjects and predicates, of course, are the heart of a sentence, for together they produce the statement that makes a sentence comprehensible to readers. In many instances, however, the basic subject and predicate, by themselves, cannot perform the work a writer wants a sentence to do. Writers use modification to add meaning to their sentences in the form of needed details and specific information.

The following sentences are drawn from a paragraph in Barbara Tuchman's essay "History as Mirror," in which she writes about fourteenth-century Europe. Notice how the opening sentences establish the paragraph's focus of attention:

> The gaudy extravagence of noble life was awesome. . . . [I]t was pure ostentation and conspicuous consumption.

Here is one of the sentences that follow in the paragraph, presenting evidence for Tuchman's claim. Notice how modification adds details and specific information to what would otherwise be the rather dull and uninformative sentence, "Charles V owned crowns and sets of furnishings."

> Charles V of France owned forty-seven jeweled and golden crowns and sixty-three complete sets of chapel furnishings, including vestments, gold crucifixes, altarpieces, reliquaries, and prayer books.

Tuchman concludes her paragraph with the following sentence:

> For the entry into Paris of the new Queen, Isabel of Bavaria, the entire length of Rue St. Denis was hung with a canopy representing the firmament twinkling with stars from which sweetly singing angels descended bearing a crown, and fountains ran with wine, distributed to the people in golden cups by lovely maidens wearing caps of solid gold.

To see how Tuchman has used modification in this sentence, we can diagram it to show how statements modify other statements:

For the entry
into Paris
of the new Queen
Isabel of Bavaria
the entire length(subject)
of Rue St. Denis
was hung (verb)

with a canopy
representing the firmament
twinkling with stars
from which sweetly singing angels descended
bearing a crown

and fountains ran(subject + verb)

with wine
distributed to the people
in golden cups
by lovely maidens
wearing caps
of solid gold.

Notice here that statements move along both a horizontal and a vertical axis. Along the horizontal axis (from left to right), the movement is from general statements to more particular ones that support or modify the general statement, while the vertical axis (up and down) represents accumulating depth and detail.

WORKING TOGETHER: Diagramming Modification

Working together with two or three other students, diagram these sentences from Gretel Ehrlich's essay "The Solace of Open Spaces" as the sentence from Barbara Tuchman's "History as Mirror" has been diagrammed.

Seventy-five years ago, when travel was by buckboard or horseback, cowboys who were temporarily out of work rode the grub line—drifting from ranch to ranch, mending fences or milking cows, and receiving in exchange a bed and meals. Gossip and messages traveled this slow circuit with them, creating an intimacy between ranchers who were three and four weeks' ride apart.

- Identify the subject and verb in each sentence. Write this at the left margin of a page.

- Identify the modifying phrases and clauses. Write them on the page so that they move left to right, from general to particular.

- Connect the modifiers to the elements they modify.

Active and Passive Voice.

You may have heard the advice that writers should, whenever possible, use active instead of passive voice. There is a good deal of truth to this advice. Active voice in many cases makes sentences easier to read because it follows the natural order of events in which somebody does something by making the actor into the subject of the sentence. Compare these sentences:

Passive voice: The ability to write well has traditionally been included as one of the goals of a college education.

Active voice: Educators, parents, and employers have traditionally included the ability to write well as one of the goals of a college education.

Notice in the first version you can't tell who includes the ability to write well as one of the goals of a college education and therefore the significance of the sentence is hard to evaluate. There is an action going on, but no one to do it. In the second version, active voice puts the actors in the subject position and thereby makes it easier for the reader to understand and evaluate what the sentence is saying.

Many sentences can be switched from the passive to active voice with little difficulty and, usually, with a gain in clarity and emphasis.

Passive voice: The teacher said that the essays we wrote last week would be returned to us tomorrow   (Who's returning the essays?)

Active voice: The teacher said tomorrow he would return the essays we wrote last week.   (The teacher is.)

Passive voice: The dog was run over by a car that was driven by a man who was drunk.   (Unnecessarily wordy)

Active voice: The drunk driver ran over the dog.

In these sentences, as you can see, using the active voice not only makes the sentences easier to read. It also more clearly assigns responsibility to the actor who performs the action. Passive voice is used widely in government and business to avoid designating responsibility:

Bombs were dropped on civilian targets for the third day in a row.

The Smith family was denied housing assistance.

The workforce was reduced to enhance the company's competitive position in the market.

On the other hand, there are some instances in which the passive voice makes sense, depending on where you want the emphasis in a sentence to fall. Compare these sentences:

Passive voice: In 1938, the former Bolshevik leader Leon Trotsky was murdered by Stalinist goons. This murder brought to a close Trotsky's tragic struggle against the consolidation of Stalin's one-man rule in the Soviet Union.

Active voice: In 1938, Stalinist goons murdered the former Bolshevik leader Leon Trotsky. By eliminating Trotsky, Stalin took another step toward consolidating his one-man rule in the Soviet Union.
Notice that the first sentences begins a topic chain by focusing on Trotsky's murder, while the second does the same by focusing on Stalin as the murderer. In this case, the decision whether to use active or passive depends on how the writer plans to develop the paragraph.

WORKING TOGETHER: Choosing Active and Passive Voice

Notice in the following passage that the verbs are underlined. In some but not all the sentences, the use of active and passive voice has been altered from what appears in the original version. Work together in groups of three or four. Identify the verbs as active or passive. Then consider whether active or passive voice is more suited in the context of the sentence and passage. What changes in voice would you make? Which verbs would you leave as they are? How would you explain your choices? Once you have completed your work, compare the results to what other groups have done.

Love is believed by Americans to be the basis for enduring relationships. A 1970 survey found that the ideal of two people sharing a life and home together was held by 96 percent of all Americans. When the same question was asked in 1980, the same percentage agreed. Yet when a national sample was asked in 1978 whether "most couples getting married today expect to remain married for the rest of their lives," no was said by 60 percent.
—*Robert N. Bellah, et al. Habits of the Heart, p. 90*

DICTION AND THE USE OF JARGON

Diction refers to the word choices a writer makes in composing sentences. These choices give a piece of writing its particular tone of voice—formal, informal, or something in between. As a rule of thumb, it's helpful to think of diction as a way of adjusting your choice of words to your purpose and to your readers' needs.

For example, the diction in the following sentence is too informal for a college paper:

The deal about Moby Dick is that America's heaviest word-slinger, Mr. Herman Melville, uses that awesome white whale to pose some really bold questions about the nature of reality.

A more appropriate sense of word choice might lead to something like this:

In Moby Dick, Melville uses the white whale to pose searching questions about the nature of reality.

On the other hand, you can veer too far in the direction of a formal style and your word choice can come off sounding inflated (and a bit silly):

In his magisterial work Moby Dick, our master literary helmsman Herman Melville uses the white leviathan of the watery depths to pose profound and eternally perplexing questions about the nature of reality.

The term jargon refers to the specialized language a group or profession uses to accomplish its purposes. Because it is specialized, jargon by definition excludes some people. The following sentences, for example, may be difficult for many ordinary readers to understand:

The novel feature of the structure is the manner in which the two chains are held together by the purine and pyrimidine bases.

—*James Watson and Francis Crick,*

"A Structure for Deoxyribose Nucleic Acid"

To give a text an Author is to impose a limit on that text, to furnish it with a final signified, to close the writing.

—*Roland Barthes, "The Death of the Author"*

And yet, people actively involved in science and in literary theory will recognize immediately the terminology used. In fact, they would not be able to do their work without such a jargon. So if jargon seems impenetrable to outsiders, it seems an essential tool of the trade to insiders—to use in agreed-on ways such concepts as "purine" and "pyrimidine," "Author" and "signified."

This doesn't mean, of course, that jargon is forever closed off to all but an initiated few. One of the points of a college education is to gain some access to the specialized vocabularies and ways of using words that characterize the various fields of study. From this perspective, there is no reason you should not use technical terms when you are writing within a community of specialists. To speak and write that vernacular is a sign of membership.

For example, if you were writing to a friend or general reader, you probably wouldn't write:

The migration of birds proceeds southward every winter.

It sounds stuffy and uses a noun—migration—to name the main action in the sentence. You'd probably write instead:

Birds migrate south in the winter.

But if you were writing a paper in a course on animal behavior, the following sentence might well be appropriate:

The annual winter migration of certain bird species follows well-determined flightpaths to the southern hemisphere.

Using the abstract noun—"migration"—as the subject (instead of the birds who do the migrating) makes sense in this case because the concept of migration and its connection to "flightpaths" is the focus of the sentence.

Academic and professional jargon rely heavily on nominalization —nouns that are created from other words by adding -tion, -ity, -ness, -ance, -ment, and -ism. As you can see from the example, "migration"—the nominalized form of the verb "migrate"—enables us to see the idea of birds' seasonal movement as the focus of the sentence. In this case, nominalization provides a concept to think with.

In other cases, however, nominalization just clogs up sentences by making things sound more complicated than they actually are. Often called overnominalization, this style is widespread in the professions, government, and business. For example, this sentence

The recent investigation of the staff's observance of personal wellness habits provides indication of a marked reduction in the consumption of tobacco products and alcoholic beverages.

could be revised to read:

According to a recent study, the staff are smoking and drinking less.

ETHICS OF WRITING

Doublespeak

The use of jargon to exclude, obfuscate, and mystify readers is often called "doublespeak." This style of writing typically uses not only passive voice (to evade responsibility) and overnominalization (to make the simple sound complex), it also uses euphemisms that avoid saying what things really are. The town dump, for example, becomes a "sanitary land fill," bad handwriting becomes "deficient grapho-motor skills," and students taking courses over television are called "low resi-dency students." A good deal of doublespeak, of course, comes from writers who are simply trying to sound like they belong in a particular profession, government agency, or corporate position—and who do not intend to deceive their readers. The problem, though, is that the style of doublespeak, with its evasions and inflated language, is misleading. When government agencies refer to budget cuts as "advanced downward adjustments" or employers call strikebreakers "replacement workers," you can be sure they aren't trying to tell you the whole truth.

WORKING TOGETHER: Analyzing Jargon

The following two paragraphs come from the writer and editor Malcolm Cowley's essay "Sociological Habit Patterns in Linguistic Transmogrification," in which he pokes fun at inflated and jargon-laden prose. The first paragraph is a sample of sociological writing. The second is Cowley's translation of the passage into a plain and straightforward style. Work together in groups of three or four. Read the two paragraphs. Determine how Cowley has translated the original passage. Consider carefully what he has gained in his translation and whether anything has been lost. Don't just assume that Cowley's version is better. Explain who it is better for and on what terms it is better. Can you think of other ways to translate the passage that would be appropriate for a particular audience? Explain your response and compare it to the responses of other groups.

A. Original:

In effect, it was hypothesized that certain physical data categories including housing types and densities, land use characteristics, and ecological location constitute a scalable content area. This could be called a continuum of residential desireability. Likewise, it was hypothesized that several social data categories, describing the same census tracts, and referring generally to the social stratification of the city, would also be scalable. This scale would be called a continuum of socio-economic status. Thirdly, it was hypothesized that there would be a high positive correlation between the scale types on each continuum.

B. Malcolm Cowley's Translation

Rich people live in big houses set further apart than those of poor people. By looking at an aerial photograph of any American city, we can distinguish the richer from the poorer neighborhoods.

EDITING SENTENCES

Editing involves working with sentences and sequences of sentences to enhance their clarity, emphasis, and variety. In this section, we look at editing strategies writers use for these purposes.

Editing for Clarity.

There are a number of common problems that interfere with the clarity of sentences—confusing sentence structure, wordiness, and vagueness. In the following sections, you'll find examples of each problem and strategies for editing.

• Confusing sentence structure

 Confusing sentence structure is characteristic of early drafts, when writers are trying to sort out their ideas and get them down on paper. Notice in the following example how much the writer has packed into one sentence and the demands it puts on readers.

Original:

Immigration, defense of the border, and undocumented workers became political issues in the 1996 elections, if the response to Proposition 187 in California and Pat Buchanan's presidential campaign are any indication, along with politicians such as Pete Wilson (the governor of California) proposing tough policies and congressmen and senators debating whether education and other benefits should be cut off to illegal immigrants.

One thing that makes this sentence confusing is that the opening groups together a series of related but distinct items as one political issue. The following clause also puts together two distinct events—the response to Proposition 187 and Buchanan's presidential campaign—without really clarifying how they illustrate or explain the first part of the sentence. Then the last part of the sentence focuses on Pete Wilson's role and how Congress has been debating changes in immigration law. As readers, we get a certain sense of urgency here—that the writer has a lot of information and something he or she wants to say. But it is garbled and impacted.

The task here is for the writer to sort out the elements of this sentence and devise a way to present them in more manageable chunks. First of all, the writer needs to decide what it is exactly that makes up the hot political issue. Then the writer needs to explain how the following information illustrates the issue. A revision might look like this:

Edited:

With the attention given to Proposition 187 in California, immigration became one of the hottest political issues in the 1996 elections. Pete Wilson, governor of California, was instrumental in defining the terms of the national debate by seeking to cut off illegal immigrants from any of the state's social services, except emergency medical care. At the same time, Congress was debating whether states should be required to provide education for illegal immigrants, and presidential candidate Pat Buchanan campaigned on a get tough policy to defend the borders against undocumented workers.

- **Wordiness**

Wordiness means what it says: too many words to express what the writer has to say. Here are some wordy sentences, followed by revised versions.

Original:

As far as I have been able to tell, after doing thorough research on the matter, I conclude that the kind of popular music being broadcast today—whether rap, alternative, grunge, or metal—does not hold up to the music people used to hear when they were listening to the underground radio stations of the late sixties.

Edited:

The popular music on the radio today—whether rap, alternative, grunge, or metal—does not hold up well compared to the music underground radio stations played in the late sixties.

Original:

As a result of the fact that the Chicago Bulls acquired Dennis Rodman, who is the perennial rebounding leader, they got the power forward which was the missing piece in the puzzle to complement all-stars Michael Jordan and Scottie Pippin.

Edited:

When the Chicago Bulls acquired perennial rebounding leader Dennis Rodman, they got the power forward needed to complement all-stars Michael Jordan and Scottie Pippin.

- **Vagueness**

Words are vague when they don't convey with adequate precision and specificity what the writer is trying to say. Take this sentence, for example.

My roomate is a weird guy who does strange things sometimes.

From what is available to us, it is difficult to tell exactly what the writer means by "weird" or what the "strange things" might be. Clearly the writer is trying to convey an impression of his roomate, but we don't have enough information to know what he means or whether his sense of "weird" and "strange" matches our own. Here's how the writer could eliminate vagueness:

Edited:

My roomate studies a lot. He rarely parties during the week and never starts the weekend like the rest of us do by draining a keg on Thursday night.

Those two sentences would certainly clear things up, though as readers we may or may not see the roomate's behavior as "weird."

In most cases of vagueness, editing is largely a matter of unpacking the actual meaning that is lurking behind the use of vague words like "weird" and "strange." There are a number of other adjectives writers sometimes fall into using on early drafts—"awful," "fantastic," "great," "marvelous," "nice," "peculiar," "terrific," and "wonderful."

In other instances, writers use words such as "aspect," "factor," or "situation" when they could be much more specific.

Original:

Some aspects of the movie were lame, but in general the romantic situation with the characters was terrific.

Edited:

Despite the sentimentality and macho posturing inherited from the novel, the love affair between Clint Eastwood and Meryl Streep heated up the screen in the film version of Bridges of Madison County.

As this revision shows, specific words and phrases enhance the clarity of a sentence.

EDITING FOR EMPHASIS

Editing for emphasis is a way of directing your readers' attention to the most important parts of a sentence. Writers know that the places of greatest emphasis are the beginning and the end of sentences, and so they structure their sentences accordingly, locating less important information in the middle. You can edit sentences for emphasis by paying attention to 1) word order, 2) the use of parallelism and emphatic repetition, and 3) the use of climactic order.

• Emphatic word order

Make use of readers' tendencies to focus on the opening and closing of sentences. Notice in the following example how the most important material is buried in the middle of the sentence.

Original:

With its headquarters in Washington, D.C., the National Breast Cancer Coalition, which is an advocacy group promoting research and treatment of breast cancer, was founded in 1992.

Edited:

Founded in 1992, the National Breast Cancer Coalition, an advocacy group based in Washington, D.C., promotes research and treatment of breast cancer.

• Parallelism and repetition

Parallelism and repetition are useful techniques to create emphasis in a sentence by focusing the reader's attention on key elements. Notice in the following well known line how parallel phrases emphasize the main points:

. . . and that government of the people, by the people, and for the people shall not perish from the earth.

—*Abraham Lincoln, "Gettysburg Address"*

Writers can also use parallel sentences to create emphasis, as in these examples:

Ask not what your country can do for you; ask what you can do for your country.
—*John F. Kennedy, "Inaugural Address"*

You have read the horrifying stories. You have seen the gruesome pictures. You have heard of the unspeakable atrocities.
—*Doctors Without Borders, "Letter of Appeal"*

As you can see from these examples, the effective use of parallelism depends on the repetition of grammatical elements. In some cases, writers enhance emphasis by repeating key words and phrases, as in this example:

I said that it was intended that you should perish in the ghetto, perish by never being allowed to go behind the white man's definitions, by never being allowed to spell your proper name.
—James Baldwin, "The Dungeon Shook"

When you edit, look for opportunities to create emphasis by using parallelism and repetition.

Original:

To increase the odds that more lives will be saved, we need to send surgeons, anesthetists, doctors, and nurses. Surgical kits are important to provide. Also antiobiotics are necessary.

Edited:

Every surgeon, anesthetist, doctor, and nurse that we can send, every surgical kit that we can provide, every antibiotic we will administer increases the odds that more lives will be saved.
—*Doctors Without Borders, "Letter of Appeal"*

- **Climactic order**

Climactic order moves to a climax at the end of a sentence by reserving the final position for an especially important idea. Such sentences build up descriptive phrases and clauses to create suspense that is resolved only toward the end of the sentence. Here's an example:

> But really, as we envision soaring and swooping, extending, refining the combat zone of basketball into a fourth, outer, other dimension, the dreamy ozone of flight without wings, of going up and not coming down till we're good and ready, then it's Michael Jordan we must recognize as the truest prophet of what might be possible.
>
> —*John Edgar Wideman, "Michael Jordan Leaps the*
> *Great Divide"*

Notice how the following series of sentences can be combined to create climactic word order.

Original:

The Puritans were virtuous, hardworking, and pious. Schoolbooks idealize the Puritans as a "hardy band" of no-nonsense patriarchs. They were disciplined. They razed the forest and brought order to the New World. Occasionally, though, they would wander off after some fancy clothes, or rendezvous in the woods with the town prostitute.

Edited:

Virtuous, hardworking, pious, even though they occasionally would wander off after some fancy clothers, or rendezvous in the woods with the town prositute, the Puritans are idealized in our schoolbooks as a "hardy band" of no-nonsense patriarchs whose discipline razed the forest and brought order to the New World.
—Ishmael Reed, "America: The Multinational Society"

ETHICS OF WRITING

Using Nonsexist and Nondiscriminatory Language

The way people use certain words reflects and shapes attitudes about social groups and the roles of men and women. For example, to refer to women as "the ladies," "the girls," or "the weaker sex" conveys the attitude that women are not equal to men and thereby perpetuates the subordination of women, whether intended or not. Similarly, to emphasize a woman's appearance conveys the attitude that women (but not men) should be judged by their looks and what they wear. It is easy enough, for instance, to see the inappropriateness of writing

> IBM president George Smith, looking elegant in a charcoal pin-striped Armani suit, set off by platinum cuff links and British handmade calfskin

shoes, spoke to financial reporters about the company's third-quarter economic report.

So using the same standard, it treats women unfairly to write

> Executive director of the Modern Language Association Hazel Sims, looking elegant in a muted plaid suit, set off by silk scarf and alligator heels, testified before Congress yesterday about proposed cuts in the National Endowment for the Humanities.

And by the same token, to identify a woman as wife or mother when she is appearing in a professional role conveys the attitude that women's identities are based on these domestic roles instead of the role they play in public life. It seems ludicrous to write

IBM president George Smith, married for thirty-three years to high school sweetheart Wanda Smith and devoted father of four, spoke to financial reporters about the company's third-quarter economic report.

So using the same standard, it is inappropriate to write

Executive director of the Modern Language Association Hazel Sims, married for eighteen years to successful oral surgeon Ralph Moriconi and mother of two teenage girls, testified before Congress yesterday about proposed cuts in the National Endowment for the Humanities.

It is also the case that certain words and phrases convey attitudes about racial, ethnic, and other social groups. For example, to refer to African Americans as "colored people" or "Negroes" uses terms that carry a history of segregation and racial oppression with them and reinforces stereotypes about racial inequality. Moreover, to use the older terms denies African Americans the right to determine their own collective identity and the terms by which they will be known. Similarly, people from Central and South America are increasingly using the terms Latina and Latino to replace the older term Hispanic. And many gays and lesbians prefer these designations to the older term homosexual.

To write responsibly means to be sensitive to the ways in which language can perpetuate stereotypes and exclude and insult people. Here are some guidelines for using nonsexist and nondiscriminatory
language:

• Replace masculine nouns with more inclusive words when you are referring to people in general. To use masculine terms when you are talking about both sexes suggests that men are the standard by which human beings are known. There are available alternatives that are more inclusive.

Example	Alternative
mankind	humanity, human beings, people
the best man for the job	the best person, the best man or woman
man-made	synthetic, manufactured, crafted
the common man	the average person, ordinary peopl
forefathers	ancestors

• Replace masculine pronouns when you are referring to people in general. Here are a number of strategies.

Original:
Each taxpayer must file his annual federal return by April 15.

Edited by changing to plural:
Taxpayers must file their annual federal return by April 15.

Edited by eliminating unnecessary gender reference:
Each taxpayer must file an annual federal return by April 15.

Edited by using he or she:
Each taxpayer must file his or her annual federal return by April 15.
(Note: Use this strategy sparingly and avoid s/he or his/her forms.)

• Use non-gendered terms to refer to occupations and social roles. Otherwise, it will seem that certain jobs and roles are reserved for men.

Example	Alternative
chairman, congressman	chair, chairperson, representative, member of congress
coed, freshman	student, first-year student
mailman, fireman, policeman	mail carrier, firefighter, police officer
newsman,	journalist, reporter,
salesman	sales representative, sales clerk

• Replace language that reinforces stereotypes or perpetuates discriminatory attitudes. The responsible approach is to find language that is inclusive and avoids offending.

Original:
The public library should provide literacy programs for foreigners who don't speak English.
Edited:
The public library should provide programs for recent immigrants who don't speak English.

Original:
The abnormal sexual orientation of homosexuals makes some straight people feel uncomfortable.
Edited:
The sexual orientation of gays and lesbians makes some straight people feel uncomfortable.

Original:
White trash families have started to move into the neighborhood where I grew up.
Edited:
Poor working-class families have started to move into the neighborhood where I grew up.

Editing for Variety

If a series of sentences are similar in length, type, and structure, the writing is likely to get monotonous and to lack any sense of rhythm. The strategies for enhancing emphasis that you have just reviewed also tend to produce greater variety among sentences. In this section, we look at two further editing strategies to increase variety by 1) varying sentence length and 2) adding an element of surprise.

• Sentence length

To vary sentence length effectively depends on understanding the roles that sentences of different lengths can play in a passage of writing. Short sentences are particularly useful for emphasis and dramatic contrast. Longer sentences enable you to establish relationships among the ideas in a sentence and to add rhythmic variation. Middle-length sentences typically do the main work in a passage of writing, providing description and explanation. The trick is to find effective combinations of all three. Notice in the edited version below how combining some sentences and compressing others provides greater variety of sentence length and thereby enhances the message in the passage.

Original:

There was a time when people wanted to keep the peace and the crockery intact at the dinner table. They held to a strict dinner-table rule. The rule was never to argue about politics or religion. I don't know how well it worked in American dining rooms. It worked pretty well in school, where we dealt with religion by not arguing about it.

Children came out of diverse homes. They carved up the turf in their neighborhoods. They turned the playgrounds into religious battlefields. But intolerance wasn't tolerated in the common ground of the public classroom.

Edited:

There was a time when people who wanted to keep the peace and keep the crockery intact held to a strict dinner-table rule: Never argue about politics or religion. I don't know how well it worked in American dining rooms, but it worked pretty well in our schools. We dealt with religion by not arguing about it.

Children who came out of diverse homes might carve up the turf of their neighborhood and turn the playgrounds into a religious battlefield, but the public classroom was common ground. Intolerance wasn't tolerated.

—*Ellen Goodman, "Religion in the Textbooks"*

- **Surprise**

Another way of adding variety to your sentences is to put in new information or a twist of thought at the end. Changing direction at the end of sentence can be effective if it is used sparingly to create dramatic effects and set up transitions to the next sentence or paragraph. Here are some examples of sentences that use this technique.

When I left the Buffalo Bill Historical Center I was full of moral outrage, an indignation so intense it made me almost sick, though it was pleasurable, too, as such emotions usually are.

—*Jane Tompkins, "At the Buffalo Bill Museum"*

Thus the American Center of PEN, the organization of novelists, poets, essayists, editors, and publishers, finds it necessary to distribute each year a poster entitled WRITERS IN PRISON. This poster, which is very large, simply lists the writers who are currently locked in cells or insane asylums or torture chambers in various countries around the world—who are by their being and profession threats to the security of political regimes.

—*E. L. Doctorow, "False Documents"*

PROOFREADING SENTENCES: Ten Common Problems

The final editing writers do is proofreading their manuscript to identify and correct any errors that may remain. Of course, writers often eliminate sentence level problems as they revise and edit to clarify their meaning. But still there is the necessary final step of careful proofreading to make sure the writing is grammatically correct, observes the conventions of standard usage, and contains no misspelled words.

Proofreading differs from the kind of editing you've just reviewed that focuses on enhancing the clarity and emphasis of sentences and passages. In contrast, the purpose of proofreading is to make sure everything is technically correct. For this reason, when you are proofreading, it helps NOT to read for the content or meaning of the writing but instead to concentrate exclusively on recognizing grammatical or spelling errors. Some writers like to begin at the end of a manuscript, proofreading the last sentence first and then working backwards, looking carefully at each sentence. Others place a rule or blank piece of paper under the line they are proofreading to focus their attention.

In this section, we review ten common problems that you should watch for when you are proofreading your writing.

1. Sentence fragments

We look at sentence fragments first because they are the sentence-level error readers consider the most serious. College faculty and professionals are more likely to notice sentence fragments than other errors and to make judgments based on them about a writer's abilities. To put it another way, there is no grammatical reason why sentence fragments are worse than other errors. But their impact on readers does seem to be strong and to undermine confidence in the writer. For this reason, it is key to find and correct sentence fragments.

A sentence fragments is easy to define: it is a part of sentence presented as a complete sentence. Notice in the following sentence how a fragments occurs when a sentence part is detached and made to stand on its own:

Original:

I have not been happy. Since my family moved to a new neighborhood miles away from my friends.

Edited:

I have not been happy since my family moved to a new neighborhood miles away from my friends.

Editing strategy: Connect the detached part.

In the following example, an incomplete sentence part stands alone.

Original:

Basketball fans have been arguing for years about whether the Boston Celtics or the Los Angeles Lakers were the team of the 1980s. Which is an argument no one will ever finally resolve.

Edited:

Basketball fans have been arguing for years whether the Boston Celtics or the Los Angeles were the team of the 1980s. No one will ever finally resolve this argument.

Editing strategy: Make detached part into a complete sentence.

Sometimes verbals that modify nouns are taken to be the main verb in a sentence, thereby creating a fragment.

Original:

The committee charged with deciding which plants to close and which employees to lay off.

Edited: The committee was charged with deciding which plants to close and which employees to lay off.

Editing strategy: Change the modifier "charged" into a verb "was charged."

or

Edited:

The committee charged with deciding which plants to close and which employees to lay off will present their recommendations next week.

Editing strategy: Keep the modifier and add a main verb.

2. Comma splices and fused sentences

Comma splices join two complete sentences together by using a comma. Fused sentences join complete sentences together without using any punctuation. The same editing strategies work in either case—separate the sentences, use a conjunction (and, or, but, for, nor, so, yet), use a semicolon, subordinate one sentence to the other.

Original (comma splice):

At seven in the evening, the City Council members filed into the auditorium to begin the meeting, however the mayor was not there because had been arrested that afternoon for taking bribes.

Edited:

At seven in the evening, the City Council members filed into the auditorium to begin the meeting. However, the mayor was not there because he had been arrested that afternoon for taking bribes.

Editing strategy: Separate into two sentences. However, by itself, is not a conjunction and therefore cannot join two sentences together.

or

Edited:

At seven in the evening, the City Council members filed into the auditorium to begin the meeting; however, the mayor was not there because he had been arrested that afternoon for taking bribes.

Editing strategy: Use a semi-colon to join the sentences.

Original (fused sentence):

The Basque language spoken in parts of France and Spain puzzles linguists it appears to be unrelated to other European languages.

Edited:

The Basque language spoken in parts of France and Spain puzzles linguists, for it appears to be unrelated to other European languages.

Editing strategy: Use a conjunction—for—to join the sentences.

or

Edited:

The Basque language spoken in parts of France and Spain puzzles linguists because it appears to be unrelated to other European languages.

Editing strategy: Subordinate one sentence to the other.

3. Subject verb agreement

Subjects and verbs need to agree in number. Singular verbs go with singular nouns, and plural verbs go with plural nouns.

It is unlikely to create subject verb disagreement in a sentence such as this one:
Bill and Jim consider football the most important thing in life.
But when a subject is separated from its verb by an intervening phrase or clause, writers sometimes lose track of agreement, as in this sentence.

Bill and Jim, who have been competing all season for the starting position at quarterback, considers football the most important thing in life.

Note: when a phrase beginning with along with, as well as, together with, or in addition to follows the subject, it does not become part of the subject and does not make a singular subject plural.

Bill, along with his best friend Jim, was competing for the starting position at quarterback.

The best editing strategy in sentences like these is to ignore the intevening phrase in order to concentrate on the subject of the sentence and its agreement with the verb. Here are two further examples of how intervening phrases can cause confusion.

Original:
The feelings of a teenager often mystifies adults.

Edited:
The feelings of a teenager often mystify adults.

Editing strategy: Ignore for a moment the prepositional phrase "of a teenager" to concentrate on the subject "feelings."

Original:
The behavior of their children sometimes drive parents crazy.

Edited:
The behavior of their children sometimes drives parents crazy.

Editing strategy: Don't mistake "children," which is part of a prepositional phrase, for the subject because it is closer to the verb than the actual subject "behavior."

Collective nouns refer to groups of individuals—team, staff, family, audience, tribe, etc. When the collective noun acts as a single unit, use a singular verb:

The team has achieved its greatest victory.

But when members of the group act or are referred to as individuals

in the sentence, use a plural verb:

The faculty were praised for their many accomplishments.

4. Verb shift
Watch for shifts in verb tense that are inconsistent and illogical.

Original:
Jane and Margot went to the party last Friday, but when they saw it was a drunken mess, they decide to leave.

Edited:
Jane and Margot went to the party last Friday, but when they saw it was a drunken mess, they decided to leave.

Editing strategy: Keep the tense of "decided" consistent with the time of the action—in the past, last Friday.

Note: When you are writing about events in a work of literature, a film, or a television show, use the present tense consistently.

Original:
Hamlet clearly agonizes about whether he should take his fate into his own hands. As he said: "To be or not to be. That is the question."

Edited:

Hamlet clearly agonizes about whether he should take his fate into his own hands. As he says: "To be or not to be. That is the question."

Editing strategy: Note that Hamlet is not a person who spoke at some time in the past. He is a character in a play. Treat he does and says in the present tense.

Note: But if you are writing a writer or artist who lived in the past, treat what they did accordingly.

Shakespeare wrote his plays to be performed. He was not writing literature. He was working as the playwright of a theater company to put plays on stage. The written versions came later.

5. Pronoun agreement

Just as subjects need to agree with their verbs, so do pronouns need to agree with their antecedents (the word a pronoun stands in for). In many sentences, the relationship between pronouns and antecedents is easy to see:

Jane always drinks milk with her meals.

Jim drinks milk with his meals, too.

Things can become confusing when the antecedent of the pronoun is a collective noun. When the collective noun acts a single unit, use a singular pronoun:

The Northwood Unified School District always serves milk with its breakfast program.

When you emphasize the individual actions of group members, use a plural pronoun:

The staff left their hotel rooms and gathered together in the lobby.

6. Pronoun reference

Pronouns not only need to agree in number with their antecedents. They also need to make it easy for readers to see how pronouns refer to a particular antecedent. Watch for instances in which the reference of a pronoun to its antecedent is ambiguous.

Original:

After fertilizing the flower beds and pruning the dead branches from the apple tree, I watered them thoroughly.

Edited:

After fertilizing the flower beds and pruning the dead branches from the apple tree, I watered the beds thoroughly.

Editing strategy: Eliminates ambiguous reference (Did you water the beds, the dead branches, or both in the original?) by substituting a noun for the ambiguous pronoun.

Or a pronoun can be used so vaguely that readers will find it difficult to see what the pronoun refers to.

Original:

Workers are laid off, corporations are relocating their plants in other countries, but profits and executive salaries are soaring. This is why people are so angry at corporate America.

Edited:

Recent trends in industry have caused a popular uproar against corporate America: workers are laid off, corporations are relocating their plants in other countries, but profits and executive salaries are soaring.

Editing strategy:

Provide a name "recent trends in industry" for what "this" means in the original sentence. Notice that the edited sentences clarify a question readers might have about the original sentence, namely does "this" refer to all or just some of what appears in the preceding sentence.

7. Modifiers

Modifiers can be tricky at times. Dangling modifiers, misplaced modifiers, and disruptive modifiers can cause confusion for readers.

Original (dangling modifier):

Driving home from work today, a cat dashed in front of my car and was nearly run over.

Edited:

When I was driving home from work today, a cat dashed in front of my car, and I nearly ran it over.

or

Edited:

When I was driving home from work today, I nearly ran over a cat that dashed in front of my car.

Editing strategies: Cats can't drive cars, which is what the original sentence implies. The two edited versions eliminate the dangling modifiers by using a clause rather than a phrase that will modify the noun that appears next to it.

Original (misplaced modifier):

I found an old Duke Ellington album in the record store that I have wanted to buy for years.

Edited:

In the record store, I found an old Duke Ellington album that I have wanted to buy for years.

Editing strategy: Presumably it is the Duke Ellington record the writer wants to buy—not the record store.

Original (disruptive modifier):

Some politicians, even though reliable scientific studies have demonstrated the dangers of second-hand tobacco smoke, still minimize the health risks.

Edited:

Even though reliable scientific studies have demonstrated the dangers of second-hand tobacco smoke, some politicians still minimize the health risks.

Editing strategy: Relocate the modifying phrase so that subject and verb are closer together.

8. Mixed construction

Mixed construction refers to sentences that begin with one sentence structure but shift to another. This will cause readers to do a double take.

Original:

Since the most experienced writers make grammatical errors means all writers need to edit carefully.

Edited:

Even the most experienced writers make grammatical errors, and this fact suggests that all writers need to edit carefully.

Editing strategy: Separates the mixed parts of the sentence into two complete sentences joined by a conjunction.

Original:

When Shaquille O'Neal made both free throws is why the game went into overtime.

Edited:

When Shaquille O'Neal made both free throws, he sent the game into overtime.

Editing strategy: Combines the mixed parts by subordinating one to the other.

9. Faulty predication

Faulty predication occurs when subjects and verbs are not matched properly. Notice in the following example how the subject can't perform the action described by the verb.

Original:

Maria's love of opera wanted to go to Julliard for voice training.

Edited:

Because of her love of opera, Maria wanted to go to Julliard for voice training.

Editing strategy: A "love of opera" can't want to go to Julliard. Maria does.

Original:

Nationalism is when people identify emotionally with their country.

Edited:

Nationalism is a sentiment that arises when people identify emotionally with their country.
or

Edited:

Nationalist sentiments arise when people identify emotionally with their country.
Editing strategies: "Is when" is a non-standard construction writers sometimes use to define terms. The abstract term "nationalism" needs to be defined by another term or set of terms.

10. Parallelism

When you have series of items, make sure they appear in parallel form.

Original:

A backpacking trip requires the proper equipment, to be physically fit, and that you know about the wilderness.

Edited:
A backpacking trip requires the proper equipment, physical fitness, and knowledge about the wilderness.

or

Edited:
A backtripping requires that you have the proper equipment, that you are physically fit, and that you know about the wilderness.

Editing strategies: Both edited versions put the items in parallel order. The first is more succinct with its focus on noun phrases, while the second focuses more on the reader.

Original:
The New York Knicks want to draft a power forward who can rebound, with strong defensive skills, and who can score.

Edited:
The New York Knicks want to draft a power forward who can rebond, play strong defense, and score.

Editing strategy: Here the edited version creates a parallel sequence of verbs and drops the repetition of "who can."

TEN COMMON PROBLEMS FOR SECOND LANGUAGE WRITERS

In this section, we look at ten editing problems second language writers of English often encounter.

1. Subject/Pronoun Repetition

In some languages pronouns repeat the subject. In English, however, this repetition is not permitted.

Original:
Celia Cruz she is one of the most famous Cuban singers.

Edited:
Celia Cruz is one of the most famous Cuban singers.

Original:
The person who did the most to encourage me in school he was my grandfather.

Edited:
The person who did the most to encourage me in school was my grandfather.

2. Articles

Deciding when to use the indefinite articles a and an or the definite article the can pose some problems. There are general guidelines you can follow for proper, count, and noncount nouns.

- **Singular and plural proper nouns**
Proper nouns are the capitalized name of a specific person, place, group, or thing. Singular proper nouns rarely use an article. On the other hand, plural proper nouns usually do.

Original (singular):

The Disney World is a popular tourist attraction.

Edited:

Disney World is a popular tourist attraction.

Original (plural):

Himalayas are the youngest of the world's mountain chains.

Edited:

The Himalayas are the youngest of the world's mountain chains.

- **Singular and plural count nouns**

  Count nouns refer to people and things that can be counted—one baseball player, two automobiles, several friends, many tomatoes. As a general rule, use a or an before a singular count noun when it refers to something in general:

Original (singular count noun):

Modern kitchen needs a dishwasher, microwave, and food processor.

Edited:

A modern kitchen needs a dishwasher, microwave, and food processor.

But use the when you are referring to a specific thing:

Original (singular count noun):

A kitchen in our apartment has a dishwasher, microwave, and food processor.

Edited:

The kitchen in our apartment has a dishwasher, microwave, and food processor.

For plural count nouns, use no article when you refer to something in general:

Computers are changing the way people communicate.

But use the when you are referring to specific things:

The computers in the campus center are broken.

- **Noncount nouns**

  Noncount nouns name things or ideas that cannot be counted—

  electricity, silver, steel, happiness, laughter, childhood. Noncount

  nouns use either no article or the. They never take the article a or

  an. Use no article when the noncount refers to something general:

  Original (noncount nouns):

The silver is a precious metal.
A childhood is one of life's special moments.

Edited:

Silver is a precious metal.
Childhood is one of life's special moments.

But use *the* for specific noncount nouns.

Original (noncount nouns):

Silver in the bracelet was tarnished.
Childhood of Charles Dickens was a difficult time.

Edited:

The silver in the bracelet was tarnished.
The childhood of Charles Dickens was a difficult time.

3. This, That, These, and Those

This, that, these, and *those* are sometimes called demonstrative adjectives or pronouns because they point to something specific. *This* and *that* are singular. *These* and *those* are plural. Make sure they agree in number with the noun they modify.

Original:

This shoes are too big.
Those shirt is too small.

Edited:

These shoes are too big.
That shirt is too small.

4. Adjectives

The use of adjectives in English differs from their use in some other languages. Here we look at the form and sequence of adjectives.

• Adjective form

Unlike in some other languages, adjectives in English never take a plural form to agree with the noun it modifies.

Original:

Their garden is famous for its beautifuls roses.

Edited:
Their garden is famous for its beautiful roses.

• Adjective sequence

Using more than one adjective in a sequence to modify a noun can be confusing. Should you write "the green expensive new Chevrolet minivan" or "the expensive new green Chevrolet minivan"? The following list explains the order in which adjectives normally appear:

- Amount: a/an, the, that, four, several, many, a few
- Quality: good, bad, beautiful, ugly, expensive, cheap
- Physical description: large, small, tall, short, round, square, flat
- Age: young, old, new
- Color: green, blue, white, black
- Origin: German, French, Mexican, Brazilian, Vietnamese, Chinese
- Material: wood, plastic, chrome, fiberglass, ceramic
- Noun used as an adjective: Chevrolet, television (as in television program), football (as in football game)
- The noun modified: minivan, vase, etc.

Using this order, you can make up new sequences. For example:

Four beautiful old Vietnamese ceramic vases
A few ugly yellow plastic ashtrays

5. Prepositions: At, On, In

At, in, and on are prepositions that designate time and location.

- **Time**

  Use at for a specific time:

  Our class meets at 9:00.
  I was born at 5:00 a.m.
  We eat lunch at noon.

  Use on for days and dates:

  Our class meets on Mondays and Thursdays.
  I was born on April 21.

  Use in for months, years, seasons, and times during the day

  (morning, afternoon, evening):

  Our class begins in August.
  I was born in 1982.
  We eat dinner in the evening.

- **Location**

  Use at for specific addresses, named locations, general locations, or locations that involve a particular activity:

I live at 158 South Maple Street.
We plan to study at Savuth's apartment.
Jorge and Clara are at work.
The movie theater is at the mall.
Use on for names of streets, modes of transportation, floors of buildings, pages, and tracts of private land:

I live on South Maple Street.
She arrived in this country on a plane.
Our class is on the tenth floor of the Armidillo Building.
You can find that poem on page 452.
The hiking trail is on the Mohunk Nature Preserve.

Use in for the names of geographical areas of land—cities, states, countries, continents—or enclosed areas:

I was born in Bangkok.
Our college is in South Dakota.
Melissa studied in Costa Rica for a year.
Can I leave my books in your room?

6. Participles: -ing and -ed Endings

Present (-ing) and past (-ed) participles can be confusing at times. Use the present form (-ing) to describe when someone or something produces a result:

The movie was boring, but it has a surprising end.
My roomate has some annoying habits I don't want to mention.
Use the past (-ed) form to describe how someone or something experiences such results:

Bored by most of the movie, I was surprised by its end.
I am annoyed by some of my roomate's habits.

7. Present Tense: Third Person -s Endings

Check present tense verbs to make sure you add an -s or -es ending to third person singular verbs:

Original:
Maria often write to her mother in the Dominican Republic.

Edited:
Maria often writes to her mother in the Dominican Republic.

But notice with plural nouns and verbs, the -s ending goes at the end of the noun:

Original:
The two Dominican students often writes to their families.
Edited:
The two Dominican students often write to their families.

8. Auxiliary verbs: Do, Does, Did and Have, Has, Had

When you use the auxiliary verbs do, does, and did, the base form of the main verb is the correct choice. Have, has, and had always use the past participle (-ed) form:

Originals:
    They did not helped their friend.
    Gong Li has wanting to visit her family in China.
Edited:
    They did not help their friend.
    Gong Li has wanted to visit her family in China.

9. "If" or Conditional Clauses

Using "if" clauses enables a writer to state a condition and then in the main clause to describe the result. There are, however, a number of possible outcomes that can be indicated in the main clause. This section shows how the specific meanings vary depending on the verb tense you choose for the main clause. Notice the differences if the condition is A) true in the present, B) untrue or contrary to fact in the present, and C) untrue or contrary to fact in the past:

A. If clauses: True in the present

If clause	Result clause

- If the condition is generally or habitually true:

If I study hard, I get good grades.
(If + subject + present tense)   (subject + present tense verb)
- If the condition is true in the future as a one-time thing:

If I study hard, I will get good grades.
(If + subject + present tense)   (subject + future tense verb)
- If the condition is possibly true in the present as a one-time thing:

If I study hard, I might   (may, could, should) get good grades.

(If + subject + present tense)   (subject + modal + base form)

B. If clauses: Untrue in the present

If clause	Result clause

If I studied hard,   I would   (could, might) get
good grades.

(If + subject + past tense)   (subject + would, could,
     might + simple form)

C. If clauses: Untrue in the past

If clause Result clause

If I had studied hard,   I would   (could, might)
have gotten good grades.

(If + subject + past perfect)   (subject + would, could,
     might + have + past participle)

10. Idiomatic Two- and Three-Word Verbs

A number of verbs change their meanings by adding a preposition or adverb. If you are not certain about the use of idiomatic verbs, the best thing is to consult an English dictionary for second language writers or ask a native speaker. Here are a few examples.

ran into someone means "encountered a person by chance"

ran away from somewhere means "fled or escaped"

ran over a curb, person, cat, dog, etc. means "drive a car (or other vehicle) over"

ran up a bill means "spent a lot of money"

ran around with friends, a group, a gang, etc. means

look into means "investigate"

look out for means "watch carefully"